THE
ECONOMIC
CRISIS
READER

Second Edition

READINGS IN ECONOMICS, POLITICS, AND SOCIAL POLICY FROM
DOLLARS&SENSE

EDITED BY GERALD FRIEDMAN, FRED MOSELEY, CHRIS STURR,

AND THE *DOLLARS & SENSE* COLLECTIVE

THE ECONOMIC CRISIS READER, Second Edition

ISBN: 978-1-878585-84-4

Published by:
Economic Affairs Bureau, Inc. d/b/a *Dollars & Sense*
29 Winter Street, Boston, MA 02108
617-447-2177; dollars@dollarsandsense.org.
For order information, contact Economic Affairs Bureau or visit: www.dollarsandsense.org.

The Economic Crisis Reader is edited by the *Dollars & Sense* Collective, which also publishes *Dollars & Sense* magazine and the classroom books *Real World Macro, Real World Micro, Current Economic Issues, Real World Globalization, Real World Latin America, Real World Labor, Real World Banking and Finance, The Wealth Inequality Reader, The Environment in Crisis, Introduction to Political Economy, Unlevel Playing Fields: Understanding Wage Inequality and Discrimination, Striking a Balance: Work, Family, Life,* and *Grassroots Journalism.*

The 2010 *Dollars & Sense* Collective:
Arpita Banerjee, Ben Collins, Katharine Davies, Amy Gluckman, Ben Greenberg, Mary Jirmanus, Vera Kelsey-Watts, James McBride, John Miller, Larry Peterson, Linda Pinkow, Paul Piwko, Smriti Rao, Alejandro Reuss, Dave Ryan, Bryan Snyder, Chris Sturr, Ramaa Vasudevan, and Jeanne Winner.

Co-editors of this volume: Gerald Friedman, Fred Moseley, and Chris Sturr
Editorial assistance: Katharine Davies, Amy Gluckman, and Lauren Price

Cover design: Chris Sturr, based on a design by David Garrett, dgcommunications.com.

Cover photo: Copyright © Getty Images, gettyimages.com. Used with permission.

Production: Chris Sturr and Katharine Davies.

Printed in U.S.A.

CONTENTS

CHAPTER 8 • INDUSTRIAL AND EMPLOYMENT POLICY

CHAPTER 9 • LABOR ACTIVISM

CHAPTER 10 • THE INTERNATIONAL CRISIS

CONTRIBUTORS   *407*

INTRODUCTION

A year has passed since the publication of the first edition of this *Economic Crisis Reader*. After a period of incipient recovery in 2009, the economy has slowed again since early 2010 raising the possibility of a "double-dip," or a return to recession. It now appears that the stronger growth of 2009 was largely due to temporary factors, especially the expansionary fiscal policies of the incoming Obama administration and the rebuilding of business inventories after the initial crash. With these effects now fading, so fades the hope that by themselves they will be sufficient to generate a strong, lasting recovery.

Liberals and leftists would address this deteriorating economic situation with a substantial second round of stimulus, including more fiscal stimulus as well as continued monetary stimulus. But such calls face strong opposition from a Republican Party energized by Tea Party activists and encouraged by the Obama administration's lagging popularity. Economic policy is likely to remain a central political issue in the years ahead. We may have reached a point where the Obama administration's declining political position will not allow it to conduct the aggressive economic policies needed to revive the economy, even if it had the will to do so.

Meanwhile, the official rate of unemployment remains stuck at almost 10%, remaining below that level only because so many are no longer counted as unemployed because they have given up looking for jobs or have taken part-time work. (Including those who have given up looking or are working part-time involuntarily, the Bureau of Labor Statistics U6 measure places the unemployment rate at almost 17%.) Especially alarming is the growing number of long-term unemployed, including many who have exhausted any unemployment insurance benefits. The share of the unemployed who have been without work for more than 26 weeks is almost 50%, the highest by far of the postwar period. If the unemployment rate is to remain high for at least several more years, and perhaps even longer, it is likely that the ranks of these long-term unemployed will only grow.

In sum, we have a very serious unemployment crisis on our hands. If anything, the unemployment crisis is more serious today than it was a year ago, when it was hoped that a stronger economic recovery would quickly bring unemployment down.

1

The housing industry has mirrored the rest of the economy—signs of recovery early in the year, due mainly to government policies, especially the $7,000 tax credit given first-time homebuyers. But since the tax credit expired in June, home sales have fallen precipitously along with housing prices. The outlook for the near-to-medium term future does not look good because of the cumulative effect of mounting decline. One main determinant of the demand for houses is employment; if employment remains depressed in the years ahead (as appears likely), so will the housing market. Furthermore, falling employment and declining housing values are driving more homes into foreclosure, discouraging potential homebuyers.

Nor has there been much recovery in the home mortgage market, the initial locus of the financial market collapse. The mortgage market is now almost entirely dependent on government support. The newly nationalized housing finance agencies, Fannie Mae and Freddie Mac, now own or guarantee 90% of all new mortgages, and the Federal Reserve has purchased $1.2 trillion of Fannie-Freddie mortgages and debt. As with the stimulus program, the Obama administration can take some credit for stabilizing the economy; without this massive government assistance to the mortgage market, few mortgages would be issued, housing prices would have dropped further, the construction industry would be even more depressed, and the economy would be correspondingly much worse. But federal intervention has been too limited to reverse the housing market collapse. Foreclosures have continued at a rate of about one million a year, and the worst may be yet to come with the cumulative effects of unemployment and falling home values. Without progress on employment and a revival of economic activity, it may yet be that the limited measures taken by the Obama administration have only postponed the full foreclosure crisis rather than avoided it. The recent controversies about fraudulent processing of foreclosure cases by big mortgage lenders only complicates the ongoing crisis.

One possible bright spot seems to be the banking sector, which no longer appears to be on the verge of collapse. Bank profits have increased sharply, allowing executive salaries to return to their multi-million dollar levels. But before we break out the champagne to celebrate Wall Street's recovery, note that bank profits have been inflated by the Federal Reserve's readiness to lend to banks at 0% interest rates even when the banks themselves merely leave the money at the Fed as excess reserves on which they collect interest of 0.25%! While inflated bank profits have relieved concerns for the complete collapse of the financial system, the banks still hold trillions of dollars of bad mortgages on their books along with a growing portfolio of delinquent loans moving towards default by businesses and individuals suffering from the economic recession. A double-dip or return to recession would turn many of these bad loans into losses, perhaps provoking a new banking crisis.

The stalled recovery is also causing growing distress for states and localities. FY 2010 has been the hardest yet for state and local governments that had exhausted past savings and the federal assistance from the Obama stimulus. Government services have been cut dramatically in most states; thousands of public employees have been furloughed; teachers, and even police and fire fighters, have been laid off. Without a more vigorous recovery or more federal assistance, we can only anticipate more cuts in the future, contributing further to the risk of another economic downturn.

In sum, we continue to face a very serious economic crisis. This makes it more essential than ever that all of us get a better understanding of the fundamental causes of this crisis so that we can get a better idea of what should be done to overcome the crisis in an equitable and sustainable way. We think that the articles in this collection help to develop this collective understanding, and we hope that readers will find them interesting and illuminating. Our own recommendations remain essentially the same as in the first edition: a big second stimulus program, with an emphasis on jobs, help for the unemployed, and aid to state and local governments; redistribution of income in favor of workers through support for labor unions and progressive taxation; aid to homeowners facing foreclosure; the strict regulation of banks and other financial institutions, including the nationalization or break-up of the "too-big-to-fail" megabanks; and the permanent nationalization of Fannie Mae and Freddie Mac. None of this is likely to happen, however, without sustained left organizing among working people in the United States to counter the reactionary activism of the Tea Party and the outsized political and economic clout of capital and the superrich. ❏

INTRODUCTION TO
THE FIRST EDITION

The economic downturn that began at the end of 2007 has been the most severe since the Great Depression. Between mid 2007 and late 2009, the official unemployment rate more than doubled to 10.2%. U.S. workers lost nearly 7 million jobs over this span. The official U.S. poverty rate has climbed to 13.2%, the highest level since 1997. Total wage income has dropped by 5% in the last year, and by 7% in the private sector. This economic decline has been driven by a sharp drop in all categories of demand except for government spending. Driven by the loss of stock market and housing wealth, consumption has fallen: spending on non-durable goods (such as food and clothing) is down by 2.5% since the beginning of the crisis, while consumption of durables (such as washing machines and refrigerators) is down by almost 8%. Private investment (spending on new structures, machinery, etc.) in the fall of 2009 is falling at an annual rate of 30%, with residential construction (a component of investment) falling even faster. Since the recession began, gross domestic product (GDP), the sum of output of all goods and services, has fallen by 3%. While GDP appears to be growing again, and the pace of job loss has eased, high levels of unemployment and falling spending by local and state governments almost guarantee that consumption and investment will remain depressed for at least the next few years.

Beyond declines in economic activity, there has been a dramatic decline in wealth (measured in monetary terms) due to falling stock and real-estate values. The Dow Jones Industrial Average lost nearly half its value between its 2007 peak and the end of 2008. While the fall in housing prices, down a third from their peak in 2006, has been smaller, it has affected many more people in the United States as homeowners, investors, and even renters. Overall, fifteen trillion dollars of wealth seemingly "disappeared" in the first year of the recession, the sharpest wealth decline in over 50 years of modern records. The talk of wealth "disappearing" should be taken with a grain of salt. A house's market price can increase or decrease dramatically without its physical characteristics or usefulness in satisfying human needs changing at all. The crisis has not destroyed nearly so much wealth—thought

5

of in terms of useful objects—as the statistics suggest, any more than the preceding housing and stock-market bubbles "created" trillions in wealth. The consequences of the crash, however, have been real, and severe.

Falling wealth has hit many Americans particularly hard because many households had maintained living standards by borrowing heavily during the 2002-2007 boom. Rising debt levels, including both home equity loans and consumer and credit-card debt, have made more families vulnerable to any drop in income or wealth. Household debt doubled between 1999 and 2007. The ratio of debt to income, meanwhile, soared by 40% in just seven years (to double the rate of the mid-1970s). Home mortgages accounted for 90% of the increase in debt, as some homeowners went into debt to buy real estate in anticipation of rising values and others borrowed against home equity to finance consumption spending. Both groups are now struggling, with nearly a third of all home mortgages "under water" (with the value of the home less than what is owed on the mortgage). At the end of 2008, 11% of mortgages were delinquent or in foreclosure. Personal bankruptcy filings for 2009 are expected to hit 1.5 million, 50% above the already-high rate of 2008.

The current economic crisis has challenged a comfortable consensus among economists around the idea of a "great moderation" in economic activity. Through the 1990s, and even after the collapse of the dot-com bubble in 1999, many spoke admiringly of Federal Reserve chief Alan Greenspan for orchestrating a "Goldilocks" economy that was neither "too hot," so as to provoke inflation, nor "too cold," so as to drive up the unemployment rate. As has happened during previous booms, mainstream economists concluded that governments had finally mastered the art of economic management by providing just enough support to let markets do their thing—operate efficiently and thereby maintain full employment.

Greenspan's economy rested on two pillars of "neoliberal" economics (the pro-business, "free-market" economic policy framework of the last few decades):

• Growing inequality: Ever-rising shares of income and wealth were going to the rich while wages and salaries stagnated for most Americans.

• Decreasing regulation: Less redistributive taxation, weakened social-welfare programs, less protections for workers and unions, less regulation of private industry and financial markets.

While stagnating wages sound like good news for business—and to a great extent, they have been—they also posed a threat. Workers are also consumers, and their stagnating incomes might make it hard for businesses to find buyers for their products. This is where debt came to the rescue: Deregulated financial markets established new instruments that allowed Americans to increase their borrowing and so keep their spending high.

Anyone could have seen that a boom fueled by rising debt, issued by an increasingly leveraged and unregulated financial market, could not be sustained and would end in a crisis. Anyone, that is, except an economist trained in neoclassical orthodoxy. Two major pillars of orthodox economic theory prevented mainstream economists from foreseeing the crisis:

- The "natural" state of the economy is full employment, where everyone who wants work at the going wage will be hired and the only people without jobs will be those between jobs or those who have compelling reasons to remain out of the workforce. Mainstream economists do not deny that there is unemployment, but assume that any serious recession is caused by "exogenous shocks" (external factors, such as bad government policies, bad weather, or an increase in the price of oil). Once this shock passes, the economy is expected to recover on its own and return more or less quickly to its "natural" state of full employment.

- People behave "rationally" to advance their interests, and this will ensure that financial markets will price all assets properly, discouraging the development of risky products, such as sub-prime mortgages. A risky loan, mainstream economists believe, will always fetch a high enough interest rate to compensate the lender for the additional risk, or the lender would not be willing to make it.

Seeing the world in this way, orthodox economists ignored the warning signs. They dismissed rising debt levels by assuming that both borrowers and lenders had an incentive not to allow borrowers to accumulate more debt than they could manage. Instead, orthodox economists hailed rising debt levels as a sign that deregulated financial markets were providing the boon of new financial products to meet consumer needs.

Of course it all exploded. A rising tide of defaults and foreclosures in the sub-prime mortgage market in 2007 soon spread through the banking system to other mortgage markets, commercial real estate, and corporate bonds. Overleveraged themselves, banks reduced their lending. This made it harder (and more expensive) for consumers and businesses to borrow, driving down consumption and investment, and forcing many healthy businesses to reduce employment and production. Thus, the excessive debt that had kept the economy growing earlier in the decade caused a full-fledged recession at the end.

Not only did orthodox economists fail to anticipate the crisis, they have been unable to understand it since it began and unable to recommend effective policies to ameliorate it. Thinking of financial markets as efficient, they ignore debt, and the tendency of indebtedness to increase during a period of expansion. Thinking of the economy as fundamentally self-correcting, they believe the key adjustments necessary to bring about this automatic adjustment and return to full employment are falling wages and prices (i.e. "deflation"). Once debt levels become high (and debt levels in the United States today are much higher than they have ever been before, about twice as high overall as in 1929), however, deflation—the supposed key to the return to full employment—risks disaster. Declining prices and wages and declining incomes raise the already-too-high burden of debt payments. This forces even more households and businesses into bankruptcy, further undermining the banks and the financial system. The potential disaster resulting from deflation in a heavily indebted economy is widely recognized by economists in an ad hoc way in their policy recommendations, but it is completely missing in mainstream macroeconomic theory. As chair of the Federal Reserve, Ben Bernanke is terrified of deflation, and has done everything he can to avoid it. But his macroeconomic textbook (the latest edition was published in 2008) presents the orthodox theory, in which deflation is a solution to recessions and the only problem is if it comes too slowly!

Fortunately, there are heterodox economists and other social scientists outside the mainstream who recognize that capitalism is an inherently unstable economic system in which recurring severe crises are to be expected. Many of these economists recognize that debt is a crucial variable in a theory of capitalism, especially in a theory of crises in capitalism. The economists represented in this collection belong to this group of non-mainstream macroeconomists; the other authors—scholars from other disciplines, as well as activists, organizers, and journalists—have been influenced by heterodox economics. Some have been predicting a severe economic crisis for some time, and were not taken by surprise.

The heterodox economic theories that underlie the articles in this collection deny that recessions and crises are unusual events caused by "exogenous shocks." Instead crises are endogenous to a capitalist economy: they come from within the economic system. Far from accidents, recessions and crises are the result of capitalism's own internal structure and dynamics, especially the contradiction between the concentration of power and income and the need for capitalist firms to market their products widely. The authors in this reader therefore explain the current economic crisis in terms of internal causes—such as falling profits, stagnant wages, increasing inequality, and increasing debt of all kinds.

If crises are the expected result of unregulated capitalism, conscious government intervention is needed to bring about a recovery and to limit future recessions. High wages and full employment did not cause the crisis, and recovery should not be at the expense of workers. A crisis that has been caused by rising inequality that undermined consumer demand and drove up household debt cannot be cured by cutting wages and laying off workers. Instead, we need to raise wages and to protect people from the consequences of the crisis with extended unemployment benefits, public-service job creation, and programs to reduce mortgage debt and stop foreclosures. To emerge from the crisis, we need to reorder our priorities and level the distribution of income to allow healthy and sustainable growth with a reduction in the burden of debt.

Almost all of the articles in this reader were originally published in *Dollars & Sense*, with three from *The Nation* and one from *New Politics* (whose permission for publication in this collection is gratefully acknowledged). The articles are divided into eight chapters: general explanations of the current crisis, warning signs, the housing crisis, the financial crisis, monetary policy, fiscal policy, the international crisis, and workers and the crisis.

The important events of the current economic crisis will be studied for years. We think that the articles in this collection (and other articles by these and other heterodox economists) will help ordinary people understand the causes of crises in capitalism. We also hope that mainstream economists will read these articles and learn how to incorporate capitalism's endogenous crises into their theories. ❏

Chapter 1

GENERAL EXPLANATIONS
OF THE CRISIS

Article 1.1

THE GREED FALLACY
You can't explain a change with a constant.

BY ARTHUR MacEWAN
November/December 2008

Various people explain the current financial crisis as a result of "greed." There is, however, no indication of a change in the degree or extent of greed on Wall Street (or anywhere else) in the last several years. Greed is a constant. If greed were the cause of the financial crisis, we would be in financial crisis pretty much all the time.

But the financial markets have not been in perpetual crisis. Nothing close to the current crisis has taken place since 1929. Yes, there was 1987 and the savings-and-loan debacle of that era. But the current crisis is already more dramatic—and threatens to get a good deal worse. This crisis emerged over the last decade and appeared full-blown only at the beginning of 2008 (though, if you were looking, it was moving up on the horizon a year or two earlier). The current mess, therefore, is a change, a departure from the normal course of financial markets. So something has to have changed to have brought it about. The constant of greed cannot be the explanation.

So what changed? The answer is relatively simple: the extent of regulation changed.

As a formal matter, the change in regulation is most clearly marked by the Gramm-Leach-Bliley Act of 1999, passed by the Republican-dominated Congress and signed into law by Bill Clinton. This act in large part repealed the Glass-Steagall Act of 1933, which had imposed various regulations on the financial industry after the debacle of 1929. Among other things, Glass-Steagall prohibited a firm from being engaged in different sorts of financial services. One firm could not be both an investment bank (organizing the funding of firms' investment activities) and a commercial bank (handling the checking and savings accounts of individuals and firms and making loans); nor could it be one of these types of banks and an insurance firm.

However, the replacement of Glass-Steagall by Gramm-Leach-Bliley was only the formal part of the change that took place in recent decades. Informally, the relation between the government and the financial sector has increasingly become one of reduced regulation. In particular, as the financial sector evolved new forms of operation—hedge funds and private equity funds, for example—there was no attempt on the part of Washington to develop regulations for these activities. Also, even where regulations existed, the regulators became increasingly lax in enforcement.

The movement away from regulation might be seen as a consequence of "free market" ideology, the belief as propounded by its advocates that government should leave the private sector alone. But to see the problem simply as ideology run amok is to ignore the question of where the ideology comes from. Put simply, the ideology is generated by firms themselves because they want to be as free as possible to pursue profit-making activity. So they push the idea of the "free market" and deregulation any way they can. But let me leave aside for now the ways in which ideas come to dominate Washington and the society in general; enough to recognize that deregulation became increasingly the dominant idea from the early 1980s onward. (But, given the current presidential campaign, one cannot refrain from noting that one way the firms get their ideas to dominate is through the money they lavish on candidates.)

When financial firms are not regulated, they tend to take on more and more risky activities. When markets are rising, risk does not seem to be very much of a problem; all—or virtually all—investments seem to be making money. So why not take some chances? Furthermore, if one firm doesn't take a particular risk—put money into a chancy operation—then one of its competitors will. So competition pushes them into more and more risky operations.

The danger of risk is not simply that one investment—one loan, for example—made by a financial firm will turn out badly, or even that a group of loans will turn out badly. The danger arises in the relation between its loans (obligations to the firm), the money it borrows from others (the firm's obligations to its creditors) and its capital (the funds put in by investors, the stockholders). If some of the loans it has made go bad (i.e., if the debtors default), it can still meet its obligations to its creditors with its capital. But if the firm is unregulated, it will tend to make more and more loans and take on more and more debt. The ratio of debt to capital can become very high, and, then, if trouble with the loans develops, the bank cannot meet its obligations with its capital.

In the current crisis, the deflation of the housing bubble was the catalyst to the general crumbling of financial structures. The housing bubble was in large part a product of the Federal Reserve Bank's policies under the guidance of the much-heralded Alan Greenspan, but let's leave that issue aside for now.

When the housing bubble burst, many financial institutions found themselves in trouble. They had taken on too much risk in relation to their capital. The lack of regulation had allowed them to get in this trouble.

But the trouble is much worse than it might have been because of the repeal of the provisions of Glass-Steagall that prevented the merging of investment banks, commercial banks, and insurance companies. Under the current circumstances, when trouble develops in one part of a firm's operations, it is immediately transmitted throughout the other segments of that firm. And from there, the trouble spreads to all the other entities to which it is connected—through credits, insurance deals, deposits, and a myriad set of complicated (unregulated) financial arrangements.

AIG is the example *par excellence*. Ostensibly an insurance company, AIG has morphed into a multi-faceted financial institution, doing everything from selling life insurance in rural India to speculating in various esoteric types of investments on Wall Street. Its huge size, combined with the extent of its intertwining with other financial firms, meant that its failure would have had very large impacts around the world.

The efforts of the U.S. government may or may not be able to contain the current financial crisis. Success would not breathe life back into the Lehman Brothers, Bear Stearns, and who knows how many other major operators that are on their deathbeds. But it would prevent the financial crisis from precipitating a severe general depression; it would prevent a movement from 1929 to 1932.

The real issue, however, is what is learned from the current financial mess. One thing should be evident, namely that greed did not cause the crisis. The cause was a change in the way markets have been allowed to operate, a change brought on by the rise of deregulation. Markets, especially financial markets, are never very stable when left to themselves. It turns out that the "invisible hand" does some very nasty, messy things when there is no visible hand of regulation affecting the process.

The problem is that maintaining some form of regulation is a very difficult business. As I have said, the firms themselves do not want to be regulated. The current moment may allow some re-imposition of financial regulation. But as soon as we turn our backs, the pressure will be on again to let the firms operate according to the "free market." Let's not forget where that leads. ❑

Article 1.2

INEQUALITY, POWER, AND IDEOLOGY
Getting It Right About the Causes of the Current Economic Crisis

BY ARTHUR MacEWAN
March/April 2009

It is hard to solve a problem without an understanding of what caused it. For example, in medicine, until we gained an understanding of the way bacteria and viruses cause various infectious diseases, it was virtually impossible to develop effective cures. Of course, dealing with many diseases is complicated by the fact that germs, genes, diet, and the environment establish a nexus of causes.

The same is true in economics. Without an understanding of the causes of the current crisis, we are unlikely to develop a solution; certainly we are not going to get a solution that has a lasting impact. And determining the causes is complicated because several intertwined factors have been involved.

The current economic crisis was brought about by a nexus of factors that involved: a growing concentration of political and social power in the hands of the wealthy; the ascendance of a perverse leave-it-to-the-market ideology which was an instrument of that power; and rising income inequality, which both resulted from and enhanced that power. These various factors formed a vicious circle, reinforcing one another and together shaping the economic conditions that led us to the present situation. Several other factors were also involved—the growing role of credit, the puffing up of the housing bubble, and the increasing deregulation of financial markets have been very important. However, these are best understood as transmitters of our economic problems, arising from the nexus that formed the vicious circle.

What does this tell us about a solution? Economic stimulus, repair of the housing market, and new regulation are all well and good, but they do not deal with the underlying causes of the crisis. Instead, progressive groups need to work to shift each of the factors I have noted—power, ideology, and income distribution—in the other direction. In doing so, we can create a *virtuous* circle, with each change reinforcing the other changes. If successful, we not only establish a more stable economy, but we lay the foundation for a more democratic, equitable, and sustainable economic order.

A crisis by its very nature creates opportunities for change. One good place to begin change and intervene in this "circle"—and transform it from vicious to virtuous—is through pushing for the expansion and reform of social programs, programs that directly serve social needs of the great majority of the population (for example: single-payer health care, education programs, and environmental protection and repair). By establishing changes in social programs, we will have impacts on income distribution and ideology, and, perhaps most important, we set in motion *a power shift* that improves our position for preserving the changes. While I emphasize social programs as a means to initiate social and economic change, there are other ways to intervene in the circle. Efforts to re-strengthen unions would be especially important; and there are other options as well.

Causes of the Crisis: A Long Time Coming

Sometime around the early 1970s, there were some dramatic changes in the U.S. economy. The twenty-five years following World War II had been an era of relatively stable economic growth; the benefits of growth had been widely shared, with wages rising along with productivity gains, and income distribution became slightly less unequal (a good deal less unequal as compared to the pre-Great Depression era). There were severe economic problems in the United States, not the least of which were the continued exclusion of African Americans, large gender inequalities, and the woeful inadequacy of social welfare programs. Nonetheless, relatively stable growth, rising wages, and then the advent of the civil rights movement and the War on Poverty gave some important, positive social and economic character to the era—especially in hindsight!

In part, this comparatively favorable experience for the United States had depended on the very dominant position that U.S. firms held in the world economy, a position in which they were relatively unchallenged by international competition. The firms and their owners were not the only beneficiaries of this situation. With less competitive pressure on them from foreign companies, many U.S. firms accepted unionization and did not find it worthwhile to focus on keeping wages down and obstructing the implementation of social supports for the low-income population. Also, having had the recent experience of the Great Depression, many wealthy people and business executives were probably not so averse to a substantial role for government in regulating the economy.

A Power Grab

By about 1970, the situation was changing. Firms in Europe and Japan had long recovered from World War II, OPEC was taking shape, and weaknesses were emerging in the U.S. economy. The weaknesses were in part a consequence of heavy spending for the Vietnam War combined with the government's reluctance to tax for the war because of its unpopularity. The pressures on U.S. firms arising from these changes had two sets of consequences: slower growth and greater instability; and concerted efforts—a power grab, if you will—by firms and the wealthy to shift the costs of economic deterioration onto U.S. workers and the low-income population.

These "concerted efforts" took many forms: greater resistance to unions and unionization, battles to reduce taxes, stronger opposition to social welfare programs, and, above all, a push to reduce or eliminate government regulation of economic activity through a powerful political campaign to gain control of the various branches and levels of government. The 1980s, with Reagan and Bush One in the White House, were the years in which all these efforts were solidified. Unions were greatly weakened, a phenomenon both demonstrated and exacerbated by Reagan's firing of the air traffic controllers in response to their strike in 1981. The tax cuts of the period were also important markers of the change. But the change had begun earlier; the 1978 passage of the tax-cutting Proposition 13 in California was perhaps the first major success of the movement. And the changes continued well after the 1980s, with welfare reform and deregulation of finance during the Clinton era, to say nothing of the tax cuts and other actions during Bush Two.

Ideology Shift

The changes that began in the 1970s, however, were not simply these sorts of concrete alterations in the structure of power affecting the economy and, especially, government's role in the economy. There was a major shift in ideology, the dominant set of ideas that organize an understanding of our social relations and both guide and rationalize policy decisions.

Following the Great Depression and World War II, there was a wide acceptance of the idea that government had a major role to play in economic life. Less than in many other countries but nonetheless to a substantial degree, at all levels of society, it was generally believed that there should be a substantial government safety net and that government should both regulate the economy in various ways and, through fiscal as well as monetary policy, should maintain aggregate demand. This large economic role for government came to be called Keynesianism, after the British economist John Maynard Keynes, who had set out the arguments for an active fiscal policy in time of economic weakness. In the early 1970s, as economic troubles developed, even Richard Nixon declared: "We are all Keynesians now."

The election of Ronald Reagan, however, marked a sharp change in ideology, at least at the top. Actions of the government were blamed for all economic ills: government spending, Keynesianism, was alleged to be the cause of the inflation of the 1970s; government regulation was supposedly crippling industry; high taxes were, it was argued, undermining incentives for workers to work and for businesses to invest; social welfare spending was blamed for making people dependent on the government and was charged with fraud and corruption (the "welfare queens"); and so on and so on.

Alan Greenspan, Symbol of an Era

One significant symbol of the full rise of the conservative ideology that became so dominant in the latter part of the 20th century was Alan Greenspan, who served from 1974 through 1976 as chairman of the President's Council of Economic Advisers under Gerald Ford and in 1987 became chairman of the Federal Reserve Board, a position he held until 2006. While his predecessors had hardly been critics of U.S. capitalism, Greenspan was a close associate of the philosopher Ayn Rand and an adherent of her extreme ideas supporting individualism and *laissez-faire* (keep-the-government-out) capitalism.

When chairman of the Fed, Greenspan was widely credited with maintaining an era of stable economic growth. As things fell apart in 2008, however, Greenspan was seen as having a large share of responsibility for the non-regulation and excessively easy credit (see article) that led into the crisis.

Called before Congress in October of 2008, Greenspan was chastised by Rep. Henry Waxman (D-Calif.), who asked him: "Do you feel that your ideology pushed you to make decisions that you wish you had not made?" To which Greenspan replied: "Yes, I've found a flaw. I don't know how significant or permanent it is. But I've been very distressed by that fact."

And Greenspan told Congress: "Those of us who have looked to the self-interest of lending institutions to protect shareholders' equity, myself included, are in a state of shocked disbelief."

Greenspan's "shock" was reminiscent of the scene in the film *Casablanca* in which Captain Renault (played by Claude Rains) declares: "I'm shocked, shocked to find that gambling is going on in here!" At which point, a croupier hands Renault a pile of money and says, "Your winnings, sir." Renault replies, *sotto voce*, "Thank you very much."

On economic matters, Reagan championed supply-side economics, the principal idea of which was that tax cuts yield an increase in government revenue because the cuts lead to more rapid economic growth through encouraging more work and more investment. Thus, so the argument went, tax cuts would reduce the government deficit. Reagan, with the cooperation of Democrats, got the tax cuts—and, as the loss of revenue combined with a large increase in military spending, the federal budget deficit grew by leaps and bounds, almost doubling as a share of GDP over the course of the 1980s. It was all summed up in the idea of keeping the government out of the economy; let the free market work its magic.

Growing Inequality

The shifts of power and ideology were very much bound up with a major redistribution upwards of income and wealth. The weakening of unions, the increasing access of firms to low-wage foreign (and immigrant) labor, the refusal of government to maintain the buying power of the minimum wage, favorable tax treatment of the wealthy and their corporations, deregulation in a wide range of industries, and lack of enforcement of existing regulation (e.g., the authorities turning a blind eye to off-shore tax shelters) all contributed to these shifts.

Many economists, however, explain the rising income inequality as a result of technological change that favored more highly skilled workers; and changing technology has probably been a factor. Yet the most dramatic aspect of the rising inequality has been the rapidly rising share of income obtained by those at the very top, who get their incomes from the ownership and control of business, not from their skilled labor. For these people the role of new technologies was most important through its impact on providing more options (e.g., international options) for the managers of firms, more thorough means to control labor, and more effective ways—in the absence of regulation—to manipulate finance.

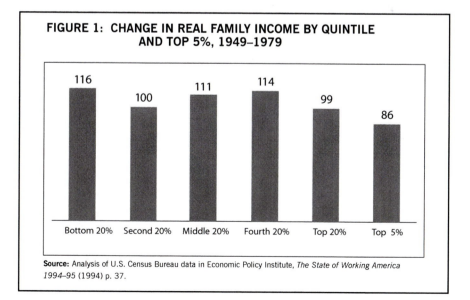

FIGURE 1: CHANGE IN REAL FAMILY INCOME BY QUINTILE AND TOP 5%, 1949–1979

Bottom 20%	Second 20%	Middle 20%	Fourth 20%	Top 20%	Top 5%
116	100	111	114	99	86

Source: Analysis of U.S. Census Bureau data in Economic Policy Institute, *The State of Working America 1994–95* (1994) p. 37.

All of these gains that might be associated with new technology were also gains brought by the way the government handled, or didn't handle (failed to regulate), economic affairs.

Several sets of data demonstrate the sharp changes in the distribution of income that have taken place in the last several decades. Most striking is the changing position of the very highest income segment of the population. In the mid-1920s, the share of all pre-tax income going to the top 1% of households peaked at 23.9%. This elite group's share of income fell dramatically during the Great Depression and World War II to about 12% at the end of the war and then slowly fell further during the next thirty years, reaching a low of 8.9% in the mid-1970s. Since then, the top 1% has regained its exalted position of the earlier era, with 21.8% of income in 2005. Since 1993, more than one-half of all income gains have accrued to this highest 1% of the population.

Figures 1 and 2 show the gains (or losses) of various groups in the 1947 to 1979 period and in the 1979 to 2005 period. The difference is dramatic. For example, in the earlier era, the bottom 20% saw its income in real (inflation-adjusted) terms rise by 116%, and real income of the top 5% grew by only 86%. But in the latter era, the bottom 20% saw a 1% decline in its income, while the top 5% obtained a 81% increase.

The Emergence of Crisis

These changes, especially the dramatic shifts in the distribution of income, set the stage for the increasingly large reliance on credit, especially consumer and mortgage credit, that played a major role in the emergence of the current economic crisis. Other factors were involved, but rising inequality was especially important in effecting the increase in both the demand and supply of credit.

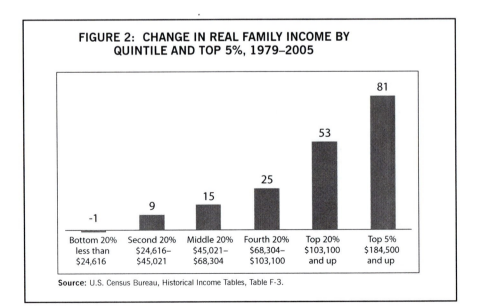

FIGURE 2: CHANGE IN REAL FAMILY INCOME BY QUINTILE AND TOP 5%, 1979–2005

Source: U.S. Census Bureau, Historical Income Tables, Table F-3.

Credit Expansion

On the demand side, rising inequality translated into a growing gap between the incomes of most members of society and their needs. For the 2000 to 2007 period, average weekly earnings in the private sector were 12% below their average for the 1970s (in inflation-adjusted terms). From 1980 to 2005 the share of income going to the bottom 60% of families fell from 35% to 29%. Under these circumstances, more and more people relied more and more heavily on credit to meet their needs—everything from food to fuel, from education to entertainment, and especially housing.

While the increasing reliance of consumers on credit has been going on for a long time, it has been especially marked in recent decades. Consumer debt as a share of after-tax personal income averaged 20% in the 1990s, and then jumped up to an average of 25% in the first seven years of the new millennium. But the debt expansion was most marked in housing, where mortgage debt as a percent of after-tax personal income rose from 89% to 94% over the 1990s, and then ballooned to 140% by 2006 as housing prices skyrocketed.

On the supply side, especially in the last few years, the government seems to have relied on making credit readily available as a means to bolster aggregate demand and maintain at least a modicum of economic growth. During the 1990s, the federal funds interest rate averaged 5.1%, but fell to an average of 3.4% in the 2000 to 2007 period—and averaged only 1.4% in the 2002 to 2004 period. (The federal funds interest rate is the rate that banks charge one another for overnight loans and is a rate directly affected by the Federal Reserve.) Corresponding to the low interest rates, the money supply grew twice as fast in the new millennium as it had in the 1990s. (And see the box on the connection of the Fed's actions to the Iraq War.)

The increasing reliance of U.S. consumers on credit has often been presented as a moral weakness, as an infatuation with consumerism, and as a failure to look beyond the present. Whatever moral judgments one may make, however, the expansion of the credit economy has been a response to real economic forces—inequality and government policies, in particular.

The Failure to Regulate

The credit expansion by itself, however, did not precipitate the current crisis. Deregulation—or, more generally, the failure to regulate—is also an important part of the story. The government's role in regulation of financial markets has been a central feature in the development of this crisis, but the situation in financial markets has been part of a more general process—affecting airlines and trucking, telecommunications, food processing, broadcasting, and of course international trade and investment. The process has been driven by a combination of power (of large firms and wealthy individuals) and ideology (leave it to the market, get the government out).

The failure to regulate financial markets that transformed the credit expansion into a financial crisis shows up well in three examples:

The 1999 repeal of the Glass-Steagall Act. Glass-Steagall had been enacted in the midst of the Great Depression, as a response to the financial implosion following the

---

Joseph Stiglitz on the War and the Economy

On October 2, 2008, on the Pacifica radio program "Democracy Now!," Amy Goodman and Juan Gonzalez interviewed Joseph Stiglitz about the economic situation. Stiglitz was the 2001 winner of the Nobel Prize in Economics, former chief economist at the World Bank, and former chair of President Clinton's Council of Economic Advisers. He is a professor at Columbia University. Following is an excerpt from that interview:

AMY GOODMAN: Joseph Stiglitz, you're co-author of *The Three Trillion Dollar War: The True Cost of the Iraq Conflict.* How does the bailout [of the financial sector] connect to war?

JOSEPH STIGLITZ: Very much. Let me first explain a little bit how the current crisis connects with the war. One of the reasons that we have this crisis is that the Fed flooded the economy with liquidity and had lax regulations. Part of that was this ideology of "regulations are bad," but part of the reason was that the economy was weak. And one of the reasons the economy was weak was oil prices were soaring, and part of the reason oil prices were soaring is the Iraq war. When we went to war in 2003, before we went, prices were $23 a barrel. Futures markets thought they would remain at that level. They anticipated the increase in demand, but they thought there would be a concomitant increase in supply from the low-cost providers, mainly in the Middle East. The war changed that equation, and we know what happened to the oil prices.

Well, why is that important? Well, we were spending—Americans were spending hundreds of millions—billions of dollars to buy—more, to buy imported oil. Normally, that would have had a very negative effect on our economy; we would have had a slowdown. Some people have said, you know, it's a mystery why we aren't having that slowdown; we repealed the laws of economics. Whenever anybody says that, you ought to be suspect.

It was actually very simple. The Fed engineered a bubble, a housing bubble to replace the tech bubble that it had engineered in the '90s. The housing bubble facilitated people taking money out of their . . . houses; in one year, there were more than $900 billion of mortgage equity withdrawals. And so, we had a consumption boom that was so strong that even though we were spending so much money abroad, we could keep the economy going. But it was so shortsighted. And it was so clear that we were living on borrowed money and borrowed time. And it was just a matter of time before, you know, the whole thing would start to unravel.

---

stock market crash of 1929. Among other things, it required that different kinds of financial firms—commercial banks, investment banks, insurance companies—be separate. This separation both limited the spread of financial problems and reduced conflicts of interest that could arise were the different functions of these firms combined into a single firm. As perhaps the most important legislation regulating the financial sector, the repeal of Glass-Steagall was not only a substantive change but was an important symbol of the whole process of deregulation.

The failure to regulate mortgage lending. Existing laws and regulations require lending institutions to follow prudent practices in making loans, assuring that borrowers have the capacity to be able to pay back the loans. And of course fraud—lying about the provisions of loans—is prohibited. Yet in an atmosphere where regulation was "out," regulators were simply not doing their jobs. The consequences are illustrated in a December 28, 2008, *New York Times* story on the failed Washington Mutual Bank. The article describes a supervisor at a mortgage processing center as having been "accustomed to seeing babysitters claiming salaries worthy of college presidents, and schoolteachers with incomes rivaling stockbrokers'. He rarely questioned them. A real estate frenzy was under way and WaMu, as his bank was known, was all about saying yes."

One may wonder why banks—or other lending institutions, mortgage firms, in particular—would make loans to people who were unlikely to be able to pay them back. The reason is that the lending institutions quickly combined such loans into packages (i.e., a security made up of several borrowers' obligations to pay) and sold them to other investors in a practice called "securitization."

Credit-default swaps. Perhaps the most egregious failure to regulate in recent years has been the emergence of credit-default swaps, which are connected to securitization. Because they were made up of obligations by a diverse set of borrowers, the packages of loans were supposedly low-risk investments. Yet those who purchased them still sought insurance against default. Insurance sellers, however, are regulated—required, for example, to keep a certain amount of capital on hand to cover possible claims. So the sellers of these insurance policies on packages of loans called the policies "credit-default swaps" and thus were allowed to avoid regulation. Further, these credit-default swaps, these insurance policies, themselves were bought and sold again and again in unregulated markets in a continuing process of speculation.

The credit-default swaps are a form of derivative, a financial asset the value of which is derived from some other asset—in this case the value of packages of mortgages for which they were the insurance policies. When the housing bubble began to collapse and people started to default on their mortgages, the value of credit-default swaps plummeted and their future value was impossible to determine. No one would buy them, and several banks that had speculated in these derivatives were left holding huge amounts of these "toxic assets."

Bubble and Bust

The combination of easy credit and the failure to regulate together fueled the housing bubble. People could buy expensive houses but make relatively low monthly payments. Without effective regulation of mortgage lending, they could get the loans even when they were unlikely to be able to make payments over the long run. Moreover, as these pressures pushed up housing prices, many people bought houses simply to resell them quickly at a higher price, in a process called "flipping." And such speculation pushed the prices up further. Between 2000 and 2006, housing prices rose by 90% (as consumer prices generally rose by only 17%).

While the housing boom was in full swing, both successful housing speculators and lots of people involved in the shenanigans of credit markets made a lot of money. However, as the housing bubble burst—as all bubbles do—things fell apart. The packages of loans lost value, and the insurance policies on them, the credit-default swaps, lost value. These then became "toxic" assets for those who held them, assets not only with reduced value but with unknown value. Not only did large financial firms—for example, Lehman Brothers and AIG—have billions of dollars in losses, but no one knew the worth of their remaining assets. The assets were called "toxic" because they poisoned the operations of the financial system. Under these circumstances, financial institutions stopped lending to one another—that is, the credit markets "froze up." The financial crisis was here.

The financial crisis, not surprisingly, very quickly shifted to a general economic crisis. Firms in the "real" economy rely heavily on a well-functioning financial system to supply them with the funds they need for their regular operations—loans to car buyers, loans to finance inventory, loans for construction of new facilities, loans for new equipment, and, of course, mortgage loans. Without those loans (or with the loans much more difficult to obtain), there has been a general cut-back in economic activity, what is becoming a serious and probably prolonged recession.

What Is to Be Done?

So here we are. The shifts in power, ideology, and income distribution have placed us in a rather nasty situation. There are some steps that will be taken that have a reasonable probability of yielding short-run improvement. In particular, a large increase in government spending—deficit spending—will probably reduce the depth and shorten the length of the recession. And the actions of the Federal Reserve and Treasury to inject funds into the financial system are likely, along with the deficit spending, to "un-freeze" credit markets (the mismanagement and, it seems, outright corruption of the bailout notwithstanding). Also, there is likely to be some re-regulation of the financial industry. These steps, however, at best will restore things to where they were before the crisis. They do not treat the underlying causes of the crisis—the vicious circle of power, ideology, and inequality.

Opportunity for Change

Fortunately, the crisis itself has weakened some aspects of this circle. The cry of "leave it to the market" is still heard, but is now more a basis for derision than a guide to policy. The ideology and, to a degree, the power behind the ideology, have been severely weakened as the role of "keeping the government out" has shown to be a major cause of the financial mess and our current hardships. There is now widespread support among the general populace and some support in Washington for greater regulation of the financial industry.

Whether or not the coming period will see this support translated into effective policy is of course an open question. Also an open question is how much the turn away from "leaving it to the market" can be extended to other sectors of the economy. With regard to the environment, there is already general acceptance of the principle that the government (indeed, many governments) must take an active role in regulating economic activity. Similar principles need to be recognized with regard to health care, education, housing, child care, and other support programs for low-income families.

The discrediting of "keep the government out" ideology provides an opening to develop new programs in these areas and to expand old programs. Furthermore, as the federal government revs up its "stimulus" program in the coming months, opportunities will exist for expanding support for these sorts of programs. This support is important, first of all, because these programs serve real, pressing needs—needs that have long existed and are becoming acute and more extensive in the current crisis.

Breaking the Circle

Support for these social programs, however, may also serve to break into the vicious power-ideology-inequality circle and begin transforming it into a virtuous circle. Social programs are inherently equalizing in two ways: they provide their benefits to low-income people and they provide some options for those people in their efforts to demand better work and higher pay. Also, the further these programs develop, the more they establish the legitimacy of a larger role for public control of—government involvement in—the economy; they tend to bring about an ideological shift. By effecting a positive distributional shift and by shifting ideology, the emergence of stronger social programs can have a wider impact on power. In other words, efforts to promote social programs are one place to start, an entry point to shift the vicious circle to a virtuous circle.

There are other entry points. Perhaps the most obvious ones are actions to strengthen the role of unions. The Employee Free Choice Act may be a useful first step, and it will be helpful to establish a more union-friendly Department of Labor and National Labor Relations Board. Raising the minimum wage—ideally indexing it to inflation—would also be highly desirable. While conditions have changed since the heyday of unions in the middle of the 20th century, and we cannot expect to restore the conditions of that era, a greater role for unions would seem essential in righting the structural conditions at the foundation of the current crisis.

Shifting Class Power

None of this is assured, of course. Simply starting social programs will not necessarily mean that they have the wider impacts that I am suggesting are possible. No one should think that by setting up some new programs and strengthening some existing ones we will be on a smooth road to economic and social change. Likewise, rebuilding the strength of unions will involve extensive struggle and will not be accomplished by a few legislative or executive actions.

Also, all efforts to involve the government in economic activity—whether in finance or environmental affairs, in health care or education, in work support or job training programs—will be met with the worn-out claims that government involvement generates bureaucracy, stifles initiative, and places an excessive burden on private firms and individuals. We are already hearing warnings that in dealing with the financial crisis the government must avoid "over-regulation." Likewise, efforts to strengthen unions will suffer the traditional attacks, as unions are portrayed as corrupt and their members privileged. The unfolding situation with regard to the auto firms' troubles has demonstrated the attack, as conservatives have blamed the United Auto Workers for the industry's woes and have demanded extensive concessions by the union.

Certainly not all regulation is good regulation. Aside from excessive bureaucratic controls, there is the phenomenon by which regulating agencies are often captives of the industries that they are supposed to regulate. And there are corrupt unions. These are real issues, but they should not be allowed to derail change.

The current economic crisis emerged in large part as a shift in the balance of class power in the United States, a shift that began in the early 1970s and continued into the new millennium. Perhaps the present moment offers an opportunity to shift things back in the other direction. Recognition of the complex nexus of causes of the current economic crisis provides some guidance where people might start. Rebuilding and extending social programs, strengthening unions, and other actions that contribute to a more egalitarian power shift will not solve all the problems of U.S. capitalism. They can, however, begin to move us in the right direction. ❑

Article 1.3

RECESSION, DEPRESSION, REPRESSION: WHAT'S IN A NAME?

BY JOHN MILLER
July/August 2009

A frightening financial panic, a virulent housing bust, and plummeting economic output have left global capitalism facing its worst crisis since the Great Depression.

Economies across the globe are in trouble. The European and Japanese economies shrank at double-digit rates in the first three months of this year; even China's growth rate is slowing precipitously. U.S. autoworkers, European and U.S. finance workers, Japanese electronics workers, Chinese garment workers, and Indian software workers are losing their jobs as their economies slow and world export markets dry up.

In the United States, where the crisis hit first, the downturn that began in December 2007 is now the longest since World War II, with the greatest job losses and, by some measures, the highest unemployment of the postwar period.

Housing prices, the fountainhead of the crisis, have now fallen more than they did during the housing bust of the Great Depression. Record levels of mortgage defaults and foreclosures have spread panic through a rickety global financial system. In a six-month span, three of the five largest U.S. investment banks disappeared. Leading U.S. mortgage company Countrywide bit the dust. Washington Mutual collapsed, the largest commercial bank failure in U.S. history.

The stock market has crashed as well. Stock prices fell to below one-half of their peak value in most indices, matching the initial declines in 1929.

In brief, the current contraction is no run-of-the-mill recession. But neither, at least at this point, is it comparable to the decade-long Great Depression, in which output fell by one-quarter and more than one-quarter of the U.S. workforce went without work.

So what is it? A recession or a depression? Truth is, economists make no precise distinction between the two other than that recessions are mild and depressions are more severe.

Even with their imprecision, neither term properly fits our current economic decline at this point, although it may yet become inarguably a depression. What term would fit? "The Great Recession," the name favored by former Fed chair Paul Volcker among others, is one candidate. "The Panic of 2008-2009" is another.

But better yet is "The Repression," a name suggested by University of Massachusetts economist Arthur MacEwan. Part recession, part depression, today's economic meltdown is very much a product of the large dose of economic repression that preceded it. Deregulatory, pro-rich, anti-labor public policy guaranteed that the benefits of economic growth, at least what we had of it this decade, went almost exclusively to the most well-to-do among us, leaving many vulnerable. The latest business cycle, both its expansion beginning in 2001 and its catastrophic downturn now underway, make those consequences clear for all to see. In a very real way, the

Repression of 2008 and 2009 has now pushed many people out of the frying pan and into the fire. And not only does the term "repression" describe the causes of the current crisis; it also points us toward its consequences, and toward prospective cures for today's economic woes.

The Frying Pan: The Expansion of 2001–07

Economic expansions are supposed to improve our life chances, not just swell the economy. For some time now, however, economic upswings have done less to improve the lot of most people than they used to.

During the first two decades after World War II, the U.S. economy grew rapidly, lifted incomes and wages, reduced inequality, and alleviated poverty. With its global dominance, the U.S. economy grew an average of 5.0% a year during the expansions between 1950 and 1969. Strong trade unions and expanding government programs helped to protect workers, fight poverty, and spread the benefits of economic growth widely, at least by today's standards.

No subsequent expansion has met those standards. But in this decade the capacity of economic growth to make most people better off all but evaporated. First off, the U.S. economy has grown more slowly in this decade than in any of the earlier postwar decades, even before accounting for the current crisis. Beginning in November 2001, the economy grew for 73 months or just over six years, reaching a peak in December 2007. That is longer than the 57-month average duration of postwar expansions. But GDP grew at an anemic annual rate of 2.5% in the 2001–07 expansion, far below the 4.3% average for postwar expansions. (See Table 1.)

Along with slower growth that failed to engage the productive capacity of the U.S. economy, successive economic expansions have created fewer and fewer jobs. In the last three business cycles, the economy has continued to lose jobs even after an economic recovery was underway. On top of that, recoveries have taken longer and longer to replace the jobs lost in the downturn. (See Table 2.)

TABLE 1: SIZING UP THE 2001–2007 EXPANSION

	2001–07 Expansion	Postwar Expansion
Length of Expansion	73 Months	57 Months
GDP Growth	2.5%	4.3%
Employment Gains	0.9%	2.5%
Wage and Salary Growth	1.8%	3.8%
Corporate Profits	10.8%	7.4%

Notes: GDP, employment, wages and salaries, and corporate profits are all measured as annual rates of change and corrected for inflation. The average for postwar expansions is calculated for the six expansions from 1961 to 2001.

Sources: Bureau of Economic Analysis, Bureau of Labor Statistics, and Federal Reserve Board.

**TABLE 2: JOB MARKET DECLINE AND RECOVERY
IN SIX POSTWAR RECESSIONS** (NUMBERS IN MONTHS)

Recession	Recession	Losses	Recovery
Nov. 1969 – Nov. 1970	12	14	19
Dec. 1973 – March 1975	16	16	25
Jan. 1980 – July 1980	6	6	11
July 1981 – Nov. 1982	16	19	29
July 1990 – March 1991	8	11	30
March 2001 – Nov. 2001	8	32	48

Source: Bureau of Labor Statistics.

In this decade, "the great American jobs machine" truly met its maker. Shockingly, the economy continued to lose jobs *for the first two and half years* of this last expansion. A full four years passed before the economy had added back the jobs lost during the 2001 recession, more than twice as long as in the average expansion since 1970.

The economic expansion from 2001 to the end of 2007 added jobs more slowly than any other expansion since World War II. The number of jobs in the economy increased by just 0.9% a year, about one-third of the 2.5% rate posted by the average postwar expansion.

Sluggish economic growth left employers with little need for new hires. Another drain on U.S. job creation was the increasing number of jobs lost to global outsourcing. Not only manufacturing jobs went abroad, but so did white collar work from backroom office operations (bookkeeping, customer service, and marketing) to engineering and computer software design.

All told, during the eight years of the George W. Bush administration, job growth averaged a meager 0.28% annually. That's just 378,000 new jobs a year, a total we would expect a growing economy to add in a single month.

Expansion and Repression

The sluggish economic growth of the first six years of this decade not only created fewer jobs than earlier postwar expansions, it also, not surprisingly, did less to lift incomes, alleviate poverty, or improve the economic well-being of all but the best-off. Those lopsided results are easily documented:

  • For the first time in the postwar period, median household income (corrected for inflation) at the peak of this expansion was still below its level at the previous peak in 2000.

- By 2007, 5.9 million more people were without health insurance than when the expansion began in 2001.

- For the first time in a postwar expansion, the poverty rate failed to decline. In 2007 at the peak of this expansion, the U.S. poverty rate stood at 12.5%, well above the 11.7% rate when the expansion began.

- After correcting for inflation, wages and salaries grew just 1.8% a year during this expansion, less than half the 3.8% rate during the average postwar expansion.

- At the same time, real corporate profits skyrocketed, increasing 10.8% a year, after adjusting for inflation, compared to the 8.3% average growth rate in other postwar growth periods.

Not surprisingly, inequality, which by 2001 was already unprecedented by postwar standards, continued to worsen during the decade. But just how much of the population missed out on the benefits of economic growth was astonishing. The average real income of the poorest 20% of households declined, but so did that of the best-off 20% of households. The incomes of the three quintiles in between stagnated; none grew by more than 1.1% over the entire period. Even the average income of the richest 5% declined during this expansion.

The top one percent of households, on the other hand, continued to make out like bandits. Their real income grew by 10.9% each year from 2002 to 2006, reports economist Emmanuel Saez using the most recent data available. That small sliver of the population monopolized 73% of the income growth during those years. In contrast, the bottom 99% of households saw their real incomes grow just 1.0% in each of those years.

As these figures make clear, the combination of sluggish economic growth, few new jobs, stagnant wages and incomes, and extreme inequality left many people behind long before the economy collapsed in 2008.

Bubbles Bursting

The economic collapse, however, began before 2008 with the bursting of the housing bubble. Despite spanning the 2001 recession, that ten-year bubble, from 1996 to 2006, drove up housing prices further and for longer than in any period since 1890. According to Yale economist Robert Shiller's long-term U.S. home price index, real (i.e., inflation-adjusted) housing prices increased an unprecedented 84.5% in that period.

Skyrocketing housing prices allowed homeowners to use their homes as ATMs, as economics journalist Doug Henwood first put it, taking out loans on the rising value of their houses. The volume of these so-called mortgage equity withdrawals more than doubled from 2000 to the peak of the housing bubble in 2005-6 and financed about one-third of the growth in consumption over those years.

U.S. housing prices are now down by more than one-quarter from their peak in late 2005. That is not only the sharpest decline of the postwar period, it is the biggest drop in housing prices since the 32.3% drop from 1914 to 1921—including the housing bust during the Great Depression. The collapse of housing prices put the kibosh on consumer spending, precipitated a crisis of mortgage defaults and foreclosures, and punched a hole in the financial system.

The crash of the stock market is unprecedented by postwar standards as well. By March 2, 2009, the Dow Jones Industrial Average of 30 blue-chip stocks had fallen 53.2% from its October 2007 peak. Broader stock indices, such as the Standard & Poor's 500, had registered even sharper declines. In comparison, the high-tech stock market crash earlier this decade had knocked 35.2% off the price of blue-chip stocks at its low point; the bear market of 1973, 42.2%. Only the Great Depression took more out of stock prices. At their low point in June 1932, stocks had lost a stunning 88.8% of their October 1929 value. While the stock market lately has shown some life, the turnaround in stock prices is unlikely to be rapid even if the stock market has already seen its bottom. It took 6 years, 9 years, and 25 years respectively for the stock market to replace the value lost in the 2001, 1973, and 1929 crashes.

The Fire: Increased Repression in 2007–09

Dismal labor market conditions were the cutting edge of the economic downturn proper. The economy began shedding jobs long before economic growth plummeted. Even the National Bureau of Economic Research (NBER), which determines the turning points of U.S. business cycles, took notice. In 2008 the economy lost jobs every month of the year for the first time since the Great Depression. The mounting monthly job losses convinced the NBER to declare the recession's start-date December 2007, even though at that point the economy had not yet suffered two consecutive quarters of negative economic growth—the standard definition of a recession.

In other words, in this downturn job losses are no lagging indicator. But don't expect employment to be a leading indicator of the recovery either. Job losses will almost certainly continue even after economic growth returns. Before things are

TABLE 3: THE DEPTH OF THE CURRENT DOWNTURN

	2007-09 Recession to Date	Average Postwar Recession
Length of Downturn	17 Months	10 Months
Economic Output Loss	-2.4 (1st five quarters)	-2.05%
Industrial Production	-13.6%	-4.0%
Retail Sales	-11.8%	-3.5%
Employment Losses	-4.1%	-2.1%

Notes: Economic output loss is the cumulative loss of output over a recession measured as the decline of GDP corrected for inflation. The industrial production index is again the cumulative decline in the index over the recession. Retail sales are measured as the total decline in retail sales corrected for inflation. Employment losses are measured as the drop in total employment over the recession. The averages for industrial production, retail sales, and employment losses are for the six recessions from 1969 to 2001. The GDP average is for 10 recessions from 1948 to 2001.

Sources: Bureau of Economic Analysis, Bureau of Labor Statistics, and Federal Reserve Board.

over, the labor market downturn and the suffering endured by all those looking for work will have persisted far longer than the contraction of economic output.

The U.S. economy is losing jobs as never before in the postwar period. Seventeen months into the downturn, the economy has lost more jobs than in any previous downturn and has lost nearly twice the share of its employment base as in the typical postwar recession. (See Table 3.) Construction, manufacturing of all sorts, and the financial industry, all male-dominated employments, have been especially hard hit. But even software giant Microsoft and major law firms are now laying off workers.

The fact that the 2001–2007 economic expansion created so few jobs heightens the effects of this extreme job loss. With few new jobs, especially full-time ones, workers' connection to the labor force is ever more tenuous. By the first quarter of 2009, marginally attached workers (those who want a job and have looked for work in the last year but not in the last month, hence are not counted as unemployed) formed a larger share of the labor force than in the 2001 recession. (Data are available only from 1994 on.) Also, the proportion of the labor force forced to work part-time because they could not find full-time jobs was higher than in any recession since 1970, including the severe 1974–75 and 1982 recessions. (Data are available from 1968 on.) By April 2009, forced part-time workers made up twice the share of the labor force as in the 2001 recession.

The failure of the 2001 expansion to lift incomes is also intensifying the suffering in this crisis. In the nearly decade-long expansion of the 1960s, the income of the median household, corrected for inflation, rose nearly 4% a year. But the 2001 to 2007 expansion added a measly 0.2% a year to real median incomes.

As income stagnated with increasingly repressive economic growth, households went deeper into debt. In the 1982 recession, 10.7% of U.S. households' disposable income went to service debt payments. In December 2007, at the onset of this downturn, that figure had reached 14.3%. It dipped slightly in 2008 as worried households began to cut back on their borrowing, but it is no longer dropping as mounting unemployment has pushed down households' disposable income.

This downturn has already gone on longer than even the two longest postwar downturns, in 1973–75 and 1981–1982, both of which lasted 16 months. Even if the economy begins to recover in the last quarter of 2009, the downturn would have lasted 22 months, more than twice as long as the 10-month average length of postwar recessions.

To date, the loss of output has not matched that in the worst postwar recessions. Through its first five quarters, inflation-adjusted GDP in the current downturn has fallen 2.4%—more than the average loss of output during all postwar recessions of 2.05% but less than the steeper declines in output during the 1974–75 and 1982 recessions. In the first half of 2008 the economy continued to grow slowly even as it shed jobs. Then the contraction began; output fell at annual rates of over 6% in the last quarter of 2008 and the first quarter of 2009. Even the most optimistic forecasts do not see a return to economic growth until the last quarter of 2009. By that time the loss of output over the last two years will surely have outdistanced that of any postwar downturn.

In specific sectors the current loss of output has already outdistanced all postwar recessions. Industrial production, which includes hard-hit manufacturers of automobiles, home electronics, and construction supplies, has fallen off at double-digit rates—more than three times its decline in the average postwar recession. Today's loss of industrial output has already matched the shredding of industry in the 1982 recession, the worst previous case (see Table 3).

Retail sales have been decimated as well. In the typical postwar recession, retail sales dropped off by about 3.5%, stabilizing within half a year after the onset of the downturn. But this time, retail sales have dropped 12.9% and are still falling. Circuit City, the electronics giant, closed its doors; Filene's Basement, the venerable department store, laid off workers; and even eBay, the internet retailer, issued pink slips.

Fighting Repression

The cure to the Repression is to fight repressive policies. Public policy must make the fight by promoting genuine full employment, legalizing card check union drives by passing the Employee Free Choice Act, enforcing labor laws already on the books by expanding the workplace inspection staff of the Department of Labor, and extending health insurance to all. Reducing payroll taxes, the bulk of most people's federal tax bill, will help, along with letting the Bush tax cuts targeted at the wealthy expire in 2010. Those policies would do much to enhance workers' bargaining power, lessen labor abuse, and arrest today's worsening inequality—or if you will, to undo repression.

Realizing those goals would take active and progressive government intervention into the labor markets and substantial funding for government programs that will put people to work repairing our decaying infrastructure and making it greener, restoring the social services cut out of state budgets in the crisis, and providing relief to those who have lost their homes or their jobs. And that spending would also get the economy going and counteract the Repression.

None of that will happen without massive public pressure. The Obama administration must not succumb to the calls of deficit hawks to slash government spending. Their do-nothing strategy, or worse yet more tax cuts for the wealthy, would saddle the federal government with even larger deficits as the economy and tax revenues fell through the floor. And unlike a program of progressive government spending, which holds the potential to spark a period of economic growth that could pay the public debt, a do-nothing strategy would likely lead us into a depression that would impose costs far more serious than a rise in government debt.

In addition, the Obama administration will need to impose strict controls on a financial industry to which it has close ties: one of its most senior economic advisors played a key role in deregulation. It will also have to convert its stress tests of troubled banks into a lever to take over any distressed bank, mortgage house, or insurer that is too big to fail and then run them as mutual savings banks for the benefit of the public.

Those steps will help to end the Repression by getting the economy going and to disable the drivers that have shaped economic growth so lopsidedly in favor of so few while repressing so many. Without them we will see either a return of the kind of economic growth that creates few jobs and does little to alleviate economic repression, or worst yet a decade-long period of economic stagnation and worsening economic suffering. ❑

Sources: Kelly Evans and Robert Guy Matthews, "Manufacturing Tumbles Globally," *Wall Street Journal*, Jan. 3, 2009; *Left Business Observer* #118, Dec. 22, 2008; Josh L. Bivens and John Irons, "A Feeble Recovery: The Fundamental Economic Weaknesses of the 2001-2007 Expansion," Economic Policy Institute Briefing Paper #214, May 1, 2008; Jon Hilsenrath and Kelly Evans, "Mixed Economic Data Show a Changing Business Cycle," *Wall Street Journal*, September 8, 2008; National Bureau of Economic Research, "Determination of the 2007 Peak in Economic Activity," December 11, 2008; John Schmitt and Dean Baker, "What We're In For: Projected Economic Impact of the Next Recession," Center for Economic and Policy Research, January 2008; Marcus Walker et al., "Global Slump Seen Deepening," *Wall Street Journal*, Jan. 1, 2009; Tom Lauricella and Annelena Lobb, "Stocks Hit '97 Level, Signaling Long Slump," *Wall Street Journal*, March 3, 2009; Sudeep Reedy, "Jobless Rate Hits 8.5%," *Wall Street Journal*, April 4, 2009; Charles Gascon, "The Current Recession: How Bad Is It?" Economic Synopsis No. 4, St. Louis Federal Reserve Bank, 2009; Kevin Klieson, "Recession or Depression," *Economic Synopsis* No. 15, St. Louis Federal Reserve Bank, 2009; Robert Shiller, "Online Data," at www.econ.yale.edu/~shiller/data.htm.

Article 1.4

THAT '70S CRISIS
What can the crisis of U.S. capitalism in the 1970s teach us about the current crisis and its possible outcomes?

BY ALEJANDRO REUSS
November/December 2009

A capitalist economy is like a very complex machine. It involves millions of individuals and capitalist firms, all making decisions that are not deliberately coordinated beforehand. The many gears of this machine do not automatically mesh. When some people decide to save part of their incomes, it does not automatically mean that they will find others who want to borrow and invest. When some people decide to invest, it does not automatically mean that they will find buyers for the goods produced as a result. Whether the gears of a capitalist economy mesh or not depends on the institutional framework in which capitalist companies operate. If the institutional framework does not work, and the gears do not mesh, the result is a crisis.

Radical political economists in the United States have termed the whole set of conditions and institutions that shape the process of capitalist profit-making, in a particular society at a particular time, a "social structure of accumulation." Capital accumulation, the process of capitalist companies making profits and re-investing them to expand their operations, is essential to capitalist economies. Capitalist firms that cannot turn a profit will not have an incentive to invest. If capitalist companies do not invest, factories will be shuttered and workers unemployed. Capitalist economies always go through boom-and-bust cycles, with recessions interrupting the process of capital accumulation and economic growth. Most of the time, these crises are shallow enough that "normal" economic growth resumes without major changes in framework institutions. However, severe crises, exposing serious defects in the existing "social structure of accumulation," may result in the overturn of the old framework and the establishment of a new one.

The most severe crises may actually threaten not only the established framework, but even the continued existence of the capitalist system itself. In the last century, there have been three periods of profound crisis in the framework institutions of U.S. capitalism: the Great Depression of the 1930s, the crisis of the 1970s, and the current crisis. Of these three, the Depression was the most profound, though it did not come close to threatening the capitalist system in the United States (it came much closer in other capitalist countries). Both the Depression and the crisis of the 1970s, however, resulted in major changes in the framework institutions of U.S. capitalism. The Depression ushered in an era in which the framework included a relatively large government role and powerful unions in the most important industries. This is sometimes known as the period of "regulated capitalism." The crisis of the 1970s ended this era and ushered in another, characterized by a new framework in which the government role diminished and unions were gravely weakened. This is sometimes known as the era of "neoliberal capitalism."

A retrospective look at the crisis of the 1970s—as a pivot between two different eras in the history of U.S. capitalism—is not just an exercise in nostalgia. Rather, it is an opportunity to try to extract lessons from the history of U.S. capitalism, including this and other crises, to apply to the current crisis and its possible outcomes.

The "Golden Age" of U.S. Capitalism

Mainstream ("neoclassical") economists often act as if capitalist economies operate according to unchanging universal laws, and that any violation of these "laws of the market" (such as government macroeconomic intervention, industrial regulation, social welfare spending, unions, etc.) inevitably spells disaster. The performance of the U.S. economy during the so-called "Golden Age," from the late 1940s to the early 1970s, belies this view.

Our first key lesson: *Capitalist economies can operate under a wide variety of institutional frameworks that foster capital accumulation and economic growth.*

By most conventional measures, the U.S. economy performed better during the "Golden Age" than during comparable periods in U.S. history, combining high rates of economic growth along with low rates of unemployment and inflation. From the late 1940s to the early 1970s, the U.S. economy grew at an average annual rate of nearly 4%. The annual unemployment rate only exceeded 6% twice in the 25 years between 1949 and 1973. The annual inflation rate, too, only topped 6% twice, and was actually under 2% for 14 of the 25 years in this period. The average hourly earnings of production workers increased at an average rate of over 2% per year.

During this period, the U.S. economy was less characterized by the "free market" policies favored by today's mainstream economists than during the periods before or since. A much broader consensus existed among economists and policymakers of the need for government intervention to stabilize the overall economy, prevent recessions, and maintain full employment. Government spending on consumption and investment (which excludes transfers) was somewhat higher (generally 21-23% of GDP) from the late 1950s to the early 1970s than it has been since (generally less than 21%, and less than 19% between the early 1990s and the current recession). Several major business sectors, including transportation, communications, utilities, and, most importantly, banking and insurance, were highly regulated. The regulation of the financial sector, in particular, was a response to the Depression and an attempt to reduce the financial instability that had helped precipitate it. Unions had a much larger and more secure place in the U.S. economy. The unionization rate peaked at over one-fourth of the labor force in the mid 1950s, and remained over 20% into the mid 1970s (for nonagricultural workers, it peaked at nearly 35% and remained over 25% into the mid 1970s).

The radical economists Samuel Bowles, David Gordon, and Thomas Weisskopf, in their influential book *Beyond the Waste Land*, identified three key pillars of the postwar social structure of accumulation, which they termed the "limited capital-labor accord," the "capitalist-citizen accord," and the "Pax Americana."

The limited capital-labor accord included the willingness of large employers to recognize unions and bargain collectively, and the unions' acceptance of management control over the production process in exchange for wage increases tied to productivity growth, health and retirement benefits, and job security. Radical econo-mists speak of a *limited* capital-labor accord since these arrangements excluded the majority of U.S. workers, who were not employed by large companies in the "core" industries (auto, steel, trucking, etc.). In addition, the idea of the accord should not be interpreted to mean that industrial conflict ended. Even in the core industries, employers only grudgingly accepted unions and, unable to destroy them by frontal assault, adopted strategies akin to low-intensity warfare.

The capitalist-citizen accord included the government commitment to prevent-ing mass unemployment and the establishment of the social welfare state. These were responses to the Great Depression and the upsurge in social protest during the 1930s, and helped moderate the levels of social protest in the late 1940s and 1950s. Again, the idea of an "accord" requires serious qualification. In the era before the main advances of the Civil Rights and women's liberation movements, most of the U.S. population was excluded from any accord. These grievances would give rise to the explosive social protests of the 1960s.

The "Pax Americana" refers to the dominant position of the United States in the capitalist world. In the early postwar period, the leading U.S. companies had little to fear from international competitors, then only beginning to emerge from the ruin of the Second World War. U.S. political and military power, meanwhile, helped secure sources of cheap raw materials and energy. The U.S. government propped up friendly dictators whom it could count on to "fight communism," maintain the security of U.S. companies' investments, and quash efforts at labor organization. When this strategy failed, as when socialist or nationalist governments came to power and threatened U.S. companies' property or access to cheap labor, the U.S. government engineered coups or intervened militarily.

Capitalists found plenty to complain about in the postwar social structure of accumulation, especially the large role of government and the relative strength of the labor movement. Government macroeconomic stabilization policies, the welfare state, and large powerful unions in the core industries, however, were part of an institutional framework that fostered capitalist profitability and economic growth. Government macroeconomic stabilization policies helped to prevent recessions, and the loss of sales and profits they entail. Social welfare programs, like unem-ployment insurance, acted as "automatic stabilizers" by moderating the decline in incomes and spending during recessions. The existence of unions and the steady increase in real wages helped to fuel booming demand for the products churned out by growing mass-production industries.

The Demise of the Golden Age

In the 1970s, the United States' position as the unchallenged colossus of the capi-talist world was suddenly threatened from multiple directions: rising international competition, spiking energy prices, declining productivity and profitability, and soaring inflation and unemployment. The United States' trade deficit crept up in the course of the 1960s, and government deficits emerged late in the decade and persisted through the 1970s. Declining international confidence in the dollar led to the deple-tion of U.S. government gold reserves, as international holders of dollars demanded redemption of their dollars for gold. (The Nixon administration responded by ending the fixed-rate convertibility of the dollar for gold.) Inflation picked up in the late 1960s, ratcheting up from about 3% in 1966 to nearly 6% in 1971. While these rates may not look that high now, they were alarming at the time, coming on the heels of a seven-year period in which the annual inflation rate never exceeded 1.6%. (Nixon responded to the threat of inflation with unprecedented peacetime wage and price controls.) In 1973-1974, the first of two major "oil shocks" increased the price of petroleum four-fold, dramatically raising energy costs for both consumers and businesses. Workers' wage demands outpaced the rate of productivity growth, driving up unit labor costs for businesses. The annual inflation rate spiked to over 10% in 1974 and again in each of the three years from 1979 to 1981. The annual unemployment rate topped 8% in 1975 and would reach nearly 10% in 1982.

The economy seemed trapped in the new nightmare of "stagflation," so called because it combined low economic growth and high unemployment ("stagnation") with high rates of inflation. Traditional macroeconomic policy tools seemed powerless to deal with this new beast. In the 1960s, the idea of a stable inverse relationship between unemployment (known as the "Phillips curve") became part of the economic-policy orthodoxy. If the unemployment rate was high, inflation was likely to be low, and vice versa. This "tradeoff" left policymakers with the means to combat unemployment or inflation when either appeared separately. When facing a recession, policymakers could lower interest rates, increase government spending, or lower taxes to stimulate demand and bring down the unemployment rate, at the cost of some increase in the inflation rate. When dealing with inflation, they could raise interest rates, lower spending, or raise taxes to reduce demand and "cool off" the economy, at the cost of some increase in unemployment. When high rates of inflation and unemployment appeared simultaneously, however, orthodox policy seemed to lack a solution.

What brought the "Golden Age" to such an inglorious end? The conditions that fostered successful capital accumulation and economic growth in the United States during the "Golden Age" broke down toward the end of this period. The postwar institutional framework, so successful in conventional terms for a quarter century, gave way to crisis not only because conditions changed around it, but because its own operation undermined its continued viability.

Our second key lesson: *As conditions change, an institutional framework that had fostered capital accumulation and economic growth may come to hinder them.*

All three pillars of the postwar framework were shaken during the 1960s and 1970s. Internationally, the United States no longer enjoyed uncontested economic, political, and military dominance over the capitalist world. The U.S. government had encouraged the reconstruction of the economies of Western Europe and Japan, both to undermine the appeal of communism in those countries and to demonstrate the superiority of capitalism to the rest of the world. The revival of manufacturing in Europe and Japan, however, also meant increased competition for U.S. firms in "core" manufacturing industries like steel and auto. Resistance to U.S. dominance in the global South, meanwhile, undermined U.S. companies' access to cheap materials and energy resources. The 1973 embargo of Western buyers by petroleum-producing countries and the ensuing oil-price hike coincided with a low point in the

United States' ability to project its military and political power internationally, just after the defeat of the U.S. military in Vietnam. "If instead of in 1973, OPEC had tried to raise prices and restrict production in 1953 or in 1963," radical economist Stephen A. Marglin argues, "American marines would almost certainly have been dispatched." In other words, under other political circumstances, the "oil crisis" of the 1970s would likely not have occurred.

Domestically, the so-called capitalist-citizen accord broke down in the politically explosive 1960s. Mass social movements—civil rights, women's liberation, anti-war, environmental—were part of this change. Increased pressure for social reform also gave rise to increased government regulation of private business. Under the old "economic" regulation, government agencies had overseen specific industries such as railroads, trucking, telecommunications, utilities, or banks. In contrast, the "new social regulation," including environmental, consumer-protection, occupational safety and health, and anti-discrimination laws, affected companies across all industries. Regulation was a way, in the late 1960s and early 1970s, for the government to respond to increasing demands for reform without increasing government spending (already surging for both domestic and war purposes). Capitalist corporations railed against the new regulations as imposing onerous new costs of doing business.

Meanwhile, the relatively low unemployment of the postwar period meant that, by the 1960s, most active workers had no direct experience (or ingrained fear) of mass unemployment. In the late 1960s, the unemployment rate actually dipped lower (below 4% for each of the four years from 1966 to 1969). Marglin argues that low unemployment, along with the cushion offered by the welfare state in the event of unemployment, resulted in a declining "cost of job-loss." Declining fear of unemployment emboldened workers to demand larger wage increases while reducing capitalists' authority on the shop floor, their ability to enforce a high pace of work, and therefore the rate of productivity growth. Radical economist James Crotty points to the combined effects of rising wages and declining productivity growth in driving large increases in labor costs per unit of output. Unit labor costs, constant in the first half of the 1960s, grew at nearly 2% per year from 1966 to 1967, and at over 6% per year from 1968 to 1969. These rising costs, in turn, ate into capitalists' profits—the "full employment profit squeeze."

It may seem strange that radical economists, whose sympathies lie with the working class, attribute the crisis to increasing wages and declining profits. They do not, however, mean to "blame" workers for the crisis. Rather, they are making two points:

First, unemployment is not just a sickness from which capitalist economies can be "cured," to the benefit of all concerned. Unemployment is one of the cogs that capitalist economies require to function. Going back to Karl Marx, radical economists have understood the importance of unemployment in ensuring the conditions for profitability in capitalist economies. Capitalists are more able to resist demands for wage increases (or even to impose wage cuts) if there are many unemployed people seeking work, and the employers can credibly threaten to replace current workers with unemployed job-seekers. Capitalists' ability to enforce a high pace of work also depends on the existence of substantial unemployment. The threat of firing, a key means for disciplining workers, is more credible if employers can easily replace fired workers and if workers losing their jobs would likely face a long and costly period of unemployment. Long periods of very low unemployment threaten capitalist profitability for both these reasons.

Second, profits are the lifeblood of capitalism. If capitalists do not expect to make a profit, they will not invest (purchase buildings, machinery, etc.) or hire workers. This is not to say that what is in the interests of capitalists (profits) is also in the interests of workers, except perhaps in the way one could say it is in the interest of an armed robber to get the victim's money and it is in the victim's interest to hand it over. Rather, it means that capitalists use their control of the means of production to extract a tribute, in the form of profit, from what the workers produce. The power of the capitalists over investment and employment in a capitalist economy means that, if the capitalists cannot extract their tribute, the rest of society will suffer.

The Capitalist Mobilization

The crisis of the 1970s marked the end of the "Golden Age" framework and the advent of "neoliberal" capitalism. The triumph of an economic policy agenda hostile to government economic intervention, social welfare programs, and labor organization was part of a broader shift to the right in U.S. politics. The right drew on currents in U.S. political culture pining for an imagined past of individual independence and blaming government regulation, taxation, and social programs for the perceived economic and moral decay of society. It tapped into and fueled a backlash against the civil rights and women's liberation movements. Conservatives channeled this rage into attacks on social programs and affirmative action. It also drew on the power of nationalism, and the identification of many ordinary people with the superpower status of the United States. It promised to reverse recent blows to the national self-image—the defeat in the Vietnam War, the rise of OPEC and the oil shocks, the Iranian Revolution and hostage crisis, the apparent loss of economic dominance to international competitors—and to restore the country to its rightful place of worldwide supremacy. These were the pillars of right-wing "populism" in the 1970s and 1980s, and to a great extent remain so today.

As important as this "populist" appeal was, however, the "right turn" in U.S. economic policy also had distinctly elite sources. Facing multiple threats during the crisis of the 1970s, capitalists (especially the very largest capitalist corporations) mobilized in extraordinarily effective ways to ensure that the crisis was resolved in a way that was favorable to their shared class interests.

There were three major prongs in the capitalist mobilization. First, they financed policy organizations (or "think tanks") which helped develop the conservative economic policy agenda. Capitalists channeled financial support to existing conservative think tanks, like the Hoover Institution and the American Enterprise Institute, which until then had limited resources and influence. They also supported new policy organizations, founded in the early 1970s, like the Institute for Contemporary Studies and the Heritage Foundation. This support helped vault both older and newer conservative think tanks to national prominence.

Second, they stepped up the scale and effectiveness of their lobbying efforts. Capitalists swelled the membership of existing business organizations, such as the U.S. Chamber of Commerce, and large corporations created a major new organization, the Business Roundtable. Founded in 1972 (merging two earlier organizations), the Business Roundtable brought together the largest U.S. industrial companies. By 1974, its 150 members included 60 of the largest 100 industrial companies in the United States and 90 of the largest 200. During the late 1960s and early 1970s, large corporations had been on the defensive, facing a rising tide of environmental, occupational safety and health, and consumer-protection regulation. By the late 1970s, two major pieces of reform legislation, a labor-law reform proposal backed by the AFL-CIO and a bill to establish a consumer-protection agency, went down in defeat, largely due to the business mobilization against them. As political scientist David Vogel put it, "business turned the tide" politically, even before the watershed 1980 election brought a slew of new conservatives to Congress and Reagan into the White House.

Third, they directed support to conservative candidates for public office. Capitalist corporations do not always direct campaign contributions only to candidates they perceive as ideologically "pro-business." Individual corporations also use campaign contributions to gain influence with elected officials and may contribute to candidates they do not regard as generally pro-business, but who they think are likely to win election and repay the favor of a campaign contribution. Companies in highly regulated industries and those highly dependent on government contracts are especially likely to engage in this kind of "pragmatic" campaign giving. By the 1978 election cycle, corporate political action committees began to shift away from pragmatic and toward ideological contributions. Rather than contribute to powerful incumbents large corporations increasingly directed their contributions to conservative challengers. This support helped shift the ideological composition of Congress in a "pro-business" direction, especially in the 1980 elections, and helped conservatives defend their gains in 1982.

The capitalist mobilization of the 1970s played a big role in bringing about a sea change in economic policy, sometimes known as the "right turn," beginning late in the decade and continuing with the "Reagan Revolution" in the 1980s:

The "full employment profit squeeze" ended in the late 1970s, when Federal Reserve Chair Paul Volcker, appointed by President Carter, engineered a dramatic increase in interest rates. This detonated a deep recession and pushed the average annual (official) unemployment rate near 10% in both 1982 and 1983. Massive unemployment was not an unintended consequence of this policy, but the chosen means to finally break the power of workers to push for wage demands. By the 1980s, power of the labor movement had been waning for years, and individual capitalist corporations had adopted an increasingly aggressive stance toward labor. This employer offensive intensified after Reagan broke the air-traffic controllers' strike in 1982, widely interpreted as a signal to capitalists of "open season" on unions. Union decline accelerated, and strikes (which had become virtually unwinnable in the new anti-union climate) dropped off dramatically.

For all their railing against the evils of "big government," conservatives did not slash federal expenditures during the 1980s. Rather, the priorities changed. Conservatives attacked social programs (though the "end of welfare as we know it" would have to wait for the 1990s and the Clinton administration) while the Reagan administration pursued an unprecedented peacetime military build-up. This spending spree was not only a boon to defense contractors, but also part of the administration's program of rebuilding U.S. military power globally.

Meanwhile, corporations and the rich enjoyed a bonanza of tax cuts, abetted by "supply side" economists who argued that high marginal tax rates were destroying incentives to work and invest. Tax reforms in 1981 and 1986 cut the marginal tax rate on the highest personal incomes from 70% to 34%, raised the threshold for the estate tax, and cut corporate income tax rates.

Both the Carter and Reagan administrations pursued the rollback of industry-specific regulation on sectors like telecommunications, transportation, and finance. The deregulation of finance was mostly accomplished in the early 1980s (leaving only regulatory separations, dating back to the Depression, between commercial banking, investment banking, stock brokering, and insurance, to be repealed under Clinton during the 1990s). The Reagan administration also had a strategy for defanging the "new social regulation," even when it could not repeal the regulatory legislation, by slashing funding and staffing of enforcement agencies.

The so-called Reagan Revolution was more than just a set of policies pursued by one administration. Reagan-era policies were not reversed—and in many ways were deepened—by subsequent administrations, Republican and Democratic. Like the New Deal in the 1930s, the Reagan era laid the groundwork of a new set of relatively stable framework institutions. The so-called neoliberal social structure of accumulation, monstrous though it was, functioned as a framework for capital accumulation and economic growth for nearly three decades. Now it has fallen into crisis.

Where to From Here?

When looking at history retrospectively, it is sometimes hard to remember that the outcome was not a foregone conclusion—that things did not have to turn out the way they did. That the postwar framework was "interventionist," however, does not automatically mean that its demise would give rise to a "free market" framework, as if economic policy swung like a pendulum between two fixed positions. Multiple policy proposals contended as possible ways out the 1970s crisis. Among these were proposals that would have *increased* the role of government in economic life: "incomes policy" (in which the government plays a much larger role in determining the distribution of income between labor and capital at a national level, as in many Western European social democracies) and "industrial policy" (in which the government plays a much larger role in directing investment to particular sectors of the economy, an idea given traction in the 1970s and 1980s by the success of Japan with such policies). The triumph of "neoliberal" capitalism in the wake of the 1970s crisis was not inevitable.

Our third key lesson: *The outcome of a crisis is not preordained by the characteristics of the preexisting framework or the details of the crisis itself, but determined by the balance of power among different social groups with conflicting interests.*

This last lesson is, perhaps, the most important in understanding the current economic crisis and its possible outcomes. Consider the last two profound crises of the U.S. economy, the Great Depression and the crisis of the 1970s. In the United

States, the Depression resulted in a major upsurge in union organizing. Major industries like automobiles, steel, and long-haul trucking were organized for the first time. The national unionization rate more than tripled—from less than 7% to nearly 24% of the labor force between 1930 and 1947. This upsurge from below both benefited from and helped to force policy changes from above, including the creation of the modern welfare state. In other countries, where the balance of forces was different, the consequences of the Depression were different—including, of course, the rise of Nazism. During the crisis of the 1970s, capitalists, especially the largest capitalist corporations, mobilized with extraordinary effectiveness and used the crisis to help bring about policy changes they wanted. Again, the outcomes were not the same in all countries. The neoliberal policy agenda that took hold in the United States and the United Kingdom has not gone nearly so far in other rich capitalist countries.

The current crisis has created a "fluid" situation in economic policy. In response to the current recession, the most severe for the United States since the 1930s, the federal government has adopted "counter-cyclical" (anti-recession) policies that mainstream economists claimed were neither necessary nor desirable. It has extended large bailouts to private companies, mostly to financial institutions, though also to the ailing auto industry that was once the crown jewel of U.S. capitalism. The crisis has given rise to calls for new financial regulation, which would begin to reverse the de-regulating trends of the last thirty years. Major new regulation or reforms to the energy and health-insurance sectors are also possible. Some of these measures have met with sharp opposition, both from big capitalist corporations (e.g., health-insurance companies) and from reactionary populist movements. There has been little or no indication, however, of any resurgence in labor organizing or any mass mobilization in favor of new regulation, an expanded social-welfare state, a shift in labor-relations policy back in favor of workers, or other reforms, to say nothing of a more radical social agenda.

Few people outside the rabid right believe that capitalism faces imminent abolition in the United States. For those of us who would like to see the capitalist system replaced with a society based on workers' control of their own workplaces, democratic control over the economy-wide allocation of resources, guaranteed access to basic goods (like adequate nutrition, shelter, health care, and education) as human rights, and a generally egalitarian distribution of wealth—to use the fashionable term, "socialism"—the outcomes of the present crisis are, nonetheless, a matter of great importance. The directions taken in economic policy at critical junctures in history can have a big effect on the conditions of life for millions of people and the conditions of political struggle for decades to come. These outcomes are unlikely to be positive without a resurgence of social movements—the labor movement and others—to counter the power of large corporations and right-wing populism.

If new movements do emerge, they should not become the foot soldiers of a particular government administration or political party (as, unfortunately, the union movement became for the Democratic Party after the New Deal). Independent grassroots movements might support some reform proposals from a particular party or administration, pressure for others to go further than its sponsors would want, and oppose still others. They could develop reform proposals of their own, to challenge not just this or that economic policy, but the foundations of the capitalist system itself. They could spawn not only new organizations in workplaces and communities, but also new political parties, unbeholden to capitalist patrons. These are ways to fight for and win positive reforms, to be sure, but also, more importantly, to rebuild the fighting capacity of movements for radical social change. ❏

Sources: David M. Kotz, Terrence McDonough, and Michael Reich, *Social Structures of Accumulation: The Political Economy of Growth and Crisis*, Cambridge University Press, 1994; Stephen A. Marglin and Juliet B. Schor, *The Golden Age of Capitalism: Reinterpreting the Postwar Experience*, Clarendon Press, 1990; Bureau of Economic Analysis, National Economic Analysis, Current Dollar and Real GDP, www.bea.gov; Bureau of Labor Statistics, Labor Force Statistics from the Current Population Survey, Annual Averages, Unemployment Rate, Historical Data, www.bls. gov; Samuel Bowles, David Gordon, and Thomas Weisskopf, *Beyond the Waste Land: A Democratic Alternative to Economic Decline*, Anchor Press/Doubleday, 1983; Michael Goldfield, The Decline of Organized Labor in the United States, University of Chicago Press, 1987; David Vogel, *Fluctuating Fortunes: The Political Power of Business in America*, Basic Books, 1989; James Crotty, "Review: *Turbulence in the World Economy*, by Robert Brenner," *Challenge*, Vol. 42, No. 3, 1999; Dan Clawson and Mary Ann Clawson, "Reagan or Business: Foundations of the New Conservatism," in Michael Schwartz (ed.), *The Business Elite as a Ruling Class*, Holmes and Meier, 1987; Joseph G. Peschek, *Policy-Planning Organizations: Elite Agendas and America's Rightward Turn*, Temple University Press, 1987; Val Burris and Games Salt, "The Politics of Capitalist Class Segments: A Test of Corporate Liberalism Theory," *Social Problems*, Vol. 37 No. 3, 1990; United States Department of the Treasury, "History of the U.S. Tax System," www.treas.gov; Tax Foundation, "U.S. Federal Individual Income Tax Rates History, 1913-2009" www.taxfoundation.org; Internal Revenue Service, "Corporation Income Tax Brackets and Rates, 1909-2002," www.irs.gov.

Article 1.5

CRISIS AND NEOLIBERAL CAPITALISM

BY DAVID KOTZ
November/December 2008

The Financial Crisis and the Real Economy

It is impossible to predict the course of the financial crisis. The effects of the crisis on the real economy could be very large, especially if it engulfs more and more of the financial sector. But even if the financial crisis is contained, the bursting of the housing bubble—which began in 2007 and is bound to continue for some time—will have a powerful downward impact on the economy.

A speculative "bubble" arose in the housing sector of the U.S. economy starting around 2002. By the summer of 2007, housing prices had risen by 70% since 1995 corrected for inflation. Yet since 2002 the real value of home rents had been flat. By 2006 the ratio of the Housing Price Index to the Homeowners Equivalent Rent had risen sharply to an all-time high of 168.3, compared to 110.0 in 1995. This is clear evidence of a huge asset bubble in the U.S. housing market. This bubble created an estimated $8 trillion in inflated new wealth, which was about 38% of the peak total housing wealth of $21 trillion. When this bubble started to collapse in 2007, it set the stage for both a financial crisis and a recession in the "real" economy.

There are two ways in which the collapsing housing bubble affects the real economy. First, there is a downward wealth effect on housing investment and consumer spending. The collapse of the bubble in the housing sector has led to a sharp drop in residential investment. Since the second quarter of 2007, it has been falling at 21.6% annual rate. Second, falling home values are causing a reduction in consumer spending. Since 2002 households had been borrowing against their homes to get funds for consumer spending. One study estimated that during 2004-06 Americans took $840 billion per year from their home equity through borrowing and capital gains from the sale of housing. This was almost 10% of disposable personal income in the United States.

Suddenly, in 2007, people could no longer supplement their income with funds borrowed against their home, which has now led to a large drop in consumer spending, at a 3.1% per year rate in the third quarter of 2008. This happened *before* the financial crisis had begun to affect consumer spending. If all of the estimated $8 trillion of inflated home value disappears, the estimated effect on aggregate consumption would be a reduction of about $320 billion to $480 billion per year, or about 5% of total consumption. Dean Baker, co-director of the Center for Economic and Policy Research and a respected analyst of the financial crisis, estimated the total effect of the collapsing housing bubble to be a decline of between 3.1% and 7.0% of GDP.

The collapse of the bubble also affects investment in new plant and equipment by business. After several quarters of little growth, business investment fell at a 1%

annual rate in the first quarter of 2008. The bubble-propelled and debt-financed expansions of 1991-2000 and 2001-2007 produced a growing amount of productive capacity, relative to ordinary income. As the current crash develops, industry will find it has substantial excess productive capacity. As a result, the incentive for business investment may be depressed for some time. In the last recession in the United States, in 2001, business fixed investment fell for two consecutive years, at an accelerating rate, for this reason.

A severe recession was averted in 2001–2002 by the start of the housing bubble. It does not seem possible for a new bubble to arise and avert a serious recession this time. Also, the financial crisis is likely to make the coming recession more severe. One way this happens is that banks' reluctance to lend to business due to the financial crisis will worsen the recession. Secondly, the stock market collapse precipitated by the financial crisis will have effects similar to the effects of the housing price collapse—it will tend to reduce consumer and investment demand. The only bright spot for the U.S. economy has been exports, but they are not likely to continue to do well in the face of a spreading global recession.

The Restructuring Is Just Beginning

Every form of capitalism has contradictions that eventually bring about a structural crisis of that form of capitalism. In the 1970s the system of state-regulated capitalism, having produced rapid growth and high profits for a few decades, stopped working effectively and went into structural crisis. The predominant form of capitalism changed to the "neoliberal" form, which means a type of capitalism in which the state plays a limited role in the economy, particularly withdrawing from activities that benefit ordinary people. It now appears that neoliberal capitalism can no longer overcome two key problems and is entering a structural crisis of its own. First, the high and rising inequality it generates means that the majority has insufficient income to buy the growing output of the economy without relying on an unsustainable buildup of household debt. Second, the deregulated financial system of neoliberal capitalism is inherently unstable, as we have so clearly seen in recent months.

From 1945 to 1973, a regulated form of capitalism predominated in the world, including in the United States. Regulated capitalism here included extensive government regulation of business and finance, regulation of the macroeconomy (aimed partly at achieving a relatively low unemployment rate), social programs that amounted to a modest welfare state, relatively cooperative relations between big business and trade unions, restrained competition between big corporations, and trade and capital flows regulated by governments and international institutions.

The shift to neoliberal capitalism in the United States involved the deregulation of business and finance, the reduction of active government macroeconomic policy (and a shift of aim to assuring low inflation, not low unemployment), sharply reduced social programs, a big business and government attack against labor unions, unrestrained ("cutthroat") competition among large corporations, and relatively free movement of goods, services, and capital across national boundaries. This neoliberal transformation of capitalism was relatively thorough in the United

States, the United Kingdom, and in international financial institutions such as the International Monetary Fund and World Bank.

As neoliberal capitalism enters a period of crisis, we can see the rapid loss of legitimacy of the previously reigning dominant "free market" ideology. This is similar to the sudden demise of the previously dominant Keynesian ideology of regulated capitalism in the 1970s. Capitalism is going to be restructured, in the United States and globally, during the coming years. The outcome of this restructuring process, however, is not pre-determined.

So far the bankers have led the initial stage of restructuring. Treasury Secretary Henry Paulson, the former CEO of Wall Street giant Goldman Sachs, has been succeeding so far in getting the government to rescue the banks in ways that mainly benefit the bankers. This process has encouraged rapidly growing concentration of the financial sector, as the largest banks merge with one another and get big cash infusions and new federal backing.

However, the restructuring is just beginning. We can fight for changes that would benefit the majority rather than the bankers. First, the underlying reason for the financial crisis is all those people unable to make the payments on their mortgages. The government should pass an emergency measure to ease mortgage terms to reflect the declining values of homes and the declining economy. This would impose a one-time loss on the financial institutions that invested in the risky new mortgage-based securities, but it would also make it easier to know the value of the mortgage-backed securities, eliminating a source of great uncertainty in the financial system.

Second, millions of people have learned the important lesson that banks and other financial institutions are not ordinary private companies. If General Mills loses money, or even goes bankrupt, it harms its shareholders and workers—but its competitors gain. But if a few major banks lose money and are in danger of going under, this threatens the entire financial system, and with it the economy as a whole.

The obvious conclusion is that the financial sector cannot be operated on a profit and loss basis. Instead, it should become part of the public sector, operated to serve the public interest. If banks, which are granted the power to create our money supply, and whose credit is essential to the welfare of the entire public, were made public institutions, then public policy aims could guide their actions. They could be directed to stay away from speculative activities and instead make loans for socially valuable purposes. This would include steering credit into renewable energy technologies, fuel-efficient vehicles, low cost housing, and other good purposes. An advantage of public ownership of the banks over another cycle of government regulation of private banks is that reregulated private banks would simply press for the elimination of the regulations—as they did successfully starting in the early 1980s.

The developing financial and economic crises have exposed the high-flying financial operators for what they always were—thieves who got rich without doing anything productive. This has also exposed their fallacious free-market ideology. This is a promising time to build popular movements that can fight for progressive changes in our economy. ❏

Article 1.6

CAPITALISM HITS THE FAN

BY RICHARD D. WOLFF
November/December 2008

Let me begin by saying what I think this crisis is not. It is not a *financial* crisis. It is a systemic crisis whose first serious symptom happened to be finance. But this crisis has its economic roots and its effects in manufacturing, services, and, to be sure, finance. It grows out of the relation of wages to profits across the economy. It has profound social roots in America's households and families and political roots in government policies. The current crisis did not start with finance, and it won't end with finance.

From 1820 to around 1970, 150 years, the average productivity of American workers went up each year. Average workers produced more stuff every year than they had the year before. They were trained better, they had more machines, and they had better machines. So productivity went up every year.

And, over this period of time, the wages of American workers rose every decade. Every decade, real wages—the amount of money you get in relation to the prices you pay for the things you use your money for—were higher than the decade before. Profits also went up.

The American working class enjoyed 150 years of rising consumption, so it's not surprising that it would choose to define its own self-worth, measure its own success in life, according to the standard of consumption. Americans began to think of themselves as successful if they lived in the right neighborhood, drove the right car, wore the right outfit, went on the right vacation.

But in the 1970s, the world changed for the American working class in ways that it hasn't come to terms with—at all. Real wages stopped going up. As U.S. corporations moved operations abroad to take advantage of lower wages and higher profits and as they replaced workers with machines (and especially computers), those who lost their jobs were soon willing to work even if their wages stopped rising. So real wages trended down a little bit. The real hourly wage of a worker in the 1970s was higher than what it is today. What you get for an hour of work, in goods and services, is less now that what your parents got.

Meanwhile, productivity kept going up. If what the employer gets from each worker keeps going up, but what you give to each worker does not, then the difference becomes bigger, and bigger, and bigger. Employers' profits have gone wild, and all the people who get their fingers on employers' profits—the professionals who sing the songs they like to hear, the shareholders who get a piece of the action on each company's profits—have enjoyed a bonanza over the last thirty years.

The only thing more profitable than simply making the money off the worker is handling this exploding bundle of profits—packaging and repackaging it, lending it and borrowing it, and inventing new mechanisms for doing all that. That's called the finance industry, and they have stumbled all over themselves to get a hold of a piece of this immense pot of profit.

What did the working class do? What happens to a population committed to measuring people's success by the amount of consumption they could afford when the means they had always had to achieve it, rising wages, stop? They can go through a trauma right then and there: "We can't anymore—it's over." Most people didn't do that. They found other ways.

Americans undertook more work. People took a second or third job. The number of hours per year worked by the average American worker has risen by about 20% since the 1970s. By comparison, in Germany, France, and Italy, the number of hours worked per year per worker has dropped 20%. American workers began to work to a level of exhaustion. They sent more family members—and especially women—out to work. This enlarged supply of workers meant that employers could find plenty of employees without having to offer higher pay. Yet, with more family members out working, new kinds of costs and problems hit American families. The woman who goes out to work needs new outfits. In our society, she probably needs another car. With women exhausted from jobs outside and continued work demands inside households, with families stressed by exhaustion and mounting bills, interpersonal tensions mounted and brought new costs: child care, psychotherapy, drugs. Such extra costs neutralized the extra income, so it did not solve the problem.

The American working class had to do a second thing to keep its consumption levels rising. It went on the greatest binge of borrowing in the history of any working class in any country at any time. Members of the business community began to realize that they had a fantastic double opportunity. They could get the profits from flat wages and rising productivity, and then they could turn to the working class traumatized by the inability to have rising consumption, and give them the means to consume more. So instead of paying your workers a wage, you're going to lend them the money—so they have to pay it back to you! With interest!

That solved the problem. For a while, employers could pay the workers the same or less, and instead of creating the usual problems for capitalism—workers without enough income to buy all the output their increased productivity yields—rising worker debt seemed magical. Workers could consume ever more; profits exploding in every category. Underneath the magic, however, there were workers who were completely exhausted, whose families were falling apart, and who were now ridden with anxiety because their rising debts were unsustainable. This was a system built to fail, to reach its end when the combination of physical exhaustion and emotional anxiety from the debt made people unable to continue. Those people are, by the millions, walking away from those obligations, and the house of cards comes down.

If you put together (a) the desperation of the American working class and (b) the efforts of the finance industry to scrounge out every conceivable borrower, the idea that the banks would end up lending money to people who couldn't pay it back is not a tough call. The system, however, was premised on the idea that that would not happen, and when it happened nobody was prepared.

The conservatives these days are in a tough spot. The story about how markets and private enterprise interact to produce wonderful outcomes is, even for them these days, a cause for gagging. Of course, ever resourceful, there are conservatives who will rise to the occasion, sort of like dead fish. They rattle off twenty things the government did over the last twenty years, which indeed it did, and draw a line from those things the government did to this disaster now, to reach the conclusion that the reason we have this problem now is too much government intervention. These days they get nowhere. Even the mainstream press has a hard time with this stuff.

What about the liberals and many leftists too? They seem to favor regulation. They think the problem was that the banks weren't regulated, that credit-rating companies weren't regulated, that the Federal Reserve didn't regulate better, or differently, or more, or something. Salaries should be regulated to not be so high. Greed should be regulated. I find this astonishing and depressing.

In the 1930s, the last time we had capitalism hitting the fan in this way, we produced a lot of regulation. Social Security didn't exist before then. Unemployment insurance didn't exist before then. Banks were told: you can do this, but you can't do that. Insurance companies were told: you can do that, but you can't do this. They limited what the board of directors of a corporation could do ten ways to Sunday. They taxed them. They did all sorts of things that annoyed, bothered, and troubled boards of directors because the regulations impeded the boards' efforts to grow their companies and make money for the shareholders who elected them.

You don't need to be a great genius to understand that the boards of directors encumbered by all these regulations would have a very strong incentive to evade them, to undermine them, and, if possible, to get rid of them. Indeed, the boards went to work on that project as soon as the regulations were passed. The crucial fact about the regulations imposed on business in the 1930s is that they did not take away from the boards of directors the freedom or the incentives or the opportunities to undo all the regulations and reforms. The regulations left in place an institution devoted to their undoing. But that wasn't the worst of it. They also left in place boards of directors who, as the first appropriators of all the profits, had the *resources* to undo the regulations. This peculiar system of regulation had a built-in self-destruct button.

Over the last thirty years, the boards of directors of the United States' larger corporations have used their profits to buy the president and the Congress, to buy the public media, and to wage a systematic campaign, from 1945 to 1975, to evade the regulations, and, after 1975, to get rid of them. And it worked. That's why we're here now. And if you impose another set of regulations along the lines liberals propose, not only are you going to have the same history, but you're going to have the same history faster. The right wing in America, the business community, has spent the last fifty years perfecting every technique that is known to turn the population against regulation. And they're going to go right to work to do it again, and they'll do it better, and they'll do it faster.

So what do we do? Let's regulate, by all means. Let's try to make a reasonable economic system that doesn't allow the grotesque abuses we've seen in recent decades. But let's not reproduce the self-destruct button. This time the change has to include the following: The people in every enterprise who do the work of that enterprise will become collectively their own board of directors. For the first time in American history, the people who depend on the survival of those regulations will be in the position of receiving the profits of their own work and using them to make the regulations succeed rather than sabotaging them.

This proposal for workers to collectively become their own board of directors also democratizes the enterprise. The people who work in an enterprise, the front line of those who have to live with what it does, where it goes, how it uses its wealth, they should be the people who have influence over the decisions it makes. That's democracy.

Maybe we could even extend this argument to democracy in our political life, which leaves a little to be desired—some people call it a "formal" democracy, that isn't real. Maybe the problem all along has been that you can't have a real democracy politically if you don't have a real democracy underpinning it economically. If the workers are not in charge of their work situations, five days a week, 9 to 5, the major time of their adult lives, then how much aptitude and how much appetite are they going to have to control their political life? Maybe we need the democracy of economics, not just to prevent the regulations from being undone, but also to realize the political objectives of democracy. ❏

Article 1.7

WE'RE ALL MINSKYITES NOW

BY ROBERT POLLIN
November 2008, The Nation

As the most severe financial crisis since the 1930s Depression has unfolded over the past 18 months, the ideas of the late economist Hyman Minsky have suddenly come into fashion. In the summer of 2007, the *Wall Street Journal* ran a front-page article describing the emerging crisis as the financial market's "Minsky moment." His ideas have since been featured in the *Financial Times, BusinessWeek* and *The New Yorker,* among many other outlets. Minsky, who spent most of his academic career at Washington University in St. Louis and remained professionally active until his death, in 1996, deserves the recognition. He was his generation's most insightful analyst of financial markets and the causes of financial crises.

Even so, most mainstream economists have shunned his work because it emerged out of a dissident left Keynesian tradition known in economists' circles as post-Keynesianism. Minsky's writings, and the post-Keynesian tradition more generally, are highly critical of free-market capitalism and its defenders in the economics profession—among them Milton Friedman and other Nobel Prize-winning economists who for a generation have claimed to "prove," usually through elaborate mathematical models, that unregulated markets are inherently rational, stable and fair. For Friedmanites, regulations are harmful most of the time.

Minsky, by contrast, explained throughout his voluminous writings that unregulated markets will always produce instability and crises. He alternately termed his approach "the financial instability hypothesis" and "the Wall Street paradigm."

For Minsky, the key to understanding financial instability is to trace the shifts that occur in investors' psychology as the economy moves out of a period of crisis and recession (or depression) and into a phase of rising profits and growth. Coming out of a crisis, investors will tend to be cautious, since many of them will have been clobbered during the just-ended recession. For example, they will hold large cash reserves as a cushion to protect against future crises.

But as the economy emerges from its slump and profits rise, investors' expectations become increasingly positive. They become eager to pursue risky ideas such as securitized subprime mortgage loans. They also become more willing to let their cash reserves dwindle, since idle cash earns no profits, while purchasing speculative vehicles like subprime mortgage securities that can produce returns of 10% or higher.

But these moves also mean that investors are weakening their defenses against the next downturn. This is why, in Minsky's view, economic upswings, proceeding without regulations, inevitably encourage speculative excesses in which financial bubbles emerge. Minsky explained that in an unregulated environment, the only way to stop bubbles is to let them burst. Financial markets then fall into a crisis, and a recession or depression ensues.

Here we reach one of Minsky's crucial insights—that financial crises and recessions actually serve a purpose in the operations of a free-market economy, even while they wreak havoc with people's lives, including those of tens of millions of innocents who never invest a dime on Wall Street. Minsky's point is that without crises, a free-market economy has no way of discouraging investors' natural proclivities toward ever greater risks in pursuit of ever higher profits.

However, in the wake of the calamitous Great Depression, Keynesian economists tried to design measures that could supplant financial crises as the system's "natural" regulator. This was the context in which the post-World War II system of big-government capitalism was created. The package included two basic elements: regulations designed to limit speculation and channel financial resources into socially useful investments, such as single-family housing; and government bailout operations to prevent 1930s-style depressions when crises broke out anyway.

Minsky argues that the system of regulations and the bailout operations were largely successful. That is why from the end of World War II to the mid-1970s, markets here and abroad were much more stable than in any previous historical period. But even during the New Deal years, financial market titans were fighting vehemently to eliminate, or at least defang, the regulations. By the 1970s, almost all politicians—Democrats and Republicans alike—had become compliant. The regulations were initially weakened, then abolished altogether, under the strong guidance of, among others, Federal Reserve chair Alan Greenspan, Republican Senator Phil Gramm and Clinton Treasury Secretary Robert Rubin.

For Minsky, the consequences were predictable. Consider the scorecard over the twenty years before the current disaster: a stock market crash in 1987; the savings-and-loan crisis and bailout in 1989-90; the "emerging markets" crisis of 1997-98—which brought down, among others, Long-Term Capital Management, the super-hedge fund led by two Nobel laureates specializing in finance—and the bursting of the dot-com market bubble in 2001. Each of these crises could easily have produced a 1930s-style collapse in the absence of full-scale government bailout operations.

Here we come to another of Minsky's major insights—that in the absence of a complementary regulatory system, the effectiveness of bailouts will diminish over time. This is because bailouts, just like financial crises, are double-edged. They prevent depressions, but they also limit the costs to speculators of their financial excesses. As soon as the next economic expansion begins gathering strength, speculators will therefore pursue profit opportunities more or less as they had during the previous cycle. This is the pattern that has brought us to our current situation—a massive global crisis, being countered by an equally massive bailout of thus far limited effectiveness.

Minsky's Wall Street paradigm did not address all the afflictions of free-market capitalism. In particular, his model neglects the problems that arise from the vast disparities of income, wealth and power that are just as endemic to free-market capitalism as are its tendencies toward financial instability, even though he fully recognized that these problems exist.

Yet Minsky's approach still provides the most powerful lens for understanding the roots of financial instability and developing an effective regulatory system.

Minsky understood that his advocacy of comprehensive financial regulations made no sense whatsoever within the prevailing professional orthodoxy of free-market cheerleading. In his 1986 magnum opus, *Stabilizing an Unstable Economy*, he concluded that "the policy failures since the mid-1960s are related to the banality of orthodox economic analysis ... Only an economics that is critical of capitalism can be a guide to successful policy for capitalism." ❑

Article 1.8

THE "CREDIT TSUNAMI"
Explaining the inexplicable with debt and deleveraging.

BY STEVE KEEN
September 2009

In his October 2008 testimony to the House Committee on Oversight and Government Reform, Alan Greenspan described the financial crisis as a "once-in-a-century credit tsunami." Like most of his utterances while chairman of the Federal Reserve, the phrase is pungent, evocative—and utterly misleading.

Though geologists understand the cause of a tsunami—a large undersea earthquake triggered by movements in the earth's tectonic plates—they also know that its timing is inherently unpredictable, and nothing can be done to prevent one. Once a tsunami has occurred, the forces that caused it are dissipated, and another may well take a century to develop.

The global financial crisis is an entirely different kind of beast. First, unlike a tsunami, the force that gave rise to the crisis—excessive private debt—is still with us. If not addressed by deliberate policy, it will plunge the U.S. economy into a "lost decade" that will be far more painful than that which crippled Japan in the 1990s.

Second, geologists understand what causes tsunamis. As Greenspan's convoluted words nonetheless make clear, he and most economists do not understand why the global financial crisis occurred:

> To exist, you need an ideology. The question is, whether it … is accurate or not. What I am saying to you is, yes, I found a flaw … in the model that I perceived is the critical functioning structure that defines how the world works, so to speak.

Third, though geologists understand tsunamis, they do not cause them. In contrast, the policies implemented by neoclassical economists like Greenspan, former Treasury Secretary Larry Summers, and current Fed chair Ben Bernanke in the last two decades made this crisis at least twice as severe as it would otherwise have been. Completely oblivious to the dangers, these powerful official economists—and the vast majority of their colleagues in academia—encouraged a debt-financed speculative bubble in asset prices that financed 20 years of illusory prosperity but was doomed to burst and usher in a sustained economic downturn.

The Economy that Leverage Built

I am one of the handful of economists who did predict the crisis, as listed by Dutch economist Dirk Bezemer. Bezemer noted that though we came from varied ideological backgrounds (to use Greenspan's phrase), we shared four concerns: "with financial assets as distinct from real-sector assets, with the credit flows that finance both forms of wealth, with the debt growth accompanying growth in financial wealth, and with the accounting relation between the financial and real economy."

My own analysis uses a theory of monetary dynamics known as "circuit theory" to extend the financial instability hypothesis developed by economist Hyman Minsky in the 1960s. Both played a key role in helping me identify that a crisis was imminent. From Minsky I focus on the debt-to-GDP ratio as the key indicator of financial fragility, while circuit theory helped me to develop a purely monetary model of the economy in which changes in debt play a crucial role in determining the level of aggregate demand.

The debt-to-GDP ratio—which effectively shows how many years it would take to reduce debt to zero if all of GDP were devoted to debt repayment—has been in danger territory, not merely since the subprime crisis began, but ever since the stock market crash of 1987. In the early 1990s, the ratio approached 175%, the level that caused the last Great Depression.

Figure 1: U.S. Private Debt-to-GDP Ratio and Inflation Rate

Sources: Pre-1953 debt data are derived from the Statistical Abstract of the United States (census.gov/compendia/statab/past_years.html); post-1953 data come from the Federal Reserve Flow of Funds (federalreserve.gov/releases/zl/Current/data.htm). Inflation data from Bureau of Labor Statistics (ftb.bls.gov/pub/special.requests/epi/epiai.txt).

Had the Federal Reserve not intervened to rescue Wall Street in 1987, it is quite possible that we would have had a mild depression back then. De-leveraging (that is, devoting part of income to reducing debt rather than to spending) would have depressed economic activity, and it would have been a mild one because inflation would have helped reduce the debt burden. Instead, the Fed's rescues encouraged the financial sector to move from one debt-financed bubble to another—first the savings-and-loan bubble, then the dot-com, and finally the subprime.

As bubble gave way to rescue and a subsequent bigger bubble, the debt ratio grew from a Depression-level 165% of GDP in 1987 to an unprecedented 298% by March 2009. The unwinding of this huge debt burden, coupled with an inflation rate that has now fallen below zero, is causing a deleveraging-led economic downturn that will rival the Great Depression in severity.

Leverage and Economic Activity

The economic ideology that Greenspan now concedes is false asserts—among many other false propositions—that money has no long-lasting impact on the real economy. In fact, we live in a fundamentally monetary credit-based economy, and in such an economy, aggregate demand is the sum of income *plus the change in debt*.

When the debt-to-GDP ratio is small, so too is the contribution that an increase in debt can make to demand, and changes in debt are relatively unimportant. But as debt grows relative to GDP, then even a small change in debt can constitute a major proportion of aggregate demand. Figure 2 illustrates the rising role of debt in driving demand by showing the correlation between the debt-financed fraction of demand and unemployment.

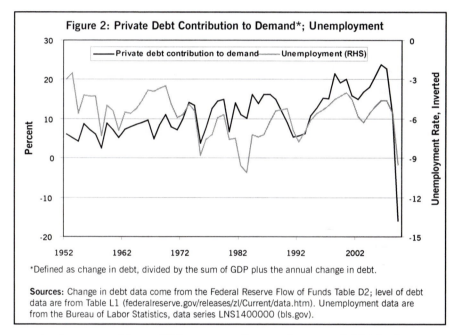

Figure 2: Private Debt Contribution to Demand*; Unemployment

*Defined as change in debt, divided by the sum of GDP plus the annual change in debt.

Sources: Change in debt data come from the Federal Reserve Flow of Funds Table D2; level of debt data are from Table L1 (federalreserve.gov/releases/zl/Current/data.htm). Unemployment data are from the Bureau of Labor Statistics, data series LNS1400000 (bls.gov).

As the private debt-to-GDP ratio rose from under 50% of GDP back in 1950 to six times that today, the share of aggregate demand that came from an increase in debt rose from as little as 2% in 1954, to as much as 28% in mid-2007. In the '50s and '60s, when the debt ratio was below 100%, debt's contribution to demand had little impact upon unemployment. But from 1975 on, this contribution explained most of the movement in unemployment: when debt-financed spending went up, unemployment went down (the correlation coefficient between the two series since 1990 is -0.83). Our economy had become debt-dependent, and the Fed's rescues simply extended this period of debt dependence for another two decades.

This fundamentally monetary contribution to demand was completely ignored by conventional neoclassical economists like Greenspan and Bernanke, yet it was primarily responsible for the illusory prosperity of the last fifteen years—which, before the bubble burst, they happily attributed to their own good economic management in what they called "The Great Moderation." Throughout that period, the increase in private debt was responsible for over 18% of aggregate demand.

Unfortunately, leverage is a factor that cuts both ways: while a debt-financed speculative bubble drives up demand, the deleveraging that happens after the bubble bursts subtracts from it. Deleveraging by the private sector is now reducing aggregate demand by over 10% and driving unemployment up as a result. Given the scale of debt today, at 70% above that of 1929, it could take much more than a decade of deleveraging to reduce debt to levels at which its contribution to economic activity is minor.

That period will be one in which aggregate demand is substantially below GDP, since debt will be reduced by households and businesses spending less than they earn. This contrasts with the last six decades, when debt grew almost every year, and the increase in debt each year financed spending in excess of earned income. With deleveraging, growth in demand will be less than the growth in output, and growth will fall below the level needed to sustain employment.

Can Bernanke Do It?

Having helped caused this mess by ignoring and effectively encouraging the growth of debt-financed asset bubbles, Bernanke is now attempting to ward off deflation via "quantitative easing"—a dramatic increase in the level of base money (currency and commercial bank accounts with the Federal Reserve)—in an attempt to cause a substantial expansion in the money supply, and hence cause inflation. He explained the strategy in 2002: "prevention of deflation remains preferable to having to cure it. If we do fall into deflation, however, we can take comfort that the logic of the printing press example must assert itself, and sufficient injections of money will ultimately always reverse a deflation." Bernanke is certainly being true to his theory. The problem is that his theory is false.

In the model he employs, the money supply is determined by (a) the central bank's injections of "base money" into the economy, and (b) the "reserve requirement" it sets—in the United States, 10%. So an injection of $1 trillion into bank reserves via "quantitative easing" should result in a total of $10 trillion being

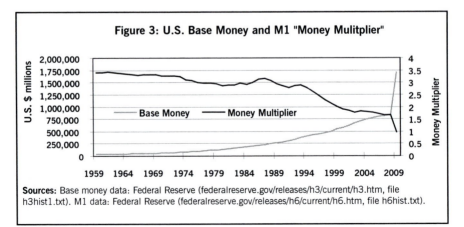

Figure 3: U.S. Base Money and M1 "Money Mulitplier"

Sources: Base money data: Federal Reserve (federalreserve.gov/releases/h3/current/h3.htm, file h3hist1.txt). M1 data: Federal Reserve (federalreserve.gov/releases/h6/current/h6.htm, file h6hist.txt).

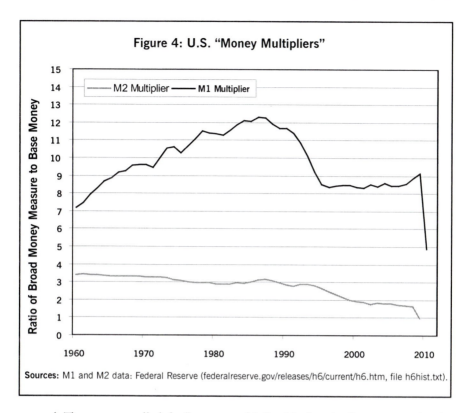

Figure 4: U.S. "Money Multipliers"

Sources: M1 and M2 data: Federal Reserve (federalreserve.gov/releases/h6/current/h6.htm, file h6hist.txt).

created. The process, called the "money multiplier," is that the first recipient banks keep 10% of the deposited money ($100 billion) and lend the rest—creating $900 billion of debt as well. Then the borrowers deposit that $900 billion in other banks, who keep 10% of this ($90 billion) and lend out the rest ($810 billion). This process repeats until $9 trillion additional credit money—and debt—has been created.

This model sees lending as being constrained by banks' limited capital, so that providing them with reserves in excess of their needs will spur a lending and credit creation process that will in turn increase the money supply and cause inflation.

As the data emphatically show, that is *so* not what is happening. Instead reserves are filling up and *not* being lent—and with good reason. Bank lending is constrained not by any lack of cash, but by the unwillingness of banks to lend, and the unwillingness of a public that is already $45 trillion in debt to take on the additional $9 trillion in debt that this vision of the money creation process requires.

Not only is aggregate private debt higher than at any time in history, it is also spread more widely than ever before. Non-financial businesses have a debt burden (as a share of GDP) just 20% below the level of 1930; households are carrying 2.5 times that level, and the financial sector tops the polls with six times its 1930 level. Even government, whose debt should move counter-cyclically to private debt, has twice the debt-to-GDP level it had in 1930.

There is simply no one left to lend money to.

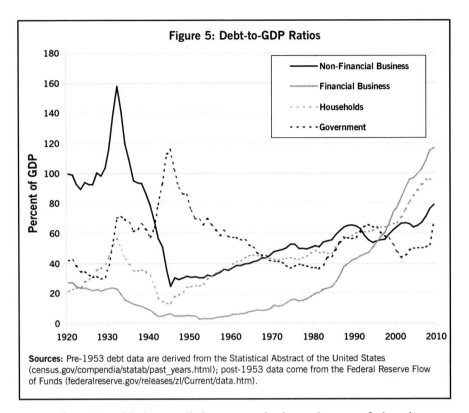

Figure 5: Debt-to-GDP Ratios

Sources: Pre-1953 debt data are derived from the Statistical Abstract of the United States (census.gov/compendia/statab/past_years.html); post-1953 data come from the Federal Reserve Flow of Funds (federalreserve.gov/releases/zl/Current/data.htm).

In this real world, the so-called money multiplier—the ratio of a broader measure of the money supply like M1 or M2 to base money—is collapsing. The ratio has collapsed to below 1 for M1, and for M2 the ratio has virtually halved in the last year.

This is striking confirmation that the money multiplier model is false, as claimed long ago by Canadian economist Basil Moore, and that the "loans create deposits" perspective of the European monetary circuit school is correct. The basic proposition of this model is that the banking sector is effectively unconstrained in its lending, and the act of a bank creating a loan simultaneously creates a deposit of the same size—thus "loans create deposits." Thus rather than banks being powerless to create money until they receive deposits from the public, the very act of giving a loan simultaneously creates deposits.

I have developed a mathematical model of the process of money creation in a pure credit economy without a government sector. The simplest possible version is described in the table below, which shows the financial flows that would exist in a simple credit-driven economy in which there had been a single loan from the banking sector to the firm sector.

The loan obliges the firm sector to pay interest (A), which is a transfer from the firm's deposit account at the bank to the bank's account. The firm then hires and pays workers, creating a flow of funds from its account to households (B). Finally bankers and workers consume, and pay for what they consume by transferring money from their accounts to the firm's account (C & D).

In this "bare bones" model, A is the interest rate times the outstanding debt, B is a function of the amount in the firm's deposit account reflecting its need for workers, and C and D are functions of the amount in the bank's and households' accounts respectively reflecting their consumption rates. A dynamic model with 3 variables (technically a system of coupled "Ordinary Differential Equations" with 3 system states) is derived simply by adding up the entries in each column, and it describes a self-sustaining "toy" economy with a constant credit money stock, constant economic activity, and constant wages, profits, and interest earnings for the three sectors. (This contrasts with works in the Circuitist tradition that erroneously claim that a constant rate of economic activity would require continuous injections of new money.)

Bank Balance Sheet	Assets	Liabilities (Deposits)		
	Loans	Firm	Bank	Household
Interest on Loan		-A	+A	
Hire workers		-B		+B
Consume		+C+D	-C	-D

An extended version of this model simulates a "credit crunch" (see my article "Bailing out the Titanic with a Thimble," available online at cap-journal.com.au, for the technical details). When three key parameters change suddenly—the rate of loan repayment jumps, and the rates of re-lending of reserves and new money creation drop dramatically—the results include a collapse in deposits and a dramatic rise in bank reserves, just as we are experiencing now (see Figure 6).

Bernanke's quantitative easing simply throws more money into a pool from which banks are extremely reluctant to lend. Though the sums involved are

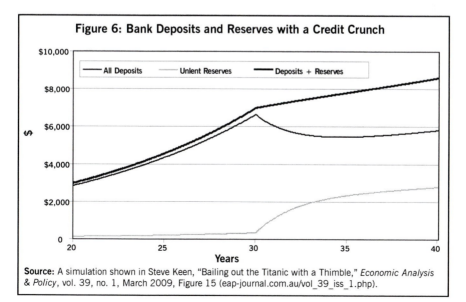

Figure 6: Bank Deposits and Reserves with a Credit Crunch

Source: A simulation shown in Steve Keen, "Bailing out the Titanic with a Thimble," *Economic Analysis & Policy*, vol. 39, no. 1, March 2009, Figure 15 (eap-journal.com.au/vol_39_iss_1.php).

enormous—of the order of $1 trillion—they amount to less than six month's interest on the current level of U.S. private debt, and less than half the amount by which the private sector has reduced its leverage in the past year. The private sector is taking money out of the economy at a far faster rate than Bernanke and Obama together are throwing money into it.

My prognosis is therefore that the U.S. economy will continue to suffer a prolonged deleverage-driven downturn until such time as the level of outstanding debt is tackled directly—either by a never-ending wave of bankruptcies amid rising unemployment, or by the abolition of debt that should never have been created in the first place. ❏

Sources: Ben S. Bernanke, "Deflation: Making Sure 'It' Doesn't Happen Here', Federal Reserve Board, 2002; Ben S. Bernanke, "The Great Moderation," remarks by Governor Ben S. Bernanke at the meetings of the Eastern Economic Association, Washington, DC February 20, 2004; Dirk Bezemer, "'No One Saw This Coming': Understanding Financial Crisis Through Accounting Models," Faculty of Economics, University of Groningen, The Netherlands; A. Graziani, *The Monetary Theory of Production*, Cambridge University Press, 2009; Alan Greenspan, "Testimony of Dr Alan Greenspan to the Committee on Oversight and Government Reform," in *The Financial Crisis and the Role of Federal Regulators*, U.S. Congress, Washington, 2008; "Hearing on the Role of Federal Regulators in the Financial Crisis," House of Representatives, C. o. O. a. G. R. 2008, in Committee on Oversight and Government Reform, U.S. Congress, Washington; Steve Keen, "Finance and Economic Breakdown: Modeling Minsky's 'Financial Instability Hypothesis'" *Journal of Post Keynesian Economics*, vol. 17, no. 4, 1995; Steve Keen, "Keynes's 'revolving fund of finance' and transactions in the circuit," in *Keynes and Macroeconomics after 70 Years*, R. Wray and M. Forstater, eds., Edward Elgar, 2008; Steve Keen, "Bailing out the Titanic with a Thimble," *Economic Analysis & Policy*, vol. 39, no. 1, 2009; Hyman P. Minsky, "The Financial Instability Hypothesis: An Interpretation of Keynes and an Alternative to 'Standard' Theory," *Nebraska Journal of Economics and Business*, vol. 16, no. 1, 1977; B.J. Moore, B. J. 1979, "The Endogenous Money Stock," *Journal of Post Keynesian Economics*, vol. 2, no. 1, 1979.

Article 1.9

PROFITS, THE BUSINESS CYCLE, AND THE CURRENT CRISIS

BY PAUL MATTICK
August 2009

As last year's economic slowdown turned into a financial crisis, and then into a global recession, there has been more and more reference to the Great Depression of the 1930s, as well as to the less severe downturns that have punctuated the decades since World War II. There is little mention, however, of the fact that business depressions have been a recurrent feature of the capitalist economy since the early nineteenth century, inspiring a vast literature of theoretical attempts to understand them and statistical materials for identifying and tracking them.

Among many suggested explanations for this cyclical pattern the most plausible emerged from the major survey of economic data carried out over many decades at the National Bureau of Economic Research by Wesley C. Mitchell and his associates. Since a business must regularly turn a profit to continue to prosper, Mitchell wrote, "the making of profits is of necessity the controlling aim of business management" and decisions about where to invest and so what to produce are regulated by the quest for profit. At some times businesses do better across the economy as a whole, earning more profit on the average, than at other times. And when average profits are high society enjoys prosperity, but declining profits can lead to depression.

What determines these changes in the profitability of capital investment? This question—which Mitchell did not really answer—bears on capitalists' ability to invest, since the money available for investment is either drawn from existing profits or borrowed against future profits, which must then come into existence if loans are to be repaid. As Mitchell explained the regulation of business decisions by the need for profit, "industry is subordinated to business, the making of goods to the making of money." But what determines the size of the difference between money costs and sales prices that is collected as profit?

Money is basic to capitalism because this is the first social system in which most productive activity is wage labor, performed in exchange for money. Most people, lacking access to land, tools, and raw materials, or enough money to purchase these, cannot produce the goods—housing, clothes, food—they need; they must work for others who have the money to hire them as well as to supply materials and tools. This money flows back to the employers when employees purchase goods they—as a class—have produced. Meanwhile, employers buy and sell goods—raw materials, machinery, consumer goods—from and to each other. Thus flows of money connect all the individuals involved in one social system.

The workers in bakeries and automobile factories do not know who will buy the bread and the cars they make, or what quantities they want and can afford. The same is true of their employers. Though capitalist businesses produce to meet the needs of anyone who can pay, they are linked to the rest of society only by the exchange of goods for money, when they buy materials and labor and when they sell their products. It is only when products are sold and consumed that the labor that has made them counts as part of the total work performed under the employer-employee system that is the dominant form of production.

Like all forms of representation, money is an abstracting device: by being exchangeable for any kind of product, money transforms the different kinds of work that make these products into elements of an abstraction, "social productive activity." The abstract character of modern production is not only an idea, but has social reality: for businesses, the particular product they sell is of interest only as a means to acquire money that, as a representation of social productive activity in general, can be exchanged for any sort of thing. Executives move capital from one area of business to another not because they care more about automobiles than soybeans or stuffed animals, but to make money.

The fact that money is the most important practical way in which the social aspect of productive activity is represented allows it to misrepresent social reality as well. By being exchanged for money, natural resources like land and oil deposits are represented in the same terms—as worth sums of money—as humanly produced things. Interest—more money—must be paid for the use of someone else's money. Things that are simply symbols of money, like IOUs, including complicated IOUs like banknotes and stocks and bonds issued by companies, can be bought and sold, since they entitle their owners to money incomes and so can be treated as if they were saleable products. And since goods must be priced so that their sale allows businesses to make a profit, even in the case of actual products the amount something costs is affected by the amount people are able and willing to spend on it.

As a result, profit, as a portion of the sales price, misleadingly appears to be generated by the activities of particular firms, especially because it is appropriated by individual businesses, who compete with each other to get as much of it as possible. In reality, profit—*because it exists in the abstract form of money, rather than in that of particular kinds of product*—must be produced by the whole network of productive activities held together by the exchange of goods for money. It is with the goal of making money that employers buy equipment and materials from each other and labor from employees, who in turn buy back the portion of their product not used to replace or expand the productive apparatus and—let's not forget—to provide the employers with their own, generally expensive, consumables. The capitalistically-desired output of this whole process, profit, is the money-representation of the labor performed beyond that required to reproduce the class of employees (paid in the form of wages) and to provide the goods required for production. That is, profit is the difference between the money-price of the goods and services produced by employees and the wages they are paid.

It is the whole social system that produces profit, though individual companies get to keep it. The social character of profit can be seen in the very fact that the level of profitability on capital investment alters over time, independently of the wishes of businessmen, who, like everyone else, must adapt to the price movements that determine how well they do (it is this that gives rise to the idea of "the economy" as a set of impersonal forces like the laws of nature.) Competition for shares of the socially-produced profit forces businesses to charge similar prices for similar products; since they must themselves buy goods (labor and materials), their ability to compete by lowering prices depends on the production techniques they employ. In this way, the social character of the system asserts itself through pressure on individual firms to raise productivity. Though the individual firms are not thinking about the whole system, but only about their own competitive position, increasing productivity increases profits because it can reduce the price of the goods employees consume and thereby enable employers to reduce wages or increase wages at a slower rate, leaving more of the money-equivalent of the total product as profit (while at the same time maintaining or even increasing the employees' standard of living). Thanks to the stress on productivity, by the end of the twentieth century most production had become mechanized mass production, requiring less and less labor relative to a growing quantity of machinery and, of course, raw materials.

If profit is the money-representation of the labor performed in all of society's businesses in excess of the work required to replace raw materials, tools, and those employees themselves, then it will decline relative to total investment if businesses increasingly invest more of their money in machines and materials than in labor. Karl Marx, who first figured this out, called it "the most important law of modern political economy": the tendency of the rate of profit to fall. Marx's explanation of this tendency is a controversial one, to say the least. But it led to a prediction that has proved all too correct: that the history of capitalism would take the form of a cycle of depressions and prosperities. And it explains the correlation Mitchell demonstrated between changes in profitability and the business cycle.

Marx pointed out that the growth of capitalism, with its bias towards mechanization, led to an increase in the amount of money needed to continue to expand production, and so to the increasing size of individual companies. (For the largest 100 firms in the United States, for instance, in real terms the amount of money invested in equipment per worker doubled between 1949 and 1962.) And, of course, as increasing mechanization raised labor productivity, growing amounts of raw materials must be paid for. One consequence of this is that if the profitability of capital falls, at some point the amount of profit will be insufficient for further expansion of the system.

Slowing investment means a shrinking market for produced goods. Employers neither invest capital in the purchase of buildings, machinery, and raw materials nor pay the wages which workers would have spent on consumer goods. A slowdown in investment is experienced by workers as a rise in unemployment and by businessmen as a contraction of markets. This is a self-magnifying process, as declining demand causes business failures, higher unemployment, and further contraction of demand. At the same time, since businessmen (and other borrowers) are increasingly unable to meet financial obligations, the various forms of IOUs issued by banks and brokerage houses lose value, causing a financial crisis, while falling stock prices reflect the declining value of business enterprises. Individuals and institutions hoard money, rather than invest it. In short, capitalism finds itself in a depression.

But in a capitalist economy, what causes suffering for individuals can be good for the system. As firms go bankrupt and production goods of all sorts go unsold, the surviving companies can buy up buildings, machinery and raw materials at bargain prices, while land values fall. There is market pressure for the design of new, more efficient and cheaper machinery. As a result, the cost of capital investment declines. At the same time, rising unemployment drives down wages. Capitalists' costs are thus lower while the labor they employ is more productive than before, as people are made to work harder and on newer equipment. A depression, that is, is the cure for insufficient profits; it is what makes the next period of prosperity possible, even as that prosperity will in turn generate the conditions for a new depression.

Like earlier crises, the Great Depression of the 1930s, together with the enormous destructive force of the Second World War, laid the foundations for the postwar boom economists call the Golden Age. It was not surprising, in view of the history of the business cycle, that this new prosperity began to decline by the end of the 1960s, when economists noted a drop in profitability in the United States and Europe. By the mid-1970s, the world economy had entered a period of decidedly slower growth. Yet the depression one might have expected then did not materialize. The reason for this is that, while capitalism remained at base the same system, the economic policy practiced by governments had changed. On the one hand, the political dangers threatened by the mass social movements unleashed by the previous depression were unacceptable to the governing elite of the capitalist states, especially in the context of what was believed to be an epic confrontation with Communism. On the other hand, it was also imagined that Keynesian methods of deficit financing could control the ravages of the business cycle. And in fact the continuously growing level of government spending on military and civilian projects after 1945, which increased the demand for goods and services beyond that produced by the capitalist economy proper, created prosperous conditions despite declining profitability.

In addition, the money that governments—the U.S. government above all—printed to pay for all this spending, together with the credit private financial establishments were encouraged by central banks to extend to corporate and individual borrowers, made possible the debt expansion that underwrote individual consumption, corporate acquisitions and, especially from the 1980s on, ever more forms of speculation, in real estate, the stock market, and (with the refinement of derivatives) the ups and downs of speculation itself. This ever-increasing public, business, and individual debt appeared on bank and other business balance sheets as profits, despite their missing foundation in productive enterprise. Contrary to what is commonly claimed today, it was precisely the deregulation of finance that made possible what passed for prosperity during the last two decades.

Meanwhile, just as in earlier periods of economic decline, pressure was put on workers to work harder, while labor costs were lowered by moving plants from high wage to low wage areas or simply by using the threat of such moves to cut wages and benefits. Starting in the 1980s, spending on the socialized wage payments constituted by welfare-state programs was cut, freeing up money for corporate use. All this may have contributed to an actual increase in profits, but evidently not by enough to make possible a new round of capital investment on a scale able to challenge the charms of speculation's short-run high returns. But the lack of actual profits sets a limit to speculation. As a result, we are now confronting, more or less, the depression that should have come much earlier, but which political-economic policy was able to delay—in part by displacing it to poor parts of the world, but largely by an historically unprecedented creation of debt in the rich parts—for thirty-odd years.

Government deficit financing did not solve this problem, and will not solve it in the future, because government-financed production does not produce profit. This is hard to grasp, not only because it violates a basic presupposition of the past seventy-five years of economic policy, but because a company that sells goods to the state, as when Boeing provides bombers for the Air Force, does receive a profit, and usually a good one, on its investment. But the government has no money of its own; it pays with tax money or with borrowed funds that will eventually have to be repaid out of taxes.

Tax money appears to be paid by everyone. But despite the appearance that business is undertaxed, only business actually pays taxes. To understand this, think of the total income produced in a year as the money available for all social purposes. Some of this money must go to replace producers' goods used up in the previous year; some must go as wages to buy consumer goods so that the labor force can reproduce itself; the rest appears as profit, interest, rent—and taxes. The money workers actually get is their "after tax" income; from this perspective, tax increases on employee income are just a way of lowering wages. The money deducted from paychecks, as well as from dividends, capital gains, and other forms of business income, could appear as business profits—which, let us remember, is basically the money generated by workers' activity that they do not receive as wages—if it didn't flow through paychecks (or other income) into government coffers. So when the government buys goods or services from a corporation (or simpler yet, hands agribusiness a subsidy or a bank a bailout) it is just giving a portion of its cut of profits back to business, collecting from all and giving to some.

Furthermore, the situation today is rather different from that at the outset of the last great depression. The United States had a government debt of $16 billion in 1930; today it is $11 trillion and climbing. In terms of percentage of GDP, the federal debt had already reached 37.9% by 1970; in 2004 it was 63.9%. The federal government is already responsible for about 35% of economic output (as measured by GDP, the value of all goods and services produced in a year). When this number hit 50% at the height of the Second World War, the growth of private capital came more or less to a halt. All of which is to say, the Keynesian means for depression-fighting have been largely used up, unless the state is to displace private enterprise completely to create a state-run economy like that of the old Soviet Union, a goal favored by no actual political force.

Whatever mix of stimulus and respect for market freedom governments decide upon, the working-class majority will pay for it, with greater unemployment or lower wages and benefits—in fact, as we can already see, it will be with both. No doubt, as in the past, Americans will demand that industry or government provide them with jobs, but perhaps it will also occur to people that the factories, offices, farms, and other workplaces will still exist, even if they cannot be run profitably, and can be set into motion to produce goods that people need. Even if there are not enough *jobs*—paid employment, working for business or the state—there is work aplenty to be done if people organize production and distribution *for themselves*, outside the constraints of the business economy.

When the financial shit hit the fan last fall, everyone with access to the media, from the President to left-wing commentators like Doug Henwood of the *Left*

Business Observer, agreed that it was necessary to save the banks with infusions of government cash lest the whole economy collapse. But, aside from the fact that the economy is collapsing anyway, the *opposite* is closer to the truth: if the whole financial system fell away, and money ceased to be the power source turning the wheels of production, the whole productive apparatus of society—machines, raw materials, and above all working people—would still be there, along with the human needs it can be made to serve. The fewer years of suffering and confusion it takes for people to figure this out, the better. ❏

This essay is based on four essays published in the Brooklyn Rail *in October and November 2008 and January and April 2009; they can be found at brooklynrail.org.*

Article 1.10

SAME OUTPUT + FEWER HOURS = ECONOMIC CRISIS?

Today's economic crisis is less about the quantity of output than the distribution of income and leisure.

BY ALEJANDRO REUSS
September/October 2010

During the current crisis, real (inflation-adjusted) GDP per capita for the U.S. economy declined for six consecutive quarters. It has since increased for four consecutive quarters, though the figure for the second quarter of 2010 remains well below the pre-crisis peak. This might seem like an indication that real GDP per capita is a good measure of economic well-being. We're in a severe crisis, everyone thinks things are bad, and GDP is down. Even though GDP has been growing again recently, we're still not back to the level of prosperity before the crisis.

Consider, however, that real GDP per capita for the second quarter of 2010 was higher than it was in the second quarter of 2005—and in fact for every previous quarter in U.S. history. Now, hardly anyone thinks that things are better in the United States today, economically, than they were in 2005—or that, excepting about three years between 2005 and 2008, things are better economically now than they have ever been before. It can't be that our only problem is having fewer goods and services (as measured by real GDP per capita), since similar levels back in 2005 were not considered a disaster.

One alternative explanation is that the level of GDP does not matter as much as the change in GDP. Maybe we've gotten used to higher levels of affluence, and now miss the extra goods and services. At first blush, that doesn't seem like the issue

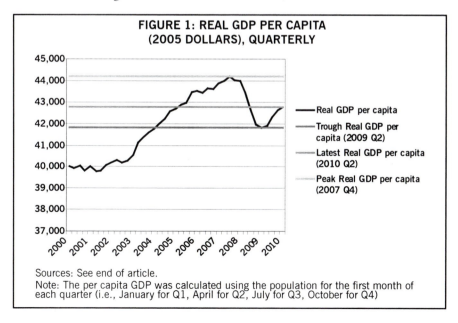

FIGURE 1: REAL GDP PER CAPITA
(2005 DOLLARS), QUARTERLY

Real GDP per capita

Trough Real GDP per capita (2009 Q2)

Latest Real GDP per capita (2010 Q2)

Peak Real GDP per capita (2007 Q4)

Sources: See end of article.
Note: The per capita GDP was calculated using the population for the first month of each quarter (i.e., January for Q1, April for Q2, July for Q3, October for Q4)

either. The difference between the pre-crisis peak in real per capita GDP and even the trough of the recession is surprisingly small, less than 6%. Many people, counting on their incomes not only to remain at the higher (pre-crisis) level but to keep increasing, however, undoubtedly made spending decisions that are now difficult to reverse—like buying a house of a certain size and location or sending one's children to a certain college. Even if the decline in incomes were spread evenly across the population, for those living close to the limits of their means, it might be difficult to "scale back."

Of course, the impact of the recession has not fallen equally on everyone, and that is much closer to the crux of the problem. The unemployed have borne the brunt of the recession. The official number of unemployed people in the U.S. labor force dipped below 6.5 million just before the recession, in the first half of 2007. Today, it stands at nearly 15 million. For the unemployed themselves, this means not only a loss of income but also of an important source of personal identity and self-esteem, of a major part of their social lives, and of future career prospects. For millions of others, mass unemployment means increased insecurity and anxiety about their own futures.

Real U.S. GDP in 2009 was nearly the same as for 2006—just under $13 trillion. (The Bureau of Economic Analysis reports figures of $12.8806 trillion (in 2005 dollars) for 2009 and $12.9762 trillion for 2006). While these measures of total output produced are nearly identical, the figures for the number of workers employed and the number of work hours required to produce that output are strikingly different. In 2006, about 138.7 million workers (16 years and over) were employed, compared to only about 134.4 million in 2009. The total time spent at work, by all workers 16 and over, was about 18 billion hours less in 2009 than in 2006.

Producing the same quantity of output in fewer hours means that labor productivity has increased. There are several possible causes: increased intensity or pace of work (or "speed up"), increased worker skill, improved production methods, or greater quantity or quality of tools used. During the current crisis, multiple factors may have been involved. High unemployment itself reduces workers' bargaining power. Employers know that there are plenty of unemployed workers who

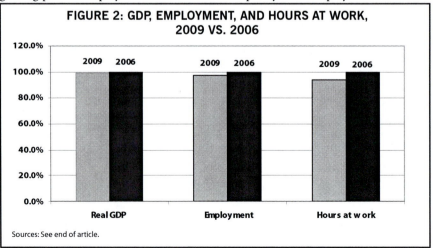

FIGURE 2: GDP, EMPLOYMENT, AND HOURS AT WORK, 2009 VS. 2006

Sources: See end of article.

are desperate for a job. Meanwhile, workers who do have jobs are desperate to keep them. This makes it relatively easy for employers to push down wages or demand a faster pace of work. It may also be that workers' average skill level has increased, if for no other reason than that less-skilled workers are disproportionately represented among those laid off. There may also have been innovation in production methods and technology that explain part of this productivity increase.

Increased productivity is not intrinsically a bad thing. It can mean being able to produce more goods—and a higher "standard of living"—without additional work hours. Increases in productivity have been a major source of economic growth in capitalist economies. As long as demand for goods and services keeps pace with rising productive capacity, productivity increases generally fuel rising real output. In principle, increased productivity can also mean being able to produce the same amount of goods in fewer work hours. Fewer work hours can mean more leisure time and a higher quality of life.

The increase in productivity over the last few years, however, has not been matched by an increase in demand for goods. Overall demand now stands around the same level as a few years ago and at a significantly lower level than at the peak of the last boom, even as overall productive capacity has increased. The managers of capitalist enterprises do not set workers to produce goods just because they can, but because they (the managers) believe that this output can be sold at a profit. The decline in demand, then, means that some productive resources go unused—in the form of shuttered factories and idle machinery, and a dramatic decrease in employment and work hours.

This decline in work hours has not been distributed sensibly or equitably among all members of the population—in the form of a shorter regular working week, more vacation time, or an earlier retirement. Therefore, we have the strange paradox that today the U.S. economy produces about as much output (real goods and services) as it did in 2006, and requires billions fewer work hours to do so, which sounds like a good thing. And yet, as a result, we find ourselves in a disastrous crisis—millions have lost their jobs and main sources of income, while uncounted millions live in fear of a similar fate.

Karl Marx and Friedrich Engels wrote, over 150 years ago, that capitalist economies, in which goods are produced only if they can be sold, and will not be produced at all if they cannot be sold for a profit, had created a new kind of economic crisis: "an epidemic that, in all earlier epochs, would have seemed an absurdity—the epidemic of over-production." Economic crises in previous societies, Marx and Engels understood, had been caused by an inadequate supply of goods, the results of drought, flood, war, and the like. In capitalist societies, for the first time in human history, there appeared crises as a result not of too little productive capacity, but of too much—"too much civilization, too much means of subsistence, too much industry, too much commerce."

Marx and Engels spoke of "too much means of subsistence, too much industry" with a sort of grim irony. They did not mean that there was really too much productive power compared to peoples' needs or wants, but compared to their buying power (what later economists termed "effective demand"). It is certainly questionable whether endlessly producing more goods and services is really the key to making us better off—as opposed to enjoying greater leisure time, a more pleasant environment, greater economic security, less economic inequality, greater autonomy at work, etc. However, there's no reason that the development of greater productive power must exact the enormous toll of human suffering that it can—and, very often, does—in a capitalist economy. ❏

Sources: Bureau of Labor Statistics, Labor Force Statistics (CPS), Table A-1, "Employment status of the civilian population by sex and age," www.bls.gov/webapps/legacy/cpsatab1.htm; Bureau of Labor Statistics, "Persons at work in agriculture and related and in nonagricultural industries by hours of work," 2006, ftp.bls.gov/pub/special.requests/lf/aa2006/aat19.txt; Bureau of Labor Statistics, "Persons at work in agriculture and related and in nonagricultural industries by hours of work," 2009, ftp.bls.gov/pub/special.requests/lf/aat19.txt; Bureau of Economic Analysis, Table 1.1.6. Real Gross Domestic Product, Chained Dollars (A) (Q), bea.gov/national/nipaweb/SelectTable.asp; Census Bureau, Table 1. "Monthly Population Estimates for the United States, April 1, 2000, to July 1, 2010," www.census.gov/popest/national/NA-EST2009-01.html; Karl Marx and Friedrich Engels, *The Communist Manifesto.*

Article 1.11

WHY WON'T THE ECONOMY SPRING BACK?
Historical Perspective on the Downturn of 2007-2010

BY JAMES M. CYPHER
October 2010

According to dominant economic ideas, massive government interventions beginning in 2007—by way of Keynesian fiscal stimulus programs of the Bush and Obama administrations, the TARP (Wall Street bailout) program, and unprecedented interventions by the Federal Reserve—should have reset the economy. The stimulus and rescue programs did prevent an even greater avalanche of interlocking bankruptcies from reverberating via Wall Street to Main Street and back again—as occurred for years during the Great Depression of the 1930s. Yet as of the fall of 2010, the general state of the U.S. economy looks bleak. With the economy losing over 443,000 jobs from June through September and unemployment rising again in August to an official rate of 9.6%, attention shifted toward further stimulus. By September, with most of his original $787 billion stimulus plan now spent, President Obama urged $50 billion for new infrastructure projects. There is a bit of buzz about a "manufacturing strategy"—a belated attempt to address the long-term collapse of the manufacturing sector from nearly 30% of the economy in 1953 to only 11% in 2009. Here, Obama has offered only increased funding for the Export-Import Bank in order to meet his goal of doubling U.S. exports by 2015. In short, the administration proffers small and unimaginative policies as the economy stagnates and weakens.

These interventions have not addressed the economy's huge *structural* issues. Wage increases were tightly linked to productivity increases from the end of World War II through the early 1970s. Since then, in a new era of deregulation, globalization, and de-unionization, labor productivity has nearly doubled, but real hourly wages for non-supervisory workers—over 80% of the workforce—have stagnated or fallen slightly for over 30 years. This has left the working class without any viable strategy as jobs were offshored and outsourced. Instead, women flooded into the workforce, workers sought second jobs, money was pumped into 401(k)s in the hope that stock market plays could make up for declining labor opportunities, household debt reached record levels, and the dream of windfall gains from house-flipping became a major focus for millions of working-class and middle-class families. From 2007 onward, the unprecedented interventions of the Bush and Obama administrations were designed to meet the immediate needs of elite financial institutions, leaving largely unaddressed the sorry plight of the dwindling middle and working classes, now marginalized in the new era of neoliberalism.

Still, the interventions *have* served the purpose of putting a squishy floor underneath the collapsing edifice. All available evidence tends to support the Obama administration's claim that its fiscal interventions have saved or created some 2.7 million jobs. But these numbers constitute a counterfactual that is hard to demonstrate to the general public: the job growth owing to the stimulus has taken place in a broader context of massive job cuts—roughly 8 million jobs lost—since the downturn began. Economists Alan Blinder and Marc Zandi estimate that had it not been for a range of extremely active monetary and fiscal interventions beginning in the closing months of 2008, GDP in 2010 would have been 10.5% lower and an additional 8.5 million Americans would be out of work. Nonetheless, the public mostly rejects the assertions of Obama's economic spokespersons, either because most Americans have never learned of Keynesian economics or because they have been stampeded by a well-greased juggernaut financed by people like Pete Peterson, the Koch brothers, and the many others who would like to return the U.S. political economy to the good old days of 19th-century Social Darwinism.

Neoclassical to Neoliberal: Economic Theory in a Circular Process

The new era of neoliberalism, which has reigned since the late 1970s, has been anchored in an attempt to sweep away the New Deal policies that had guided the economy during the Keynesian interlude (1933-1978). Prior to the Great Depression economists strongly embraced the neoclassical doctrine of self-adjusting markets seamlessly functioning to bring about a full employment "equilibrium." Any time the economy tended to slow down—causing unemployment to rise as profit, production, and general business activity declined—wages would decline, raw material prices would drop, wholesale prices would plummet, etc. According to received neoclassical dogma, cheap wages, cheap raw materials, readily available credit and under-priced machinery and equipment would all combine to create a seductive combination for business interests who would then jump back into the market—hiring workers, building new plants, buying up raw materials, taking on bank loans in order to enjoy an unbeatable profit-making situation. Other things remaining the same, went the argument, the deflation of the economy would create its own recovery momentum as sharp traders availed themselves of a once-in-a-lifetime opportunity.

This approach assumed the economic system functioned as if it were a mechanical apparatus that was somehow "invested with a tendency to an equilibrium." Equilibrium was noted in the fall of 1929, shortly before the great stock market crash, by the most acclaimed economist of the day, Dr. Irving Fisher. Fisher stated that stock prices had reached a "permanently high plateau," adding in September of 1929, as stocks began to crater, that there could not be "anything in the nature of a crash." In the same month President Hoover's powerful Treasury Secretary Andrew Mellon—scion of the robber baron financiers who ran the Pittsburgh-based "House of Mellon"—proclaimed that the "high tide of prosperity will continue." So ended what was, until then, the longest continuous expansion in U.S. history. Prior to the crash the era was dubbed the "New Economy," wherein recession and downturns were understood as things of the past. So, too, the information technology boom of the 1990s was dubbed a "New Economy." In the 1990s, across the United States, congenitally blind economics departments scrapped almost all of their few remaining courses on business cycles.

When the depression of 1929-1939 began, Treasury Secretary Mellon—known as a financial prodigy—ecstatically championed the neoclassical theory of downwardly flexible prices: "liquidate labor, liquidate stocks, liquidate farmers, liquidate real estate ... Values will adjust ... "! In other words, after a brief bought of deflation, the economy would in machine-like fashion quickly restore its balance; the inevitable forces of the New Economy would spring back into motion and the U.S. economic ascent would resume.

Indeed, as the real value of the GDP dropped like a stone from late 1929 through 1933, wages and prices did fall. Autoworkers' money wages fell by 64%, miners' wages plummeted by 74%, steelworkers wages dropped by 62%, and the wages of agricultural workers—one-quarter of the economy was engaged in this sector—fell by 50%. Meanwhile prices in general fell by about 25%. (However, wage and *salary* income—crucially including managerial and executive incomes—apparently fell by *less* than the price level. For a few privileged employees with outsized salaries the standard of living *rose*.)

According to neoclassical theory, the dramatic drop in real wage income—spread throughout the vast manufacturing sector—should have been an inducement for businesses to invest. Along with cheap money, cheap machinery, and cheap commodities, lower wages should have been more than sufficient inducement to restore the economy to high levels of employment at lower price levels. The New York Federal Reserve Bank—the most important in the system—dropped its interest rate from 6% in 1929 to a record low of 1.5% in May 1931. But business cut and cut its investment level: while investment accounted for only 19.3% of GDP in 1929, 56% of the total drop in GDP from 1929 through 1933 was due to *the decline* in investment! The leading sector of the New Economy of the 1920s had been the auto industry. By 1933 real auto production had fallen by 65%—hardly a situation that would encourage the expansion of plants and equipment, the lost cost of labor, machinery, materials, and loans notwithstanding. Left to its own devices and the tepid interventions of the Hoover administration, the economic system became ever more dysfunctional—no mechanical apparatus was at work to bring the system back to any semblance of equilibrium.

Surprisingly, by 1933 Fisher had reflected deeply on the idea that the economy would quickly spring back to full employment. In a 180-degree turn, he now argued that the Depression had unleashed forces that were sending the economy ever downward. The U.S. economy of the 1920s had been built on mountains of business, farm, mortgage, and personal debt. Now deflation was creating its own momentum. The burden of that debt was growing greater and greater as incomes shrank under the relentless pressures of deflation. As farm and business income fell, an ever-larger portion of income was shifted to the financial sector to pay debts that had been contracted when prices were much higher. In short, the growing debt burden was driving farmers and businesses into bankruptcy, thereby leading to further layoffs and more unemployment. Those households that had accumulated mortgage debt or consumer debt were in the same boat. As wages fell, families could not possibly pay an ever-growing share of their shrinking income to make debt payments *that did not deflate with the rest of the economy*. This was Fisher's all-important debt-deflation theory; it explained how a situation of over-indebtedness would lead to declining overall demand as the economy now favored creditors over debtors.

In neoclassical theory the fact that more of the total income was now shifting to creditors should not have impeded the economy's recovery. What debtors no longer spent, went the argument, creditors would now spend. This symmetrical model, however, just did not apply in the real and non-mechanical world of economic institutions. Banks and other creditors found that their income from debt repayments gave them greater power as money *increased* in value while wages and all other components of the economy *declined* in value. But the banks did not then lend out more money because they were fearful of the endless chain of bankruptcies the Depression had unleashed. They wanted to hold lots of funds in reserve against future losses. And to the degree that the income from the creditor institutions was passed through to managers, owners, and shareholders, these well-off groups were less likely to spend the additional income than were the workers, farmers, and owners of small- and medium-sized businesses who suffered growing losses. In sum, shifting a greater share of total income into the hands of wealthy creditors served only to push the economy further downward because (1) banks hoarded funds against future losses, (2) businesses seeing low and falling sales refused to take on any more debt, and (3) the rich did not put much of their new, more powerful, dollars back into the spending stream due to what Keynes later referred to as a their "low marginal propensity to consume." Far from adjusting "values" toward equilibrium, as Andrew Mellon had predicted, *deflation had a supercharger effect—downward movement in the macro-economy unleashed powerful forces that led to further, perhaps accelerating, downward movement.*

Today, Fisher is far less well known than another economist who took on neoclassical economics orthodoxy in the 1930s, John Maynard Keynes. Keynes challenged the neoclassicals with his interpretation of how total final demand determined the level of production and employment. He sought to show that the macro-economy could be caught up in a "special case" wherein equilibrium was established at very high levels of unemployment. In this situation, economic forces were aligned and balanced in a way that—whatever the rate of unemployment and excess capacity—the economy could do no more than simply reproduce itself year after year. Monetary policy would not revive the economy. Keynes famously urged massive government intervention to "prime the pump," thereby inducing the economic system to return to its normal state.

Yet Fisher's model of a debt-deflation disequilibrium is much more compelling than Keynes' idea of a high-unemployment equilibrium. Inflation-adjusted GDP fell by 9.5% from 1929 to 1930, and then fell by 7%, 15%, and 2.7% in the following three years. This was a downward spiral, not an equilibrium process.

The Structural Problem

The Great Depression signaled a moment when the U.S. economic system had met with structural barriers to its own expanding reproduction. The period from the 1870s to the 1920s saw the birth and consolidation of the giant corporation and the end of competitive capitalism based on small units of production, as economist Richard Du Boff has documented. By the 1920s, competitive capitalism could be found only in the minds of economists and in the texts and lectures they fed to generations of misinformed students. Along with the consolidation of a new structure of monopoly capitalism, the dynamic engine of the system had shifted from the production of producers' goods to the production of consumer durables such as washing machines and radios. The 1920s were fueled above all by exploding consumer demand for autos and their backward linkages to the oil industry, the auto parts companies, machine-tool firms, mining corporations, and producers of other raw materials such as rubber.

But growing income inequality, of a magnitude precisely equal to that which occurred in the run-up to the financial meltdown of 2007, undermined the future growth of the U.S. auto industry. (The top 1% in the household income distribution received an incredible 24% of all income in both 1928 and 2007.) Investment in the auto industry peaked in 1926, after which stagnating demand forestalled the building of more auto plants. Weak-to-nonexistent union power was a major reason why the economy began to totter both in 1927, and again in 2006 when the housing boom peaked—a crucial matter ignored by both Fisher and Keynes.

Deeply embedded in the popular consciousness is the idea that the stock-market crash of 1929 *caused* the depression of the 1930s. The same was true of the most severe 19th century downturn: conventional accounts of the Panic of 1873 claimed that the depression was due to the collapse of the largest financier of the time, Jay Cooke & Company, causing losses to reverberate through the financial centers, particularly New York. Similarly, many of today's commentators pin the current economic crisis on *financialization*—the growing weight of the finance, insurance and real estate sector—which, the story goes, led to Ponzi finance, excessive leverage and the collapse of Bear Stearns, Lehman Brothers, and (effectively) A.I.G.

In short, the depressions of 1873, 1929, and the borderline depression that began in 2007 are all widely assumed to have been caused by the alchemy of financial wizards. Those who take this view generally restrict their focus to the complex world of finance, without giving due attention or weight to underlying structural changes that have resulted in unsustainable tensions among the non-financial foundational components of the economy.

In recent years, the pace of structural change has been determined by (1) the realignment of capital-labor relations resulting in the effective de-unionization of the U.S. economy; (2) the outsourcing and offshoring of millions of jobs coupled with the threat of such actions, which has caused a dramatic tilt in the distribution of national income toward capital (partly buried as the greater part of the "salary" portion of the largest national income category, "wages and salaries"); (3) the subsequent delinking of productivity increases from wages, leaving a growing mass of profits to be redirected both to conspicuous consumption on a scale never before imagined and to predatory financial gamesmanship championed by Nobel Prize-winning neoclassical economists who argued that all the madness conformed to an efficient-markets hypothesis which "demonstrated" that markets could neither over- nor under-value stocks or houses or other commodities sold in them. In brief, a profound process of capital restructuring has taken place, giving rise to a new system of globally integrated production that has left the U.S. working class puzzled, powerless, and leaderless.

A Fisher Forecast?

According to the general perspective of the economics profession, depressions are a thing of the past: clever monetary policy and/or dynamic fiscal policy can reverse any downturn. Through massive injections of cheap credit and/or some combination tax cuts, automatic countercyclical outlays (such as unemployment benefits), and discretionary expenditures (including especially those that boost the income of military contractors), federal policymakers can induce a recovery. All this is to be financed by deficit spending. Since 2007 the United States has followed exactly this prescription: the Federal Reserve has undertaken interventions of breathtaking magnitude while the federal deficit will average approximately 10% of GDP for three consecutive years in 2009, 2010, and 2011—more than double President Roosevelt's peak New Deal deficits in 1935 and 1936.

We can credit these massive interventions with curbing the forces unleashed as a result of the overcapacity problems—particularly in construction and auto production. Keynesian fiscal stimulus, however, has not resuscitated the Keynesians' prime focus: employment. The U-6 unemployment rate—the best measure of the health of the labor market—includes the officially registered unemployed and also those who are working part-time but are seeking full-time employment and those "discouraged" workers who are not actively seeking employment but would if they thought jobs were available. In the aftermath of the last two recessions (1990-1991 and 2001), the U-6 unemployment rate reached 10.8% in 1994 and 10.1% in 2003. In other words, the rate rose at the close of the recession when workers not counted by it flooded back into the labor market because they perceived the recoveries, however slow, as potentially offering them an employment opportunity. This time the U-6 rate started to climb in late 2007 and had already hit 10.6% in 2008. It then soared on to 16.3% in 2009 and 16.7% in the first six months of 2010. If we take these data at face value, the U.S. economy is in a borderline depression, and one that is deepening.

Of course, unemployment is not the only factor. GDP has grown at an anemic annual rate of 3.2% in the past four quarters. Recoveries entail at first merely the reestablishment of previous levels of output, yet second quarter 2010 GDP (constant dollar) was still some $52 billion below levels attained in the third quarter of 2007. In the most recent nine-month period (fourth quarter 2009 through second quarter 2010) much of the growth has been in inventories, not in final demand. In fact, in the second quarter of 2010 final demand grew at an annual rate of only 1.3%.

The $64 question is this: what will happen after the third quarter of 2010 when the Obama administration's fiscal stimulus will rapidly drop off? Even though the federal fiscal year 2011 (beginning October 1, 2010) will entail deficit spending of roughly 10% of GDP—constituting massive stimulus—it will be partially counteracted by declining spending on the part of most state and local governments. The total effect of massive cuts at the state and local level in 2011 will be to *withdraw* funds in relatively labor-intensive areas such as education and health care. An estimated 500,000 local government employees are scheduled to be terminated in 2010 and 2011. To this group should be added another 900,000 public and private sector jobs currently sustained by the 34 states that will face the need to trim their budgets to accommodate falling tax revenues in fiscal years 2011 and 2012. Although federal legislation to inject $26 billion into the states' budgets might momentarily save up to 300,000 state and local jobs, this is a policy of short-term support. The roughly 1.4 million threatened state and local layoffs could eventually have a much larger impact, potentially forcing twice that number or even more into unemployment. That is, the negative job multiplier effects would cause other workers—those who depend on state workers' spending—to lose their jobs. Even with the emergency one-year funding that passed the Congress, sizeable state and local layoffs and wage cuts will occur in fiscal year 2011. In September local government layoffs hit their highest rate in over 30 years.

In addition, a large amount of the federal deficit in 2011 will, once again, bleed away as imports. That is, a significant portion of government stimulus funds received by households via unemployment insurance payments, food stamps, tax cuts, jobs saved in construction, etc., will be sent abroad to pay for imported consumer goods, oil, machinery and equipment. Further, the major share of the federal debt (54% of marketable treasury bonds in December 2009) is now owned by foreigners—so most tax payments for interest must be shipped abroad to service the debt accumulated in past years.

One of the oddest features of the current "recovery" is how heavily it has been fueled by a drop in the savings rate of households with incomes above $210,000— the top 5%. This echelon generally accounts for one-third of all consumption spending. The rich responded to the strong recovery of the stock market in 2009 by dropping their savings rate from approximately 23% in late 2008 to -7% in early 2010! In early 2010 the spending of the most affluent households was 33% higher than it had been in the previous twelve months. But the fragile spending boom that had boosted Mercedes sales by 26% leveled off in June 2010.

Another odd feature is the fact that major corporations have continued avidly restructuring their production processes, laying off workers right and left. For example, consider Ford. Ford's North American division posted huge a second quarter 2010 profit of $1.9 billion—this after cutting its labor force by 50% and seeing its revenue drop by $20 billion since 2005. The new corporate formula is higher profits from lower sales. All this is being done with fewer and fewer workers who are under the gun to ramp up their productivity. Real Gross Investment (new capital spending plus replacement spending for worn-out equipment, adjusted for inflation) fell by 30% from the third quarter of 2007 to the first quarter of 2009. In the second quarter of 2010 overall investment was still 17.4% below the level achieved in late 2007.

Investment, then, is weak, while profits are high. The true profit rate (per unit of real value added) for domestic non-financial corporations can be measured after making adjustments for taxes, depreciation, and inventory adjustment. This profit rate rose by almost 30% from its recent low in the first quarter of 2008 through the first quarter of 2010. Indeed, the profit rate is now so high—thanks to the great squeeze on workers—that it exceeds the level achieved in the third quarter of 2007, close to the peak of the last business cycle, by about 13%. *If* these bloated profits were channeled back into investment, then the economy would have a tendency to recover. But they are not. Corporations are taking their profits and sitting on them—cash holdings are at their highest levels since the early 1960s.

On average, for the past 18 months unit labor costs have been falling because labor productivity increases have greatly exceeded (minuscule) wage increases. Across the United States in both the public and private sectors, in union and non-union workplaces, wage cuts have become a front-line strategy. A 2010 survey of U.S. cities found that 51% were either cutting or freezing existing wages. A wage squeeze continues even at highly profitable corporations such as General Motors, where all new hires make one-half the rate of senior workers. As federal government spending stalls out in late 2010, as the rich pull back from their recent spending binge, as corporations pocket much of their fat profits instead of plowing them back into expanded capacity, as wages stagnate or fall, and as most state and local governments retrench further, it is very difficult to foresee a continuation of what is conventionally called a "recovery"—even if the Obama administration succeeds in enacting its tepid proposals for further stimulus.

Waving his magic wand over this witch's brew, the chair of the Federal Reserve claims that monetary policy can still do a great deal to improve the situation. Will the Fed buy more trash with its cash? Will its attempt to lower long-term interest rates work to induce more investment? Keynesians of yesteryear were very leery of such tactics. They argued that under the delicate conditions outlined above, giving financial intermediaries more money while lowering interest rates would not do the trick. Banks would bulk up on cash or secure short-term assets—they would not lend very much. Businesses facing overwhelming excess capacity would not be prone to borrow much even if long-term interest rates fell. Under the sway of the Chicago School, Fed Chair Bernanke suffers from a perception problem.

The larger question, however, relates to the weak response from three years of huge federal deficits in fiscal years 2009, 2010 and 2011. Keynesians assume that massive federal stimulus will somehow cause the forward gears of the capitalist system to mesh—but they do not explain how or why. So far, Keynesianism has gained no forward traction, although it has prevented a backward slide. This stalemate is not unprecedented. The New Deal was largely stuck in place after 1936 because of the political resistance of the captains of industry and finance to further and larger deficits. Likewise, political opposition to further huge deficits likely explains some of the current situation of stagnation and slippage. But when World War II spending ended the Depression, more was involved that just spending. The war industries created a new industrial base that generated a host of major technological changes, for example in petrochemicals, aircraft engineering, and plastics. The war broke a power logjam and financed the industrial restructuring of the U.S. economy.

Since 2008 the government has prioritized policies to push the profit rate up, thereby benefiting the top 5 million (3.7%) of all households, those with incomes above $250,000, while shrugging off the plight of the working and middle classes and the structural problems that have created the current impasse. Millions in these classes are now caught in a Fisher-style debt trap, with their incomes falling, their debt-service payments constant or growing, and their debt-to-income ratios rising. Aside from some largely symbolic gestures, neither the Bush nor the Obama administration's stimulus efforts have addressed the drag effect that Fisher highlighted. This has stalemated the stimulus programs and the easy-money efforts of the Fed, leaving the majority in the United States in a condition of crushing economic precariousness. ❑

Sources: Alan Blinder and Marc Zandi, "How the Great Recession was Brought to an End" (July 27, 2010; www.economy.com/mark-zandi/documents/End-of-Great-Recession.pdf); Bureau of Labor Statistics, BLS Data Series: Labor Force Statistics, Table A-15, "Alternative Measures of Labor Underutilization" (www.bls.gov); Susan Carter *et al.*, *Historical Statistics of the United States,* Cambridge: Cambridge University Press, Tables Aa9-14, Ba4218 and Ca208-212 (2006); Lester Chandler, *America's Greatest Depression.* New York: Harper & Row (1970); Richard Du Boff, *Accumulation and Power: An Economic History of the United States*, Armonk, New York: M.E. Sharpe (1989); Rendig Fels, "American Business Cycles 1865-1879,"*American Economic Review* v. 41 no. 3 (June 1951); Irving Fisher, "The Debt-Deflation Theory of Great Depression," *Econometrica* v.1, no. 4 (October 1933); John K. Galbraith, *The Great Crash.* Boston: Houghton Mifflin (1954); Steven Greenhouse, "More Workers Face Pay Cuts, not Furloughs," *New York Times* (August 8, 2010); Nicholas Johnson *et al.*, "An Update on State Budget Cuts," Center on Budget and Policy Priorities (August 4, 2010; cbpp.org/cms); J. M. Keynes, *Economic Consequences of the Peace*, New York: Harcourt, Brace & Howe (1920); J. M. Keynes, *The General Theory of Employment, Interest and Money*, New York: Harcourt, Brace & World (1936); David Leonhardt, "Biggest Local Cuts in 30 Years," *New York Times* Economix blog (October 8, 2010, economix. blogs.nytimes.com); Cathrine Rampell, "Recovery Slows; Outlook on Jobs Grows Dimmer," *New York Times* (July 31, 2010); Motoko Rich, "Wealthy Sector of Buying Public is Cutting Back," *New York Times* (July 17, 2010); Emanuel Saez, "Striking it Rich," (August 5, 2010; elsa.berekley. edu/-saez/saez-UStopincomes-2007.pdf); William Selway, "US Cities and Counties Poised to Cut 500,000 Jobs," (July 27, 2010; Bloomberg.com/news/2010-07-27); Nelson Schwartz, "Industries Find Surging Profits in Deeper Cuts," *New York Times* (July 26, 2010); Louis Uchitelle, "A White House Campaign for Factories," *New York Times* (September 10, 2010); U.S. Department of Commerce, Bureau of Economic Analysis, *National Income and Product Accounts*, Table 3-b (2010); Thorstein Veblen, "Why is Economics not an Evolutionary Science?" in *The Portable Veblen,* Max Lerner, ed., New York: Viking (1948), reprinted from the *Quarterly Journal of Economics,* (July 1898); Francis Warnock, "How Dangerous Is U.S. Government Debt?" *Capital Flows Quarterly* (Council on Foreign Relations, 2010).

Chapter 2

WARNING SIGNS

Article 2.1

BUBBLE TROUBLE
Talk about irrational exuberance. Housing is the new bull market.

BY DEAN BAKER
January/February 2005

As lukewarm as the economic recovery [from the 2001 recession] has been, it would have been far chillier if not for the housing market. Throughout the recession and recovery, overheated housing prices have kept the economy simmering.

Since late 1995, housing prices have risen nationwide by almost 35% after adjusting for inflation. In some regions, real home prices have risen by more than 50%. Such a steep run-up is abnormal. Prior to 1995, home prices had closely tracked the inflation rate.

By borrowing against the inflated values of their homes throughout the economic slowdown, families spurred consumption growth—despite the weak job market and stagnant wages—providing much of the lift for the current recovery. Since Bush took office in 2000, the amount of outstanding mortgage debt has risen a remarkable 50.4%. As a result, the ratio of mortgage debt to home equity hit a record high in 2003.

Some argue there's no need to worry; the rise in housing prices is not a bubble, but is founded on genuine factors such as scarce urban land, immigration, and income growth—but these explanations don't make sense. Vacant land in many urban areas has long been scarce, but this never before led to such a surge in prices. And most immigrants are not in the market for the half-million dollar homes that are driving the bubble in several regions. Income doesn't get us far in explaining the bubble, either; income growth during the late 1990s pales in comparison to the period between 1951 and 1973, when there was no bubble. Plus, the housing bubble has continued to grow over the past 3.5 years, when income growth was leveling off.

The housing bubble most likely has its origins in another bubble—the stock bubble of the late 1990s, when investors used their Wall Street returns to buy pricier homes. The increased demand began to drive up prices; soon, homebuyers came to expect continued price increases and based their purchase decisions on that expectation. Homebuyers who may otherwise have viewed a $200,000 home as too costly

79

became willing to pay that much in the expectation that the home would sell for far more down the road. Expectations of ever-rising prices drive speculative bubbles.

Sound familiar? Indeed, the current housing bubble is not unlike the run-up in stock prices to which it owes its origins. If and when this bubble bursts, as the stock bubble did, the economy will likely find itself in another recession, and millions of families will see their net worth disappear as their homes, particularly those in over-inflated housing markets, plummet in value. With nearly 40% of new homebuyers choosing adjustable-rate mortgages, and interest rates on the rise, some homebuyers could face increased mortgage payments even as the values of their homes fall. Those with high debt-to-equity balances could face negative equity, or the prospect of owing more than they own.

The recent rise in mortgage rates has begun to slow the four-year refinancing frenzy, but the middle class is now so laden with mortgage debt that the damage when the bubble bursts will be widely felt. ❑

Article 2.2

A HOUSE OF CARDS
Current levels of household debt are unsustainable.

BY TAMARA DRAUT AND ADRIA SCHARF
January/February 2005

As the Federal Reserve continues its "measured" interest rate increase, borrowers nationwide are bracing for the impact. Families are more burdened by debt than ever before, owing nearly $9 trillion in mortgages, car loans, credit card balances, home equity lines of credit, and other loans—more than $30,000 per person. From both the perspective of families struggling to make ends meet and that of the larger macroeconomy, consumers are leveraged to the hilt.

Twenty-five years ago, the total debt of U.S. households equalled half of GDP. Today, the figure is 80%. Between 2000 and 2004, the ratio of household debt to household assets spiked from 14% to 18%. For the first time, total consumer debt now exceeds aggregate annual disposable income, meaning that families owe more on average than they earn after taxes. Poor households are particularly burdened; very low-income households spend a staggering 40% of take-home earnings on debt payments, according to the Federal Reserve's Survey of Consumer Finances.

At the end of 2003, families owed on average $12,000 in credit card debt per indebted household—far more than they owed 15 years ago. Analysis of Federal Reserve data by the public policy organization Demos shows that middle-class families' credit card debt increased by 75% between 1989 and 2001. Very low-income families' credit card debt grew by a whopping 184% over the same period.

This level of debt is unsustainable, and the warning signs of collapse are clear. Delinquencies have risen steadily over the last three years. Personal bankruptcy filings reached record highs in 2003. Over 1.6 million households collapsed financially that year, an 11% increase over 2001 and more than double the bankruptcies in 1990. More children today will see their parents go through bankruptcy than divorce.

About one-fifth of all consumer debts, including 40% of new mortgages, have adjustable-rate financing. For borrowers with rate-sensitive loans such as adjustable-rate mortgages, home equity lines of credit, and many credit cards, the new year bodes financial strain, as more of their disposable income will go to interest payments. The Federal Reserve, the nation's central bank, has raised the federal funds rate, which influences the interest-rate cost of household and commercial debt, by a quarter point five times since June, and is expected to continue to edge the rate upward in 2005. While each rate increase has been small, these mini-hikes will, cumulatively, have a big impact on borrowers' bottom lines, and on consumer spending—income spent to service debt will be siphoned away from forms of spending that better stimulate the economy.

This all invites the question: why are so many families sinking into debt? It's not simply that Americans are spending willy-nilly. The problem is more serious.

Almost two-thirds of economic output is driven by consumer spending, so economic growth hinges on Americans buying, buying, and buying some more. But over the last decade, wages grew slowly, and actually stagnated or declined for some categories of workers. At the same time, the average family saw dramatic increases in health premiums, housing costs, college tuition, and child care costs. Then the new decade brought a double whammy for working families: rising unemployment and state funding cuts. Households are using credit cards to fill in the gap between their costs and their income. Then they're transferring that debt to their mortgages by refinancing and using the cash to pay down their credit card balances, a move that can cut interest costs but will put their homes at risk if hard times return or if the housing bubble bursts. And because the underlying economic pressures on families have not been addressed, many families will eventually rack up credit card debt once again. They'll pay dearly as credit card companies impose escalating rates and fees that push balances upward—making it more difficult for consumers to climb out of the hole. A recent *New York Times* report exposed credit card companies' aggressive new tactics to exact penalties for minor financial transgressions. For example, the major cards now raise interest rates for late payments on other bills, including utility bills, and have increased late fees to $39, up from $10 eight years ago, according to the *Times*. Unless incomes surge, consumers will have trouble keeping up with payments, especially now that the era of ultra-low interest rates is coming to an end.

Should we be worried? Not according to Federal Reserve chairman Alan Greenspan. In a speech in October [2004], Greenspan argued that despite the dangerous ratio of household debt to after-tax incomes, it was unlikely that the high level of household debt represented a serious threat to the economy. "Household finances appear to be in reasonably good shape," Greenspan said. He made no mention of the epidemic of delinquencies or the spike in bankruptcies. A growing chorus of economists disagree. They warn that an economy so reliant on credit may be built on a house of cards. ❏

Article 2.3

(MIS)UNDERSTANDING A BANKING INDUSTRY IN TRANSITION

Under deregulation the industry became dysfunctional—but economists still won't revise their anti-regulation script.

BY WILLIAM K. BLACK
November/December 2007

The U.S. financial system is, once again, in crisis. Or, more precisely, twin crises—first, huge numbers of defaults among subprime mortgage borrowers, and second, massive losses for the holders of new-fangled investments comprised of bundles of loans of varying risk, including many of those subprime mortgages.

These crises should shock the nation. Our largest, most sophisticated financial institutions have followed business practices that were certain to produce massive losses—practices so imprudent, in precisely the business task (risk management) that is supposed to be their greatest expertise, that they have created a worldwide financial crisis.

Why? Because their CEOs, acting on the perverse incentives created by today's outrageous compensation systems, engaged in practices that vastly increased their corporations' risk in order to drive up reported corporate income and thereby secure enormous increases in their own individual incomes. And those perverse incentives follow them out the door: CEOs Charles Prince, at Citicorp, and Stanley O'Neal, at Merrill Lynch, had dismal track records of similar failures prior to the latest disasters, but they collected massive bonuses for their earlier failures and will receive obscene termination packages now. Pay and productivity (and integrity) have become unhinged at U.S. financial institutions.

As this goes to print, Treasury Department officials are working with large financial institutions to cover up the scale of the growing losses. This is the same U.S. Treasury that regularly prates abroad about the vital need for transparency. And a former Treasury Secretary, Robert Rubin, who failed utterly in his fiduciary duty as lead board member at Citicorp to prevent the series of recent abuses, will become Citicorp's new CEO.

To even begin to understand events in the U.S. and global banking industries, you have to look back at the seismic shifts in the industry over the past 30 to 40 years, and at the interplay between those shifts and government policy. The story that continues to unfold is one of progressively worse policies that make financial crises more common and more severe.

These policies have their boosters, though. Chief among them are neoclassical banking and finance economists, whose ideology and methodologies lead them into blatant misreadings of the realities of the industry and the causes of its failures. When the history of this crisis-ridden era in global finance is written, the economists will no doubt be given a significant share of the blame.

A New Era of Crisis

The changes in the U.S. banking industry in recent decades have been so great that a visitor from the 1950s would hardly recognize the industry. Over two decades of intense merger and acquisition activity has left a far smaller number of banks, with assets far more concentrated in the largest ones. Between 1984 and 2004, the number of banks on the FDIC's rolls fell from 14,392 to 7,511; the share of the U.S. banking industry's assets held by the ten largest banks rose from 21% in 1960 to nearly 60% in 2005. At the same time, nonbank businesses that lend, save, and invest money have proliferated, as have the products they sell: a vast array of new kinds of loans and exotic savings and investment vehicles. And the lines have blurred between all of the different players in the industry—between banks and thrifts (e.g., savings and loans), between commercial banks and investment banks.

These changes were made possible by the deregulation of the industry. Bit by bit, beginning in the 1970s, the banking regulations put into place in the wake of the Great Depression were repealed, culminating in the Gramm-Leach-Bliley Act in 1999, which removed the remaining legal barriers to combining commercial banking, investment banking, and insurance under one corporate roof. The

---

Deposit Insurance Spreads Despite Economists' Protests

Banking economists now overwhelmingly criticize deposit insurance. This represents a major change. The prior consensus, shared by Milton Friedman and John Kenneth Galbraith alike, praised deposit insurance for ending the periodic runs on uninsured banks that helped cause the Great Depression. Today, however, the conventional economic wisdom is that deposit insurance may stop runs, but at the expense of encouraging banks to make imprudent loans and take excessive risks. (Neoclassical economists widely view insurance as inherently creating an incentive for insured parties to act in unduly risky ways because of the safety net that insurance provides—a phenomenon termed "moral hazard.")

This claim is dubious: economists do not offer a credible mechanism whereby deposit insurance could lead to the ills they claim it causes. Deposit insurance does not protect the shareholders or the CEO—the two groups (the first, in theory; the second, in practice) that control a bank. It is the depositors who are insured. Thus, they must be the ones who are subject to moral hazard—in other words, the argument against deposit insurance must be based on the claim that it reduces the incentive of depositors to exercise "private market discipline" by pulling their money out of a bank they believe is being poorly run or looted. But there is no credible evidence that depositors are capable of either discerning frauds or avoiding runs on healthy banks based on false rumors. Indeed, studies have shown that even private-sector financial experts who specialize in evaluating the health of banks cannot do so effectively.

Proponents of the view that deposit insurance causes banking failures display an unrecognized logical inconsistency. Their proposed reform is to rely on private market discipline to prevent management from looting the bank or lending imprudently in a bubble. But, if we assume hypothetically that private market discipline is effective against CEOs who would be so inclined, then it should normally be effective despite the presence of deposit insurance. Deposit insurance does not remove private market discipline where the bank is owned by shareholders (unless the CEO owns all the stock) or where the bank issues uninsured subordinated debt. Yet during the S&L crisis, control fraud (the looting of an institution by its own managers or owners) was most common in S&Ls owned in stock form, with the largest losses overwhelmingly among stock S&Ls. In these cases deposit insurance did not

new world of combined financial services is exemplified by the deal, inked (but ostensibly illegal) before the 1999 law was passed, that merged the insurance and investment-banking giant Travelers with Citibank, at the time the nation's number-one commercial bank.

These transformational changes in domestic banking, along with the related effects of economic globalization both in the United States and abroad, have produced recurrent crises in the financial sector. Indeed, the current era has seen over 100 major banking crises, in countries around the globe. Thomas Hoenig, head of the Kansas City Federal Reserve Bank, emphasized the remarkable and disturbing facts in a meeting with fellow heads of supervision:

> A 1996 survey by the IMF [International Monetary Fund] ... found that 73 percent [133 of 181] of their member countries had experienced significant banking problems during the preceding 15 years. Many of these problems led to substantial declines in GDP [and] serious disruptions in credit and capital markets. ...

To date none of these crises has led to a global Great Depression. Only a few were larger in absolute terms than the 1980s S&L debacle in the United States. Yet

preclude private market discipline; market discipline was simply inadequate to prevent control fraud. Some opponents of deposit insurance proclaim the S&L debacle to be their primary example—a flat misreading of the facts.

The empirical evidence economists use to support their critique of deposit insurance is inconsistent. Moreover, even where the adoption of deposit insurance is correlated with a rise in bank failures, the causal relationship may be just the opposite of what economists claim. Nations with early signs of an impending banking crisis may adopt deposit insurance to reduce the risks of runs. Developing nations tend to adopt deposit insurance in conjunction with privatization—which itself often prompts a banking crisis. More broadly, in part because of the fall of the Soviet Union and the rise of the neoliberal "Washington Consensus," the number of nations adopting deposit insurance increased sharply in the last two decades. Banking crises have indeed been far more common over this same period—precisely because these radical transitions have been occurring in nations with weak institutions, too few regulators with too little experience, patterns of bank ownership that maximize conflicts of interest, and substantial corruption.

In addition, empirical studies rely on subjective coding of different countries' deposit insurance policies, often done by economists who oppose deposit insurance. In countries with no formal deposit insurance, implicit government guarantees for banks are common. There are good theoretical and historical reasons to argue that such implicit guarantees—common in crony capitalism and kleptocracies—create greater moral hazard than explicit deposit insurance does because they can be structured to bail out a bank's shareholders and CEO as well as its creditors (as was done in Chile). But there is no way to code accurately for whether there was an implicit guarantee (or whether bank CEOs believed there was an implicit guarantee) in a particular country at a particular time.

Despite these weaknesses in both evidence and analysis, World Bank economists draw firm conclusions, opposing the adoption of deposit insurance in any nation and clearly hoping for its elimination. But the world has rejected their advice. By 2006, 95 countries had deposit insurance, over four times the number in 1983. Moreover, economists' suggestions on how to "improve" deposit insurance (require banks to issue subordinated debt, charge variable rates for deposit insurance, or require private insurance of accounts) are rarely adopted and have proven unsuccessful in practice.

many imposed a much greater relative cost, measured as a percentage of the country's GDP. Some caused severe, depression-like economic problems in the affected nation. Some produced contagion effects that caused severe crises in other nations. And acute banking crises can cause long-term harm. Japan is a rich nation and can afford a 15-year banking crisis—but the world economy cannot. The crisis cut Japan's economic growth to near-zero for a decade, in turn creating contagion effects in the many countries for whom Japan was a major trading partner or a significant source of capital investment. Tens of millions of people remain in poverty in Asia and Africa as a result.

The recurrent banking crises have come as a shock to the United States, given the dearth of bank failures over the first three decades after World War II. The first severe postwar U.S. banking crisis was stemmed from the large loans that top U.S. banks made to sovereign borrowers (i.e., nations), largely in Latin America. The banks had claimed that sovereign loans offered high returns with minimal default risk because the nation could always repay the loan by printing more money. Citibank head Walter Wriston notoriously implied that countries could not go broke. The claim was absurd. However, banking regulators took no effective action to restrain this lending.

The 1982 Mexican default led to contagion and fears of an international meltdown, but the Federal Reserve and the Bank for International Settlements (BIS) took effective action. Brazil experienced a long economic slowdown that contributed to an imminent default on its loans from major U.S. banks. A Brazilian default could have rendered several of our largest banks insolvent. The banks were rescued by a combination of bailouts to Brazil through the IMF and the World Bank and flawed (albeit permissible under so-called Generally Accepted Accounting Principles, or GAAP) "troubled-debt restructuring" to cover up the losses. Brazil used the bailouts to pay minimal interest on the U.S. bank loans and ultimately recovered; while several U.S. banks took serious losses, none failed.

On the heels of this crisis came the savings and loan crisis, an unprecedented debacle which saw the collapse of some 1,000 S&Ls and which cost U.S. taxpayers about $125 billion dollars—primarily the cost of repaying to depositors money that criminal S&L heads had literally stolen from their institutions.

The causes of these crises are varied. They typically occur, however, when large banks are in essence looted by their owners and managers (a phenomenon known as "control fraud") or when there are financial bubbles in which assets become massively overvalued.

Economists who conduct case studies of banking crises commonly report the existence of substantial control fraud. Looting played a prominent role in the S&L debacle. Here is the conclusion of the National Commission on Financial Institution Reform, Recovery and Enforcement (NCFIRRE):

> The typical large failure was a stockholder-owned, state-chartered institution in Texas or California where regulation and supervision were most lax. ... The failed institution typically had experienced a change of control and was tightly held, dominated by an individual with substantial conflicts of interest. ... In the typical large failure, every accounting trick available was used to make the institution look profitable, safe, and solvent. Evidence of

fraud was invariably present as was the ability of the operators to "milk" the organization through high dividends and salaries, bonuses, perks and other means. In short, the typical large failure was one in which management exploited virtually all the perverse incentives created by government policy.

Looting has played a significant role in banking crises around the world. It became so prevalent in the states of the former Soviet Union that it inspired a new term of art, "tunneling," to describe the process of the CEO and owners converting a company's funds to their private benefit.

In addition to the national banking crises, fraud has caused spectacular failures of large banks. The Bank for Credit and Commerce International (BCCI—known informally as the "Bank for Crooks and Criminals International"), Barings Bank, and Continental Bank all stunned the public when they failed. BCCI was the largest bank in the developing world, Barings was England's oldest bank, and Continental was America's third largest bank. Each one collapsed with minimal public warning.

And, of course, more recently control fraud played a role in a number of spectacular business failures outside of the banking industry including Enron, WorldCom, and Tyco. This fact makes it obvious that the conventional economic wisdom, which blames this era's wave of bank failures and banking crises on regulation and deposit insurance (which are specific to the banking industry) is just wrong. Despite this, mainstream economists persist in their diagnosis, rarely scrutinizing the deregulation and privatization that many observers believe in fact triggered these crises.

...They First Make Proud

Economists have dominated the creation of public policies to prevent banking crises. Their track record has been abysmal. They designed and implemented the disastrous deregulation that produced the U.S. S&L debacle, they praised Japan's and East Asia's banking structures just before they collapsed, and they designed the IMF's crisis intervention strategy that intensified losses and human misery. They also designed and praised privatization programs in many transition economies that led to banking crises; they planned (and in some cases profited from) the catastrophic

---

Offshore Banks

One particularly dark side of globalization is the rise of new offshore banks. While Switzerland now has reasonably workable procedures for tracking the funds of kleptocrats and drug traffickers, several small nations have adopted extreme forms of bank secrecy designed to cater to the needs of criminals and tax evaders. Corporations often incorporate in a tax haven because of the extremely low tax rates. In the late 1990s, the Organisation for Economic Co-operation and Development, an organization of the world's industrialized countries, created an initiative to try to curtail these abuses. Conservative think tanks sought to kill the OECD plan and convinced President Bush to block its implementation as one of his earliest actions. The administration reduced its opposition to the OECD initiative after the 9/11 attacks, when it became clear that terrorists used the offshore banks as their preferred means to move funds.

failure of "shock therapy" in Russia. The irony is that when financial experts were most confident in their consensus, they erred the most grievously. As Mark Twain remarked: "It's not the things you *don't* know that cause disasters; it's the things you *do* know, *but aren't true.*"

This record of failure is disappointing and has caused great human suffering. Remarkably, the economists' hubris is unaffected by it. They are now engaged in a war against deposit insurance and regulation. At this juncture, they are losing that war, but they are persevering in their effort to reclaim their domination over banking policy.

Neoclassical banking economists are failing in this arena for three reasons. First, they neither study nor understand fraud mechanisms and the institutions that are essential to limit fraud and corruption. Second, they are shackled by an ideology that *presumes* that unfettered markets always produce the best outcomes and that government intervention is always bad. For instance, in their writings many of the World Bank's banking economists display a passionate contempt for democratic government and banking regulators. Third, they are mono-disciplinary. They rarely cite (and no doubt rarely examine) the literature in other relevant fields such as political science, sociology, and white-collar criminology.

Indeed, although it should be central to their study of crisis prevention, they rarely even cite the work of economist and 2001 Nobel Prize winner George Akerlof. Based on their study of the S&L crisis, which found that looting was a major cause of total S&L losses, Akerlof and Paul Romer developed an economic model of the looting control fraud.

Looters use accounting fraud to make a company *appear* extraordinarily profitable. Consider the S&L crisis. The worst S&L control frauds were the ones reporting

They Just Never Learn

Today's financial crisis offers a superb example of how their methods lead mainstream economists to endorse both private practices and public policies that are perverse. The current crisis exemplifies a variant of accounting control frauds—one in which the CEO and top managers "skim" rather than loot the company—and demonstrates the unrecognized economic costs of obscenely high CEO pay. The incentives created by typical CEO compensation packages in the financial services industry produce bad investment decisions, decisions that increase the CEO's ability to skim, but that expose the financial institution to losses and the nation and world to recurrent financial crises.

Consider the plight of the honest chief financial officer (CFO) in the modern financial world. His counterparts at rival firms are earning record returns by investing in subprime mortgages. Economists trumpet studies showing that banks' income is boosted by practices he questions, including:

- Making more subprime mortgages
- Making more of the worst mortgages such as "Ninja" loans (no verification of income, job or assets), also known as "liars' loans"
- Making subprime loans at particularly high interest rates—which draws in the riskiest borrowers because only the worst credit risks and frauds will apply
- Making loans as quickly as possible
- Growing as quickly as possible
- Reducing internal controls against fraud
- Making loans in cities known to be "hot spots" for mortgage fraud
- Qualifying borrowers by offering "teaser" interest rates that will soon increase substantially

the highest profitability. Moreover, the control frauds were routinely able to get a Big 8 audit firm to give them "clean" GAAP (or Generally Accepted Accounting Principles, the official standard of review in the U.S. accounting industry) opinions for false financial statements.

Economists, in turn, relied on *reported* accounting profits and share prices (which rose along with reported profits) to determine whether a given S&L was well run. But relying on reported accounting earnings or stock prices *must* lead to perverse results when a wave of looting control frauds is expanding. Thanks to their fraudulent accounting, whatever strategies control frauds follow will look profitable, and hence praiseworthy. In the S&Ls, this led economists to praise (1) domination by an owner/CEO; (2) extremely rapid growth; (3) changes of control; and (4) large investments in acquisition, development, and contruction (ADC) loans and direct investments. Lo and behold, these factors turned out to characterize the worst failures. In other words, standard econometrics techniques led economists to praise that which was fraudulent and fatal. The error was so great that they identified the worst S&L in the nation as the best.

Worse, economists persist in the same error. During the recent expansion of the even larger wave of looting control frauds such as Enron, economists touted (1) conflicts of interest at the top audit firms (which they euphemistically restyled as "synergies"); (2) using a top-tier auditor; (3) rapid growth; and (4) granting the CEO greater stock options as positive factors that were leading to increased profits and higher share prices. It was only after the looters began to collapse that variables like these reversed their sign (from a positive to a negative correlation) and displayed their true relationship to business failure. Economists are doomed to

---

- Making loans in areas with rapidly inflating housing bubbles
- Purchasing and holding in portfolio high-yield CDOs (collateralized debt obligations, the investment instruments backed by bundles of mortgages and other loans, often of high risk)
- Keeping minimal reserves against losses

When a housing bubble is expanding, these practices dramatically increase fees and other noninterest income, minimize expenses, and produce relatively few losses. (Losses remain low as long as house prices are rising because borrowers who get in trouble can sell their house for more than they owe or else refinance based on its market value.) Note that this pretty income picture requires accounting and securities fraud, though: reserving properly for the future losses inherent in subjecting the financial institution to this vastly increased default risk would remove the fictional accounting gain.

The combination of dramatically increased revenue, moderately reduced expenses, and minimal loss means that financial institutions that invest heavily in subprime mortgages and CDOs must report record profits while the bubble is hyperinflating.

So what is our honest CFO to do? If she does not follow the pack, her company will report substantially lower income. Its stock price will fall relative to its rivals. The CEO's and CFO's compensation and wealth will fall sharply as raises disappear, bonuses decline, and the value of their shares and stock options falls. The CFO may be fired.

The upshot is that modern compensation systems and the short-term perspective of investors and senior managers all result in perverse incentives to make grossly imprudent investments in those assets experiencing the worst bubbles. This creates a destructive cycle in which large numbers of financial institutions follow the same dysfunctional strategy, which in turn extends and inflates the bubble and produces even more accounting control frauds.

repeat these mistakes until they adopt statistical techniques that cannot be gamed by accounting fraud.

The Economists' War against Banking Regulation

In keeping with their skewed analysis of the recent wave of bank failures and banking crises, banking economists, including those at the World Bank and the IMF, have been waging a war against banking regulation. It is a curious assault that rests on implicit and false dichotomies between market and regulation and between types of regulation.

The World Bank economists recognize that regulation is vital to mandate accurate disclosure of corporate financial information and aid private market enforcement, but appear to believe that regulatory strength is unnecessary to induce banks to provide accurate information. That view is illogical and incorrect. Obtaining accurate information about banks is the heart of banking examination. Regulators use their powers primarily to pry out accurate information from the fraudulent; control frauds do not cooperate voluntarily.

Economists' rationale for opposing strong banking regulators typically rests on public choice theory, which holds that the actors in political systems act to maximize their own self-interest. This analysis paints politicians as corrupt and regulators as "captured" by the industries they are supposed to be regulating. World Bank economist Thorsten Beck and his colleagues summed up this view in 2003 and 2006 working papers:

> Politicians may induce banks to divert the flow of credit to politically connected firms, or powerful banks may "capture" politicians and induce official supervisors to act in the best interest of banks … .

> Government solutions to overcome market failures … have been proven wrong in Bangladesh as across the developed and developing world. … Indeed, powerful regulators are worse than futile—they are corrupt and harmful.

Again, this analysis is nonsensical. If banks can dominate politicians and strong regulators, they can certainly dominate the design of the disclosure standards they face. In that case, pursuant to the economists' own logic, the banks will submit, and politicians beholden to them will permit, deceptive financial reports that grossly overstate banks' value. (This has, in fact, been done in many cases.) Accounting fraud, in turn, renders markets deeply inefficient and causes private market discipline to become perverse. The looters report record profits. Credit is supposed to flow to the most profitable banks. So private markets *aid* the CEOs looting their banks by providing them with the funds to expand rapidly. Again, the failure to understand bank accounting fraud mechanisms, which have been well explained by Akerlof and Romer, leads to a deeply flawed analysis. (In lieu of Akerlof and Romer, the anti-regulation economists frequently cite work sponsored by Michael Milken's institute. Milken was the notorious junk-bond king and looter who caused large losses during the S&L crisis by recruiting and funding several of the worst control frauds, such as Charles Keating. Today, Milken's institute blames the S&L debacle on regulation and seeks to rehabilitate his reputation.)

This overarching logical error, their hostility to democracy, and their view of public officials as inevitably rapacious leads economists to a claim that only *private* parties should exert discipline against banks. The view has a number of problems. First, it is overstated. Regulators in some nations do resist political pressure. In the S&L crisis, many regulators did their job despite intense political pressure and saved over a trillion dollars in the process. On the other hand: if, over time, people are taught to believe that it is normal and rational for public officials to be rapacious, this can become a self-fulfilling prophecy as those who aim to enrich themselves sign on to become officials.

Moreover, the argument proves too much. If the banks (or politicians) are powerful enough to act illegitimately *through* regulators, they are powerful enough to act illegitimately *without* regulators to achieve the same result. The argument is also based on a fundamental misunderstanding of control frauds. It is not the "powerful banks" Beck and his coauthors refer to that put pressure on regulators or politicians—it is the CEOs or their agents who do. They do not coerce regulators "to act in the best interest of banks." They coerce them in an attempt to act to help the CEO loot the bank.

In fact, the evidence shows that private parties are *more* subject to capture than public officials. Looting control frauds are routinely able to get top-tier audit firms to give their blessing to massive accounting fraud. The ratings agencies do no better against control fraud. Our most prestigious law firms have helped CEOs loot and destroy their clients. Private deposit insurance funds for thrifts used to exist in many states. None do now. The Maryland, Ohio, and Utah funds were each destroyed by the very first thrift that collapsed in their state thanks to control fraud. No private insurer made more than a feeble effort to exercise discipline. Instead, they acted as boosters for the CEOs who looted and destroyed their own thrifts and brought down the insurance funds with them.

Finally, the empirical studies on banking regulation rely on coding of data by economists who typically oppose regulation, rendering the results unreliable. The risks of subjective bias are acute. There is no objective measure of "strong" regulation, or capture, or "rent seeking behavior." We know that economists have claimed that the Bank Board under Chairman Edwin Gray was captured during the S&L crisis. Not so. In fact, *private* experts were routinely captured by the S&L control frauds. Plus, the studies focus on formal supervisory power, yet informal banking supervision is widespread and often a regulator's most effective tool.

Overall, empirical studies find that better quality regulation (again, to be fair, a subjective concept) reduces banking losses.

International Convergence

Despite the flawed logic and lack of empirical support for their views, conventional banking economists, including those at the World Bank, continue to voice opposition to the creation of strong supervisory agencies. For now, however, their call has been rejected.

In the 1980s, the U.S. government reacted to Japan's emergence as the new (apparent) dominant financial power by claiming that Japan gained an unfair advantage because its banks were permitted to operate with lower capital reserves. If all other factors are held constant, a bank held to a lower capital reserve requirement can grow more quickly, lend more cheaply, and finance greater economic growth. Complaining that the playing field was not level, the United States insisted on an international agreement to set minimum bank capital standards. The U.S. effort succeeded in 1988, when the largest industrial nations adopted the Basel Accord. More recently, the accord was revised and expanded ("Basel II") to include more closely calibrated minimum capital requirements as well as a supervisory strategy of "prompt corrective action" against banks that fail to meet the capital requirements and a strategy to make private market discipline more effective by requiring banks to disclose more information.

The Basel Accord was a major step towards greater international uniformity of banking regulation ("convergence") among developed nations. The expansion of the European Union is another major force for convergence, as candidate nations must adopt modern banking laws and regulatory structures meeting the EU's minimum standards.

Banks are also subject to an increasing number of international treaties designed to restrict money laundering and bribery. There are, however, very few enforcement actions or prosecutions, so enforcement does not appear to be effective at this time. In addition, offshore banks remain an enormous loophole limiting the effectiveness of convergence.

New banking crises have diminished substantially in nations complying with the Basel accords. Of course, it is too early to judge whether the Basel process is responsible for this success. However, we do have cross-country evidence showing that weak regulation leads to recurrent waves of control fraud. Tests of Basel's effectiveness by one of the World Bank economists find positive relationships between stronger regulation and bank health. (These tests employed a methodology that posed less risk of subjective bias by the economists conducting the studies, but they remain inherently subjective.)

The economists' frustration, however, is understandable. They are skilled research scientists for whom econometric studies are the epitome of proof. Contrary case studies are mere "anecdotal evidence" that are fully encompassed within their data and, therefore, require no refutation. Moreover, their worldview is shaped by public choice theory. They view banking regulators as corrupt, "rent seeking" parasites who merely pretend to virtue. Alternatively, in their "capture" model, regulators are cowards who roll over to aid the control frauds. They have not been banking regulators, so they are uncontaminated and can see the truth as the empirical data reveal it to them.

Regulators, however, dominate much of the Basel process. They view the economists' disdain as an inaccurate and insulting caricature that indicates their ignorance of the real-world banking business. Regulators tend to believe in their experiences, which overwhelmingly teach that control frauds exploit regulatory weaknesses and that normally honest, sober bankers act like frat boys on spring break during financial bubbles. Imprudent lending is the norm in bubbles. Regulators have seen many econometric "proofs" of propositions they know to be false from experience. Some of them have a reasonably sophisticated understanding of the illusion of precision in empirical work and the many opportunities for subjective coding to lead even the best scholars into error. To date, the regulators have staved off the economists' war against banking regulation, and even the World Bank's economists have had to concede that the *initial* results of the Basel process are extremely positive.

Basel II does have a worrying component. It encourages the large banks to value their assets (which implicitly means evaluating their risk) using their own proprietary models. It is easy for these models to be designed so as to dramatically overstate asset values. The problem is compounded by the nature of proprietary models: they are secret, complex, and (perhaps) subject to frequent adjustment. That makes them a nightmare to try to regulate. And in what is essentially a form of control fraud, modern compensation systems, especially in the United States, create powerful incentives for top managers to overstate banks' asset values in order to puff up their own pay packages. Such abuse is so common that instead of "mark to market," the usual term for bringing the valuation of an asset into line with its market price, the process is often known to insiders as "mark to myth."

In the United States, the word "deregulation" still has a positive ring for many despite the disastrous results of this country's experiment in loosening the reins on the banking industry. So perhaps it is ironic that it was the United States that instigated an international effort to develop convergent banking regulations worldwide. International convergence is moving forward, and for now the pace of new financial crises has slowed. The Basel process is indeed leveling the playing field among financial services companies around the world. But what kind of field will emerge? Does the Basel process offer any hope of reshaping the new world of banking into one that better meets consumer needs and better serves the broader public interest? If the banking economists, with their ideological commitment to oppose any regulation, are kept at bay, then at least we may find out. ❑

Sources. C.E.V Borio and R. Filosa, "The Changing Borders of Banking: Trends and Implications," *BIS Working Paper* 23, 10/94; Center for International Private Enterprise, "Financial Reform: Paving the Way for Growth and Democracy," *Economic Reform Today*, 1995; J. Bisignano, "Precarious Credit Equilibria: Reflections on the Asian Financial Crisis," *BIS Working Papers*, 3/99; W. K. Black, The Best Way to Rob a Bank is to Own One, 2005; L.J. White, T*he S&L Debacle: Public Policy Lessons for Bank and Thrift Regulation*, 1991; Federal Home Loan Bank Board, "Agenda for Reform: A Report on Deposit Insurance," 1983; K. Calavita et al., *Big Money Crime: Fraud and Politics in the Savings and Loan Industry*, 1997; W. K. Black et al., "The Savings and Loan Debacle of the 1980's: White-Collar Crime or Risky Business?" *Law & Policy* 17; G. Akerlof and P. M. Romer, "Looting: The Economic Underworld of Bankruptcy for Profit," *Brookings Papers on Econ Activity*, 1993; M. Mayer, *The Greatest-Ever Bank Robbery*, 1990; T. Curry and L. Shibut, "The Cost of the Savings and Loan Crisis: Truth and Consequences," *FDIC Banking Review*, Fall 2000; W. K. Black, "Reexamining the Law-and-Economics Theory of Corporate Governance," *Challenge*, 1993; C-J Lindgren et al., "Bank Soundness and Macroeconomic Policy," IMF, 1996; T. M. Hoenig, "Exploring the Macro-Prudential Aspects of Financial Sector Supervision," speech to the Meeting for Heads of Supervision, BIS, Basel, Switzerland, 4/27/04; V. A. Atanasov et al., "The Anatomy of Financial Tunneling in an Emerging Market," McCombs

School of Business, Research Paper Fin-04-06; N. Passas, "The Genesis of the BCCI Scandal," *J Law and Soc*, 3/66; P. L. Zweig, *Belly Up: The Collapse of the Penn Square Bank*, 1986; R. J. Herring, "BCCI & Barings: Bank Resolutions Complicated by Fraud and Global Corporate Structure"; H.R. Davia et al., *Accountant's Guide to Fraud Detection and Control* (2nd ed.), 2000; P. Blustein, "The Chastening: Inside the Crisis that Rocked the Global Financial System and Humbled the IMF," *Public Aff*, 2001; W. K. Black, "A Tale of Two Crises," Kravis Leadership Inst Rvw, Fall 2002; Federal Reserve Bank of San Francisco, *Economic Letter*, 3/06; B. H. Soral et al., "Fraud, banking crisis, and regulatory enforcement: Evidence from micro-level transactions data," *European Journal of Law and Econ*, 4/06; J. L. Pierce, *The Future of Banking*, 1991; E. J. Kane, *The Gathering Crisis in Federal Deposit Insurance*, MIT Univ Press, 1985; A. Demirguc-Kunt and E. Detragiache, "Does Deposit Insurance Increase Banking System Stability? An Empirical Investigation," *J Monetary Econ*, 10/02; D. Pyle, review of "The Gathering Crisis in Federal Deposit Insurance" in *J Econ Lit*, 9/86; J. Santos, "Bank Capital Regulation in Contemporary Banking Theory: A review of the literature," in *Financial Markets, Institutions & Instruments*, 2001; A.B. Ashcraft, "Does the Market Discipline Banks? New Evidence from Regulatory Capital Mix," 10/2/06; T. Beck et al., "Bank Supervision and Corporate Finance," *World Bank Policy Research Working Paper*, 5/03; D. R. Brumbaugh, Jr, *Thrifts Under Siege: Restoring Order to American Banking*, 1988; T. Beck et al., "Bank Supervision and Corruption in Lending," 9/3/05; A. Demirguc-Kunt et al., "Banking on the Principles: Compliance with Basel Core Principles and Bank Soundness," *IMF Working Paper* 10/06; R. La Porta et al., "Related Lending," *Quarterly J Econ*, 2003; S. Johnson et al., "Tunnelling," Am Econ Assoc Papers & Proceedings, 2000; R. Haselmann et al., "How Law Affects Lending," *Columbia Law and Economics Working Paper*, 9/06; J. D. Edwards and J. H. Godwin, "Why Sound Accounting Standards Count," *Econ Reform Today*, 1995; J. R. Barth, *The Great Savings and Loan Debacle*, 1991.

Article 2.4

AMERICA'S GROWING FRINGE ECONOMY

HOWARD KARGER
November/December 2006

Financial services for the poor and credit-challenged are big business.

Ron Cook is a department manager at a Wal-Mart store in Atlanta. Maria Guzman is an undocumented worker from Mexico; she lives in Houston with her three children and cleans office buildings at night. Marty Lawson works for a large Minneapolis corporation.* What do these three people have in common? They are all regular fringe economy customers.

The term "fringe economy" refers to a range of businesses that engage in financially predatory relationships with low-income or heavily indebted consumers by charging excessive interest rates, superhigh fees, or exorbitant prices for goods or services. Some examples of fringe economy businesses include payday lenders, pawnshops, check-cashers, tax refund lenders, rent-to-own stores, and "buy-here/pay-here" used car lots. The fringe economy also includes credit card companies that charge excessive late payment or over-the-credit-limit penalties; cell phone providers that force less creditworthy customers into expensive prepaid plans; and subprime mortgage lenders that gouge prospective homeowners.

The fringe economy is hardly new. Pawnshops and informal high-interest lenders have been around forever. What we see today, however, is a fringe-economy sector that is growing fast, taking advantage of the ever-larger part of the U.S. population whose economic lives are becoming less secure. Moreover, in an important sense the sector is no longer "fringe" at all: more and more, large mainstream financial corporations are behind the high-rate loans that anxious customers in run-down storefronts sign for on the dotted line.

The Payday Lending Trap

Ron and Deanna Cook have two children and a combined family income of $48,000—more than twice the federal poverty line but still $10,000 below Georgia's median income. They are the working poor.

To make ends meet, the Cooks borrow from payday lenders. When Ron and Deanna borrow $300 for 14 days they pay $60 in interest—an annual interest rate of 520%! If they can't pay the full $360, they pay just the $60 interest fee and roll over the loan for another two weeks. The original $300 loan now costs $120 in interest for 30 days. If they roll over the loan for another two-week cycle, they pay $180 in interest on a $300 loan for 45 days. If the payday lender permits only four rollovers, the Cooks sometimes take out a payday loan from another lender to repay the original loan. This costly cycle can be devastating. The Center for Responsible Lending tells the tale of one borrower who entered into 35 back-to-back payday loans over 17 months, paying $1,254 in fees on a $300 loan.

The Cooks take out about ten payday loans a year, which is close to the national average for payday loan customers. Although the industry claims payday loans are intended only for emergencies, a 2003 study of Pima County, Ariz., by the Southwest Center for Economic Integrity found that 67% of borrowers used their loans for general non-emergency bills. The Center for Responsible Lending found that 66% of borrowers initiate five or more loans a year, and 31% take out twelve or more loans yearly. Over 90% of payday loans go to borrowers with five or more loans a year. Customers who take out 13 or more loans a year account for over half of payday lenders' total revenues.

The Unbanked

Maria Guzman and her family are part of the 10% of U.S. households—more than 12 million—that have no relationship with a bank, savings institution, credit union, or other mainstream financial service provider. Being "unbanked," the Guzmans turn to the fringe economy for check cashing, bill payment, short-term pawn or payday loans, furniture and appliance rentals, and a host of other financial services. In each case, they face high user fees and exorbitant interest rates.

Without credit, the Guzmans must buy a car either for cash or through a "buy-here/pay-here" (BHPH) used car lot. At a BHPH lot they are saddled with a 28% annual percentage rate (APR) on a high-mileage and grossly overpriced vehicle. They also pay weekly, and one missed payment means a repossession. Since the Guzmans have no checking account, they use a check-casher who charges 2.7% for cashing their monthly $1,500 in payroll checks, which costs them $40.50 a month or $486 a year.

Like many immigrants, the Guzmans send money to relatives in their home country. (Money transfers from the United States to Latin America are expected to reach $25 billion by 2010.) If they sent $500 to Mexico on June 26, 2006, using Western Union's "Money in Minutes," they would have paid a $32 transfer fee. Moreover, Western Union's exchange rate for the transaction was 11.12 pesos for the U.S. dollar, while the official exchange rate that day was 11.44. The difference on $500 was almost $14, which raised the real costs of the transaction to $46, or almost 10% of the transfer amount.

Without a checking account, the Guzmans turn to money orders or direct bill pay, both of which add to their financial expenses. For example, ACE Cash Express charges 79 cents per money order and $1 or more for each direct bill payment. If the Guzmans use money orders to pay six bills a month, the fees total nearly $57 a year; using direct bill pay, they would pay a minimum of $72 in fees per year.

All told, the Guzmans spend more than 10% of their income on alternative financial services, which is average for unbanked households. To paraphrase James Baldwin, it is expensive to be poor and unbanked in America.

The Cooks and the Guzmans, along with people like Marty Lawson caught in a cycle of credit card debt (see sidebar on next page), may not fully appreciate the economic entity they are dealing with. Far from a mom-and-pop industry, America's fringe economy is largely dominated by a handful of large, well-financed multinational corporations with strong ties to mainstream financial institutions. It is a comprehensive and fully formed parallel economy that addresses the financial needs of the poor and credit-challenged in the same way as the mainstream economy meets the needs of the middle class. The main difference is the exorbitant interest rates, high fees, and onerous loan terms that mark fringe economy transactions.

The Scope of the Fringe Economy

The unassuming and often shoddy storefronts of the fringe economy mask the true scope of this economic sector. Check-cashers, payday lenders, pawnshops, and rent-to-own stores alone engaged in at least 280 million transactions in 2001, according to Fannie Mae Foundation estimates, generating about $78 billion in gross revenues. By comparison, in 2003 combined state and federal spending on the core U.S. social welfare programs—Temporary Aid to Needy Families (AFDC's replacement), Supplemental Security Income, Food Stamps, the Women, Infants and Children (WIC) food program, school lunch programs, and the U.S. Department of Housing and Urban Development's (HUD) low-income housing programs—totaled less than $125 billion. Revenues in the combined sectors of the fringe economy—including subprime home mortgages and refinancing, and

---

Credit Cards, College Students, and the Fringe Economy

Marty Lawson is one of the growing legions of the credit poor. Although he earns $65,000 a year, his $50,000 credit card debt means that he can buy little more than the essentials. This cycle of debt began when Marty received his first credit card in college.

Credit cards are the norm for today's college students. A 2005 Nellie Mae report found that 55% of college students get their first credit card during their freshman year; by senior year, 91% have a credit card and 56% carry four or more cards.

College students are highly prized credit card customers because of their high future earnings and lifetime credit potential. To ensnare them, credit card companies actively solicit on campus through young recruiters who staff tables outside university bookstores and student centers. Students are baited with free t-shirts, frisbees, candy, music downloads, and other come-ons. Credit card solicitations are stuffed into new textbooks and sent to dormitories, electronic mailboxes, and bulletin boards. According to Junior Achievement, the typical college freshman gets about eight credit card offers in the first week of the fall semester. The aggressiveness of credit card recruiters has led several hundred colleges to ban them from campus.

Excited by his newfound financial independence, Marty overlooked the fine print explaining that cash advances carried a 20% or more APR. He also didn't realize how easily he could reach the credit limit, and the stiff penalties incurred for late payments and over-the-credit-limit transactions. About one-third of credit card company profits come from these and other penalties.

Marty applied for a second credit card after maxing out his first one. The credit line on his second card was exhausted in only eight months. Facing $4,000 in high-interest credit card bills, Marty left college to pay off his debts. He never returned. Dropping out to repay credit card debt is all too common, and according to former Indiana University administrator John Simpson, "We lose more students to credit card debt than academic failure." Not coincidentally, by graduation the average credit card debt for college seniors is almost $3,000. Credit card debt worsens the longer a student stays in school. A 2004 Nellie Mae survey found the average credit card debt for graduate students was a whopping $7,831, a 59% increase over 1998. Fifteen percent of graduate students carry credit card balances of $15,000 or more.

used car sales—would inflate the $78 billion several times over and eclipse federal and state spending on the poor.

There can be no doubt that the scope of the fringe economy is enormous. The Community Financial Services Association of America claims that 15,000 payday lenders extend more than $25 billion in short-term loans to millions of households each year. According to Financial Service Centers of America, 10,000 check-cashing stores process 180 million checks with a face value of $55 billion.

The sheer number of fringe economy storefronts is mind-boggling. For example, ACE Cash Express—only one of many such corporations—has 68 locations within 10 miles of my Houston zip code. Nationwide there are more than 33,000 check-cashing and payday loan stores, just two parts of the fringe economy. That's more than the all the McDonald's and Burger King restaurants and all the Target, J.C. Penney, and Wal-Mart retail stores in the United States combined.

ACE Cash Express is the nation's largest check-casher and exemplifies the growth and profitability of the fringe economy. In 1991 ACE had 181 stores; by 2005 it had 1,371 stores with 2,700 employees in 37 states and the District of Columbia. ACE's revenues totaled $141 million in 2000 and by 2005 rose to $268.6 million. In 2005 ACE:

- cashed 13.3 million checks worth approximately $5.3 billion (check cashing fees totaled $131.6 million);
- served more than 40 million customers (3.4 million a month or 11,000 an hour) and processed $10.3 billion in transactions;
- processed over 2 million loan transactions (worth $640 million) and generated interest income and fees of $91.8 million;
- added a total of 142 new locations (in 2006 the company anticipates adding 150 more);
- processed over $410 million in money transfers and 7.6 million money orders with a face value of $1.3 billion;
- processed over 7.8 million bill payment and debit card transactions, and sold approximately 172,000 prepaid debit cards.

Advance America is the nation's leading payday lender, with 2,640 stores in 36 states, more than 5,500 employees, and $630 million this year in revenues. Dollar Financial Corporation operates 1,106 stores in 17 states, Canada, and the United Kingdom. Their 2005 revenues were $321 million. Check-into-Cash has more than 700 stores; Check N' Go has 900 locations in 29 states. Almost all of these are publicly traded NASDAQ corporations.

There were 4,500 pawnshops in the United States in 1985; now there are almost 12,000, including outlets owned by five publicly traded chains. In 2005 the three big chains—Cash America International (a.k.a Cash America Pawn and SuperPawn), EZ Pawn, and First Cash—had combined annual revenues of nearly $1 billion. Cash America is the largest pawnshop chain, with 750 locations; the company also makes payday loans through its Cash America Payday Advance, Cashland, and Mr. Payroll stores. In 2005, Cash America's revenues totaled $594.3 million.

The Association of Progressive Rental Organizations claims that the $6.6 billion a year rent-to-own (RTO) industry serves 2.7 million households through 8,300 stores in 50 states. Many RTOs rent everything from furniture, electronics, major appliances, and computers to jewelry. Rent-A-Center is the largest RTO corporation in the world. In 2005 it employed 15,000 people; owned or operated 3,052 stores in the United States and Canada; and had revenues of $2.4 billion. Other leading RTO chains include Aaron Rents (with 1,255 stores across the United States and Canada and gross revenues of $1.1 billion in 2005) and RentWay (with 788 stores in 34 states and revenues of almost $516 million in 2005).

These corporations represent the tip of the iceberg. Low-income consumers spent $1.75 billion for tax refund loans in 2002. Many lost as much as 16% of their tax refunds because of expensive tax preparation fees and/or interest incurred in tax refund anticipation loans. The interest and fees on such loans can translate into triple-digit annualized interest rates, according to the Consumer Federation of America, which has also reported that 11 million tax filers received refund anticipation loans in 2000, almost half through H&R Block. According to a Brookings Institution report, the nation's largest tax preparers earned about $357 million from fringe economy "fast cash" products in 2001, more than double their earnings in 1998. All for essentially lending people their own money!

The fringe economy plays a big role in the housing market, where subprime home mortgages rose from 35,000 in 1994 to 332,000 in 2003, a 25% a year growth rate and a tenfold increase in just nine years. (A subprime loan is a loan extended to less creditworthy customers at a rate that is higher than the prime rate.) According to Edward Gramlich, former member of the Board of Governors of the Federal Reserve System, subprime mortgages accounted for almost $300 billion or 9% of all mortgages in 2003.

While the fringe economy squeezes its customers, it is generous to its CEOs. According to Forbes, salaries in many fringe economy corporations rival those in much larger companies. In 2004 Sterling Brinkley, chairman of EZ Corp, earned $1.26 million; ACE's CEO Jay Shipowitz received $2.1 million on top of $2.38 million in stocks; Jeffrey Weiss, Dollar Financial Group's CEO, earned $1.83 million; Mark Speese, Rent-A-Center's CEO, made $820,000 with total stock options of $10 million; and Cash America's CEO Daniel Feehan was paid almost $2.2 million in 2003 plus the $9 million he had in stock options.

Fringe-economy corporations argue that the high interest rates and fees they charge reflect the heightened risks of doing business with an economically unstable population. While fringe businesses have never made their pricing criteria public, some risks are clearly overstated. For example, ACE assesses the risk of each check-cashing transaction and reports losses of less than 1%. Since tax preparers file a borrower's taxes, they are reasonably assured that refund anticipation loans will not exceed refunds. To further guarantee repayment, they often establish an escrow account into which the IRS directly deposits the tax refund check. Pawnshops lend only about 50% of a pawned item's value, which leaves them a large buffer if the pawn goes unclaimed (industry trade groups claim that 70% of customers do redeem their goods). The rent-to-own furniture and appliance industry charges well above the "street price" for furniture and appliances, which is more than enough to offset any losses. Payday lenders require a post-dated check or electronic debit to assure repayment. Payday loan losses are about 6% or less, according to the Center for Responsible Lending.

Much of the profit in the fringe economy comes from financing rather than the sale of a product. For example, if a used car lot buys a vehicle for $3,000 and sells it for $5,000 cash, their profit is $2,000. But if they finance that vehicle for two years at a 25% APR, the profit jumps to $3,242. This dynamic is true for virtually every sector of the fringe economy. A customer who pays off a loan or purchases a good or service outright is much less profitable for fringe economy businesses than customers who maintain an ongoing financial relationship with the business. In that sense, profit in the fringe economy lies with keeping customers continually enmeshed in an expensive web of debt.

A Glossary of the Fringe Economy

- **Payday loans** are small, short-term loans, usually of no more than $1,500, to cover expenses until the borrower's next payday. These loans come with extremely high interests rates, commonly equivalent to 300% APR. The Center for Responsible Lending conservatively estimates that predatory payday lending practices cost American families $3.4 billion annually.
- **Refund anticipation loans (RALs)**, provided by outlets of such firms as H&R Block, Western Union, and Liberty Tax Service, are short-term loans, often with high interest rates or fees, secured by an expected tax refund. Interest rates can reach over 700% APR-equivalent.
- **Check cashing stores** (ACE Cash Express is the biggest chain) provide services for people who don't have checking accounts. These stores are most often located in low-income neighborhoods and cash checks for a fee, which can vary greatly but is typically far higher than commercial banks charge for the same service. Check cashing fees have steadily increased over the past ten years.
- **Money Transfer companies** (outlets of such companies as Western Union, Moneygram, and Xoom) allow people to make direct bill payments and send money either to a person or bank account for a fee, typically 10% of the amount being sent, not including the exchange rate loss for money sent internationally. the total cost can reach up to 25% of the amount sent.
- **Pawnshops** give loans while holding objects of value as collateral. The pawnbroker returns the object when the loan is repaid, usually at a high interest rates. If the borrower doesn't repay the loan within a specified period, the pawnbroker sells the item. For example, the interest charge on a 30-day loan of $10 could be $2.20, equivalent to a 264% APR. Most pawnshops are individually owned but regional chains are now appearing.
- **Rent-to-own (RTO) stores**—two leading chains are Rent-A-Center and Aaron Rents—rent furniture, electronics, and other consumer goods short-term or long-term. The consumer can eventually own the item after paying many times the standard retail price through weekly rental payments with an extremely high interest rate, commonly around 300% APR. If the consumer misses a payment, the item is repossessed.
- **Buy here/pay here (BHPH) car lots** offer car loans on used cars on-site, with interest rates much higher than auto loans issued by commercial banks. Customers are often saddled with high-interest loans for high-mileage, overpriced vehicles. If a customer misses one payment, the car is repossessed. The largest BHPH company is the J.D. Byrider franchise, with 124 dealerships throughout the country.

Funding and Exporting America's Fringe Economy

Fringe economy corporations require large amounts of capital to fund their phenomenal growth, and mainstream financial institutions have stepped up to the plate. ACE Cash Express has a relationship with a group of banks including Wells Fargo, JP Morgan Chase Bank, and JP Morgan Securities to provide capital for acquisitions and other activities. Advance America has relationships with Morgan Stanley, Banc of America Securities LLC, Wachovia Capital Markets, and Wells Fargo Securities, to name a few. Similar banking relationships exist throughout the fringe economy.

The fringe economy is no longer solely a U.S. phenomenon. In 2003 the HSBC Group purchased Household International (and its subsidiary Beneficial Finance) for $13 billion. Headquartered in London, HSBC is the world's second largest bank and serves more than 90 million customers in 80 countries. Household International is a U.S.-based consumer finance company with 53 million customers and more than 1,300 branches in 45 states. It is also a predatory lender. In 2002, a $484 million settlement was reached between Household and all 50 states and the District of Columbia. In effect, Household acknowledged it had duped tens of thousands of low-income home buyers into loans with unnecessary hidden costs. In 2003, another $100 million settlement was reached based on Household's abusive mortgage lending practices.

HSBC plans to export Household's operations to Poland, China, Mexico, Britain, France, India, and Brazil, for starters. One shudders to think how the fringe economy will develop in nations with even fewer regulatory safeguards than the United States. Presumably, HSBC also believes that predatory lending will not tarnish the reputation of the seven British lords and one baroness who sit on its 20-member board of directors.

What Can be Done?

The fringe economy is one of the few venues that credit-challenged or low-income families can turn to for financial help. This is especially true for those facing a penurious welfare system with a lifetime benefit cap and few mechanisms for emergency assistance. In that sense, enforcing strident usury and banking laws to curb the fringe economy while providing no legal and accessible alternatives would hurt the very people such laws are intended to help by driving these transactions into a criminal underground. Instead of ending up in court, non-paying debtors would wind up in the hospital. Simply outlawing a demand-driven industry is rarely successful.

One strategy to limit the growth of the fringe economy is to develop more community-based lending institutions modeled on the Grameen Bank or on local cooperatives. Although community banks might charge a higher interest rate than commercial banks charge prime rate customers, the rates would still be significantly lower than in the existing fringe sector.

Another policy option is to make work pay, or at least make it pay better. In other words, we need to increase the minimum wage and the salaries of the lower middle class and working poor. One reason for the rapid growth of the fringe economy is the growing gap between low and stagnant wages and higher prices, especially for necessities like housing, health care, pharmaceuticals, and energy.

Stricter usury laws, better enforcement of existing banking regulations, and a more active federal regulatory system to protect low-income consumers can all play a role in taming the fringe economy. Concurrently, federal and state governments can promote the growth of non-predatory community banking institutions. In addition, commercial banks can provide low-income communities with accessible and inexpensive banking services. As the "DrillDown" studies conducted in recent years by the Washington, D.C., non-profit Social Compact suggest, low-income communities contain more income and resources than one might think. If fringe businesses can make billions in low-income neighborhoods, less predatory economic institutions should be able to profit there too. Lastly, low and stagnant wages make it difficult, if not impossible, for the working poor to make ends meet without resorting to debt. A significant increase in wages would likely result in a significant decline in the fringe economy. In the end, several concerted strategies will be required to restrain this growing and out-of-control economic beast. ❑

Sources: "2003 Credit Card Usage Analysis" (2004) and "Undergraduate Students and Credit Cards in 2004" (2005) (Nellie Mae); Alan Berube, Anne Kim, Benjamin Forman, and Megan Burns, "The Price of Paying Taxes: How Tax Preparation and Refund Loan Fees Erode the Benefits of the EITC" (Brookings Institution and Progressive Policy Institute, May 2002); James H. Carr and Jenny Shuetz, "Financial Services in Distressed Communities: Framing the Issue, Finding Solutions," Financial Services in Distressed Communities: Issues and Answers (2001, Fannie Mae Foundation); "Making the Case for Financial Literacy: A Collection of Current Statistics Regarding Youth and Money" (Junior Achievement); Amanda Sapir and Karen Uhlich, "Pay Day Lending in Pima County Arizona" (Southwest Center for Economic Integrity, 2003); Keith Urnst, John Farris, and Uriah King, "Quantifying the Economic Cost of Predatory Payday Lending" (Center for Responsible Lending, 2004).

Resources: Organizations working on these issues include U.S. Public Interest Research Group, www.uspirg.org; Association of Community Organizations for Reform Now (ACORN), www.acorn.org; Coalition for Responsible Credit Practices, www.responsible-credit.net; Community Financial Services Association of America, www.cfsa.net; Consumer Federation of America, www.consumerfed.org; Harvard University, Joint Center for Housing Studies, www.jchs.harvard.edu; National Consumer Law Center, www.consumerlaw.org.

Article 2.5

FINANCIALIZATION: A PRIMER

BY RAMAA VASUDEVAN
November/December 2008

You don't have to be an investor dabbling in the stock market to feel the power of finance. Finance pervades the lives of ordinary people in many ways, from student loans and credit card debt to mortgages and pension plans.

And its size and impact are only getting bigger. Consider a few measures:

- U.S. credit market debt—all debt of private households, businesses, and government combined—rose from about 1.6 times the nation's GDP in 1973 to over 3.5 times GDP by 2007.

- The profits of the financial sector represented 14% of total corporate profits in 1981; by 2001-02 this figure had risen to nearly 50%.

These are only a few of the indicators of what many commentators have labeled the "financialization" of the economy—a process University of Massachusetts economist Gerald Epstein succinctly defines as "the increasing importance of financial markets, financial motives, financial institutions, and financial elites in the operation of the economy and its governing institutions."

In recent years, this phenomenon has drawn increasing attention. In his latest book, pundit Kevin Phillips writes about the growing divergence between the real (productive) and financial economies, describing how the explosion of trading in myriad new financial instruments played a role in polarizing the U.S. economy. On the left, political economists Harry Magdoff and Paul Sweezy had over many years pointed to the growing role of finance in the operations of capitalism; they viewed the trend as a reflection of the rising economic and political power of "rentiers"—those whose earnings come from financial activities and from forms of income arising from ownership claims (such as interest, rent, dividends, or capital gains) rather than from actual production.

From Finance to Financialization

The financial system is supposed to serve a range of functions in the broader economy. Banks and other financial institutions mop up savings, then allocate that capital, according to mainstream theory, to where it can most productively be used. For households and corporations, the credit markets facilitate greatly increased borrowing, which should foster investment in capital goods like buildings and machinery, in turn leading to expanded production. Finance, in other words, is supposed to facilitate the growth of the "real" economy—the part that produces useful goods (like bicycles) and services (like medical care).

In recent decades, finance has undergone massive changes in both size and shape. The basic mechanism of financialization is the transformation of future streams of income (from profits, dividends, or interest payments) into a tradable asset like a stock or a bond. For example, the future earnings of corporations are transmuted into equity stocks that are bought and sold in the capital market. Likewise, a loan, which involves certain fixed interest payments over its duration, gets a new life when it is converted into marketable bonds. And multiple loans, bundled together then "sliced and diced" into novel kinds of bonds ("collateralized debt obligations"), take on a new existence as investment vehicles that bear an extremely complex and opaque relationship to the original loans.

The process of financialization has not made finance more effective at fulfilling what conventional economic theory views as its core function. Corporations are not turning to the stock market as a source of finance for their investments, and their borrowing in the bond markets is often not for the purpose of productive investment either. Since the 1980s, corporations have actually spent more money buying back their own stock than they have taken in by selling newly issued stock. The granting of stock options to top executives gives them a direct incentive to have the corporation buy back its own shares—often using borrowed money to do so—in order to hike up the share price and allow them to turn a profit on the sale of their personal shares. More broadly, instead of fostering investment, financialization reorients managerial incentives toward chasing short-term returns through financial trading and speculation so as to generate ballooning earnings, lest their companies face falling stock prices and the threat of hostile takeover.

What is more, the workings of these markets tend to act like an upper during booms, when euphoric investors chase the promise of quick bucks. During downturns these same mechanisms work like downers, turning euphoria into panic as investors flee. Financial innovations like collateralized debt obligations were supposed to "lubricate" the economy by spreading risk, but instead they tend to heighten volatility, leading to amplified cycles of boom and bust. In the current crisis, the innovation of mortgage-backed securities fueled the housing bubble and encouraged enormous risk-taking, creating the conditions for the chain reaction of bank (and other financial institution) failures that may be far from over.

Financialization and Power

The arena of finance can at times appear to be merely a casino—albeit a huge one—where everyone gets to place her bets and ride her luck. But the financial system carries a far deeper significance for people's lives. Financial assets and liabilities represent claims on ownership and property; they embody the social relations of an economy at a particular time in history. In this sense, the recent process of financialization implies the increasing political and economic power of a particular segment of the capitalist class: rentiers. Accelerating financial transactions and the profusion of financial techniques have fuelled an extraordinary enrichment of this elite.

This enrichment arises in different ways. Financial transactions facilitate the reallocation of capital to high-return ventures. In the ensuing shake-up, some sectors of capital profit at the expense of other sectors. More important, the capitalist class as a whole is able to force a persistent redistribution in its favor, deploying its newly expanded wealth to bring about changes in the political-economy that channel even more wealth its way.

The structural changes that paved the way for financialization involved the squashing of working-class aspirations during the Reagan-Thatcher years; the defeats of the miners' strike in England and of the air traffic controllers' (PATCO) strike in the United States were perhaps the most symbolic instances of this process. At the same time, these and other governments increasingly embraced the twin policy mantras of fighting inflation and deregulating markets in place of creating full employment and raising wages. Corporations pushed through legislation to dismantle the financial regulations that inhibited their profitmaking strategies.

Financialization has gathered momentum amid greater inequality. In the United States, the top 1% of the population received 14.0% of the national after-tax income in 2004, nearly double its 7.5% share in 1979. In the same period the share of the bottom fifth fell from 6.8% to 4.9%.

And yet U.S. consumption demand has been sustained despite rising inequality and a squeeze on real wages for the majority of households. Here is the other side of the financialization coin: a massive expansion of consumer credit has played an important role in easing the constraints on consumer spending by filling the gap created by stagnant or declining real wages. The credit card debt of the average U.S. family increased by 53% through the 1990s. About 67% of low-income families with incomes less than $10,000 faced credit card debt, and the debt of this group saw the largest increase—a 184% rise, compared to a 28% increase for families with incomes above $100,000. Offered more and more credit as a privatized means of addressing wage stagnation, then, eventually, burdened by debt and on the edge of insolvency, the working poor and the middle class are less likely to organize as a political force to challenge the dominance of finance. In this sense, financialization becomes a means of social coercion that erodes working-class solidarity.

As the structures created by financial engineering unravel, the current economic crisis is revealing the cracks in this edifice. But even as a growing number of U.S. families are losing their homes and jobs in the wake of the subprime meltdown, the financial companies at the heart of the crisis have been handed massive bailouts and their top executives have pocketed huge pay-outs despite their role in abetting the meltdown—a stark sign of the power structures and interests at stake in this era of financialization. ❑

Sources: Robin Blackburn, "Finance and the Fourth Dimension," *New Left Review* 39 May-June 2006; Robert Brenner, "New Boom or Bubble," *New Left Review* 25 Jan-Feb 2004; Tamara Draut and Javier Silva, "Borrowing to make ends meet," *Demos*, Sept 2003; Gerald Epstein, "Introduction" in G. Epstein, ed., *Financialization and the World* Economy, 2006; John Bellamy Foster, "The Financialization of Capitalism," *Monthly Review*, April 2007; Gretta Krippner, "The financialization of the US economy," *Socio-Economic Review* 3, Feb. 2005; Thomas Palley, "Financialization : What it is and why it matters," Political Economy Research Institute Working Paper #153, November 2007; A. Sherman and Arin Dine, "New CBO data shows inequality continues to widen," Center for Budget Priorities, Jan. 23, 2007; Kevin Phillips, *Bad Money: Reckless Finance, Failed Politics, and the Global Crisis of American Capitalism*, 2008.

Article 2.6

PRIVATE EQUITY EXPOSED
An insider gives a peek at a notoriously secretive industry.

BY ORLANDO SEGURA, JR.
July/August 2008

Today, private equity seems to be everywhere. Enter a Dunkin' Donuts, and you experience private equity. Scan your radio dial, and you're likely to encounter private equity. Purchase gifts for your children at Toys "R" Us, and you engage with private equity. The private equity industry, like other alternative investment industries that have risen to prominence over the last two decades, exerts tremendous economic and political influence in the United States and globally. It is important, then, to understand how this industry works and thrives. For the past three years, I have had the opportunity to see firsthand the inner workings of the industry—first as a consultant to large buyout firms, and then as a financial analyst for one of the firms themselves. Drawing on these experiences, I will try to shed some light on this notoriously secretive industry and answer three important questions: How do private equity firms make money? How do private equity firms affect the distribution of financial risk in society as a whole? And how does the regulatory landscape in the United States give private equity firms an advantage in the market?

How Do Private Equity Firms Make Money?

Specialized transactions called leveraged buyouts are central to what private equity firms do, and it is important to be familiar with the mechanics of these transactions in order to understand how these firms generate profit. Private equity firms are private partnerships that raise money from large investors—pension funds, other investment funds, and wealthy individuals (often the same people who are running the private equity firms)—and use that money to purchase other companies. This is the "buyout" part.

The "leveraged" part is the more important one, however. Private equity firms do not simply employ the money they raise on their own to buy companies. They borrow money from investment banks to complete the transactions. In most instances, this borrowed money constitutes the majority of the funding needed to pay for the company. At one point in the industry's infancy, firms were able to borrow 90% or more of the purchase price of the "target" companies. Today, as credit markets have tightened, that number is lower, but on average it still exceeds 50% of purchase price. When the buyout transaction is completed, the payback for this debt becomes the responsibility of the acquired company and is placed on its balance sheet as a liability. Most private equity firms retain ownership of the businesses they buy for three to five years and then sell them for a profit, often to other private equity firms.

The ability to use such leverage vastly increases the potential returns on private equity firms' investments. A simple analogy helps show how this works. Imagine you decide to buy a house that costs $100,000 in a neighborhood where property values are appreciating. You put a very small $1,000 down payment on the house and borrow the other $99,000 from the bank. In three years' time, the house has doubled in value and you are now able to sell it for $200,000. After you repay the loan, you have $100,000 in profit—a return of 100 times your original $1,000 investment. Now, imagine if you had only been able to borrow $1,000 from the bank; you would have had to make a $99,000 down payment. The house still appreciates to a value of $200,000, but in this scenario you have turned your original $99,000 investment into a $100,000 profit, generating only a return roughly equal to your original investment. In the first scenario, you put much less of your own equity at risk, yet you generate the same absolute profit as in the second scenario. This simple example illustrates the power of leverage, and why private equity firms would want to maximize the share of borrowed money they invest.

Why have investment banks been willing to lend private equity firms so much money? Part of the reason is that they are able to pass the debt along by selling, or "syndicating," it. Banks package the debt into securities called collateralized debt obligations, or CDOs, which they sell on the open market. CDOs have existed since 1987, but did not achieve prominence in the markets until 2001, when banks began devising sophisticated models that allowed them to rapidly price and sell these securities.

The benefit banks derive from their ability to segment and distribute the risks associated with the debt they underwrite for private equity firms cannot be overstated. They lower their downside risk associated with default on these loans because they only hold onto a small portion of the entire loan package, or "facility." So banks can underwrite more debt than they would be able to if they held onto the loans in full. And they can take in more lucrative fees, too. The banks get most of their revenues from fees for originating the loans, generally 2% to 3% of the amount of the loan.

All told, such large amounts of capital being used to purchase companies creates hefty profits for the investment banks and the private equity firms, not to mention the ancillary professional service industries required to complete the deals, including accountants, lawyers, and consultants.

This is simply the tip of the profit iceberg for private equity firms, however. The real money comes in what is called "carry"—the share of profits that the funds' managers are entitled to when they sell a business. Remember, the more these firms borrow for a transaction—the more they "leverage"—the more any increase in value translates into equity profit. The industry norm is for private equity partnerships to keep 20% of the profit that they make when they sell a company.

And apart from the über-profits they "earn" from selling the highly leveraged businesses they own, private equity firms charge hefty management fees to *both* the investors in the fund and to the companies they buy. The "market" management fee that private equity firms charge their investors ranges between 2% and 2.5% of the total fund size. The companies they purchase must likewise pay a quarterly "management fee," usually around 2% of the purchase price of the company. Effectively, private equity firms earn money in return for being given money *and* for spending money. As the value of many of the companies that private equity firms buy can soar into the hundreds of millions, or even billions, of dollars, this represents a low-risk, assured stream of income. On a fund of $10 billion, these fees alone can translate into hundreds of millions of dollars in revenue a year.

How do private equity firms affect the distribution of financial risk in society?

The profits that financial players like private equity firms and investment banks enjoy come at a price. Today, there are hundreds of billions of dollars in CDOs that are spread throughout the economy, most owned by individual investors. Of course, it is the businesses private equity firms own that are carrying the underlying loans that were bundled to create the CDOs. These businesses risk default if they are not able to make the payments on these debts. And the more the private equity firm was able to borrow to purchase the company, the greater the risk the business faces because it will have to manage larger debt payments on an ongoing basis. An ordinary business downturn that the business might have been able to weather may now thrust it into default if it cannot manage the high debt payments resulting from the leveraged buy-out. And if enough of these businesses get into trouble, the holders of the CDOs will see the value of their investments tumble. We are seeing this happen now with the sub-prime crisis, which was fueled by devaluation in mortgage-backed securities.

The ability of banks and private equity firms to siphon the benefits while distributing the risks of leverage is rooted in the legal frameworks that "incentivize" such behavior (to use the industry jargon). Private equity firms are shielded from the extreme downside financial risks because of their peculiar form of corporate governance. Private equity firms set up each company they buy as a separate corporation with limited liability. This means that if one of the highly leveraged businesses experiences a downturn and is unable to pay its loans, the only equity that is at stake is what was used to purchase that business. Thus, a private equity fund can still post healthy returns even if some businesses in its portfolio go bankrupt.

As we've seen, private equity firms have an incentive to leverage their business buyouts as much as possible. But this increases the risk of default for the individual businesses they own because they are forced to pay such large principal and interest payments to support the debt that has been placed on their shoulders. Thus, not only do private equity firms increase the systemic risk across the economy by issuing publicly traded CDOs that provide their leverage, they also increase the more immediate risk for those who work for the businesses they own by saddling them with heavy debt obligations.

The "loosening" of the credit markets, fueled partly through the ascendance of CDOs, predictably led private equity firms to execute ever-larger transactions. In 2007, the Blackstone Group purchased Equity Office Properties for $39 billion and in one fell swoop became one of the largest holders of real estate in the world. Currently, Bain Capital is in the process of completing the purchase of Clear Channel Communications, the largest owner of radio stations in the United States. These are but two of many multi-billion dollar transactions by private equity firms that have occurred over the past decade, and which until now have largely gone unnoticed by the general public. These colossal companies, like all businesses bought up by private equity firms, are now at an increased risk should their profit margins weaken or interest rates rise in a cyclical downturn of the economy. To ensure that their requisite loan payments are made, the new managers of these companies, appointed by and acting on behalf of the private equity firm owner, may cut costs by simply laying off workers and offshoring certain functions. The market implications of contractions in the economy are thus amplified by the actions of private equity firms.

How does the regulatory landscape give private equity firms a market advantage?

With the profits that can be earned in private equity, it is no surprise that the industry has grown as much as it has recently, and it is no surprise that private equity firms are able to attract some of the brightest business minds in the market. Predictably, self-interested individuals are drawn to these firms, aiming to maximize the amount of money they can earn. But that is not the whole story. The regulatory landscape in the United States has given private equity firms a number of advantages in the market—limited transparency into the business dealings of the firms and the businesses they own, capital-gains tax advantages, a lack of consumer protection in the credit markets, lax antitrust law enforcement, among others. In effect, the legal landscape is ripe for private equity firms to thrive.

Since private equity firms have at their disposal all these levers for generating profit so seamlessly, one would imagine that the government would tax their earnings at an effectively higher tax rate than normal business earnings. This could not be further from the truth. Owners of corporations in the United States are afforded numerous tax breaks and incentives from writing off "losses" or deducting "business expenses" from taxable earnings. On this front, private equity firms have cleverly found ways to go above and beyond the call of duty. Virtually all private equity firms are structured as limited liability partnerships, or LLPs. This confers two explicit benefits to the partners. First, they are protected from any downside in their equity investments, meaning that if one of their investments goes bust, they will only lose the equity that they put into that specific business. Second, they are protected under a tax shelter that allows the majority of their profits to be taxed at a very low rate. Because they are partnerships that technically earn "capital gains" on the profitable sale of a business, they are taxed at a flat 15% rate, as opposed to the 28% to 33% income tax rate that ordinary individuals pay. Thanks to this loophole, private equity managers are taxed at lower rates than their secretaries and administrative assistants who make as much money in a year as their bosses make in a day.

Many European countries have recently instituted laws in recognition of the legal and regulatory advantages that private equity owners have enjoyed since the industry's inception. In the UK this past year, for example, Parliament passed a law that took away private equity firms' tax advantages, which incidentally were very similar to what currently exists in the United States. Here, House Democrats recently introduced a bill to do away with the capital gains tax structure for private equity firms and tax them at ordinary income tax rates. This would have raised private equity firms' tax rates on their carry from a flat 15% to a flat 35%. But Charles Schumer (D-N.Y.), head of the Senate Finance Committee, came out against the bill, killing it for now.

It is no coincidence that, as a senator from New York, Schumer receives tens of thousands of dollars from private equity bosses and relies on their support for an ever-increasing portion of his campaign funding. Of course, he is not alone. The private equity industry created its own PAC in 2007, the Private Equity Council, to lobby against efforts to increase taxes on the industry. To date, they have succeeded; there is every reason to believe they will continue to succeed. Schumer's fellow senator from New York, Hillary Clinton, is a loyal recipient of private equity money and joined him in opposing the bill. On the Republican side, former New York City mayor Rudy Giuliani has taken a predictable pro-private-equity stance, as did his competitor in the Republican presidential primaries, Mitt Romney, who made hundreds of millions of dollars as a partner of Bain Capital, one of the leading private equity firms in the world. The political muscle of the industry is as strong as its economic success.

The legal framework that actively encourages this industry to thrive has spawned a new breed of capitalism, one in which businesses are treated as assets to be bought and sold rather than as social institutions that are sources of people's livelihood. Perhaps we should ask: What value do these firms confer upon the economy, and through it, on society? Private equity firms do not foster innovation in the economy, they do not create jobs, and for the most part they do not actively manage the businesses they own. Rather, they redirect the benefits of equity ownership to a small and insular group of people instead of creating social value for everyone. It is time to learn more about how and why these institutions exert their power and, at the very least, to demand more transparency, thoughtful regulation, and fairer taxation in return for the privilege of being able to operate in our economy. ❑

Sources: Tomas Krüger Andersen, "Legal Structure of Private Equity and Hedge Funds," 2007 (available at isis.ku.dk/kurser/blob.aspx?feltid= 155330); Martin Arnold, "Doubt Cast on Buy-Out Firms' Huge Profits," *Financial Times*, November 23, 2007; Neil Hodge, "Private Equity: A Debt to Society?" *Financial Management*, September 2007.

Article 2.7

HEDGE FUNDS

BY ARTHUR MacEWAN
July/August 2008

> Dear Dr. Dollar:
> *When one hedge fund makes $3 billion, who has lost $3 billion? Where does the money come from that hedge funds capture? Who produced the value?*
> — Peter Marcuse, Waterbury, Conn.

As with any "winnings" in the financial markets, the money obtained by hedge funds comes directly from some losers who are also operating in the financial markets. On the surface, the situation might appear like a poker game: when one player wins the pot, some other players lose. Those of us not sitting at the table neither win nor lose.

However, while financial markets do involve a lot of gambling, the analogy to a poker game is limited. Those of us who are not sitting in on "the game" do suffer some substantial losses from the operations of hedge funds. Hedge fund operators, along with other operators in the financial system, have taken an active role in increasing the size of their "pot"—that is, in shifting the income distribution upward, moving money from lower-income workers to business owners and high-salaried professionals. So value created by the rest of us becomes the hedge funds' billions.

Contrary to their popular image, however, hedge funds are not making billions and billions of dollars for their investors. In fact, the performance of hedge funds is not significantly better than the performance of other types of investment funds. Nonetheless, although the investors in hedge funds are not doing especially well, the *managers* of the hedge funds are making off with billions.

The key to the incomes of hedge fund managers lies more in the nature of what the funds are than in how well they do. After all, aside from some notable exceptions, hedge funds as a group have not done especially well.

So what are hedge funds? Hedge funds are a category of mutual funds. In all mutual funds, the money of multiple investors is pooled and invested according to the decisions of the funds' managers. Regular mutual funds are subject to various government regulations, as are some other financial institutions, for example, commercial banks. The rationale for these regulations is that they protect the individual investors.

Hedge funds, however, avoid most regulations by limiting participation to a small number of "qualified" individuals and institutions (e.g., pension funds or college endowment funds) with large sums of money. To be "qualified," an investor must have a net worth of at least $5 million, excluding his or her home. Because they have large sums of money, these wealthy investors supposedly do not need the protection that regulation is assumed to provide.

Largely unregulated, hedge funds can undertake highly risky types of investments that would be off limits to regular mutual funds. With these more risky investments, they are *sometimes* able to obtain very high returns. They can also operate with a good deal of secrecy, exempt from the reporting requirements of regular mutual funds.

Like other investment funds, hedge funds charge a fee to the individuals and institutions that provide them with money. But hedge funds have been able to charge relatively high fees, including performance fees on top of the basic management fees. The basic fees run 1.5% to 2% of the total investment, and the performance fees typically run 20% of positive returns—sometimes higher. In some cases, management fees run to 5% combined with performance fees of over 40%. Furthermore, while hedge fund managers get their hefty performance fees when their funds achieve positive returns, they do not lose anything when their funds have negative returns. In effect, they are saying to their investors: If I perform well, we both win; if I perform poorly, you lose. So it is not difficult to see why the managers of hedge funds do so well.

It is difficult, however, to see why so many investors put their money into hedge funds. Part of the explanation lies in the fact that rich individuals are often not smart investors, and they are drawn in by the popular image, the billions made by some funds, and the aura of success surrounding the stories of hedge fund managers who take home billions. And the institutional investors in hedge funds—local pension funds or college endowment funds, for example—are not especially "smart" either. Perhaps it is also the case that investors with large sums of money are willing to put at least some of their money into hedge funds, looking for the higher returns that the funds do sometimes obtain.

But whatever returns are obtained "sometimes," overall hedge funds do not do significantly better than other types of investment funds. While the secrecy of hedge funds makes it difficult to determine their overall returns, one 2006 study concludes: "...overall performance of hedge funds … is about the same as that of U.S. equities [as measured by the Standard and Poor's Index of 500 equities] …[H]edge funds underperformed the stock market … during the six year, 'bull market' run-up to 1999, while on average they outperformed the stock market during the six year 'bear market' (or lull period) through 2005."

And recently the story has been quite poor: in the period from January 2007 up to May of 2008, hedge funds returned on average 3.1% and were out-performed by rich-world corporate bonds. (These figures are only for hedge funds that are open to new investors and thus, presumably, report how they have been doing. Hedge funds that are not accepting new investors are more opaque.) One might conclude that hedge funds are an undistinguished group of investments.

There are, however, some things that distinguish hedge funds—most particularly the huge payments that are often obtained by the people who run the funds. The most outstanding recent example is John Paulson, who in 2007 took in $3.7 billion running his Paulson & Co. hedge funds. Several others did pretty well also: George Soros was number two last year, at $2.9 billion, and James Simons was third at $2.8 billion

The top 25 hedge fund managers got themselves $22.3 billion in 2007, up substantially from a meager $14 billion in 2006. It is, we may assume, the stories of these individuals that generates the aura of success surrounding hedge funds.

How did hedge fund managers do so well when the economy was moving into bad times? In Paulson's case, according to Bloomberg.com, "Paulson & Co., which oversees about $28 billion, made money betting on the collapse of subprime mortgages in 2007. The Paulson Credit Opportunities Fund soared almost sixfold, helped by bets on slumping housing and subprime mortgage prices, according to investor letters obtained by Bloomberg." More generally, the hedge fund managers rely on their fee structure, as described above, to assure that, regardless of bad times, they come out well.

If rich individuals and institutional investors were the only ones to take the hit when the John Paulsons take home their astronomical fees, perhaps the rest of us could shrug it off. If they want to pay excessive fees to take part in the glitter—and possible large returns—of high stakes finance, that's their problem.

But the rest of us do pay a price. First of all, there is the ridiculously favorable tax treatment that hedge fund managers have been able to garner. Most important, they are allowed to classify their payments as capital gains rather than as salaries, and thereby they pay a low tax rate on their incomes—typically only 15%, compared to the top tax rate of 35%.

There is simply no good reason for this favorable treatment of hedge fund managers' incomes—other than the apparent power they are able to wield. The result is that the rest of us either pay more in taxes or get by with fewer public services.

Also important, hedge fund managers are not passive investors. They do not accept as a given the current profit levels of the companies they invest in, and simply try to claim a larger share of those profits. Instead, at least at times (but their secrecy makes it difficult to determine how often and to what extent), they take an active role in attempting to push up their profits. Along with private equity funds, with which the hedge funds are closely associated and sometimes overlap, they can push firms to downsize and reorganize, lay off workers, outsource, or alter their overall investment strategies.

For instance, according to a May 15, 2008 report in the "Silicon Alley Insider," John Paulson, who through his funds owns 4% of Yahoo stock, has joined corporate raider Carl Icahn in a proxy fight, an attempt to force Yahoo to accept a Microsoft buy-out offer.

There is no reason to think that any general social interest is served when hedge fund managers attempt to affect the operation of the firms in which they have holdings. In the Yahoo example, the impact on the rest of us may be obscure, but when it comes to layoffs, downsizing, outsourcing, and the like, it is clear that many people outside of the financial markets—people who have no seat at the gambling tables—pay a large price for the gains of hedge funds, and especially of fund managers.

Stagnant wages of workers in recent decades and the increased share of total national income going to corporate profits are the consequence of large, long-run economic forces—the decline of unions, globalization, conservative government policies, and technological shifts to name a few. But the hedge funds are one of the instruments by which these forces have their impact on the rest of us, shifting the value that we create into the financial markets and then taking as large a share as they can. ❑

Sources: Andy Baker, "Better than beta? Managers' superior skills are becoming harder to prove," *The Economist*, February 28, 2008; Arindam Bandopadhyaya and James L. Grant, *A Survey of Demographics and Performance In the Hedge Fund Industry*, Working Paper 1011, Financial Services Forum, College of Management, University of Massachusetts Boston, July, 2006; "Hedge-Fund Performance," *The Economist*, May 15, 2008; Tom Cahill and Poppy Trowbridge, "Paulson's $3.7 Billion Top Hedge Fund Pay, Alpha Says," Bloomberg.com, April 16, 2008; Henry Blodget, "Hedge-Fund Mogul Paulson Joins Icahn in Yahoo Siege; 30% of Proxy Vote in Bag," Silicon Alley Insider, May 15, 2008.

Article 2.8

THE FED AND AMERICA'S DISTORTED EXPANSION

BY THOMAS I. PALLEY
November/December 2007

The U.S. economy has been in expansion mode since November 2001. Though of reasonable duration, the expansion has been fragile and unbalanced. Now, with the subprime mortgage crisis and the ongoing deflation of the house price bubble, there are signs that the expansion may be ending.

Many observers blame the recent crises on the Federal Reserve, claiming the Fed promoted excess in the credit and housing markets by keeping interest rates too low for too long. However, the reality is that low interest rates were needed to sustain the expansion. Instead, the root problem has been a distorted expansion caused by record trade deficits and manufacturing's failure to fully participate in the expansion.

If the Fed deserves criticism, it is for endorsing the policy paradigm underlying these distortions. That paradigm rests on disregard of manufacturing and neglect of the adverse real consequences of trade deficits.

By almost every measure the current expansion has been fragile and shallow compared to previous business cycles. Following an extended period of jobless recovery, private sector job growth has been below par. Though the headline unemployment rate has fallen significantly, the percentage of the working age population that is employed remains far below its previous peak. Meanwhile, inflation-adjusted wages have barely changed despite rising productivity.

This gloomy picture justified the Fed in keeping interest rates low. But why the economic weakness—despite historically low interest rates, massive tax cuts in 2001, and huge increases in military and security spending triggered by 9/11 and the Iraq war?

The answer is the overvalued dollar and the trade deficit, which more than doubled between 2001 and 2006 to $838 billion or 6.5% of GDP. Increased imports have shifted spending away from domestic manufacturers, which explains manufacturing's weak participation in the expansion. Some firms have closed permanently, while others have grown less than they would have otherwise. Additionally, many have cut back on investment owing to weak demand or have moved their investment to China and elsewhere. These effects have then multiplied through the economy, with lost manufacturing jobs and reduced investment causing lost incomes that have further weakened consumer demand and, hence, job creation.

The evidence is clear. Manufacturing has lost an unprecedented 1.8 million jobs during the current expansion. Before 1980, manufacturing employment hit new peaks with every expansion. Since 1980 it has trended down, but it at least recovered somewhat during expansions. In this business cycle, manufacturing employment has fallen during the expansion. The business investment numbers tell a similar dismal story, with much weaker capital spending than in previous expansions.

These conditions compelled the Fed to keep interest rates low in order to maintain the expansion. That policy worked, but only by stimulating loose credit and a house price bubble that triggered a construction boom. Thus, residential investment never fell during the recession and has been stronger than normal during the expansion. Construction, which accounted for 5% of total employment, has provided over 12% of job growth. Meanwhile, higher house prices have fuelled a home-equity borrowing boom that has enabled consumption spending to grow despite stagnant wages. This explains both increased imports and job growth in the service sector.

The overall picture is one of a distorted expansion in which manufacturing continued to shrivel while imports and services expanded. The expansion was carried by the bubble in house prices and the rising burden of consumer debt, both unsustainable. That contradiction has surfaced with the implosion of the subprime mortgage market and deflation of the house price bubble.

The Fed is now trying to assuage markets to keep credit flowing. It has recently lowered interest rates and will lower them further if the economy continues to slow. On one level that is the right response, and it may even work again—though more and more it is coming to seem like sticking a finger in the dike. But the deeper problem is the policy paradigm behind the distorted expansion; this is where the Fed—along with a wide swath of federal policymakers and politicians—is at fault.

The ideological and partisan Alan Greenspan wholeheartedly endorsed corporate globalization and promoted the unbalanced expansion policies coming out of the White House and the Treasury Department. The Fed's professional economists also seem to have endorsed corporate globalization in the name of free trade, dismissing the sharp drop-off of domestic manufacturing as inconsequential. Thus, the Fed has tacitly supported the underlying policy paradigm that has given rise to the U.S. economy's distorted expansion. Despite talk about reducing global financial imbalances, the Fed under Chairman Ben Bernanke still seems locked into this paradigm, which is where constructive criticism should now be directed. ❑

Article 2.9

WHO CARES IF BEAR STEARNS FAILS?

BY ARTHUR MacEWAN
May/June 2008

> Dear Dr. Dollar:
> *Who cares if Bear Stearns fails? Or the Carlyle Group? Or Merrill Lynch? Or one of the other big financial companies? They've made their profits. So what's the problem?*
> —Julia Willebrand, New York, N.Y.

When Bear Stearns, the large New York investment bank, closed its doors in March [2008], some people lost money. Even with the bailout of Bear Stearns engineered by the Federal Reserve, the stockholders of the company paid dearly.

Of course long-term holders of Bear Stearns stock didn't lose so much relative to what they had invested, perhaps years ago. But they lost a lot relative to what they thought they had one year ago.

Then the stock was selling for about seventeen times what they ended up getting when, under the tutelage of the Fed, JPMorgan Chase bought Bear Stearns at $10 a share. Recent buyers of Bear Stearns stock, however, were big losers; if they bought a year ago at $170 a share, they ended up taking losses of 94%. Life is tough.

Then there are the employees of Bear Stearns. Hundreds of people are losing their jobs. And right now is not a good time to be looking for work in the financial industry!

But what about the rest of us? It turns out that the rest of us get hurt too when a large financial firm—or, for that matter, any large firm—goes under. We see the bad impacts of a firm's failure most clearly in a small town where a single employer plays a major role. When the firm fails, people lose their jobs. The fall in their incomes means they buy less, and other firms and other workers in the town feel the pinch. The impact spreads.

When large financial firms like Bear Stearns fail, the impacts can be very far reaching. These firms have extensive financial connections to other firms, which in turn are dependent on payments of obligations from the failing firms to meet their own obligations. If firm A fails, it doesn't meet its payments to firm B, which then can't meet is obligations to firm C, and so on. Any one of these firms that is close to the edge can be pushed over it by this failure of payments.

But the problem goes beyond these very tangible connections. The financial industry works on confidence. People loan money and buy stocks and bonds based on their confidence that these investments will pay off—that the firms to which they provide the money will return their money at a profit. When a large financial firm fails, they start to get worried; they lose their confidence. Not only do they fear the consequences of that firm's failure spreading (from A to B to C). They also worry that the same underlying problems that affected that company will affect others and ultimately their investments. Losing confidence, they are reluctant to supply money.

Loss of confidence is especially understandable when the causes of the problems that afflicted Bear Stearns are so well known and widespread. An era of excessively risky investments—with the sub-prime mortgage mess as the most visible part of the crisis—is now readily apparent.

But loans make the world go round. Without ready access to loans, firms are forced to cut back their investments and home-buyers find it more difficult—or more expensive—to obtain credit for their purchases. Even the student loan market is being affected by the current lack of credit—this "credit crunch." How many students from middle- and low-income families will not go to college next fall because they cannot get the funds?

So the rest of us can pay a dear price when a large financial firm fails. This is the rationale that the Fed offered when it stepped in to arrange for Bear Stearns to avoid actual failure. Its obligations will be taken over by JPMorgan Chase. But the takeover affects confidence roughly like a failure.

Even when the threat to the rest of us is real, this doesn't mean there has to be a bailout—or even a partial bailout as took place with Bear Stearns. For example, early this year, the British government nationalized Northern Rock bank when it could not meet its obligations. The government will run the bank, providing extra funds to the extent needed, and, when it is solvent again, will sell it off to private interests. The original stockholders will get money from the sale of the bank, but only after the government gets all of its money back.

Equally important, because the government, operating through the Fed, has to step in when financial firms fail, the government also has to set rules by which those firms operate. Increasingly, regulations have been removed from the financial sector and new sorts of financial firms have been created to avoid existing regulations. But the financial sector is too important, and too volatile, to be left on its own. ❏

Article 2.10

CAN THE FED HANDLE A SYSTEMIC CRISIS? *MAYBE.*

BY JANE D'ARISTA
May/June 2008

The Federal Reserve's bailout in March [2008] of 85-year-old Bear Stearns, one of the world's largest investment banks, gave a clear signal that the U.S. financial system was facing a systemic crisis.

Bear Stearns was highly leveraged. Like Carlyle Capital Corp., a Carlyle Group subsidiary which had collapsed shortly before, Bear's leverage was over 30 to 1; in other words, these firms had invested over 30 borrowed dollars for each dollar of their own. And they were emblematic of excessive borrowing across the financial sector: borrowing by all U.S. financial institutions soared from 62% of GDP in 1997 to 114% of GDP at the end of 2007. Such massive borrowing made the whole system vulnerable to disruption when economic circumstances changed.

The boom in leveraged investing had been facilitated by the creation of huge and poorly understood markets for derivatives. Derivatives are investment vehicles that derive their value from changes in the prices of underlying assets such as foreign exchange deposits, bank loans, or the now notorious mortgage-backed securities built on the income stream from large "bundles" of mortgages. Derivatives are commonly traded not on organized exchanges such as the New York Stock Exchange, but rather in so-called over-the-counter (OTC) markets.

Americans hear daily, even hourly, about price changes in the stock market. In contrast, OTC markets are nontransparent: they do not provide the timely information on price and volume that markets need to function efficiently. But the OTC markets are now much larger than the traditional exchanges and are the locus of problems in the current crisis. And while few Americans have even heard of these markets, millions are experiencing the fallout. As these markets quake, the prices of assets on the books of financial institutions drop, forcing them to constrict their lending. Tighter credit spills over into declines in house prices and thus in households' net worth—and not only for homeowners with subprime mortgages. Moreover, analysts predict that over two million more families will lose their homes before the current crisis subsides. This bout of failed loans and foreclosures will continue to push home prices down. And, needless to say, it is an ongoing tragedy, for families and entire communities.

The growth of nontransparent OTC markets in derivatives and the explosion in leverage both point to what went wrong in the U.S. financial system over the last two decades. The Federal Reserve loosened the reins on bank practices, then overlooked the resulting excesses. It refused to try to curtail the stock bubble in the late 1990s by raising margin requirements so as to limit the amount of stock purchased with borrowed funds. It ignored the explosion in debt that fueled the more recent housing bubble. Ultimately, the Fed intervened only when those excesses had created a severe disruption.

And, after both Congress and the Fed acquiesced to the industry's demands and rescinded many Depression-era banking regulations that had delimited the structure of the industry for over 50 years, the Fed failed to foresee that the new financial landscape would require new regulation. For instance, if different kinds of institutions would now be allowed to engage in a single function such as mortgage lending, regulations appropriate to that function would have to apply to all of them. It was only last December that the Fed—acting under authority Congress had granted it 13 years earlier—belatedly proposed (modest) rules for *all* mortgage lenders.

The Fed also overlooked the implications of a major shift in the country's financial structure. Beginning in the 1980s, households increasingly channeled their savings into pension and mutual funds rather than into banks. These funds, in turn, sought places to invest this expanded flow of savings; their demand for investment opportunities encouraged business borrowers to issue securities rather than borrow from banks. (The issuer of securities such as bonds is essentially borrowing from those who buy them.) Banks themselves contributed to this shift as they removed loans from their books, packaged them into pools, and issued securities against them. The result of these trends has been to shift the financial system's center of gravity away from banks and toward capital markets.

The Fed's governors failed to acknowledge that this shift, in conjunction with other factors, had gravely weakened its ability to modulate the swings of the business cycle. Meanwhile, banks account for a far smaller share of total credit than they used to—their share of credit market assets fell from 56% in 1977 to 24% at year-end 2007—further undermining the Fed's influence over either the expansion or contraction of credit, as the policy tools at its disposal were designed primarily to operate on banks.

What the Fed is trying to do by cutting interest rates is to slow sales of assets in order to stabilize prices, and to encourage a resumption of lending. If successful, its efforts will benefit homeowners and families with savings invested in financial institutions. If it can restore the flow of credit to businesses, its actions will help stem the loss of jobs and cushion the slowdown in economic activity. But we are learning that, in the midst of this systemic crisis, the Fed may be far less able to act systematically than many have supposed. Falling asset prices, particularly the ongoing decline in house prices, have eroded the capital cushion that underpins the entire financial system; so that at this point, the Fed's interventions must be aimed at preventing a financial-sector meltdown. But how effective a central bank designed for a bank-dominated system will be in protecting the far less bank-centric financial system we have today remains to be seen.

Congress has its hands full. At least some members are trying to provide effective aid to homeowners and others who have been hurt by the credit crunch. This may require the creation of agencies similar to the Depression-era Reconstruction Finance Corporation to recapitalize financial institutions and revive lending to Main Street businesses. Congress also needs to work its way through a full menu of regulatory reforms, including placing curbs on leverage, making OTC markets transparent, and ensuring that the same rules and regulations apply to all institutions engaged in a given financial function.

But Congress has another critical job to do: reform the Fed itself to ensure that it has the tools to moderate excessive credit expansion and contraction across the entire financial system and thus create the conditions needed for stable and sustainable economic growth. And, while it's at it, Congress should take steps to ensure that its own Constitutional responsibility for effective oversight of the Fed will no longer be woefully ignored. ❑

Chapter 3

THE HOUSING BUBBLE AND BUST

Article 3.1

THE HOMEOWNERSHIP MYTH

BY HOWARD KARGER
Spring 2007

Anyone who has given the headlines even a passing glance recently knows the subprime mortgage industry is in deep trouble. Since 2006 more than 20 subprime lenders have quit the business or gone bankrupt. Many more are in serious trouble, including the nation's number two subprime lender, New Century Financial. The subprime crisis is also hitting Wall Street brokerages that invested in these loans, with reverberations from Tokyo to London. And the worst may be yet to come. At least $300 billion in subprime adjustable-rate mortgages will reset this year to higher interest rates. CNN reports that one in five subprime mortgages issued in 2005-2006 will end up in foreclosure. If these dire predictions come true, it will be the equivalent of a nuclear meltdown in the mortgage and housing industries.

What's conspicuously absent from the news reports is the effect of the subprime lending debacle on poor and working-class families who bought into the dream of homeownership, regardless of the price. Sold a false bill of goods, many of these families now face foreclosure and the loss of the small savings they invested in their homes. It's critical to examine the housing crisis not only from the perspective of the banks and the stock market, but also from the perspective of the families whose homes are on the line. It is also critical to uncover the systemic reasons for the recent burst of housing-market insanity that saw thousands upon thousands of families getting signed up for mortgage loans that were highly likely to end in failure and foreclosure.

Like most Americans, I grew up believing that buying a home represents a rite of passage in U.S. society. Americans widely view homeownership as the best choice for everyone, everywhere and at all times. The more people who own their own homes, the common wisdom goes, the more robust the economy, the stronger the community, and the greater the collective and individual benefits. Homeownership is the ticket to the middle class through asset accumulation, stability, and civic participation.

For the most part, this is an accurate picture. Homeowners get a foothold in a housing market with an almost infinite price ceiling. They enjoy important tax benefits. Owning a home is often cheaper than renting. Most important, homeownership builds equity and accrues assets for the next generation, in part by promoting forced savings. These savings are reflected in the data showing that, according to the National Housing Institute's Winton Picoff, the median wealth of low-income homeowners is 12 times higher than that of renters with similar incomes. Plus, owning a home is a status symbol: homeowners are seen as winners compared to renters.

Homeownership may have positive effects on family life. Ohio University's Robert Dietz found that owning a home contributes to household stability, social involvement, environmental awareness, local political participation and activism, good health, low crime, and beneficial community characteristics. Homeowners are better citizens, are healthier both physically and mentally, and have children who achieve more and are better behaved than those of renters.

Johns Hopkins University researchers Joe Harkness and Sandra Newman looked at whether homeownership benefits kids even in distressed neighborhoods. Their study concluded that "[h]omeownership in almost any neighborhood is found to benefit children. ... Children of most low-income renters would be better served by programs that help their families become homeowners in their current neighborhoods instead of helping them move to better neighborhoods while remaining renters." (Harkness and Newman also found, however, that the positive effects of homeownership on children are weaker in unstable low-income neighborhoods. Moreover, the study cannot distinguish whether homeownership leads to positive behaviors or whether owners were already predisposed to these behaviors.)

Faith in the benefits of homeownership—along with low interest rates and a range of governmental incentives—have produced a surge in the number of low-income homeowners. In 1994 Bill Clinton set—and ultimately surpassed—a goal to raise the nation's overall homeownership rate to 67.5% by 2000. There are now 71 million U.S. homeowners, representing close to 68% of all households. By 2003, 48% of black households owned their own homes, up from 34.5% in 1950. Much of this gain has been among low-income families.

Government efforts to increase homeownership for low-income families include both demand-side (e.g., homeowner tax credits, housing cost assistance programs) and supply-side (e.g., developer incentives) strategies. Federal housing programs insure more than a million loans a year to help low-income homebuyers. Fannie Mae and Freddie Mac—the large, federally chartered but privately held corporations that buy mortgages from lenders, guarantee the notes, and then resell them to investors—have increasingly turned their attention to low-income home-buyers as the upper-income housing market becomes more saturated. Banking industry regulations such as the Community Reinvestment Act and the Home Mortgage Disclosure Act encourage homeownership by reducing lending discrimination in underserved markets.

The Housing and Urban Development department (HUD) has adapted some of its programs originally designed to help renters to focus on homeownership. For instance, cities and towns can now use the federal dollars they receive through HOME (the Home Investment Partnerships Act) and Community Development

Block Grants to provide housing grants, down payment loans, and closing cost assistance. The American Dream Downpayment Initiative, passed by Congress in 2003, authorized up to $200 million a year for down payment assistance to low-income families. Private foundations have followed suit. The Ford Foundation is currently focusing its housing-related grants on homeownership rather than rental housing; the foundation views homeownership as an important form of asset-building and the best option for low-income people.

While homeownership has undeniable benefits, that doesn't mean it is the best option for everyone. For many low-income families, buying a home imposes burdens that end up outweighing the benefits. It is time to re-assess the policy emphasis on homeownership, which has been driven by an honest belief in the advantages of homeownership, but also by a wide range of business interests who stand to gain when a new cohort of buyers is brought into the housing market.

The Downsides of Homeownership

Low-income families can run into a range of pitfalls when they buy homes. These pitfalls may stem from the kinds of houses they can afford to buy (often in poor condition, with high maintenance costs); the neighborhoods they can afford to buy in (often economically distressed); the financing they can get (often carrying high interest rates, high fees, and risky gimmicks); and the jobs they work at (often unstable). Taken together, these factors can make buying a home a far riskier proposition for low-income families than it is for middle- and upper-income households.

Most low-income families only have the financial resources to buy rundown houses in distressed neighborhoods marked by few jobs, high crime rates, a dearth of services, and poor schools. Few middle-class homebuyers would hitch themselves to 30-year mortgages in these kinds of communities; poor families, too, have an interest in making the home-buying commitment in safe neighborhoods with good schools.

Homeownership is no automatic hedge against rising housing costs. On the contrary: lower-end affordable housing stock is typically old, in need of repair, and expensive to maintain. Low-income families often end up paying inflated prices for homes that are beset with major structural or mechanical problems masked by cosmetic repairs. A University of North Carolina study sponsored by the national nonprofit organization NeighborWorks found that almost half of low-income homebuyers experienced major unexpected costs due to the age and condition of their homes. If you rent, you can call the landlord; but a homeowner can't take herself to court because the roof leaks, the plumbing is bad, or the furnace or hot water heater quits working.

Besides maintenance and repairs, the expenses of homeownership also include property taxes and homeowners insurance, both of which have skyrocketed in cost in the last decade. Between 1997 and 2002 property tax rates rose nationally by more than 19%. Ten states (including giants Texas and California) saw their property tax rates rise by 30% or more during that period. In the suburbs of New York City, property tax rates grew two to three times faster than personal income from 2000 to 2004.

Nationally, the average homeowner's annual insurance premiums rose a whopping 62% from 1995 to 2005—twice as fast as inflation. Low-income homeowners in distressed neighborhoods are hit especially hard by high insurance costs. According to a Conning and Co. study, 92% of large insurance companies run credit checks on potential customers. These credit checks translate into insurance scores that are used to determine whether the carrier will insure an applicant at all, and if so, what they will cover and how much they will charge. Those with poor or no credit are denied coverage, while those with limited credit pay high premiums. Needless to say, many low-income homeowners do not have stellar credit scores. Credit scoring may also partly explain why, according to HUD, "Recent studies have shown that, compared to homeowners in predominantly white-occupied neighborhoods, homeowners in minority neighborhoods are less likely to have private home insurance, more likely to have policies that provide less coverage in case of a loss, and are likely to pay more for similar policies."

THE NEW WORLD OF HOME LOANS

The new home loan products, marketed widely in recent years but especially to low- and moderate-income families, are generally adjustable-rate mortgages (ARMs) with some kind of twist. Here are a few of these "creative" (read: confusing and risky) mortgage options.

Option ARM: With this loan, borrowers choose each month which of three or four different—and fluctuating—payments to make:

- full (principal+interest) payment based on a 30-year or 15-year repayment schedule.
- interest-only payment—does not reduce the loan principal or build homeowner equity. Borrowers who pay only interest for a period of time then face a big jump in the size of monthly payments or else are forced to refinance.
- minimum payment—may be lower than one month's interest; if so, the shortfall is added to the loan balance. The result is "negative amortization": over time, the principal goes up, not down. Eventually the borrower may have an "upside down" mortgage where the debt is greater than the market value of the home.

According to the credit rating firm Fitch Ratings, up to 80% of all option ARM borrowers choose the minimum monthly payment option. So it's no surprise that in 2005, 20% of option ARMs were "upside down." When a negative amortization limit is reached, the minimum payment jumps up to fully amortize the loan for the remaining loan term. In other words, borrowers suddenly have to start paying the real bill.

Even borrowers who pay more than the monthly minimums can face payment shocks. Option ARMs often start with a temporary super-low teaser interest rate (and correspondingly low monthly payments) that allows borrowers to qualify for "more house." The catch? Since the low initial monthly payment, based on interest rates as low as 1.25%, is not enough to cover the real interest rate, the borrower eventually faces a sudden increase in monthly payments.

With few cash reserves, low-income families are a heartbeat away from financial disaster if their wages decline, property taxes or insurance rates rise, or expensive repairs are needed. With most—or all—of their savings in their homes, these families often have no cushion for emergencies. HUD data show that between 1999 and 2001, the only group whose housing conditions worsened—meaning, by HUD's definition, the only group in which a larger share of households spent over 30% of gross household income on housing in 2001 than in 1999—were low- and moderate-income homeowners. The National Housing Conference reports that 51% of working families with critical housing needs (i.e., those spending more than 50% of gross household income on housing) are homeowners.

Most people who buy a home imagine they will live there for a long time, benefiting from a secure and stable housing situation. For many low-income families,

Balloon Loan: This loan is written for a short 5- to 7-year term during which the borrower pays either interest and principal each month or, in a more predatory form, interest only. At the end of the loan term, the borrower must pay off the entire loan in a lump sum—the "balloon payment." At that point, buyers must either refinance or lose their homes. Balloon loans are known to real estate pros as "bullet loans," since if the loan comes due—forcing the owner to refinance—during a period of high interest rates, it's like getting a bullet in the heart. According to the national organizing and advocacy group ACORN, about 10% of all subprime loans are balloons.

Balloon loans are sometimes structured with monthly payments that fail to cover the interest, much less pay down the principal. Although the borrower makes regular payments, her loan balance increases each month: negative amortization. Many borrowers are unaware that they have a negative amortization loan until they have to refinance.

Shared Appreciation Mortgage (SAM): These are fixed-rate loans for up to 30 years that have easier credit qualifications and lower monthly payments than conventional mortgages. In exchange for a lower interest rate, the borrower relinquishes part of the future value of the home to the lender. Interest rate reductions are based on how much appreciation the borrower is willing to give up. SAMs discourage "sweat equity" since the homeowner receives only some fraction of the appreciation resulting from any improvements. Not surprisingly, these loans have been likened to sharecropping.

Stated-Income Loan: Aimed at borrowers who do not draw regular wages from an employer but live on tips, casual jobs that pay under the table, commissions, or investments, this loan does not require W-2 forms or other standard wage documentation. The trade-off: higher interest rates.

No-Ratio Loan: The debt-income ratio (the borrower's monthly payments on debt, including the planned mortgage, divided by her monthly income) is a standard benchmark that lenders use to determine how large a mortgage they will write. In return for a higher interest rate, the no-ratio loan abandons this benchmark; it is aimed at borrowers with complex financial lives or those who are experiencing divorce, the death of a spouse, or a career change.   —*Amy Gluckman* this is not what happens. Nationwide data from 1976 to 1993 reveal that 36% of low-income homeowners gave up or lost their homes within two years and 53% exited within five years, according to a 2005 study by Carolina Katz Reid of the University of Washington. Reid found that very few low-income families ever bought another house after returning to renting. A 2004 HUD research study by Donald Haurin and Stuart Rosenthal reached similar conclusions. Following a national sample of African Americans from youth (ages 14 to 21) in 1979 to middle age in 2000, the researchers found that 63% of the sample owned a home at some point, but only 34% still did in 2000.

Low-income homeowners, often employed in unstable jobs with stagnant incomes, few health care benefits, limited or no sick days, and little vacation time, may find it almost impossible to keep their homes if they experience a temporary job loss or a change in family circumstances, such as the loss of a wage earner. Homeownership can also limit financial opportunities. A 1999 study by economists Richard Green (University of Wisconsin) and Patric Hendershott (Ohio State University) found that states with the highest homeownership rates also had the highest unemployment rates. Their report concluded that homeownership may constrain labor mobility since the high costs of selling a house make unemployed homeowners reluctant to relocate to find work.

Special tax breaks have been a key selling point of homeownership. If mortgage interest and other qualifying expenses come to less than the standard deduction ($10,300 for joint filers in 2006), however, there is zero tax advantage to owning. That is one reason why only 34% of taxpayers itemize their mortgage interest, local property taxes, and other deductions. Even for families who do itemize, the effective tax saving is usually only 10 to 35 cents for every dollar paid in mortgage interest. In other words, the mortgage deduction benefits primarily those in high income brackets who have a need to shelter their income; it means little to low-income homeowners.

Finally, homeownership promises growing wealth as home prices rise. But the homes of low-income, especially minority, homeowners generally do not appreciate as much as middle-class housing. Low-income households typically purchase homes in distressed neighborhoods where significant appreciation is unlikely. Among other reasons, if financially stressed property owners on the block can't afford to maintain their homes, nearby property values fall. For instance, Reid's longitudinal study surveyed low-income minority homeowners from 1976 to 1994 and found that they realized a 30% increase in the value of their homes after owning for 10 years, while middle- and upper-income white homeowners enjoyed a 60% jump.

"Funny Money" Mortgages And Other Travesties

Buying a home and taking on a mortgage are scary, and people often leave the closing in a stupor, unsure of what they signed or why. My partner and I bought a house a few years ago; like many buyers, we didn't retain an attorney. The title company had set aside one hour for the closing. During that time more than 125 single-spaced pages (much of it in small print) were put in front of us. More than 60 required our signature or initials. It would have been difficult for us to digest these documents in

24 hours, much less one. When we asked to slow down the process, we were met with impatience. After the closing, Anna asked, "What did we sign?" I was clueless.

Yet buying a home is the largest purchase most families will make in their lifetimes, the largest expenditure in a family budget, and the single largest asset for two-thirds of homeowners. It's also the most fraught with danger.

For low-income families in particular, homeownership can turn out to be more a crushing debt than an asset-building opportunity. The primary reason for this is the growing chasm between ever-higher home prices and the stagnant incomes of millions of working-class Americans. The last decade has seen an unprecedented surge in home prices, which have risen 35% nationally. While the housing bubble is largely confined to specific metropolitan areas in the South, the Southwest, and the two coasts (home prices rose 50% in the Pacific states and 60% in New England), there are also bubbles in midwestern cities like Chicago and Minneapolis. And although the housing bubble is most pronounced in high-end properties, the prices of low-end homes have also spiked in many markets.

Current incomes simply do not support these inflated home prices. For example, only 18% of Californians can afford the median house in the state using traditional loan-affordability calculations. Even the fall in mortgage interest rates in the 1990s and early 2000s was largely neutralized by higher property taxes, higher insurance premiums, and rising utility costs.

This disparity might have put a dent in the mortgage finance business. But no: in 2005, Americans owed $5.7 trillion in mortgages, a 50% increase in just four years. Over the past decade the mortgage finance industry has developed creative schemes designed to squeeze potential homebuyers, albeit often temporarily, into houses they cannot afford. It is a sleight of hand that requires imaginative and risky financing for both buyers and financial institutions.

Most of the "creative" new mortgage products fall into the category of subprime mortgages—those offered to people whose problematic credit drops them into a lower lending category. Subprime mortgages carry interest rates ranging from a few points to ten points or more above the prime or market rate, plus onerous loan terms. The subprime mortgage industry is growing: lenders originated $173 billion in subprime loans in 2005, up from only $25 billion in 1993. By 2006 the subprime market was valued at $600 billion, one-fifth of the $3 trillion U.S. mortgage market.

Subprime lending can be risky. In the 37 years since the Mortgage Bankers Association (MBA) began conducting its annual national mortgage delinquency survey, 2006 saw the highest share of home loans entering foreclosure. In early 2007, according to the MBA, 13.5% of sub-prime mortgages were delinquent (compared to 4.95% of prime-rate mortgages) and 4.5% were in foreclosure. By all accounts, this is just the tip of the iceberg. However, before the current collapse the rate of return for subprime lenders was spectacular. *Forbes* claimed that subprime lenders could realize returns up to six times greater than the best-run banks.

In the past there were two main kinds of home mortgages: fixed-rate loans and adjustable-rate loans (ARMs). In a fixed-rate mortgage, the interest rate stays the same throughout the 15- to 30-year loan term. In a typical ARM the interest rate varies over the course of the loan, although there is usually a cap. Both kinds of loans traditionally required borrowers to provide thorough documentation of their finances and a down payment of at least 10% of the purchase price, and often 20%.

Adjustable-rate loans can be complicated, and a Federal Reserve study found that fully 25% of homeowners with ARMs were confused about their loan terms. Nonetheless, ARMs are attractive because in the short run they promise a home with an artificially low interest rate and affordable payments.

Even so, traditional ARMs proved inadequate to the tasks of ushering more low-income families into the housing market and generally keeping home sales up in the face of skyrocketing home prices. So in recent years the mortgage industry created a whole range of "affordability" products with names like "no-ratio loans," "option ARMS," and "balloon loans" that it doled out like candy to people who were never fully apprised of the intricacies of these complicated loans. (See box for a glossary of the new mortgage products.) These new mortgage options have opened the door for almost anyone to secure a mortgage, whether or not their circumstances auger well for repayment. They also raise both the costs and risks of buying a home—sometimes steeply—for the low- and moderate-income families to whom they're largely marketed.

Beyond the higher interest rates (at some point in the loan term if not at the start) that characterize the new "affordability" mortgages, low-income homebuyers face other costs as well. For instance, predatory and subprime lenders often require borrowers to carry credit life insurance, which pays off a mortgage if the homeowner dies. This insurance is frequently sold either by the lender's subsidiary or else by a company that pays the lender a commission. Despite low payouts, lenders frequently charge high premiums for this insurance.

As many as 80% of subprime loans include prepayment penalties if the borrower pays off or refinances the loan early, a scam that costs low-income borrowers about $2.3 billion a year and increases the risk of foreclosure by 20%. Pre-payment penalties lock borrowers into a loan by making it difficult to sell the home or refinance with a different lender. And while some borrowers face penalties for paying off their loans ahead of schedule, others discover that their mortgages have so-called "call provisions" that permit the lender to accelerate the loan term even if payments are current.

And then there are all of the costs outside of the mortgage itself. Newfangled mortgage products are often sold not by banks directly, but by a rapidly growing crew of mortgage brokers who act as finders or "bird dogs" for lenders. There are approximately 53,000 mortgage brokerage companies in the United States employing an estimated 418,700 people, according to the National Association of Mortgage Brokers; *BusinessWeek* notes that brokers now originate up to 80% of all new mortgages.

Largely unregulated, mortgage brokers live off loan fees. Their transactions are primed for conflicts of interest or even downright corruption. For example, borrowers pay brokers a fee to help them secure a loan. Brokers may also receive kickbacks from lenders for referring a borrower, and many brokers steer clients to the lenders that pay them the highest kickbacks rather than those offering the lowest interest rates. Closing documents use arcane language ("yield spread premiums," "service release fees") to hide these kickbacks. And some hungry brokers find less-than-kosher ways to make the sale, including fudging paperwork, arranging for inflated appraisals, or helping buyers find co-signers who have no intention of actually guaranteeing the loan.

Whether or not a broker is involved, lenders can inflate closing costs in a variety of ways: charging outrageous document preparation fees; billing for recording fees in excess of the law; "unbundling," whereby closing costs are padded by duplicating charges already included in other categories.

All in all, housing is highly susceptible to the predations of the fringe economy. Unscrupulous brokers and lenders have considerable latitude to ply their trade, especially with vulnerable low-income borrowers.

Time to Change Course

Despite the hype, homeownership is not a cure-all for low-income families who earn less than a living wage and have poor prospects for future income growth. In fact, for some low-income families homeownership only leads to more debt and financial misery. With mortgage delinquencies and foreclosures at record levels, especially among low-income households, millions of people would be better off today if they had remained renters. Surprisingly, rents are generally more stable than housing prices. From 1995 to 2001 rents rose slightly faster than inflation, but not as rapidly as home prices. Beginning in 2004 rent increases began to slow—even in hot markets like San Francisco and Seattle—and fell below the rate of inflation.

In the mid-1980s, low- and no-downpayment mortgages led to increased foreclosures when the economy tanked. Today, these mortgages are back, along with a concerted effort to drive economically marginal households into homeownership and high levels of unsustainable debt. To achieve this goal, the federal government spends $100 billion a year for homeownership programs (including the $70-plus billion that the mortgage interest deduction costs the Treasury).

Instead of focusing exclusively on homeownership, a more progressive and balanced housing policy would address the diverse needs of communities for both homes and rental units, and would facilitate new forms of ownership such as community land trusts and cooperatives. A balanced policy would certainly aim to expand the stock of affordable rental units. Unfortunately, just the opposite is occurring: rental housing assistance is being starved to feed low-income homeownership programs. From 2004 to 2006, President Bush and the Congress cut federal funding for public housing alone by 11%. Over the same period, more than 150,000 rental housing vouchers were cut.

And, of course, policymakers must act to protect those consumers who do opt to buy homes: for instance, by requiring mortgage lenders to make certain not only that a borrower is eligible for a particular loan product, but that the loan is suitable for the borrower.

The reason the United States lacks a sound housing policy is obvious if we follow the money. Overheated housing markets and rising home prices produce lots of winners. Real estate agents reap bigger commissions. Mortgage brokers, appraisers, real estate attorneys, title companies, lenders, builders, home remodelers, and everyone else with a hand in the housing pie does well. Cities raise more in property taxes, and insurance companies enroll more clients at higher premiums. Although housing accounts for only 5% of GDP, it has been responsible for up to 75% of all U.S. job growth in the last four years, according to the consulting firm Oxford Analytica. Housing has buffered the economy, and herding more low-income families into homes, regardless of the consequences, helps keep the industry ticking in the short run. The only losers? Renters squeezed by higher rents and accelerating conversion of rental units into condos. Young middle-income families trying to buy their first house. And, especially, the thousands of low-income families for whom buying a home turns into a financial nightmare. ❏

Sources: Carolina Katz Reid, *Studies in Demography and Ecology: Achieving the American Dream? A Longitudinal Analysis of the Homeownership Experiences of Low-Income Households,* Univ. of Washington, CSDE Working Paper No. 04-04; Dean Baker, "The Housing Bubble: A Time Bomb in Low-Income Communities?" *Shelterforce Online,* Issue #135, May/June 2004, www.nhi.org/online/issues/135/bubble.html; Howard Karger, *Shortchanged: Life and Debt in the Fringe Economy* (Berrett-Koehler, 2005); National Multi Housing Council (www.nmhc.org).

Article 3.2

WHAT WERE THE BANKERS THINKING?

BY ARTHUR MACEWAN
March/April 2010

Dear Dr. Dollar,
As I understand it, the main cause of the current economic mess was that banks made a lot of bad housing loans. When the people who took out those loans couldn't make their payments, the banks got in trouble and then the whole economy got in trouble. So why did the bankers make all those bad loans? What were they thinking!?
—Sara Boyle, Manchester, Conn.

They were thinking they could make a lot of money. To a large extent, they were right. Sure, they finally started losing. But you won't see many bankers in soup-kitchen lines.

Here's how it worked. The actual makers of the mortgage loans were willing to make high-risk loans because they quickly put these loans into bundles (electronic bundles) and sold the bundles to investors. So the makers of the mortgages—mortgage companies, commercial banks, savings and loans, and credit unions—were not harmed when someone stopped payment on a mortgage. These bundles are called mortgage-backed securities, a form of Collateralized Debt Obligations (CDOs). CDOs are a type of derivative—a financial instrument (i.e., a vehicle for financial investment) the value of which is derived from some other financial instrument, in this case the set of mortgages in the bundle.

The underwriters—the financial firms handling the marketing of these CDOs, usually large investment banks—then had to get them rated by one of the rating agencies. Moody's, Standard & Poor's, and Fitch are the three big firms, controlling 85% of the market, that evaluate the risk involved in financial instruments. The rating agencies, however, are paid by the underwriters, so they have a conflict of interest that gave them an incentive to rate the CDOs too high, indicating less risk than was really involved. Also, the underwriters could shop among the rating agencies to get the best rating. In general, the rationale for good ratings was that the mortgage-based CDOs were relatively safe because they included many mortgages, creating at least an aura of diversity. Diversity is always taken as implying low risk. (Except, of course, when there is a general failure.)

Also, buyers of the CDOs could buy insurance on these investments, just in case something did go wrong. The insurance policies on the CDOs are called "credit default swaps"—another set of derivatives, the value of which is derived from the value of the CDOs. The credit default swaps, like the CDOs themselves, were then treated in the financial market as another type of financial instrument.

Many investment banks made a lot of money in holding these derivatives as well as in buying and selling them. The banks got high returns on the derivatives they held and they got fees for buying and selling derivatives. Bear Stearns and Lehman

Brothers, the two investment banks that went under in 2008, had made lots of money on these activities between 2002 and 2006.

To understand the actions of the banks, it is important to recognize that the salaries and, especially, the large bonuses that the bankers obtained in these operations were based on the immediate, short-run profits that they generated. If in one year (say in 2005) they made lots of money through the fees on buying and selling the derivatives and through the returns on holding the derivatives, then it didn't matter that things fell apart soon after (in 2007). None of the bankers had to give back their salaries or bonuses. (These operations were facilitated by the general lack of regulation of derivative trading.)

Of course when things did fall apart, no one would buy the CDOs or the credit default swaps. These were the "toxic assets" that were held by many large banks and other investors and which "poisoned" the financial system. Some of the people who had made lots of money in salaries and bonuses also held stock in, for example, Bear Stearns or Lehman Brothers, and they lost money on those stocks.

There was, however, still a problem. Lots of financial institutions had taken out loans for which these CDOs and credit default swaps were collateral. With the value of these derivatives collapsing, it looked as though the creditors might lose their money. This was when people started talking about a collapse of the financial system.

Not to worry. The government stepped in and made sure that the creditors got their money.

So, it turns out that a whole set of arrangements—from the initial making of the mortgage to the salary-bonus system to the government bailout—protected the bankers and other actors from the risks of their actions. The arrangements encouraged excessively risky behavior that ultimately placed a huge cost on the rest of us.

But the bankers? They pretty much came out OK. No, you won't see many bankers in soup-kitchen lines. ❏

Article 3.3

RENTERS IN THE CROSSHAIRS

BY DANIEL FIRESIDE
March/April 2009

The United States is in the midst of a national foreclosure crisis that threatens to wreak havoc not just on homeowners, but also tenants, urban neighborhoods, and entire cities. Community organizers and legal activists are working hard to stop it.

Over 2 million properties went into foreclosure proceedings last year, a number that experts fear could jump to 10 million in the next few years. Foreclosures aren't just pushing owners into the street. According to the National Low Income Housing Coalition, renters make up an estimated 40% of families facing eviction because of foreclosure. And because the shakiest loans are concentrated in inner cities, the impact of vacant buildings on already fragile neighborhoods can be devastating.

Lenders and lawmakers have been slow to respond to this growing crisis. The Obama administration's mortgage rescue plan announced in February offers limited help to some individual homeowners at risk of foreclosure, but almost completely overlooks the plight of renters in foreclosed buildings. Families facing eviction are left to fend for themselves, often with little understanding of their legal rights or other options. But an array of community organizers and legal advocates have been pushing back—organizing tenants, pressuring policymakers and lenders, and throwing wrenches into the legal system.

Steve Meacham, a tenant organizer with City Life/Vida Urbana, a Boston-based social-justice organization, has been on the front lines of the foreclosure battle. Traditionally, CL/VU had mainly organized tenants facing eviction into unions in order to negotiate with landlords. "About a year ago, we noticed something strange," explains Meacham. "Most of the evictions were being pushed by the banks and lenders."

Now the group scans the latest foreclosure listings and goes door to door to alert tenants. They host meetings with people at risk of eviction, provide assistance and advice about negotiating with lenders, and organize demonstrations outside banks. They also work with former owners who hope to renegotiate their loans with the banks and keep renting out their properties.

Renters are usually the last to learn about a foreclosure. "Tenants will get a letter from a bank offering them a few hundred dollars if they leave in two weeks, and threatening to evict them within a month if they refuse and give them nothing," says Meacham. Those who leave usually lose their security deposits and any prepaid rent. "Most banks depend on people getting scared and leaving. When people resist, especially tenants and former owners, the banks don't know what to do with that and back off."

Thanks to the group's tactics, scores of tenants and former owners have stalled foreclosures, negotiated higher payout deals, and even forced banks to cut mortgages.

Housing advocates are also taking the battle to state and federal policymakers. In December, New Haven Legal Assistance (NHLA) threatened to sue Fannie Mae and Freddie Mac for illegally evicting tenants in buildings the federal lenders had foreclosed on. The agencies backed down and drew up new rules that stopped the practice. Now activists are pressing for the same rules to apply to private lenders.

"The current situation is lose-lose for everyone right now," says NHLA's Amy Eppler-Epstein. "Banks can make more money on a full building than an empty one that's trashed. Shareholders, neighborhoods, communities, and tenants are suffering. It's crazy and it's got to change." ❑

Article 3.4

HOW TO STOP THE FORECLOSURES
A Review of the Policy Proposals

BY FRED MOSELEY
July/August 2008; updated October 2010

O ver one million U.S. homeowners have already lost their homes due to foreclosures since the mortgage crisis began last summer. Another one million homeowners are 90 days past due on their mortgages (foreclosure notices usually go out
after 90 days) and two million more are 30 days past due, so three million more
households may face foreclosure in the months ahead. If current policies do not
change, it is estimated that up to five million homeowners would lose their homes
due to foreclosure over the next few years. Five million is roughly 10% of the total
number of homes U.S. with mortgages. This is clearly the worst housing crisis since
the Great Depression, and will wreack havoc in the lives of millions of families
unless something is done. A high foreclosure rate also has a deteriorating effect on
surrounding neighborhoods, further depressing housing prices and quality of life.

Many of those facing foreclosure are low- to middle-income homeowners who
were enticed into buying houses by fraudulent mortgage companies and low "teaser"
interest rates that are adjusted up ("reset") after two to three years. As long as housing prices were increasing, homeowners could always refinance their mortgages and
get a new teaser rate for another few years. However, now that house prices are falling, these homeowners can no longer refinance, and many of them cannot afford to
pay the higher interest rates when they are reset. Falling prices also mean that many
of these homeowners owe more on their mortgage than the current value of their
house (i.e. they have "negative equity" in their house). The recession is also resulting
in declining employment and income, meaning even more homeowners are struggling to make their monthly mortgage payments. The further housing prices decline,
and the worse the recession is, the worse the foreclosures will be, in a vicious cycle.

Clearly, the federal government must take some positive actions to stop the spreading foreclosures, especially for low- and middle-income families, who would suffer the
most. But what should those actions be? At a minimum, policies should apply only to
owner-occupied homes, and not to "investor" or "speculative" homeowners (those who
buy houses in order to sell them later at a higher price). But beyond this, various policies have been proposed, and not all of them would truly help homeowners at risk.

Workouts, Not Bailouts

There are two main types of anti-foreclosure policies: bailouts and workouts. In bailouts, the government gives aid either to lenders (e.g., by purchasing bad mortgages
at their full original value) or to homeowners (e.g., by giving them loans so they can
repay their lenders). Of course, aid to homeowners indirectly bails out the lenders as
well. In workouts, the terms of the original mortgage contract are modified, either by
reducing the rate of interest or reducing the principal owed, or both, in order to make

the loan more affordable. So far, most of the proposals to deal with the foreclosure crisis have been workouts more than bailouts, although there are elements of bailout in some of them as well. The lenders made fortunes on these risky mortgages during the housing bubble, so if someone has to suffer losses now, it should be the lenders. There should be no bailouts of the lenders in any way.

Lender-Initiated Workouts

There are two types of workouts, depending on whether they are initiated by the lenders or the homeowners. Most of the policies proposed and enacted so far have been initiated by the lenders, i.e., they are voluntary on the part of the lenders. The main policy of the Bush administration is called "Hope Now," in which the lenders voluntarily postpone the resets of interest rates that are scheduled to take place in the months ahead, and leave the principal of the loan unchanged (or sometimes the foregone interest is added to the principal). The Bush administration claims that over 500,000 mortgages have been modified in this way in recent months, and estimates that another 500,000 mortgages will be modified in the months ahead. However, critics argue that these numbers are exaggerated and that many of these modifications have been simply allowing homeowners more time to make the same payments. It is likely that in the months ahead, many of these homeowners still will not be able to make their payments, and many of them will be foreclosed on, which has led some critics to call this the "No Hope" plan. The only lasting solution is to reduce the mortgage principal owed to more affordable levels. The main problem now is not the reset of interest rates, but rather declining housing prices, which has the effect that more and more homeowners now owe more money on their mortgage than their house is worth.

The House and Senate have recently passed two versions of a similar bill that is primarily a workout, but also is potentially part bailout, and is also lender-initiated. The bill would replace existing mortgages with new mortgages that would have a value of 85% of the current market value of the houses, and these refinanced mortgages would be guaranteed by the Federal Housing Administration (how this "current market value" is to be determined is a crucial detail which so far has not been specified). For example, a homeowner with an original mortgage of $300,000 would have the principal reduced to $225,000, and the monthly payments reduced by a similar proportion. This 15% "write-down" of the principal, plus the prior 10% decline of prices, means that the total write-down for lenders will be a maximum of approximately 25% (and less to the extent that the borrower made a down payment or has accumulated equity through monthly payments). The bill would permit FHA to guarantee up to $300 billion in new mortgages, which it estimates could help up to 1.5 million homeowners. President Bush initially threatened a veto, but has since promised to sign the bill. In any case, it remains unclear how many lenders will voluntarily implement this refinancing.

Another problem with this bill is that housing prices in some areas are likely to fall more than an additional 15%. Mortgages on these houses are likely to be the ones that the lenders will voluntarily refinance, and any further losses would be borne by the government (i.e., by the taxpayers). This will be a partial bailout of the lenders.

Homeowner-Initiated Workouts

Another bill has been introduced into the House (H.R. 3609) and Senate (S. 26360) that would provide workouts that would be initiated by the homeowners and would be mandatory for the lenders. These bills would allow bankruptcy judges to modify mortgage contracts (by reducing the principal and/or by reducing the interest rate) in order to make monthly payments more affordable for homeowners. It used to be possible for bankruptcy judges to modify mortgage contracts, but this was explicitly prohibited in a 1993 bankruptcy law. One can see the hand of the mortgage bankers in the writing of that provision. Modifications on other types of loans are allowed: for investment properties, for vacation homes, and even for boats, but no modifications allowed for primary residences! So all that needs to be done is to delete this one phrase in the law which prohibits modifications for primary residences. A significant advantage of this plan is that it would not cost taxpayers anything.

One problem with this bill is that homeowners would have to declare bankruptcy, which is expensive (about $2,000) and would hurt their credit rating in the future. But at least they would still have their home, with an affordable mortgage, and thus would have the chance to restore their credit rating.

This bill is supported by the AFL-CIO, SEIU, NAACP, ACORN, the Center for Responsible Lending, and many other consumer protection groups. It is of course strongly opposed by the Mortgage Bankers Association, and does not seem to have enough support for passage at the present time.

Another homeowner-initiated plan has been proposed by Dean Baker of the Center for Economic and Policy Research. According to this "own-to-rent" plan, homeowners faced with foreclosure would have the option to stay in their houses as tenants, rather than as owners, and would pay the prevailing rental rates, which are generally much lower than mortgage payments. Eligibility for the plan would be capped at the median house price in a metropolitan area and thus would not benefit high-income homeowners. This plan also would not cost taxpayers anything. A bill along these lines was recently introduced in the House (H.R. 6116).

Looking Ahead

The presidential candidates have had disappointingly little to say about the foreclosure crisis and anti-foreclosure policies. Senator Barack Obama has expressed support for the FHA guarantee bill, but not yet for the bankruptcy modification bill. In good Republican tradition, McCain advocates "no government intervention." But the foreclosure crisis is likely to worsen in the coming months, and the public may well demand more policies to address this growing problem. The homeowner-initiated policies are preferable because they provide the most protection for homeowners against foreclosure. Both of these options should be available to homeowners facing foreclosure, especially for those with low or moderate incomes.

The guiding principles of government anti-foreclosure policies should be: (1) homeowners should be allowed to stay in their homes; and (2) there should be no bailouts for the lenders. And the long-run objective of government housing policies should be: decent affordable housing for all.

Update on the Foreclosure Crisis, October 2010

More than two years after this article was originally published, the foreclosure crisis continues and threatens to get worse. So far, over 3 million homeowners have lost their homes due to foreclosure since the crisis began. In addition, over 2 million mortgages are now in the process of foreclosure and another 5 million are 30 to 90 days delinquent. Eleven million mortgages are "underwater," i.e., the holder owes more than the current value of the house. Estimates of the total number of foreclosures under current policies range from 6 million to 10 million (12% to 20% of all mortgages). If unemployment remains very high for several more years, as seems very likely, foreclosures will reach the high end of these estimates. It takes a paycheck to make a mortgage payment.

The main policy of the Obama administration to deal with foreclosures—the Home Affordable Modification Program or HAMP, which offers to pay lenders part of the cost of the modifications—has not been very effective. As of July 2010, only about 420,000 homeowners have received permanent modifications of their mortgages (after a three-month period of temporary modifications), and it is likely that a majority of these will probably end in foreclosure in the years ahead because the modifications were not significant enough. (The ratings agency Fitch forecasts that the default rate of modified mortgages will be 75%; the financial services company Barclays forecasts 60%.)

Therefore, the main effect of HAMP so far has been to delay foreclosures, due to temporary modifications, rather than to stop foreclosures. This delay has been beneficial for homeowners, but it means that the worst is yet to come unless government policies change significantly.

The main problem with HAMP, as with the earlier Bush policies, is that it is voluntary on the part of lenders, and lenders have generally not been very willing to "volunteer." Almost half of the modifications so far have been by Fannie Mae and Freddie Mac, which are owned by the government.

The best way to avoid this escalating foreclosure crisis remains to require that lenders participate in modifications initiated by homeowners or the government and that these modifications reduce the principle (the amount owed) of mortgages "underwater" to their current market value, rather than just reduce interest rates or delay payments. Bankruptcy judges should be allowed to modify mortgage contracts. Special judgeships should be created to adjudicate mortgage modifications. As long as participation is voluntary on the part of lenders, participation will be minimal and insufficient. There should also be a general moratorium on foreclosures until appropriate policies can be worked out and implemented.

Finally, the government should not pay lenders for any of their losses. The lenders made plenty of profit on these mortgages in the good times, and there is no good reason why taxpayers should suffer the losses from the lenders' bad loans.

As this second edition goes to press (October 2010), the foreclosure crisis has taken a significant turn for the worse. It was disclosed recently that major mortgage servicers who carry out the foreclosures (GMAC, JPMorgan Chase, and Bank of America) have skirted the rules for providing documentation to justify foreclosures in an attempt to rush the process as quickly as possible. Their employees have routinely signed thousands of legal affidavits that the companies have the titles to the houses that are being foreclosed, even though they are not certain that this is true. The term "robo-signer" has entered the lexicon of the financial crisis. These four mortgage servicers have halted foreclosures in the 23 states that require court approval of foreclosures, and they face likely opposition in other states as well, including investigations by state attorneys general. It looks like the federal government will probably impose some kind of moratorium on foreclosures in order to review all these procedures. The Obama administration should use this moratorium to institute mandatory mortgage modifications. ❑

Resources: For more information about H.R. 3609 and S. 26360, visit the website of the Center for Responsible Lending (www.responsiblelending.org). For more information about Dean Baker's "own-to-rent" plan (introduced in the House as H.R. 6116), visit the website of the Center for Economic and Policy Research (www.cepr.net).

Article 3.5

THE BAILOUT OF FANNIE MAE AND FREDDIE MAC

BY FRED MOSELEY
September/October 2008

O n Sunday, September 7 [2008], Treasury Secretary Henry Paulson announced that the U.S. government was taking control of Fannie Mae and Freddie Mac, the two giant home mortgage companies, which together either own or guarantee almost half of the mortgages in the United States. This takeover stands in striking contrast to the generally laissez-faire philosophy of the U.S. government, especially the Republican Party. Why did Paulson take this highly unusual action? And what will be the future of Fannie and Freddie? To delve into these questions is to underscore the critical fault line between private profits and public aims—in this case, the aim of making homeownership affordable—a fault line that ran right through the hybrid structure of Fannie and Freddie.

A Brief History

Fannie Mae (short for the Federal National Mortgage Association) was created as an agency of the federal government in 1938 in an attempt to provide additional funds to the home mortgage market and to help the housing industry recover from the Great Depression. Fannie Mae purchased approved mortgages from commercial banks, which could then use the funds to originate additional mortgages. It continued to fulfill this function on a modest scale in the early postwar years.

Fannie Mae was privatized in 1968, in part to help reduce the budget deficit caused by the Vietnam War (a short-sighted goal, if ever there was one). In 1970, Freddie Mac (Federal Home Loan Mortgage Corporation) was created as a private company in order to provide competition for Fannie Mae. Chartered by the federal government, both are (or were, until the takeover) so-called government-sponsored enterprises: private enterprises whose main goal is to maximize profit for the shareholders who own them, but also quasi-public enterprises with a mandated goal of increasing the availability of affordable mortgages to families in the United States. In the end, this dual mandate proved to be untenable.

In order to obtain funds to purchase mortgages, Fannie and Freddie sell short-term bonds. In other words, their business plan involves borrowing short-term and lending long-term, because interest rates are higher on long-term loans than on short-term loans. However, such "speculative finance" is risky because it depends on the willingness of short-term creditors to continue to loan to Fannie and Freddie by rolling over or refinancing their short-term loans. If creditors were to lose confidence in Fannie and Freddie and refuse to do so, then they would be in danger of bankruptcy. This is what almost happened in the recent crisis.

Beginning in the 1970s, Fannie and Freddie began to develop and sell "mortgage-backed securities"—hundreds of mortgages bundled together and sold to investors as a security, similar to a bond. They also guaranteed these securities (so that if a mortgage defaulted, they would repurchase it from the investors) and made money by charging a fee for this guarantee (like an insurance premium). This major financial innovation enabled the two companies to buy more mortgages from commercial banks, thereby increasing the supply of credit in the home mortgage market, which in turn was supposed to push mortgage interest rates lower, making houses more affordable. These early mortgage-backed securities consisted entirely of "prime" mortgages—that is, loans at favorable interest rates, typically made to cred-itworthy borrowers with full documentation and a substantial down payment.

The securities that Fannie and Freddie sold were widely perceived by investors to carry an implicit government guarantee: if Fannie or Freddie were ever in dan-ger of bankruptcy, then the federal government would pay off their debts (even though this government guarantee was explicitly denied in legislation and in the loan agree-ments themselves). This perceived guarantee enabled Fannie and Freddie to borrow money at lower interest rates because loans to them were viewed as less risky.

In the 1980s, Wall Street investment banks also began to package and sell mortgage-backed securities. In the 1990s and 2000s, these "private label" mort-gage-backed securities expanded rapidly in volume and also in reach, coming to include "subprime" mortgages—loans at higher interest rates with less favorable terms, geared toward less credit-worthy borrowers and typically requiring little or no documentation and little or no down payment.

The subprime innovation was entirely the work of the investment banks; as of 2000, Fannie and Freddie owned or guaranteed almost no subprime mortgages. This innovation greatly increased the supply of credit for home mortgages and led to the extraordinary housing boom of the last decade, and also eventually to the crisis. As a result of these changes, the share of mortgage-backed securities sold by Fannie and Freddie fell to around 40% by 2005.

In the recent housing boom, the companies—especially Freddie—began to take greater risks. While continuing to bundle prime mortgages into securities and sell them to investors, Fannie and Freddie began to buymortgage-backed securities issued by investment banks, including some based on subprime and Alt-A (between prime and subprime) mortgages. Why did they begin buying as well as selling mort-gage-backed securities? Buying these private-label securities gave Fannie and Freddie a way to get in on the subprime action—while still avoiding direct purchases of sub-prime mortgages from the banks and mortgage companies that originated them. It was a way both to increase their profits at the behest of their shareholders, and, in response to pressure from the government, to make more mortgages available to low- and middle-income families. Of course, it also opened them up to the risks of the subprime arena. Moreover, the prime mortgages they continued to buy and guarantee were increasingly at inflated, bubble prices, making them vulnerable to the eventual bust and the decline of housing prices.

Anatomy of a Crisis

When the subprime crisis began in the summer of 2007, Fannie and Freddie at first appeared to be relatively unaffected, and were even counted on to increase their pur-chases of mortgages in order to support the mortgage market and help overcome the crisis. Congress facilitated this by relaxing some of its regulations on the two companies: the maximum value of mortgages that they could purchase was increased substantially; their reserve capital requirements, already much lower than for commercial banks, were reduced further; and restrictions on their growth were lifted. As a result of these changes and the drying up of private label mortgage-backed securities, the share of all mortgage-backed securities sold by Fannie and Freddie doubled to approximately 80%. Without Fannie and Freddie, the mortgage and housing crises of the last year would have been much worse.

As the overall crisis unfolded, however, the financial situation of Fannie and Freddie deteriorated. Delinquency and foreclosure rates for the mortgages they own or guarantee, while lower than for the industry as a whole, increased rapidly and beyond expectations. The two companies together reported losses of $14 billion in the last year. Their actual losses have been much worse. As of mid-2008, the two had lost about $45 billion due to the decline in the value of their mortgage-backed securities, mostly those backed by subprime and Alt-A mortgages. But by labeling that decline "temporary," they could leave the losses off their balance sheets. If these losses were counted, as they should be, then Freddie's capital would be completely wiped out (a value of -$5.6 billion), and Fannie's would be reduced to a razor-thin margin of $12.2 billion (less than 2% of its assets), likely becoming negative in the coming quarters. In addition, both Fannie and Freddie count as assets "tax deferred losses" that can be used in future years to offset tax bills—if they make a profit. Without this dubious (but legal) accounting trick, the net assets of both Fannie and Freddie would be below zero, -$20 billion and -$32 billion respectively.

The financial crisis of Fannie and Freddie worsened in early July. The price of their stock, which had already fallen by more than half since last summer, declined another 50% in a few weeks, for a total decline of over 80%. Fear spread that Fannie and Freddie's creditors would refuse to roll over their short-term loans to the two. If that were to happen, then the U.S. home mortgage market and the housing construction industry probably would have collapsed completely, and the U.S. economy would have fallen into an even deeper recession. Furthermore, approximately 20% of the mortgage-backed securities and debt of Fannie and Freddie are owned by foreign investors. Mainly these are foreign governments, most significantly China. If these foreign investors became unwilling to continue to lend Fannie and Freddie money, this would have precipitated a steep fall in the value of the dollar which, on top of recent significant declines, would have dealt another blow to the U.S. economy. Clearly, the potential crisis here was serious enough to spur government action.

In late July, Congress passed a law authorizing the Treasury to provide unlimited amounts of money to Fannie and Freddie, either by buying new issues of stock or by making loans, and also to take over the companies in a conservator arrangement if necessary.

Government Takeover

Through August [2008] the financial condition of Fannie and Freddie continued to deteriorate (especially Freddie), and confidence in their ability to survive waned. Foreign investors in particular reduced their purchases of the companies' debt, and mortgage rates increased. The Treasury concluded that it had to implement a takeover in order to reassure creditors and restore stability to the home mortgage market.

The Treasury plan has three main components:

• It commits up to $200 billion over the next 15 months for purchases of preferred shares of Fannie and Freddie as necessary to keep the companies solvent;

• It establishes a special lending facility that will provide emergency loans in case of a liquidity crisis;

• It commits to purchase unspecified amounts of Fannie and Freddie's mortgage-backed securities "as deemed appropriate."

The day after Paulson's announcement, William Poole, ex-president of the Federal Reserve Bank of St. Louis, estimated that the total cost to taxpayers would be in the neighborhood of $300 billion.

The top managers and the boards of directors of both companies will be dismissed and replaced by new, government-appointed managers. Other than that, the Treasury hopes that day-to-day operations at Fannie and Freddie will be "business as usual." They will continue to borrow money from creditors, now reassured by the government's intervention and more willing to lend to them, and they will continue to purchase and guarantee prime mortgages. In fact, Treasury Department plans call for the volume of mortgages purchased by the two companies to increase over the next year in order to push the supply of mortgage loans up and mortgage interest rates down.

The Treasury plan is a complete bailout of the creditors of Fannie and Freddie, who will be repaid in full, with taxpayer money if necessary. In contrast, owners of Fannie or Freddie stock will lose to some degree: dividends will be suspended for the foreseeable future, and their stock is now worth very little. But their stock was not expropriated. Nor was it wiped out entirely; it could regain value in the future as the home mortgage market recovers. Without the intervention, both companies would have gone bankrupt and the stockowners would have lost everything. So the intervention does represent at least a modest bailout for shareholders.

The most controversial issue in the months ahead will be the future of Fannie and Freddie. Should they become public enterprises permanently? Should they be re-privatized? Should they be sold off in pieces and cease to exist? Secretary Paulson made it clear that the government's current conservatorship is a holding action, and that decisions about the companies' ultimate status will only be made once the next administration and the next Congress are in office. Paulson said that Fannie and Freddie's current structure is unworkable because of its dual and conflicting goals of making housing affordable and maximizing profit—a radical statement, if you think about it! And he suggested that the two should either be fully public enterprises, or else they should be fully private enterprises without any government backing.

In the upcoming debate, the left should advocate forcefully for a public home mortgage agency, one whose sole purpose is to provide affordable housing without the conflicting purpose of maximizing profit. This would stabilize the home mortgage market and help it avoid the boom/bust cycle of private mortgage markets that has brought on the current crisis.

More fundamentally, because decent affordable housing is a basic economic right, providing credit for home purchases should be a function of the government rather than of private businesses whose primary goal is maximum profit. The provision of credit for housing should not be an arena where enormous profits are made, as has been the case in recent years. Without these huge profits, mortgages would be cheaper and houses more affordable. Plus, the kinds of fraudulent lending practices that played a significant role in the recent housing boom would be minimized.

With the presidential election just weeks away, the crisis of Fannie, Freddie, and the whole home lending market is poised to become a major campaign issue. McCain has said that he wants Fannie and Freddie to "go away"—i.e., to be broken up and disappear, leaving the mortgage market entirely to private enterprises. Obama has emphasized the conflict between the public aim of making housing widely affordable and the private aim of making a profit, but so far he has not come down on one side or the other. Now he will have to decide. I hope that he will be a strong advocate of a public home mortgage agency, and I think this would help him to get elected. ❑

Update on the Future of Fannie Mae and Freddie Mac, October 2010

As it turned out, the future of Fannie Mae and Freddie Mac was not an issue in the 2008 presidential campaign. Neither candidate (or party) knew what to do about Fannie and Freddie, especially in the midst of the worst housing crisis since the Great Depression, so they avoided the subject. And the Obama administration continued to avoid the subject, at least in public, as a lower priority than health-care reform and financial reform—until August 17, when Treasury Secretary Geithner convened a one-day conference on "The Future of Housing Finance." The Obama administration has promised their proposal by next January. So the moment of decision on the future of Fannie and Freddie is approaching.

Indications are that Obama will propose that Fannie and Freddie be restructured into a public mortgage insurance agency, which would provide insurance for mortgages owned by private banks, and would not buy and hold any mortgages in its own portfolio. The private banks would pay a premium for the insurance in order to limit taxpayer risk, similar to the insurance premiums they pay to the FDIC. Stricter regulation and eligibility requirements for mortgages will probably also be included.

Geithner argues that the main advantage of a government insurance agency over a strictly private mortgage market (without government guarantees) is that it would increase the availability of credit for mortgages at a lower rate of interest, especially in times of economic downturns, like the current crisis. Without the government guarantee, investors would generally charge a higher rate of interest to finance 30-year fixed rate mortgages for households, and may not be willing to lend at all in economic downturns. The interest rate spread in normal times between a purely private mortgage system (e.g., jumbo loans which exceed the maximum for Fannie-Freddie mortgages) and a mortgage system with government insurance in recent decades has been between 0.25% and 0.5%. However, in the current recession, this spread increased sharply to 1.5% and is still today almost 1%. The current recession has clearly demonstrated that private banks and other investors will flee the mortgage market in a serious recession unless there are government guarantees. Only about 10% of new mortgages since the recession began have been without government guarantees. Where would the mortgage market and the economy be today without Fannie and Freddie? The mortgage market would be about one-tenth of its present size, and the economy would be in correspondingly much worse shape.

In spite of these obvious risks, Republicans want to do away with the government role in the mortgage market altogether. They argue that private banks would increase competition, which would lower costs and lower mortgage rates. But this argument is disingenuous, to say the least; everyone but free-market true-believers recognizes that, without explicit government backing, mortgage rates would be higher and in a crisis would be much higher. In such a Republican world, houses would be less affordable and homeownership would decline. And in a crisis, new home-buying would become almost impossible. Because of their blind allegiance to the "free market," Republicans are willing to play reckless with our economy and our lives. Obviously, we should not allow them to do this.

Although a government insurance agency would be much better than a purely private mortgage market, there is an even better way to reduce interest rates on mortgages to levels even lower than the Obama insurance plan would: transform Fannie and Freddie into a public mortgage bank (rather than an insurance company) that would buy eligible mortgages from originators and hold them in their own portfolio. Actually, this would be a "return to the past" and to the original structure of Fannie Mae from its beginning in the Great Depression (to provide more affordable mortgages) until its privatization in 1968 (to help pay for the Vietnam War). This public bank option was not discussed at the August conference, but should be part of the discussion.

Such a public bank could charge lower interest rates than private banks (even with government insurance) because the main goal of private banks is to maximize profit and maximize shareholder value, and also to allow for multimillion-dollar salaries of bank executives. A public mortgage bank would have a different objective: not to maximize profit, shareholder value, and executive salaries, but to increase the availability of affordable housing. This goal would not be pursued to the point of losing money, but the profit margin could be less. And the executive salaries would be more in line with high civil servant salaries. Public bank mortgages would also have an upper limit, perhaps $500,000. The public bank provision of low-interest mortgages would not apply to more expensive houses or to second homes.

A relevant comparison is with student loans. The explicit argument of the Obama administration for their "direct lender" model is that they can provide student loans more cheaply than the private companies they have been subsidizing, and can also use the savings to fund more Pell grants for low-income students. What a great idea! The same logic could be applied to housing.

Another related advantage of a public bank over private banks is that its profit would not have to go to private shareholders (there would be none), but would instead become public income that could be used to pursue public policy goals, such as building more affordable housing.

Another advantage of a public bank over the Obama insurance plan is that it would eliminate the risk (which is probably significant) that the insurance premium charged to banks would be too low, and that in the next serious crisis, taxpayers would once again suffer the losses, rather than the private banks that profited from the mortgages during the good times.

A public bank would raise funds to buy mortgages by borrowing money in the capital market (i.e., by selling bonds), the same way that private banks raise funds to finance their mortgages. But this borrowed money would not add to the government deficit, because the money would be invested in mortgages, which would eventually be recovered, together with a modest profit.

The future of Fannie and Freddie will be one of the most important economic policy issues in 2011. The Left should attempt to put the public bank option on the table for discussion, and should advocate its adoption, as the best way to achieve the objective of more affordable housing for all Americans and a more stable economy. ❏

Article 3.6

WHO GETS THOSE TRILLIONS?

BY ARTHUR MacEWAN
January/February 2009

Dear Dr. Dollar:
As housing prices have fallen, it seems that people have lost a huge amount in terms of the value of their homes. We are told that, over the whole country, trillions of dollars in home equity have been lost. Who gets those trillions? And, likewise, what about the trillions lost in the stock market?
—Carlos Rafael Alicea Negrón, Bronx, N.Y.

The simple answer to your question is that no one gets the lost trillions; they are simply gone. But, like all simple answers, this one doesn't explain very much.

Suppose that seven years ago, you bought your house for $200,000. Housing prices continued to rise, and at the beginning of 2007 you saw that other people in your neighborhood were selling houses similar to yours for $400,000. So you, quite reasonably, figured that your house was worth $400,000.

But now the housing bubble has burst. Similar houses in your neighborhood are selling for "only" $300,000 and thus it is now quite reasonable to figure that the value of your house has dropped by $100,000 as compared to the beginning of 2007. (Multiply this $100,000 by roughly 75 million homes across the country, and you have losses of $7.5 trillion.)

Your house, however, was not involved in any actual transaction at this lower value. So no one has gained the value you lost. If, for example, last year one of your neighbors had sold an equivalent house for $400,000 and now buys your house for $300,000 this neighbor would have gained what you lost. But most houses are not bought and sold in any given year. Their value is determined by those equivalent (or similar) houses that are actually bought and sold.

Moreover, even if someone bought your house at $300,000, that person would gain the value you lost only in the special case of the example above, where the person was lucky enough to have sold an equivalent house at $400,000. If instead that person was a new entrant to the housing market or a person who had just sold a similar house elsewhere for $300,000, then no one would be gaining what you lost.

Thus in the great majority of cases, the $100,000 value would simply be gone, and no one would have gotten it.

The situation on the stock market is similar. The values of stocks are determined by the sales that actually take place. When we hear that today the value of Mega Corporation's stock fell from $100 a share to $75 dollars a share, this means that the price of shares that were traded today were selling at $75 while those that were traded yesterday were selling for $100. But most shares of Mega Corporation were not actually traded either day. Their value fell—just like the value of your house fell when neighbors sold their houses—but no one gained this lost value. As in the housing market, the values of stocks have declined by trillions, but the trillions are simply gone.

Of course as with the situation in the housing market, some actual gains of value can take place when stock prices fall. If someone sold a share of Mega Corporation yesterday for $100 and bought it today for $75, this person obtained a gain. But with most of the declines in stock values, no one gets a gain.

To understand what has happened recently, it is useful to keep in mind that the high housing values of recent years were the result of a speculative bubble. The values increased not because there was some real change in the houses themselves. The houses were not providing more living services to the degree that their prices rose. The prices of housing rose because people expected them to rise more. The situation was a speculative bubble, and housing prices rose far above their historical trend.

And just as, in general, the loss of value when prices fell was not balanced by a gain, the gains that people saw when the bubbles expanded were not balanced by losses. As the bubble grew and the value of your house rose from $200,000 to $400,000, no one experienced an equivalent loss. Virtually all home buyers and owners were winners.

But speculative bubbles do not last. ❏

Article 3.7

DON'T BLAME THE CRA

Far from causing the subprime crisis, the Community Reinvestment Act, suitably expanded, might have prevented it.

BY JIM CAMPEN
October 2010

At an American Bankers Association convention in the early 1980s, bank consultant Ken Thomas was surprised to hear howls of laughter emerge from one of the meeting rooms. He stepped in to find the speaker ending his presentation with a flourish, pointing to the initial letters of the words projected behind him. "In conclusion," he shouted above the laughter and applause, "you can have your Community Reinvestment Act Programs, you can have your Community Reinvestment Act Policies, you can have your Community Reinvestment Act Personnel. But—as you can see—it's all just ... CRAP!"

The bankers' laughter may have been justified at the time, as the Reagan administration and its bank regulators ignored the law that a nationwide grassroots movement of community activists had successfully pushed Congress to enact in 1977. But the CRA went on to be a huge success, encouraging banks to invest in low-income communities. The notion, propounded by the right, that the CRA was responsible for the subprime crisis ignores the fact that subprime lending was *less* likely in areas covered by the CRA.

The CRA was enacted in 1977 because banks were collecting deposits in inner-city neighborhoods but failing to reinvest the funds back into those same areas. For this reason, CRA performance evaluations were focused on "assessment areas" defined in terms of where bank branches were located. At that time, this covered the great majority of all mortgage lending.

In fact, the CRA was one of the most remarkable success stories of the 1990s. Under strong pressure from a second wave of grassroots activism, many banks recognized the potential for profitable business in neighborhoods that they had written off without a second thought not so long before. Mortgage loans to minority and low-income homebuyers soared. Hundreds of local partnerships among banks, community-based organizations, and government agencies resulted in tens of thousands of new units of affordable housing. The CRA acquired broad and deep support, due to the difference that it made in hundreds of communities throughout the United States. This support paid off in 1996 when the CRA emerged intact from a determined attempt by congressional Republicans, following their 1994 electoral victory, to gut the law.

But when Congress passed the Financial Services Modernization Act of 1999, capping a decades-long process of deregulating banks and other financial companies, it rejected the compelling arguments by community groups that the CRA needed to be "modernized" as well. The industry-friendly Republicans who controlled the Senate Banking Committee adamantly opposed any strengthening of the CRA.

As a result, the impact of the CRA continued to erode, as an ever-greater share of total mortgage lending fell outside its reach. By 2005, according to the Federal Reserve, only one in four home-purchase loans (26%) were made by banks in their CRA assessment areas. The rest of the loans were made by banks in areas where they didn't have branches (Wells Fargo Bank makes loans in all 50 states, although it only has branches in 24), by affiliated companies that didn't have to be included in CRA evaluations (such as CitiBank's sister company, CitiFinancial, that specialized in high-cost loans), and by independent mortgage companies not related to banks (including many, such as Ameriquest and New Century, that focused on high-cost predatory lending).

Within this shrinking area of coverage, the CRA continued to have an important impact, encouraging banks to make responsible home loans that borrowers could afford to repay and discouraging predatory subprime loans. The Federal Reserve found that only 7% of the loans that banks made in 2005 in their assessment areas were high-cost loans, compared to 24% of the loans that they made elsewhere, and 38% of the loans made by mortgage companies. My own research in Massachusetts found that in 2006, at the height of the subprime boom, banks whose local lending was covered by the CRA accounted for only 655 out of 40,173 subprime loans in the state (just 1.6% of the total). Conservative claims that the CRA was responsible for the subprime lending crisis have things exactly backwards. If CRA had been expanded to cover the entire mortgage lending industry as part of the 1999 "financial modernization" law, the subprime lending crisis might never have happened.

In the aftermath of the crisis, it is even more vital to finally update the CRA— both to prevent predatory lending from re-emerging once the current crisis is over, and to ensure that those responsible for the crisis provide the credit and capital that local communities need to recover. Accordingly, community-based organizations have stepped up their campaigns for expanding and modernizing CRA. Last year, National People's Action and the PICO National Network (together representing more than 70 community-based organizations nationwide) got the Federal Reserve to agree to hold a series of day-long meetings with local leaders and hundreds of activists in nine hard-hit cities across the country, from Richmond, Calif., to Brockton, Mass. In Washington, D.C., meanwhile, the National Community Reinvestment Coalition has led a broad collection of local, regional, and national groups in bringing pressure to bear on regulators and elected officials.

The most important proposals for updating and strengthening the CRA include: extending CRA coverage to bank lending in all of the communities where they do business and to all lending by all affiliated companies; extending CRA coverage to independent mortgage companies; extending CRA-like responsibilities to Wall Street firms such as investment banks and hedge funds; increasing emphasis on basic banking services, including convenient branch offices, affordable small-dollar loans, and inexpensive checking and savings accounts for lower-income families; and expanding the attention given to evaluating performance in meeting the credit and banking needs of people and communities of color.

Some of these long-overdue measures to expand the CRA's coverage and operation would require legislation, such as the American Community Investment

Reform Act of 2010, introduced in the House of Representatives in September. But many others could be implemented under the current law, by the bank regulators charged with implementing the CRA. The struggle continues, on both fronts. ❏

Resources: Revisiting the CRA: Perspectives on the Future of the Community Reinvestment Act, Federal Reserve Banks of Boston and San Francisco, 2009 (www.bos.frb.org/commdev/cra/Revisiting-the-CRA.htm); the National Community Reinvestment Coalition (www.ncrc.org); National People's Action (www.npa-us.org); PICO National Network (www.piconetwork.org).

Article 3.8

UPDATE ON MORTGAGE LENDING DISCRIMINATION
After a disastrous detour, we're back where we started.

BY JIM CAMPEN
October 2010

In the 1980s and early 1990s, racial discrimination in mortgage lending resulted in less access to home loans for predominantly black and Latino borrowers and neighborhoods. Home mortgages were a fairly standardized product, and the problem was that banks avoided lending in minority neighborhoods (redlining) and denied applications from blacks and Latinos at disproportionately high rates compared to equally creditworthy white applicants (lending discrimination).

Soon afterwards, however, a different form of lending discrimination rose to prominence as high-cost subprime loans became increasingly common. Precisely because borrowers and neighborhoods of color had limited access to the traditional prime loans, they were vulnerable for exploitation by predatory lenders pushing the new product.

Redlining was soon over-shadowed by "reverse redlining." Instead of being ignored, borrowers and neighborhoods of color were now aggressively targeted for high-cost subprime loans. Community groups documented and aggressively publicized the problem, and the U.S. Department of Housing and Urban Development (HUD) reported in 2000 that "subprime loans are five times more likely in black neighborhoods than in white neighborhoods." By the final year of the Clinton administration, government regulators were mobilizing to take action against this plague. But once the Bush administration took over in 2001, predatory lenders had nothing to fear from the federal government.

In the early 2000s, predatory lending began to take on a new and more explosive form. Mortgage brokers earned high fees for persuading borrowers to take on high-cost loans from lenders, who then sold the loans to big Wall Street firms, who in turn packaged them into "mortgage-backed securities" that were sold to investors. Everybody earned big fees along the way—in fact, the worse the deal was for borrowers, the bigger the fees for everyone else—and so the system gathered incredible momentum. Wall Street's demand for loan volume led ultimately to a complete lack of lending standards and millions upon millions of loans were made to borrowers who had no realistic prospect of repaying them.

For present purposes, the most important aspect of this appalling story is that these exploitative high-cost loans were strongly targeted to borrowers and neighborhoods of color. My own research on lending in Greater Boston during 2006, the peak year of the subprime lending boom, found that 49% of all home-purchase loans to blacks, and 48% of all home-purchase loans to Latinos, were high-cost loans, compared to just 11% of all loans to whites—and that the share of high-cost loans in predominantly minority neighborhoods was 4.4 times greater than it was in predominantly white neighborhoods. Similar racial and ethnic disparities were documented in numerous studies all across the country. Echoing what researchers at the Boston Fed did fifteen years earlier, the Center for Responsible Lending made use of industry data to demonstrate that these disparities could be only partially accounted for by differences in credit scores and other legitimate measures of borrower risk. In other words, they proved that racial discrimination was at least partly responsible for the observed racial disparities.

Nevertheless, federal regulators again did virtually nothing in response to the abundant evidence of violations of fair housing laws. Their most vigorous action was when the Comptroller of the Currency, the principal regulator of the nation's largest banks, actually went to court to stop New York's attorney general from enforcing that state's anti-discrimination laws against big national banks.

Finally, in 2007, the housing bubble popped and subprime lenders collapsed. Millions of homeowners who had received high-cost subprime loans either lost their homes to foreclosure or are in danger of being foreclosed upon soon. Because they were targeted by the predatory lenders, blacks and Latinos have been hit the hardest by this foreclosure tsunami. For example, researchers at the Center for Responsible Lending estimated that among recent mortgage borrowers, "nearly 8% of both African Americans and Latinos have lost their homes to foreclosures, compared to just 4.5% of whites."

By 2008, borrowers and neighborhoods of color were no longer being targeted by predatory lenders, as that industry had all but disappeared in the aftermath of the subprime meltdown. Instead, the more traditional form of discrimination again rose to the foreground. A recent report by a group of community-based organizations from seven cities across the country found that between 2006 and 2008 prime mortgage lending decreased 60.3% in predominantly minority neighborhoods while falling less than half that much (28.4%) in predominantly white neighborhoods. Home Mortgage Disclosure Act data for 2009, as tabulated by the Federal Reserve, showed that the denial rate for black applicants for conventional mortgage loans was 2.48 times greater than the denial rate for their white counterparts (45.7% vs. 18.4%; the denial rate for Latinos was 35.9%). This denial rate ratio is even higher than those which created such outrage when denial rate data first became public in the early 1990s.

Geoff Smith, senior vice president of Chicago's Woodstock Institute, summed up the new situation this way: "After inflicting harm on neighborhoods of color through years of problematic subprime loans, banks are now pulling back at a time when these communities are most in need of responsible loans and investment. We are concerned that we have gone from a period of reverse redlining to a period of re-redlining." ❏

Sources: U.S. Dept. of Housing and Urban Development, "Unequal Burden: Income & Racial Disparities in Subprime Lending in America," 2000 (archives.hud.gov/reports/subprime/subprime. cfm); Jim Campen, "Changing Patterns XIV: Mortgage Lending to Traditionally Underserved Borrowers & Neighborhoods in Boston, Greater Boston, and Massachusetts, 2006," Massachusetts Community and Banking Council (www.mcbc.info/files/ChangingPatternsXIV_0.pdf); Center for Responsible Lending, "Unfair Lending: the Effect of Race and Ethnicity on the Price of Subprime Mortgages," 2006, and "Foreclosures by Race and Ethnicity: The Demographics of a Crisis," 2010 (both available at www.responsiblelending.org); California Reinvestment Coalition and six other groups, "Paying More for the American Dream IV: The Decline of Prime Mortgage Lending in Communities of Color," 2010 (available at: www.woodstockinst.org).

Chapter 4

THE FINANCIAL MELTDOWN AND BAILOUT

Article 4.1

FROM TULIPS TO MORTGAGE-BACKED SECURITIES

BY GERALD FRIEDMAN
January/February 2008

Thirty years ago, economist Charles Kindleberger published a little book, *Manias, Panics, and Crashes*, describing the normal tendency of capitalist financial markets to fluctuate between speculative excess (or "irrational exuberance" in the words of a recent central banker) and panic. Kindleberger describes about 40 of these panics over the nearly 260 years from 1720–1975, or one every seven years. Following Kindleberger's arithmetic, we were due for a panic because it had been seven years since the high-tech bubble burst and the stock market panic of 2000–1. And the panic came, bringing in its wake a tsunami of economic woe, liquidity shortages, cancelled investments, rising unemployment, and economic distress.

Of course, more than mechanics and arithmetic are involved in the current financial panic. But there is a sense of inevitability about the manias and panics of capitalist financial markets, a sense described by writers from Karl Marx to John Maynard Keynes, Hyman Minsky, John Kenneth Galbraith, and Robert Shiller. The problem is that financial markets trade in unknown and unknowable future returns. Lacking real information, they are inevitably driven by the madness of crowds.

Unlike tangible commodities whose price should reflect its real value and real cost of production, financial assets are not priced according to any real returns, nor even according to some expected return, but rather according to expectations of what others will pay in the future, or, even worse, expectations of future expectations that others will have of assets' future return. Whether it is Dutch tulips in 1637, the South Sea Bubble of 1720, Florida real estate in the 1920s, or mortgage-backed securities today, it is always the same story of financial markets floating like a manic-depressive from euphoria to panic to bust. When unregulated, this process is made still worse by market manipulation, and simple fraud. Speculative markets like these can make some rich, and can even be exciting to watch, like a good game of poker; but this is a dangerous and irresponsible way to manage an economy.

There was a time when governments understood. Learning from past financial disasters, the United States established rules to limit the scope of financial euphoria and panic by strictly segregating different types of banks, by limiting financial speculation, and by requiring clear accounting of financial transactions. While they were regulated, financial markets contributed to the best period of growth in American history, the "glorious thirty" after World War II. To be sure, restrictions on speculative behavior and strict regulations made this a boring time to be a banker, and they limited earnings in the financial services sector. But, limited to a secondary role, finance served a greater good by providing liquidity for a long period of steady and relatively egalitarian economic growth.

Of course, over time we forgot why we had regulated financial markets, memory loss helped along by the combined efforts of free-market economists and self-interested bankers and others on Wall Street. To promote "competition," we lowered the barriers between different types of financial institutions, widening the scope of financial markets. We moved activities such as home mortgage lending onto national markets and allowed a rash of bank mergers to create huge financial institutions too large to be allowed to fail, but never too large to operate irresponsibly. Despite the growing scope and centralization of financial activity, the government accepted arguments that we could trust financial firms to self-regulate because it was in their interest to maintain credible accounting.

So we reap the whirlwind with a market collapse building to Great Depression levels. Once again, we learn history's lesson from direct experience: capitalist financial markets cannot be trusted. It is time to either re-regulate or move beyond. ❏

Article 4.2

PONZI SCHEMES AND SPECULATIVE BUBBLES

BY ARTHUR MacEWAN
July/August 2009

Dear Dr. Dollar:
What is the difference between a Ponzi scheme and the way the banks and other investors operated during the housing bubble?
—Leela Choiniere, Austin, Texas

As badly as our banking system operated in recent years, the housing bubble was not a Ponzi scheme. In some respects, however, it was even worse than a Ponzi scheme!

A Ponzi scheme is based on fraud. The operators of the scheme deceive the participants, telling them that their money is being used to make real or financial investments that have a high return. In fact, no such investments are made, and the operators of the scheme are simply paying high returns to the early participants with the funds put in by the later participants. A Ponzi scheme has to grow—and grow rapidly—in order to stay viable. When its growth slows, the early participants can no longer be paid the returns they expect. At this point, the operators disappear with what's left of the participants' funds—unless the authorities step in and arrest them, which is what happened with Charles Ponzi in 1920 and Bernard Madoff this year.

Fraud certainly was very important in the housing bubble of recent years. But the housing bubble—like bubbles generally—did not depend on fraud, and most of its development was there for everyone to see. With the principal problems out in the open and with the authorities not only ignoring those problems but contributing to their development, one might say that the situation with the housing bubble was worse than a Ponzi scheme. And Madoff bilked his marks out of only $50 billion, while trillions were lost in the housing bubble.

Bubbles involve actual investments in real or financial assets—housing in the years since 2000, high-tech stocks in the 1990s, and Dutch tulips in the 17th century. People invest believing that the price of the assets will continue to rise; as long as people keep investing, the price does rise. While some early speculators can make out very well, this speculation will not last indefinitely. Once prices start to fall, panic sets in and the later investors lose.

A bubble is similar to a Ponzi scheme: early participants can do well while later ones incur losses; it is based on false expectations; and it ultimately falls apart. But there need be no fraudulent operator at the center of a bubble. Also, while a Ponzi scheme depends on people giving their money to someone else to invest (e.g., Madoff), people made their own housing investments—though mortgage companies and banks made large fees for handling these investments.

Often, government plays a role in bubbles. The housing bubble was in part generated by the Federal Reserve maintaining low interest rates. Easy money meant readily obtainable loans and, at least in the short run, low monthly payments. Also,

Fed Chairman Alan Greenspan denied the housing bubble's existence—not fraud exactly, but deception that kept the bubble going. (Greenspan, whose view was ideologically driven, got support in his bubble denial from the academic work of the man who was to be his successor, Ben Bernanke.)

In addition, government regulatory agencies turned a blind eye to the highly risky practices of financial firms, practices that both encouraged the development of the bubble and made the impact all the worse when it burst. Moreover, the private rating agencies (e.g., Moody's and Standard and Poor's) were complicit. Dependent on the financial institutions for their fees, they gave excessively good ratings to these risky investments. Perhaps not fraud in the legal sense, but certainly misleading.

During the 1990s, the government made tax law changes that contributed to the emergence of the housing bubble. With the Taxpayer Relief Act of 1997, a couple could gain up to $500,000 selling their home without any capital gains tax liability (half that for a single person). Previously, capital gains taxes could be avoided only if the proceeds were used to buy another home or if the seller was over 55 (and a couple could then avoid taxes only on the first $250,000). So buying and then selling houses became a more profitable operation.

And, yes, substantial fraud was involved. For example, mortgage companies and banks used deceit to get people to take on mortgages when there was no possibility that the borrowers would be able to meet the payments. Not only was this fraud, but this fraud depended on government authorities ignoring their regulatory responsibilities.

So, no, a bubble and a Ponzi scheme are not the same. But they have elements in common. Usually, however, the losers in a Ponzi scheme are simply the direct investors, the schemer's marks. A bubble like the housing bubble can wreak havoc on all of us. ❑

Article 4.3

CONFIDENCE TRICK

BY JOHN MILLER
September/October 2008

Hyman Minsky, the theorist of financial fragility whose work has enjoyed a revival as U.S. financial institutions crumble, always maintained that "there is nothing wrong with macroeconomics that another depression wouldn't cure."

Whatever salutary effects today's financial crisis, undoubtedly the worst since the Great Depression, might be having on macroeconomics, it has yet to improve economic policymaking. The Bush administration exploited a financial panic, vastly exaggerating its dangers for the broader economy, to extort $700 billion from a Congress only too willing to open taxpayer's wallets to bail out those who benefited from the speculative excesses of an $8 trillion housing bubble.

Whatever this massive public purchase of bad debt will do to patch up the credit system, the bailout will not counteract the downward spiral in housing prices that brought on the credit crisis and will undoubtedly continue. The bailout will do little to make bad mortgage debt more viable or to provide relief to homeowners behind in their mortgage payments or facing foreclosure. Nor does the bailout place effective limits on CEOs' pay or their golden parachutes, erect the regulatory safeguards that will curb future financial excesses, or counteract the worsening recession. Worse yet, the bailout swells the federal budget deficit and for that reason will likely sap whatever political will could have been mustered to make the massive public investments necessary to prevent the economy from falling into a prolonged depression.

For the policy maestros to do better than this disgraceful, already-failed, confidence trick of a bailout package that entirely ignores the elephant in the room (as economists Nouriel Roubini, Paul Krugman, Joseph Stiglitz, and Glen Hubbard have described it), the crisis will have to put an end to the illusion of self-regulating markets, much as Minsky envisioned a depression might.

But neoliberal prestidigitation continues. Even as the *Wall Street Journal* reports that the financial system has been "shaken to the core," its editors steadfastly maintain that the "sins of deregulation" are "a political fairy tale" in an attempt to absolve the market from blame for the crisis. The government-sponsored enterprises Fannie Mae and Freddie Mac, complain the editors, "turbo-charged the credit mania" by subsidizing rates of return for mortgage-backed securities and increasing the number of mortgages available to risky low-income borrowers.

The *Journal* editors' latest free-market sleight of hand notwithstanding, unregulated and deregulated financial markets combined with new, harder-to-regulate financial instruments and ever-present greed to unleash today's pernicious economic instability. As the economy teeters, we must challenge the antidemocratic dictates of an inflation-phobic Wall Street to demand that government effectively regulate the entire range of financial institutions through strict capital requirements and a tax on speculative turnover intended to encourage long-term productive investment. We must build institutions of regulatory enforcement that will remain strong when the next bubble comes and its beneficiaries pour buckets of money into the political system to move their deregulatory agenda forward. Likewise, massive public spending is needed to put the nearly one million people who will have lost their jobs this year back to work and to jump-start the economy. Public policy must also be dedicated to spreading the benefits of renewed economic growth widely through progressive taxes and by putting the interests of people before the profits of those who have recklessly polluted the economy with toxic debt.

Without those measures, Wall Street will continue to be, as Woody Guthrie put it in the midst of the Great Depression, the street that keeps the rest of us off Easy Street. ❑

Article 4.4

DERIVATIVES AND DEREGULATION

BY MARTY WOLFSON
November/December 2008

I t has become commonplace to describe the current financial crisis as the most serious since the Great Depression. Although we have more tools now to avoid a depression, the current crisis presents in some ways more significant challenges than did the banking crises of the 1930s.

And it's not over.

The form of the current crisis is similar to others we have seen in the past: a speculative increase in asset prices, overly optimistic expectations, and an expansion of debt sustainable only if the speculative bubble continues. Then the bubble pops, debt can't be repaid, and losses mount at financial institutions. The risk of bank failures rises and lenders get scared. They panic, refuse to lend to anyone that seems at all risky, and seek safety in cash or super-safe assets.

In the early 1930s, there was no federal deposit insurance and little federal government intervention. Depositor runs took down the banking system.

In more recent crises, though, the Federal Reserve successfully developed and used its powers as a lender of last resort. Deposit insurance helped to reassure small depositors and, if needed, the Federal Deposit Insurance Corporation stepped in and bailed out threatened banks. It could guarantee all liabilities of a failing bank and arrange mergers with healthier banks. These tools generally worked to reduce panicked reactions and prevent the freezing up of credit.

But this time, after the collapse of the speculative bubble in housing prices, the course of events has been different. The Federal Reserve was forced to expand the concept of a lender of last resort in unprecedented ways. It has lent to investment banks and insurance companies, not just regulated depository institutions. It has taken all kinds of assets as collateral for its loans, not just the high-grade securities it traditionally accepted. It has even lent to nonfinancial corporations (by buying their commercial paper).

What is surprising is that these dramatic actions and expensive bailouts of financial institutions, such as American International Group (AIG) and even Fannie Mae and Freddie Mac, were insufficient to reassure lenders about the ability of financial institutions to honor their repayment commitments. Treasury Secretary Paulson's plan to use $700 billion to buy "toxic assets" from financial institutions, signed into law by President Bush on October 3rd, failed to stop what had become by then a generalized panic and freeze-up of credit. It took a coordinated global initiative to inject capital directly into financial institutions, plus a federal guarantee on bank debt and unlimited FDIC insurance on non-interest-bearing (mostly business) accounts at banks, announced on October 12th, to begin to have an effect on unfreezing credit markets.

The "TED spread," a widely watched measure of credit risk that had spiked sharply during the panic, began to reverse its path following the October 12 announcement. The TED spread measures the difference between an interest rate that banks charge when lending to each other (the London Interbank Offered Rate, or LIBOR) and the interest rate on U.S. Treasury bills. Because the Treasury is assumed to be "risk-free," the difference between it and LIBOR measures the perceived relative risk of lending to banks.

Why has this panic been so much more difficult to control? The answer has to do with the widespread use of complicated and opaque securities, known as derivatives, in a deregulated, interconnected, and global financial system.

A derivative is a financial contract that derives its value from something else, such as an asset or an index. At the root of the current crisis are derivatives known as mortgage-backed securities (MBSs). MBSs are claims to payments from an underlying pool of mortgages. The ability of MBS issuers to repay their debt, and thus the value of the MBS, is derived from the ability of homeowners to meet their mortgage payments.

In the process leading up to the crisis, a mortgage broker typically extended a mortgage to a borrower, and then turned to a commercial bank to fund the loan. The bank might sell the loan to Fannie Mae, which would pool a group of mortgages together and sell the resulting MBS to an investment bank like Lehman Brothers. Lehman, in turn, repackaged the MBS in various ways, and issued even more complicated derivatives called collateralized debt obligations (CDOs). Buyers of the CDOs might be other banks, hedge funds, or other lenders.

At the base of this complicated pyramid of derivatives might be a subprime borrower whose lender did not explain an adjustable-rate loan, or another borrower whose abilityto meet mortgage payments depended on a continued escalation of home prices. As subprime borrowers' rates reset, and especially as housing price speculation collapsed, the whole house of cards came crashing down.

Why were mortgage loans made that could not be repaid? And why did supposedly sophisticated investors buy MBSs and CDOs based on these loans? First of all, the mortgage brokers and commercial banks that made and funded these loans quickly sold them off and no longer had any responsibility for them. Second, rating agencies like Moody's and Standard & Poor's gave these derivatives stellar AAA ratings, signifying a credit risk of almost zero. Recent Congressional hearings have highlighted the conflict of interest that these rating agencies had: they were being paid by the issuers of the derivatives they were rating. Third, financial institutions up and down the line were making money and nobody was limiting what they could do. In the deregulated financial environment, federal regulators stood aside as housing speculation spun out of control and did little to regulate, or even document, the growth of complicated derivatives.

Finally, financial institutions' concerns about the creditworthiness of the derivatives they held were eased because they thought they could protect themselves against possible loss. For example, by using another type of derivative known as a credit default swap, holders of MBSs and CDOs could make periodic premium payments to another financial institution, like American International Group (AIG), to insure themselves against default by the issuers of the MBSs and CDOs. (This insurance contract was technically classified as a derivative rather than insurance in order to escape regulation.) However, if an insurer like AIG is unable to honor all its insurance contracts, then the protection against loss is illusory.

The total value of all the securities insured by credit default swaps at the end of 2007 was estimated by the Bank of International Settlements to be $58 trillion, and by the International Swaps and Derivatives Association to be $62 trillion. (The estimates could vary by as much as $4 trillion because unregulated credit default swaps do not have to be officially reported to regulatory agencies. Moreover, even greater ambiguity surrounds these contracts because insurers can transfer their liability to other parties, and the insured party may be unaware of the creditworthiness or even the identity of the new insurer.)

Surprisingly, though, the value of the actual securities that form the basis of these credit default swaps was only about $6 trillion. How could $6 trillion worth of assets be insured at ten times that amount? The discrepancy is due to the fact that it is possible to speculate on the likelihood of default of a security without actually owning the security: all the speculator has to do is enter into a credit default swap contract with an insurer. The total volume of "insured securities" can thus escalate dramatically.

Because derivatives are so complex, because so much speculation and debt are involved, and because it is so hard to know how much is at risk (and exactly who is at risk), regulators are unsure of the implications of the failure of a particular financial institution. That is why they have been so fearful of the consequences of letting a troubled institution fail.

The exception that did indeed prove the rule was Lehman Brothers. The Federal Reserve and Treasury did not bail it out, and its failure led to an intensification of the problems in credit markets. A money market fund, the Reserve Primary Fund, announced that it would only pay 97 cents on the dollar to its investors, because its investments in Lehman Brothers could not be redeemed. The Treasury moved quickly to announce that it would insure money market funds, in order to prevent a run on the funds. However, the Lehman failure raised further concerns that lenders had about the derivatives portfolios of other banks, and about the possibility that the banks would not have enough capital to cover potential losses.

Secretary Paulson's initial plan to buy "toxic" assets (including MBSs and CDOs) from financial institutions was designed to address these concerns about bank capital. However, his plan was probably also negatively affected by uncertainty. Because these "toxic" assets are complex and nobody wants to buy them, there is no market for them and their value is uncertain. And because the Paulson plan's unstated objective was to boost bank capital by overpaying for these assets, the difficulties in pricing the assets raised the prospects of long delays and questions about whether the plan to increase bank capital would be successful. Lenders continued to hold back. They may also have hesitated because of concern about a political backlash against a taxpayer subsidy for the very banks that many people blamed for the crisis.

By injecting capital directly into the banks, the global initiative announced on October 12th raised the prospect of returns on the capital investment for taxpayers. It also avoided the uncertainties of buying individual assets and helped to reduce the panic.

But the crisis isn't over. Reducing the panic is only the first step. There is now likely to be a longer-term credit crunch that will continue to threaten the broader economy. Banks and other lenders will be wary for quite some time. Losses on mortgage-related assets will continue as years of housing speculation—financed with heaps of borrowed money—continues to unwind. Bank lending will lag as banks rebuild their capital and overcome their pessimistic expectations.

It will be up to the federal government to pick up the slack that the banks will leave. We will need programs to enable people to stay in their homes and stabilize their communities. We will need to create jobs by investing in infrastructure, renewable energy, and education. We will need a "trickle-up" approach that puts people first and raises living standards and opportunities.

At the same time, we need a regulatory structure for the financial system that puts limits on risk and manipulation. It is clear that deregulation, and the entire neoliberal model that has dominated economic policy for the past 30 years, has run aground. It has sown the seeds of financial crisis, and this crisis has led us to the edge of an abyss. Only by dramatically reorienting our economic and financial structure can we avoid the abyss and create the kind of society that meets our needs. The nature of that new structure should be the subject of intensive democratic discussion and debate in the days to come. ❑

Article 4.5

DEALING WITH A ROTTEN TOOTH

BY ARTHUR MacEWAN
November/December 2008

> Dear Dr. Dollar:
> *Isn't the "bailout" of Wall Street like having a rotten tooth extracted? The extraction is very unpleasant, but it beats the alternative. Even if the dentist charges an unreasonably high fee, I am still going to pay and have the job done. Later I will worry about taking better care of my teeth. So shouldn't people quit complaining about the bailout, suck it up, and get the job done?*
> —Peter Wagner, Weston, Mass.

I do like thinking about the mess in the financial markets as a "rotten tooth," for something is certainly "rotten" in the current situation. And there is a way in which the analogy is useful: just as we are heavily dependent on the dentist to deal with our teeth, we are heavily dependent on the banks and other financial institutions for the operation of our economy. But if we are going to use the dentist-finance analogy, we need to take it a bit further.

In particular, if the dentist who tells me I need my tooth yanked out in an emergency extraction is the same dentist who for years has been telling me that my teeth are fine, then I get suspicious. This dentist has been making money from me all along, and now, when the crisis of a rotten tooth emerges, the dentist stands to make more money while I incur the pain. The situation is similar to the bailout of the financial system: the banks keep their profits in good times, but the losses are imposed on the rest of us in bad times. At the very least, when the people responsible for a problem—dentists or bankers—tell me to solve the problem in a way that benefits them, I want to get a second opinion, figure out the options, and proceed with caution.

As we have been learning in recent weeks, there is more than one option for dealing with the "rotten tooth." In part because of public pressure (i.e., complaining), the Treasury shifted away from its initial plan to buy up the bad assets in the financial system and is now taking partial ownership of the banks by providing them with capital. Not only is the second plan more likely to work (in the sense of preventing a breakdown of the financial system), but it is also more likely to cost the rest of us less over the long run (because as the banks recover and start to earn profits, the government will share in those profits).

There are other options that the U.S. government might follow as well. For example, the main reason we care about what happens to the banks is that their failures could spread to the rest of us, causing a severe depression. But instead of working simply from the top down, the U.S. government would do well to work from the bottom up—by focusing on the problems of people losing their homes due to foreclosures and by providing a large economic stimulus program through spending on schools, infrastructure, health care, and other real economic needs.

And, just as with my tooth, if the problem really did arise because of the bad practices of those who were supposed to take care of the situation (wasn't this the dentist who had been telling me all was well?), then we should give some immediate attention to proper regulation. The current financial crisis could have been avoided but for the deregulation craze of recent decades. Fixing the deregulation disaster should not be put off to the distant future.

Regulation is not a panacea. There can certainly be bad regulations, sometimes brought about by the firms themselves in an effort to use regulation to secure their power and profits. Establishing good regulations is a constant battle, as the large firms devote huge amounts of their resources to get deregulation or to shape regulation in their favor. Yet without regulation, markets—especially financial markets—are prone to instability, and at times that instability can have severe impacts on the rest of us.

While the dentist analogy may be incomplete, it does bring out a very important point. Because we are excessively dependent on the operations of a relatively small number of very large firms, when they get in trouble, we can be forced to bail them out. Not a good situation. Indeed, the situation is made worse as the current crisis is leading to more consolidation of the banking industry; with the encouragement of the Federal Reserve and the Treasury, big banks are being taken over by even bigger banks. At the very least, if we are going to allow some firms to become "too big to fail," then we would do well to watch them pretty carefully—that is, to regulate them and thus do all we can to prevent them from operating in ways that put us all at risk.

[Full disclosure: Last month I had a tooth extracted and it wasn't all that bad—certainly not as painful as the current Wall Street bailout! —A.M.] ❑

Article 4.6

TIME FOR *PERMANENT* NATIONALIZATION!
If the big banks are "too big to fail," they should be public.

BY FRED MOSELEY
March/April 2009

The Treasury Department's recent bailouts of major U.S. banks will result in a massive transfer of income from taxpayers to those banks' bondholders.

Under the government's current bailout plan, the total sum of money transferred from taxpayers to bondholders will probably be at least several hundred billion dollars and could be as much as $1 trillion, which is about $3,300 for each man, woman, and child in the United States. These bondholders took risks and made lots of money during the recent boom, but now taxpayers are being forced to bail them out and pay for their losses.

This trillion-dollar transfer of income from taxpayers to bondholders is an economic injustice that should be stopped immediately, and it can be stopped—if the government fully and permanently nationalizes the banks that are "too big to fail."

The TARP program ("Troubled Asset Relief Program") has gone through several incarnations. It was originally intended to purchase high-risk mortgage-backed securities from banks. But this plan floundered because it is very difficult in the current circumstances to determine the value of these risky assets and thus the price the government should pay for them. The main policy for the first $350 billion spent so far has been to invest government capital into banks by buying preferred stock (which is the equivalent of a loan), which receives a 5% rate of return (Warren Buffet gets a 10% rate of return when he buys preferred stocks these days) and has no voting rights. Managers of the banks are not being replaced, and there are usually cosmetic limits on executive pay, unlikely to be enforced. So these bank managers, who are largely responsible for the banking crisis, will continue to be rewarded with salaries of millions of dollars per year, paid for in part with taxpayer money. Existing bank stock loses value as the bank issues stock secured by TARP funds.

But the main beneficiaries of the government bailout money are the bondholders of the banks (see sidebar, "Bank Bonds," below). In the event of future losses, which are likely to be enormous, the government bailout money will be used directly or indirectly to pay off the bondholders. This could eventually take all of the available TARP money, and perhaps even more. So the government bailout of the banks is ultimately a bailout of the banks' bondholders, paid for by taxpayers.

The Bush administration's rationale for this approach to the bailout was that if the government did not bail out the banks and their bondholders, then the whole financial system in the United States would collapse. Nobody would lend money to anybody, and the economy would seize up (in the memorable words of George W. Bush: "this sucker would go down"). Bush Treasury Secretary Paulson presented us with an unavoidable dilemma—either bail out the bondholders with taxpayers' money or suffer a severe recession or depression.

If Paulson's assertion were correct, it would be a stinging indictment of our current financial system. It would imply that the capitalist financial system, left on its own, is inherently unstable, and can only avoid sparking major economic crises by being bailed out by the government, at the taxpayers' expense. There is a double indictment here: the capitalist financial system is inherently unstable and the necessary bailouts are economically unjust.

But there is a better alternative, a more equitable, "taxpayer friendly" option: Permanently nationalize banks that are "too big to fail" and run these banks according to public policy objectives (affordable housing, green energy, etc.), rather than with the objective of private profit maximization. The nationalization of banks, if it's done right, would clearly be superior to current bailout policies because it would not involve a massive transfer of wealth from taxpayers to bondholders.

Besides providing a more equitable response to the current banking crisis, nationalizing the biggest banks will help ensure that a crisis like this never happens again, and we never again have to bail out the banks and their bondholders to "save the economy." Once some banks have become "too big to fail" and everyone understands that the government will always bail out these large banks to avoid a systematic collapse, it follows that these banks should be nationalized. Otherwise, the implicit promise of a bailout gives megabanks a license to take lots of risks and make lots of money in good times, and then let the taxpayers pay for their losses in the bad times. Economists call this dilemma the "moral hazard" problem. In this case, we might instead call it the "economic injustice" problem.

The best way to avoid this legal robbery of taxpayers is to nationalize the banks. If taxpayers are going to pay for banks' losses, then they should also receive their profits. The main justification for private profit is to encourage capitalists to invest and to invest wisely because they would suffer the losses if their investment fails. But if the losses fall not on capitalists, but instead on the taxpayers, then this justification for private profit disappears.

Freed from the need to maximize short-term profit, nationalized banks would also make the economy more stable in the future. They would take fewer risks during an expansion to avoid debt-induced bubbles, which inevitably burst and cause so much hardship. For example, there would be fewer housing bubbles; instead, the deposits of these megabanks would be invested in decent affordable housing

Bank Bonds

Bank bonds are loans to banks by the bondholders, in contrast to common stocks, which are capital invested in banks by their owners. Bank bonds are a relatively new phenomenon in the U.S. economy (and the rest of the world). Until the 1980s, almost all loans by banks were financed from money deposited in the banks by depositors. Then in the 1980s, banks began to borrow more and more money by selling bonds to bondholders; this became a primary way that banks financed their loans. This debt strategy of banks enabled them to invest ever larger sums and make more profits. However, this debt strategy left the banking system more unstable and vulnerable to collapse because banks would have to repay their bondholders. And when major banks were unable to do so, the banking system fell into crisis.

available to all. With housing more affordable, mortgages would be more afford-able and less risky.

The newly nationalized banks could also increase their lending to credit-worthy businesses and households, and thereby help stabilize the economy and lessen the severity of the current recession. As things stand, banks do not want to increase their lending, since the creditworthiness of any borrower is difficult to determine, especially that of other banks that may also hold toxic assets. They have suffered enormous losses over the last year, and they fear that more enormous losses are still to come. Banks prefer instead to hoard capital as a cushion against these expected future losses.

What the government is doing now is giving money to banks in one way or another, and then begging them to please lend this money to businesses and house-holds. Nationalization is clearly the better solution. Instead of giving money to the banks and begging them to lend, the government should nationalize the banks in trouble and lend directly to credit-worthy businesses and households.

How would the nationalization of banks work? I suggest the following general principles and guidelines:

(1) The federal government would become the owner of any "systemically significant" bank that asks for a government rescue or goes into bankruptcy pro-ceedings. The value of existing stock would be wiped out, as it would be in a normal bankruptcy.

(2) The government would itself operate the banks. Top management would be replaced by government banking officials, and the managers would not receive "golden parachutes" of any kind.

(3) Most importantly, the banks' long-term bonds would be converted into common stock in the banks. This would restore the banks to solvency, so they could start lending again. The private common stock would be subordinate to the government preferred stock in the capital structure, which would mean that any future losses would be taken out of the private stock before the government stock. Bondholders could also be given the option of converting their stocks back to bonds at a later date, with a significant write-down or discount, determined by bankruptcy judges.

These "bonds-to-stocks" swaps (often called "debt-to-equity" swaps), or par-tial write-downs if the bondholders so choose, are a crucial aspect of an equitable nationalization of banks. The bondholders lent their money and signed contracts that stipulated that if the banks went bankrupt, they might suffer losses. Now the banks are bankrupt and the bondholders should take the losses.

This process of accelerated bankruptcy and nationalization should be applied in the future to any banks that are in danger of bankruptcy and are deemed to be "sys-temically significant." This would include the next crises at Citigroup and Bank of America. Other banks in danger of bankruptcy that are not systemically significant should be allowed to fail. There should be no more bailouts of the bondholders at the expense of taxpayers. In addition, the banks who received some of the first $350 bil-lion should be subject to stricter conditions along the lines that Congress attached to the second $350 billion—that banks should be required to increase their lending to businesses and consumers, to fully account for how they have spent the government capital, and to follow strict limitations on executive compensation. The government should withdraw its capital from any banks that fail to meet these standards.

There is one other acceptable option: the government could create entirely new banks that would purchase good assets from banks and increase lending to credit-worthy borrowers. These government banks are sometimes called "good banks," in contrast to the "bad bank" proposals that have been floated recently, according to which the government would set up a bank to purchase bad ("toxic") assets from banks. The term "good bank" is no doubt more politically acceptable than "government bank," but the meaning is the same. The only difference between the "good bank" proposal and the nationalization proposal I've outlined here is that my proposal would start with existing banks and turn them into government banks.

In recent weeks, there has been more and more talk about and even acceptance of the "nationalization" of banks. the *Washington Post* recently ran an op-ed by NYU economists Nouriel Roubini and Matthew Richardson entitled "Nationalize the Banks! We Are All Swedes Now," and *New York Times* business columnist Joe Nocera has written about how more and more economists and analysts are beginning to call for nationalization: "Nationalization. I just said it. The roof didn't cave in."

Even former Fed chair Alan Greenspan, whom many regard as one of the main architects of the current crisis, recently told the *Financial Times* that (temporary) nationalization may be the "least bad option." He added, "I understand that once in a hundred years this is what you do."

But there are three crucial differences between such pseudo-nationalizations and full-fledged, genuine nationalization:

(1) The pseudo-nationalizations are intended to be temporary. In this, they follow the model of the Swedish government, which temporarily nationalized some major banks in the early 1990s, and has subsequently almost entirely re-privatized them. Real nationalization would be permanent; if banks are "too big to fail," then they have to be public, to avoid more crises and unjust bailouts in the future.

(2) In pseudo-nationalizations, the government has little or no decision-making power in running the banks. In real nationalization, the government would have complete control over the banks, and would run the banks according to public policy objectives democratically decided.

(3) In pseudo-nationalizations, bondholders don't lose anything, and the loans owed by the banks to the bondholders are paid in full, in large part by taxpayers' money. In real nationalization, the bondholders would suffer their own losses, just as they reaped the profits by themselves in the good times, and the taxpayers would not pay for the losses.

In mid-February, Treasury Secretary Timothy Geithner announced the Obama administration's plans for the bank bailout—renamed the "Financial Stability Plan." This plan is very similar to Paulson's two versions of TARP: it includes both purchases of high-risk mortgage-backed securities from banks and also investing capital in banks. The main new feature is that government capital is supposed to be invested together with private capital. But in order to attract private capital, the government will have to provide sufficient guarantees, so most of the risks will still fall on taxpayers. So Geithner's Financial Stability Plan has the same fundamental flaw as Paulson's TARP: it bails out the banks and their bondholders at the expense of taxpayers.

The public should demand that the Obama administration cancel these plans for further bank bailouts and consider other options, including genuine, permanent nationalization. Permanent nationalization with bonds-to-stocks swaps for bondholders is the most equitable solution to the current banking crisis, and would provide a better basis for a more stable and public-oriented banking system in the future. ❏

Sources: Dean Baker, "Time for Bank Rationalization," cepr.net; Willem Buiter, "Good Bank/ New Bank vs. Bad Bank: a Rare Example of a No-Brainer," blogs.ft.com/maverecon; Krishna Guha and Edward Luce, "Greenspan Backs Bank Nationalization," Financial Times, February 18, 2008; Joe Nocera, "A Stress Test for the Latest Bailout Plan," New York Times, February 13, 2009; James Petras, "No Bailout for Wall Street Billionaires," countercurrents.org; Matthew Richardson and Nouriel Roubini, "Nationalize the Banks! We're All Swedes Now," Washington Post, February 15, 2009; Joseph Stiglitz, "Is the Entire Bailout Strategy Flawed? Let's Rethink This Before It's Too Late," alternet.org.

Article 4.7

TRUST YOUR GUT

BY WILLIAM GREIDER
March 2009, The Nation

Areassuring new story line is emanating from our leaders. I heard Representative Barney Frank, chair of the House Banking Committee, explain it. Then I read the same line in a *Washington Post* news story. That tells me people in high places are selling it. Dynamic capitalism, they explain, invents ways to create greater wealth, but sometimes it goes a little too far. Then government has to step in to correct things. This need typically occurs every generation or so, all in a day's work. The Obama administration is proposing "sweeping" new regulatory laws so that capitalism can continue its good works.

The story makes disturbing current events sound practically normal. But what are the storytellers leaving out? They aren't saying that this financial catastrophe was not merely an inevitable development of history but a man-made disaster. Greedheads on Wall Street did their part, but so did Washington. The reason we need new rules is that a generation of Democrats and Republicans systematically repealed or gutted the old ones—the regulatory controls enacted 80 years ago to remedy the last breakdown of capitalism (better known as the Great Depression).

The White House executed a nifty two-step this week to re-educate the public and deflect anger. On Tuesday Treasury Secretary Timothy Geithner re-launched the massive bailout of banking and finance. Knowing how unpopular this is with the people at large, Geithner followed on Thursday with his "sweeping" plans to re-regulate the bankers and financiers. Whenever official plans are called "sweeping," it indicates that they really, really mean it this time.

Most Americans are not financial experts. It's very difficult, nearly impossible, for normal mortals to sort through the dense policy talk and conflicting opinions to figure out if the rhetoric of reform is real. Confusion is widespread in the land. Most Americans want to believe this president is leading us out of the swamp, but how can they know? I say, trust your gut feelings. They are as reliable as the learned experts.

Many Americans want to believe because they think that returning to "normal" means their decimated 401(k) accounts might somehow recover the 30-40% that disappeared during the past year. If it takes monster bank bailouts to restore stock-market prices, let's have bailouts. Good luck with that. The Dow has regained 21% in two weeks of rallies, but I remind friends that steep, short bursts in the stock market do not foretell the future of the economy. Banks may be relieved of their losses without changing the general economic outlook. After the crash of 1929, there were occasional stock rallies, followed by fierce bears. It took 25 years (until 1954) for the Dow to regain its old peak. Another way to assess the Obama plan for reform is ask: who likes it? The verdict was swift and sure after Geithner's twin announcements. Wall Street likes it. The blueprint for regulatory reforms was applauded by the Securities Industry and Financial Markets Association; the American Insurance Association; and the Private Equity Council, the trade group for the major private funds that will get public money and backup insurance to buy the banking system's rotten assets. This could be born-again patriotism. Or it could be the animal appetites of financiers smelling gorgeous opportunity for returns.

This may be one of those moments where people can find some guidance from their moral convictions. They do not need to know all the details to ask simple questions. Does the outline of what's happening to rescue major financial institutions seem morally wrong? Or is it justified by the larger necessities of the national predicament? Is the government insufficiently tough in demanding reciprocal commitments from the beneficiaries? Should Washington pursue larger structural changes in the banking system?

Trying to imagine alternatives to the bankers-first bailouts is a good place to start. What follows are suggestions I produced at the request of young people organizing demonstrations around the country for April 11. They call themselves A New Way Forward. I hope they light lots of bonfires.

This rough outline leaves out lots of particular regulatory issues, but the core goal of reform is to create a banking and financial system that serves the society and the economy, not the other way around. Everything being done to rescue and restore the old order gets in the way of creating something truly new and valuable for the future. Those of us throwing logs in the path of the bailouts are dismissed as naysayers or worse, but the financial titans are trying to foreclose just solutions by stampeding Congress and the president to adopt ill-considered ideas.

If Wall Street gets its way, the "reforms" may further consolidate power and ratify a corporate state—a grotesque hybrid that combines the worst aspects of socialism and capitalism. The reform ideas announced by Geithner would plant the seeds by creating a "systemic risk" regulator, presumably the Federal Reserve, to oversee the largest, most politically adept banks and financial firms that qualify as "too big to fail." Capitalism, with its inherent tendency toward monopoly, would have the means to monopolize democracy.

My new book, *Come Home, America,* asks people to enunciate their versions of "patriotic realism." That is the essence of an alternative vision: de-concentrate power, liberate people and smaller enterprises, workers and middle managers and investors, to help shape the country's future from many different perspectives. This is how democracy was supposed to work. It can again.

Some points I recommend people consider:

1. Euthanasia for insolvent banks. Transferring their losses to the public will not restore the trillions in capital the bankers helped destroy. It would merely relieve the banks, their creditors and shareholders of the pain. Government must take control of the system to supervise a just unwinding of the mess—whether we call it nationalization or something else. Handing out money and leaving bankers in control of how it's spent is nutty and morally wrong. People everywhere understand this. Only Washington seems oblivious to the irrationality of what it is attempting.

2. The Federal Reserve must be democratized and effectively stripped of its peculiar antidemocratic status as an unaccountable island of power within the government. A new federal agency—accountable to Congress and the president—can

be refashioned from the working parts of the Fed. Call it a central bank or something else, but its governing power must not rest with heavyweight bankers on the board of directors at the twelve regional banks. (To understand why, consider that the New York Federal Reserve Bank was headed until recently by Geithner.)

3. The reformed Fed would be confined to conducting monetary policy and stripped of its regulatory functions. A different section of the Treasury or a new freestanding regulatory agency can assume responsibility for regulation and be armed with strong antitrust laws and other rules to ensure that "too big to fail" institutions are redefined as "too big to save."

4. The federal law against usury can be restored to halt predatory lending. Persistent violators would not be fined with trivial penalties, as they are now, but stripped of their government protections and subsidies—that is, doomed.

5. A new banking system—smaller and more diverse and responsible to the public interest—can fill the hole left by the demise of major banks like Citigroup. Vast public resources should be devoted to creating this system, not to saving the mastodons. Public banks (like the North Dakota State Bank) and nonprofit savings and lending cooperatives can also serve as an important cross-check on private commercial banking—a competitive model that offers credit on non-usurious terms and keeps the big boys honest.

6. Once the Federal Reserve is domesticated in a democratic fashion, then it can be reformed to assume broad supervision of the nonbank financial firms in the "shadow banking system"—hedge funds, private equity firms, pension funds, mutual funds, insurance companies.

7. Our first political challenge is to disturb business as usual in Washington and prevent Congress from taking hasty action to adopt Wall Street's "reform" agenda. Congress is rattled by the exploding popular anger and listening nervously. The people need to speak louder—loud enough for the president to hear. ❑

Article 4.8

NOT TOO BIG ENOUGH
How the "too-big-to-fail" banks got that way, and why the current banking reform won't solve the problem.

BY ROB LARSON
July/August 2010

T he government bailout of America's biggest banks set off a tornado of public anger and confusion. With a price tag in the trillions of dollars, rescuing the biggest American banks has left the public resentful over the bailout of banks considered "too big to fail." But two years later, the Senate has rejected a proposal to break up today's "megabanks" into smaller institutions, claiming that tougher reserve requirements and higher insurance premiums will prevent future large-scale bank failures.

Dealing with the collapse of these "systemically important banks" is a difficult policy issue, but the less-discussed issue is how the banking industry got to this point. If the collapse of just one of our $100 billion megabanks, Lehman Brothers, was enough to touch off an intense contraction in the supply of essential credit, we need to know how some banks became "too big to fail" in the first place. The answer lies in certain incentives for bank growth, which after the loosening of crucial industry regulations drove the enormous waves of bank mergers in the last thirty years.

Geographical Growth and Economies of Scale

Before the 1980s, American commercial banking was a small-scale affair. State-chartered banks were prohibited by state laws from running branches outside their home state, or sometimes even outside their home county. Nationally chartered banks were likewise limited, and federal law allowed interstate acquisitions only if a state legislature specifically decided to permit out-of-state banks to purchase local branches. No states allowed such acquisition until 1975, when Maine and other states began passing legislation allowing at least some interstate banking. The trend was capped in 1994 by the Riegle-Neal Act, which removed the remaining restrictions on interstate branching and allowed direct cross-state banking mergers.

This geographic deregulation allowed commercial banks to make extensive acquisitions, in-state and out. When Wells Fargo acquired another large California bank, Crocker National, in 1986 it was the largest bank merger in U.S. history. Since "the regulatory light was green," a single banking company could now operate across the uniquely large U.S. market, opening up enormous new opportunities for economies of scale in the banking industry.

Economies of scale are savings that companies enjoy when they grow and produce more output. The situation is similar to a cook preparing a batch of cookies for a Christmas party and then preparing a batch for New Year's while all the ingredients and materials are already out. Producing more output (cookies) in one afternoon is more efficient than taking everything out again later to make the New Year's batch separately. In other words, there's less effort per cookie if you make them all at once. In enterprise, this corresponds to spreading the large costs of startup investment over more and more output, and is often thought of as lower per-unit costs as the level of production increases. Economies of scale, when present in an industry, create a strong incentive for firms to grow larger, since profitability will improve. But they also give larger, established firms a valuable cost advantage over new competitors, which can put the brakes on competition.

Once unleashed by the policy changes, these economies of scale played a major role in the industry's seemingly endless merger activity. "In order to compete, you

Economies of Scale in Banking and Finance

Economies of scale are savings that companies benefit from as they grow larger and produce more output. While common in many industries, in banking and finance, these economies drove bank growth after industry deregulation in the 1980s and 90s. Some of the major scale economies in banking are:

- **Spreading investment over more output.** With the growth in importance of large-scale computing power and sophisticated systems management, the costs of setting up a modern banking system are very large. However, as a firm grows it can "spread out" the cost of that initial investment over more product, so that its cost per unit decreases as more output is produced.

- **Consolidation of functions.** The modern workforce is no stranger to the mass firings of "redundant" staff after mergers and acquisitions. If one firm's payroll staff and computer systems can handle twice the employees with little additional expense, an acquired bank may see its payroll department harvest pink slips while the firm's profitability improves. When Citicorp merged with the insurance giant Travelers Group in 1998, the resulting corporation laid off over 10,000 workers—representing 6% of the combined company's total workforce and over $500 million in reduced costs for Citigroup. This practice can be especially lucrative in a country like the United States, with a fairly unregulated labor market where firms are quite free to fire. Despite the economic peril inflicted on workers and their families, this consolidation is key to increasing company efficiency post-merger. Beyond back-office functions, core profit operations may also benefit from consolidation. When Bank of America combined its managed mutual funds into a single fund, it experienced lower total costs, thanks to trimming overhead from audit and prospectus mailing expenses. Consolidating office departments in this fashion can yield savings of 40% of the cost base of the acquired bank.

- **Funding mix.** The "funding mix" used by banks refers to where banks get the capital they then package into loans. Smaller institutions, having only limited deposits from savers, must "purchase funds" by borrowing from other institutions. This increases the funding cost of loans for banks, but larger banks will naturally have access to larger pools of deposits from which to arrange loans. This funding cost advantage for larger banks relative to smaller ones represents another economy of scale.

- **Advertising.** The nature of advertising requires a certain scale of operation to be viable. Advertising can reach large numbers of potential customers, but if a firm is small or local, many of those customers will be too far afield to act on the marketing. Large firm size, and especially geographic reach, can make the returns on ad time worth the investment.

need scale," said a VP for Chemical Bank when buying a smaller bank in 1994. Of course, in 1996 Chemical would itself merge with Chase Manhattan Bank.

Spreading big investment costs over more output is the main source of generic economies of scale, and in banking, the large initial investments are in sophisticated computer systems. The cost of investing in new computer hardware and systems is now recognized as a major investment obstacle for new banks, but once they are installed by banks large enough to afford them, they are highly profitable. The *Financial Times* describes how "the development of bulk computer processing and of electronic data transmission ... has allowed banks to move their back office operations away from individual branches to large remote centers. This has helped to bring real economies of scale to banking, an industry which traditionally has seen diseconomies set in at a very modest scale."

Economies of scale are common in manufacturing, and in the wake of deregulation the banking industry was also able to exploit a number of them. Besides spreading out the cost of computer systems, economies of scale may be present in office consolidation, in the funding mix used by banks, and in advertising. (See box.)

Industry-to-Industry Growth

BusinessWeek's analysis is that the banking industry "has produced large competitors that can take advantage of economies of scale ... as regulatory barriers to interstate banking fell," although not until the banks could "digest their purchases." The 1990s saw hundreds of bank purchases annually and hundreds of billions in acquired assets.

But an additional major turn for the industry came with the Gramm-Leach-Bliley Act of 1999 (GLB), which further loosened restrictions on bank growth, this time not geographically but industry-to-industry. After earlier moves in this direction by the Federal Reserve, GLB allowed for the free combination of commercial banking, insurance, and the riskier field of investment banking. These had been separated by law for decades, on the grounds that the availability of commercial credit was too important to the overall economy to be tied to the volatile world of investment banking.

GLB allowed firms to grow further, through banks merging with insurers or investment banks. The world of commercial credit was widened, and financial mergers this time exploited economies of scope—where production of multiple products jointly is cheaper than producing them individually. As commercial banks, investment banks, and insurers have expanded into each others' fields in the wake of GLB, their different lines of business can benefit from single expenses—for example, banks perform research on loan recipients that can also be used to underwrite bond issues. Scope economies such as these allow the larger banks to both run a greater profit on a per-service basis and attract more business. Thanks to the convenience of "one stop shopping," Citigroup now does more business with big corporations, like IT giant Unisys, than its component firms did pre-merger.

Exploiting economies of scope to diversify product lines in this fashion can also help a firm by reducing its dependence on any one line of business. Bank of America weathered the stock market downturn of 2001 in part because its corporate-debt-underwriting business was booming. Smaller, more specialized banks can become "one-trick ponies" as the *Wall Street Journal* put it—outdone by larger competitors with low-cost diversification thanks to scope economies.

These economies of scope are parallel to the scale economies, since both required deregulatory policy changes to be unleashed. Traditionally, banking wasn't seen as an industry with the strong economies of scale seen in, say, manufacturing. But the deregulation and computerization of the industry have allowed these firms to realize returns to greater scale and wider scope, and this has been a main driver of the endless acquisitions in the industry in recent decades.

Market Power

The enormous proportions that the banking institutions have taken on following deregulation have meant serious consequences for market performance. A number of banks have reached sufficient size to exercise market power—the ability of firms to influence prices and to engage in anticompetitive behavior. The market power of the enormous banks allows them to take positions as price leaders in local markets, where large firms use their dominance to elevate prices (i.e., increase fees and rates on loans, and decrease interest rates on deposits). Large firms can do this because smaller firms may perceive that lowering their prices to take market share could be met by very drastic reductions in prices from the larger firm in retaliation. Large firms, having deeper pockets, may be able to withstand longer periods of operating at a loss than the smaller firms.

Small banks are likely to perceive that the colossal size and resources of the megabanks make them unprofitable to cross—better to follow along and charge roughly what the dominant, price-leading firm does. Empirical research by Federal Reserve Board senior economist Steven Pilloff supported this analysis, finding that the arrival of very large banks in local markets tended to increase bank profitability for reasons of price leadership, due to the larger banks' economies of scale and scope, financial muscle, and diversification.

Examples of the use of banking industry market power are easy to find. Several bills now circulating in Congress deal with the fees retail businesses pay to the banks and the credit-card companies. When consumers make purchases with credit cards, two cents of each dollar goes not to the retailer but to the credit-card companies that run the payment network and the banks which supply the credit for cards branded Visa and MasterCard. These "interchange fees" bring in over $35 billion in profit in the United States alone, and they reflect the strong market power of the banks and credit-card companies over the various big and small retailers. The 2% charge comes to about $31,000 for a typical convenience store, just below the average per-store yearly profit of $36,000; this has driven a coalition of retailers to press for congressional action.

Visa has about 50% of the debit and credit-card market, and MasterCard has 25%, which grants them profound market power and strong bargaining positions. Federal Reserve Bank of Kansas City economists found the United States "maintains the highest interchange fees in the world, yet its costs should be among the lowest, given economies of scale and declining cost trends." The *Wall Street Journal's* description was that "these fees … have also been paradoxically tending upward in recent years when the industry's costs due to technology and economies of scale have been falling." Of course, there's only a paradox if market power is omitted from the picture. The dominant size and scale economies of the banks and the credit-card oligopoly allow for high prices to be sustained—bank muscle in action against a less powerful sector of the economy. The political action favored by the retailers includes proposals for committees to enact price ceilings or (interestingly) collective bargaining by the retailers. As is often the case, the political process is the reflection of the different levels and positions of power of various corporate institutions, and the maneuvering of their organizations.

Market power brings with it a number of other advantages. A powerful company is likely to have a widespread presence, make frequent use of advertising, and be able to raise its profile by contributing to community organizations like sports leagues. This allows the larger banks to benefit from stronger brand identity—their scale and resources make customers more likely to trust their services. This grants a further advantage in the form of customer tolerance of higher prices due to brand loyalty.

Political Clout

Crucially, large firms with market power are free to participate meaningfully in politics—using their deep pockets to invest in electoral campaigns and congressional lobbying. The financial sector is among the highest-contributing industries in the United States, with total 2008 campaign contributions approaching half a billion dollars, according to the Center For Public Integrity. So it's unsurprising that they receive so many favors from the state, since they fund the careers of the decision-making state personnel. This underlying reality is why influential Sen. Dick Durbin (D-Ill.) said of Congress, "The banks own the place."

Finally, banks may grow so large by exploiting scale economies and market power that they become "systemically important" to the nation's financial system. In other words, the scale and interconnectedness of the largest banks are considered to have reached a point where an abrupt failure of one or more of them may have "systemic" effects—meaning the broader economic system will be seriously impaired. These are the banks called "too big to fail," which were bailed out by act of Congress in the fall of 2008. Once a firm becomes so enormous that the state must prevent its collapse for the good of the economy, it has the ultimate advantage of being free to take far greater risks. Riskier investments come with higher returns and profits, but the accompanying greater risk of collapse will be less intimidating to huge banks that have an implied government insurance policy.

Some analysts have expressed doubt that such firms truly are too large to let fail, and that the banks have pulled a fast one. It might be pointed out in this connection that in the past the banks themselves have put their money where their mouths are—they have paid out of pocket to rescue financial institutions they saw as too large and connected to fail. An especially impressive episode took place in 1998, when several of Wall Street's biggest banks and financiers agreed to billions in emergency loans to rescue Long Term Capital Management (LTCM), a high-profile hedge fund that had borrowed enormous sums of capital to make billion-dollar gambles on financial markets.

America's biggest banks aren't in the habit of forking over $3.5 billion of good earnings, but they had loaned heavily to LTCM and feared losing their money if the fund went under. The Federal Reserve brought the bankers together, and in the end, they paid up to bail out their colleagues; the *Wall Street Journal* reported that it was the Fed's "clout, together with the self-interest of several big firms that already had leant billions of dollars to Long-Term Capital, that helped fashion the rescue." Interestingly, the banks insisted on real equity in the firm they were pulling out of the fire, and they gained a 90% stake in the hedge fund. Comparing this to the less-valuable "preferred stock" the government settled for in its 2008 bailout package of the large banks is instructive. The banks also got a share of control in the firm they rescued, again in stark contrast to the public bailout of some of the same banks.

Even Bigger?

In fact, the financial crisis and bailout led only to further concentration of the industry. The crisis gave stronger firms an opportunity to pick up sicker ones in another "wave of consolidation," as *BusinessWeek* put it. And a large part of the government intervention itself involved arranging hasty purchases of failing giants by other giants, orchestrated by the Federal Reserve. For example, the Fed helped organize the purchase of Bear Stearns by Chase in March 2008 and the purchase of Wachovia by Wells Fargo in December 2008. Even the bailout's "capital infusions" were used for further mergers and acquisitions by several recipients. The Treasury Department was "using the bailout bill to turn the banking system into the oligopoly of giant national institutions," as the *New York Times* reported.

The finance reform bill, still emerging as Congress' response to the financial crisis, has had most of its tougher elements rejected. Notably, a proposal to pay for future bailouts by a special tax on the megabanks was dropped from the bill, and no provisions remain that would actively break up the systemically important institutions. The main thrust is to oblige banks to hold somewhat more reserve capital, and other small reforms, many influenced by the Basel Committee, which is negotiating international banking accords. The goal is to prevent another megabank bailout with the public's money, but as Tony Jackson wrote in the *Financial Times*, "Governments may swear blind they will not stand behind bank creditors. But if the market correctly surmises official nerve will crack in a crisis, these protestations are worthless."

The monumental growth of the largest banks owes a lot to the industry's economies of scale and scope that developed once regulations were relaxed so firms could exploit them. While certainly not unique to finance, these dynamics have brought the banks to such enormous size that their bad bets can put the entire economy in peril. Banking therefore offers an especially powerful case for the importance of these economies and the role of market power, since it's left the megabanks holding all the cards.

In fact, many arguments between defenders of the market economy and its critics center on the issue of competition vs. power—market boosters reliably insist that markets mean efficient competition, where giants have no inherent advantage over small, scrappy firms. However, the record in banking clearly shows that banks have enjoyed a variety of real benefits from growth. The existence of companies of great size and power is a quite natural development in many industries, due to the appeal of returns to scale and power. This is why firms end up with enough power to influence state policy, or such absurd size that they can blackmail us for life support—and leave us crying all the way to the bank. ❏

Sources: Judith Samuelson and Lynn Stout, "Are Executives Paid Too Much?" *Wall Street Journal*, February 26, 2009; Tom Braithwaite, "Geithner Presses Congress for Action on Reform," *Financial Times*, September 23, 2009; Phillip Zweig, "Intrastate Mergers Between Banking Giants Might Not Be Out of the Question Anymore," *Wall Street Journal*, March 25, 1986; Bruce Knecht, "Chemical Banking plans acquisition of Margaretten," *Wall Street Journal*, May 13, 1994; Eric Weiner, "Banks Will Post Good Quarterly Results," *Wall Street Journal*, January 10, 1997; Gabriella Stern, "Four Big Regionals To Consolidate Bank Operations," *Wall Street Journal*, July 22, 1992; "Pressure for change grows," *Financial Times*, September 27, 1996; Tracy Corrigan and John Authers, "Citigroup To Take $900 million charge: Cost-cutting Program to Result in Loss of 10,400 Jobs," *Financial Times*, December 16, 1998; Eleanor Laise, "Mutual-Fund Mergers Jump Sharply," *Wall Street Journal*, March 9, 2006; Steven Pilloff, "Banking, commerce and competition under the Gramm-Leach-Bliley Act," *The Antitrust Bulletin*, Spring 2002; David Humphrey, "Why Do Estimates of Bank Scale Economies Differ?" *Economic Review of Federal Reserve Bank of Richmond*, September/October 1990, note four; Michael Mandel and Rich Miller, "Productivity: The Real Story," *Business Week*, November 5, 2001; John Yang, "Fed Votes to Give 7 Bank Holding Firms Additional Power in Securities Sector," *Wall Street Journal*, July 16, 1987; "Banking Behemoths—What Happens Next: Many companies Like to Shop Around For Their Providers of Financial Services," *Wall Street Journal*, September 14, 2000; Carrick Mollenkamp and Paul Beckett, "Diverse Business Portfolios Boost Banks' Bottom Lines," *Wall Street Journal*, July 17, 2001; *Journal of Financial Services Research*, "Does the Presence of Big Banks Influence Competition in Local Markets?" May 1999; "Credit-Card Wars," *Wall Street Journal*, March 29, 2008; *Economic Review of the Federal Reserve Bank of Kansas City*, "Interchange Fees in Credit and Debit Card Markets: What Role for Public Authorities," January-March 2006; "Credit Where It's Due," *Wall Street Journal*, January 12, 2006; Keith Bradsher, "In One Pocket, Out the Other," *New York Times*, November 25, 2009; Center For Public Integrity, *Finance/Insurance/Real Estate: Long-Term Contribution Trends*, opensecrets.org; Dean Baker, "Banks own the US government," *Guardian*, June 30, 2009; Anita Raghavan and Mitchell Pacelle, "To the Rescue? A Hedge Fun Falters, So the Fed Persuades Big Banks to Ante Up," *Wall Street Journal*, September 24, 1998; Theo Francis, "Will Bank Rescues Mean Fewer Banks?" *Business Week*, November 25, 2008; Joe Nocera, "So When Will Banks Give Loans?" *New York Times*, October 25, 2008; Edward Wyatt, "Bill Drops Fund to Shut Failed Banks," *New York Times*, May 4, 2010; Sewell Chan, "Financial Debate Renews Scrutiny on Banks' Size," *New York Times*, April 20, 2010; Tony Jackson, "'Too big to fail' debate makes move in right direction," *Financial Times*, April 12, 2010.

Article 4.9

BONANZAS AS USUAL

The megabanks' denial about bad loans unleashes profit and pay.

BY ROB LARSON
November/December 2010

Since the catastrophic bank collapses of 2008 and the government rescue of the finance industry, Wall Street has staged a dramatic comeback. Since the bailout, profits are up, capital reserves are up, stock prices are up, government direct aid has been paid back, and executive compensation is exploding. But a closer look shows bank stability is just skin-deep, and dense accounting rules hide a powder keg of bad debt and mounting funding issues. While the recent paper-thin re-regulation of finance was a major political victory, the banks' core business is headed downhill and even worse trouble seems to lie ahead.

All of the big four U.S. megabanks—Bank of America, Citigroup, Chase, and Wells Fargo—reported either decreases or very modest increases in their massive profitability during 2010. But this surprisingly weak performance would have been even more disappointing without a pair of accounting maneuvers. One was a bookkeeping measure allowing banks to book projected profit from buying back their debt when their bonds become cheaper. But the banks rarely buy back their debt, so this is essentially a paper gain. The other penstroke that boosted profit was consumption of money set aside to protect against losses on loans—as banks have grown more outwardly confident about the economic recovery, they have lowered their stated expectations of bad loans and designated some of their capital cushions as profit.

But these shallow techniques for elevating profit weren't enough to compensate for the decline in banks' core business—interest income, the money collected from loans minus that paid out to depositors. That income has consistently dropped this year, mainly due to falling loan volume. Banks are making fewer loans to consumers and businesses, citing a "lack of demand," which obscures the quite favorable credit rating now required to get a loan. The lower supply of qualified applicants as job losses persist, combined with locking out applicants with spottier credit history and a general consumer preference to reduce total debt, have all caused bank loan books to continue to shrink in the feeble recovery.

The market has not rewarded the banks for the elaborate camouflage of this core weakness, and their stock prices have lately sagged as a result. But executive compensation is another story, and traders' pay is also rebounding into the $200,000-to-$500,000 range, while tens of millions of Americans struggle to keep food on the table. Meanwhile Obama's much-hailed "pay czar" in charge of monitoring finance-executive compensation, Kenneth Feinberg, has reported that within three months of receiving their bailouts, the megabanks had paid out $1.6 billion in bonuses—up to a quarter of their TARP rescue totals. However, the "czar" has no formal power to rescind exorbitant pay now that the majors have repaid their government capital infusions, and compensation will now be monitored by a rather unintimidating consortium of regulators. With the CEOs of the bank majors making about a million a year each in straight salary, no upward limit is in sight for financier compensation. But the banking institutions themselves may have some bumpy days ahead.

Extend and Pretend and Descend

While the banking majors were relieved of much of their bad home mortgage-based investments by government purchases in the course of the financial crisis and aftermath, large loans related to commercial real estate remained on their books. Many of these loans went to growing businesses and overoptimistic developers, and have frequently failed to perform as the recession has rendered projects unprofitable, reducing borrowers' ability to repay.

But the loans are often for sobering amounts, upwards of tens of millions of dollars, and rather than foreclose on such large credit lines, banks large and small are engaging in what has come to be called "extend and pretend." The practice involves not taking legal measures on underperforming commercial real-estate loans, but rather "restructuring" loans with new, more favorable terms for the borrowers, like below-market interest rates or extended timelines for repayment. The goal of the practice is to prevent foreclosure on large loans, with the hope that extending maturities will give borrowers enough time to recover their business and repay.

There are several problems with this practice. First, it conceals the real condition of the commercial real-estate market. Second, the restructured loans are usually still foreclosed upon in the end—in the first quarter of fiscal year 2010, 44% of restructured loans were still a month or more delinquent, a fact related to the startling two-thirds of commercial real-estate loans maturing by 2014 that are underwater—meaning that the property is worth less than the bank loan itself. Finally, the bad loans take up space on bank balance sheets that could go to real lending. This suggests that the banks' current predicament may lead to a miniature version of 1990s Japan, where refusal to accept real-estate loan losses led to a decade of slow growth, in part due to banks' inability to make fresh loans when demand recovered.

However, the "extend and pretend" policy presents one major benefit to the big banks: restructuring these loans allows banks to count them as "performing" rather than delinquent or worse, which means banks may reduce their capital reserves against losses. This enables banks to claim their capital cushions as profit; banks remain in denial about their bad loans, and this itself allows the recent profit increases. And when banks are one day obliged to confront these serious losses, they may find they no longer have the capital cushion to absorb the damage.

This ominous hidden liability is on top of the better-publicized problem of banks' under-performing residential mortgage holdings. The mortgage delinquency rate is now hovering around 10% nationwide, and including those behind on payments and those on the verge of eviction, fully one U.S. mortgage in seven is in some kind of trouble. Importantly, the bad mortgage debt on banks' books has ceased to be a primarily "subprime" phenomenon of low-income loan recipients; over a third of new foreclosures early this year were prime fixed-rate loans, as the layoff-intensive recovery pulls the rug out from under mortgage recipients.

One Hand Regulates the Other

July's Wall Street Reform and Consumer Protection Act was expected to be a return to at least moderate finance regulation, even if a far cry from the more sweeping controls of the 1930s. But the slap-on-the-wrist nature of the bill became clear when stock prices of the megabanks *rose* 3% on its passage. The bill delegates dozens of important decisions, from what constitutes a systemically important bank to credit ratings disclosure, to the regulatory agencies themselves. Crucially, bank regulators are expecting what the press calls a "lobbying blitz," as former employees of the regulators are bankrolled by Wall Street to lobby for industry discretion and relaxed standards on every rule. Highlights include:

- While now stuck with limits on overdraft fees and the "interchange fees" charged to merchants for debit-card processing, banks are phasing out free checking accounts and elevating fees elsewhere, since they have the market power to do so. Many depositors are unable to afford checking account fees, of course, but the *New York Times* expects the banks to "jettison unprofitable customers."

- The Volcker Rule would limit banks' "proprietary trading," investments made with a bank's own money rather than clients' funds. The practice was damaging during the financial crisis, but banks have already found a work-around for the new rule. Banks are moving star proprietary traders to client desks, where they will primarily conduct derivatives trade for clients, but will also be able to engage in the barred practice on the side, further blurring the client/proprietary distinction.

- Derivatives will now be listed on established indexes and will require collateral as a cushion against losses, having previously been traded ad-hoc by individual banks. This removes significant risk from the banks themselves, reducing them to competing on service rather than generating large securitization fees. Importantly, businesses that use derivatives for legitimate purposes, such as farmers buying futures contracts to secure favorable grain prices, are exempted from the bill's indexing and collateralizing requirements.

- The bill includes a resolution authority that gives regulators a procedure to "unwind" a bank—overseeing its bankruptcy in an orderly fashion and at its creditors' expense. Additionally, the Kanjorski amendment to the bill gives regulators the authority to break up any financial institution considered to be a systemic threat to the financial system. But it seems unlikely that regulators, typically close to the firms they regulate, would let a titan go down regardless of their resolution authority.

- The new Consumer Financial Protection Bureau requires more information transparency from banks in their communications with customers. However, despite apocalyptic predictions from bank spokespeople, it is notable that banks with under $10 billion in assets are exempt from its rules. This excludes the small and medium-sized lenders that make up 98% of U.S. banks, but does include the large proportion of the industry run by the majors.

Sources: Congressional Oversight Panel, Small Banks In the Capital Purchase Program, July 14, 2010; Eric Dash and Nelson Schwartz, "Banks Seek to Keep Profits as New Oversight Rules Loom," *New York Times,* July 15, 2010; Aaron Lucchetti and Jenny Strasburg, "What's a 'Prop' Trader Now?—Banks Move Those Who Wager With Firms' Money to Client-Focused Jobs," *Wall Street Journal,* July 6, 2010; Randall Smith and Aaron Luchetti, "The Financial-Regulation Overhaul," *Wall Street Journal,* June 26, 2010; Damian Paletta, "Late Change Sparks Outcry Over Finance-Overhaul Bill," *Wall Street Journal,* July 2, 2010; Michael Phillips, "Finance Overhaul Casts Long Shadow on the Plains," *Wall Street Journal,* July 14, 2010; "Killing Them Softly," *The Economist,* August 26, 2010; "Not All On the Same Page," *The Economist,* July 1, 2010; Eric Lichtblau, "Ex-Regulators Get Set to Lobby on New Financial Rules," *New York Times,* July 27, 2010.

Notably, the home mortgages still held by the banks are listed on bank balance sheets at inflated values since they are for homes bought at the housing bubble peak, and government has not forced the banks to account them at any reasonable value. And beside this additional hidden weakness and the space taken up on bank balance sheets by this bad mortgage debt, the banking majors are vulnerable to moves by insurers and other investors to force the banks to repurchase securitized home loans sold to them at wildly inflated prices. So far, losses on affected and expected repurchases have cost the biggest four U.S. banks nearly $10 billion, with further losses anticipated.

Meanwhile, the banks have allowed extremely few mortgage borrowers to modify their mortgages or reduce their principal—the National Bureau of Economic Research has found that just 8% of delinquent borrowers received any modification, while a pitiful 3% have received reductions in their total owed principal. However, about half of all seriously delinquent borrowers have had foreclosure proceedings brought by their bank. Of course, banks ultimately benefit more from a renegotiated loan that is paid off than from a foreclosure, but the long timeline required in the foreclosure process allows the banks to once again push back acknowledgement of the loss.

The banks' rush to foreclose is reflected in the recent suspension of the practice by several megabanks, after discovery that foreclosure standards were not being followed, with single employees overseeing upwards of 400 foreclosures daily, far more than can be properly reviewed according to legal standards. The investigation by state attorneys general adds to the legal swamp that may slow down the flood of foreclosures, but also testifies to the large banks' preference for foreclosure over loan modification.

Lending on Borrowed Time

Banks face other market difficulties in the near future. One involves the increased reliance of the large banks on short-term borrowing to fund their loan portfolios. While banks have issued bonds to raise loan capital for years, in recent years they have grown increasingly dependent on short-term borrowing—the average maturity of recent bank bond issues is under five years, the shortest in decades. This is in fact why the seizing up of the credit markets in 2008 was such a big deal—banks were in immediate trouble if they couldn't borrow. Of course, the government bailout included guarantees for short-term bonds, leading the banks to become even more reliant upon them.

This means banks must "turn over" their debt more frequently—they must issue fresh bonds to raise capital to pay off the maturing older bonds—and U.S. banks must refinance over a trillion dollars through 2012. The problem is that the banks will be competing with huge bond rollovers from state and federal government, which are heavily indebted because of upper-class tax cuts, as well as expensive wars and recent rounds of stimulus at the federal level. Even the powerful megabanks may struggle in this environment—as the *New York Times* puts it, "The cost of borrowing is likely to rise faster than banks can pass it on to customers." The total demand for institutional credit may significantly spike in coming years, meaning perhaps higher interest rates as states and finance houses compete for the bond market's favor, or a further decline in lending by banks due to prohibitive funding costs.

Meanwhile, smaller banks have experienced a different post-crisis environment. Despite some TARP bailout crumbs, they have gone under in record numbers—140 failed in 2009, with 2010 on track for a yet larger figure. Most of these smaller fry succumb to losses or suffocate under bad loans following the real-estate bubble of the last decade. This sector of the industry is ironically on track to cause more taxpayer losses from non-repayment of bailout funds than the majors, which have attracted the most scorn for taking TARP funds.

Compounding these stabilized but still shaky banking positions, the industry is now subject to a significantly reshaped regulatory environment. In addition to the major finance reform bill enacted in July, banks face new international capital standards in the Basel Rules and new regulatory scope for the Federal Reserve as

Basel Faulty

The Basel III bank guidelines are meant to be the G-20's coordinated global response to the crisis of 2008, establishing consistent rules limiting banking risk. But as with the U.S. bill, lightweight standards were greeted by stock jumps for the bank majors, since the process was heavily influenced by massive financial industry lobbying and other, nationalist factors.

Perhaps most notably, the biggest banks' minimum leverage ratio—how much hard capital banks must hold to cushion against sudden losses—has been set at a modest 7% of assets. However, banks need not meet this requirement until 2019, with only a 2.5% requirement by 2015. Further, the Basel Committee has caved to industry demands to count assets like deferred-tax funds, mortgage-service rights, and investments in other firms as capital. These are now allowed to make up 15% of a bank's capital cushion, despite being illiquid and thus not very helpful in a crisis. Notably, some U.S. megabanks had reserve levels close to these on the eve of the finance crisis, and of course found them to be insufficient.

A related issue is how much long-term funding (vs. short-term bonds) the banks issue, making them less-vulnerable to sudden credit-market lockups as in 2008. The committee failed to reach agreement on this issue, and the rule has been postponed until 2015, along with many others, including "calibration," the specific required reserve level banks must maintain based on their importance to the overall finance system.

One obstacle to progress is the distinctly nationalist approach taken by the regulators, who aim to minimize the weight of regulations that will affect the banks based in their home countries. The United States has pushed aggressively for broader definitions of capital, since U.S. banks still hold large volumes of mortgage securitization rights. Germany wants "flexible" enforcement of the reserve requirements for its undercapitalized banks; France wants allowances for its banks to continue to own insurers, and so on. The result is banking regulators fighting tooth and nail against regulating their own banks.

In this way, the standards meant to prevent banks from reverting to their old systemically risky ways have been heavily diluted, diminishing Basel to a fig leaf. As the *Wall Street Journal* accurately predicted, "significant moves by the Basel Committee to back away from its initial proposals...[are] likely to provoke criticism that regulators are caving to industry pressure and missing a chance to impose restraints that could reduce the risk of future costly crises."

Sources: Damian Paletta and David Enrich, "Banks Gain in Rules Debate," *Wall Street Journal*, July 15, 2010; Damian Paletta and David Enrich, "Risks Rulebooks Is Nearly Done—Key Aspects of Banks' New Restraints Are Agreed Upon," *Wall Street Journal*, July 27, 2010; Damien Paletta, "Banks Get New Restraints," *Wall Street Journal*, September 13, 2010.

well. But all these reforms have been limited by massive lobbying spending by Wall Street, coming to over $700 million in the last 18 months alone, as estimated by the Center For Responsive Politics. (See boxes.)

A crucial part of the picture is the uncertainty caused by the notorious secrecy of the financial world. Large parts of the modern finance system do not accept deposits as commercial banks do, and therefore face far less regulation, allowing them to disclose much less information about their investments and leverage. Additionally, even the commercial banks are not obliged to report changes to the terms of their commercial real-estate holdings, obscuring the full extent of "extend-and-pretend" practices. And the Federal Reserve, for its part, has fought to preserve its own institutional secrecy. The Wall Street reform bill does include provisions for limited audits of the Fed's open-market operations and discount window, the basic monetary policy tools used to manipulate interest rates and to modulate economic activity. But this casts little light on the Fed's expansive holdings in mortgage securities and other paper bought from the banks in the course of the 2008-9 bailout. From the banks to the regulators, secrecy—and thus uncertainty—colors the picture.

In the end, moderately higher capital requirements and the public listing and indexing of derivatives may take the financial system back to short-term stability, but banks remain stuck with significant bad loans limiting core interest income, and continue to rely on market bubbles and on their outsized political power. They also face a difficult short-term bond market in the near future in addition to some higher regulatory costs, and crucially, their core business is further limited by weak credit demand in the low-expectations recovery. Unsurprisingly, compensation has rocketed back into seven figures in spite of these circumstances.

So while ordinary Americans limp along in a jobless recovery, the banks have their execs instead of Hell to pay. ❑

Sources: Eric Dash, "JPMorgan Chase Profit Rises as Loans Provisions Fall," *New York Times*, October 13, 2010; Eric Dash, "Citigroup Reports $2.2 Billion Profit in Third Quarter," *New York Times*, October 18, 2010; Bradley Keoun, "Bank Profits Are Worse Than They Look," *Bloomberg Businessweek*, July 22, 2010; Matthias Rieker and Marshall Eckblad, "Banks Generate Profits, but Struggle to Lend," *Wall Street Journal*, July 22, 2010; Eric Dash, "Federal Report Faults Banks on Huge Bonuses," *New York Times*, July 22, 2010; "Bankers' Pay," *New York Times*, July 27, 2010; Carrick Mollenkamp and Lingling Wei, "To Fix Sour Property Deals, Lenders 'Extend and Pretend,'" *Wall Street Journal*, July 7, 2010; David Streitfeld, "Mortage Data Leaves Bankers Uncertain of Trend," *New York Times*, May 19, 2010; Floyd Norris, "Banks Stuck With Bill for Bad Loans," *New York Times*, August 19, 2010; Manuel Adelino et al, "Why Don't Lenders Renegotiate More Home Mortgages? Redefaults, Self-Curse and Securitization," NBER, July 2009; Jack Ewing, "Crisis Awaits World's Banks as Trillions Come Due," *New York Times*, July 11, 2010; AP, FDIC Closes 6 Banks, Including 3 in Florida," *New York Times*, July 16, 2010; Randall Smith and Robin Sidel, "Banks Keep Failing, No End in Sight," *Wall Street Journal*, September 27, 2010; Binyamin Appelbaum, "Mortgage Securities It Holds Pose Sticky Problem for Fed," *New York Times*, July 22, 2010; Peter Goodman, "Policy Options Dwindle as Economic Fears Grow," *New York Times*, August 28, 2010; Center For Responsive Politics, Lobbying Spending Database, FIRE 2010, opensecrets.org.

Article 4.10

THE SAD FUTURE OF BANKING
Reforms fail to address the "control fraud" that caused the financial crisis.

BY WILLIAM K. BLACK
October 2010

A truly amazing thing has happened in banking. After the worst financial crisis in 75 years sparked the "Great Recession," we have

- Failed to identify the real causes of the crisis;
- Failed to fix the defects that caused the crisis;
- Failed to hold the CEOs, professionals, and anti-regulators who caused the crisis accountable—even when they committed fraud;
- Bailed out the largest and worst financial firms with massive public funds;
- Covered up banking losses and failures—impairing any economic recovery;
- Degraded our integrity and made the banking system even more encouraging of fraud;
- Refused to follow policies that have proved extremely successful in past crises;
- Made the systemically dangerous institutions (SDIs) even more dangerous;
- Made our financial system even more parasitic, harming the real economy.

And pronounced this travesty a brilliant success.

The Bush and Obama administrations have made an already critically flawed financial system even worse. The result is that the banking industry's future is bad for banking, terrible for the real economy, horrific for the public—and wonderful for the top executives at the largest banks. This is significantly insane. It appears that we will need to suffer another great depression before we are willing to put aside the crippling dogmas that have so degraded the financial system, the real economy, democracy, and the ethical standards of private and public elites.

The Economics Blindfold

Why did most of the experts neither foresee nor understand the forces in the U.S. banking industry that caused this meltdown? The short answer is: their dogmatic belief in neoclassical economic theory that is impervious to the facts, or what I like to call theoclassical economics.

Neoclassical economics is premised on the asserted effectiveness of private market discipline. This (oxymoronic) discipline is the basis for the "efficient markets" and "efficient contracts" hypotheses that are the pillars of faith supporting modern finance theory and much of neoclassical microeconomics. Collectively, these hypotheses lead to absolute faith that markets exclude fraud. "A rule against fraud is not an essential or even necessarily an important ingredient of securities markets," wrote eminent corporate law scholars Frank Easterbrook and Daniel

Fischel in their 1991 *The Economic Structure of Corporate Law*, in a typical statement of that faith.

How are markets supposed to exclude fraud? Easterbrook and Fischel offer two reasons. The first, a circular argument, lies in theoclassical economists' core belief that markets are by nature efficient. Markets that allow frauds cannot be efficient. Therefore, markets must exclude fraud.

The other argument rests on "signaling" theory. The logical premise is that honest firms have a financial incentive to signal to investors and creditors that they are honest. The false premise is that honest firms have the unique ability to signal that they are honest. Easterbrook and Fischel claim that there are three signals of honesty that only honest firms can transmit: hiring a top-tier audit firm, having the CEO own substantial stock in the firm, and operating with extreme leverage, i.e., a high ratio of debt to capital. The reality, which Fischel knew before he co-authored the treatise, was that firms engaging in so-called control fraud can mimic each of these signals. Control fraud occurs when the executives at a seemingly legitimate firm use their control to loot the firm and its shareholders and creditors. In banking, accounting is the weapon of choice for looting. Accounting control frauds have shown the consistent ability to get "clean" accounting opinions from top tier audit firms; their CEOs use their stock ownership to loot the firm; and they love to borrow extensively, as that allows them to loot the firm's creditors.

In fact, the claim that markets inherently exclude fraud runs contrary to all of our experience with securities markets. The role of epidemics of accounting control frauds in driving recent financial crises is well documented. The national commission that investigated the causes of the savings and loan debacle found that at the "typical large failure," "fraud was invariably present." Similarly, the Enron and WorldCom scandals were shown to be accounting control frauds. Savings and loan regulators used their hard-won understanding of accounting control fraud to stop a developing pattern of fraud in California in 1990-1991, involving S&Ls making so-called liar's loans. We recognized that making mortgage loans without adequate underwriting creates intense "adverse selection," i.e., it means more lending to borrowers who are not creditworthy, and that such lending was guaranteed to result in high reported (albeit fictional) income and high real losses. Theoclassical economists, however, refused to acknowledge these frauds because recognizing the existence of control fraud would challenge the assumptions underlying their faith-based economic theories.

This economic dogma was so dominant that it drove regulatory policy in the United States, Europe, and Japan during the last three decades. Regulations ignored control fraud and assumed that paper profits produced by fraud were real. The result, from the mid-1990s on, was regulatory complacency endorsed by economists who actually praised the worst of the emerging control frauds because of their high reported profits. So it is no surprise that the recent U.S. banking crisis was driven by an epidemic of lending fraud, primarily mortgage lenders making millions of "liar's loans" annually. According to Credit Suisse, for instance, 49% of all mortgage originations in 2006 were stated-income loans, meaning loans based on applicants' self-reported incomes with no verification. MARI, the Mortgage Bankers Association experts on fraud, warned in 2006 that these loans caused endemic fraud:

> Stated income and reduced documentation loans … are open invitations to fraudsters. It appears that many members of the industry have little historical appreciation for the havoc created by low-doc/no-doc products that were the rage in the early 1990s. Those loans produced hundreds of millions of dollars in losses for their users.
>
> One of MARI's customers recently reviewed a sample of 100 stated income loans upon which they had IRS Forms 4506. When the stated incomes were compared to the IRS figures, the resulting differences were dramatic. Ninety percent of the stated incomes were exaggerated by 5% or more. More disturbingly, almost 60% of the stated amounts were exaggerated by more than 50%. These results suggest that the stated income loan deserves the nickname used by many in the industry, the "liar's loan."

Why would scores of lenders specialize in making liar's loans after being warned by their own experts and even by the FBI that such loans led to endemic fraud? (Not that they needed any warnings. Bankers have known for centuries that underwriting is essential to survival in mortgage lending. Even the label "liar's loan," widely used in the industry, shows that bankers knew such loans were commonly fraudulent.) How could these fraudulent loans be sold to purportedly the most sophisticated underwriters in the history of the world at grossly inflated values blessed by the world's top audit firms? How could hundreds of thousands of fraudulent loans be pooled into securities, the now-infamous collateralized debt obligations (CDOs), and receive "AAA" ratings from the top rating agencies? How could markets that are supposed to exclude all fraud instead accommodate millions of fraudulent loans that hyper-inflated the largest financial bubble in history and triggered the Great Recession?

The answer is that making bad loans allows lenders to grow extremely rapidly and charge premium yields. This maximizes reported accounting income, which in turn boosts executive compensation and optimizes looting. The financial system is riddled with incentives so perverse that it is criminogenic—it creates fraud epidemics instead of preventing fraud. When compensation levels for banking executives and professionals are very large and based substantially on reported short-term income, financial firms become superb vehicles for control fraud. Add in deregulation and desupervision, and the result is an environment ripe for a fraud epidemic.

Accounting is the weapon of choice for financial-sector control frauds. The recipe for a lender to maximize (fictional) reported accounting income has four ingredients:

1. Extremely rapid growth
2. Lending regardless of borrower creditworthiness, at premium yields
3. Extreme leverage
4. Minimal loss reserves

The first two ingredients are related. A U.S. housing lender operates in a mature, reasonably competitive industry. A mortgage lender cannot grow extremely rapidly by making high quality mortgages. If it tried to do so, it would have to cut its yield substantially in order to gain market share. Its competitors would respond by cutting their yields and the result would be modest growth and a serious loss of yield, reducing reported profits. Any lender, however, can guarantee extremely rapid growth and charge borrowers a premium yield simply by making loans to borrowers who most likely cannot repay them. Worse, hundreds of lenders can follow this same recipe because there are tens of millions of potential homebuyers in the United States who would not able to repay their loans. Indeed, when hundreds of firms follow the same recipe, they hyper-inflate the resultant financial bubble, which in turn allows borrowers to refinance their loans and thereby delay their defaults for years.

Economists George Akerlof and Paul Romer explained in 1993 that accounting fraud is a "sure thing" and explained why it caused bubbles to hyper-inflate, then burst. Note that the same recipe that produces record fictional income in the short-term eventually produces catastrophic real losses. The lender will fail (unless it is bailed out or able to sell to the "greater fool"), but with their compensation largely based on reported income, the senior officers can walk away wealthy. This paradox—the CEO prospers by causing the firm's collapse—explains Akerlof and Romer's title, "Looting: The Economic Underworld of Bankruptcy for Profit."

Senior executives can also use their ability to hire, promote, compensate, and fire to suborn employees, officers, and outside professionals. As Franklin Raines, chairman and CEO of Fannie Mae, explained to *BusinessWeek* in 2003:

> Investment banking is a business that's so denominated in dollars that the temptations are great, so you have to have very strong rules. My experience is where there is a one-to-one relation between if I do X, money will hit my pocket, you tend to see people doing X a lot. You've got to be very careful about that. Don't just say: "If you hit this revenue number, your bonus is going to be this." It sets up an incentive that's overwhelming. You wave enough money in front of people, and good people will do bad things.

Raines knew what he was talking about: he installed a compensation system at Fannie Mae that produced precisely these perverse incentives among his staff and made him wealthy by taking actions that harmed Fannie Mae.

In an earlier work, Akerlof had explained how firms that gained a competitive advantage through fraud could cause a "Gresham's" dynamic in which bad ethics drove good ethics from the marketplace. The national commission that investigated the savings and loan debacle documented this criminogenic dynamic: "[A]busive operators of S&L[s] sought out compliant and cooperative accountants. The result was a sort of 'Gresham's Law' in which the bad professionals forced out the good." The same dynamic was documented by N.Y. Attorney General Andrew Cuomo's 2007 investigation of appraisal fraud, which found that Washington Mutual blacklisted appraisers who refused to inflate appraisals. An honest secured lender would never inflate, or permit the inflation of, appraisals.

Failure to Respond

The U.S. government's response to the meltdown has been not merely inadequate, but actually perverse. The Bush and Obama administrations' banking regulators have left frauds in charge of failed banks and covered up the banks' losses, allowed the behemoths of the industry to become even larger and more dangerous, and passed a "reform" law that fails to mandate the most critical reforms.

In March 2009, Congress, with the explicit encouragement of Federal Reserve Board Chairman Bernanke and the implicit acceptance of the Obama administration, successfully extorted the Financial Accounting Standards Board on behalf of the banking industry to force it to change the banking rules so that banks did not have to recognize losses on their bad assets until they sold them. Normal accounting rules sensibly require banks to recognize losses on bad loans when the problems with the loans are not "temporary." The losses at issue in the recent crisis were caused by system-wide fraud and the collapse of the largest financial bubble in world history. They were not temporary—moreover, they were (and are) massive. If banks had recognized these losses as they were required to do under pre-existing accounting rules, many of them would have had to report that they were unprofitable, badly undercapitalized, or even insolvent.

Gimmicking the accounting rules so bankers could lie about their asset values has caused the usual severe problems. First, it allows CEOs to pretend that unprofitable banks are profitable and so continue to pay themselves massive bonuses. This is not only unfair; it contributes to a broadly criminogenic environment. Second, it leads banks to hold onto bad home loans and other assets at grossly inflated prices, preventing markets from clearing and prolonging the recession. This is the Japanese scenario that led to the country's "lost decade" (now extended). Third, it makes it harder for regulators to supervise vigorously, should they try to do so, because many regulatory powers are triggered only when losses occur with the resulting failure to meet capital requirements. Indeed, the assault on honest accounting was launched with the express purpose of evading the Prompt Corrective Action law, passed in 1991 on the basis of bitter experience: when savings-and-loan CEOs who had looted "their" institutions were allowed to remain in control of them by using fraudulent accounting, the losses and the fallout of the S&L crisis kept growing. Fourth, it embraces dishonesty as an official policy. Indeed, it implies that the solution to the accounting fraud that massively inflated asset valuations is to change the accounting rules to encourage the massive inflation of those same asset values. Effective regulation is impossible without regulatory integrity; lying about asset values destroys integrity.

Even in the case of the roughly 20 massive U.S. financial institutions considered "too big to fail," the public policy response has been perverse. (The Bush and Obama administrations and their economists have claimed that if any of these giant banks were to fail, it would cause a systemic global crisis, hence the "too big to fail" moniker. I am dubious that a systemic crisis would inevitably result, but I agree that these banks are so large that they pose a systemic danger to the global economy.) The terminology itself demonstrates how economists err in their analysis—and how much they identify with the CEOs who helped cause the Great Recession. They refer to the largest banks as "systemically important institutions," as if these banks deserved gold stars. By the prevailing logic, however, the massive banks are the opposite. They are ticking time bombs that can take down the global financial system if they fail. So "systemically dangerous institutions," or SDIs, would be more apt.

It should be a top public policy priority to end the ability of any single bank to pose a global systemic risk. That means that the SDIs should be forbidden to grow, required to shrink over a five-year period to a size at which they no longer pose a systemic risk, and intensively supervised until they shrink to that size. In particular, regulation of the SDIs must end the existing perverse incentives that are so criminogenic—executive compensation systems tied to short-term reported income, the accounting cover-up which has gutted the Prompt Corrective Action law, the use of compensation and hiring and firing powers to create a "Gresham's" dynamic among the SDIs' personnel and outside professionals, and the use of political contributions to impair effective regulation. These reforms are vital for all banks but particularly urgent for the SDIs, with their potential to cause massive damage.

Instead, the opposite has been done. Both administrations have responded to the financial crisis by allowing (indeed, encouraging) SDIs, even insolvent ones, to acquire other failed financial firms and become even larger and more systemically dangerous to the global economy. The SDIs' already perverse incentives were made worse by giving them a bailout plus the accounting cover-up of their losses on terms that made the U.S. Treasury and the Federal Reserve the "fools" in the market.

With small- and medium-size banks likely to continue to fail in high numbers due to residential and commercial real estate losses, the financial crisis has increased the long-term trend toward extreme concentration in the financial industry. The SDIs will pursue diverse business strategies. Some will continue their current strategy of borrowing short-term at extremely low interest rates and reinvesting the proceeds primarily in government bonds. They will earn material, not exceptional, profits but will do little to help the real economy recover. Others will invest in whatever asset category offers the best (often fictional) accounting income. They will drive the next U.S.-based crisis.

What about the long-awaited bank reform law, which Congress finally delivered in July 2010 in the form of the Dodd-Frank Act? The law does not address the fundamental factors that have caused recurrent, intensifying financial crises: fraud, accounting, executive and professional compensation, and regulatory failure. Instead, it deals primarily with the excuses Treasury Secretary Paulson and Federal Reserve Chairman Bernanke offered for their failures. The new law gives regulators (weak) authority to place a failing SDI in receivership. Paulson and Bernanke claimed they had no legal authority to place Lehman in receivership, but they did not place insolvent megabanks over which they had clear legal authority in receivership either. The Bush administration's problem was always a lack of regulatory will, not a lack of authority. The Dodd-Frank Act also creates a regulatory council that is supposed to identify systemic risks. The council, however, will be dominated by economists of the same theoclassical stripe who not only failed to identify the systemic risks that produced the modern financial crises that this essay discusses, but actually praised the criminogenic incentives that caused those crises. The most hopeful part of the Dodd-Frank Act is the creation of a bureau with the mission of protecting financial consumers. No one can predict at this juncture whether it will accomplish its mission.

The chief international reform, the Basel III accord, shares the fundamental deficiency of the Dodd-Frank Act. Dominated as they were by theoclassical economists, the Basel negotiations not surprisingly produced an agreement that ignores the underlying causes of the crisis. Instead, it focuses on one symptom of the crisis—extreme leverage, the third ingredient of the recipe for optimizing accounting control fraud. The remedy was to restore capital requirements to roughly the levels required under Basel I (Basel II eviscerated European banks' capital requirements). Fortunately, the U.S. did not fully implement the Basel II capital reserve reductions, which means that the leverage of non-fraudulent U.S. banks has been significantly lower than their European counterparts.

However, capital requirements only have meaning under honest accounting. Once one takes into account the fictional "capital" produced by the accounting fraud that first massively inflated asset values and now hides the losses—along with the revised accounting rules that will be exploited to create fictional income in the future—the irrelevance of the proposed Basel III capital requirements becomes clear.

If the Dodd-Frank Act of 2010 and the Basel III proposals are the limits of our response to the crisis, then the most probable outcome in the near- and medium-term is the Japanese scenario—a weak, delayed, and transitory recovery followed by periodic recessions. Banks will remain weak and a poor provider of capital for economic expansion.

With private market "discipline" having become criminogenic, the only hope for preventing the current crisis was vigorous regulation and supervision. Unfortunately, the dogmatic belief that markets automatically prevent fraud led to complacency and the appointment of anti-regulators chosen for their willingness to praise and serve their banking "customers." (The "reinventing government" initiative championed by former Vice President Al Gore and by George W. Bush when he was Texas' governor indeed instructed banking regulators to refer to bankers as their "customers.") President Obama has generally left in office, reappointed, or promoted the heads (or their "acting" successors) of the Office of the Comptroller of the Currency, the Office of Thrift Supervision, the Federal Reserve, the Federal Reserve Bank of New York, and the Federal Housing Finance Agency. Several of these leaders did not simply fail as federal regulators; they actually made things worse by aggressively preempting state regulatory efforts against fraudulent and predatory mortgage lenders.

None of the reforms to date addresses the fundamental criminogenic incentive structures that have produced recurrent, intensifying financial crises. True, liar's loans have been largely eliminated, and in 2008 the Federal Reserve finally used its regulatory authority under the Home Ownership and Equity Protection Act of 1994 to regulate mortgage bankers (after most of the worst ones had failed), but none of this came soon enough to contain the current crisis and none of it will prevent the next one. The accounting control frauds merely need to switch to a different asset category for a time. ❑

Sources: George A. Akerlof, "The Market for 'Lemons': Quality Uncertainty and the Market Mechanism," *Quarterly Journal of Economics* 84(3):488–500 (1970); George A. Akerlof and Paul G. Romer, "Looting: The Economic Underworld of Bankruptcy for Profit," in W. Brainard and G. Perry, eds., *Brookings Papers on Economic Activity* 2:1-73 (1993); William K. Black, "Reexamining the Law-and-Economics Theory of Corporate Governance," *Challenge* 46(2):22-40 (2003); William K. Black, *The Best Way to Rob a Bank Is to Own One: How Corporate Executives and Politicians Looted the S&L Industry*, Austin: University of Texas Press (2005); Frank Easterbrook and Daniel Fischel, *The Economic Structure of Corporate Law*, Cambridge, Mass.: Harvard University Press (1991); National Commission on Financial Institution Reform, Recovery and Enforcement (NCFIRRE), "Origins and Causes of the S&L Debacle: A Blueprint for Reform,"Washington, D.C.:Government Printing Office (1993).

Chapter 5

MONETARY POLICY:
THE FED AND THE MONEY SUPPLY

Article 5.1

PUSHING ON STRINGS
*The explosion of U.S. banks' excess reserves since last fall
illustrates the dramatic failure of monetary policy.*

BY GERALD FRIEDMAN
May/June 2009

Monetary policy is not working. Since the economic crisis began in July 2007, the Federal Reserve has dramatically cut interest rates and pumped out over a trillion dollars, increasing the money supply by over 15% in less than two years. These vast sums have failed to revive the economy because the banks have been hoarding liquidity rather than investing it.

The Federal Reserve requires that banks hold money on reserve to back-up deposits and other bank liabilities. Beyond these required reserves, in the past banks would hold very small amounts of excess reserves, holdings that they minimized because they earn very little or no interest. Between the 1950s and September 2008,

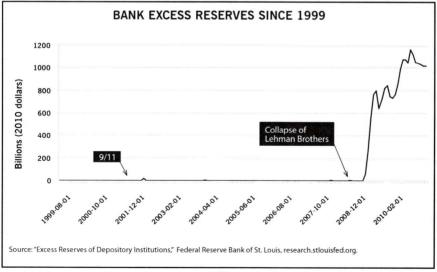

BANK EXCESS RESERVES SINCE 1999

Source: "Excess Reserves of Depository Institutions," Federal Reserve Bank of St. Louis, research.stlouisfed.org.

all the banks in the United States held more than $5 billion in excess reserves only once, after the September 11 attacks. This changed with the collapse of Lehman Brothers. Beginning with less than $2 billion in August 2008, excess reserves soared to $60 billion in September and then to $559 billion in November before rising to $798 b. in January 2009. They hovered around that level for nearly a year until jumping again in the winter of 2009-10.

This explosion of excess reserves represents a signal change in bank policy that threatens the effectiveness of monetary policy in the current economic crisis. Aware of their own financial vulnerability, even insolvency, frightened bank managers responded to the collapse of major investment houses like Lehman Brothers by grabbing and hoarding cash. (The spike in excess reserves also coincides with a change in Federal Reserve policy to begin paying interest on required and excess reserves. The rate paid, however—about 0.25%—is so low that it would not deter banks from making real investments and loans. On the other hand, the payment of interest amounts to a subsidy to banks by the Federal Reserve, and, ultimately, the United States Treasury, worth tens of billions of dollars.) At the same time, a general loss of confidence and spreading economic collapse persuaded banks that in any case there are few to whom they could lend with good confidence that they will be repaid. Clearly, our banks have decided that they need, or at least want, the money more than do consumers and productive businesses.

Banks could have been investing this money by lending to businesses needing liquidity to buy inventory or pay workers. Had they done so then monetarist economists would be shouting from the rooftops, at least in the university halls, about how monetary policy prevented another Great Depression. Instead, even the *Wall Street Journal* is proclaiming that "We're All Keynesians Again" because monetary policy has failed. Monetary authorities, the *Journal* explains, can create money but they cannot force banks to lend or to invest it in productive activities. The Federal Reserve confronts a reality shown in the graph above: it can't push on a string.

If the banks won't lend, then we need more than monetary policy to get out of the current crisis. The Obama stimulus was an appropriate response to the failure of string-pushing. But to solve a crisis this large will need much more government stimulus, and we will need programs to move liquidity from bank vaults to businesses and consumers. It may be time to stop waiting on the banks, and to start telling them what to do with our money. ❏

Article 5.2

BERNANKE'S BAD TEACHERS

BY GERALD FRIEDMAN
July/August 2009

Addressing a conference honoring Milton Friedman on his 90th birthday in 2002, the future chairman of the Federal Reserve Board, Ben Bernanke, praised Friedman's 1963 book, written with Anna J. Schwartz, *A Monetary History of the United States*. Before Friedman and Schwartz, most economists saw the Great Depression of the 1930s as proof that capitalist economies do not tend towards full-employment equilibrium. But Friedman and Schwartz restored the prior orthodoxy by blaming the Great Depression on bad monetary policy by the Federal Reserve while exonerating American capitalism. The Great Depression was "the product of the nation's monetary mechanism gone wrong."

It is significant that Friedman and Schwartz never use the phrase "the Great Depression"; instead, they speak of "the Great Contraction" of the 1930s, addressing the reduction in the money supply while treating the fall in employment and output as a secondary matter, the consequence of bad government policy that caused "the Great Contraction." By flattering the prejudices of economists who want to believe in the natural stability of free markets, Friedman and Schwartz's story has become the accepted explanation of America's worst economic disaster.

Bernanke, for one, confesses that he was inspired by their work; "hooked" in graduate school, "I have been a student of monetary economics and economic history ever since." Pushing on an open door, Friedman and Schwartz persuaded most orthodox economists, and that part of the political elite that listens to economists, that the economic collapse that began in 1929 was an accident that would have been avoided by reliance on free markets and competent Federal Reserve monetary policy.

Bernanke closed his 2002 remarks with a promise. "Let me end my talk," he said, "by abusing slightly my status as an official representative of the Federal Reserve. I would like to say to Milton and Anna: Regarding the Great Depression. You're right, we did it. We're very sorry. But thanks to you, we won't do it again."

Bernanke had five years to ponder this promise before he faced a worthy challenge; and then he acted with the vigor of a Friedman/Schwartz acolyte. When this decade's housing bubble began to deflate in early 2007, major financial firms like New Century Financial and Bear Stearns reported major losses, and confidence in the U.S. financial system began to collapse as swiftly as in 1929–33. In early August, the rising tide reached tsunami dimensions when the International Monetary Fund warned of a trillion dollars in bank losses from bad mortgages. This was Bernanke's moment. Channeling Friedman and Schwartz, careful to avoid the mistakes of 1929–33, the Federal Reserve moved quickly in early August 2007 to provide liquidity to financial markets. It acted again on August 17 by cutting mortgage rates. More cuts came on September 18, on October 31, and on December 11. Then, on December 12, the Fed announced the creation of a new facility formed with the Europeans (Term Auction Facility, or TAF) to provide $24 billion in additional liquidity to financial markets. After still more interest-rate cuts in January 2008, a new special lending facility, with $100 billion, was established on March 2, along with another $75 billion for the TAF. Then, on March 11, another new facility was created, the Term Securities Lending Facility, with $200 billion. And all this was long before the bailouts of Fannie Mae, Freddie Mac, AIG, or the federal government's trillion-dollar Troubled Asset Relief Program (TARP).

If insanity consists of doing the same thing over and over again and expecting different results, then the Federal Reserve went insane after the summer of 2007. Never before has it acted this aggressively in trying to get ahead of a financial market meltdown. Under Bernanke, the Fed has increased the money supply by over 16% in less than two years, nearly mirroring the 18% drop in the money supply in the same period after the stock market collapse of 1929. Had he lived, Milton Friedman would have been proud.

The one thing that has not changed between the crisis of 1929 and the crisis of 2007 has been the behavior of the real economy. Bernanke has avoided his predecessors' monetary policy mistakes, but he has not prevented a sharp economic downturn. Since 2007, the economy has lost nearly 6 million jobs, including over half a million in the last month. At 8.9%, the April 2009 unemployment rate unnervingly equals the 1930 figure. We have a long way to go before we hit Great Depression level unemployment; but we are only in the second year of this collapse. And monetary policy is not helping.

Here, then, we see the legacy of Friedman and Schwartz. Confident that capitalist free markets naturally move towards a full-employment equilibrium, Bernanke and his allies saw the need for only one type of government action: providing liquidity to the banks in order to strengthen confidence in the financial markets. Guided by Friedman and Schwartz, Bernanke has provided nearly unlimited aid to the Wall Street bankers and financiers responsible for our current economic collapse. And he has starved the real economy—businesses, workers, and homeowners—to avoid interfering in free markets.

Bernanke has conducted an economic policy as cruel as it has been ineffective. But the blame here goes beyond Milton Friedman and Anna Schwartz. It lies squarely on the economics profession. ❏

Article 5.3

THE BAILOUTS REVISITED
Who gets bailed out and why? Is there any alternative to "Too Big to Fail"?

BY MARTY WOLFSON
September/October 2009

Bank of America got bailed out, but Lehman Brothers was allowed to fail. The insurance company American International Group (AIG) was rescued, but in July federal authorities refused to bail out a significant lender to small and medium-sized businesses, the CIT Group (not to be confused with Citigroup, which did get bailed out).

What is the logic behind these decisions? Who is being bailed out—and who should be? The AIG story offers an instructive case study, one that sheds light on these and other questions.

Last September, the Federal Reserve Board announced that it was lending AIG up to $85 billion to prevent the firm's collapse. Unless it bailed out AIG, the Fed warned, financial markets could panic, loans could become more difficult to get, and many more businesses, jobs, and homes could be lost. To counter public anger over the bailout, the Fed argued that the ultimate beneficiaries would be the American people.

Citing proprietary information, AIG initially released few details about how it paid out the money it received. But this March, AIG's plan to pay $165 million in bonuses to employees at its Financial Products unit hit the headlines. An angry firestorm erupted: why should public bailout money be used to pay excessive bonuses to the very people who had caused the problem? U.S. officials and AIG CEO Edward Liddy denounced the payments as outrageous, but claimed they could not rescind the bonuses because they were bound by legal contracts. As it turned out, many AIG employees returned the bonuses voluntarily. And in a rare display of bipartisanship, the House of Representatives voted 328 to 93 to enact a 90% tax on bonuses paid to executives at companies that had received at least $5 billion in bailout money.

But the AIG bailout involved billions of dollars. The Financial Products employees only got millions. Who got the rest of the money? Under mounting public pressure, and after consulting with the Federal Reserve, AIG finally revealed who the beneficiaries were.

It's the Banks!

Yes, the money went primarily to large banks, those same banks that took their own large risks in the mortgage and derivatives markets and that are already receiving billions of dollars in federal bailout money. The banks are using AIG's bailout money to avoid taking losses on their contracts with the company.

Why did AIG, an insurance company, have such extensive dealings with the large banks, and why did those transactions cause so much trouble for AIG?

The story begins with AIG's London-based financial products unit, which issued a large volume of derivatives contracts known as credit default swaps (CDSs).

These were essentially insurance contracts that provided for payments to their purchasers (known as "counterparties") in the event of losses on collateralized debt obligations (CDOs), another kind of derivative. Many of the CDOs were based in complicated ways on payments on home mortgages. When the speculative housing bubble popped, mortgages could not be repaid, the CDOs lost value, and AIG was liable for payment on its CDSs.

By September 2008, AIG's situation had deteriorated to the point where its credit ratings were downgraded; this meant the company was required to post collateral on its CDS contracts, i.e., to make billions of dollars in cash payments to its counterparties to provide some protection for them against possible future losses. Despite its more than $1 trillion in assets, AIG did not have the cash. Without assistance it would have had to declare bankruptcy. After attempts to get the funding from private parties, including Goldman Sachs and JPMorgan Chase, failed, the Federal Reserve stepped in. The initial $85 billion credit line was followed by an additional $52.5 billion in credit two months later. By March 2009 the Treasury had invested $70 billion directly in the company, after which the Fed cut back its initial credit line to $25 billion.

AIG paid out those billions in several categories. Between September and December of 2008, $22.4 billion went to holders of CDSs as cash collateral. This cash was paid not only to those who sought insurance for CDOs they actually held, but also to speculators who purchased CDSs without owning the underlying securities. (Data to evaluate the extent of speculation involved have not been published.) The largest beneficiaries of these payments were Société Générale, Deutsche Bank, Goldman Sachs, and Merrill Lynch.

Second, in an effort to stop the collateral calls on these CDSs, AIG spent $27.1 billion to purchase insured CDOs from its counterparties in return for their agreement to terminate the CDSs. Again, the largest beneficiaries of this program were Société Générale, Goldman Sachs, Merrill Lynch, and Deutsche Bank.

Third, it turned out that a significant cash drain on AIG was its securities lending program. Counterparties borrowed securities from AIG and in turn posted cash collateral with AIG. When AIG got into trouble, though, the counterparties decided that they wanted their cash back and sought to return the securities they had borrowed. However, AIG had used the cash to buy mortgage-backed securities, the same securities that were falling in value as the housing market crashed. So $43.7 billion of AIG's bailout money went to those counterparties—chiefly Barclays, Deutsche Bank, BNP Paribas, Goldman Sachs, and Bank of America, with Citigroup and Merrill Lynch not too far behind.

Necessary Bailouts?

Without all that bailout money going to the banks via AIG, wouldn't the financial system have crashed, the banks have stopped lending, and the recession have gotten worse? Well, no.

At least, the banks did not need to receive all the money they did. If a regulatory agency such as the Federal Reserve or the Federal Deposit Insurance Corporation had taken over AIG, it could have used the appropriate tools to, as Fed chair Ben Bernanke told a House committee this March, "put AIG into conservatorship or receivership, unwind it slowly, protect policyholders, and impose haircuts on creditors and counterparties as appropriate. That outcome would have been far preferable to the situation we find ourselves in now." (A haircut in this context is a reduction in the amount a claimant will receive.)

A sudden and disruptive bankruptcy of AIG could indeed have caused a crash of the financial system, especially as it would have come just one day after the sudden fall of Lehman Brothers on September 15. It is the element of surprise and uncertainty that leads to panic in financial markets. On the other hand, an orderly takeover of AIG such as Bernanke described, with clear information on how much counterparties would be paid, likely could have avoided such a panic.

So why didn't the Federal Reserve take over AIG? It said it did not have the legal authority to take over a nonbank financial institution like AIG. Indeed, to his credit, Bernanke frequently asks for such authority when he testifies to Congress. So why didn't the Fed demand it last September? Wasn't such authority important enough to make it a condition of the bailout? And couldn't Congress have passed the necessary legislation as quickly as it passed the bank bailout bill last fall and the tax on AIG bonuses? Even if that took a few weeks, the Fed could have lent money to AIG to keep it from failing until it had the authority to take the company over.

Of course, the Fed already has the authority to take over large troubled banks—but refuses to use it. Now, Fed and Treasury officials claim that since all the major banks passed the recently administered "stress test," such takeovers are unnecessary. However, even some of the banks that passed the test were judged to be in need of more capital. If they can't get it from private markets then, according to Treasury Secretary Timothy Geithner, the government is prepared to supply them with the capital they need.

In other words, the federal government's strategy of transferring extraordinary amounts of public money to large banks that lose money on risky deals will continue. In fact, the same strategy is evident in the Treasury's proposed Public Private Investment Program, which uses public money to subsidize hedge funds and other private investors to buy toxic assets from the banks. The subsidy allows the private investors to pay a higher price to the banks for their toxic assets than the banks could have received otherwise.

Bail Out the People

The consistent principle behind this strategy is that no large bank can fail. This is why the relatively small CIT Group wasn't rescued from potential bankruptcy but Bank of America was. The decision not to bail out Lehman Brothers, which led to panic in financial markets, is now considered a mistake. However, policymakers drew the wrong lesson from the Lehman episode: that all large bank failures must be prevented. They failed to recognize the important distinction between disruptive and controlled failures.

Yes, there are banks that are too big to fail suddenly and disruptively. However, any insolvent bank, no matter what its size, should be taken over in a careful and deliberative way. If this means nationalization, then so be it. Continental Illinois National Bank, at the time the 11th largest bank in the United States, was essentially nationalized in 1984, ending the turmoil in financial markets that Continental's difficulties had created.

This "too big to fail" strategy equates stabilizing the financial system and promoting the people's welfare with saving the corporate existence of individual large banks. Likewise the auto companies: while GM and Chrysler have been treated much more harshly than the banks, the auto bailout was similarly designed to keep these two corporate entities alive above all else, even at the expense of thousands of autoworker jobs.

The federal government's current bank-bailout strategy may be well-meaning, but there are four problems with it. It uses public money unnecessarily and is unfair to taxpayers. It may not work: it risks keeping alive "zombie banks" that are really insolvent and unwilling to lend, a recipe for repeating Japan's "lost decade" experience. It makes financial reform going forward much more difficult. Protecting the markets for derivative products like CDOs and CDSs allows for a repeat of the risky practices that got us into the current crisis. And finally, by guaranteeing the corporate existence of large banks, we are maintaining their power and priorities and thus are not likely to see gains on predatory lending, foreclosure abuse, and other areas where reform is sorely needed.

If we want to help the people who are suffering in this crisis and recession, then we should make financial policies with them directly in mind. Just throwing money at the banks will not get the job done. ❑

Article 5.4

OF BUBBLES AND BAILOUTS

New Wall Street bailout accounting puts the numbers in perspective.

BY MARY BOTTARI
July/August 2010

The collapse of the U.S. housing bubble led directly to the largest industry bail-out in U.S. history. While it will be many years yet before we can put a hard number to the amount of taxpayer dollars actually lost in the bailout, the Center for Media and Democracy (CMD) has developed an assessment of the dollars disbursed in the bailout that graphically illustrates the extraordinary lengths to which the federal government has gone to bail out the financial sector. This original Wall Street bailout accounting includes all the major bailout programs of the U.S. Treasury Department, the Federal Reserve, and other government agencies including the FDIC and the Federal Housing Authority. The tally is updated monthly and does not include stimulus funds, unemployment insurance payments, student loans, the auto-industry bailout, or other initiatives to create jobs or support ordinary people, as other bailout tallies do. CMD's total for taxpayer dollars that have gone out the door to date: $4.7 trillion, with $2 trillion still outstanding as of June 2010. The chart below puts this extraordinary expenditure of $4.7 trillion into perspective.

This assessment of dollars disbursed demonstrates that the hotly contested $700 billion Troubled Asset Relief Program (aka "TARP") was only a small por-tion of the funds that the U.S. government rapidly deployed to aid the financial sector. Without Congressional discussion or debate, the Fed has provided the

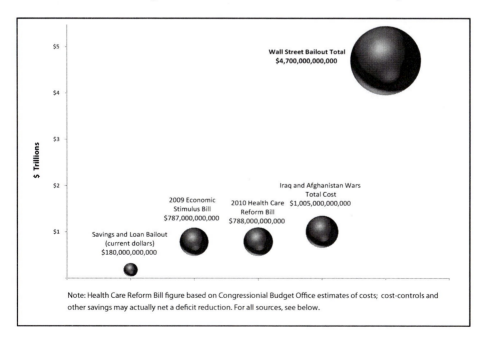

Note: Health Care Reform Bill figure based on Congressional Budget Office estimates of costs; cost-controls and other savings may actually net a deficit reduction. For all sources, see below.

bulk of the money in the form of loans and purchases of toxic assets and other securities that may—or may not—be sellable, amounting to 80% of the $4.7 trillion. And contrary to popular belief, the bailout continues unabated as the Fed pumps money into Fannie Mae and Freddie Mac, amounting to a $1.6 trillion "stealth" bailout. The full accounting for the various Fed programs is still murky, as the Fed has fought court battle after court battle to prevent the release of information regarding certain programs. Hopefully the unprecedented Federal Reserve audit provided for in the 2010 financial-reform package will finally shed light on these "Secrets of the Temple." ❏

Sources: S&L bailout: "Financial Audit: Resolution Trust Corporation's 1995 and 1994 Financial Statements" (adjusted here to 2010 dollars), gao.gov; *Economic Stimulus Bill:* Track the Money, recovery.gov; *Health Care Reform:* Congressional Budget Office, Final Reconciliation, www.cbo.gov; *Wars:* National Priorities Project, nationalpriorities.org; *Wall Street bailout:* Total Wall Street Bailout Cost Table, sourcewatch.org.

Article 5.5

FIXING THE FED

BY WILLIAM GREIDER
March 2009, The Nation

Congress and the Obama administration face an excruciating dilemma. To restore the crippled financial system, they are told, they must put up still more public money—hundreds of billions more—to rescue the largest banks and investment houses from failure. Even the dimmest politicians realize that this will further inflame the public's anger. People everywhere grasp that there is something morally wrong about bailing out the malefactors who caused this catastrophe. Yet we are told we have no choice. Unless taxpayers assume the losses for the largest financial institutions by buying their rotten assets, the banking industry will not resume normal lending and, therefore, the economy cannot recover.

This is a false dilemma. Other choices are available. Throwing more public money at essentially insolvent banks is like giving blood transfusions to a corpse and hoping for Lazarus—or, as banking analyst Christopher Whalen puts it, pouring water into a bucket with a hole in the bottom. So far Washington has poured nearly $300 billion into the bucket, and Treasury Secretary Timothy Geithner has suggested it may take another $1 trillion or more to complete the banks' resurrection. The president has budgeted $750 billion for the task. Morality aside, that sounds nutty.

Here is a very different way to understand the problem: to restore the broken financial system, Washington has to fix the Federal Reserve. Though this is not widely understood, the central bank has lost its ability to govern the credit system—the nation's overall lending and borrowing. The Fed's control mechanisms have been severely undermined by a generation of deregulation and tricky innovations that have substantially shifted credit functions from traditional banks to lightly regulated financial markets. When the Fed tried to apply its old tools, starting in the 1980s, the credit system perversely produced opposite results—an explosion of debt the policy-makers could not restrain. In its present condition, the Fed may even make things worse.

Instead of frankly acknowledging the problem, Fed governors proceeded in the past two decades to engineer exaggerated swings in monetary policy—raising interest rates, then lowering them, in widening extremes. This led to the series of bubbles in financial prices—first stocks, then housing and commodities—that collapsed with devastating consequences, climaxing in the present crisis. In other words, the central bank's weakened condition and its misguided policy decisions have been a central factor in destabilizing the American economy. More to the point, the Fed's operating disorders are directly threatening to recovery; the economy is not likely to get well if the dysfunctional Fed is not also reformed.

In this crisis the central bank has so far flooded credit markets and financial institutions with trillions of dollars in new liquidity and loan guarantees, which may help to stabilize credit markets. But the Fed has been unable to engineer what the economy desperately needs—renewed lending to companies and consumers that can finance renewed growth. The confused purpose of monetary policy stands in the way. The Fed could not restrain credit expansion when it was exploding, and now it cannot stimulate credit expansion when it is frozen.

This analysis is drawn from the work of Jane D'Arista, a reform-minded economist and retired professor with a deep conceptual understanding of money and credit. D'Arista proposes operating reforms at the central bank that would be powerfully stimulative for the economy and would also restore the Fed's role as the moderating governor of the credit system. The Fed, she argues, must create a system of control that will cover not only the commercial banks it already regulates but also the unregulated nonbank financial firms and funds that dispense credit in the "shadow banking system," like hedge funds and private equity firms. These and other important pools of capital displaced traditional bank lending with market securities and collaborated with major banks in evading prudential rules and regulatory limits. "Shadow banking" is, likewise, frozen by crisis.

Once the central bank has established balance-sheet connections to all the important financial institutions, including insurance companies and mutual funds, it can engineer the balance-sheet conditions that will virtually compel them to unfreeze lending and restart the flows of credit. This does not require spending vast sums of taxpayers' money. It does require the government to abandon the pretense that it is merely assisting troubled private enterprises in these difficult times. Government has to step up to this financial crisis and take charge of the solution, regardless of how it disposes of the so-called zombie banks. Otherwise, Washington, including the Fed, will be restoring a dysfunctional system that can lead to the same scandalous errors.

D'Arista, who taught at Boston University and years ago was on the staff of the House banking committee, is barely known among exalted policy-makers. But her work has a strong following among progressive economists, who recognize the originality of her thinking. For nearly fifteen years with the Financial Markets Center, a monetary policy think tank, D'Arista identified the systemic disorders emerging in domestic and international finance. She proposed timely reforms while admiring economists congratulated the Fed for creating an era of "great moderation." D'Arista, I should add, is also a published poet. Formal economists will scoff, but poets often see realities the bean counters fail to recognize.

Leaning With the Wind

To understand D'Arista's reform ideas, start with her devastating critique of the central bank. The Federal Reserve, she explains, has failed in its most essential function: to serve as the balance wheel that keeps economic cycles from going too far. It is supposed to be a moderating force in American capitalism on the upside and on the downside, the role popularly described as "leaning against the wind." By applying its leverage on the available supply of credit, the Fed can slow down a boom that is dangerously overwrought or, likewise, stimulate the economy if it is sinking into recession. The Fed's job, a former chairman once joked, is "to take away the punch bowl just when the party gets going." Economists know this function as "counter-cyclical policy."

The Fed not only lost control, D'Arista asserts, but its policy actions have unintentionally become "pro-cyclical"—encouraging financial excesses instead of countering the extremes. "The pattern that has developed over the last two decades," she wrote in 2008, "suggests that relying on changes in interest rates as the primary tool of monetary policy can set off pro-cyclical foreign capital flows that tend to reverse the intended result of the action taken. As a result, monetary policy can no longer reliably perform its counter-cyclical function—its *raison d'être*—and its attempts to do so may exacerbate instability."

Anyone familiar with the back-and-forth swings of monetary policy during recent years will recognize her point. On repeated occasions, the Fed set out to tighten the availability of credit but was, in effect, overruled by the credit markets, which instead expanded their lending and borrowing. The central bank would raise short-term interest rates to slow things down, only to see long-term borrowing rates fall in financial markets and negate the Fed's impact. These recurring contradictions were familiar to financial players but not to the general public. Fed chair Paul Volcker was stymied by expanding credit when he raised rates in 1982-84. His successor, Alan Greenspan, experienced the same frustration in 1994-95 (the beginning of the great debt bubble) and again at the end of the decade. The contradiction became more visible in 2005: Greenspan kept raising short-term interest rates in gradual steps, yet long-term rates kept falling, feeding the bubble of borrowing and inflating prices.

"Rather than restore its ability to exert direct influence over credit expansion and contraction," D'Arista wrote, "the Fed adhered to outdated tools and policies that became increasingly counterproductive. Too often its actions tended to exacerbate cyclical behavior in financial markets rather than exert countercyclical influence."

Most politicians do not even know the Fed is broken. The central bank's awesome authority is an intimidating mystery to most elected officials, and they typically defer to its oracular pronouncements. But the Federal Reserve, like all human institutions, is subject to folly and error. In fact, it has experienced colossal failure once before in its history. After the stock-market crash of 1929, the Fed was utterly disgraced because its response led directly to the Great Depression. Fed governors were motivated by conservative orthodoxy and their desire to protect the profitability of the largest banks, but they misunderstood the mechanics of monetary policy and also stuck to outdated theory that produced the disastrous results. D'Arista's analysis is chilling because she suggests the modern central bank, albeit in very different circumstances, may again be pursuing wrongheaded theory, blinded by similar political biases and obsolete doctrine (for the history, see my book *Secrets of the Temple: How the Federal Reserve Runs the Country*).

When deregulation began nearly thirty years ago, some leading Fed governors, including Volcker, were aware that it would weaken the Fed's hand, and they grumbled privately. The 1980 repeal of interest-rate limits meant the central bank would have to apply the brakes longer and harder to get any response from credit markets. "The only restraining influence you have left is interest rates," one influential governor complained to me, "restraint that works ultimately by bankrupting the customer." Yet the Fed supported deregulation, partly because its most important constituency, Wall Street banking and finance, pushed for it relentlessly. Working Americans felt greater pain as a result. The central bank braked the real economy's normal growth continually in a roundabout attempt to slow down the credit markets.

The central bank was undermined more gravely by further deregulation, which encouraged the migration of lending functions from traditional bank loans to market securities, like the bundled mortgage securities that are now rotten assets. Greenspan became an aggressive advocate of the so-called modernization that created Citigroup and the other hybridized mega-banks—the ones in deep trouble. Old-line banks lost market share to nonbanks, but they were allowed to collaborate with unregulated market players as a way to evade the limits on borrowing and risk-taking. In 1977 commercial banks held 56% of all financial assets. By 2007 the banking share had fallen to 24%.

The shrinkage meant the Fed was trying to control credit through a much smaller base of lending institutions. It failed utterly—witness the soaring debt burden and subsequent defaults. Greenspan, celebrated as the wise wizard, never acknowledged Wall Street's inflation of debt. Indeed, he attempted to slow down the economy in order to constrain the financial system's bubbles. That did not succeed either. As *Nation* readers may recall, I have more than once blistered the Fed's inept performance and blamed Greenspan's "free-market" ideological bias. D'Arista's analysis goes deeper and attributes the systemic malfunctioning to the Fed's weakened control mechanisms.

Central bankers attempted to fix the problem, but they may have made it worse. In the late '80s, the Fed and Wall Street leaders, joined by foreign central banks, created an international regulatory regime that requires banks to hold greater levels of capital instead of bank reserves. Reserves are the Fed's traditional cushion for ensuring the "safety and soundness" of the system. Banks were required to post non-interest-bearing accounts on their balance sheets to backstop deposits and as the means for the central bank to brake bank lending. It was assumed that the new capital requirements would do the same. Instead, the so-called Basel Accords (named for the Bank of International Settlements in Basel, Switzerland) applied very little restraint on lending but created an unintended vulnerability for banking. The new rules have acted like a pro-cyclical force—driving banks into a deeper hole as the crisis has spread because bank capital is destroyed directly by the mounting losses from market securities. The more banks lose on their rotten assets, the more capital they have to borrow from wary investors, who understandably refuse to play. That spreads the panic and failure that governments are trying to cure with public money.

Meanwhile, acting at the behest of bankers, the Fed has practically eliminated the old safety cushion by allowing reserve levels to fall nearly to zero. Bankers complained that reserves were a drag on profits and were no longer needed given the capital rules. In a shocking new arrangement, the Fed, with approval from Congress, has started to pay interest to the banks on their reserves. The commercial banks already enjoyed privileges and protections from the government that were unavailable to any other business sector. Now they insist on getting paid for their public subsidy.

How to Restore Credit—and Credibility

In the past six months, the Fed seems to have reversed course, because bank reserves suddenly jumped tenfold in September, then doubled again by December. Skeptics may conclude that it has created a safe haven for bankers. When everything else is collapsing, banks are given risk-free assets by the Fed; then they collect income from the central bank instead of lending the funds to risky customers. If reserve balances keep growing, the deal will begin to look like hoarding.

These distorted arrangements are what D'Arista thinks must be changed to break out of the downward spiral. The all-encompassing requirement she proposes— liability reserves—would give the central bank the mechanism to inject stimulus into the credit system, into banks and nonbanks alike, funding the Fed can withdraw later if the economy no longer needs a boost. The Fed would first purchase a variety of sound financial instruments from the lending institutions and create an interest-free account that would be posted as a "liability" on the institutions' balance sheets—an obligation owed to the Fed. In order to balance this liability against the loss of income-earning assets on their books, the banks and other firms would have to use the Fed-injected money to make new loans to companies and consumers or to other banks. Either way, the Fed injection would spur lending and help unlock the paralysis in credit markets.

In this arrangement, the Fed would remain in control, because all these transactions would be covered by a repurchase agreement requiring the bank to buy back what it sold to the Fed, on a fixed date and at the same price. The Fed could demand its money back or renew the repurchase contract at its choosing (a standard practice in Fed open-market operations). Thus, if the bank does nothing with its newly injected funds to create loans and generate more income, it will be in trouble when the repurchase contract comes due. The Fed is likewise inhibited from buying worthless junk from banks because that would ruin its balance sheet, the base for the money supply. Instead of earning risk-free income by holding idle reserves, the banking industry would abruptly feel the lash of the central bank's policy decisions—open up your wallets and start lending to more borrowers, or face consequences down the road.

But where does the Fed find the money to make all these transactions? Essentially, it creates the money. That is basically what occurs routinely whenever the central bank decides to inject new reserves into the banking system. It is accomplished with a computer keystroke crediting the money to the private bank's account (and money is extinguished whenever the Fed withdraws reserves). The mystery of money creation defies common reason, but it works because people believe in the results. The money supply relies on the "full faith and credit" of the society at large—pure credit from the people who use the currency. The public's faith can be enlisted in the national recovery, a far better option than spending the hard-earned money that comes from taxpayers.

D'Arista's solution would create the scaffolding to impose many other regulations on the behavior of lending and borrowing. But it does not resolve the problem of what to do with zombie banks. Some of them deserve to die—right now— because they are "too big to save," as the Levy Institute puts it. Other institutions in trouble can be tightly supervised by regulators for years to come, without relieving them of their rotten assets. This will require a kind of silent forbearance that lets the bankers slowly work off their losses, but it does not dump the losses on the public. D'Arista points out that the government has done this many times in the past. The closest comparison is the Third World debt crisis during the 1980s, when some of the same major banks were under water as Latin American nations threatened massive loan defaults. A lengthy, methodical workout was managed by the Fed under Paul Volcker. It wasn't pretty, nor was it just, but the public was not really aware of the deal-making. This time, the deal is too big to hide. People see it happening and are rightly enraged.

The great virtue of D'Arista's approach is that it's forward-looking. Her focus is not on saving the largest and most culpable names at the pinnacle of the financial system but on creating the platform for a financial order composed of thousands of smaller, more deserving institutions that can serve the country more reliably. To achieve this, the Federal Reserve will have to submit to its own reckoning. By its very design, the cloistered central bank is an offense to democratic principles—and now the Fed's secretive, unaccountable political power has failed democracy again. The question of how to democratize the temple or whether to tear it down has to be on the table too, the subject of future discussion. ❏

Article 5.6

KEYNES AND THE LIMITS OF MONETARY POLICY

BY ALEJANDRO REUSS

May/June 2009

As the United States has plunged into financial crisis and the deepest recession since the Great Depression, the U.S. Federal Reserve (the "Fed") has pursued an aggressively "expansionary" monetary policy. Monetary policy refers to government policies affecting the money supply or interest rates. Expansionary monetary policy is aimed at increasing the money supply or lowering interest rates. The idea is that, by lowering interest rates, the government can stimulate investment (such as firms' purchases of new equipment and construction of new plant). Projects that would not be profitable for a company if it had to borrow at a higher interest rate could be profitable if borrowing were less costly. Fed policymakers hope, then, that lower interest rates will encourage investment and bring about renewed economic growth.

The main interest rate the Fed targets is the "federal funds rate," the interest rate that banks charge each other for overnight loans. For all of 2006 and 2007, the federal funds rate stood at over 4%. In the course of 2008, as the financial crisis and recession grew deeper, the Fed moved aggressively to cut interest rates. By the end of the year, the federal funds rate was 0.0-0.25%, where it remains today. Even with the federal funds rate basically at zero, however, the economy has spiraled deeper into recession. GDP shrank at an annual rate of 6.2% in the fourth quarter of 2008 and the official unemployment rate climbed to 8.5% by March 2009.

Are Interest Rates Coming Down?

Firms and consumers cannot borrow at the federal funds rate. Then why does the Fed try to bring down the federal funds rate when it wants to stimulate economic activity? Fed policymakers hope that by pulling down very short-term interest rates that do not directly affect firms and consumers, they can indirectly pull down longer-term interest rates that are important to firms and consumers.

Interest rates on 30-Year Fixed-Rate mortgages have declined, reaching historic lows under 5% in March 2009. The low mortgage rates, however, may be deceptive. Mortgage lenders have generally tightened lending standards, and the low rates are only available to borrowers that banks consider very safe. Other borrowers may pay rates several percentage points higher, or be unable to borrow at all. Meanwhile, banks have raised credit-card interest rates and dramatically tightened borrowing limits.

Key corporate interest rates have not come down. Moody's AAA bond rate, an index of the interest rates on long-term bonds for low-risk corporate borrowers, was about the same in March 2009 as in January 2008 (about 5.3%). Moody's Baa bond rate, the equivalent index for higher-risk corporate borrowers, has gone from about 6.5% in January 2008 to over 8% in March 2009. The spreads between these rates and the federal funds rate have increased dramatically as the federal funds rate has fallen.

That would come as no surprise to John Maynard Keynes. Keynes argued, in *The General Theory of Employment, Interest, and Money* (1936), that during boom periods the general estimation of risk by both lenders and borrowers is "apt to become unusually and imprudently low." Lenders loan out money freely, even recklessly, accepting a low rate of interest relative to the risk involved. During crisis periods, on the other hand, lenders often become much more risk-averse, parting with their money less freely, and insisting on a higher rate of interest in exchange for the risk of not being paid back. This is sometimes known as the "flight to liquidity" or "flight to safety."

Keynes' analysis suggests that during economic crises the interest rates on assets that are considered very safe—like government bonds—are apt to go down, since people are looking to avoid losses and willing to accept a low rate of return to do so. But the interest rates on riskier assets may go up. A rise in the interest rates that firms or consumers pay would tend to deepen—rather than correct—an economic downturn.

Can't the Fed Do More?

If interest rates are not low enough to turn the economy around, then why doesn't the Fed increase the money supply some more—until interest rates are low enough? The answer is that nominal interest rates can reach a lower bound below which they cannot decline further. (The "nominal" interest rate, in contrast to the "real" interest rate, does not account for changes in the purchasing power of the dollar due to inflation.) This lower bound can be greater than 0%, but cannot be lower than 0%. The federal funds rate is now about 0%. When interest rates reach this lower limit, the economy is commonly described as being caught in a "liquidity trap."

People hold their wealth in the form of bonds rather than money because they can earn interest on bonds. For example, you may be able to buy a bond for $100 that promises a payment of $110 in one year. That gives you a 10% annual interest rate (you loaned the bond issuer $100 for a year, and at the end of the year get your $100 back plus $10 interest). That is the incentive to buy the bond instead of just holding money.

Suppose the Fed wants to lower interest rates to stimulate spending. It offers to buy government bonds (previously sold to the public) at a higher price, driving down the interest rate. For instance, the Fed might offer $110 for bonds that promise $110 in one year. If you were to buy such a bond at the new price of $110, you would receive the same amount of money back a year later. The interest rate on that bond is now 0%. The idea of the policy is that banks will sell their government bonds to the Fed at the new higher price, take the money and buy other bonds (such as those issued by corporations), driving up their price and lowering the interest rate on those bonds.

Imagine that the Fed, however, decided that an interest rate of 0% was not low enough, and decided instead to pay banks $120 for bonds that promise $110 in a year. The banks would gladly sell their bonds, so the money supply would increase. But they would not loan out the money they received at a negative interest rate (paying consumers or firms to borrow from them). They would be better off just keeping the money in their vaults. In other words, once the interest rate reaches 0%, there is nothing more that the government can do with conventional expansionary monetary policy. That is the liquidity trap—any extra liquidity (money) the Fed makes available gets trapped, instead of being loaned out.

Monetary Policy and Interest Rates Today

Economic journalists and commentators have inaccurately described "interest rates" as being at or near 0% these days. The federal funds rate has hit rock bottom, but other interest rates clearly have not. Keynes was acutely aware that, when monetary authorities limit themselves to buying short-term securities, the "effect may ... be mainly confined to the very short-term rate of interest and have but little reaction on the much more important long-term rates of interest."

In a famous passage in *The General Theory*, Keynes notes the possibility that "after the rate of interest has fallen to a certain level ... almost everyone prefers cash to holding a debt which yields so low a rate of interest." This passage is often taken to be Keynes' description of the liquidity trap. He goes on to say that he did not know of any case when this had actually happened and notes that it is not likely to happen "owing to the unwillingness of most monetary authorities to deal boldly in debts of long term." It is clear from this passage that Keynes was not describing merely a situation in which certain short-term interest rates targeted by the government (such as the federal funds rate) were pushed to their lower limits, but rather one in which all interest rates hit rock bottom—a different situation from what is commonly referred to as a "liquidity trap" today.

Keynes viewed monetary policymakers' focus on certain short-run interest rates not as an inherent limitation in monetary policy, but as a limitation in the ways monetary policy was conventionally practiced. He notes that governments did not usually buy long-term bonds and drive down long-term interest rates, but that there was no reason they could not. In March, the Fed actually began to do just that, buying billions in long-term government securities in an attempt to bring down long-term rates. The 10-Year Treasury bond rate dropped dramatically (from about 3% to 2.5%) the day the purchases began. It has increased somewhat since then, but remains lower than it was before November 2008.

Any attempt to revive private investment by manipulating interest rates, however, faces at least two additional barriers:

First, the interest rates consumers and firms pay do not move in lockstep with interest rates on government securities, either short-term or long-term. The contrast between short-term and long-term bonds is not the same as the difference between relatively safe government bonds and riskier corporate bonds or consumer loans. As we have seen, interest rates on corporate bonds have failed to decline, even as rates on long-term government bonds have declined. Banks' consumer lending standards, likewise, have tightened even as the Fed has driven down interest rates on government bonds.

Second, economic activity simply may not change dramatically in response to changes in interest rates, especially during a recession. Expectations of future sales and profits are extremely negative, so firms are dramatically slashing payrolls and investment spending. Total employment has decreased by over half a million people for each of five consecutive months from November 2008 to March 2009. Nonresidential fixed investment decreased by over 20% in the last quarter of 2008; investment in nonresidential structures by nearly 10%. Firms have inventories they cannot sell, are laying off workers, and are producing below their existing productive capacity. Most of them are not going to make large investments in new plant and equipment under such conditions.

For these reasons, Keynesian economists have advocated a very large fiscal stimulus. Fiscal policy, in contrast to monetary policy, involves government spending and taxation. A fiscal stimulus program involves increases in government spending or reductions in taxes. Keynesian economists, believing that monetary policy is not adequate to pull the economy out of its current crisis, have argued especially for a dramatic increase in government spending as the surest way to revive overall spending, production, and employment. ❑

Sources: John Maynard Keynes, *The General Theory of Employment, Interest, and Money*, First Harvest/Harcourt, 1964; The Federal Reserve Bank, Intended federal funds rate, Change and level, 1990 to present; Bureau of Economic Analysis, "News Release: Gross Domestic Product (GDP) and Corporate Profits," March 26, 2009; Bureau of Labor Statistics, Table A-12, Alternative measures of labor underutilization; Luke Mullins, "Banks Tighten Mortgage Lending Standards," *U.S. News and World Report*, February 2, 2009; Jeannine Aversa and Alan Zibel, "Mortgage rates down, but standards remain high," Associated Press, *Press-Telegram* (Long Beach, CA), March 19, 2009; Bob Tedeschi, "Mortgages: 'Cashing Out' is Now Harder," *New York Times*, March 19, 2009; Kathy Chu, "Changing credit card terms squeeze consumers," *USA Today*, December 16, 2008; Jane J. Kim, "BofA to Boost Rates on Cards With Balances," *Wall Street Journal*, April 9, 2009; Federal Reserve Bank of St. Louis, Moody's Seasoned Aaa Corporate Bond Yield; Federal Reserve Bank of St. Louis, Moody's Seasoned Baa Corporate Bond Yield; Paul Krugman (blog), Spreads, January 19, 2009; Jon Hilsenrath, *Wall Street Journal*, "Fed in Bond-Buying Binge to Spur Growth," March 19, 2009; Paul Krugman (blog), Return of depression economics, March 4, 2009; Federal Reserve Bank of St. Louis, Ten-Year Treasury Constant Maturity Rate; Bureau of Labor Statistics, Payroll Employment; Bureau of Economic Analysis, News Release: Gross Domestic Product (GDP) and Corporate Profits, March 26, 2009.

Article 5.7

BAD NEWS, GOOD NEWS, AND CLASS CONFLICT

BY JOHN MILLER
January/February 2010

SOFT ECONOMY? NO PROBLEM
Stocks have surged despite a steady increase in the unemployment rate.

First the bad news: The economy is weak. And now the good news: The economy is weak... Oddly, the same problem that worries many investors over the longer term is what encourages some for the short term: a soft economy. The reason is that an ailing economy requires the Federal Reserve to keep its short-term interest-rate targets near zero and continue pumping billions of dollars into the financial system.
  —E. S. Browning, "For Stock Investors, Bad Economy Isn't Bad,"
  Wall Street Journal, November 9, 2009

So the *Journal* has noticed that bad news on Main Street is good news on Wall Street. What's next—will the *Journal* report that "the history of all hitherto existing societies is the history of class struggle"?

But the *Journal*'s reporters still have some work to do before they earn their merit badges in Marxism. First off, any economist worth her salt will tell you that stock prices are a leading economic indicator that goes up ahead of an economic recovery. Stock prices (measured in the chart to the right as the change in the Dow Jones Industrial Average) rise in anticipation of improved corporate profits, as investors want to buy in early. And the unemployment rate is a lagging economic indicator that goes down only after the economy heats up.

Employment lags because employers do not want to hire more workers until they are sure that the expansion will hold, and in the meantime they push the existing workforce harder and expand hours. So it's not surprising to see stock prices and unemployment rates moving together as the economic recovery is just getting under way.

Second, the *Journal* attributes the correlation between rising stock prices and unemployment rates to the Fed's prodigious expansion of the money supply that pushed down interest rates. With few other good investment outlets, the plentiful supply of funds found its way into the stock market igniting a speculative boom.

There is something to that. Low interest rates have especially benefited hard-hit financial corporations. Cheap money brought these banks back to life. Rock-bottom interest rates widened their margins, the gap between short-term rates at which banks borrow and long-term interest rates at which they lend, boosting bank profits. And the price of their stocks has risen at twice the rate of the nearly year-long upswing in the market.

But that is only part of the story. As any class-conflict theorist would quickly add, the Fed could not have cut interest rates so drastically unless the threat of inflation had been tamed—especially the threat of higher wages, the largest cost of most corporations. Stock prices are up because the weak economy has put a damper on wage increases and allowed corporate cost-cutting to boost profits. As the 1970s demonstrated, inflation wipes out stock market gains.

Nothing knocks the stuffing out of workers' ability to push for higher wages more than a weak economy. Double-digit official unemployment rates have battered workers' bargaining power. As of October 2009, there were 6.3 officially unemployed workers for every job opening, the highest number since the Bureau of Labor Statistics began tracking that ratio in 2000. This is surely not the time to be asking the boss for a raise.

Don't expect the economic recovery to break the correlation between rising stock market gains and unemployment rates anytime soon by lowering unemployment rates—unless the stock market boom fizzles. A jobless recovery, a hallmark of the economic downturns of the last two decades, has transformed the correlation between rising unemployment rates and stock market prices to something other than a statistical oddity.

Even though the economy has begun growing again, the prospects for more jobs anytime soon remain bleak. Following the 2001 economic downturn, the U.S. economy continued to lose jobs for another two years and it took more than three years before the economy had replaced the jobs lost in the recession. If the current sluggish recovery creates jobs at the same pace as the last recovery, it would take 86 months, or more than 7 years, to replace the far greater number of jobs lost in this downturn than in the 2001 recession.

Now that's enough to make anyone, even a *Journal* reporter, a Marxist. ❏

Sources: E. S. Browning, "For Stock Investors, Bad Economy Isn't Bad," *WSJ*, 12/9/09; Tom Lauricella, "For Bank-Stock Gains, Hope for a Slow Recovery," *WSJ*, 11/29/09; Connor Dougherty, "Jobs Data Cloud Recovery," *WSJ*, 11/3/09; Heidi Shierholz, "6.3 job seekers per job opening in October," Economic Policy Institute, 12/08/09.

Article 5.8

PRESSURE FROM THE BOND MARKET

BY ARTHUR MacEWAN
May/June 2010

Dear Dr. Dollar:
With the crisis in Greece and other countries, commentators have said that governments are "under pressure from the bond market" or that bond markets will "punish" governments. What does this mean?
—Nikolaos Papanikolaou, Queens, N.Y.

It means that money is power.

The people and institutions that buy government bonds have the money. They are "the bond market." By telling governments the conditions under which they will make loans (i.e., buy the governments' bonds), they are able to greatly influence governments' policies.

But let's go back to some basics. When a government spends more than it takes in as taxes, it has to borrow the difference. It borrows by selling bonds, which are promises to pay. So the payments for the bonds are loans.

A government might sell a bond that is a promise to pay $103 a year from the date of sale. If bond buyers are confident that this promise will be kept and if the return they can get on other forms of investments is 3%, they will be willing to pay $100 for the bond. That is, they will be willing to loan the government $100 to be paid back in one year with 3% interest. This investment will then be providing the same return as their other investments.

But what if they are not confident that the promise will be kept? What if the investors ("the bond market") think that the government of Greece, for example, may not be able to make the payments as promised and will default on the bonds? Under these circumstances the investors will not pay $100 for the bonds that return $103 next year. They may be willing to pay only $97.

If the government then does meet its promise, the bond will provide a 6.2% rate of return. But if the "bond market's" fear of default turns out to be correct, then these bonds will have a much lower rate of return—or, in the extreme case, they will be a total loss. The "bond market" is demanding a higher rate of return to compensate for the risk. (The 3% - 6.2% difference was roughly the difference between the return on German and Greek bonds in March, when this column was written.)

However, if the Greek government—or whatever government is seeking the loans—can sell these bonds for only $97, it will have to sell more bonds in order to raise the funds it needs. In a year, the payments (that 6.2%) will place a new, severe burden on the government's budget.

So the investors say, in effect, "If you fix your policies in ways that we think make default less likely, we will buy the bonds at a higher price—not $100, but maybe at $98 or $99." It is not the ultimate purchasers of the bonds who convey this message; it is the underwriters, the large investment banks—Goldman Sachs for example. As underwriters they handle the sale of the bonds for the Greek government (and take hefty fees for this service).

Even if the investment banks were giving good, objective advice, this would be bad enough. However, the nature of their advice—"the pressure from the bond market"—is conditioned by who they are and whom they represent.

Foremost, they push for actions that will reduce the government's budget deficit, even when sensible economic policy would call for a stimulus that would be provided by maintaining or expanding the deficit. Also, investment bankers will not tell governments to raise taxes on the rich or on foreign corporations in order to reduce the deficit. Instead, they tend to advocate cutting social programs and reducing the wages of public-sector workers.

It does not require great insight to see the class bias in these sorts of actions.

Yet the whole problem does not lie with the "pressure from the bond market." The Greek government and other governments have followed policies that make them vulnerable to this sort of pressure. Unwilling or unable to tax the rich, governments borrowed to pay for their operations in good times. Having run budget deficits in good times, these authorities are in a poor position to add more debt when it is most needed—in the current recession in particular. So now, when governments really need to borrow to run deficits, they—and, more important, their people—are at the mercy of the "bond markets."

Popular protests can push back, saving some social programs and forcing governments to place a greater burden on the wealthy. A real solution, however, requires long-term action to shift power, which would change government practices and reduce vulnerability to "the pressure from the bond market." ❑

Chapter 6

FISCAL POLICY:
STIMULUS AND DEFICITS

Article 6.1

STIMULATING WHINING
The prospect of bigger government sets some in the business press howling.

BY JOHN MILLER
March/April 2009

> "Bridges to Everywhere: Making Ted Stevens jealous" (12/26/08)
>
> "Feel Like a Trillion Bucks: Only WWII was pricier than Obama's stimulus plans" (1/5/09)
>
> "States of Distress: Our local politicians want $200 billion without any shaping up" (1/26/09)
>
> "A 40-Year Wish List: You won't believe what's in that stimulus bill" (1/28/09)
>
> "The Entitlement Stimulus: More giant steps toward government health care" (1/29/09)
>
> "The Real Stimulus Burden: We'll be paying for this in many ways, for many years" (2/12/09)
>
> —Recent *Wall Street Journal* editorials opposing the Obama stimulus package

If former Senator Phil Gramm had been talking about the editors of the *Wall Street Journal*, he might have had a point when he dismissed those complaining about the recession as whiners.

To be fair, it is not the recession proper, but the prospect of a massive economic stimulus package that has set the *Journal*'s editors to whining in editorial after editorial, some seventeen and counting since December [2008].

This two-month-long crying jag seems to boil down to two central claims. First, that the package will expand public spending too much and leave us too deep in debt. Second, that government spending, inevitably wasteful, will also be ineffectual as economic stimulus when compared to tax cuts. Both these claims are misleading and at some points just plain wrong.

221

Too Big and Too Much in Debt?

At $789 billion, the final economic stimulus bill *is* big. But it's smaller than the $1.3 trillion Bush tax cut of 2001, wholeheartedly endorsed at the time by the *Journal* and other business publications. And making the Bush 2001 and 2003 tax cuts permanent, a *Journal* editorial-page mantra if there is one, would open a far larger hole in the federal budget than the stimulus package: it would cost the federal government $889 billion in lost tax revenues from 2010 to 2014, and $2.4 trillion by 2020.

If anything, the Obama stimulus package is too small. With over 3.6 million jobs already lost during the recession and more job losses sure to follow—and with over a million new entrants into the job market each year—the plan will need to provide more than its promised 3.5 million jobs.

The editors are also wringing their hands over the record federal budget deficit. Without the stimulus package, the Congressional Budget Office was already projecting the 2009 deficit to reach $1.2 trillion, or 8.4% of GDP. With the stimulus package, the deficit could reach 11% of GDP. Those are indeed record numbers for "peacetime" deficits. The Reagan deficits in their worst year reached 6% of GDP. Only World War II spending pushed the federal deficit to qualitatively different levels—30.3% of GDP in the midst of the war.

But those numbers must be viewed in context. A do-nothing strategy would saddle the federal budget with yet larger deficits as the economy and federal tax revenues fell through the floor. "Without fast action," worries Allen Sinai, chief economist at Decision Economics, "federal debt levels could soon reach 100% of GDP." And unlike World War II spending, which sparked a quarter-century boom that helped pay down that debt, a do-nothing strategy today would be followed by a depression that would impose costs far more serious than a rise in government debt.

Pork, Stimulus, and Multipliers

What is really bugging the *Journal* editors is the *content* of the stimulus package, which they describe as a 40-year Democratic Party pork wish list. Of course, pork is in the eye of the beholder. Replacing the current fleet of government vehicles with more energy-efficient ones may look to some like pure pork, as one *Journal* editorial labeled it, but to others it's worthwhile spending.

More important, these editorials claim, the spending side of the package will just not provide a stimulus. Government spending, or so the argument goes, cannot result in net economic growth because the money the government spends has to come from somewhere and that somewhere is the private sector: "For every $1 the government 'injects,' it must take $1 away from someone else—either in taxes or by issuing a bond. In either case this leaves $1 less available for private investment or consumption."

The truth of the matter is far different. Government spending, pork or otherwise, *is* stimulus.

Now, the editors are correct that the money for such spending comes from the private sector. And, private spending could provide much-needed stimulus in today's economy. What they fail to mention is that in a period of economic distress, especially one accompanied by a financial crisis, that private spending is seldom forthcoming. Workers are unemployed but so too is capital. Factories, stores, and businesses of all kinds are cutting back or shutting their doors. With the economy in dire straits, the financial system teetering, and economic anxiety widespread, businesses balk at investing, and consumers are so cautious they are retiring debt for the first time in decades.

With capital and labor standing idle, government taxing or borrowing will not create a drag on private spending. On the contrary, government spending compensates for the lack of private spending and provides the jolt necessary to bring the coding economy back to life. The real issues are how much stimulus any spending program (or tax cut) provides and how quickly it kicks in.

The amount of stimulus is exactly what is measured by Keynesian multipliers, which estimate the bang for each buck of government spending or tax cuts in terms of what it will add to GDP within a year. The multipliers above were submitted to Congress last summer by Mark Zandi, chief economist at Moody's Economy.com and an informal advisor to the McCain campaign—hardly a "tax-and-spend liberal."

Zandi's figures show that the very items championed by the *Journal*, such as making the Bush tax cuts permanent or reducing the corporate income tax, would do the least to stimulate economic growth. It's a tall order to get a corporation to invest in a crumbling economy. And personal income tax cuts, especially the Bush ones, go overwhelmingly to wealthy families who can and likely will save, rather than spend, the extra cash.

It is the programs the editors inveigh against, such as aid to state and local governments, that have the highest multipliers. These programs have the additional advantage of quick start-up and can immediately stem job losses. Sadly, it is this timely and effective spending, including on health care for the unemployed and on education, that the "centrist" Senators demanded be cut from the stimulus package, with the result that 35% of the final version is tax cuts rather than actual spending.

In addition to their disastrous social consequences, these cuts fly in the face of the lessons from Japan's prolonged economic stagnation in the 1990s. There, every dollar spent on social services like elder care and pension payments added $1.64 in additional output and every dollar of financing for schools and education delivered an even bigger $1.74 boost in output, according to a 1998 Japanese think-tank report.

The evidence is clear: Doing good—expanding health care spending, improving schools, and reducing the payroll tax burden on workers—is good for a flagging economy.

Much more needs to be done to stimulate economic justice and not just economic growth. But that surely would be life-threatening for the *Journal* editors and their ilk, whose blood pressure is already spiking from the few important but ultimately disappointing steps in that direction included in the stimulus package. ❑

Sources: Mark Zandi, "A Second Quick Boost From Government Could Spark Recovery," testimony before the U.S. House Committee on Small Business, July 24, 2008; Martin Fackler, "Japan offers lessons on stimulus spending," *New York Times*, Feb. 6, 2009; "Budget and Economic Outlook," Congressional Budget Office, Jan. 9, 2009; "Preliminary Analysis of Obama's Stimulus Tax Cuts: Could Be Worse, Could Be a Lot Better," Citizens For Tax Justice, Jan. 9, 2009.

Article 6.2

HOW I LEARNED TO STOP WORRYING
AND LOVE THE DEFICIT

BY JOHN MILLER
November/December 2009

> THE PELOSI-OBAMA DEFICITS
> [C]urrent U.S. fiscal policy is "borrow and spend" on a hyperlink. The ...
> deficit for 2009 will be "only" $1.58 trillion ... . But the Obama fiscal plan
> envisions $9 trillion in new borrowing over the next decade.
>
> We've never fretted over budget deficits, at least if they finance tax
> cuts to promote growth or spending to win a war. But these deficit esti-
> mates are driven entirely by more domestic spending and already assume
> huge new tax increases.
>
> [T]he White House still hasn't ruled out another fiscal stimulus. ...
> Obamanomics has turned into an unprecedented experiment in runaway
> government with no plan to pay for it, save, perhaps, for a big future toll
> on the middle class such as a value-added tax.
> —from an op-ed in the *Wall Street Journal*, 9/26/09

You would have thought the federal budget deficit had morphed into Dr.
Strangelove's doomsday machine from the howling that followed the publication of the Congressional Budget Office (CBO) projections in August. The *Wall
Street Journal* editors were happy to join in despite assuring readers that they are
not deficit-phobic.

But the truth is, government spending and the budget deficit it engendered
are what stood between us and an economic doomsday that would have rivaled
the Great Depression of the 1930s. In that context, the Obama budget deficits are
neither all that big nor all that bad, although they sure could have been better had
the spending priorities been more progressive. And even larger deficits could have
done—and still could do—more to alleviate the economic suffering that continues
unabated even as the economy begins to stabilize.

How Big Is It?

Even after correcting for inflation, $1.58 trillion is a record federal budget deficit.
But this eye-popping number needs to be seen in context.

A trillion and a half dollar deficit will equal 11.2% of Gross Domestic Product
(GDP) for 2009, according to CBO estimates. That too is a record for "peacetime"
deficits. The Reagan deficits in their worst year reached 6% of GDP. During World
War II, however, military spending pushed the federal deficit to qualitatively different levels, reaching 31.3% of GDP and never dropping below 14.5% during the war
years 1942 to 1945.

Whatever its size, before pinning the 2009 deficit on runaway government spending, it's important to assess how much the collapsing economy contributed to the deficit. Big government bashers like the *Journal* editors would have you believe that the entire budget deficit was brought on by reckless government spending.

That is hardly the case. The collapsing economy added more to the deficit from 2007 to 2009 than any other factor. As economic activity dried up, personal and corporate income tax revenues plummeted: this year government revenues will drop to 14.9% of GDP, their lowest level since 1950. Plus, the crashing economy automatically pushed government spending on unemployment insurance and food stamps up, further widening the deficit. Even the financial-sector bailout and the Obama stimulus package taken together did less to swell the deficit than the economic collapse did.

To control for the effect of the business cycle on the budget deficit, economists look at the so-called standardized, or cyclically adjusted, deficit—the deficit that would occur if the economy was always operating at the peak of the business cycle, in other words, at its "potential GDP." Standardized deficit figures indicate that the 2009 budget is highly stimulative but hardly disproportionate to the economic emergency it confronted. In 2009 the cyclically adjusted deficit will reach 8.6% of potential GDP, and then shrink to 3.4% by 2011, according to CBO estimates. The previous high was 4.7% in 1986 (with data back to 1962), in the midst of the "borrow and squander" Reagan years when the only emergencies facing the nation were the desire of the rich for a tax cut and the drive to expand cold-war military spending. Under George W. Bush, tax cutter to the rich *extraordinaire*, the cyclically adjusted deficit reached 3.1% in 2004, the near equal of the projected 2011 figure.

The CBO projected deficits will add $9 trillion in the next decade to the national debt, the cumulative amount of money the government will have borrowed to finance its annual deficits.

That is another frightening number, but it too needs to be seen in context. For instance, publicly held federal-government debt will reach 67.8% of GDP in 2019, according to CBO projections. That number would be the largest ratio of debt to national output since 1952, but still not in the same ballpark as the 120% figure at the end of World War II.

But absent the stimulus, the federal government would face yet larger deficits as the economy and federal tax revenues fell further. And unlike World War II spending that sparked a 20-year economic boom, a do-nothing strategy would be followed by a depression that would impose far greater costs than escalating government debt.

Domestic Spending Gone Wild?

The *Journal*'s editors are correct that it is not the size of the deficit that is worrisome, but its content—the spending and taxing policies that brought it about. But on that count they really should not be complaining, because it was the tax cuts and military spending they favor that played a decisive role in pushing the federal budget out of the black and into the red.

When the Bush administration took office in 2001, the CBO projected the federal government would run a budget *surplus* of $710 billion in FY 2009. The CBO now projects a $1.6 trillion budget deficit. The Economic Policy Institute found that the bad economy (slow growth and then the crisis) and Bush administration tax and spending policies (from the 2001 and 2003 tax cuts, to spending on Afghanistan and Iraq, to Medicare prescription drug coverage) each caused about 42% of that $2.3 trillion budget swing. Following by quite a distance were the Obama stimulus package and the TARP bailout, accounting for 7.6% and 7.7% of the budget swing respectively. Supplemental defense allocations for the Iraq and Afghanistan wars accounted for more of the increase in the deficit (9.3%) than either program.

Nor do the CBO numbers justify the editors' claim that we are about to enter a period of runaway government and deficits "driven entirely by more domestic spending." Discretionary domestic spending (federal government spending on education, housing, infrastructure, and the like) will average 3.7% of GDP over the 2010 to 2019 period—no higher than in 2008, the last year of the Bush administration. Mandatory domestic spending (including Social Security, Medicare, Medicaid, and unemployment insurance) will average 12.8% of GDP over the next ten years, 1.6 percentage points more than in 2008. Even that jump in what is, after all, already-obligated spending will account for just two-fifths of the federal deficits that the CBO projects for the next ten years. That is hardly domestic spending gone wild.

The True Test

Obama administration policies might not have been the chief cause of the 2009 deficit or the $2.3 trillion budget swing from black to red ink over this decade, nor will they commission runaway domestic spending as the editors allege.

But that alone does not make the president's policies successful. The true test of any deficit spending policy is whether it makes people better off. The policies endorsed by the editors have failed that test miserably. Worse yet, they saddled us with large deficits that now block the very spending proposals that might pass that test. Whether it is spending for universal health care, green technology, infrastructure repair, or school renovations—or help for those who have lost their homes—the new refrain is that spending must not add one dime to "the deficit."

A second dose of deficit-financed stimulus spending, a notion the editors dismiss out of hand, would create jobs desperately needed as even official unemployment rates are likely remain at double-digit levels through much of 2010.

In a very real way, our jobs and our prospects for living in a fair society depend upon learning to stop worrying and love the deficit. ❏

Sources: The Pelosi-Obama Deficits," *Wall Street Journal*, Sept. 26, 2009; "The Budget and Economic Outlook: An Update," Congressional Budget Office, August 2009; "Measuring the Effects of the Business Cycle on the Federal Budget: An Update," Congressional Budget Office, September 1, 2009; John Irons, Kathryn Edwards, and Anna Turner, "The 2009 Budget Deficit: How did we get here?" Economic Policy Institute, August 20, 2009.

Article 6.3

RESPONDING TO REVISIONISM
Fiscal stimulus and recovery during the Great Depression.

BY GERALD FRIEDMAN
May/June 2009

"THERE IS NO DISAGREEMENT THAT WE NEED ACTION BY OUR GOVERNMENT,
A RECOVERY PLAN THAT WILL HELP TO JUMPSTART THE ECONOMY."

—PRESIDENT-ELECT BARACK OBAMA, JANUARY 9, 2009

With all due respect, Mr. President, that is not true.

*Notwithstanding reports that all economists are now Keynesians and
that we all support a big increase in the burden of government, we the
undersigned do not believe that more government spending is a way to
improve economic performance. More government spending by Hoover
and Roosevelt did not pull the United States economy out of the Great
Depression in the 1930s. More government spending did not solve Japan's
"lost decade" in the 1990s. As such, it is a triumph of hope over experience to believe that more government spending will help the U.S. today. To
improve the economy, policymakers should focus on reforms that remove
impediments to work, saving, investment and production. Lower tax rates
and a reduction in the burden of government are the best ways of using
fiscal policy to boost growth.*
  —Full-page Cato Institute ad in the *New York Times* and other
  major newspapers, signed by 200 economists, late January 2009

In the 1930s, the Great Depression discredited laissez-faire capitalism, and
President Franklin Roosevelt's New Deal showed the world how an active government could restore economic vitality and improve life. Since then, the claim that
the New Deal failed to end the Great Depression of the 1930s has become central
to conservative attacks on government fiscal policy. "More government spending by
Hoover and Roosevelt," the Cato Institute claims in a recent advertisement, "did not
pull the United States economy out of the Great Depression in the 1930s."

Such claims have some superficial credibility; official statistics, not including
workers on federal emergency employment, report an unemployment rate of over 9%
at the end of Roosevelt's first term, and over 12% in 1938. Indeed, economic historians
have long recognized that New Deal fiscal policy did not end the Great Depression; E.
Cary Brown concluded in 1956, for example, that fiscal policy "seems to have been an
unsuccessful recovery device in the 'thirties." But he adds that this was "not because
it did not work but because it was not tried." Christina D. Romer, now head of the
President's Council of Economic Advisers, reached similar conclusions, also finding
that fiscal policy was applied too timidly to end the Depression.

It is a nice piece of rhetoric for the Cato Institute and other conservatives to equate FDR with the failed policies of Herbert Hoover. Yes, FDR was not fiscally aggressive enough, but Hoover did not try to stimulate the economy with government spending at all. Instead, he greeted the onset of the Great Depression by trimming government spending to maintain budget balance. He ran surpluses during the early Depression years, 1929–30, only reversing course in 1932 when plunging revenues, which fell to half the 1930 level, forced a significant deficit. On the spending side, federal consumption and investment remained stuck at 1.8% of Gross Domestic Product (GDP) throughout the Hoover years.

Thus Cato is right: Hoover's policy of budget balance and spending restraint did not stem economic collapse. Instead, under Hoover, investment fell by 81%, consumption by 18%, and the GDP by over 25%. Unemployment rose from 2.9% of the civilian labor force to 23% and 8 million jobs disappeared. By the end of his term, collapse had spread to the banking system. The economy spiraled down when banks, fearing insolvency due to mortgages and loans unlikely to be repaid in a collapsing economy, further cut back on their lending. Depositors lined up to withdraw their money, driving the banks another step towards insolvency, and dragging the economy down further.

Arriving in office in March 1933, Roosevelt intervened aggressively in financial markets, averting further panic by closing all banks for a week. Eventually, only the stronger banks were allowed to reopen, and they were backed with a new federal system of depositor insurance to prevent further bank panics. Roosevelt pressed the Federal Reserve to inaugurate a policy of monetary ease. He also significantly increased government spending, running deficits that averaged 4.8% of GDP throughout his first term. Unlike Hoover's inadvertent 1932 deficit, Roosevelt's New Deal deficits reflected significantly increased spending even with rising revenues. During FDR's first term, real federal spending was over twice the Hoover level.

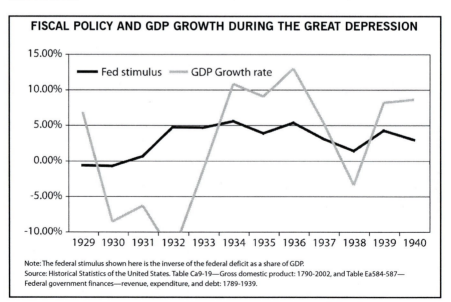

FISCAL POLICY AND GDP GROWTH DURING THE GREAT DEPRESSION

Note: The federal stimulus shown here is the inverse of the federal deficit as a share of GDP.

Source: Historical Statistics of the United States. Table Ca9-19—Gross domestic product: 1790-2002, and Table Ea584-587—Federal government finances—revenue, expenditure, and debt: 1789-1939.

Critics who charge that Roosevelt's fiscal policy failed to cure the Depression ignore the very rapid economic recovery that came with the New Deal. Stimulated by his aggressive fiscal policy, the economy boomed during Roosevelt's first term at rates about double the size of the federal deficit. GDP growth averaged over 10% a year from 1934 to 1936, and the economy grew from 62% of its trend level in 1933 to 76% in 1936. By 1937, FDR's stimulus policies had lowered unemployment to 9%, less than half the rate when he assumed office.

While the New Deal did not end the Depression, had FDR remained on course through his second term, the Depression may have ended by 1940. But instead of continuing aggressive fiscal policy, FDR reversed course in 1937, dramatically reducing the federal deficit after 1936. This plunged the economy back into a severe depression. Unemployment shot up three points to 12% in 1938. Roosevelt quickly reversed course with enough deficit spending from 1939 to 1941 to revive the economy after the 1938 dip. But it was the massive Keynesian stimulus of WWII, with deficits as high as 27% of GDP in 1943, that finally ended the Great Depression.

Even this casual examination of the 1930s discredits conservative claims about the New Deal. But there are positive lessons here as well. Far from contradicting Keynesian expectations, the New Deal shows the power of fiscal policy, both to promote recovery (1933–37 and 1939–45) and to exacerbate depression (1929–30 and 1938). The New Deal could have done better with a larger deficit. Nonetheless, when combined with reform of the financial sector and the banks, the New Deal produced four years of rapid growth that by 1937 had more than halved the unemployment rate.

Cato is right that there are lessons for the Obama administration in the New Deal experience. But the lessons are the opposite of those they would preach. First, we will need a very large stimulus, probably significantly larger than the deficit of 6–8% of GDP planned for now. Between a sharp drop in consumption with falling housing and stock market prices, falling exports, and declining investment due to the financial crisis, we may have a decline in aggregate demand of as much 20% of GDP. This would suggest the need for a deficit of between 10% and 14% of GDP, significantly more than is currently planned by the administration.

Lesson two: facing a serious economic downturn, don't declare victory prematurely. An economic collapse builds a great deal of depressing inertia that may require a long period of sustained stimulus to overcome. By prematurely moving towards budget balance in 1937–38, the Roosevelt administration prolonged the Great Depression by several years. We may hope that the Obama administration will be in a position to make that mistake in 2010 or 2011; and let us hope that they learn from the past. ❑

Sources: E. Cary Brown, "Fiscal Policy in the 'Thirties: A Reappraisal," *The American Economic Review* 46:5 (Dec. 1956), 857–79; John K. Galbraith, *The Great Crash of 1929* (New York, Harpers, 1955); Charles Kindleberger, *The World in Depression* (Berkeley, University of California Press, 1986); Christina D. Romer, "What Ended the Great Depression?" *The Journal of Economic History* 52:4 (Dec 1993), 757–84; Herbert Stein, *The Fiscal Revolution in America* (Chicago, University of Chicago Press, 1969); Peter Temin and Barrie Wigmore, "The End of One Big Deflation," *Explorations in Economic History* 27 (Oct. 1990), 483-502; Peter Temin, *Did Monetary Forces Cause the Great Depression?* (New York, Norton, 1976); Peter Temin, *Lessons from the Great Depression* (Cambridge, MIT Press, 1989).

Article 6.4

FISCAL POLICY AND "CROWDING OUT"

BY ALEJANDRO REUSS
May/June 2009

In response to the deepest recession in the United States since the Great Depression, the Obama administration proposed a large fiscal "stimulus" plan. (Fiscal policies involve government spending and taxation. A fiscal stimulus involves increases in government spending or tax cuts, or both.) The current stimulus plan, after some compromises between the Obama administration and Republicans in Congress, included both substantial tax cuts and increases in government spending. Together, they would increase the federal government deficit by over $700 billion.

A fiscal stimulus is a standard "Keynesian" response to a recession. The logic behind these policies is that recessions can be caused by insufficient total demand for goods and services. If saving (a "leakage" from demand) exceeds investment (an "injection" of demand), there will not be enough demand to buy all the goods and services that the economy is capable of producing at the "full employment" level. Some goods will go unsold, and firms will reduce output. They will cut jobs, cancel supply orders, and even close production facilities. The economy will spiral into a recession.

In standard Keynesian models, either tax cuts or increased government spending can increase total demand, and therefore total output and employment. An initial increase in spending (by either the government or the recipients of the tax cuts) results in new income for other individuals, who then go on to spend part (not all) of this income, which results in new income for still other individuals, and so on. Ultimately, this series of additions to income results in a total increase in GDP greater than the original increase in government spending or reduction in taxes. The increase in real GDP divided by the initial spending increase is called the "multiplier." The standard Keynesian view implies a multiplier greater than one.

The Conservative Critique

Conservative economists, whose intellectual heritage includes decades-old attempts to refute Keynesian theory, disagree with this view. They argue that government spending cannot possibly increase overall economic activity, and that the stimulus plan is therefore doomed to fail. This position is sometimes known as the "Treasury view" (because it mirrors the arguments of the British Treasury Department during the Great Depression) or the theory of "crowding out." The new government spending, these economists argue, "has to come from somewhere," either from higher taxes or increased government borrowing. Either way, the increase in government spending will come at the expense of private spending.

If the spending is financed by tax increases, conservative economists argue, this will reduce individuals' after-tax incomes and therefore reduce their spending. If it is financed through borrowing, the increased government demand for loans will drive up interest rates, and this will "crowd out" private investment. (Some private investment projects that would have been profitable at lower interest rates would not be profitable at the higher rates, and therefore would not be undertaken.) Extreme versions of this theory, known as "dollar-for-dollar" crowding out, argue that the decrease in private investment will exactly offset the increase in government spending, and there will be no change in the overall output of goods and services.

Government intervention is not only incapable of pulling the economy out of a recession, conservative economists argue, it is also unnecessary. If there is more saving than investment, the quantity of funds people are willing to loan out will exceed the quantity that people are willing to borrow at the current interest rate. The surplus of loanable funds will drive down the interest rate. People will save less (since the reward to saving is lower) and borrow more and invest more (since the cost of borrowing is lower), until the injection of investment and the leakage of saving are equal. In short, if insufficient demand ever caused a recession, the economy would quickly pull itself back to full employment without any need for government intervention.

Keynes' Rejoinder

Keynes agreed with the idea that saving equals investment. In his view, however, this is true not only when the economy is producing at its full-employment capacity, but also when it is producing at far less than its capacity. Keynes argued that the "classical" economists (as he called the conservative orthodoxy of his time) had an incorrect view of the relationship between interest rates and savings, and that this was at the heart of their errors about the possibility of prolonged recessions.

The classicals believed that as interest rates increased, savings would increase, and that as interest rates declined, savings would decline. Keynes agreed that this was true at "a given income," but that a change in the interest rate would also affect the amount investment and therefore the level of income. A higher interest rate, he argued, was associated with lower investment, lower incomes, and therefore lower saving; a lower interest rate, with higher investment, higher incomes, and therefore higher saving. (As people's incomes increase, they spend more *and* save more; as their incomes decline, they spend less *and* save less.) In Keynes' view, saving will equal investment whether investment and saving are both high (at or near the full employment level of output) or if investment and saving are both low (in a low-output, high-unemployment economy). In the latter case, Keynes believed, there was no guarantee that the economy would pull itself back to full employment.

Keynes was also well aware, long before his critics, that government borrowing could crowd out some private investment. In *The General Theory* itself, he noted that the effects of the government directly increasing employment on public works may include "increasing the rate of interest and so retarding investment in other directions." This does not imply, however, dollar-for-dollar crowding out. Keynes still believed, and the empirical evidence confirms, that under depression conditions an increase in government spending can result in an increase in total output larger than the initial spending increase (a multiplier greater than one).

Of Spending and Multipliers

In a recent article in the *Wall Street Journal*, conservative economist Robert Barro declares, as a "plausible starting point," that the multiplier actually equals zero. That's what the dollar-for-dollar crowding-out theory means—an increase in government spending will be matched by equal decreases in private spending, and so will have zero effect on real GDP. When it comes to estimating the multiplier, based on historical data from 1943-1944, however, Barro finds that it is not zero, but 0.8.

First, contrary to Barro's intent, this is actually a disproof of dollar-for-dollar crowding out. It means that increased government spending brought about increased real GDP, though not by as much as the spending increase. It increased the production of public-sector goods by (much) more than it reduced the production of private-sector goods. Unless one views private-sector goods as intrinsically more valuable than public-sector goods, this is not an argument against government spending.

Second, Barro chose to base his study on two years at the height of the U.S. mobilization for World War II. When the economy is at or near full employment, the multiplier is bound to be small. If all resources are already being used, the only way to produce more of some kinds of goods (say, tanks and war planes) is to produce less of some others (say, civilian cars). Keynesian economists certainly understand this. Their point, however, is that government spending creates a large multiplier effect when the economy is languishing in a recession, not when it is already at full employment.

Economist Mark Zandi of Moody's Economy.com reports much higher multipliers for government spending. Zandi estimates multipliers between 1.3 and 1.6 for federal aid to states and for government infrastructure expenditures. The multipliers are even larger for government transfers (such as food stamps or unemployment compensation) to the hardest-hit, who are likely to spend all or almost all of their increase in income. Zandi estimates these multipliers at between 1.6 and 1.8. Tax cuts for high income individuals and corporations, who are less likely to spend their additional disposable income, have the lowest multipliers—between 0.3 and 0.4.

Why the General Theory?

The conservative case against standard Keynesian fiscal stimulus policy rests on the assumption that all of the economy's resources are already being used to the fullest. Keynes titled his most important work *The General Theory* because he thought that the orthodox economics of his time confined itself to this special case, the case of an economy at full employment. He did not believe that this was generally the case in capitalist economies, and he sought to develop a theory that explained this.

The argument conservatives make against government spending—"it has to come from somewhere"—is actually no less true for private investment. If dollar-for-dollar crowding out were true, therefore, it would be just as impossible for private investment to pull the economy out of a recession. This, of course, would be nonsense unless the economy was already at full employment (and an increase in one kind of production would have to come at the expense of some other kind of production).

If the economy were already operating at full capacity—imagine a situation in which all workers are employed, factories are humming with activity 24/7, and no unused resources would be available to expand production if demand increased—the argument that increased government spending could not increase overall economic output might be plausible. But that is manifestly not the current economic situation.

Real GDP declined at an annual rate of 6.3% in the fourth quarter of 2008. The official unemployment rate surged to 8.5%, the highest rate in 30 years, in March 2009. Over 15% of workers are unemployed, have given up looking for work, or can only find part-time work. Employment is plummeting by more than half a million workers each month. A theory that assumes the economy is already at full employment can neither help us understand how we got into this hole—or how we can get out. ❑

Sources: John Maynard Keynes, *The General Theory of Employment, Interest, and Money*, 1964; Associated Press, "Obama: Stimulus lets Americans claim destiny," February 17, 2009; Paul Krugman, "A Dark Age of macroeconomics (wonkish)," January 27, 2009; J. Bradford DeLong, "More 'Treasury View' Blogging," February 5,2009; J. Bradford DeLong, "The Modern Revival of the 'Treasury View,'" January 18, 2009; Robert J. Barro,"Government Spending is No Free Lunch," *Wall Street Journal*, January 22, 2009; Paul Krugman, "War and non-remembrance," January 22, 2009; Paul Krugman, "Spending in wartime," January 23, 2009; Mark Zandi, "The Economic Impact of a $750 Billion Fiscal Stimulus Package," Moody'sEconomy.com, March 26, 2009; Bureau of Labor Statistics, Alternative measures of labor underutilization; Bureau of Labor Statistics Payroll Employment.

Article 6.5

WHY ARE THINGS GETTING WORSE AND WORSE?

BY ARTHUR MacEWAN
March/April 2009

Dear Dr. Dollar:
I learned in my economics classes that in a market economy, problems tend to be self-correcting: when a recession starts, demand weakens; then prices drop, people and firms start to buy more and the economy picks up again. So why don't we see this kind of self-correction now? Why does it seem as if things are getting worse and worse? —Corina Chio, Los Angeles, Calif.

Life, it turns out, is more complicated than the way it is presented in many economics classes. "More complicated" means different.

One of the key differences between reality and the standard fare of some economics classes is that the standard fare does not take sufficient account of the time lapses between one event and another. These time lapses don't simply mean that adjustments take longer; they mean that the nature of those adjustments can be very different from what one learns in class.

When demand weakens, prices do tend to drop, but they don't drop immediately. So, for example, when demand weakens and people buy fewer cars, candy, cardigans, and computers, the prices of these goods don't fall right away. But, facing the fall-off in purchases, the firms that make these products cut back on production and lay off workers. So demand falls further because the unemployed have less money to buy all these products. In this situation, things can get worse and worse instead of being turned around by the falling prices. Which way things go is not automatic, but depends on the seriousness of the initial fall-off in demand and the speed with which that fall-off occurs.

A further problem with the simplistic analysis presented in some classes is that people's buying decisions are based on expectations about the future as well as on current prices. If auto dealers try to get me to buy a new car by lowering the price, I am not likely to respond positively if I think I may well lose my job soon and be unable to make the monthly payments. And if my main use for a car is to get to and from work, my expectation of lack of work will make me even less likely to buy a new car regardless of the price.

Firms behave similarly. Why should a firm hire more labor or invest in new plants and equipment if the firm expects that people will be cutting back on demand for the firm's products? Even if interest rates and the prices of labor and raw materials are all falling, firms are unlikely to expand operations if they do not think the demand will be there. Indeed, it is precisely the falling prices that signal to firms that a recession is developing—which means that demand will not be there.

Worse: as prices fall, both consumers and firms are likely to delay purchases, expecting that things will be even cheaper if they wait. But by waiting (i.e., by not spending) they create even more downward pressure. So falling prices (deflation) can make things worse, not better.

And even worse still: because consumers and firms act quite rationally in this manner—cutting back expenditures because they expect things to get worse—things do get worse! When each firm and consumer acts rationally in response to negative expectations, as a group they tend to insure that those negative expectations will become reality. Individual rationality and social rationality come in conflict with one another. This phenomenon is often referred to as "the paradox of thrift." People respond to the situation by being thrifty, doing what is good for them individually. But the outcome for society as a whole is bad. Under these circumstances, there is a need for collective action—that is, government action.

This collective action—this government action—will be most effective when it takes the form of deficit spending. And this is exactly what is meant when people talk about a "stimulus package." By engaging in deficit spending the government is increasing demand more by its spending than it is reducing demand through taxes. The difference is made up by borrowing, and the "stimulus" is greatest when the borrowed money would not have been spent—and it would not have been spent precisely because the private firms and individuals who have the money (the money the government is borrowing) also have poor expectations about the future.

Not every economic downturn gets worse and worse. There can be a process of self-correction. But when a serious downturn develops—as is the case right now—self-correction is not going to solve our problems. The collective action that we can take through government is essential to avoid economic disaster. ❏

Article 6.6

THE ECONOMIC CRISIS IN THE STATES

BY GERALD FRIEDMAN
October 2009

In recent recessions, state and local governments have been among the few sources of economic stability and employment growth. This is why the recent fall in government employment, including a loss of 37,000 local government jobs in September 2009, has alarmed, even shocked, observers. But without serious action, a sharp drop in government employment, with a loss of a million jobs or more, is what we can expect over the next year. This has implications for the economy as a whole and also for the well-being of large parts of the American public who depend on state and local government services. Two intrinsic features of the American system of government come together to threaten a social disaster: the limited capacity of state and local governments to spend beyond their immediate revenues even in the harshest economic crises, and our peculiar federal system in which education and social services are largely funded by local and state authorities rather than by the federal government, with its deep pockets and ability to spend beyond its revenues as needed to maintain existing services.

When tax revenues fall and demands for services rise during an economic downturn, the federal government sells bonds to cover its expenses, bonds often paid for with money printed by the Federal Reserve. States cannot do this. In 49 states, state constitutions requires a balanced budget, a requirement further enforced by bond-rating agencies and financial institutions, which threaten to lower the rating and raise the interest rate on bonds issued by states facing declining revenues and rising spending.

Together, constitutional requirements and the pressure of bond-raters require that state governments respond to economic recessions and declines in revenue with budget cuts. This makes state and local spending *pro-cyclical,* moving up or down *with* the economy, reinforcing downturns rather than acting *counter-cyclically* to

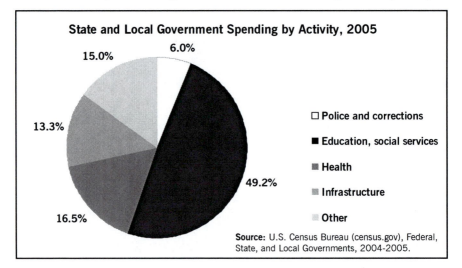

State and Local Government Spending by Activity, 2005

- 6.0%
- 15.0%
- 13.3%
- 49.2%
- 16.5%

□ Police and corrections

■ Education, social services

▨ Health

▨ Infrastructure

▨ Other

Source: U.S. Census Bureau (census.gov), Federal, State, and Local Governments, 2004-2005.

ameliorate economic recessions. Not only is pro-cyclical spending by states and localities bad macroeconomic policy, but a peculiar feature of American federalism ensures that reducing spending during economic downturns is especially hard on investments in infrastructure, human capital, and the welfare of needy Americans. This is because problematic funding of states and local governments parallels a division of labor in the American system. With its deep pockets and elastic spending, the federal government is responsible for the military and for a few special programs, notably retirement pensions and health care for the elderly. States and localities, with rigid restrictions on spending, are responsible for education, local infrastructure, and social services. Federal spending, for example, accounts for only 8% of education spending in the United States, compared with nearly 83% from states and localities. When economic circumstances drive down tax revenues and increase the need for services, there is always money for the federally-funded military; but states and localities have to scramble to coordinate spending cuts and tax increases to balance budgets. They reduce social services, hitting the poor and middle-class, the young, the needy, and the disabled, just when the need for services is greatest.

The crisis facing the states has just begun and threatens to get worse, much worse. Special circumstances delayed the collapse of state and local government services in the current crisis. While state tax revenues are running more than 10% below last year's level, and have already fallen to the 2005 level, most states have been able to balance their budgets without draconian cuts because of two special circumstances. First, heading into the recession, 41 states had "rainy day" funds with an average balance of nearly 3% of revenue. These funds, mostly exhausted now, helped to cushion the initial decline in revenue. Second, the federal government came to the rescue with the American Recovery and Reinvestment Act (ARRA). Under the ARRA, the "Obama Stimulus" program, the federal government in effect shared its elastic borrowing capacity with states by granting them nearly $100 billion in immediate fiscal relief with another $230 billion in supplemental and competitive grants.

Rainy day funds and ARRA allowed most states to balance their budgets in the past two fiscal years with cuts of "only" $168 billion. Unfortunately, both the rainy

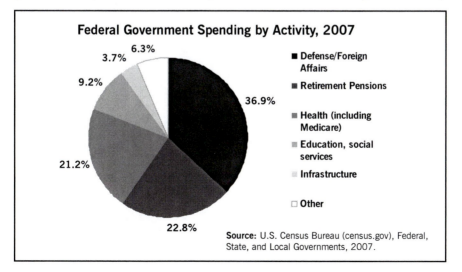

Federal Government Spending by Activity, 2007

6.3%
3.7%
9.2%
21.2%
22.8%
36.9%

- Defense/Foreign Affairs
- Retirement Pensions
- Health (including Medicare)
- Education, social services
- Infrastructure
- Other

Source: U.S. Census Bureau (census.gov), Federal, State, and Local Governments, 2007.

day funds and the ARRA will be exhausted long before the recovery of state and local revenues. Under an optimistic forecast, the combination of declining revenues, rising demand for services, and the withdrawal of ARRA aid will force states to cut as much as 4% of their spending each fiscal year through 2013; if the economic recovery slows the cuts will have to be as much as 8% of spending. Even this forecast may be too optimistic. A recent report by the Center on Budget and Policy Priorities finds that revenue shortfalls in the *current* fiscal year are forcing 26 states to reopen their budgets and cut an additional $16 billion, or 4%. In the current fiscal year, 48 states have already reduced spending or increased revenues by $178 billion, or 26%, the largest budget gap on record. In the next fiscal year, 2011, budget gaps are projected to be $80 billion for 35 states, or 14%, and this total is likely to grow to over $180 billion as revenues continue to deteriorate. Deficits of this magnitude will require further state and local spending cuts and revenue enhancements made even more punishing than previous rounds because of the exhaustion of rainy-day funds and ARRA aid. Ironically, by reducing employment and spending, cuts of these magnitudes will slow any recovery, making the less-optimistic forecast more likely.

The division of labor in American federalism creates the fiscal pressure causing these draconian budget cuts and places them squarely on the infrastructure investments and education and social services financed at the state and local levels. There is nothing new in this depressing analysis. Early-19th-century politicians like John Quincy Adams and Henry Clay, for example, wanted the federal government to use its more elastic and expansive revenue stream to provide more adequate funding for education and welfare as part of a broad national program of internal improvements. Before the Civil War, their proposals were rejected by southern politicians who dominated the federal government. Southern secession in 1860-61 opened the door to a more active federal role. Under the Morrill Act of 1862, the federal government provided land grants to establish public universities in every state, and in 1867, a federal Department of Education was formed building on the work of the Freedman's Bureau and charged with promoting education and learning.

Over the next 20 years, measures were proposed to expand the federal role in education, including the 1870 Hoar Bill, sponsored by Massachusetts Senator

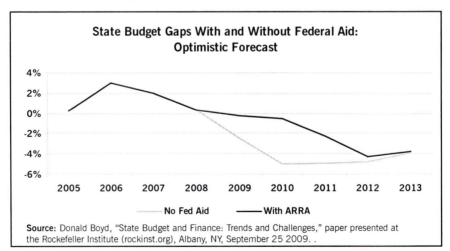

State Budget Gaps With and Without Federal Aid: Optimistic Forecast

Source: Donald Boyd, "State Budget and Finance: Trends and Challenges," paper presented at the Rockefeller Institute (rockinst.org), Albany, NY, September 25 2009. .

George Hoar, to "compel by national authority the establishment of a thorough and efficient system of public instruction throughout the whole country." The most sustained efforts were led by Senator Henry W. Blair of New Hampshire whose so-called Blair Bill would have provided federal funds to states for education with extra funds provided states with high levels of illiteracy. Despite this provision, that would have sent additional funds to the South, white southern Democrats repeatedly voted down Blair's bill because it required that funds be expended on free common schools to *all children* without distinction of race or color. Some northerners resisted this expansion of federal spending, especially on southern schools. The Blair Bill was anathema to southern planters and politicians who feared, as one put it, "the difficulty of controlling more educated Negroes."

The determination of southern politicians to control their African American and poor white labor force led them to stymie efforts to use federal funds to expand access to education and, later, to social welfare benefits. The Hoar Bill or the Blair Bill *could* have been enacted; we *could* finance education or welfare nationally using the relatively abundant and elastic federal tax system. Their defeat, and the defeat of later measures, left the financing of education and welfare on the state and local level because it was a decision made by politicians to accommodate entrenched local oligarchs, especially southern planters. Had the American left been politically stronger or legislatively more astute, we could have had a different fiscal regime. Maybe we still can. And then maybe we'll have adequate financing of education and human services; and the Pentagon will have to hold bake sales to buy bombers.

The mismatch of needs and revenues on the state and local level threatens social services and endangers needed investments in health, in transportation, in green technology, and elsewhere. If we allow this to happen, cuts in state and local spending will chase the economy down the hill to economic recession or worse. All of us, including the needy, the poor, the young, the disabled, and the sick will pay the price. Building on the ARRA program, we can insist on a renewed program of federal support for states and localities. This would avoid the worst effects of the current crisis but it would be better to eliminate the problem, the standing threat of local fiscal failure to essential programs of social insurance and investment, with a renewed

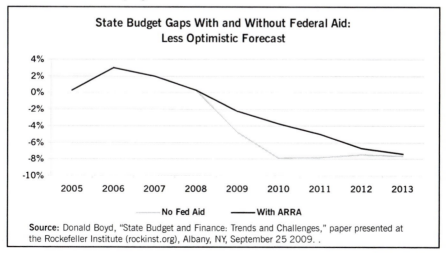

State Budget Gaps With and Without Federal Aid: Less Optimistic Forecast

No Fed Aid   With ARRA

Source: Donald Boyd, "State Budget and Finance: Trends and Challenges," paper presented at the Rockefeller Institute (rockinst.org), Albany, NY, September 25 2009. .

revenue sharing program which would place a floor under state revenues. Even better would be to fund these programs with federal dollars, spreading the umbrella of the federal government's elastic revenue stream over them so as to give all Americans equal access to schooling and social services, regardless of what states they live in. In this way, we would give education, health care, the environment, and other services the same fiscal priority we now give the military.

For two centuries, racists used a "states' rights" to block national programs. By dismantling segregation, the Civil Rights movement eliminated this obstacle. We now have the opportunity to bring Lincoln's "new birth of freedom" to all Americans by moving our federal system away from the shadow of states' rights and, as the late Hubert Humphrey said, to "walk forthrightly into the bright sunshine of human rights." It is only our political failure that leaves infrastructure, social services, and education on the chopping block to be decimated by state and local budget balancers who are bound to match expanding spending needs with shrinking revenues. ❑

Sources: Richard Franklin Bensel, *Yankee Leviathan: The Origins of Central State Authority in America, 1859-1877*, Cambridge University Press, 1990; Michael K. Browon, *Race, Money, and the American Welfare State*, Cornell University Press, 1999; R. Freeman Butts, *A History of Education in American Culture*, Holt, 1953; Lawrence A. Cremin, *The American Common School: An Historic Conception*, Teachers College, Columbia University, 1951; Donald Boyd, "Coping with Effects of Recession in the States," Nelson A. Rockefeller Institute, www.rockinst.org, July 27, 2009; Hubert Humphrey, "Hubert Humphrey's 1948 Speech on Civil Rights," available through the Minnesota Historical Society, www.mnhs.org; Gordon Canfield Lee, *The Struggle for Federal Aid, First Phase; a History of the Attempts to Obtain Federal Aid for the Common Schools, 1870-1890*, Teachers College, Columbia University, 1949; Jill S. Quadagno, *The Color of Welfare: How Racism Undermined the War on Poverty*, Oxford University Press, 1994; Jill S. Quadagno, *The Transformation of Old Age Security: Class and Politics in the American Welfare State*, University of Chicago Press, 1988; Center on Budget and Policy Priorities, "Recession Continues to Batter State Budgets; State Responses Could Slow Recovery," October 20, 2009, www.cbpp.org; Elaine Maag and Alison McCarthy, "State Rainy Day Funds," the Urban Institute, www.urban.org; Donald J. Boyd and Lucy Dadayan, "State Tax Decline in Early 2009 Was the Sharpest on Record," Nelson A. Rockefeller Institute of Government, www.rockinst.org, July 17, 2009; "10 Facts About K-12 Education Funding," U.S. Department of Education, www.ed.gov.

Article 6.7

STATE BUDGET BLUES
Looking for Funds in All the Wrong Places

BY MARIANNE HILL
November/December 2009

California's fiscal woes may have grabbed the national headlines, but states across the nation are slashing budgets to close gaps that are averaging a jaw-dropping 24% this year. Even before the economy nose-dived in late 2008, the Government Accountability Office (GAO) was warning states to expect growing revenue short-falls over the coming decade. The recession and the staggering increase in the federal debt have worsened the GAO's predictions.

The GAO now estimates that, if programs are maintained at current levels, state and local revenues will fall short by an average of 7.6% annually over the coming decade.

To close the yawning gaps in their budgets, states are currently relying on stimulus funds and budget cuts. But fewer federal funds will be there to help as the country begins to pay down the huge national debt. Experts anticipate that federal dollars going to state programs will be scaled back, with funding levels increasing only in targeted areas such as health care and energy. So shortfalls in state budgets will continue for years to come unless states either enact more cuts or update their antiquated tax systems.

In fact, it is past time to overhaul current tax systems. Neither the federal government nor state and local governments are adequately capturing revenue from the high-income, high-growth segments of the economy. At the same time, lower- and middle-income families are unfairly burdened.

Trends in expenditures account for part of the problem. State and local spending on health care for Medicaid, employees, and retirees is projected to significantly outpace revenues. Federal grants-in-aid, which finance about 20% of state and local budget outlays, are dominated by grants to Medicaid. Half of federal grants-in-aid go to Medicaid and this proportion has been increasing with rising enrollment and the growing cost of health care. By 2012, 60% of grants-in-aid will be going to Medicaid, leaving fewer federal dollars for other programs.

Health care reform that succeeds in reducing the cost of medical services while expanding coverage could improve the states' budgetary outlook, but the outlook for revenue collections would remain problematic. The major factor is the erosion of state tax bases, particularly of the sales tax, which accounts for about a third of state and local revenues.

The fiscal crisis in the states will have a long-term impact on our quality of life since state and local governments, with federal assistance, provide most of the public services we receive. They employ almost seven times as many people as does the federal government, and state and local expenditures on public services are greater than federal expenditures, if Medicare and military spending are excluded.

The growing demands on the states are not taken into account by the GAO study, by the way, which only considers the cost of maintaining current service levels. The future scenario for state budgets, then, is likely to be more dire than the GAO predicts. Even with health care reform and improvements in revenue collection and program efficiency, the states will need new revenue sources, better aligned with their income bases, to carry out their vital role in the economy.

Traditionally, states have turned to the sales tax when seeking additional funds. The sales tax is the largest single revenue source for state and local budgets, accounting for a third of tax receipts. Statewide sales tax rates range from a low of 0% in the five states with no general sales tax to 7.25% in California. Recent expansions of the sales tax include the increased taxation of services and of Internet sales.

This reliance on the sales tax is increasingly a liability, however, since the most rapidly expanding industries are in services that are often not subject to the sales tax, such as health care, education. and financial services (credit cards, loans, etc.). A few states are now taxing gross receipts of all businesses to capture service industries, but economists are generally appalled: firms with high input costs but low profit margins can be crippled by a tax on receipts rather than on income net of costs.

Personal and corporate incomes, other potential revenue sources, offer an expanding tax base, but increases in exemptions and deductions have cut into taxable income. (Personal income taxes accounted for about 24% of state and local tax receipts, corporate income taxes 5%, and property taxes 30%, in 2007.)

How states raise needed revenues can be as critical as how they are spent. Equity—basing taxes on the ability to pay—is a prime concern: equity aids both revenue collections and the economic well-being of families. It is especially urgent given recent income trends.

Since the 1980s, progress in raising living standards has been hindered both in the states and nationally by rising income inequality. Output per employee more than doubled in the United States from 1960 to 2005, but earnings did not. In fact, real hourly earnings in 2005 were lower than in 1967, after adjusting for inflation.

The picture is very different for those at the top of the corporate ladder. The typical S&P 500 CEO had an income about 42 times as high as that of the average worker in 1980, but now this CEO gets 344 times as much, according to the Institute for Policy Studies. The top 5% of families currently have incomes about 20 times as high as the bottom 20% at present, up from 11 times as high in 1979.

These figures help to explain why the poverty rate in 1988, 1998, and 2008 remained stubbornly at 13%, despite rising average incomes.

Taxes can increase inequality. Sales taxes, for example, absorb a greater percentage of the income of low-income families than of high-income families, and so increase inequality. Figures on federal corporate taxation are especially disturbing for this reason: 30% of U.S. corporations with gross receipts of $50 million or more paid no taxes over the 1998-2005 period, according to the GAO. If smaller corporations are included as well, 65% paid no U.S. corporate income tax.

Corporations also avoid state taxes. The Multistate Tax Commission found that large, multi-state corporations avoided about $7 billion in state corporate taxes, due to such tactics as shifting their reported profits from high-tax states to low-tax states.

To combat such problems, 20-plus states have banded together and use combined reporting. This requires a multi-state corporation to add together the profits of all its subsidiaries, regardless of their location, into one report. The report provides each state with information needed to levy the appropriate tax, based on individual state tax provisions.

Combined reporting also makes it more difficult for companies to avoid reporting income altogether: one study of 252 large corporations found that in 2003 those companies on average failed to include two-thirds of their actual U.S. pretax profits on their state tax returns. The study found, for example, that Wal-Mart reported $77 billion in pretax profits to its shareholders but paid state income taxes on about half that sum.

The National Association of State Budget Officers suggests another reform: monitoring tax breaks offered to corporations. It notes that some states impose a surcharge on tax breaks offered under business incentive programs if the return to the state from these tax breaks is not as great as expected.

Other reforms could improve the states' revenue outlook. Currently, the personal income tax rate paid by those in the top bracket ranges from Vermont's 9.5% to zero: there are nine states with no personal income tax. An increase in the number of brackets and in rates could boost revenues, while increasing basic exemptions at the same time would protect middle-income families. The tax break on capital gains should be examined.

There are nontraditional means of raising funds as well. For example, penalties and fines for fraud and violations of labor and environmental regulations can be imposed or increased. A carbon emissions tax could be a major revenue source.

Stable, equitable revenue sources are found when taxes are levied in line with the distribution of income and wealth in a state. Taxes like the sales tax that push low-income families further into poverty don't make sense when alternative revenue sources are available that are both more lucrative and more equitable. It is time to look to these sources to close shortfalls in state and local budgets. ❏

Sources: Center for Budget and Policy Priorities; Citizens for Tax Justice; Economic Policy Institute, Institute on Taxation and Economic Policy, *State of Working America 2007*; *Economic Report of the President 2008*; Federation of Tax Administrators; GAO documents GAO-09-210T, GAO-08-957 and GAO-07-1080SP.

Article 6.8

MYTHS OF THE DEFICIT

BY MARTY WOLFSON
May/June 2010

Nearly 15 million people are officially counted as unemployed in the United States, and more than 6 million of these have been unemployed for more than 26 weeks. Another 11 million are the "hidden" unemployed: jobless workers who have given up looking for work and part-time workers who want full-time jobs. Unemployment has especially affected minority communities; the official black teenage unemployment rate, for example, stands at 42%.

The *moral* case for urgently addressing the unemployment issue is clear. The costs of unemployment, especially prolonged unemployment, are devastating. Self-worth is questioned, homes are lost, families stressed, communities disrupted. Across the land, the number one issue is jobs, jobs, jobs.

The *economic* case for how to address the jobs issue is also clear. As Keynes argued during the Great Depression, federal government spending can directly create jobs. And the $787 billion stimulus package approved by Congress in February 2009 did help pull the economy back from disaster, when it was shedding 20,000 jobs *a day* in late 2008 and early 2009.

But we still have a long way to go. To get back just to where we were when the recession began in December 2007, the economy would need to create 11.1 million jobs: 8.4 million to replace the jobs lost and 2.7 million to absorb new workers who have entered the labor market since then.

Despite a pickup of economic activity recently, long-term projections are that the unemployment rate will fall only gradually over the next several years. The Congressional Budget Office forecast for the unemployment rate for 2012 is a stubbornly high 8%. So why are we not moving more aggressively to reduce unemployment?

The *ideological* opposition to government spending remains a major obstacle. There are those who see an increase in the role of government as something to be avoided at all costs—even if the cost is the jobs of the unemployed.

Even among those who are not subject to such ideological blinders, there is still a *political* argument that resonates strongly. The argument is that government spending to create jobs will create large budget deficits, which will have terrible consequences for the American people. Politicians, pundits, and other commentators—in a frenzied drumbeat of speeches, op-eds, and articles—have asserted that the most urgent priority *now* is to reduce the budget deficit.

It is important to note that this argument is focused on current policy, not just the long-term budgetary situation. There is room for debate about long-term budget deficits, but these are affected more by the explosive growth of health-care costs than by government discretionary spending to create jobs.

Why, then, are people taken in by an argument that says it is more important to reduce the budget deficit now than for the government to spend money to create jobs? Two myths constantly repeated in the public debate have contributed to this situation:

1) *Families can't spend more than they have; neither should the government.*

It seems to be common sense that a family can't spend more than it has. But of course that is exactly what the family does when it takes out a car loan or a student loan, or does any other kind of borrowing. The government, just like families, should be able to borrow. The real issue is whether or not the debt is affordable. For families, and for the government, that depends on the size of the debt relative to the income available to service the debt; it also depends on the nature of the borrowing.

For the federal government, the relevant debt-income measure is the ratio of outstanding debt of the federal government to gross domestic product. (*Outstanding debt* is the total amount owed at a particular time, roughly the result of debt accumulated over time by annual budget deficits; GDP, the value of goods and services produced, is equal to total income.) In 2009, this ratio was 53%. Although higher than the recent low point of 33% at the end of the 1990s expansion, the ratio in 2009 was still far lower than the record peak of 109% in 1946—after which the U.S. economy in the post-World War II period experienced the strongest economic growth in its history.

The U.S. ratio of 53% actually compares favorably to those of other advanced industrial countries. For example, IMF data indicate the following debt-to-GDP ratios for 2009: France (67%), Germany (70%), Japan (105%), and Italy (113%).

The nature of the borrowing also affects affordability. If a family runs up credit-card debt to finance a lavish lifestyle, after the fancy dinners are eaten the family still needs to figure out how to pay its debt. But if a family member borrows to buy a car to get to work, presumably the job will help provide the income to service the debt.

Likewise for the federal government: If the government borrows to finance tax cuts for the rich, and the rich use their tax cuts to purchase imported luxury goods, then the government still needs to figure out how to pay its debt. On the other hand, if the government borrows to put people to work creating long-term investments that increase the productivity of the U.S. economy, like infrastructure and education, then it is in a much better situation. The income generated by the more productive economy, as well as by the newly employed workers, can help to provide the tax revenue to service the debt.

So it is a myth to say that families can't spend more than they have. They can, and so can the government. And both are justified in borrowing if the size of the debt is manageable and if so doing helps to provide the income necessary to service the debt.

2) *Large budget deficits create a burden for our grandchildren.*

This is the issue that probably resonates most forcefully with public opinion. If we in the current generation run up a big debt, it may be left to our grandchildren to repay. The only difficulty with this reasoning is that the grandchildren who may be asked to repay the debt are paying it to other grandchildren. When the government incurs a debt, it issues a bond, an obligation to repay the debt to the holder of the bond. If the holders of the bond are U.S. residents, then paying off the debt means paying money to U.S. residents. In other words, debt that is an obligation of future U.S. taxpayers is also a source of income to the U.S. holders of that debt. Thus there is not a generational burden that we today are imposing on "our grandchildren" as a collective entity.

Of course, the obvious exception to this reasoning is the debt held by non-U.S. residents. In that case, it is indeed true that future generations of Americans will need to pay interest to foreign holders of U.S. debt. But the basic reason for this situation is the trade deficit, not the budget deficit. When we pay more for imports than we receive from exports, and when U.S. multinational companies ship production abroad to take advantage of low-cost labor, foreigners are provided with dollars that they can use to invest in U.S. assets. And the real burden that this causes is the same whether foreigners invest in U.S. government debt or whether they invest in U.S. companies, real estate, the U.S. stock market, etc.

Borrowing by the federal government can in some situations create a real burden, but it has less to do with generational transfers and more to do with distributional issues and the nature of economic growth (discussed above). If the grandchildren who are taxed in the future to pay off government debt are poorer than the grandchildren who are paid, the distribution of income becomes more unequal.

Also, cutting taxes for the rich and spending money on wars in Iraq and Afghanistan do not lead to the kind of productive economic growth that generates strong tax revenue. So financing these by debt *does* create a real distributional burden: The rich and military contractors benefit, but the losers are those who might be taxed, or those whose government programs might be squeezed out of the budget, because of the need to pay interest on the debt.

Borrowing money to put people back to work does make sense. It helps people most in need, the unemployed. It provides them with income that they can use to pay taxes and to buy goods and services that create more jobs, more income, and more tax revenue. Indeed, our inability thus far to seriously tackle the unemployment problem is what has worsened the budget problem, as tax receipts have fallen and spending for unemployment benefits and food stamps have risen. An analysis by the Economic Policy Institute reveals that the largest source of the 2009 budget deficit (42%) was actually the recession itself.

We *will* leave a burden for our grandchildren if we don't address the urgent problem of unemployment, if we let parents and grandparents suffer the indignities and financial hardships of lost jobs. We *will* leave a burden for our grandchildren if we don't rebuild our aging infrastructure, break our reliance on fossil fuels, and provide all our children with an excellent education. It makes perfect sense to borrow money now to address these problems, and we shouldn't let myths about budget deficits get in the way of meeting these real needs. ❑

Sources: Congressional Budget Office, "The Budget and Economic Outlook: Fiscal Years 2010 to 2020," January 2010; John Irons, Kathryn Edwards, and Anna Turner, "The 2009 Budget Deficit: How Did We Get Here?" Economic Policy Institute, August 20, 2009; Dean Baker, "The Budget Deficit Scare Story and the Great Recession," Center for Economic and Policy Research, February 2010; Office of Management and Budget, "The President's Budget For Fiscal Year 2011, Historical Tables: Table 7.1, Federal Debt at the End of Year: 1940-2015," February 2010.

Article 6.9

DEFICITS: REAL ISSUE, PHONY DEBATES
What's at Stake on Either Side of the Class Divide

BY RICHARD D. WOLFF
November/December 2010

Deficits have now risen, yet again, to headline status. Conservatives inside and right of the Republican Party frame the national debates by attacking deficits. They want to reduce them by cutting government spending. Liberals respond, as usual, by insisting that overcoming the crisis requires big government spending ("stimulus") and hence big deficits. Most Americans watch the politicians' conflicts with mixtures of confusion, disinterest, and disdain. Yet deficits pose a real issue for all citizens, even though the debates among politicians and their economist advisors miss, ignore, or hide that issue.

When the federal government raises less in taxes than it spends, it must borrow the difference. Such annual borrowing is each year's deficit. The U.S. Treasury borrows that money by selling bonds, federal IOUs, to the lenders. The accumulation of annual deficits comprises the national debt, the total of outstanding U.S. treasury bonds. So the first and simplest questions about deficits are (1) why does the federal government choose to borrow rather than to raise taxes? and (2) why does it borrow rather than cut its expenditures? The twin answers are profoundly political. Elected officials are afraid to raise taxes on business and the rich because their profits and great personal wealth can then finance the defeat of officials who do that. Cutting government spending that benefits business and the rich is avoided for the same reason. As the tax burden shifted increasingly onto middle- and lower-income citizens for decades, elected officials have faced rising tax revolts over recent years coupled with demands for more government services and supports.

In the United States—as in most capitalist countries—business and the rich, on one side, and the middle-income and poor on the other, have placed the same demands on the government budget. Each side has wanted *more* government spending on what it needs and *less* taxes on its incomes. Both parties thus fear raising taxes or cutting spending on the masses because that risks electoral defeats. This has been a very real, basic, and socially disruptive contradiction built into capitalist systems.

These days, business and the rich want *both* massive government supports to overcome the current crisis *as well as* their usual government benefits. The latter include government activities abroad—including wars—that secure export markets and access to crucial imports (e.g., the needed quantities and prices of business inputs and means of consumption not domestically available). They also demand the subsidies typically provided to agricultural enterprises, transport companies, defense producers, and so on, as well as tax reductions offered for various kinds of investments. Businesses press government to maintain or expand roads, harbors, airports, schools, mass transportation systems, and research institutes crucial for their enterprises' profits. Wealthy individuals want government spending on the police and judicial systems that protect their wealth.

Business and the rich likewise want the government not to raise their taxes. Businesses seek to keep in place their legal opportunities to evade taxes on profits (by means of offshore operations, internal transfer invoicing, etc.). Business and the rich in the United States want donations to their own foundations, to rich universities, art institutions, and their favorite charities to remain subsidized by generous federal tax reductions granted for such donations. They also currently demand the continuation of Bush-era tax exemptions and reductions on taxes on their incomes and on the estates they leave.

Middle-income and poorer Americans demand government spending for their unemployment insurance, to prevent or soften the blow of home foreclosures, to provide low-interest mortgage money for their home purchases or refinancing, and to guarantee low-interest educational loans for their children. They want public schools well financed to function as means of advancement for their children. They support government regulation to guarantee safe and honestly labeled consumer goods and services and likewise health and safety on their jobs. They demand Social Security retirement benefits and Medicare. There is broad support even for Medicaid, food stamps, and welfare despite some demonization of those programs and their poor recipients. The middle-income and poor alike demand no more taxes nor higher Medicare and Social Security deductions from their incomes.

In all capitalist countries, more or less, the contradiction between these conflicting financial demands on the government's budget has shaped politics. Elected officials have neither raised taxes nor cut spending enough to bring them into balance. Instead they have increasingly resorted to borrowing, running budget deficits. The officials like deficits because they reap immediate political benefits—"satisfying" business, the rich, and all the rest by holding down taxes and maintaining spending—while shifting the political costs of repaying rising national debt and its rising interest costs onto office-holders coming after them (today's equivalent of Louis XV's remark, "après moi le deluge").

Government borrowing also benefits businesses and the rich by offering them an attractive investment. They lend money to the government, which then repays those sums with interest. Instead of losing a portion of their wealth by paying taxes, those groups keep that portion (in the form of a purchased government bond) and earn more with it. Businesses and the rich are usually major lenders to their governments; workers rarely are. The same U.S. business leaders who advise governments to "live within their means" simultaneously fill their business and personal portfolios with government bonds.

Each country's unique history, culture, and politics determine how much its government borrows. In the United States, as elsewhere, successive governments (usually of both left and right) have borrowed so much that further borrowing is becoming increasingly difficult. One obstacle looms, because the more a government pays in interest and debt repayment, the less funds it has to undertake the spending business and the public demand. Over the last five years, annual interest payments on the United States' national debt have averaged over $400 billion. Political opposition to continuing those interest payments, and perhaps anger directed against lenders, may arise. Since lenders to governments are overwhelmingly businesses, rich individuals, and various government entities (foreign and domestic), such opposition may draw on deep resentments. Rising national indebtedness therefore builds its own opposition. Where and when that happens or even threatens to happen, major lenders stop risking further purchases of government bonds. Unable to borrow as before, governments return to face the original problem: which social groups are going to be taxed more and/or which will suffer government spending cuts.

Greece, Ireland, Hungary, and Spain are among countries whose people have already felt the impacts of their combinations of tax increases and spending cuts. In those countries, businesses and rich citizens have been able to impose their preferred response to the problem of deficits, what politicians call "austerity." When government borrowing must be reduced or stopped, "austerity" means sharply cut government spending on public sector jobs and services for the mass of people. Across Europe, government after government is being pressed by its businesses and its richest citizens to impose austerity on its people. However, also across Europe, slowly but steadily—because they are less well organized and financed—labor unions, left parties, and left political formations are mobilizing against austerity and for alternative plans. These involve raising taxes on business and the rich and/or reducing the government spending benefiting them.

Because the United States is the world's richest country and can borrow more and more easily than other countries, the federal government has not yet reached the limits of its borrowing capacity. However, states and municipalities are forbidden to borrow for their operating budgets, so they have already imposed austerities across the United States (especially visible in the massive spending cuts on public services in California and New York). Yet in the United States, too, there are the beginnings of signs of anti-austerity movement. For example, in January 2010, Oregon voters ratified their state's decision to respond to the economic crisis neither by borrowing nor by cutting state expenditures, but rather by raising over $700 million in taxes on businesses and on households earning over $250,000 per year.

Consider an illustrative example of this kind of alternative to austerity programs. Every year, two companies catering to rich investors survey their clients. Capgemini and Merrill Lynch Wealth Management's World Wealth Report for 2010 counts as High Net Worth Individuals (HNWIs) everyone with at least $1 million of "investible assets" *in addition to* the values of their primary residence, art works, collectibles, etc. HNWIs in the United States numbered 2.9 million in 2009: well *under 1% of U.S. citizens.* The HNWIs' investible assets totaled $12.09 trillion. For 2009, the total U.S. budget deficit was $1.7 trillion. Had the U.S. government levied an economic emergency tax of 15% on only the HNWIs' investible assets, no government borrowing would have been necessary in 2009. Obama's stimulus program would have required no deficit, no borrowing, and no additional taxes for 99% of U.S. citizens.

The real debates all along should have been—and now ought to be—about *who* pays how much in taxes and *who* benefits in what ways from government spending. Deficits are neither necessary in normal economic times nor when crises hit and require government stimulus. That business and the rich prefer lending to finance government deficits over being taxed instead is just their understandable self-interest. The rest of us have not only the right to a very different preference, but also a clear basis in economic theory and available empirical studies not to abandon our preference for theirs. We only have deficits because of who pays and who does not pay how much in taxes and who gets how much in government spending.

We should be debating the social acceptability of a capitalist class division between employers and employees that places dangerously contradictory pressures on government budgets. Had we had such debates and a democratic process of deciding them in the United States, deficits and their consequences might have been avoided or at least drastically reduced. But that never happened. Instead, the mainstream debates about deficits have simply assumed their necessity. Those debates then focus narrowly on the size of deficits—whether larger versus smaller is better—rather than on why they exist and who benefits from them. No wonder those debates never solved the deficit problem; they functioned rather to obscure the underlying issue about who pays for and who benefits from government budgets in capitalist societies.

A brief look at the two major current debates about deficits in the United States can show how they hide or obscure why we have deficits, who benefits from them, and who stands to lose now that further deficits become increasingly difficult for government budgets. The first debate rages in the world of electoral politics where the chief contenders are Republicans and Democrats. The second debate rages among professional economists (who include major advisors to both parties and their major candidates), where the chief contenders are the neoclassical and Keynesian camps.

In the United States, politicians take the blame for economic troubles more than those most clearly and directly responsible for those troubles. For example, high unemployment is *not* often blamed on the private corporations and their boards of directors who actually fire, lay off, or refuse to hire workers. Similarly, foreclosures are blamed more on politicians than on the banks and other lenders who actually choose to file the court papers ejecting families from their homes. Republican politicians therefore seek electoral gains chiefly by saying other politicians—Obama and the Democrats—caused and/or failed to overcome the economic crisis. Republicans stress how government is bad, deficit-financed big government is worse, and Democrats are worst because they favor both big government and big deficits. The Democrats counter that Bush caused or failed to overcome the crisis leaving an awful mess for Obama to fix and that Republicans keep obstructing Obama's programs that would otherwise overcome the crisis. Each side aims to channel anger, resentment, and anxiety about economic suffering (high unemployment and foreclosures, job insecurities, etc.) by blaming the other side. Neither side dares to criticize, let alone blame, the economic system and its class divisions. Neither side proposes (so neither side needs to oppose) avoiding deficits by taxing business and the rich. That option and the basic, underlying issue of who pays the taxes and who gets the government services drops out of the debates altogether.

Professional mainstream U.S. economists also debate deficits. The "left" among them (e.g., Keynesians such as *New York Times* columnist Paul Krugman) argues that ending the crisis requires more/larger government stimulus—deficit spending—than Obama undertook. Such economists want more spending on public works, greening the economy, etc. without offsetting the resulting economic stimulus by any similar rise in taxes. The resulting deficits, they insist, will only be temporary. This is because boosting government spending will increase production and employment (reducing mortgage defaults, bankruptcies, foreclosures, etc.) and that will generate more government tax revenue. The crisis will therefore pass, allowing government stimulus spending to be cut back. The temporary deficits necessitated *now* during the crisis can *then* be erased by using rising tax revenues and reduced government spending to pare down the government's outstanding debt.

The right (e.g. John B. Taylor of Stanford University's Hoover Institute) attacks bigger stimulus policies as ineffective: they cannot and will not overcome the crisis, which only the private sector can do. Moreover, higher government borrowing resulting from stimulus spending imposes increases on future taxpayers to cover the interest and repayment of mounting government debt. That, they insist, will undermine economic growth, not lift it. So they prefer minimal government intervention, tax cuts, and reliance on private enterprises to lift us out of crisis.

Like the mainstream politicians, the mainstream economists debate larger versus smaller deficits. They keep off the agenda for public discussion debate over why deficits exist, who benefits from them, and what alternative mechanisms exist (including basic changes in the economic system) to avoid their real social costs. ❑

The tensions between boss owners and workers is what leads to the two differing needs.

Chapter 7

THE JOBS CRISIS

Article 8.6

THE *REAL* UNEMPLOYMENT RATE HITS A 68-YEAR HIGH

BY JOHN MILLER
July/August 2009

Although you have to dig into the statistics to know it, unemployment in the United States is now [June 2009] worse than at any time since the end of the Great Depression.

From December 2007, when the recession began, to May of this year, 6.0 million U.S. workers lost their jobs. The big three U.S. automakers are closing plants and letting white-collar workers go too. Chrysler, the worst off of the three, will lay off one-quarter of its workforce. Heavy equipment manufacturer Caterpillar and giant banking conglomerate Citigroup have both laid off thousands of workers. Alcoa, the aluminum giant, has let workers go. Computer maker Dell and express shipper DHL have both canned many of their workers. Circuit City, the leading electronics retailer, went out of business, costing its 40,000 workers their jobs. Lawyers in large national firms are getting the ax. Even on Sesame Street, workers are losing their jobs.

The official unemployment rate hit 9.4% in May—already as high as the peak unemployment rates in all but the 1982 recession, the worst since World War II. And topping the 1982 recession's peak rate of 10.8% is now distinctly possible. The current downturn has pushed up unemployment rates by more than any previous postwar recession (see figure).

THE MAY 2009 UNEMPLOYMENT PICTURE (DATA IN THOUSANDS, NOT SEASONALLY ADJUSTED)	
Civilian Labor Force	154,336
Employed	140,363
Unemployed	13,973
Marginally Attached Workers	2,210
Discouraged workers	792
Reasons other than discouragement	1,418
Part-time for Economic Reasons	8,785
Slack work or business conditions	6,647
Could only find part-time work	1,898

Sources: Bureau of Labor Statistics, Tables A-1, A-5. A-12, A-13. Data are not seasonally adjusted because seasonally adjusted data for marginally attached workers are not available.

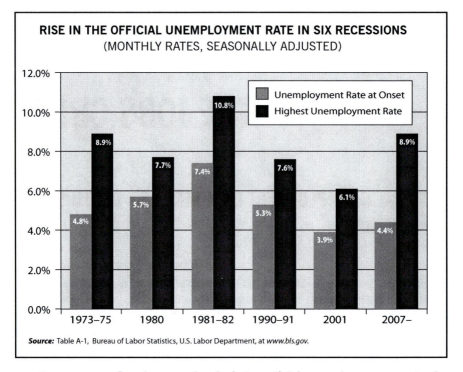

RISE IN THE OFFICIAL UNEMPLOYMENT RATE IN SIX RECESSIONS
(MONTHLY RATES, SEASONALLY ADJUSTED)

Legend:
- Unemployment Rate at Onset
- Highest Unemployment Rate

Recession	Unemployment Rate at Onset	Highest Unemployment Rate
1973–75	4.8%	8.9%
1980	5.7%	7.7%
1981–82	7.4%	10.8%
1990–91	5.3%	7.6%
2001	3.9%	6.1%
2007–	4.4%	8.9%

Source: Table A-1, Bureau of Labor Statistics, U.S. Labor Department, at *www.bls.gov.*

Some groups of workers are already facing official unemployment rates in the double digits. As of May, unemployment rates for black, Hispanic, and teenage workers were already 14.9%, 12.7% and 22.7%, respectively. Workers without a high-school diploma confronted a 15.5% unemployment rate, while the unemployment rate for workers with just a high-school degree was 10.0%. Nearly one in five (19.2%) construction workers were unemployed. In Michigan, the hardest hit state, unemployment was at 12.9% in April. Unemployment rates in seven other states were at double-digit levels as well.

Calculating the Real Unemployment Rate

The BLS calculates the official unemployment rate, U-3, as the number of unemployed as a percentage of the civilian labor force. The civilian labor force consists of employed workers plus the officially unemployed, those without jobs who are available to work and have looked for a job in the last four weeks. Applying the data found in the table yields an official unemployment rate of 9.1%, or a seasonally adjusted rate 9.4% for April 2009.

The comprehensive U-6 unemployment rate adjusts the official rate by adding marginally attached workers and workers forced to work part time for economic reasons to the officially unemployed. To find the U-6 rate the BLS takes that higher unemployment count and divides it by the official civilian labor force plus the number of marginally attached workers. (No adjustment is necessary for forced part-time workers since they are already counted in the official labor force as employed workers.)

Accounting for the large number of marginally attached workers and those working part-time for economic reasons raises the count of unemployed to 24.0 million workers for May 2009. Those numbers push up the U-6 unemployment rate to 15.9% or a seasonally adjusted rate of 16.4%.

As bad as they are, these figures dramatically understate the true extent of unemployment. First, they exclude anyone without a job who is ready to work but has not actively looked for a job in the previous four weeks. The Bureau of Labor Statistics classifies such workers as "marginally attached to the labor force" so long as they have looked for work within the last year. Marginally attached workers include so-called discouraged workers who have given up looking for job-related reasons, plus others who have given up for reasons such as school and family responsibilities, ill health, or transportation problems.

Second, the official unemployment rate leaves out part-time workers looking for full-time work: part-time workers are "employed" even if they work as little as one hour a week. The vast majority of people working part time involuntarily have had their hours cut due to slack or unfavorable business conditions. The rest are working part time because they could only find part-time work.

To its credit, the BLS has developed alternative unemployment measures that go a long way toward correcting the shortcomings of the official rate. The broadest alternative measure, called "U-6," counts as unemployed "marginally attached workers" as well as those employed "part time for economic reasons."

When those adjustments are taken into account for May 2009, the unemployment rate soars to 16.4%. That is the highest rate since the BLS began calculating the U-6 rate in 1994. While not exactly comparable, it is also higher than the BLS's earlier and yet broader adjusted unemployment rate called the U-7. The BLS began calculating the U-7 rate in 1976 but discontinued it in 1994 in favor of the U-6 rate. In the 1982 recession, the U-7 reached 15.3%, its highest level. In fact, no bout of unemployment since the last year of the Great Depression in 1941 would have produced an adjusted unemployment rate as high as today's.

Why is the real unemployment rate so much higher than the official, or U-3, rate? First, forced part-time work has reached its highest level ever, going all the way back to 1956 and including the 1982 recession. In May 2009, 8.8 million workers were forced to work part time for economic reasons. Forced part-timers are concentrated in retail, food services, and construction; about a quarter of them are young workers between 16 and 24. The number of discouraged workers is high today as well. In May, the BLS counted 2.2 million "marginally attached" workers. That matches the highest number since 1994, when the agency introduced this measure.

With the economy in the throes of a catastrophic downturn, unemployment, no matter how it's measured, will rise dramatically and impose yet more devastating costs on society and on those without a job or unable to find full-time work. ❑

Sources: U.S. Dept. of Labor, "The Unemployment Rate and Beyond: Alternative Measures of Labor Underutilization," *Issues in Labor Statistics,* June 2008; John E. Bregger and Steven E. Haugen, "BLS Introduces New Range of Alternative Unemployment Measures," *Monthly Labor Review*, October 1995.

Article 7.2

UNEMPLOYMENT: HOW BAD FOR HOW LONG?

The outlook is grim unless there is serious government intervention.

BY FRED MOSELEY
March/April 2010

How bad will unemployment be in the months and years ahead? One way to answer that question is to look at how long it took the U.S. economy to regain jobs in previous post-war recessions. By this measure, the employment outlook is quite grim.

Since the recession began in December 2007, the U.S. economy has lost 8.4 million jobs, or 6.2% of employment, over 25 months. This is the biggest decline in the postwar period, and the recession is not yet over.

In none of the other recessions since World War II has the economy lost such a large percentage of its employment base. None of the other recessions in the figure below show such a high cumulative percent decline of employment. (The vertical axis shows the percentage cumulative decline from the beginning of the recession, i.e., the month employment peaks; the horizontal axis shows the number of months from the peak of employment.)

The 1981-82 recession gives us some hint of what would happen if the U.S. economy falls into "double-dip" recession in the years ahead, which many economists consider a distinct possibility. The total decline of employment in the recession of 1981-82 was only 3% and the jobs lost in recession were recovered in just 11 months. Nonetheless, the rate of unemployment reached a peak of 10.8%, the highest of the postwar period. That was because the 1981-82 recession followed close on the heels of a recession in 1980. In this "double-dip" recession, the two declines of employment were smaller than the current decline and yet the combined effect was a rate of unemployment of almost 11%.

The two most recent recessions, 1990 and 2001, look distinctly different from the 1981-82 recession. These were mild recessions and the declines of employment were only 1.5% and 2% respectively. But for both of these recessions, the recoveries were disturbingly slow and it took much longer to replace the jobs lost in the recession than after previous recessions. It took 30 months in the early 1990s and 47 months in the early 2000s to return to the previous peak in employment. In these "jobless recoveries," the rate of unemployment continued to increase for months after the recovery of employment began.

The main causes of the slow growth of employment in these recent jobless recoveries were the slow growth of output, or Gross Domestic Product (GDP), and business emphasis on cost-cutting, especially labor costs. The latter factor led companies to force existing employees to work harder and produce more output rather than hire more workers as demand picked up. The emphasis on cost-cutting also led companies to outsource operations to low-wage areas of the world.

These factors are still very much present in the U.S. economy today. It is widely forecast that GDP growth in the years ahead will be very slow by historical comparisons (perhaps even slower than in the previous two jobless recoveries) and business seems as eager as ever to cut labor costs. In addition, as demand picks up, companies will first increase the hours of the large number of existing part-time workers before they start hiring new workers. So this is shaping up to be the mother of all jobless recoveries, which will result in high rates of unemployment for years to come.

How long will it take for employment in the U.S. economy to return to its previous peak? The graph suggests that it will take at least 48 months. Of course, returning to the previous peak would not guarantee that the rate of unemployment would decline because of the growth of the labor force. But increasing employment at least makes it possible that the rate of unemployment might start to decline.

How many months will it take to recover the 8.4 million jobs that have been lost? That depends on the average monthly increase of employment in the months and years ahead. If the average monthly increase of employment turns out to be 200,000 per month—which would be more than twice as fast as in the last recovery—then it would take 42 more months to return to the previous peak employment.

Even if the average monthly increase turns out to be 300,000—and this is surely over-optimistic—it would take 28 more months, or until mid-2012, to return to the previous peak employment. In this scenario, what would the rate of unemployment likely be in mid-2012? Employment would be the same as in December 2007. At that time, the official rate of unemployment was 5%. Assuming that the labor force increases 1% per year, it will have increased at least 4% between December 2007 and mid-2012. So the rate of unemployment in mid-2012 would be about 4% higher than in December 2007, or around 9%.

And this is the optimistic scenario. If there is a "double-dip" recession, then the official rate of unemployment will still be over 10% for years to come. This means that the true rate of unemployment—including involuntary part-time workers and marginally attached or discouraged workers who have stopped looking for jobs—would likely top 15%.

PERCENT JOB LOSSES IN THE FIVE MOST RECENT POST-WWII RECESSIONS

NUMBER OF MONTHS AFTER PEAK EMPLOYMENT

---- 1948 ········ 1980 ——— 1981 ····· 2001 —— 2007

Sources: Calculated Risk (calculatedriskblog.com).and Bureau of Labor Statistics (bls.gov).

In other words, U.S. workers will be facing a long period of very high unemployment. Already, 40% of the officially unemployed have been unemployed for six months or more—the highest since records have been kept starting in 1948—and the percentage of total unemployed (including "discouraged workers") is much higher. And these percentages will go even higher in the months ahead.

Long-term unemployment like this has very serious negative effects on workers—it makes it much harder to return to employment and it has hidden costs on families, children, and communities.

To avoid this economic disaster for working people, we should demand that Congress pass a Full Employment Law, committing the federal government to provide jobs for all workers willing and able to work any time there are not enough private sector jobs. Such a law would be based on the principle that a job with a decent income is a basic economic right.

Could we afford a full-employment law? Contrary to what the deficit hawks claim, the answer is yes. A full-employment jobs program could be paid for by higher taxes on the rich and by a significant reduction in military spending. It's not about a lack of funds—it's about priorities. If the government abandoned its current priorities of keeping tax rates on the rich low and giving the military a blank check for foreign wars, it could instead help workers cope with the long-term after-effects of recession.

Update on Unemployment: The Outlook is Even Grimmer (October 2010)

In the ten months since this article was originally written, the official estimates of the rate of unemployment in the U.S. economy have remained roughly constant at just under 10%. But the only reason the official estimates are not over 10% is that the official "labor force" has not grown at all since the beginning of the recession in December 2007. This is because many people have given up looking for jobs and therefore are not counted in the labor force. If the labor force had increased at the usual rate of about one percent a year, the rate of unemployment would be 12.5% rather than 9.7%. Plus, another 5% of the employed workers are working part-time involuntarily; if these are added, the real rate of unemployment and underemployment is over 17%.

But the most disturbing graph is still the one accompanying the article showing the percentage decline in employment in the five most recent recessions, including the current one. The upward blip in the graph this spring and summer was due to temporary Census workers, who are no longer employed now that the Census is over. The average rate of increase since the trough in January 2010 has been less than 100,000 per month. At this rate (which is about the same rate as in the two previous "jobless recoveries"), it would take 84 months to restore the 8.4 million jobs lost during the recession; that is, until January 2017! And this would only get us back to the previous level of employment in December 2007; it would not provide jobs for the roughly 15 million young workers who will have entered the labor force—or would like to—between 2007 and 2017.

If the monthly rate of increase were to accelerate in the months and years ahead to a monthly rate of 200,000 jobs, then (as discussed in the original article) it would take 42 months, until July 2013, to restore the 8.4 million jobs, and the rate of unemployment at that time (assuming a normal one percent annual increase in the labor force) would be around 10.5%. But such an acceleration of job growth does not seem very likely in the months ahead; the economy is slowing down, not speeding up.

Therefore, my conclusion now is even grimmer than before—it seems very likely that the U.S. economy will suffer from high double-digit rates of unemployment for at least four to five years, and perhaps even longer. It looks like this could be a "lost decade" for jobs in the U.S. economy—unless, that is, government policies change drastically, including the federal government as employer of last resort, in cooperation with state and local governments. ❏

Thanks to the website Calculated Risk (calculatedriskblog.com) for the idea for the graph accompanying this article and for sharing the data.

Article 7.3

UNEMPLOYMENT INSURANCE: A BROKEN SYSTEM

BY MARIANNE HILL

September/October 2009

Millions of workers have lost their jobs in the current recession. Employment is down 12% in manufacturing, 7% in professional and business services, and more than 5% overall in the private sector compared to last year. Over 5.6 million people have lost their jobs since last June. The ranks of the unemployed are continuing to grow; the unemployment rate in June hit 9.5%. Good thing that unemployment insurance provides income to help tide these workers over this rough patch, right? Not so fast.

The share of unemployed workers receiving benefits has gradually shrunk since the 1970s. In 1975, over half of unemployed workers received regular benefits. But in 2008, only 37% of the unemployed did; in some states the figure was less than 25%. And so-called "discouraged workers," those who want but are not actively seeking employment, are not considered part of the labor force and so are not even included in these figures.

Unemployment insurance, in short, is not a benefit that everyone who loses a job can count on. Several groups are working to change this. The American Recovery and Reinvestment Act (ARRA), better know as the Obama stimulus package, provides temporary funding for states that expand their unemployment coverage, and so far this year 25 states have done so. Others, however, are resisting even a temporary expansion of coverage that would be fully federally funded.

Why Unemployment Compensation?

When unemployment insurance was established as a nationwide program in 1935, it was hailed as a means of enabling workers to protect their standard of living between jobs. With it, workers are better able to keep their homes and their health. It helps to stabilize family well-being and maintain the labor force in a region. By enabling workers to engage in longer job searches, unemployment compensation also improves workers' job choices. It even enhances employers' flexibility in hiring by making lay-offs less painful.

Unemployment insurance is also an important countercyclical tool: it bolsters consumer spending during economic downturns and then automatically drops off as the economy recovers and unemployment falls. Because it reduces the need for other forms of government intervention to raise demand in a downturn, the program has supporters across the ideological spectrum.

Coverage and benefits vary by state. The average weekly benefit in 2008 was $300—about 35% of the average weekly wage. Benefits are paid from state funds that are financed by a payroll tax on employers. This tax is levied on anywhere from the first $7,000 to the first $35,300 of each worker's annual earnings depending on the state; the national average is $11,482. The tax rate ranges from 0.83% to 5% of the taxable portion of wages, with a national average of 2.42%. (Who bears the cost of this tax is debated: economists have shown that whether or not a company is able to pass the cost of payroll taxes forward to customers or back to employees depends on conditions in its particular product and labor markets.)

Shifts in employment patterns and a tightening of eligibility requirements are behind the nationwide reduction in effective unemployment insurance coverage. Today almost 30% of the U.S. work force is employed in nonstandard work arrangements, including part-time, temporary, contract or on-call work, and self-employment. Most of these jobs are subject to the payroll tax that funds unemployment benefits—yet these workers often find they are ineligible. For instance, persons who are seeking only part-time employment do not qualify for unemployment benefits in many states. This affects women in particular, including heads of households, who often work part time due to dependent care responsibilities. People who work full time but only for part of the year may also find it difficult to qualify for unemployment benefits.

Many workers who are not eligible for benefits provide income that is critical to their families. In 2007, 41% of workers worked only part-time or part-year. Among heads of households, this figure, though lower, was still sizeable: in 2007, it was 32% overall and 42% for female family heads. Besides child care, elder care can also mean part-time or part-year work for many. Nearly one-third of working adults with older parents report missing some work to care for them.

Who Are the Unemployed?

Certain industries, regions, and workers are being hit harder than others this recession. In June, 15 states and the District of Columbia had unemployment rates of over 10%, but only one, North Dakota, had an unemployment rate below 5%. Michigan, Oregon, South Carolina, and Rhode Island all had seasonally adjusted jobless rates of 12% or more.

Unemployment hits some population groups much harder than others—young people, people of color, and anyone with relatively few years of education. Among workers over 20 years of age, black men had the highest jobless rate in June at 16.4%. The rate for Hispanic women was 11.5%, for black women 11.3%, and for Hispanic men 10.7%. In contrast, the jobless rate was under 10% for both white men (9.2%) and white women (6.8%).

A combination of factors including occupational segregation, lower educational levels, and discrimination result in lower incomes for women and for black and Latino men, exacerbating the impact of higher unemployment. Data from 2005-2007 show that black women working year-round, full-time earned $15,900 a year less than white men; for Hispanic women the wage gap was $21,400.

Lower-income families have fewer assets to see them through rough economic times, and their extended families are also hard-pressed as demands upon them increase. Nonprofits, another part of the social safety net, suffer from increased demand for services and decreased donations during recession. As a result, families of blacks, women and Hispanics suffer severe setbacks during a period of recession, and unemployment insurance can be especially critical to them.

Families in which one or more wage earners lose their jobs bear costs greater than just the lost wages. Savings are exhausted; rates of illness, both mental and physical, increase; debt levels often rise (inadequate medical insurance coverage is a major factor—in 2008, 60% of the unemployed lacked health insurance); and the pursuit of a college education or other training may be postponed. Studies have documen-ted a rise in suicide rates, mental and physical illnesses, and domestic and other violence among the unemployed. These problems become widespread during recessions and become a burden on society, not just on individual families.

Promising Initiatives

Under the Obama stimulus package, states that elect to expand their programs in certain ways receive federal funds to finance these changes for at least two to three years. States can make unemployment benefits more available in a number of ways:

- Changing the base period used to determine whether a worker qualifies for benefits and if so, the amount he or she will receive.

- Making unemployment insurance available to certain individuals who are seeking only part-time work and/or to those who lost or left their jobs due to certain compelling family reasons (for example, domestic violence or a spouse relocating).

- Providing an additional 26 weeks of compensation to workers who have exhausted regular unemployment benefits and are enrolled in and making satisfactory progress in certain training programs.

- Paying an additional dependents' allowance of at least $15 per dependent per week to eligible beneficiaries.

Another potential reform relates to the extension of benefits beyond the regular 13- to 26-week period. States are required to offer extended benefits during periods of especially high unemployment (with half the cost covered by the federal government) only if certain trigger requirements are met—and that does not happen often. The ARRA offers states the option of adopting a new, less stringent trigger requirement. As of mid-July, 29 of the 30 states adopting the new trigger requirements have had extended benefits go into effect, compared with only six of the 20 states that have kept earlier triggers. Last year Congress authorized a separate program, Emergency Unemployment Compensation, to provide federally funded benefits after regular benefits are exhausted. The National Employment Law Project estimated that about 1.2 million workers would exhaust their benefits under *this* program before July 2009 and so become eligible for extended benefits.A permanent expansion of coverage to a larger share of the unemployed, with or without an increase in benefit levels, would cost more than the average $23 per month in unemployment insurance taxes currently paid per worker. This gap could be filled by expanding the portion of wages on which the tax is levied. To reduce the negative impact on low-income workers, this could be accompanied by adjustments to the earned income tax credit.

Even if the reforms contained in the Obama administration's stimulus package were fully enacted, benefits and coverage would be low in the United States in comparison to Europe. Much remains to be done to ensure minimal income security here. As the unemployment rate approaches 10%, it is time to revamp our broken system. ❑

Sources: U.S. Department of Labor, especially www.ows.doleta.gov/unemploy/finance.asp; U.S. Bureau of Labor Statistics; National Employment Law Project, www.nelp.org; William Conerly, "European Unemployment: Lessons for the United States," National Center for Policy Analysis, May 26, 2004; National Institutes of Health, www.pubmedcentral.nih.gov; Marcus Walker and Roger Thurow, "U.S., Europe Are an Ocean Apart on Human Toll of Joblessness," *Wall Street Journal*, May 7, 2009.

Article 7.4

EMPLOYERS GO ON STRIKE—BECAUSE THEY CAN

The Journal *editors support the bosses' strike demands.*

BY JOHN MILLER
July/August 2010

EMPLOYERS ON STRIKE

Congress keeps giving business reasons not to hire.

Yesterday [June 4th, 2010] Americans learned that the economy created a net total of 431,000 new jobs in May, including 411,000 temporary Census hires.

The private economy—that is, the wealth creation part, not the wealth redistribution part—gained only 41,000 jobs, down sharply from the encouraging 218,000 in April, and 158,000 in March.

Almost everything Congress has done in recent months has made private businesses less inclined to hire new workers. ObamaCare imposes new taxes and mandates on private employers. Even with record unemployment, Congress raised the minimum wage to $7.25, pricing more workers out of jobs.

The "jobs" bill that the House passed last week expands jobless insurance to 99 weeks, while raising taxes by $80 billion on small employers and U.S-based corporations. On January 1, Congress is set to let taxes rise on capital gains, dividends and small businesses.

　　　　　　　—*Wall Street Journal*, "Review & Outlook," June 5, 2010

Employers surely have been on strike, but that's hardly news. Private sector hiring through the first four months of 2010 was no higher than in 2009. What there has been for job growth in the private sector is due to the decline in layoffs (and discharges) not an uptick in hiring. As of May nearly eight million fewer workers were on private payrolls than when the recession began in Dec. 2007.

Employers may be on strike, but they haven't missed a paycheck. The same, of course, can't be said for the 17.8 million workers the striking employers failed to hire. That number includes the 15 million officially counted as unemployed, and another 2.8 million workers who gave up looking for work or who could never get their first job during the recession. And honoring the demands issued by the *Wall Street Journal* editors would not help find them a job but rather would prolong the employers' strike.

Record Long-Term Unemployment

Unemployed workers have gone longer without a paycheck than any time in the last 62 years. In May the median or typical unemployment spell was 23.2 weeks (5.4 months). And 6.8 million workers, some 46% of the unemployed, had been unemployed over six months, the highest level of long-term unemployment on record (with data back to 1948). Even in the worst months of the early 1980s recession, when the jobless rate topped 10% for ten straight months, only one in four of the unemployed was out of work for more than six months.

Unemployed black workers, manufacturing workers, and workers in the transportation, utilities, financial, and information industries have all typically endured spells of unemployment 26 weeks or longer. In addition, the median unemployment spell increases unrelentingly with age, exceeding a half year for workers 35 or older and reaching 50 weeks, or nearly a year, for workers 65 and over.

The effects have been devastating. Just under one half of the unemployed have now gone without work longer than the traditional length of unemployment benefits (26 weeks). A third of the unemployed have gone a year or longer without a job. Congress has extended jobless benefits to a maximum of 99 weeks in states with high unemployment. Still the longer people are unemployed the more likely they are to eventually give up searching and drop out of the labor force.

There are few signs that unemployment will abate or its duration shorten, or that private sector hiring will spring back to life, anytime soon. In May 2010, there were still 5.5 officially unemployed workers for every job opening counted by the Bureau of Labor Statistics. With a backlog of 2.8 million workers wanting a job not accounted for in those figures, the official unemployment rate is likely to hover at near double-digits levels for the rest of 2010. In addition, with plenty of part-time employees who want full-time jobs, far more than during previous recoveries, employers will continue to add to those workers' hours before they hire additional workers.

Employers' Strike Demands

Employment readings admittedly vary month to month in any recovery, but the evidence is overwhelming: the private sector is not hiring.

Why not? The *Wall Street Journal* editors are only too happy to tell you: That pesky public sector keeps redistributing wealth, crushing whatever incentive employers might have had to hire workers. Health care mandates and taxes, a higher minimum wage, expanded jobless benefits, and, worst of all, the prospect of letting the Bush tax cuts expire.

The problems with the editors' list of strike demands are manifold. First, each and every one of these demands would redistribute wealth, the editors' supposed complaint about the public sector. But in this case that redistribution would favor employers, not workers. Not providing health care benefits, allowing the purchasing power of the minimum wage to deteriorate, skimping on social spending, cutting taxes on capital gains and dividends, and lowering the top income-tax bracket have all contributed to a massive redistribution of income to the wealthy over the last three decades, a trend the editors are dedicated to continuing.

Second, employers already have the financial wherewithal to hire new workers. Their costs are down, their profits are up, and they are rolling in dough. Corporate profits are back to pre-recession levels. The combination of rapid productivity gains and stagnant wages have slashed unit labor costs (compensation costs per unit of output) to lower levels than before the onset of the recession. And by the end of March 2010, non-financial corporations held 7% of all their assets in cash, the highest level since 1963.

Third, government spending is the source of much of what there has been in the way of new jobs. As the editors point out, almost all the jobs created in May 2010 were temporary Census hires. In addition, according to estimates from the Congressional Budget Office, the $895 billion government stimulus passed in early 2009 created jobs for between 1.2 million and 2.8 million workers during the first quarter of 2010. Even the lower estimate exceeds the 1.15 million hires in the private sector in the same time period, some of which should be directly attributed to the stimulus package.

No Restart Button

Finally and most importantly, the policies the editors attack are not what stand between us and massive hiring and sustained economic growth. Undoing those policies, as limited as they have been, and re-instituting the Bush tax cuts, would constitute little more than hitting the restart button. And what would be restarted is nothing other than the very forces that brought on the worst crisis since the Great Depression.

Consider this: The economy has grown only about half as quickly as typically follows a deep recession. Much of the reason has been sputtering consumer spending, held back by a lack of jobs, to be sure, and by the debt consumers racked up during the last two decades. The very polices advocated by the editors kept a lid on wages and concentrated income gains among those at the top, leaving most consumers to ring up more and more debt in an effort to keep up their standard of living. That debt burden, still a third higher than that in the mid 1990s relative to household income, continues to hamstring consumption. A recent Gallup Poll reveals that the modest increase in consumer spending over the last year came exclusively from well-to-do families. Consumers with an income over $90,000 a year increased their monthly expenditures by one-third from May 2009 to May 2010, while the monthly expenditures of consumers with incomes below $90,000 remained unchanged.

More government spending is needed to help jump-start the engine of economic growth. A good place to start is the Local Jobs for America Act of 2010, introduced by Rep. George Miller (D-Cal.). It would create or save approximately 1 million jobs by protecting or creating state and local government and nonprofit sector jobs. Those jobs are much needed since state and local governments have shed 231,000 jobs since August 2008.

But the engine of economic growth needs to be rebuilt as well. Employers are not the only ones on strike; lenders are as well. In 2009 total outstanding loans at FDIC insured banks dropped an epic 7.4%, the sharpest decline in lending since 1942. Without genuine reform that breaks the power of the mega-financial institutions, protects consumers and mortgage holders, and regulates financial transactions, lending will not resume. And what there is for economic growth will reward the employers the editors are so concerned about, while the jobs machine sputters and workers continue to endure long spells of unemployment. ❏

Sources: Sara Murray, "Lending Falls at Epic Pace," by Crittenden and Eckblad, Wall Street Journal, 2/24/10; "Chronic Joblessness Takes Toll," *Wall Street Journal*, June 2, 2010; Justin Lahart, "U.S.

Firms Build Record Cash Piles," *Wall Street Journal*, June 10, 2010; Heather Boushey, "The Latest Employment Woes," Center For American Progress, June 4, 2010; "Estimated Impact of the American Recovery and Reinvestment Act on Employment and Economic Output from January 2010 Through March 2010," Congressional Budget Office; Dennis Jacobe, "Frugality Fatigue: Upper-Income Spending Surges 33%," gallup.com; Bureau of Labor Statistics, Household Data, Tables A-12, A-34, A-35, A-36, A-37, bls.gov.

Article 7.5

GENDER AND THE RECESSION
Recession Hits Traditionally Male Jobs Hardest

BY HEATHER BOUSHEY
May 2009

A woman is now the primary breadwinner in millions of families across the United States because her husband has lost his job. Three out of four jobs lost during our Great Recession, which began in December 2007, have been men's jobs. This has left women to support their families nationwide—a task made more challenging since women typically earn only 78 cents compared to the male dollar.

Men have lost more jobs than women because the industries with the largest job losses so far during the recession have been ones dominated by men. New data from the Bureau of Labor Statistics' Current Establishment Survey for March 2009 shows that since the recession began men have lost 75.0% of all nonfarm jobs and 72.7% of all private-sector jobs.

Women have become a larger share of payroll employees. As of March 2009, the latest data available, women made up nearly half the labor force: 49.7% of all workers employed in the United States are women, up from 48.7% when the recession began in December 2007.

The recession is playing out differently by gender because men and women tend to work in very different industries and occupations. Women especially predominate in financial activities—mostly because they are the majority of real estate agents, not because they are the majority of bankers—as well as in government, education, and health. (See Figure 1.) Men predominate in transportation, construction, and manufacturing, as well as in certain retail professions, such as the sale of automobiles and electronic appliances.

Larger job losses among men have occurred because the recession is hitting traditionally male working-class jobs. Half of the job losses during this recession so far have occurred in either construction or manufacturing. Another quarter of the total job losses have occurred in professional and business services, mostly among temporary workers. Even though it is the financial sector which is driving the economic crisis, the financial activities industry only accounts for 7.4% of the jobs lost so far in this recession.

Yet, it is not just that men work in industries hardest hit by the recession. Within a number of hard-hit industries, men are also losing a disproportionate share of the jobs. For example, within retail, although men accounted for half (49.8%) of all workers at the beginning of the recession, they held two-thirds (64.5%) of the jobs lost. In finance and insurance, men accounted for over a third (36.7%) of the jobs at the beginning of the recession, but have lost half (50.6%) of the jobs.

It is not unique for blue-collar workers to bear the brunt of job losses in a recession. What is notable in this recession is that while manufacturing and construction accounted for a larger share of total job losses than in prior recessions, the industries that are seeing jobs gains—education, health, and government—are seeing smaller

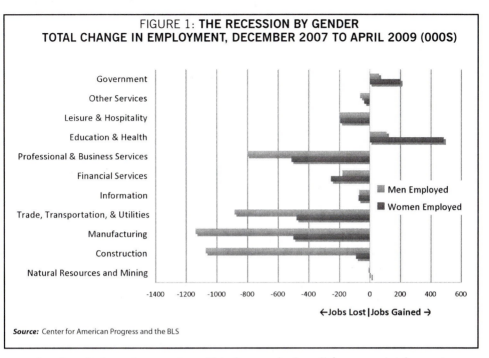

FIGURE 1: **THE RECESSION BY GENDER**
TOTAL CHANGE IN EMPLOYMENT, DECEMBER 2007 TO APRIL 2009 (000S)

Government
Other Services
Leisure & Hospitality
Education & Health
Professional & Business Services
Financial Services
Information
Trade, Transportation, & Utilities
Manufacturing
Construction
Natural Resources and Mining

Men Employed
Women Employed

-1400   -1200   -1000   -800   -600   -400   -200   0   200   400   600

← Jobs Lost | Jobs Gained →

Source: Center for American Progress and the BLS

gains than during prior recessions. This does not bode well for women's jobs moving forward, since women are concentrated in these industries.

Notably, during the 1980s recession—when the unemployment rate went above 10%—women actually gained jobs on net because of continued hiring in women-dominated industries. Clearly, that is not the case during the current recession. Women's employment is already 98.5% of its level from December 2007.

As of April 2009 the unemployment rate for adult men was 9.4%—more than double what it was in December 2007. The unemployment rate for adult women was 7.1% in April. The male unemployment rate is now 2.3 percentage points higher than women's—larger than at any other time since 1949.

Women are also less likely than men to be unemployed in married families. The unemployment rate for married men is 6.3%—higher than at any time since 1983. The unemployment rate for married women is 5.5%—the highest since 1986.

That means more and more women in millions of families across the United States will be supporting their families.

Ensuring that those women, and every woman, earn a fair day's pay could not be a more pressing issue for families. A good—and fast—place to start would be for the Obama administration to devote its efforts to simply enforcing the laws already on the books and implementing better monitoring of equal pay. That would be a down payment to help families make ends meet while the labor market is getting back on track. ❏

This article combines two "infographics" written by Heather Boushey, "Gender and The Recession," May 8, 2009, and "The Importance of Women Breadwinners," April 30, 2009. Both are available at the Center for American Progress (americanprogress.org).

Article 7.6

A DISMAL TIME TO GRADUATE
What the recession means to the class of 2009, including me.

BY KATHERINE FAHERTY
January/February 2010

The current state of the economy is hitting recent graduates hard. As a 2009 college graduate, I speak from experience. Seven months after graduating I have secured an unpaid internship and a part-time job, which puts me in the same boat as many of my classmates. Last spring one of my professors kindly reminded our assembly of scared and excited seniors that it was a dismal time to graduate. He was right. Unemployment for my age group (20-24) reached a staggering 16% in November, compared to 11.1% in November 2008.

My roommate, who has a master's degree in art history, has only been able to find an unpaid internship at an auction house plus a part-time receptionist job. Even without the part-time job, the Bureau of Labor Statistics would count her as employed because she goes to "work" at the auction house every day. She is among the hordes of recent graduates holding unpaid internships that were once the sole province of college students—a viable route only for grads with family resources to fall back on.

Another friend has been on a constant job search since March. She moved back into her parents' house and returned to her old summer job as a bank teller. Then she took a job at the local mall so she could make her student-loan payments. She gets a great discount at her store, but she's not putting her double degree in economics and psychology to use. Like almost 32% of workers under 25, she is "underemployed." Along with those who want full-time jobs but can find only part-time ones, underemployed workers are counted as employed. So

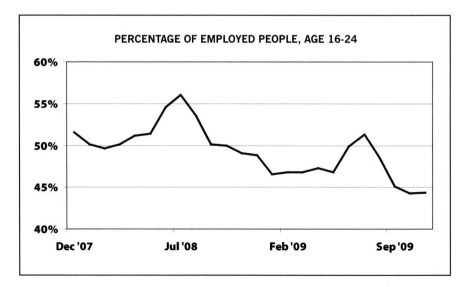

PERCENTAGE OF EMPLOYED PEOPLE, AGE 16-24

neither group shows up in the most widely reported unemployment rate (the BLS's "U-3" measure).

A few of my friends were lucky enough to find jobs in their desired fields. One deploys her dual majors at a Massachusetts economic and environmental consulting firm. She is in the minority of last year's college graduates; just 48% were employed in September, including all of those underemployed receptionists and cashiers.

While I don't personally know anyone who hasn't found something to do, New York City's Covenant House does; the organization, which serves young people facing homelessness, has seen a 25% increase in residents. Around the country, there are some 4,088,000 unemployed people ages 16 to 24 looking for work. It's a pretty dismal state, especially since there are 6.3 people vying for every available job as of October 2009, again not including all the interns, the underemployed, and the involuntary part-timers still vying for those jobs.

In October, *BusinessWeek* labeled us "the lost generation." I disagree. We're not lost, just confused and frustrated. No one wants to get stuck in a rut. According to Yale economist Lisa Kahn, recession graduates never fully recover. Early-1980s recession graduates earned 8% less than comparable graduates in non-recession years in their first year out of college and are still earning less almost 20 years later. Kahn characterized the consequences of graduating during a recession as "large, negative, and persistent."

It's clear that we need more jobs with career ladders available to entry-level candidates. But until more jobs become available, I, like my classmates, will try to move forward, hoping my internship and part-time job build character (or at least enhance my résumé) and looking for the light at the end of the tunnel. ❏

Sources: The Class of 09 Curse," *Wall Street Journal*, May 9, 2009; "The Employment Situation –November 2009," Bureau of Labor Statistics; "The Lost Generation," *BusinessWeek*, October 8, 2009; "Who's Paying for the Recession Most of All? Young Workers," alternet.org, November 9, 2009; Tony Pugh, "Recession's Toll: Most Recent College Grads Working Low-Skill Jobs," McClatchy, June 25, 2009.

Article 7.7

HOW BLACKS MIGHT FARE IN THE JOBLESS RECOVERY

BY SYLVIA A. ALLEGRETTO AND STEVEN PITTS
November/December 2010

There have been seemingly contradictory announcements recently concerning the economy. In September another 95,000 jobs were shed as the official unemployment rate remained at 9.6%. Unemployment has been at 9.5% or higher for well over a year now. About the same time this bad news about employment came out, it was announced that the recession, which began in December 2007, had actually ended in June of 2009—thus we are several months into the second year of recovery.

How could the recession be over, even amidst continued job losses and stubbornly high unemployment? And how might black workers, whose levels of unemployment have (as usual) been much higher than white workers' in this recession, fare in a "jobless recovery"?

The Dating of the Business Cycle

The task of officially declaring the start and end dates of recessions is performed by the Business Cycle Dating Committee of the National Bureau of Economic Research. The Committee is currently comprised of seven economists (an eighth is on leave) from prominent universities. The Committee examines the data trends of several economic indicators, including measures of:

- Overall output
- Overall national income
- Total employment
- Aggregate hours worked

The Committee did not say that the economy had returned to its pre-recession level of activity or that the economy was strong; it just stated that the decline in several economic measures that began in December 2007 had ended and any new decline in economic activity would represent a new recession. That the economy is not officially in recession does not mean that it doesn't feel as if it is for many workers and their families. There is often not a palpable difference between a recessionary economy and a weak recovery—this is especially true with what are called "jobless recoveries."

What Is Meant by a "Jobless Recovery"?

An economy officially in recovery that continues to shed jobs as if in recession, or experiences prolonged tepid job growth, is deemed a "jobless recovery." In a jobless recovery it takes an inordinate amount of time to recoup the jobs lost during the downturn. While the recession officially ended in June 2009, the employment picture remains quite dismal. At the lowest point for jobs, in December 2009, 8.4 million jobs were lost, which represented 6.1% of all jobs. To date job losses are still at 7.7 million, which represents 5.6% of all jobs. Since the onset of recovery, the monthly employment reports have been mixed, but the net employment level has fallen by an additional 439,000.

Figure 1 depicts the dynamics of recessionary job losses and jobless recoveries. Each line represents the trajectory of job growth from the onset of recession until jobs were finally recouped (when the line crosses the horizontal axis—which represents months since the onset of recession). The solid black line represents average job losses for recessions prior to 1990. (On average the pre-1990 recessions were about eleven months long and it took about 21 months to recoup pre-recessionary job level.)

Job losses due to the 1990 recession (the solid gray line) were just about 1.5%— quite shallow comparatively and the recession was officially just eight months long. But employment lingered at the trough for a long time and it took about 31 months to recoup those lost jobs. The downturn in 2001 (dotted black line) was also eight months long and about 2% of jobs were lost—again relatively mild—but it took 46 months to recoup those lost jobs.

It is clear from the figure that the recession that started in December 2007 (dot-ted gray line) led to a reduction in employment that far exceeded that of the previous recessions. This recession was 18 months long and ended in June 2009. Job losses were catastrophic. At its worst point jobs were down 8.4 million. Job growth turned positive in the spring of 2010—mostly due to the temporary hiring of Census work-ers. But shortly after Census workers were hired they were let go, and job growth once again turned negative. At this point it is clear that the labor market is in the realm of a jobless recovery—a prolonged period of negative or weak job growth. It will be a very long time before this economy recoups the enormous amount of jobs lost over this recession.

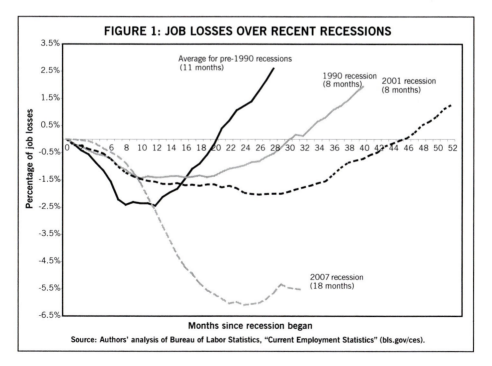

FIGURE 1: JOB LOSSES OVER RECENT RECESSIONS

Average for pre-1990 recessions (11 months)

1990 recession (8 months)

2001 recession (8 months)

2007 recession (18 months)

Percentage of job losses

Months since recession began

Source: Authors' analysis of Bureau of Labor Statistics, "Current Employment Statistics" (bls.gov/ces).

How Might Blacks Fare During a Jobless Recovery?

While it is difficult to predict exactly what might happen to black workers during this jobless recovery, it is instructive to examine what happened to black unemployment during the last jobless recovery, which followed the 2001 recession. Figure 2 provides key information.

The gray bars in the figure mark key dates of the last two recessions and recoveries. In examining the trend in black unemployment since the 2001 recession, there are six key dates:

- The beginning of the recession (March 2001)
- The official end of the recession (November 2001)
- When job creation turned positive (September 2003)
- When the employment levels returned to pre-recession level (January 2005)
- The beginning of recession (December 2007)
- The official end of the recession (June 2009)

As Figure 2 indicates, unemployment rates continued to rise after the official end of the recession in November 2001. Over the jobless recovery—from November 2001 to September 2003—unemployment increased from 9.8% to 11% for blacks and 4.9% to 5.4% for whites. Black unemployment rates did not begin to steadily fall until the total number of jobs had reached the pre-recession level (January 2005). The unemployment rates for whites started to fall just prior to September 2003—near the end of the jobless recovery.

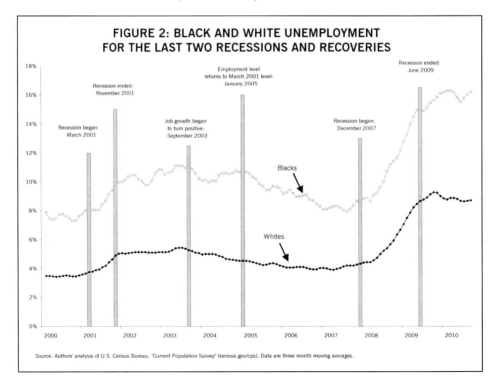

FIGURE 2: BLACK AND WHITE UNEMPLOYMENT FOR THE LAST TWO RECESSIONS AND RECOVERIES

Source: Authors' analysis of U.S. Census Bureau, "Current Population Survey" (census.gov/cps). Data are three month moving averages.

Starting with the onset of the 2007 recession, again the black unemployment rate increased at a faster rate than did that of whites. Since the onset of recovery—in June 2009—the unemployment rate of blacks has increased by 1.4 percentage points, from 14.8% to 16.2%. The rate for whites at the start of recovery was 8.7%, and after an initial increase it is back to that same rate today.

If the 2001 pattern holds, it may well be that the current black unemployment rates will not begin to significantly abate until the employment level returns to its pre-recessionary level of December 2007. This will almost certainly take several years as the shortfall in jobs is currently at 7.7 million. In order to return the national unemployment rate to its December 2007 rate, the economy would need to create 290,000 jobs per month for five years; so far this year job creation has averaged 68,000 per month, even as the last four months have averaged -98,000.

In other words, for many black workers and their families, the recovery will continue to feel like a deep recession for many years to come.

Resources: Bureau of Labor Statistics, "Current Employment Statistics" (bls.gov/ces); National Bureau of Economic Research, "The NBER's Business Cycle Dating Committee" (nber.org/cycles/recessions.html and nber.org/cycles/sept2010.html).

Chapter 8

INDUSTRIAL AND EMPLOYMENT POLICY

Article 8.1

BAIL OUT THE SAFETY NET

BY RANDY ALBELDA
January/February 2009

Even before the financial crisis and the recession, a substantial proportion of working families were not making it in America. In 2007, 20% of the population in a family with a breadwinner—that's 41 million people —did not have enough income, *including* any Food Stamps, Medicaid, housing and child care subsidies, or other public support they received, to pay their basic living expenses.

The good news that the current crisis brings for this bottom 20% is that as their plight of working hard but not making enough to pay the bills is becoming much more generalized, so should the pressure to address it. The bad news, of course, is the recession itself. The hardships these families face are growing by the day. More and more households are falling toward the social safety net.

And what about that safety net? In the 1990s, the Clinton administration ended "welfare as we know it," but at the same time promised work supports as low-wage workers moved up the ladder. Since then, employment rates for poor and low-income mothers have indeed soared, and so has the demand for affordable housing and child care assistance. But funding for them has not, with long waiting lists for both. As a result, by the early 2000s, these government work supports helped only 10% of the population in working families that couldn't meet their basic needs to actually meet them.

Despite expansions in the Earned Income Tax Credit and public health insurance for children in the 1990s, the public support programs for low-income families provide inadequate help, and even that to only a fraction of those who need it. And for workers who lose their jobs: today, only about a third of all unemployed workers receive unemployment benefits.

The safety net is not only tattered; it is nearly obsolete.

Rising unemployment is beginning to take its toll, as are draconian state budget cuts. Congress and President Obama appear ready to enact a large stimulus package to spur the economy and create jobs. Their focus so far is mostly on infrastructure, on "rebuilding our crumbling roads and bridges, modernizing schools..., building wind farms and solar panels," as Obama has said.

But bridge repair and even green jobs are not enough. Our physical infrastructure needs work, but so does our social infrastructure. And it's not just the safety net. Quality care for children and long-term care for disabled and elderly people are in short supply—and unaffordably expensive for many families. Moreover, women are disproportionately employed in these sectors, many at low wages that barely enable them to support their own families. In contrast, the construction and green-energy jobs that often pay decent wages with benefits are overwhelmingly filled by men.

So let's enact a bold recovery plan that promotes employment but also reconstructs the safety net and jump-starts the process of upgrading our social infrastructure. Here are four suggestions:

First, provide federal funding to states to prevent reductions in essential services. Now is not the time to reduce public health investments, stop transportation projects, cut higher education and lay off K-12 and early-education teachers.

Second, recreate our housing infrastructure. In exchange for buying up bad loans, secure foreclosed properties and develop an affordable housing stock.

Third, expand help for families who are struggling to pay for care for children and elders. Doing so will not only help the families struggling to care for their loved ones. It will also provide the job-creation stimulus for women workers that dollars for bridge repair will provide for men.

Fourth, replace our outdated and arbitrary poverty measure with a realistic measure of what it takes to afford basic needs and participate fully in society. This measure should be used to gauge whether the eventual economic recovery is reaching all Americans.

Economic recovery will require bold, public action. Such action isn't limited to reforming our financial system or to traditional stimulus spending. It also means upgrading our social infrastructure in ways that ensure our economy works for all. ❑

Article 8.2

CREATING DECENT JOBS: THE ROLE OF UNIONS

BY JEANNETTE WICKS-LIM
January/February 2010

The turmoil of the current recession is deflecting attention from a longer-term challenge facing the U.S. economy: how to create decent jobs. Even before the recession, nearly two-thirds of U.S. jobs failed the "decent job" test—they paid too little to cover a small family's basic needs. Between now and 2016, the strongest job growth will be largely in low-pay occupations, according to Department of Labor projections. So barring any structural changes, the U.S. economy will be no better at producing jobs that can support a worker and his or her family at a very basic living standard in 2016 than it was in 2006.

Collective bargaining through labor unions could brighten this forecast, raising the quality of future jobs even if the economy continues to produce the same types of jobs. Bringing the unionized share of the U.S. workforce back up to around its level in the 1970s—admittedly no easy task—would lift an estimated 2.5 million additional jobs over the decent-job threshold in 2016.

A reasonable definition of a decent job is one with the minimum pay and benefits necessary to provide a healthy and safe standard of living for a small family. This benchmark is substantially above the U.S. Census Bureau's official poverty threshold, widely viewed as far too low. Based on very basic family budgets the Economic Policy Institute has developed, a decent job has to pay at least $17 an hour with health and retirement benefits, or $22 an hour without.

A recent Labor Department report examines trends through 2006 to predict the jobs picture in 2016. Here are the ten occupations slated to add the most jobs: orderlies and nursing/home-health aides; registered nurses; retail salespersons; customer service representatives; food preparation and serving workers; general office clerks; personal/home-care aides; postsecondary teachers; janitors; and accounting clerks. In only two—RNs and postsecondary teachers—do the majority of existing jobs meet the decent job standard. The other eight fall short.

It's no surprise, then, that an analysis of the complete 2016 jobs projection shows little change in the overall proportion of decent jobs. By my estimates, in 2016 some 35.2% of all jobs will meet this standard, barely changed from the 2006 figure of 34.8%. These projections pre-date the current recession, and so reveal a long-term problem likely to persist well after the economy revives.

If we cannot count on a raft of novel, more lucrative occupations in the next several years, then expanding the number of decent jobs will require improving the compensation of jobs in existing occupations. Unions enable workers to do exactly that. Suppose union representation rose by a meaningful amount, say 10 percentage points to about 24%, by 2016. The proportion of decent jobs in 2016 would rise by an estimated 1.5 percentage points to 36.7%, representing an additional 2.5 million decent jobs. This is four times the projected increase if union representation levels remain the same.

But what about globalization? Forget about more decent jobs—how can U.S. workers stop decent jobs from disappearing in an increasingly integrated world economy with a large supply of labor that is cheaper than any in the United States, whether unionized or not?

One answer is to focus on jobs that are not off-shore-able and on sectors in which U.S.-based firms have a competitive edge. Clean energy initiatives fit the bill: they involve activities that can only be done locally such as retrofitting buildings, plus, renewable energy is an area where U.S.-based firms' technological edge counts.

This strategy has another potential benefit for workers: greater international solidarity. By reducing the pressure they face from the global "race to the bottom," robust clean-energy job growth would better position U.S. workers to focus on cross-border organizing that can raise the floor of the global labor market.

What would it take to bring an additional 10% of U.S. workers into unions? That is the subject of another article. But the fact that the Employee Free Choice Act, which would make it easier for workers to join unions, is under serious consideration in Congress gives reason for hope. Any policies that expand opportunities for workers to join unions would help ensure that employment growth in the coming years produces decent jobs. ❑

Sources: *Creating Decent Jobs in the United States: The Role of Labor Unions and Collective Bargaining*, peri.umass.edu; Constance F. Citro and Robert T. Michael, eds., *Measuring Poverty: A New Approach*, National Academy Press, 1995; Arlene Dohm and Lyn Shniper, "Employment outlook 2006-2016: Occupational employment projections to 2016," *Monthly Labor Review*, Nov. 2007; David Howell, Dean Baker, Andrew Glyn, and John Schmitt, "Are Protective Labor Market Institutions at the Root of Unemployment? A Critical Review of the Evidence," *Capitalism and Society* 2(1), 2007; James Heckman, "Comments on 'Are Protective Labor Market Institutions at the Root of Unemployment? A Critical Review of the Evidence'," *Capitalism and Society* (2)1, 2007; James Lin and Jared Bernstein, "What We Need To Get By," Economic Policy Institute, 2008.

Article 8.3

IS MILITARY KEYNESIANISM THE SOLUTION?

Why war is not a sustainable strategy for economic recovery.

BY HEIDI GARRETT-PELTIER
March/April 2010

The United States is currently preparing to send 30,000 additional troops to Afghanistan by summer 2010. Military contractors, deeply integrated into the U.S. economy, will continue to prosper and profit from increased military spending resulting from this surge of troops. At a time when unemployment in the domestic economy remains near 10%, it may seem convenient to fall back on the principle of military Keynesianism: War is good for the economy.

John Maynard Keynes, the British economist whose work has once again become popular in the wake of this most recent economic crisis, advocated increased government spending to lift an economy out of recession or depression. When consumers and businesses slow their spending, the government can step in to increase demand for goods and services so that businesses can continue to produce and people can remain employed. This fiscal stimulus could take the form of infrastructure projects, healthcare, education, or other productive endeavors. By this logic, military spending can lift an economy out of recession by creating demand for goods and services provided by military contractors, such as the production of tanks and ammunition or the provision of security services. Advocates of this strategy point not only to the widespread employment created by military spending, but also claim that military spending creates well-paying, stable jobs.

It is true that military spending creates jobs throughout the economy, and that many of those jobs are well-paying. But at a time when our jobless rate is high, infrastructure is crumbling, and global climate change is becoming an increasingly urgent matter, we must ask whether military spending is truly a solution to our economic woes or whether we might be able to create more jobs in productive areas that also help us meet longer-term goals.

In a recent paper that I co-authored with Robert Pollin, we show that dollar per dollar, more jobs are created through spending on clean energy, health care, and education than on the military. Further, we show that more middle-income and well-paying jobs are created in all of these areas. For each $1 billion of spending, over 17,000 jobs would be created in clean energy, close to 20,000 in health care, and over 29,000 in education. That same $1 billion would create only 11,600 jobs as a result of military spending. If we look at well-paying jobs, those that pay over $64,000 per year, these alternative domestic spending areas also outperform military spending. The same $1 billion would create 1,500 well-paying jobs in clean energy and just over 1,000 in the military—clean energy creates 50% *more* good jobs than military spending. Education, which is labor-intensive and creates many well-paying jobs per dollar of expenditure, creates close to 2,500 jobs paying over $64,000—that's 2.5 times as many as the military.

According to the National Priorities Project, military spending on the Iraq and Afghanistan wars has reached approximately $1 trillion since 2001, not including the cost of the surge of 30,000 troops. In fiscal year 2009, federal government outlays on the military were 17% of all outlays. Meanwhile, energy, resource conservation, and the environment accounted for only 1% of federal outlays, while education, training, and social services made up only 2%. Military spending is therefore *eight to seventeen times* as high as federal education- and energy-related spending.

The Obama administration is facing increased pressure to reduce the size of the fiscal deficit and the national debt, both of which have grown partly as a result of military spending. At the same time, there is an urgent need to put people back to work and to move the country toward a low-carbon future. While military Keynesianism offers one strategy for recovering from the recession, it is by no means the most effective, even putting aside the other reasons for objecting to a war economy. By reducing military spending, we can channel some of those savings to clean energy, health care, education, and other matters of national and global importance. ❏

Sources: "The U.S. Employment Effects of Military and Domestic Spending Priorities: An Updated Analysis," by Robert Pollin and Heidi Garrett-Peltier, available at www.peri.umass.edu; National Priorities Project, www.nationalpriorities.org.

Article 8.4

WE NEED A (GREEN) JOBS PROGRAM

Clean-energy investment would promote job growth for a wide swath of the U.S. workforce.

BY JEANETTE WICKS-LIM
September/October 2010

Fourteen months of an unemployment rate at or near 10% clearly calls for the federal government to take a lead role in job creation. The White House should push its clean-energy agenda as a jobs program but steer clear of all the hype about "green-collar" jobs. Green-collar jobs are widely perceived as job opportunities accessible only to an elite segment of the U.S. workforce—those with advanced degrees, such as environmental engineers, lab technicians, and research scientists. Such jobs are inaccessible to the 52% of unemployed workers with no college experience. The truth is, however, that clean-energy investments could serve as a powerful engine for job growth for a wide swath of the U.S. workforce.

My colleagues at the Political Economy Research Institute and I examined a clean-energy program that includes making buildings more energy efficient, expanding and improving mass transit, updating the national electric grid, and developing each of three types of renewable energy sources: wind, solar, and biomass fuels. Here's what we found.

First, clean-energy activities produce more jobs, dollar for dollar, than fossil fuel-related activities. This is because clean-energy activities tend to be more labor intensive (i.e., more investment dollars go to hiring workers than buying machines), have a higher domestic content (i.e., more dollars are spent on goods and services produced within the United States) and have lower average wages than fossil fuel-related activities. The figures in the table below show how a $1 million investment in clean-energy activities would create more than three times the number of jobs that would be created by investing the same amount in fossil fuels.

Second, many clean energy sector jobs would be accessible to workers with no college experience. The table also shows how the jobs created by a $1 million investment in clean energy would be spread across three levels of education: high school degree or less, some college, and B.A. or more. Nearly half of the clean energy jobs would be held by workers with a high school degree or less. These include jobs for construction laborers, carpenters, and bus drivers. Fewer than one-quarter of clean-energy jobs would require a B.A. or more. The figures for the fossil fuels sector

JOB CREATION: CLEAN ENERGY VS. FOSSIL FUELS
Number of jobs created by investing $1 million dollars in clean energy versus fossil-fuels activities, by education credentials

Education Credentials	Clean Energy	Fossil Fuels
Total	16.7 jobs (100%)	5.3 jobs (100%)
High school diploma or less	8.0 jobs (47.9%)	2.2 jobs (41.5%)
Some college, no B.A.	4.8 jobs (28.7%)	1.6 jobs (30.2%)
B.A. or more	3.9 jobs (23.3%)	1.5 jobs (28.3%)

(second column) show that they are more heavily weighted toward jobs requiring college degrees.

Does this mean green investments will just create lots of low-paying jobs? No. The figures in the table below show that investing $1 million in green activities rather than fossil fuel-related activities would generate many more jobs for workers at all three levels of formal education credentials. Compared to the fossil fuels sector, the clean energy sector would produce nearly four times the number of jobs that require a high school degree or less, three times the number of jobs that require some college experience, and 2.5 times the number of jobs that require a B.A. or more. Green investments would produce more jobs at all education and wage levels, even while generating proportionately more jobs that are accessible to workers with a high school degree or less.

Workers are right to worry about whether these high school degree jobs would offer family-supporting wages. Construction laborers, for example, average $29,000 annually—awfully close to the $22,000 official poverty line. In addition, women and workers of color have historically faced discrimination in the construction industry, which would be the source of a lot of the lower-credentialed jobs in the clean energy sector. Workers will need to do some serious organizing to put in place labor protections such as living-wage laws, strong collective bargaining rights, and affirmative action policies to ensure that these jobs pay decent wages and are equally accessible to all qualified workers. ❏

Sources: Robert Pollin, Jeannette Wicks-Lim, and Heidi Garrett-Peltier, Green Prosperity: How Clean-Energy Policies Can Fight Poverty and Raise Living Standards in the United States, Political Economy Research Institute, 2009, www.peri.umass.edu/green_prosperity.

Article 8.5

SAVING ENERGY CREATES JOBS

BY HEIDI GARRETT-PELTIER
May/June 2009

Improving energy efficiency—using less energy to do the same amount of work—saves money and cuts pollution. But today, the other benefit of investing in energy efficiency may be the best draw: saving energy creates jobs.

Let's look at energy use in residential and commercial buildings. In the United States, buildings account for 40% of all energy use and are responsible for 38% of U.S. carbon emissions. Homes and other buildings lose energy through wasted heat, air-conditioning, and electricity. Following Jimmy Carter's suddenly fashionable example, we can turn down the thermostat in the winter and put on a sweater. We can unplug appliances that aren't used and save "phantom" power.

Beyond these personal changes, though, lie massive opportunities for systematic energy efficiency gains. These include insulating buildings, replacing old windows, and updating appliances and lighting. All of these generate new economic opportunities—read, jobs—in construction, manufacturing, and other sectors.

For instance, retrofitting existing homes, offices, and schools to reduce heating- and cooling-related energy waste (also known as weatherization) creates jobs of many kinds. Recent media attention has spotlighted "green jobs" programs that are hiring construction workers to add insulation, replace windows, and install more efficient heating systems. Perhaps less visible, retrofitting buildings also creates jobs for the engineers who design the new windows and furnaces, the factory workers who build them, and the office workers who make the appointments and handle the bookkeeping.

In fact, retrofitting creates more than twice as many jobs per dollar spent than oil or coal production, according to a detailed study that my colleagues and I at the Political Economy Research Institute conducted in 2008. For each $1 million spent, retrofitting creates about 19 jobs while spending on coal creates nine jobs and oil only six. Retrofitting also creates more jobs per dollar spent than personal consumption on typical items such as food, clothing, and electronics. Personal consumption does better than fossil fuels, but not as well as retrofitting, generating about 15 jobs per $1 million spent.

Why does retrofitting create more jobs? First, retrofitting is more labor-intensive than fossil-fuel production, meaning that more of each dollar spent goes to labor and less to machinery and equipment. Retrofitting also has higher domestic content than either fossil fuels or consumer goods; in other words, more of the supplies used to retrofit buildings are produced in the United States. In fact, about 95% of spending on retrofits stays in the domestic economy, versus only 80% of spending on oil (including refining and other related activities). Since more of its inputs are produced in the United States, retrofitting employs more U.S. workers. And this raises its multiplier effect: when those workers spend their earnings, each retrofitting dollar leads to yet more demand for goods and services. To be fair, not all energy efficiency improvements will create jobs. When a more energy-efficient appliance or window design is widely adopted, the manufacturing worker who produced a less efficient good yesterday is simply producing a more efficient good today, with no net increase in employment. On the other hand, many retrofitting activities are pure job creators. Insulating attics and caulking leaky windows are activities that necessitate new workers—not just a shift from producing one good to another. With the collapse of the housing bubble and the huge rise in construction industry unemployment, retrofitting is an activity that could put tens of thousands of people back to work.

The Obama administration's stimulus package contains a wide variety of energy efficiency incentives, from 30% rebates for home insulation and for installing efficient windows, to rebates for builders of energy-efficient new homes and commercial buildings. These provisions will drive energy-saving improvements, accelerating the transition to a low-carbon economy while also creating jobs. ❑

Sources: U.S. Department of Energy, EERE Building Technologies Program; Robert Pollin, Heidi Garrett-Peltier, James Heintz, and Helen Scharber, "Green Recovery," Political Economy Research Institute, September 2008.

Article 8.6

EIGHTEEN MILLION JOBS BY 2012

BY ROBERT POLLIN
March 2010, The Nation

Unemployment in the United States stands officially at 9.7%. This represents 14.8 million people out of work. By a broader official measure that includes people employed fewer hours than they would like and those discouraged from looking for work, the unemployment rate is 16.5%, or about 25 million people in a total labor force of about 153 million. We have not seen comparable unemployment rates since 1983, 27 years ago, and before that, not since the 1930s Depression.

The job-creation proposals coming from the Obama administration, in the president's January 27 State of the Union address and elsewhere, generally point in the right direction, with more spending for clean energy, infrastructure, and support for small businesses. These proposals follow from Obama's February 2009 economic recovery program, which injected $787 billion in new spending or tax relief into the economy over two years. However, just as last February's stimulus program was too small to counteract the evaporation of $16 trillion in household wealth resulting from the financial collapse, the scope of Obama's current proposals is nowhere near large enough for the situation today.

For example, Obama has proposed $33 billion in new tax credits for small businesses. By contrast, private borrowing by businesses over the previous six months was down by $1.5 trillion relative to 2007, with the largest proportional cutbacks coming from small businesses. What's more, Obama's call to freeze discretionary federal spending in nonmilitary areas is dangerously misguided. The fiscal deficits of 2009 and 2010—at between $1.4 trillion and $1.6 trillion, or around 10% of GDP—are indeed very large. But the freeze obscures what Obama and his advisers clearly know—that deficit spending is part of the solution to our economic predicament and will remain so until we see millions of people getting hired into decent jobs.

Here is what we need: a commitment from the Obama administration to create 18 million new jobs over the remaining three years of the presidential term. That would mean an average increase of about 500,000 jobs per month, or a bit more than 4% growth in job creation over the next three years. This can be done by combining two broad types of initiatives: measures to buttress the economy's floor and thereby prevent another 2008-type collapse, and measures to inject job-generating investments into the economy. If such initiatives are successful, the official unemployment rate will stand at around 4% when Obama runs for re-election in November 2012.

Is This Realistic?

The central features of this plan can remain within the framework of proposals already established by the administration. The key is getting the scale large enough. The only way this can happen is by combining the positive energies of the public and private sectors. This public-private approach is not only practically necessary; it will also counteract right-wing claims that the government is seizing control of the economy in the name of job creation. Most of the financial heft will have to come from banks and other private financial institutions. The banks alone are hoarding cash reserves totaling about $850 billion in their accounts at the Federal Reserve. Most of that money needs to be channeled into job-generating investments. For this to happen, interest rates and the risks for lending to small businesses need to fall substantially.

But it will be necessary for the government to keep injecting spending into the economy, which will add to the deficit. Scare stories aside, the fiscal deficit is not dangerously large. The interest rates the government is paying on its borrowing—as opposed to the rates that businesses have to pay on much riskier loans—remain historically low, in the range of 2–3%. This is because the world's financial magicians of just a few years ago have chosen to protect their remaining wealth by buying up the safest possible assets they can find, which are U.S. Treasury bonds. When Ronald Reagan was running up record-breaking deficits in the early 1980s, the interest rates on the bonds were around 13%.

This huge gap in interest rates between now and the Reagan era will save the Treasury about $175 billion per year going forward. Also remember that falling unemployment rates reduce the deficit on their own, with each 1% drop generating about $90 billion in government revenues or reduced spending obligations. This is because when people are newly employed, they can support themselves and pay more taxes. We also need workers earning decent wages. Even if we didn't care about the ever-widening inequalities of wages, incomes and wealth, we would still need working people to have enough money in their pockets to boost sagging consumer markets. Conversely, when unemployment rises, the government is faced with huge extra spending burdens through unemployment insurance, food stamps, Medicaid, and related social safety net commitments. The fiscal deficit could probably be eliminated altogether if unemployment could be driven down to around 4%, even without spending cuts or increases in tax rates. Finally, we can extract about $300 billion in savings and new revenues by ending the wars in Iraq and Afghanistan and by establishing a modest tax on speculative Wall Street trading.

One argument against taking bold measures now is that, mass unemployment aside, the official indicators tell us that the recession is over. The economy did grow at a robust 5.7% over the past quarter, though that may be only a short-term blip, driven by businesses restocking their depleted inventories. But let's assume that a recovery is indeed under way at more or less the normal rate of progress relative to recent recessions. In fact, under such a "normal" scenario, unemployment would not likely fall to around 5% until early 2017. We would not likely hit 4% unemployment until mid-2018, assuming the recovery could be kept going for another eight years.

Even with a successful coordination of large-scale expansions of private and public spending, is it realistic to expect that the economy, which has been so trampled down for the past three years, could possibly create 18 million jobs over the next three years? It is an ambitious but realistic goal. This is basically the rate at which employment grew under Gerald Ford and Jimmy Carter coming out of the 1974–75 recession. The Carter years are widely derided through the lens of his 1979 "malaise" speech. Yet the first three years under Carter generated the fastest expansion of job opportunities of any comparable period since, including any three-year stretch under Reagan or Clinton.

The Carter presidency, of course, ended disastrously with the severe 1980 recession. But this was because OPEC and the oil companies doubled oil prices between 1979 and 1980. Even more important, Wall Street insisted at the time that Carter appoint Paul Volcker as chair of the Federal Reserve to stop the inflation that resulted from the oil price shock. Volcker immediately raised short-term interest rates, pushing them as high as 17% by April 1980. This brought unemployment up to 7.5% in time for Reagan's landslide victory over Carter in November 1980. (It is ironic that among Obama's top tier of economic advisers, the same Paul Volcker is taking the hardest line against Wall Street excesses.)

Of course, we need to control inflation, especially when it results from oil price jumps. But we can do this by getting serious about energy conservation and new renewable energy sources, as well as being prepared to release our strategic oil reserves as needed, to force oil prices back down amid a crisis. Pushing unemployment down to around 4% will also provoke inflation fears because it is likely to bring wage increases, as workers' bargaining power improves. But rising wages do not cause inflation on their own, as long as wage increases are in line with how much workers produce on the job. Also recall that the average wage today is about 10% below its peak level of 1972, even though average worker productivity has risen by about 90% since the early 1970s. In short, now is the time to focus on creating 18 million decent jobs and not to remain fixated—as we were from Volcker's 1979 appointment until the 2008 financial collapse—on fears of moderately rising inflation.

Reducing the Pain

Mass unemployment creates widespread human suffering. Minimizing this suffering has to be the first priority in fighting the recession. Helping people in need also contributes to countering a downward recessionary spiral and thus helps prevent another collapse. In general, the Obama administration has done reasonably well on this front, but the demands are great. More than three million homeowners have lost their homes through foreclosures or related bank actions since the crisis began, and the foreclosure rate is running at 170,000 per month, near the peak for the crisis. The African-American community, targeted as a large potential market for subprime mortgages during the bubble years, is suffering disproportionately from foreclosures. Clearly, in this case, the administration's efforts have accomplished next to nothing. Economist Dean Baker has proposed the most effective plan to keep people in their homes, which is to allow them to stay in their homes as renters, paying market rental rates. The government also needs to continue extending unemployment benefits and increase support for food stamps to compensate unemployed workers and the poor for their income losses.

In the same vein are work-sharing programs that extend unemployment compensation to workers who accept reduced hours that then enable their companies to avoid outright layoffs. Indeed, work-sharing can be even more effective and fairer than traditional unemployment insurance, since it spreads the reductions in work hours across a wide group of workers rather than concentrating the effects of the recession on the minority of workers who become completely jobless. Work-sharing programs have long been a major part of the social safety net in Western Europe. Over this recession, Germany has been especially aggressive in extending these benefits to prevent rising unemployment.

Such programs already exist on a modest scale in 17 states. Senator Jack Reed of Rhode Island has introduced a bill that would extend these programs and provide start-up funds to create measures in the remaining states. While this would be a very favorable development, we also need to recognize that work-sharing programs, similar to anti-foreclosure measures, unemployment insurance, and food stamps, do not inject any new major source of spending into the economy. They will help firm up the economy's floor. But even here they will need additional support, especially given the budgetary crisis faced by state and local governments around the country.

Bringing State and Local Governments Back to Health

California's budget is in a deep ditch, with an eye-popping 56% gap between expected revenues and spending commitments. Most other states are also staring at huge revenue shortfalls. The jobs recovery will not succeed until this situation is stabilized. How could it be otherwise? State and local governments account for about $2 trillion in annual spending, or 14% of GDP. Either directly or indirectly through their supply purchases, they generate 30 million jobs, 20% of the entire American workforce.

They are also the institutions most responsible for delivering basic needs to people—education, healthcare, support for the needy, public safety, and infrastructure.

Unlike the federal government, nearly all state and local governments are required to balance their operating budgets every year. In a recession, tax revenues decline in step with the decline in people's incomes, spending levels, and property values. This means that state and local governments almost inevitably fall into crisis in a recession. There are only two ways to avoid this within our current fiscal arrangements. The first is to build up a major surplus of "rainy-day funds." But keeping large amounts of cash on reserve is very difficult to do even during healthy economic times, given that the demands for health, education, and public safety programs are persistent. The other way for states to avoid cutbacks during a recession is to receive financial injections from the federal government.

The February 2009 recovery program provided $144 billion in support to offset that year's state budget shortfalls. This money was well spent. I know this firsthand through my own employer, the University of Massachusetts. We received around $50 million last year, which enabled us to prevent hundreds of layoffs. The layoffs would have sent shock waves throughout the region, since UMass is the largest employer in western Massachusetts. One can tell comparable stories in scores of communities around the country. Another roughly $200 billion is needed now. The Obama administration is supporting measures that would amount to perhaps $30–50 billion.

Increasing support for state and local government activities should not be seen as merely a short-term stopgap but also as a major element of a longer-term job-creation agenda. The main activities supported by state and local governments are all effective sources of job creation, in comparison for example with military spending. Thus, infrastructure projects create 40% more jobs per dollar than spending on the military, healthcare creates 70% more jobs, and education creates 240% more jobs. So if the government just moved its 2008 budget of $188 billion for Afghanistan and Iraq into support for education and infrastructure programs at the state and local levels, this alone would produce a net increase of about 2.3 million jobs per year.

Scaling Up the Green Recovery

One of the Obama administration's main jobs initiatives is retrofitting buildings, especially private homes, to make them more energy efficient. The president has described home retrofitting projects as a "sexy" way to save money. In fact, even relatively small investments in home retrofits, in the range of $2,500, can pay for themselves in three to four years, since they can lead to monthly energy bills falling by between 25 and 30%. These measures also produce rapid environmental benefits, since raising energy efficiency is the easiest way to cut greenhouse gas emissions.

Despite these attractions, private investments in retrofits have not expanded quickly enough to serve as a major jobs engine. The private market for retrofits remains underdeveloped. This is because homeowners are understandably wary about making investments when they are cash-strapped and their home values have collapsed. They are also not eager to face the hassles of dealing with banks, utility companies and work crews. This could all change rapidly if banks, utilities and community organizations could, in various combinations, figure out how to make retrofits easy and widely accessible for homeowners.

In the meantime, the government needs to take the lead by immediately advancing a major nationwide retrofitting initiative. The opportunity is enormous. There are roughly 24 billion square feet of building stock in hospitals and healthcare, education, and government buildings. This is about 20% of all U.S. building stock. Retrofitting these buildings would cost about $150 billion. If we assume this program is implemented over three years, at $50 billion per year, this would generate about 800,000 jobs per year over those three years. Retrofits are a highly efficient source of job creation, since all the work must be done within local communities, and a large proportion of the budgets go to hiring workers, as opposed to buying equipment, land, and energy.

This government-led project could be the launching point for a larger effort to build the institutional and market support for retrofitting remaining private-sector structures on an economy-wide scale. In addition to private hospitals and schools, the potential market for private retrofits for commercial and residential buildings is in the range of $650 billion. If even 20% of these buildings were retrofitted by the end of 2012, it would create another 800,000 jobs per year. Retrofitting alone could thus generate about 1.5 million of the 18 million jobs we need to create by the end of 2012. About 600,000 of them would be in construction, making up for one-quarter of the 2.6 million construction jobs lost since mid-2007.

Of course, the broader green investment project will need to expand well beyond retrofits to encompass public transportation, electrical grid upgrades, and the creation of a competitive renewable-energy manufacturing sector. These will all be major sources of job creation over time. The same is true for investments in rebuilding our traditional infrastructure of bridges, roads, and water management systems. But if we are serious about creating 18 million jobs within three years, retrofitting is the place to begin.

Making the Banks Respectable

The most powerful factor for creating 18 million jobs in three years will be the country's private financial institutions. Yes, I am referring to the same institutions— the banks, savings and loans, brokerage houses, insurance companies, and hedge funds—whose reckless practices created the economic crisis in the first place.

That is the point. Financial institutions are a formidable force for both good and bad. They were effectively regulated for roughly 30 years after World War II, in the shadow of the 1930s financial collapse and Depression. This played a major role in generating the "Golden Age" of American capitalism through the mid-1970s, with rapid growth, low unemployment rates, diminishing inequality, and historically unprecedented levels of financial stability. Without delving here into the details of today's debate on how to re-regulate finance—a debate, incredibly, still dominated by Wall Street—let's be clear on first principles. This is simple: we need regulations that will help channel credit toward productive, job-generating activities and away from hyper-speculation. For starters, that means pushing the lion's share of the banks' $850 billion in cash reserves into productive investments.

Of course, the banks need to maintain a reasonable supply of cash reserves as a cushion against future economic downturns. One of the main causes of the 2008–09 crisis and other recent financial crises was precisely that the banks' cash reserves were far too low.

In 2007 banks were holding only $21 billion in cash reserves. But increasing reserves from $21 billion to $850 billion in little more than a year is a new form of Wall Street excess. Let's say that banks should keep $200 billion in reserves as a cushion, a level roughly in line with the amounts they held during the era of regulation. The banks could still lend $650 billion to businesses just from the funds they are sitting on. At the very least, we could assume that overall new lending for productive, job-creating activities could be in the range of $700 billion or above, once we allow for funds coming from savings and loans, insurance companies, and other financial institutions in addition to the commercial banks. We would then anticipate that the financial institutions would increase business lending by comparable amounts in 2011 and 2012. Doing so would help set a level of overall lending at roughly its average level during previous economic recoveries. At the same time, expanding credit and productive business investments by around $700 billion per year could by itself deliver nearly 18 million new jobs by the end of 2012.

A big problem is not only that banks are reluctant to lend but also that businesses are unwilling to borrow. Businesses have been heavily scarred by the recession and are not eager to take on new risks. Financial market policies therefore need to focus on helping to boost business confidence and reduce the risks of job-creating investments. The first step here would be for the Federal Reserve to substantially lower the interest rates at which private businesses may borrow. The Fed has been maintaining the interest rate at which private banks borrow among themselves—the "federal funds rate"—at little more than zero for more than a year. But the rates at which non-financial businesses may borrow are at historic highs relative to the nearly zero federal funds rate.

An average solid business now has to pay about 6.5% interest for a long-term loan, roughly 6% more than the rate at which banks may borrow. The Fed needs to push the business borrowing rates down to 3–4%. The Fed has the power to make such a move, though to do so would certainly deviate from standard practice. But let's recall that nothing the Fed did during the 2008–09 crisis to bail out the banks followed the rule book. It is time for the Fed to pursue innovative policies that will directly benefit ordinary businesses and working people.

The government also needs to intervene to lower the risks facing banks making loans for productive investments and the businesses doing the investing. The policy tool to ramp up here is the government's loan guarantee programs, which support small businesses, green investments, students, rural development, and affordable housing. In 2007, the last year before the recession, the government guaranteed about $250 billion in private-sector loans.

The government should roughly double the level of support—i.e., guaranteeing another $250 billion in loans per year—to dramatically expand low-risk opportunities for a wide range of job-generating investments. The proposals being advanced to create a specialized Green Bank as well as an Infrastructure Bank fit comfortably within this broader agenda of channeling the country's financial resources to high-priority projects. At the same time, if banks decide they still can't resist pouring huge sums into the Wall Street casino, they will have to forfeit their eligibility for loan guarantees. The banks should also be required to continue holding high levels of cash reserves as a cushion against their high-stakes gambling. Keep in mind that the government holds controlling stakes in AIG—what had been the world's largest and most sophisticated financial insurance company—as well as Fannie Mae and Freddie Mac, still the most influential mortgage-lending institutions. AIG, Fannie, and Freddie could easily convert part of their operations previously devoted to hyper-speculation to supporting guaranteed loans focused on job creation.

What happens when businesses default on these guaranteed loans? Won't this blow a hole in the government's fiscal deficit? Here is what recent experience tells us. In 2007 about 4% of the government's guaranteed loans went into default. If we assume that the default rate remained at roughly the 2007 level for this expanded program, that would add about $9 billion, or 0.3%, to the federal budget. Even if, implausibly, the default rate on the new loans doubled relative to the 2007 level, that would still increase the federal budget by only 0.6%. In short, roughly doubling the government's traditional loan-guarantee programs is eminently affordable as well as an effective means of reducing risks for private businesses, which in turn would encourage them to make the $700 billion in new job-creating investments we need.

How does the set of proposals outlined here realistically get us to 18 million new jobs by the end of 2012? Starting with the $850 billion cash hoard that commercial banks are holding in their Federal Reserve accounts, we move about $700 billion in new credit into domestic employment-focused investments. Assuming we have established a firm floor for the economy through the measures discussed above, injecting $700 billion in new spending into the economy will generate about 5.5 million jobs in 2010. That's because this $700 billion will generate a 5% rate of GDP growth, which in turn translates into about 4% employment growth. My calculation here assumes that the mix of total employment will shift toward green activities and education, where the jobs per dollar of spending are significantly higher than alternatives such as fossil fuel energy and military spending. We then build from the momentum of a strong 2010 recovery to maintain the roughly 4% rate of employment growth in 2011 and 2012, which will create about 6 million jobs in 2011 and 6.5 million in 2012. By the end of 2012, about 156 million people would be employed, 18 million more than the 138 million working today (see www.peri.umass.edu for details on these and related calculations).

The necessity of advancing a jobs program on this scale follows from the fact that the crisis before us is not just 9.7% unemployment, narrowly defined, or 16.5% unemployment, more reasonably defined, though these figures obviously speak volumes about the interlocking failures of our political and economic systems. Even under a fairly favorable economic scenario, we will be saddled with deep unemployment problems well beyond the 2012 presidential election and perhaps up to the 2016 election, unless we take dramatic action now. Given the severity of the 2008–09 financial crash and recession, it would also be foolish to assume that a healthy recovery is a sure bet. Making things worse is that the Obama administration and Democratic Congress—yes, the Democrats do still hold strong majorities in both Houses—appear unwilling to take actions consistent with the depth of the problems at hand.

Perhaps one can forgive them for underestimating what was needed with the February 2009 recovery program. The full extent of the financial crash and recession were not evident then. I too underestimated what was needed at the time, writing in these pages fifteen months ago ("How to End the Recession," [*The Nation,*] November 24, 2008). The facts and choices before us are now much clearer. We can indeed create 18 million jobs and drive the unemployment rate to 4% by the end of 2012. But we have to begin now, we have to stop thinking small and we have to be willing to fight. ❑

Article 8.7

A NEW WPA?

National governments, by serving as "employers of last resort," could guarantee
full employment by providing a job for anyone ready, willing and able to work.

BY RYAN A. DODD
March/April 2008

Dark clouds are now looming over America's economic future. As first the stock market boom and then the housing boom have come to an end, along with the fountains of cheap credit that were their mainspring, the perennial gale of unemployment is blowing in. The president and Congress have addressed the downturn with tax rebates and talk of "debt relief." Meanwhile, public infrastructure is crumbling. Workers' wages are stagnating while their work hours are rising. Health insurance is becoming less and less affordable for the typical family. And as U.S. military spending escalates, government spending on essential services is drastically reduced.

All of these facts serve to remind us that capitalist economies are inherently unstable and structurally incapable of creating full employment at decent wages and benefits. While tax rebates and debt relief may provide some minor protection from the coming economic storm, these measures are temporary—and inadequate—responses to a perpetual problem. As an alternative to these ad hoc policies or, worse yet, the free-market fundamentalism still widely preached in Washington, some economists and policymakers, in the United States and abroad, are touting a policy that seeks to end unemployment via a government promise to provide a job to anyone ready, willing, and able to work.

Argentina's Experiment in Direct Job Creation

In early December 2001, following nearly two decades of neoliberal restructuring, the Argentine economy collapsed. Apparently, two decades of privatization, liberalization, and government austerity, ushered in by Argentina's brutal military junta (in power from 1976 to 1983), were not enough to sate the appetites of global financial capital: earlier that year the International Monetary Fund had withheld $1.3 billion in loans the country needed to service its $142 billion external debt. In response to the IMF's action, the government froze all bank accounts (although many wealthy Argentines managed to relocate their funds abroad before the freeze) and drastically cut government spending. As a consequence, the economy experienced a severe depression as incomes and expenditures fell through the floor. The unemployment rate shot up to a record 21.5% by May 2002, with over 50% of the population living in poverty.

The popular response to the crisis was massive. Protests and demonstrations erupted throughout the country. The government went through five presidents in the course of a month. Workers eventually reclaimed dozens of abandoned factories and created democratically run cooperative enterprises, many of which are still in operation today and are part of a growing coop movement.

Reclaiming factories was a lengthy and difficult process, however, and the immediate problem of unemployment remained. In response, in April 2002 the Argentine government put into place a direct job creation program known as *Plan Jefes de Hogar* ("Heads-of-Household Plan"), which promised a job to all heads of households satisfying certain requirements. In order to qualify, a household had to include a child under the age of 18, a person with a disability, or a pregnant woman; the household head had to be unemployed; and each household was generally limited to only one participant in the program. The program provided households with 150 pesos a month for four hours of work a day, five days a week. Program participants mainly engaged in the provision of community services and/or participated in worker training programs administered by local nonprofits.

While limited in scope and viewed by many in the government as an emergency measure, the program was incredibly successful and popular with its workers. It provided jobs and incomes to roughly two million workers, or 13% of Argentina's labor force, as well as bringing desperately needed goods and services—from community gardens to small construction projects—to severely depressed neighborhoods. The entry of many women into the program, while their husbands continued to look for jobs in the private sector, had a liberating effect on traditional family structures. And by some accounts, the program helped facilitate the cooperative movement that subsequently emerged with the takeover of abandoned factories. Not surprisingly, as Argentina's economy has recovered from the depths of the crisis, the government has recently made moves to discontinue this critical experiment in direct job creation.

"Employer of Last Resort"

The Argentine experience with direct job creation represents a real-world example of what is often referred to as the *employer of last resort* (ELR) proposal by a number of left academics and public policy advocates. Developed over the course of the past two decades, the ELR proposal is based on a rather simple idea. In a capitalist economy, with most people dependent on private employment for their livelihoods, the government has a unique responsibility to guarantee full employment. This responsibility has been affirmed in the U.N. Universal Declaration of Human Rights, which includes a right to employment. A commitment to full employment is also official U.S. government policy as codified in the Employment Act of 1946 and the Humphrey-Hawkins Act of 1976.

Although many versions of the ELR proposal have been put forward, they all revolve around the idea that national governments could guarantee full employment by providing a job to anyone ready, willing, and able to work. The various proposals differ mainly on the wage and benefit packages they would provide to participants. The most common proposal calls for paying all participants a universal basic wage and benefit package, regardless of skills, work experience, or prior earnings. This wage and benefit package would then form the effective minimum for both the public and private sectors of the economy. After fixing a wage and benefit package, the government would allow the quantity of workers in the program to float, rising and falling in response to cyclical fluctuations in private-sector employment.

As with Argentina's program, ELR proposals typically call for participants to work in projects to improve their local communities—everything from basic infrastructure projects to a Green Jobs Corps. Most ELR proponents also advocate a decentralized approach similar to Argentina's, with local public or nonprofit institutions planning and administering the projects, though it is essential that the program be funded at the national level.

This raises an important question: How will governments pay for such a large-scale program? Wouldn't an ELR program require significantly raising taxes or else result in exploding budget deficits? Can governments really afford to employ everyone who wants a job but cannot find one in the private economy? Advocates of ELR address the issue of affordability in different ways, but all agree that the benefits to society vastly outweigh the expense. Many ELR advocates go even further, arguing that any talk of "costs" to society misrepresents the nature of the problem of unemployment. The existence of unemployed workers represents a net cost to society, in terms of lost income and production as well as the psychological and social stresses that result from long spells of unemployment. Employing them represents a net benefit, in terms of increased incomes *and* enhanced individual and social wellbeing. The real burden of an ELR program, from the perspective of society, is thus effectively zero.

Most estimates of the direct cost of an ELR program are in the range of less than 1% of GDP per year. For the United States, this was less than $132 billion in 2006, or about 5% of the federal budget. (By way of comparison, in 2006 the U.S. government spent over $120 billion on the wars in Iraq and Afghanistan—and that figure does not include the cost of lives lost or ruined or the future costs incurred, for example, for veterans' health care.) Furthermore, an ELR program provides benefits to society in the form of worker retraining, enhanced public infrastructure, and increased social output (e.g., cleaner parks and cities, free child care, public performances, etc.). By increasing the productivity of those participants who attend education or training programs, an ELR program would also decrease real costs throughout the economy. Estimates of program costs take into account a reduction in other forms of social assistance such as food stamps, cash assistance, and unemployment insurance, which would instead be provided to ELR participants in the form of a wage and benefit package. Of course, those who cannot work would still be eligible for these and other forms of assistance.

Today, the ELR idea is mostly confined to academic journals and conferences. Still, proponents can point to a number of little known real-world examples their discussions have helped to shape. For example, the Argentine government explicitly based its *Jefes de Hogar* program on the work of economists associated with the Center for Full Employment and Price Stability (CFEPS) at the University of Missouri-Kansas City. Daniel Kostzer, an economist at the Argentine Ministry of Labor and one of the main architects of the program, had become familiar with the CFEPS proposal and was attempting to create such a program in Argentina a few years before the collapse provided him with the necessary political support. Similar experiments are being considered or are currently underway in India, France, and Bolivia. Advocates of ELR proposals can also be found at the Levy Economics Institute (U.S.), the Center for Full Employment and Equity (Australia), and the National Jobs for All Coalition (U.S.).

The Case for Direct Job Creation

Involuntary unemployment is a fundamental and inherent feature of a capitalist economy left to its own devices. In a society where most people depend on employment in the private sector for their livelihood, the inability of a capitalist economy to consistently create enough jobs for all who seek work is deeply troubling, pointing to the need for intervention from outside of the private sector. ELR advocates view national governments—with their unique spending abilities, and with their role as, in principle, democratically accountable social institutions—as the most logical institutions for collective action to bring about full employment. In addition, government job creation is viewed as the simplest and most direct means for overcoming the problem of involuntary unemployment in a capitalist economy.

The standard mainstream response to the problem of unemployment is to blame the victims of capitalism for lacking the necessary talents, skills, and effort to get and keep a job. Hence, the mainstream prescription is to promote policies aimed at enhancing the "human capital" of workers in order to make them more "competitive" in a rapidly globalizing economy. The response of ELR advocates is that such policies, if they accomplish anything at all, simply redistribute unemployment and poverty more equitably. For example, according to the Bureau of Labor Statistics, the number of unemployed workers (including so-called "discouraged" and "underemployed" workers) in August 2007 was 16.4 million, while the number of job vacancies was 4.1 million. No amount of investment in human capital is going to change the fact that there simply aren't enough jobs to go around.

Advocates of ELR also consistently reject the Keynesian rubric, with its focus on demand-management strategies—that is, policies aimed at increasing aggregate demand for the output of the economy. This approach has been pursued either directly, through government spending on goods and services (including transfer payments to households), or indirectly, largely through policies intended to increase private investment. Such an approach exacerbates inequality by biasing policy in favor of the already well-to-do, through tax cuts and investment credits to wealthy individuals and powerful corporations. These policies also tend to privilege the more highly skilled and better-paid workers found in the industries that generally benefit from the government's largesse (often arms manufacturers and other military-related companies). For example, much of the increase in government spending during the Cold War era went into the high-tech, capital-intensive, and oligopolized sectors of the economy. Capital-intensive industries require relatively small amounts of labor, and, thus, produce little employment growth per dollar of government expenditure. Under this policy approach, the most that lower-paid or unemployed workers could hope for would be to snatch a few crumbs from the great corporate feast as the economy expanded over time.

In contrast to both the human-capital and demand-management approaches, ELR provides a means for rapidly achieving zero involuntary unemployment. By definition, anyone who is unemployed and chooses not to accept the ELR offer would be considered voluntarily unemployed. Many individuals with sufficient savings and decent job prospects may forgo the opportunity to participate in the ELR program, but ELR always provides them with a backup option.

In addition to the immediate effects of ELR on employment, the program acts as an "automatic stabilizer" in the face of cyclical fluctuations in the private sector of the economy. During a recession, the number of participants in the program can be expected to grow as people are laid off and/or find it increasingly difficult to find private-sector employment. The opposite happens during the recovery phase of the business cycle, as people find it easier to find private-sector employment at wages above the ELR minimum. As a result, ELR advocates argue, the existence of such a program would dampen fluctuations in private-sector activity by setting a floor to the decline in incomes and employment.

A final and less discussed benefit of the program is its socializing effect. The example of Argentina is instructive in this respect. The nature of employment in the *Jefes* program, oriented as it was toward community rather than market imperatives, created a sense of public involvement and responsibility. Participants reported increases in morale and often continued to work beyond the four hours a day for which they were getting paid; they appreciated the cooperative nature of most of the enterprises and their focus on meeting essential community needs as opposed to quarterly profit targets. By expanding the public sphere, the *Jefes* program created a spirit of democratic participation in the affairs of the community, unmediated by the impersonal relations of market exchange. These are the kinds of experiences that are essential if capitalist societies are to move beyond the tyranny of the market and toward more cooperative and democratic forms of social organization.

Some economists and advocates have pressed for a similar proposal, the *basic income guarantee* (BIG). Instead of guaranteeing jobs, under this proposal the government would guarantee a minimum income to everyone by simply giving cash assistance to anyone earning below that level, in an amount equal to the gap between his or her actual income and the established basic income. (Hence this proposal is sometimes referred to as a "negative income tax.") BIG is an important idea deserving wider discussion than it has so far received. But ELR advocates have a number of concerns. One is that a BIG program is inherently inflationary: by providing income without putting people to work, it creates an additional claim on output without directly increasing the production of that output. Another is that BIG programs are less politically palatable—and hence less sustainable—than ELR schemes, which benefit society at large through the provision of public works and other social goods, and which avoid the stigma attached to "welfare" programs. Finally, a job offers social and psychological benefits that an income payment alone does not: maintaining and enhancing work skills, keeping in contact with others, and having the satisfaction of contributing to society. When, for instance, participants in Argentina's *Jefes* program were offered an income in place of a job, most refused; they preferred to work. Consequently, ELR programs meet the same objectives as basic income guarantee schemes and more, without the negative side effects of inflation and stigmatization. Nonetheless, a BIG program may be appropriate for those who should not be expected to work.

Learning from the Past

The idea that the government in a capitalist economy should provide jobs for the unemployed is not new. In the United States, the various New Deal agencies created during the Great Depression of the 1930s offer a well-known example. Organizations such as the Works Progress Administration and the Civilian Conservation Corps were designed to deal with the massive unemployment of that period. Unemployment peaked at almost 25% of the civilian labor force in 1933 and averaged over 17% for the entire decade. These programs were woefully inadequate, largely due to their limited scale. It ultimately took the massive increases in government expenditure precipitated by the Second World War to pull the U.S. economy out of depression.

The onset of the postwar "Golden Age" and the dominance of Keynesian economics sounded the death knell of direct job creation as a solution to unemployment. The interwar public employment strategy was replaced with a "demand-management" strategy—essentially a sort of trickle-down economics in which various tax incentives and government expenditure programs, mainly military spending, were used to stimulate private investment. Policymakers believed that this would spur economic growth. The twin problems of poverty and unemployment would then be eliminated since, according to President Kennedy's famous aphorism, "a rising tide lifts all boats."

In the mid-1960s, the civil rights movement revived the idea of direct job creation as a solution to the problems of poverty and unemployment. Although the Kennedy and Johnson administrations had declared a so-called War on Poverty, the movement's call for direct job creation fell on deaf ears as the Johnson administration, at the behest of its Council of Economic Advisers, pursued a more conservative approach based on the standard combination of supply-side incentives to increase private investment and assorted strategies to "improve" workers' "human capital" so as to make them more attractive to private employers.

The rise to dominance of neoliberalism since the mid-1970s has resulted in a full-scale retreat from even the mildly social democratic policies of the early postwar period. While a commitment to full employment remains official U.S. policy, the concerns of central bankers and financial capitalists now rule the roost in government circles. This translates into a single-minded obsession with fighting inflation at the expense of all other economic and social objectives. Not only is fighting inflation seemingly the only concern of economic policy, it is seen to be in direct conflict with the goal of full employment (witness the widespread acceptance among economists and policymakers of the NAIRU, or "non-accelerating inflation rate of unemployment" theory, which posits that the economy has a set-point for unemployment, well above zero, below which rapidly rising inflation must occur). Whenever falling unemployment leads to concerns about "excessive" wage growth, central banks are expected to raise interest rates in an attempt to force slack on the economy and thereby decrease inflationary pressures. The resulting unemployment acts as a kind of discipline, tempering the demands of working-class people for higher wages or better working conditions in favor of the interests of large commercial and financial institutions. The postwar commitment to full employment has finally been sacrificed on the altar of price stability.

ELR and Capitalism

As demonstrated by the history of public employment programs in the United States and the example of Argentina, direct job-creation programs do not happen absent significant political pressure from below. This is the case whether or not those calling for change explicitly demand an ELR program. Given the hegemonic position of neoliberal ideology, there are many powerful forces today that would be hostile to the idea of governments directly creating jobs for the unemployed. These forces represent a critical barrier to the implementation of an ELR program. In fact, these forces represent a critical barrier to virtually any project for greater social and economic justice. The purpose of initiating a wider discussion of ELR proposals is to build them into more comprehensive programs for social and economic justice. As is always the case, this requires the building of mass-based social movements advocating for these and other progressive policies.

A significant objection to the ELR proposal remains: it's capitalism, stupid. If you don't like unemployment, poverty, and inequality—not to mention war, environmental destruction, and alienating and exploitative work—then you don't like capitalism, and you should seek alternatives instead of reformist employment policies. ELR advocates would not disagree. In the face of the overlapping and myriad problems afflicting a capitalist economy, the achievements of even a full-scale ELR program would be limited. The political difficulties involved in establishing an ELR program in the first place, in the face of opposition from powerful elements of society, would be immense. And certainly, the many experiments in non-capitalist forms of economic and social organization currently being carried out, for example, in the factories of Argentina and elsewhere, should be championed. But it is fair to ask: shouldn't we also champion living wage laws, a stronger social safety net for those who cannot or should not be expected to work, and universal health care—as well as an end to imperialist wars of aggression, environmentally unsustainable practices, and the degradation of work? In sum, shouldn't we seek to alleviate all of the symptoms of capitalism, even as we work toward a better economic system? ❑

Sources: Joseph Halevi, "The Argentine Crisis," *Monthly Review*, April 2002; Pavlina Tcherneva, "Macroeconomic Stabilization Policy in Argentina: A Case Study of the 2002 Currency Collapse and Crisis Resolution through Job Creation," Bard College Working Paper, 2007; L. Randall Wray, *Understanding Modern Money: The Key to Full Employment and Price Stability*, Edward Elgar, 1998; Congressional Research Service, "The Cost of Iraq, Afghanistan and Other Global War on Terror Operations Since 9/11," www.fas.org/sgp/crs/natsec/RL33110.pdf, update 7/07; National Jobs for All Coalition, "September 2007 Unemployment Data," www.njfac.org/jobnews.html; Nancy Rose, "Historicizing Government Work Programs: A Spectrum from Workfare to Fair Work," Center for Full Employment and Price Stability, Seminar Paper No. 2, March 2000; Judith Russell, *Economics, Bureaucracy and Race: How Keynesians Misguided the War on Poverty*, Columbia Univ. Press, 2004; Fadhel Kaboub, "Employment Guarantee Programs: A Survey of Theories and Policy Experiences," Levy Econ. Inst., Working Paper No. 498, May 2007.

Article 8.8

CHANGING THE AUTO INDUSTRY FROM THE WHEELS UP

The problems of the U.S. auto industry call for radical solutions.

BY ALEJANDRO REUSS
May 2009

The "Big Three" U.S. auto companies are not facing a crisis—they are facing multiple interrelated crises at once. Chrysler, General Motors, and Ford have posted tens of billions in losses over the last few years. They suffer from chronic overcapacity, producing more cars than they can sell, and have ended up selling cars at a loss. Their cars are widely viewed as lagging behind those of international competitors in quality, styling, and reliability. They have focused on fighting fuel-efficiency standards rather than developing new, fuel-efficient vehicles. They have bet heavily on large, gas-guzzling models and are playing catch-up Toyota and Honda in the development of hybrid cars. They face significant cost disadvantages compared to their main competitors, mainly due to retiree health and pension "legacy costs." And, on top of all this, a deep recession has hammered car sales.

Already operating in the red before last year, the Big Three have been burning through billions in cash reserves during the current recession. General Motors, having posted losses every year since 2005, lost over $30 billion in 2008. It has reported that, in the first quarter of 2009, it lost another $6 billion (and depleted its cash reserves by over $10 billion). Ford has posted losses since 2006, including about $15 billion in 2008. Chrysler lost $8 billion last year. With their companies teetering on the edge of bankruptcy, GM and Chrysler executives appeared before Congress last November asking for a government bailout. In December [2008], the Bush administration announced $13.4 billion in loans for GM and $4 billion for Chrysler. (Since then, both companies have asked for billions more.) In April, the Obama administration offered additional loans of one-half billion to Chrysler and up to $5 billion to GM. Lacking private sources of financing, the two companies have managed to stay in business this long thanks only to the government loans.

The government has required both companies to submit restructuring plans, including concessions from workers and creditors, as a condition of the bailouts. At the end of March, the Obama administration rejected the submitted plans as inadequate. It gave Chrysler 30 days more to conclude a takeover deal with Italian auto giant Fiat, while GM got 60 days to submit a new restructuring plan. In late April, Chrysler appeared to have a deal with Fiat, with the Italian automaker set to take over operations and receive 20% of the company's stock (with a possible future increase to 35%). A United Auto Workers (UAW) retiree health-care trust would own 55% of the stock. The UAW accepted new concessions on wages and benefits, while the company's major creditors agreed to cancel billions in debt for about a third of its face value (plus less than 10% of the company's stock). When some creditors balked at the plan, however, the company filed for bankruptcy. Meanwhile, GM proposed a restructuring plan in which the federal government would own 50% of the stock (in exchange for the cancellation of about $10 billion in company debt), and the UAW retiree health-care trust nearly 40%, leaving the company's unsecured bondholders with just 10%. The plan included the shutdown of the company's Pontiac division and over 20,000 layoffs. Bondholders could still balk, however, in which case GM would go into bankruptcy as well.

No matter what the outcome of the current crisis, the "Big Three" are not likely to return to the heights of their post-World War II heyday. In the 1950s and 1960s, the Big Three dominated the U.S. auto market. As recently as the late 1990s, they accounted for over 70% of total U.S. sales of new cars and light trucks. Now, they account for less than 50%. In the mid 1950s, General Motors alone accounted for over 50% of U.S. new-car sales. Today, the company's market share is about 20%. Under the company's proposed restructuring plan, it would employ less than 40,000 union auto workers, less than one tenth the number the company employed at its peak in 1970. There is no way to put Humpty-Dumpty together again, and it does not seem that any of the major players in this drama—the companies' managements, the leadership of the UAW, or the government—really believe that there is. The real question is whether something new and better will be built from the wreckage of this industry.

Were Bailouts Necessary?

In his testimony before the Senate banking committee in November, then-GM Chairman Rick Wagoner offered an apocalyptic vision of what would happen "if the domestic industry were allowed to fail" (that is, if the government did not cough up the bailout GM and Chrysler were requesting): "The societal costs would be catastrophic: three million jobs lost within the first year, U.S. personal income reduced by $150 billion, and a government tax loss of more than $156 billion over three years… not to mention the broader blow to consumer and business confidence."

The figures, also cited by Chrysler Chairman Robert Nardelli, come from a November report by the Center for Automotive Research (CAR) predicting the consequences of "the Detroit Three automakers ceasing all operations in United States." Wagoner and Nardelli obviously chose this "100 percent contraction scenario" to make the consequences of refusing a bailout seem as bad as possible. This scenario is extremely pessimistic, assuming the disappearance of GM and Chrysler, the disappearance of Ford, which did not even ask for a bailout, and a temporary (one-year) disappearance of all U.S. auto production by international auto companies. More importantly, however, the auto CEOs' pleas snuck in the false assumption that the only way to avoid this nightmare was for the government to bail out the companies.

The current administration appears to be determined to save GM and Chrysler in one way or another. "We cannot, and must not, and we will not let our auto industry simply vanish," President Obama declared. If the companies ceased to exist, however, the workers would not vanish. The factory buildings and machinery would not vanish. If the government wanted to keep the workers employed and producing goods (whether cars or something else), it could pay the workers their wages and benefits, buy or build factories and machinery, and pay for other necessary inputs, such as materials and energy. If the government wanted to keep the workers producing cars, it could buy the auto companies themselves, or it could buy the factories and equipment (and allow the companies to cease to exist). If it wanted to put those workers to work producing something else, it could buy the factories and machinery and re-tool them as needed, or it could construct new factories or equipment (if the existing production apparatus proved unsuitable to the new purpose, or too costly to re-tool). Maintaining employment and production, in short, would not require preserving the companies in anything like their present form.

Not only were the bailouts unnecessary for saving the jobs of workers at GM and Chrysler or other companies (such as suppliers and dealers) affected by the crisis, but they have not succeeded in doing so. Auto industry employment in the United States (including vehicle and parts manufacturing and sales) has declined by about 400,000 jobs in the last year. In fact, maintenance of employment does not appear to have been the objective of government policy (under either Bush or Obama). The government has encouraged layoffs by requiring deep cuts in company costs as a condition of the bailout. The companies have sought concessions on past obligations from workers and bondholders, concessions on future wages and benefits from workers, and massive layoffs. Under GM's government-mandated restructuring plan (after the first round of bailouts), the company promised to lay off 47,000 workers worldwide by the end of 2009. Chrysler's plan promised to cut 35,000. The Obama administration rejected both plans as inadequate, saying that viable restructuring plans for both companies would require deeper cost cutting.

The Economics of Nationalization

The nationalization of large private companies has suddenly become part of mainstream U.S. political debate. Even mainstream commentators have advocated the (temporary) nationalization of major U.S. banks as a necessary fix of the financial sector. With nationalization no longer "beyond the pale" of respectable debate, talk of nationalizing the auto companies began to trickle into mainstream debate. Some commentators compared the auto companies to the bankrupt railroads of the 1970s, which were nationalized (as Conrail) and later re-privatized.

The current administration has not set out to nationalize either GM or Chrysler. "Nationalization," at least in the sense of government majority ownership, however, became a real possibility with GM's April restructuring plan. Under the plan, the government would receive a majority of the stock in the company in exchange for the cancellation of over $7 billion in the company's debt (from the bailout loans). Administration officials hastened to explain that they had not aimed to nationalize the company, that the administration had "no desire to run an auto company," and that it would not seek representation on the company's board.

From a purely economic standpoint, the government could have easily nationalized GM for much less that it gave out in bailout loans. GM stock has been trading for under $4 per share for almost all of 2009. At this price, the company's total "market capitalization"—the amount of money it would take to buy all the shares owned by members of the public—is around $2.5 billion. (This number is usually interpreted as investors' collective valuation of what a company is worth.) At the late April price of less than $2 per share, it was about $1 billion. So the government could have bought all the shares in GM for between $1 billion and $2.5 billion, depending on the timing, or a majority stake for half that. (These calculations are harder to make for Chrysler, since it is not a publicly traded company and so its stock does not have a market price, but the story would probably be quite similar.)

Had the government bought a controlling stake in either company, however, the money paid for the shares would not have been available for current production, retooling, or research and development. (This money would have gone to the shareholders, not the company.) Instead, the government could have forced the companies, which had no other place to turn for credit since no private lenders were willing to loan them money, to issue it enough new stock to give the government a majority stake. The issuance of new stock reduces the portion of a company owned by existing stockholders. If GM issued the government enough stock to give it a majority stake (just over 50%), for example, this would have reduced existing stockholders' stake by half. A one-half stake in GM would have cost about half of the company's market capitalization, or about one-half billion dollars at the late April share price. That money would have been in the possession of a company the government now controlled, and therefore available for operations. The government could have made additional financing available to the now-government-controlled company for additional shares of new stock, or as loans.

Instead of pursuing these options, the government extended bailout loans to both companies. It has handed $15.4 billion to GM so far. GM's bankruptcy plan assumes the government will extend another $11.6 billion in loans, for a total of $27 billion. The plan has the government cancelling $7.4 billion of GM's debt, and receiving a little more than half the company. In effect, if the plan goes through, the government will have paid over $7 billion for half of a company that is, right now, worth about $1 billion. The government, in effect, has become one of the creditors making dramatic concessions (taking a "haircut") in the companies' restructuring plans.

Buying the Assets

GM and Chrysler have considerable tangible assets (factories, machinery, and inventories), holdings in other companies (like GM's stake in the consumer-finance company GMAC), cash reserves (dwindling fast), and so-called intangible assets (brand names, however tarnished). They also have vast liabilities (debts)—to bondholders, suppliers, warranty holders, current workers, and retirees. Had the government bought the companies, it would have bought both the assets and the liabilities.

The government has attempted to broker a process in which the two companies' liabilities would be greatly reduced. As a condition of the bailouts, the government pushed GM and Chrysler to get concessions from both bondholders and the UAW. (The labor concessions have involved cuts in future wages and benefits, along with massive layoffs, in addition to reductions to past obligations.) If the government had bought a controlling stake in either company, it could have sought concessions from creditors (much as it has pushed the two companies to do). Some past nationalizations, such as Conrail, have also imposed harsh austerity measures on workers, so nationalization would not necessarily have been a panacea for workers.

Alternatively, the government could have bought the assets of GM or Chrysler rather than buying the company lock, stock, and barrel. In principle, it could have done this without waiting for them to burn through their remaining cash (plus the bailout funds) and declare bankruptcy. (Bankruptcy entails a great deal of uncertainty, and is usually dreaded by unions since it has been used historically by companies to cancel collective-bargaining agreements.) In late March, the Obama administration was considering plans under which both GM and Chrysler would be split into two companies, a "bad" company that would be liquidated and a viable "good" company (including most of the valuable assets) that would continue to operate. In the case of GM, the *New York Times* reported, most of the undesirable divisions and liabilities would be "left in the old company," to be subsequently sold off and used, along with proceeds from the sale of its valuable components, to pay off creditors. A new company, "financed by the government," would buy GM's valuable divisions and assets. In the case of Chrysler, the administration's plan aimed for Fiat to buy the "good" company. In neither case was the administration's plan for the government to own the new company, though there is no reason in principle that this could not have been the goal.

The government could also have bought the assets of one of the companies in the event of bankruptcy and liquidation. Bankruptcy can lead to a company's "reorganization," in which case some or all of its debts and contracts may be voided, or can end in the liquidation of the company's assets. The liquidation of a company means that the company ceases to exist, but not that its assets cease to exist—they are liquidated, not liquefied! The assets are sold off, and the proceeds are used to pay off at least some creditors. In principle, if the government wanted to get auto workers back to work producing cars, it could have bought the factories and machinery and paid the workers to produce cars. If it wanted to get them back to work producing something else, it could have still bought these factories and machinery and retooled for some other kind of production.

When a bankrupt company is liquidated, which creditors will be paid off first is always an issue. Neither Chrysler nor GM has enough assets to pay off all their creditors, so in the event of the liquidation of either company, some creditors would receive nothing. In a recent forum in the *New York Times*, UCLA law professor Lynn M. LoPucki argues that bankruptcy law gives workers "priority over the claims of ordinary creditors, including the bondholders, the suppliers, and the dealers." In practice, however, who gets paid off first (or at all) often depends on the leanings of the bankruptcy court. No matter who bought the assets in a liquidation (the government or a private buyer), the concern would be that the proceeds would be used to pay off bondholders, and leave workers and retirees in the lurch.

The creditors who balked at Chrysler's restructuring plan were "secured" lenders, meaning that they would have had first claim on the company's assets, and so were holding out for either a liquidation or a better deal. As of early May, a bankruptcy judge decided that Chrysler's restructuring could go ahead as planned, despite the creditors' objections, so a liquidation does not seem likely. (As some of the bondholders abandoned the cause, the holdout group dissolved.) It is still possible that some GM creditors will oppose its proposed restructuring, and hold out for a liquidation. Were the government to buy the assets of a bankrupt company, it should ensure, either through the terms of the particular bankruptcy or through new legislation covering all bankruptcies, that obligations to workers and retirees are honored before obligations to bondholders. In practice, this would mean that bondholders would be "wiped out."

Replacing the "Private Welfare State"

Since the Second World War, many large U.S. companies have provided benefits, such as pensions and health insurance, provided by the state in other rich capitalist countries. Under this system, sometimes known as the "private welfare state," individuals enjoy pension and health benefits by virtue of employment at a company that offers them, not as a social right. The auto industry was one of the first to offer such benefits on a large scale (during the Second World War, as a way to get around the wartime wage freeze), and these benefits grew to be very extensive in the course of the postwar period. By the 1960s, they included health coverage for retirees as well as current workers.

The UAW's objective in pushing for these benefits, especially health benefits, was not only economic, but also political. Walter Reuther, the head of the UAW in the 1940s, believed that imposing health-care costs on employers would push the companies to support a government health-care system, and so help to usher in such a system here. Obviously, that has not happened, to the detriment not only of the tens of millions left uninsured or underinsured, but even of the companies paying for such benefits. The growth of the private welfare state has resulted, for the auto companies and for other employers with longstanding retiree pension and health benefits, in enormous "legacy costs." For every $55 in current labor costs, for example, Ford pays $16 in retiree pension and health benefits.

Workers at each of the Big Three have made major concessions on retiree health-care obligations. In February, the UAW agreed to accept Ford stock in exchange for about half of the $13.6 billion the company owes a retiree health-care trust. Under GM's restructuring plan, a retiree health-care trust would receive 39% of the stock in the company. The UAW agreed to cancel about $10 billion in retiree health-care obligations, half of the total the company currently owes the trust, in exchange for this stake in the company. The trust has in effect forgiven $10 billion in debt for less than half of a company that, right now, is worth about $1 billion. Of course, the stock could end up being worth more (or less) in the future.

Under Chrysler's restructuring, the UAW has accepted, in lieu of $10.6 billion in retiree health obligations (contributions owed by the company to a retiree health-care trust), $4.6 billion as a company IOU plus 55% of the stock in the restructured company. The total value of the deal was put at $8.8 billion, with the stock being valued at $4.2 billion. Since Chrysler is not a publicly traded company, however, it is unclear what the stock is actually worth—that is, what the trust will be able to sell the stock for when it needs cash to pay out benefits. Two years ago, the venture-capital firm Cerberus paid Daimler $7.4 billion for 80% of Chrysler's stock, but $6 billion of that was retained by Chrysler and its financial arm (both controlled by Cerberus after the sale), and only $1.4 billion actually went to Daimler. Cerberus' $6 billion investment in Chrysler was worth something to Daimler, since it increased the value of the 20% of Chrysler that Daimler still owned. However, the terms of the deal do not suggest that the company was worth over $9 billion then, as some commentators have estimated. It is possible, then, that the trust's stake in Chrysler is worth less—perhaps much less—than $4.2 billion. Meanwhile, in the event that this stake ends up being worth more than $4.2 billion, under the terms of the plan the balance would go not to the trust but to the U.S. Treasury. Finally, the deal exposes retirees to additional risk since the viability of the company remains in doubt, and stock holders are last in line to be paid in the event of bankruptcy.

The auto companies signed collective-bargaining agreements promising auto workers pension and health benefits. Current and former employees have a special contractual claim on these companies for the benefits they have been promised, and should not be left without health or pension protections. (Pension benefits are insured by the government's Pension Benefit Guaranty Corporation, though in the event that any of the auto companies defaulted on their pension obligations, workers would likely get much lower pensions that they had been promised.) In the grand scheme, however, all workers—whether or not they have enjoyed the good fortune of being employed by companies that offer retirement and health benefits—have a moral claim to a comfortable retirement and access to medical care.

The failings of the private welfare state scream out for a comprehensive reform, rather than a "fix" that applies only to this or that category of workers. This system leaves tens of millions of people without health coverage. (The Centers for Disease Control reported that over 50 million people in the United States lacked coverage at some point during 2006.) Workers with health problems are afraid to change jobs, due to the danger of losing their health insurance. Workers who lose their jobs face the catastrophe of losing health coverage, as is now happening to millions of workers. (The Center for American Progress reports that over 2 million U.S. workers have lost coverage due to unemployment during the current recession.) The private welfare state, moreover, contributes to enormous administrative costs resulting from the existence of so many different health insurance plans. It narrows the pools of individuals across which risk is spread, and so makes the cost of insurance greater.

A comprehensive solution to this crisis requires the creation of a national health-care system and the revision of the public pension system to make it much more redistributive. The "private welfare state" should be replaced by a system that treats health-care and retirement benefits as economic rights, takes these factors "out of competition" for workers (so workers will not have to sacrifice retirement or health benefits to save their jobs), and broadly spreads risk across the entire society.

Industrial Conversion

The government could keep auto workers employed producing exactly what they have been producing—by nationalizing the companies, buying assets like factories and machinery, or some other policy—but that should not be the objective. Cars, especially the gas-guzzling SUVs, pickup trucks, and high-horsepower cars that the Big Three have been cranking out, are an environmental and public-health disaster. They generate tons of pollution, waste vast energy resources, require huge amounts of space and infrastructure to store and operate, and pose grave danger to other users of public roads (including other motorists, cyclists, and pedestrians).

Producing these vehicles has also turned out to be a bad business plan. The Big Three bet heavily on large, gas-guzzling vehicles that had until recently been high-profit items. All three companies actually sell substantially more "light trucks"—pickups, SUVs, vans, and minivans—than cars. In 2008, light trucks accounted for nearly 60% of GM's new vehicle sales; for Ford, nearly 65%; for Chrysler, over 70%. (Meanwhile, they accounted for about 40% of Toyota, Honda, and Nissan's new vehicle sales.) Last year's spike in fuel prices hit U.S. automakers especially hard. Both company officials and industry analysts recognized, however, that the demand for smaller, more fuel-efficient vehicles was more than just a temporary "spike." U.S. consumers were shifting permanently toward smaller vehicles, and the Big Three had been caught behind the times.

The world auto industry suffers from chronic overcapacity. Auto companies have made huge investments in plant and equipment. Once these investments have been made, the companies pay these costs regardless of the number of cars they produce, so these are referred to as "fixed" costs. (Imagine a company that has signed a lease on a factory, for example, and has to pay the rent whether it produces one vehicle or a thousand.) If an auto company does not operate near capacity, the production cost per car goes up, as those fixed costs are averaged over a smaller number of cars. As a result, the auto companies have persisted in producing too many cars, resulting in enormous inventories and, for some companies, the sale of cars at a loss.

It is not a bad thing for auto production to decline. The U.S. auto companies, however, are now cutting production in an incredibly wrenching fashion, which is decimating employment and union membership in auto manufacturing, parts manufacturing, and auto and parts sales. Employment in auto and auto-parts manufacturing in the United States has declined by over 210,000 over the last year, and at auto and auto-parts dealerships by an additional 190,000. The government, meanwhile, has encouraged layoffs by requiring deep cuts in company costs as a condition of the bailout.

Instead of overseeing this bloodletting, the government could oversee a process of shifting workers and physical resources to environmentally sustainable branches of production with a minimum of disruption, insecurity, and pain. Existing plant and equipment could certainly be used (with retooling) to produce more fuel-efficient cars, hybrid cars, or electric cars. This is already in the cards to some degree. The government made improved fuel efficiency a condition of the initial bailouts last year, and the Fiat takeover plan includes incentives that will increase the company's equity stake in Chrysler if it meets goals for the development of more fuel-efficient vehicles. GM has a primarily electric car (with a backup gasoline engine), the Chevy Volt, in the works for 2010, though some analysts have questioned design decisions that have contributed to the Volt's high projected price. The company has also promised to develop 15 hybrid models by 2012. Ford has described plans for an electric van for 2010, with other hybrid and electric vehicles to follow by 2012. Chrysler had unveiled plans for a hybrid truck in 2010, with other hybrid vehicles to follow (prior to its subsequent bankruptcy and likely takeover by Fiat). The transformation of the U.S. transportation system, however, needs to be much more dramatic, shifting toward mass transit, much smaller motorized vehicles using sustainable energy sources, and human-powered vehicles (mainly bicycles).

It might be possible to convert former auto factories and machinery to the production of locomotives and rail cars, zero-emission buses, golf-cart-like electric vehicles, electric motor scooters, and bicycles—the artifacts of a new transportation system. (Chrysler already owns a division that produces small "neighborhood electric vehicles (NEVs), though not in mass-market numbers. Meanwhile, GM has created, in collaboration with Segway, a prototype small electric vehicle. Segway officials, however, say no decision has yet been made about its commercial future.) If the government were to purchase the auto companies' assets, it could retool the factories and machinery for producing these other kinds of transportation machines. If the existing factories and machinery were not suitable for these purposes, or it would be very costly to retool, it might be preferable to scrap all or part of the old facilities and machinery and build anew. The government, in other words, would not necessarily have to buy the scraps of the auto industry to build up these other industries. Workers displaced from the auto industry could still be re-employed by deliberately directing investment toward hard-hit areas.

Building more of these other kinds of transportation machines is just one aspect of creating a sustainable transportation system. Bicycles, for example, are not exactly new inventions. Despite their enormous environmental and resource-use advantages over cars and trucks (less material required for manufacture, superior energy efficiency, far lower pollution, lower space requirements for use and storage, less wear-and-tear on infrastructure, less danger posed to other road users, etc.), however, most people in the United States still travel primarily by car. A transformation of the U.S. transportation system toward environmental sustainability would also require not only new transportation machines, but also radical changes in the use of public space, such as the creation of car-free zones, to make roads safe and welcoming for non-motorists.

Workers' Control

The Big Three managements have led the companies and their workers to the brink. As *BusinessWeek*'s Detroit bureau chief David Welch writes in his account of GM's fall from the pinnacle of the auto industry, management "just made too many mistakes for too long." The requests by GM and Chrysler for public money triggered calls for the ouster of at least top executives, and the Obama administration insisted in late March on the resignation of GM head Rick Wagoner as a condition for further government assistance. So far, however, calls for a change in the top management personnel have not come with calls for broader changes to the authoritarian system of control that pervades capitalist corporations.

The arguments for workers' control of production are, ultimately, the familiar principles of self-government: All people should be able to make for themselves the decisions that affect their lives, and should not have to accept decisions imposed on them. When such decisions affect many people, each should be able to participate equally in a system of collective decision-making. People should not to have to answer to a lord, a master, or a boss. The authoritarianism of the capitalist workplace collides with these principles. In the workplace, most people do not have—or, very often, expect—the right to make decisions for themselves or to elect representatives to whom they delegate decision-making authority (and whose authority they can revoke if they decide). Instead, they answer to a boss, whether the owner of the company where they work or a delegate of the owners, who definitely does not rule by consent of the governed. The principles of self-government are an important part of U.S. political culture, and so offer an opening to discussions of workplace democracy in this country. They are also universalistic principles, demanding the equal inclusion of all, irrespective of national borders or any other dividing lines.

Ideas of workers' control have a long history in the United States, but are no longer really part of the culture of the U.S. labor movement. During their post-World War II heyday, U.S. unions by-and-large accepted that the production process, product design, pricing, and other major decisions were "management prerogatives." In return, workers in "core" industries (like auto, steel, and trucking) got recognition of their unions, real-wage increases tied to productivity growth, steady employment, and the benefits of the private welfare state. This arrangement is often known as the "capital-labor accord," or the "limited capital-labor accord," since it never covered all—or even most—U.S. workers. Since the 1970s, employers have shredded their side of the bargain. The "management prerogatives," however, have remained.

Early reports of Chrysler's restructuring plan, under which the UAW retirees' health-care trust would get 55% of the stock in the company, suggested that the union would "own" or "control" the company. The union quickly denied that it would control Chrysler, pointing out that the retiree health-care trust was an independent entity and assuaging any fears that the union would be making managerial decisions at the company. (The UAW also announced that the trust would quickly sell off its shares to pay out benefits.) This defensiveness suggests the hostility in mainstream political culture to any hint of workers' control. In reality, though, the Chrysler deal does not involve workers' control or ownership in any meaningful way. The restructuring plan includes different categories of stock, and the category that the trust holds is defined in a way that means that the trust's 55% does not constitute a majority of the voting power. The trust would have only one (non-voting) seat on the board of directors, compared to four seats for the U.S. government and three for Fiat. The *Wall Street Journal* reported that Fiat's CEO would become the head of Chrysler or appoint someone else to the position. Under the Chrysler restructuring plan, it is Fiat, not the union or the workers, that will have operational control of the company.

As bankrupt as the current system of top-down management may be, a new system will not come about automatically, nor without a fight. For the auto industry, it is not likely to come about at all without a major upsurge in workers' resistance to the current restructuring. This may take place through the UAW and other existing unions, come from outside the existing unions (through the emergence of new workers' organizations or through "wildcat" actions), or both. The labor upsurge of the 1930s, which created the UAW and other major unions, took both forms. The fight-back today need not begin with a highly ideological commitment to a new system of workers' control. It may begin with something as basic as a refusal to accept layoffs. Workers at the Chicago-area manufacturer Republic Windows and Doors, who sat-in at their factory in December rather than accept layoffs, offer an example of such resistance. The tactic, a factory occupation, echoes the origins of the UAW itself—whose sit-down strikes unionized GM in the 1930s.

For the auto industry today, the fight-back would have to involve enormous numbers of workers, and not just in Detroit, but across the world. The auto companies are worldwide employers. Right now, to the extent that the discussion of the industry's future is about the fates of the workers, it is mainly limited to U.S. workers. A partially or fully nationalized U.S. auto company or industry (under whatever system of control), however, would not necessarily protect the interests of workers in other countries. Proponents of workers' self-management should advocate for the rights of all workers and their equal inclusion in any future system of control. Ultimately, however, whether the voices of workers, here or abroad, are heard will depend primarily on their own capacity for collective action and their own demands for real democracy. ❑

Sources: Eric Peters, "Too Many Cars, Not Enough Market," *American Spectator*, February 11, 2009; Mike Spector and Joseph B. White, "Auto Bailout Caps Flawed Relationship, *Wall Street Journal*, December 22, 2008; "Analyst: Big Three Still Lag on Fuel Efficiency," National Public Radio, June 11, 2008; "Consumer group: Big 3 dragging heels on fuel economy," CNNMoney, July 17, 2007; David Leonhardt, "$73 an Hour: Adding it Up (Figuring Autoworkers' Pay)," *New York Times*, December 10, 2008; Kevin Krolicki, "U.S. February auto sale plunge as recession deepens," Reuters, March 3, 2009; General Motors Corporation, "Analysis Tools, Financials Table, Income Statement (Annual)," *New York Times*; Nick Bunkley, "G.M. Posts a Quarterly Loss of $6 Billion, *New York Times*, May 7, 2009; Ford Motor Company, "Analysis Tools, Financials Table, Income Statement (Annual)," *New York Times*; "The Big (Troubled) Three," *New York Times*, March 30, 2009; "Billions Received, But Needing More," *New York Times*; "U.S. to give Chrysler $500 million, GM up to $5 billion in new aid," Reuters, April 21, 2009; David E. Sanger, David M. Herszenhorn, and Bill Vlasic, "Bush Aids Detroit, but Hard Choices Wait for Obama," *New York Times*, December 19, 2008; Remarks by the President on the American Automotive Industry, The White House, Office of the Press Secretary, March 30, 2009; Peter Valdes-Dapena, "Do or die for GM and Chrysler," CNNMoney, March 30, 2009; Alex P. Kellogg and Kris Maher, "UAW to Get 55% Stake in Chrysler for Concessions," *Wall Street Journal*, April 28, 2009; John Lippert and Mike Ramsey, "UAW Said to Get 55% Chrysler Ownership, Board Seats," Bloomberg, April 28, 2009; Obama Administration Auto Restructuring Initiative: Chrysler-Fiat Alliance, The White House, Office of the Press Secretary, April 30, 2009; Jim Puzzanghera, "Chrysler's major bondholders slash its debt," *Los Angeles Times*, April 29, 2009; Zachery Kouwe and Micheline Maynard, "Chrysler Bankruptcy Looms and Deal on Debt Falters," *New York Times*, April 29, 2009; Neil King Jr. and Jeffrey McCracken, "Chrysler Pushed into Fiat's Arms," *Wall Street Journal*, May 1, 2009; John D. Stoll and Sharon Terlep, "Plan Sees a Smaller, Focused—and Profitable—GM," *Wall Street Journal*, April 28, 2009; Steven Mufson, "GM's New Road Map: Partial Nationalization," *Washington Post*, April 28, 2009; John D. Stoll and Sharon Terlep, "GM Offers U.S. a Majority Stake, " *Wall Street Journal*, April 28, 2009; "America's Other Auto Industry," *Wall Street Journal*, December 1, 2008; Autodata Corporation, U.S. Light Vehicle Retail Sales, April 2009; "A brief history of General Motors Corp.," Associated Press, September 14, 2008; Bill Vlasic and Nick Bunkley, "G.M.'s Latest Plan Envisions a Much Smaller Automaker," *New York Times*, April 27, 2009; Prepared testimony by Rick Wagoner, Chairman and Chief Executive Officer, General Motors Corporation, to the United States Senate Banking, Housing, and Urban Affairs Committee, Washington, D.C., November 18, 2008, *Wall*

Street Journal; Chrysler CEO Bob Nardelli's Testimony Transcript, November 18, 2008; David Cole, Sean McAlinden, Kristin Dziczek, Debra Maranger Menk, "CAR Research Memorandum: The Impact on the U.S. Economy of a Major Contraction of the Detroit Three Automakers, Center for Automotive Research (CAR), November 4, 2008; Automotive Industry: Employment, Earnings, and Hours, Bureau of Labor Statistics, General Motors Corporation, 2009-2014 Restructuring Plan, February 17, 2009; Chrysler Restructuring Plan for Long-Term Viability, February 17, 2009; Louis Uchitelle, "Railroad Bailout May Offer a Model for Detroit," *New York Times*, March 15, 2009; Brian D. Glater, "U.S. Hopes to Ease GM to Bankcruptcy," *New York Times*, March 31, 2009; Jeffrey McCracken, Monica Langley, and John D. Stoll, "Bankruptcy Leads Possible Plans for GM, Chrysler," *Wall Street Journal*, March 30, 2009; Lynn M. LoPucki, "Legal Rights vs. Reality," in Room for Debate: "Auto Workers: Rescue Them or Not?," *New York Times*, March 9, 2009; "A Roadmap to a Chrysler Bankruptcy," *New York Times*, April 30, 2009; Michael J. de la Merced and Jonathan D. Glater, "Plan to Sell Chrysler to Fiat Clears Bar," *New York Times*, May 5, 2009; Michael J. de la Merced, "Creditors Opposing Chrysler's Overhaul Plan End Alliance," *New York Times*, May 8, 2009; Ron French, "World War II Created health insurance perk," *Detroit News*, October 25, 2006; Bill Koenig, "UAW Chief Faces Reather Legacy, 'Crashing' Industry," Bloomberg.com, July 20, 2007; Nick Bunkley, "U.A.W. Agrees to Concessions at Ford," *New York Times*, February 23, 2009; Chris Isidore, "Daimler pays to dump Chrysler," CNNMoney, May 14, 2007; Doug Henwood, "The UAW's Chrysler Stake: How 55%=0%," LBO News; Mary Williams Walsh, "Plight of Carmakers Could Upset All Pension Plans," *New York Times*, April 23, 2009; Robin A. Cohen, Ph.D., and Michael E. Martinez, M.P.H., "Health Insurance Coverage: Early Release of Estimates from the National Health Interview Survey, January—September 2006," Division of Health Interview Statistics, National Center for Health Statistics, Centers for Disease Control; Nayla Kazzi, "More Americans are Losing Health Insurance Every Day," Center for American Progress, May 4, 2009; Ken Bensinger, "Pickup truck, SUV sales run out of gas," *Los Angeles Times*, June 4, 2008; James Crotty, "Why There is Chronic Excess Capacity," *Challenge*, Vol. 45, 2002; Mike Spector and Joseph B. White, "Auto Bailout Caps Flawed Relationship," *Wall Street Journal*, December 22, 2008; Matt Vella, "Can the Chevy Volt Save GM?," *BusinessWeek*, October 29, 2008; Alex Taylor, "Taking the charge out of Chevy's Volt," *Fortune*, March 3, 2009; "Automakers Commit to Fuel Economy, Electrification in Long-Term Plans," Energy Efficiency and Renewable Energy, U.S. Department of Energy, December 3, 2008; Robert Nardelli, "Chrysler's Plan for Short-Term and Long-Term Viability," United States Senate Committee on Banking, Housing, and Urban Affairs, December 4, 2008; Sharon Terlep, "GM, Segway to Make Vehicle," *Wall Street Journal*, April 7, 2009; Jim Motavalli, "GM Conjures Up a People-Moving Pod," *New York Times*, April 6, 2009; David Welch, "How GM Lost its Sales Grown to Toyota," *BusinessWeek*, January 22, 2009; "Outside Pressure Grows for GM to Oust Wagoner," *Wall Street Journal*, December 8, 2008; Neil King Jr. and John D. Stahl, "Government Forces Out Wagoner at GM," *Wall Street Journal*, March 30, 2009; David Montgomery, *Workers' Control in America*, Cambridge University Press, 1980; Matthew Dolan, "UAW Says Won't Control Chrysler," *Wall Street Journal*, May 1, 2009; "UAW trust intends quick sale of Chrysler stake," Reuters, May 5, 2009; Alisa Priddle and David Shepardson, "UAW trust won't get control of Chrysler," *Detroit News*, April 29, 2009; Christine Tierney, "Treasury will administer VEBA's Chrysler stake," *Detroit News*, April 30, 2009; Monica Davey, "In Factory Sit-In, an Angler Spread Wide," *New York Times*, December 7, 2008; Monica Link and Larry Gabriel, "The Flint Sit-Down Strike," *UAW Solidarity*, Jan.-Feb. 2003.

Chapter 9

LABOR ACTIVISM

Article 9.1

THE GLOBAL CRISIS AND THE WORLD LABOR MOVEMENT

BY DAN LA BOTZ
Summer 2009, New Politics

The world's working people face the greatest challenge in three generations. The economic crisis that began in the banking institutions of the United States last year has rapidly spread around the globe, creating a financial and industrial disaster. In one country after another banks have failed, corporations have gone bankrupt, and millions around the world have lost their jobs. Governments from the United States, to Europe, to Asia and Latin America have responded by putting up trillions in one form or another to save the banks, to stabilize endangered corporations, and to stimulate their economies. Many nations have spent billions to create public works programs and have expanded unemployment benefits and new social programs, though no one believes that these begin to adequately deal with the problem. Working people around the world face all that goes with a crisis: joblessness, poverty, hunger, sickness, depression, drugs and alcohol, domestic abuse, and a rise in criminality, and, worst of all, the fear for their future and their children's.

The Economic Crisis

The financial collapse triggered a more profound general economic recession, what is in its fundamental features a classic overproduction crisis. Underlying what seemed to be simply the collapse of a financial bubble is a more fundamental problem, the decline of the rate of profit in manufacturing. This is not simply a minor cyclical recession, but rather it is as Marxist economists such as Anwar Shaikh argues a genuine economic depression that will be severe and long lasting. The fall in the rate of profit in manufacturing led some investors to move into real estate and finance in search of higher profits, resulting in the bubble. With the burst of the bubble, the broader and deeper economic crisis in industry has been revealed. We now appear to be entering a classical depression, likely to be accompanied by deflation, that will last until enough capital has been destroyed through the elimination of outdated plants and equipment, to once again attract investors.

If this does prove to be a deep and long lasting depression that is feared by some, that will shape and condition the nature of working class response. During the Great Depression of 1929-1939, it took four years before workers in the United States began to organize and fight back, creating a new labor movement and reshaping American politics. The depth and length of that economic crisis led to a new social compact, but also to the reincorporation of labor into the Democratic Party. Whether this crisis will also produce a working class response, and whether this time America's working people will be able to create their own political party, will only become clear in the next few years.

The central preoccupation for the labor movement is unemployment, an issue the seriousness of which has been recognized by various international organizations. The International Monetary Fund's January 28 news release read: "World Growth Grinds to Virtual Halt, IMF Urges Decisive Global Policy Response." "The ILO message is realistic, not alarmist," said Juan Somavia, Director General of the ILO, "We are now facing a global jobs crisis." The Organization for Economic Cooperation and Development (OECD) said in Paris at the end of March 2008 that the economy of its 30 developed member nations will contract 4.3% this year while unemployment across its bloc will reach 10.1% by the end of 2010. The OECD also predicted unemployment in the Group of Seven (United States, United Kingdom, France, Germany, Italy, Canada, and Japan) would reach 36 million late next year. China alone, according to some experts, could lose 50 million jobs just among its internal migrant workers. Unemployment in March was 4.4% in Japan, 10% in Indonesia, 12% in Russia, and 20% in Spain.

Working People Unprepared

Working people are hardly prepared to face this crisis. The working class does not have independent organizations with which it can fight for itself and for society at large. The so-called parties of the working class—Democrats, Labour, Socialist, and Communist—long ago gave up their role as the champions of wage labor. Labor unions in most countries have long been subordinated to capital and government, and have become thoroughly bureaucratic and unresponsive to workers' needs. In some places company and gangster unions dominate the scene, while in other countries the so-called unions are really state institutions created to control workers.

Ideologically, the mass media, government institutions, and religious organizations have convinced many working people that capitalism has no alternative. In some countries the experience of bureaucratic communism or neoliberal social democracy has given socialism a bad name. And, in terms of their capacity and willingness to struggle, the working class in most counties with some very important exceptions—Latin America and China—has not gone into motion yet. The crisis spreads like a tsunami washing away the institutional gains of decades, destroying organizations, and threatening all in its path, yet in many places the workers do not even have an organization to help them retreat to higher ground in the face of the rising water.

Not Your Great-Grandparents' Capitalism

This is not your great-grandparents' capitalism. Capitalism in the twenty-first century is, more than ever, a world system. Since the 1930s the world capitalist system has changed in several ways, all of which affect both the nature of the current crisis and the response of the working class. Capitalism has expanded, and its penetration of peoples, states, and regions of the world has deepened. At the same time, almost everywhere the system has reduced government social welfare budgets and reorganized social welfare programs. In the course of these developments, capital also transformed its relationships to unions in the workplace and to labor parties in society.

How did all of these changes come about? With the end of World War II, the process of decolonization began in Africa and Asia as former colonies became independent nations, now open to new investment and trade relationships. The fall of communism in the Soviet Union and Eastern Europe by the early 1990s also opened up that region to private capitalist investment from the West. The collapse of communism in the Soviet Union, China's evolution to a capitalist economy, and the opening up of India's economy have brought about what Thomas L. Friedman called "the great doubling" of the world capitalist labor force, adding 1.3 billion workers.

Capital simultaneously reconfigured itself, organizing world production both through multinational corporations and through extramural buyer-supplier relations, with many industrial manufacturing jobs moving from developed countries to developing countries. Throughout the post-World War II period, then, capital flowed into these vast new regions, such as Asia, and Eastern Europe which had been thrown wide open to investment. Latin America also saw significant growth in foreign investment. Africa, except for South Africa, for the most part continued to have a post-colonial economy much like the old colonial one with investment in some agricultural export products, oil and mining.

The Expansion of Capital in Asia and Latin America

Most of the capitalist economic growth in the developing world occurred in Asia—countries like Japan, South Korea, Taiwan, Hong Kong, and Singapore—though after 1980 the Chinese communist government began to oversee a transformation to a capitalist economy through the use of state capital, off-shore Chinese capital, and investment from countries such as the United States. Within little more than a decade, China had been transformed into the fastest growing capitalist industrial economy on earth, its production largely driven by the U.S. market. India, too, entered upon the path of rapid capitalist industrial development by the 1990s. In Latin America, Brazil grew into one of the world's largest ten economies, with greater industrialization also taking place in Mexico.

During this same period, capitalism changed its methods from the Taylor-Ford model of industrial production, based on scientific management and assembly line production, to the post-Fordist, Japanese or lean production model, sometimes called "management by stress." Production managers in workplaces around the world introduced just-in-time warehousing and parts delivery systems, created workplace quality circles or teams, cut the workforce, and introduced more intense supervision. At the same time, corporations reduced the size of their core facilities and workforces through subcontracting or contracting-out, a strategy which also tended to reduce the role of labor unions and collective bargaining agreement. Japanese and Korean success in the auto industry, later imitated by European and American manufacturers, was largely based on these new production models.

One of the most important new developments in world capitalism, beginning around 1980, was the growth of the worldwide manufacturing model, that is, a manufacturing system based on production of parts taking place in various countries later to be assembled in another nation, and perhaps sold in yet another. The growth of satellites, fiber optic cable, and cell phones, the computerization of communications and of production controls, the development and spread of the inter-modal containerized cargo system adaptable to trucks, trains, ships, and planes, and the creation of a world finance system facilitated by information technology made such a world production model possible.

All three of these developments—the expansion of capitalism to the post-colonial and post-communist worlds, the development of lean production, and the world production model—were accelerated by the appearance beginning in 1980 of the neoliberal economic policy. Margaret Thatcher in the UK and Ronald Reagan in the United States first began to introduce the neoliberal model based on deregulation and privatization, open markets and free trade, tight money fiscal policies, cuts in government social welfare spending, and a concerted attack on labor unions. Later the international financial institutions—the International Monetary Fund (IMF), the World Bank, the World Trade Organization (WTO—formerly the GATT), would use structural adjustment policies to press these measures on developing countries.

The Post-War Arrangement

To understand the labor movement's response to the crisis today, we have to see it in the perspective of the post-war labor and political experience. There was a radical upsurge from below led by the resistance movements in France and Italy in the last years of the war. At the war's end, the Socialist and Communist Parties, however, succeeded in keeping the movement from taking a revolutionary turn. Still, the revulsion against Fascism and Nazism and the conservative political parties in Europe, led the populations to elect the social democratic parties in Western European governments.

While the situations and the timing varied from country to country, the tendency was toward the creation of social democratic welfare states in the post-war period; moreover these institutional reforms in labor relations and social welfare remained intact even when conservatives or Christian Democrats came to power. At the same time, in most Western European nations, the government and political system tended toward the integration of the labor unions into the political system as an electoral apparatus, just as the various forms of social democratic union participation or joint-management schemes integrated the unions into the economic system as junior partners.

The general post-war prosperity of the United States and the consistent improvements in the standard of living in Europe, combined with the welfare state measures, led to a period of relative social stability lasting from 1945 to about 1965 during which the labor unions and labor parties atrophied. In the United States the post-war New Frontier, Great Society, and War on Poverty measures of Democratic presidents John F. Kennedy and Lyndon B. Johnson established a similar though narrower and weaker welfare state in America. By and large, collective bargaining became ritualized as unions traded shop floor control for wage increases, cost-of living clauses, and health and pension benefits. Automation of the plants in the 1950s and 60s led to a combination of intensified production and the gradual reduction of the size of the industrial workforce.

The Insurgency of the Late 1960s and Early 1970s

When a period of economic crisis and social conflict erupted in the late 1960s and 1970s, a New Left and a new worker insurgency in countries like Greece, Italy, France, Spain, and Portugal, and to a lesser extent in Germany, led the resistance. The French general strike of 1968, the Italian "hot autumn" of 1969-1970, and the nearly revolutionary upheavals of 1974-75 in Spain and Portugal raised the prospect of socialist revolution but proved incapable of breaking the grip of the reformist Socialist and Communist Parties and their labor federations over the largest and most strategic sections of the European working classes. Nevertheless, the tendency toward the absorption of the Socialist and Communists into the parliamentary system as moderate reformers, together with the institutionalization of labor relations, meant that the working class was too weak to stop imposition of the new capitalist order of post-Fordism, world production, and neoliberalism.

The labor insurgencies in the United States and Mexico in the same period found themselves thwarted in the first case by management and the labor bureaucracy and in the second case by the state party and its captive unions. In the United States, rebellions among miners, postal workers, teamsters, telephone workers, and African-American auto workers proved capable of overturning the old bureaucracy only in the case of the miners. In Mexico, the independent unions were created among university workers, established a small foothold in auto parts, and built a democratic current in the Mexican teachers' union. The Democratic Tendency led by the Mexican Electrical Workers, however, went down to defeat at the hands of the Army and the official union in 1975.

Neoliberalism and the Response

Throughout Europe, Japan, and the United States, with competition increasing and profits stagnating, it was the employers who in turn went on the offensive in the second half of the 1970s. The employers launched what shocked union officials called "class warfare," during a decade when every contract negotiation seemed to lead to conflict. When the economic offensive proved insufficient to recoup profits, the employers turned to political measures. The neoliberal period that began in 1980 saw the further political degeneration of left and nationalist political parties around the world. While the Labor, Social Democratic, and Communist parties of Europe had already begun in the pre-World War II or Popular Front period to play the role of reformist parties that would seek to administer the capitalist economy and its state rather than to transform or overthrow them, by the 1980s these parties had become in most cases little more than tepid center-left parties carrying out programs little different than their conservative and liberal counterparts.

The neoliberal offensive had more onerous impacts in other countries. In Mexico the Institutional Revolutionary Party stole the election of 1988 and installed Carlos Salinas de Gortari as president. It was he who privatized virtually all of the state industries except petroleum and power generation. In China in 1989, the Communist government smashed the democracy movement at the Tien An Mien square, a blow to both society at large and to the labor movement in particular.

By the 1990s, the Social Democrats of Europe and President Bill Clinton and the Democrats in the United States now converted to neoliberalism, enthusiastically privatized, deregulated, opened markets, cut the social welfare budget, and restrained labor unions. Consequently, as the working class saw its standard of living decline, its parties and unions lost their support. Throughout the neoliberal period of the 1980s and 1990s, in countries around the world, unions were driven from the halls of government, lost their weight in political party conclaves, and found themselves driven out in the cold. Unions, in fact, became the targets of a concerted attack by government and employers. In the neoliberal world, the union was at best a pathetic dependent and at worst a pariah.

Neoliberal policies affected unions in various ways: closing of older industrial plants often wiped out the strongest labor unions; direct government attacks on unions eliminated others; changes in labor legislation, particularly the promotion of "flexible" labor laws weakened union protections; contracting out (or outsourcing) replaced union workers with nonunion contract workers, while an employers' offensive debilitated unions and eroded contracts. Employers also hired immigrant workers at lower wages, often without benefits and frequently off the books.

While the government and employer attack on unions proceeded, it was often accompanied by a restructuring of production which resulted in a reconfiguration and a recomposition of the working class such that even in developing countries, industry and industrial workers tended to decline, while services and service workers grew, and casual employment multiplied. In developing nations there was a tendency for much of the workforce to become part of the underground economy. In some developing countries as much as quarter, a third, or even half of all workers labored in the informal economy without social security (health and pension), without labor unions, and without paying taxes. As the process advanced, workers often found job security imperiled, wages falling, and benefits diminishing. All of this was accompanied, of course, by a gradual and general decline in the standard of living of workers. Social inequality grew and poverty increased in developing countries.

During this period the ties between government and Communist, Social Democratic, Labor, nationalist, and populist parties and their respective labor federations were weakened. Whether in the former Soviet Union, Indonesia, or Mexico, the government-party-union connection—a connection often built on patronage and rife with corruption—was severed. In several countries—including the United

States, Mexico, and Venezuela—under the pressure of events, the old political labor federations cracked up, rival labor federations multiplied, and in some cases the unions were virtually pulverized. Unions which once found strength through their ties to a leftist party that for long periods of time controlled one or another government, now found themselves cut loose from both government and party and set adrift in the choppy economic seas.

In most countries, during this period, unions suffered damaging attacks and sometimes crushing defeats. At the same time, in Bolivia or India for example, new social movements arose, sometimes calling themselves "unions," but representing not the industrial working class or government employees, or service workers, but rather groups such as the unemployed, the self-employed, the landless, the indigenous, and women. New unions for casual workers arose in Japan, Korea, and India. Combinations of the old unions, the new movements, the indigenous groups, dissident military factions, and old left political parties created new political forces, especially in Latin America, where massive struggles eventually brought some of them to power in one or another country.

Latin America: The Neoliberal Trend Resisted

The situation was different in Latin America from that in other parts of the world. The disappointments in democratization and the failures of the economy in the 1980s and 1990s led to the rise of social movements, political parties, and candidates that opposed neoliberalism and the Washington Consensus. Latin Americans resisted neoliberalism in various countries through a series of national general strikes, popular uprising, and attempted coups. By the late 1990s the struggle found expression in political campaigns. The continental shift to the left can be seen clearly in the series of elections over the last decade which brought to power in seven Latin American nations a series of presidents with politics described as ranging from populist, to social democratic, and, in some cases, some claim, revolutionary socialist.

In Venezuela, Hugo Chávez, a charismatic military officer and coup leader was later elected in 1999 and reelected in 2000 and 2006. He proclaimed a struggle for a Bolivarian socialism, what he calls "socialism for the twenty-first century." Chávez has won support from sections of organized labor, mobilized Venezuela's poor, and has used the nation's oil wealth to finance campaigns—the Bolivarian Missions—to bring health, education, and welfare to the nation's needy. He has worked to build unity among Latin American nations to resist the United States. Chávez has in the past few years created the United Socialist Party of Venezuela (PSUV) and the National Union of Workers (UNT) as political instruments of his government's power. A charismatic populist whose methods involve a combination of direction from above and mobilization from below, Chávez's Bolivarian Revolution has been paused but not paralyzed by a reactionary bourgeois opposition, the power of the United States, and the vicissitudes of oil prices. More democratic forces with other visions of socialism tend to operate within the broad chavista movement rather than outside of it.

Ignacio "Lula" da Silva, a former steel worker, organizer of the Metalworkers Union, then of the Brazilian Labor Federation (CUT), and of the Workers Party

(PT), has pursued more cautious and traditional economic programs. His government has been aligned with the banks and big construction companies, kept its support of the CUT and PT, and created a welfare program for the nation's poor. In the international arena, he has formed an alliance with China and India to block the United States in the World Trade Organization (WTO), and he too has worked for Latin American unity under the leadership of Brazil.

Evo Morales represents the explosion of the indigenous people onto the Latin American scene. An indigenous person himself, the head of a union of coca growers, a self-proclaimed socialist and leader of the Movement to Socialism (MAS), Morales has fought both to keep control of the country's national resources (gas and lithium) and for a national land distribution. His radical program has won broad support from the country's indigenous and poor people of the altiplano and fierce opposition from the European or mestizo people of the lowlands.

Within all of these countries there exist mass labor and popular movements and revolutionary groupings, though nowhere does socialist revolution appear to be on the immediate agenda. While the most radical situations exist in Venezuela and Bolivia, to be successful there social movements would have to overcome both Chavez's personalistic model and the limits of the petroleum-based economy, while in the second it would have to surpass Morales' cautious pursuit of reform. Neither of those seems highly likely.

China in Crisis

At the new heart of contemporary world production in Guangdong Province, China, the sudden collapse of the American market and other world markets led to abrupt plant closings, layoffs, and in some cases worker protests and riots. China's growth rate fell to 6.8% in the last quarter of 2008, ending five years of growth at 10% or more. The IMF predicts China will grow by only 6.7% this year, though some think growth might only be 5%. Economists say that China needs an 8% growth rate to provide jobs to new entrants to its labor force.

Already by February there were 20 million Chinese without jobs heading home to their villages. "It's expected that 40 to 50 million or more migrant workers may lose their jobs in urban areas if the global economy keeps shrinking this year," wrote Tsinghua University's Professor Yu Qiao in a recent paper. And this does not include the permanent urban residents who will also lose jobs in this downturn. "Jobless migrant workers on this mass scale implies a severe political and social problem," said Yu. "Any minor mishandling may trigger a strong backlash and could even result in social turbulence." According to official Chinese government statistics of 2006 and 2007, the country's manufacturing industry then employed 44.5 million migrant workers and 33.5 million urban residents. The Chinese Academy of Social Sciences asserted in January that the real unemployment rate was 9.4%, and could be expected to rise.

The Chinese Ministry of Security reported that "mass incidents"—such as strikes and riots—numbered 10,000 in 1994, but by 2005, that had risen to 87,000. While the government stopped publishing the statistics, observers believe the numbers have risen even higher. "Without doubt, now we're entering a peak period for mass incidents ... In 2009, Chinese society may face even more conflicts and clashes that will test even more the governing abilities of the party and government at all levels," according to senior Xinhua agency reporter, Huang Huo.

While the state, party, and union ties broke in many countries, in China the Communist Party jealously guards its power and protects the All China Federation of Trade Unions (ACFTU).Yet even in China, the ACFTU has evolved in complex and varied ways and sometimes functions somewhat more independently and sometimes, even if rarely, in one or another situation in defense of workers. The local ACFTU union finds itself both assisted and challenged by independent workers' centers. Whether the state will be able to contain the rising tide will depend on whether or not workers can build labor and political organizations independent of the government, the Communist Party, and the ACFTU.

The Crisis, the Movement, the Left, and the Future

The left around the world finds itself in a difficult position, without in most places a strong socialist organization or a powerful labor movement. History suggests that from the onset of a depression to the beginning of a mass movement it may take years for the working class to absorb intellectually and emotionally what has happened to them and then finally assert their righteous indignation and begin to act. The key to the development of the labor and social movements and of a socialist movement in the United States and in Europe will be, as it was in the early 1930s, the development of militant minorities, ginger groups in the workplace and unions, in communities, and in the various social movements who take actions that challenge the status quo. Militant minorities, acting independently of the labor bureaucracy and of the liberal and Social Democratic parties have the capacity to set larger forces in motion. Once large numbers begin to go into motion, history suggests that that will lead suddenly to the development of new tactics and new strategies and of new political alternatives. We see perhaps the first signs of this in the appearance of the new Anti-Capitalist Party in France.

Even without forces, however, the incipient movement desires to put forward an alternative. The revolutionary left—tarred with the failures and atrocities of both social democracy and Stalinism and recognizing that programs are something to be constructed not proclaimed—hesitates to put forward a full-blown plan which it recognizes that it does not have the arguments to justify, the forces to fight for, or the power to impose. The development of a program will have to come with the development of new socialist left and, more important, of working class and popular movements.

We already begin to see such first attempts to project a program—not yet on a revolutionary basis—in the declarations of the Asia-Europe People's Forum in Beijing and the Social Forum in Belém. Their calls for socialization of finance and industry and for the administration of the economy democratically, raised by movements from below, point toward a possible future. Yet those programs and demands will be meaningless unless the labor and social movements can build labor and social movements with the power to push them forward. During this period the revolutionary left, through militant minorities and the development of its programmatic ideas, may be able to lay the basis for revolutionary organizations, and even in some countries to construct a revolutionary party. ❑

Sources: Anwar Shaikh, panel, "What is the Nature of the Economic Crisis," at the Left Forum, New York City, April 19, 2009; Jon Garnaut, "Spectre of 50m job losses looms in China," *The Age*, January 19, 2009; Tania Branigan, "China fears riots will spread as boom goes sour," *The Observer*, January 25, 2009.

Article 9.2

THE *REAL* AUDACITY OF HOPE
Republic Windows Workers Stand Their Ground

BY KARI LYDERSEN AND JAMES TRACY
January/February 2009

The 2008 holiday season is one of high hopes and high anxiety. Barack Obama's November victory raised expectations of meaningful change, while the Department of Labor estimates over a half million jobs were lost in November alone.

Workers at Chicago's Republic Windows and Doors weren't waiting for the White House when they learned that they were losing their jobs due to a plant closing. They occupied their workplace, insisted on receiving their full vacation and sick days pay—and won. Whether it be the shape of things to come or just a fleeting moment remains to be seen. Their action forced the mainstream media to show the faces behind the statistics—ones filled with pride and defiance, not pity and powerlessness.

Last fall [2008], workers at Republic noticed that important pieces of equipment had disappeared from their Goose Island warehouse. Alarmed, they notified their union, United Electrical Radio and Machine Workers of America, Local 1110 (otherwise known as UE), an independent union with a tradition of direct action. Republic's management assured the union that no plant closure was afoot; and that the equipment would be replaced with modernized pieces.

Not willing to take the company's word for it, the union covertly monitored the plant, and watched as trucks removed the very machinery needed to produce windows and doors. Meanwhile as the foreclosure crisis unfolded, Republic lost most of its contracts for new home construction.

Then on Tuesday, December 2 [2008], employees were told what they feared had been coming for a long-time. Friday, the plant would be shuttered. They were to come pick up their checks and file for unemployment. Company officials blamed the closing on the economic crisis, and on Bank of America, who they said clamped down on their credit despite a federal bailout package of $25 billion in taxpayer money.

"When we arrived to pick up our checks, we were told that we would not be getting paid for our accrued sick days," said Melvin Maclin, Local 1110's Vice President and Republic employee of seven years. Their health insurance was also cut off on Friday, December 5, despite an earlier promise it would extend until December 15. "At that point we had been told so many lies, we didn't know what to believe."

At look at Republic shows the faces of both organized labor past and present. A warehouse that produces actual products, instead of simply distributing them, is a rarity in de-industrialized America. The workers—largely Latino, many black, and a few white—reflect the shifts in Chicago's population and the composition of the blue-collar sections of the working-class. Plant closures are a common part of the Midwest experience. What makes this saga uncommon is what the workers decided to do about it.

They voted to occupy the factory in order to force the company to pay their accrued vacation time as well as comply with the federal WARN Act of 1988, which mandates that companies give 60 days notice when plants are closed or mass lay-offs are planned, or pay each employee 60 days severance. Illinois law had actually extended the required notice time to 75 days.

The workers took turns sitting on the shop floor, rotating roughly in the shifts they would have normally worked. Members of local labor and community organizations continuously visited, offering words of support and freshly cooked food. Victor Emeric, a driver with Teamsters Local 705, delivered several boxes of food and underscored what he felt as the importance of the Republic action.

"Support is very important; so is solidarity. We're hoping that the outcome of this is positive for the workers," he said. "I hope that elected officials do the right thing, I try to remain optimistic, but past experience teaches me to know better than that."

The union and company officials had reached an agreement that the workers would not be forcefully removed from the plant as long as they kept it safe and secure and only workers and union staff were allowed on the shop floor. (Supporters congregated in the small lobby and outside on the sidewalk, even in freezing rain and snow.)

Nonetheless, during the first few days of the sit-in rumors flew via text message and email that police would be ordered to evict workers from the plant. But officers keeping watch at the site seemed sympathetic to workers, perhaps another sign of how the economic crisis has affected such a wide swath of Americans and created alliances and empathy among those who wouldn't have felt it before.

One police officer, dispatched to observe the occupation from across the Republic parking lot, refused to speak on the record about his feelings, or the position of the Chicago Police Department. But from his patrol car, he then eloquently explained how the economy was destroying the futures of everyday people "just trying to survive," as plants close and pension plans disappear.

On day four of the occupation, the union began negotiations with company and Bank of America officials, as workers and supporters waited eagerly for word of the outcome. Monday evening crowds waving picket signs and chanting "Si se puede" crowded around a bonfire in a trash can and formed a line to deliver donated food hand to hand into the factory.

Donte Watson, 30, said he was furious at company officials because he was proud of all the effort he had put into this job for eight years and had assumed he would work there for decades more and then retire. He was also angry that the company would close with orders still to fill because he didn't want customers to be let down. "People put their blood, sweat, and tears into this company; it was our company too, not just the owners," he said. "They knew this was coming and they didn't say a word to us. They owed us more respect than that. We don't want anything extra, we just want what we are owed." The negotiations were continued to Tuesday, and then to Wednesday. Meanwhile during the day on Wednesday JPMorgan Chase bank offered a $400,000 line of credit to help pay the workers. Finally, on late Wednesday evening workers voted to accept a proposal from Bank of America creating $1.75 million in credit to pay health benefits for two months, severance and accrued vacation time.

It was a huge victory, a group of 260-some determined workers and their supporters convincing a major financial institution to reverse its position. But the bank didn't agree to the union's larger demand, that it finance the company to allow it to remain open. This was a tough question to tackle from political, legal and ethical standpoints: if a company is failing financially, to what extent if any is a bank—a private institution—required to subsidize them? And how does the equation change when that private institution has just received an infusion of $25 billion in public money?

The Republic Windows and Doors situation is complicated by insinuations that the owners were trying to move the plant to Iowa, perhaps to avoid having union workers. The owner had incorporated a similar business in Iowa, according to a trade journal cited in the *New York Times*, and that might explain the moving of equipment.

As this went to press, the workers were thrilled with their victory and the results of their direct action. But they also weren't satisfied with taking the money—enough to survive for several months—and still having to find new jobs in this cut-throat economy. Yet they clearly demonstrated that in a shifting economic and political context, collective action can bring real results. Protests in support of Republic workers at Bank of America branches in Philadelphia, San Francisco and Reno resulted in arrests of activists and added to the national attention of the occupation.

The tactic of a takeover evoked memories of the Flint Sit-Down Strike of 1936 that established the United Auto Workers' presence in the auto industry. Chicago has a long history of labor militancy and events there have often set the tone and tempo of the labor movement as a whole. In 1886, the Haymarket demonstrations, and subsequent massacres and trials of anarchist activists became a hallmark of the battle for the eight-hour day. Turn of the century strikes of clothing workers against Hart, Shaffner and Marx in Chicago led by Sidney Hillman later led to the founding of the Amalgamated Clothing Workers.

"With this economic crisis and unemployment, there are no other jobs," said Dagoberto Cervantes, 41, as his five-year-old son danced around with a picket sign on Monday evening.

This example has boosted the spirits of other workers facing what might be the dawn of the next depression. Across town, at the Congress Plaza Hotel, workers have been on strike for five years. Augustina Bahena, a Congress worker remarked, "Republic workers have given us all a lot of hope, and maybe some new ideas. The bailout needs to help workers. A corporation can't receive millions of dollars just to finance layoffs."

Back at Republic, the workers are talking about starting a co-op to run the factory, reminiscent of labor movements of the past and the factory takeovers by Argentine workers following the financial meltdown of the late 1990s.

Such a move would be a challenging undertaking, especially in this desperate financial climate. But the economic crisis has given people the sense they can no longer simply survive by laying low and not making waves. The status quo is no longer safe. As the workers realized when faced with the plant's closing and denial of their wages, people have no choice but to take matters into their own hands. ❑

Article 9.3

CORPORATE AMERICA'S COUNTER-STIMULUS STRATEGY
Firms decide to shut profitable plants while spurning buyers.

BY ROGER BYBEE
May/June 2009

"Is it too late? I hope not," said an exasperated Anthony Fortunato, president of the 260-worker United Steelworkers (USW) Local 2604 at an ArcelorMittal steel mill in Lackawanna, N.Y., as he and his members watched the mill being systematically taken apart.

An eager buyer has been pressing the company—the world's largest steel firm—for at least two months to sell the mill and thus keep the profitable operation open and the jobs alive. Fortunato is hoping the buyer will remain interested despite ArcelorMittal's aggressive drive to gut the mill. ArcelorMittal is rushing to dismantle complex, custom-built ovens and other equipment that will take months to replace.

Day by day, the dismantling continues relentlessly, with each step reducing the value of the mill. "Our members are getting sick watching this happen," said Fortunato.

Arcelor's plans to close the Lackawanna mill are occurring against the backdrop of a widely supported effort by President Barack Obama to stimulate the nation's flat-lining economy with the $787 billion American Recovery and Reinvestment Act. But even as Obama is moving to counter the nation's economic free-fall, major corporations are moving in the opposite direction when it comes to maintaining employment and consumer demand. A recent survey showed 71% of CEOs expecting more layoffs in the coming six months.

Not only are they accelerating the pace of outsourcing to low-wage nations like China, but there have been several recent instances of corporations closing profitable plants in the United States and then refusing to sell them to other companies interested in keeping the plants open and retaining the current workforce.

"These Jobs Aren't Coming Back"

The Lackawanna mill isn't ArcelorMittal's only closure. ArcelorMittal is also shutting down its Hennepin, Ill., steel mill, even though other firms have expressed strong interest in buying that mill, reports USW Local 7367 president David York.

At a moment when unemployment around Hennepin—about 100 miles west of Chicago—has hit 10%, ArcelorMittal is preparing to discard the 285 USW members who have performed the hard work of steel production.

The plant has been consistently profitable, earning $48.4 million even in a recessionary year like 2008. Yet ArcelorMittal is intent on shipping one product line to low-wage Brazil and another to France. Moreover, ArcelorMittal has rebuffed a proposal by another major steel company to buy the Hennepin mill and keep it running.

The Hennepin workers have little prospect of finding jobs paying anywhere close to the $70,000 their old jobs averaged, including overtime and productivity bonuses, says York. Few family-supporting jobs are available nearby.

And ArcelorMittal's strategy is not unique. Last fall, the Cerberus private equity group, through its NewPage subsidiary, shut down a highly profitable, technologically advanced paper mill in Kimberly, Wisc. Cerberus is headed by John Snow, former Treasury secretary under George W. Bush; Dan Quayle, former vice president under George H.W. Bush; and Richard Feinberg, who personally raked in $330 million in compensation from Cerberus in 2007. USW Local 2-9 President Andy Nirschl speculates that Cerberus (the name is derived from the mythological dogs who guard the gates of Hades) essentially wanted to raise paper prices by reducing capacity, regardless of the human cost to 600 workers and their families.

"This wasn't like the usual scenario we've seen again and again," says Nirschl, "where a corporation moves jobs to Mexico or China to increase their profits by paying less than a dollar an hour. This was a case of a corporation taking a productive, profitable plant and closing it, refusing to sell it to anyone." The paper mill turned a profit of $66 million in 2007, says Nirschl. Four firms showed interest in buying the plant, but Cerberus and NewPage remained uninterested, frankly admitting that it had no plan at all to market the plant to another buyer.

Meanwhile, many major firms are adopting what can best be described as a "counter-stimulus" economic program, precisely following what Nirschl called "the usual scenario." The *New York Times* reported on a massive wave of job offshoring and wholesale divesting of product lines.

"These jobs aren't coming back," John E. Silvia, chief economist at Wachovia in Charlotte, N.C., told the *Times*. "A lot of production either isn't going to happen at all, or it's going to happen somewhere other than the United States. There are going to be fewer stores, fewer factories, and fewer financial services operations. Firms are making strategic decisions that they don't want to be in their businesses."

"The decimation of employment in legacy American brands such as General Motors is a trend that's likely to continue," said Robert E. Hall, an economist at Stanford University's Hoover Institution.

Productive Base Goes Out the Window

Mark Meinster, a representative of the United Electrical Workers (UE) international, said that this latest round of job destruction is simply an intensification of trends visible in recent decades, but made all the more galling because of the wanton closing of profitable plants at a time when good jobs are increasingly scarce. "We see this every day," said Meinster. For the past 20 years, you have everything from out-and-out trickery to private equity firms transferring debt from a money-losing operation to a profitable plant, and then shutting down the plant and stripping its assets. "Meanwhile, our productive capacity completely goes out the window."

Meinster helped to coordinate the December sit-down strike at Chicago's Republic Windows and Doors. Workers there faced both an employer secretly moving equipment to a new non-union plant in Iowa and the Bank of America—which received $20 billion in grants and $118 billion in loan guarantees from the bank bailout—cutting off the firm's line of credit, which, in turn, deprived workers of vacation and severance pay.

With the plant already closed, the workers decided to take over the plant, thereby taking control of Republic's valuable inventory and holding it hostage. The result: Bank of America re-opened the financial spigot, the workers were paid, an environmentally oriented firm bought the plant and will be rehiring the workers, and the sit-down achieved worldwide fame.

The Republic sit-down also inspired non-union workers, faced with a plant closing at the Colibri Group jewelry factory in East Providence, R.I., to stage a sit-in. The action resulted in 15 arrests while intensifying pressure on the firm's owner, the Founders' Group private-equity firm.

UE Western Regional President Carl Rosen, who played a leading role in backing the sit-down strike, noted that the action—both illegal and highly unusual in the United States—ignited enormous support, including from President Obama. "We made our message everybody's message," explained Rosen. "This economy is failing because workers cannot buy back what they are making. Corporations are being bailed out and workers are being sold out."

"We're Willing to Sell"

As a Luxembourg-based firm owned by an Indian-born billionaire living in London, ArcelorMittal is clearly following the "take the money and run" model of Anglo-American capitalism. This system is far harsher than the Western European model in which employers' incentives have been more influenced by social-democratic traditions and the ongoing strength of the labor movement.

In Lackawanna, ArcelorMittal's foot-dragging on a potential sale could soon mean the loss of 260 jobs. "Until yesterday [March 26], the company was not admitting that they even had heard of any interested buyers," said USW Local 2604 president Fortunato. But the forceful intervention of Sen. Chuck Schumer (D-NY) finally produced a meeting between ArcelorMittal's U.S. CEO James Ripley and one interested buyer.

"At this point, we don't know the results of the negotiations," Fortunato told *Dollars & Sense*, the frustration and anxiety evident in his voice. The outcome of the negotiations may depend on whether ArcelorMittal's decision to aggressively dismantle the steel operation has made purchasing the existing, hollowed-out plant and re-starting production far more difficult and costly than simply beginning production from scratch.

The involvement of members of the U.S. Congress at Lackawanna—as at Hennepin and Kimberly—has forced the corporations to claim that they were willing to sell the plants and retain jobs. But once the meetings were concluded, corporate interest in selling and saving the jobs of local workers rapidly melted away. For example, a Cerberus/NewPage official was asked recently whether the company had any plans in place to market the Kimberly plant. The response: "No."

Cooperation: A One-Way Street

Particularly frustrating for Local 2604 is the fact that the union made such extensive efforts to assist the corporation. It lobbied successfully for a two-thirds reduction in their electricity costs, lined up training grants, and supported reductions in sales- and property-tax rates for the corporation. "We as a union have done a lot to help the company. They've tried to tell us we're not competitive as a plant. If that's the case, why not sell us?"

Rather than being grateful for the union's efforts to lower its costs, ArcelorMittal instead changed its internal accounting procedures so that the Lackawanna plant actually booked a loss, by charging that plant more for shipping and supplies from other ArcelorMittal plants around the United States. In that way, ArcelorMittal aimed to evade New York's higher corporate taxes, Fortunato suspects. Until ArcelorMittal made that shift in accounting, the plant had been consistently showing a profit of about $6 million a month.

With annual wages typically running in the $40,000-to-$50,000 range, his members will have a hard time finding comparable-paying work. Fortunato believes the real unemployment rate in Lackawanna, near the similarly hard-hit industrial city of Buffalo, is about 25% to 30%. "Our guys will have to work two or three jobs to make what they earn here," he said.

The process of watching the Lackawanna mill being slowly dismantled, with custom-made parts being wrecked by being disassembled or simply scrapped, is difficult for the workers who invested their lives in the plant, says Fortunato. "Our guys are getting sick at what they're scrapping."

The steelworkers in Illinois also complain of the corporation's indifference to commitments by the public to subsidize ArcelorMittal. ArcelorMittal's decision to locate its U.S. headquarters in Chicago unleashed a flow of incentives, including $2 million in assistance for furnishing corporate offices.

At the Hennepin plant, the union's current contract commits ArcelorMittal to keeping the plant open through the agreement and maintaining its viability through adequate investment. The union has taken the case to arbitration.

What Benefits? What Retraining?

As major corporations continue to undermine the impact of Obama's stimulus efforts by slashing jobs, the conventional wisdom among leading economists and elected officials in both parties is that worker retraining is the best public-policy response. As the *New York Times* put it recently, "For decades, the government has reacted to downturns by handing out temporary unemployment insurance checks, relying upon the resumption of economic growth to restore the jobs lost. This time, the government needs to place a greater emphasis on retraining workers for other careers."

But this approach, while conveniently allowing elected officials to sidestep an uncomfortable confrontation with corporations' unilateral control over the fate of workers and communities, has little empirical support as a successful strategy for "adapting" to deindustrialization and the offshoring of jobs. As the supply of family-supporting jobs is reduced, workers are essentially losing at a game of musical chairs in which good jobs are disappearing and not being replaced. When displaced workers successfully complete retraining programs, they are generally unable to find jobs comparable in pay and benefits to the ones they lost.

"Out of a hundred laid-off workers," says *New York Times* economics writer Louis Uchitelle in his book *The Disposable American: Layoffs and Their Consequences*, "27 are making their old salary again, or more, and 73 are making less, or not working at all." But even if retraining were an effective strategy, the very politicians who tout it as a solution have been unwilling to fund training in a serious way. Funding for training has plummeted from $20 billion in 1979 to just $6 billion last year (in constant dollars), according to one expert cited by the *Times*. These cutbacks in funding would seem to indicate that leading politicians, especially in the Bush era, were never quite sincere in their willingness to match their proclaimed faith in the power of retraining with an equivalent level of funding.

Further, the traditional unemployment-compensation safety net has been shredded over the past four decades, reaching a much smaller percentage of workers than in past, less severe recessions. During the 1975 recession, unemployment compensation reached 75% of the jobless and thus was a significant factor in restoring consumer demand. But thanks to radical cuts in unemployment compensation eligibility rammed through by the Reagan administration, only 45% of the unemployed received any benefits during the much more severe recession of 1982-83. The National Association of Manufacturers was delighted with the cutbacks in eligibility, crowing that under the old rules, "there was no incentive to go back to work under that program."

By 2003, the number of unemployed workers eligible for benefits had fallen further from the 1982 level of 45% down to just 41%, according to the Ohio-based

---

Corporate Royalty Ignores Workers' Years of Loyalty

Corporations are often accused of having an imperious, Marie Antoinette-style attitude toward their workers, unaware and uncaring about their daily struggles to provide for their families.

Marie Antoinette, wife of Louis XVI, was informed that the poor of Paris were too poor to afford bread. Her infamous response: "Let them eat cake." She was later beheaded in 1793 during the French Revolution.

But in the case of ArcelorMittal, which is preparing to shut down steel mills in Hennepin, Ill. and Lackawanna, N.Y., the comparison to Marie Antoinette may not be much of an exaggeration. The workers and local communities have been bewildered by the corporation's commitment to closing the profitable mills despite offers from other firms that wanted to keep them open.

Meanwhile, corporate CEO Lakshmi Mittal lives in near-royal grandeur in London in a $125 million home right next to the posh Kensington Palace. Mittal's home was constructed by combining the former Russian and Egyptian embassies. The swimming pool is inlaid with jewels, and the estate includes a 20-car garage. Lakshmi Mittal has a personal fortune estimated at $25 billion.

For the wedding of his daughter Vanisha, who is also a member of the corporation's board of directors, Mittal shelled out $55 million. If you're wondering how even the super-rich could manage to spend such a sum on a wedding, it might help to know that the five-day celebration was capped by a party—at Versailles.

That's right—Versailles, the magnificent and legendary palace that King Louis XVI gave to his 19-year-old bride, Marie Antoinette, as a wedding present. *Plus ça change...*

group Public Policy Matters. While Obama's American Recovery and Reinvestment Act may begin to reverse some cutbacks in eligibility, it remains to be seen how widely these changes will positively affect the fates of the jobless.

Needless Job Losses

The toll of unemployment extends far beyond a drop in family income, access to health care, and a loss of self-esteem for the displaced worker. Peter Dreier, a political scientist at Occidental College, recently released a study showing that each 1% increase in the national U.S. unemployment rate produces an additional 47,000 deaths, with 26,000 of the fatalities cardiac-related, 1,200 due to suicides, and 831 due to homicides.

Given these grim realities about passively accepting the consequences of deindustrialization, coupled with growing resentment about the greed and malfeasance of Wall Street, the egregious damage to workers and communities imposed by firms like Cerberus and ArcelorMittal may raise corporate investment decisions to a high-profile political issue. Corporations are closing profitable, productive plants in the midst of a severe economic crisis, and then capriciously refusing to seriously consider selling the plants to keep them open.

This would be unthinkable in a number of Western European democracies like Germany and Sweden that have long required that corporations provide a compelling rationale for shutdowns to regional government labor-market bodies. Most other Western European nations offer workers and communities some degree of protection from the effects of shutdowns, although not as extensively as in Germany or Sweden, nor with the same degree of worker and community participation in decisions about the company's plans.

In the United States, the increasingly destructive impact of arbitrary corporate decisions to close plants amidst a severe economic crisis may finally unleash public demands to place corporations' conduct under democratic constraints. ❏

Sources: Roger Bybee, "Pulp Friction: A private equity firm's decision to shut down a profitable paper mill devastates a Wisconsin community," *In These Times*, Jan. 2009; Peter S. Goodman and Jack Healy, "Job Losses Hint at Vast Remaking of Economy," *New York Times*, Mar. 7, 2009; Matt Glynn, "ArcelorMittal says it's willing to sell Lackawanna plant," *Buffalo News*, Mar. 26, 2009; Stanley Reed, "Mittal & Son: An inside look at the dynasty that dominates steel," *Business Week*, Apr. 16, 2007; New release, Northwestern University Medill News Service, Oct. 7, 2005; Making Steel.com, Feb. 21, 2007; Peter Dreier: "This Economy is a Real Killer," Huffington Post, Mar. 10, 2009, Barry Bluestone and Bennett Harrison, *The Deindustrialization of America: Plant Closings, Community Abandonment, and the Dismantling of Basic Industry* (NY: Basic Books, 1982); Lawrence Rothstein, *The Fight Against Plant Closings* (Auburn Books: Dover Mass. and London, 1986); Mark Richtel, "A Sea of Unwanted Imports, *New York Times*, Nov. 18, 2008; William K. Tabb, "Financialization Appropriation," *Z Magazine*, June 2008; William K. Tabb, "Four Crises of the Contemporary World Capitalist System," *Monthly Review*, October 2008; Vinaya Saksena, "15 arrested at EP rally," *Pawtucket Times*, Mar. 20, 2009.

Article 9.4

WORKER DIRECT ACTION GROWS IN WAKE OF FINANCIAL MELTDOWN

BY IMMANUEL NESS AND STACY WARNER MADDERN
November/December 2009

Labor-management relations have taken a dramatic turn in an era in which unions are too weak or timid to take action even as joblessness grows and companies losing financing are forced into bankruptcy by their creditors. As plants close and layoffs mount—and as workers recognize they can no longer interrupt the workflow with a strike when there is no flow to be interrupted—workers are engaging in militant action to save their jobs and livelihoods.

Over the last decade, sit-down strikes were largely confined to Latin America and elsewhere in the global South, where workers occupied factories in response to economic collapse. But the tide of direct action by workers and some unions seems to be moving north. Workers in the global North are now engaging in a wave of factory occupations and other militant actions. Many of these actions are in the syndicalist tradition of workers directly taking power—in some cases workers are acting on their own, in others they are leading lackadaisical unions to support their efforts. The current crisis in manufacturing has rendered a growing number of officially recognized unions with government-sanctioned collective bargaining agreements nearly helpless and could lay the basis for escalating direct actions by workers, possibly ushering in a more militant union movement.

In the United States and much of Europe, worker radicalism was in check for decades even as unions repeatedly offered up concessions to managers, ostensibly to save their factories. While workers have been viewed by corporate managers as docile and weak-willed, "when workers are threatened by management they seriously consider breaking the rules and fighting back," according to auto worker and activist Gregg Shotwell.

Shotwell, who worked at the Delphi auto parts plant in Flint, Mich., is a founder of Soldiers of Solidarity (SOS), a rank-and-file association that continues to resist United Auto Workers (UAW) policies of concessionary bargaining that have all but destroyed a way of life for unionized manufacturing workers in the United States. SOS formed as a worker insurgency in November 2005 following Delphi's bankruptcy filing and the union leadership's lackluster response. Workers at Delphi plants throughout the Midwest feared the worst—plant closures and abrogation of health and pension benefit agree-ments that were guaranteed after the auto parts unit was spun off by GM in 1999. Independent of the UAW, they waged a mass "work to rule" campaign as a means of sabotaging the company's plans for mass layoffs.

The 2005-2006 insurgency at Delphi was not a replay of the storied 1936-1937 Flint sit-down strike. Still, through deftly organized slow-downs and direct action on the shop floor (for instance, simply not fixing machines, thereby slowing the production process—known as "putting machines down"), and without the support of the UAW, the Delphi workers saved their health benefits and pensions. Says Shotwell, "A sit-down strike will not come out of a political philosophy, but will occur when workers feel they will lose everything if they stay complacent and take no action."

The global capitalist economic crisis that began in 2007 is unquestionably creating the kinds of conditions Shotwell describes for an increasing number of workers. This crisis has led to the devaluation of labor-management contracts that purportedly exchanged labor peace for decent wage and benefit standards and a modicum of job security. The closure of manufacturing plants in North America and Europe has swelled the ranks of distressed, frequently older, workers seeking to preserve the economic security they once took for granted. As welfare-state-based guaranteed benefits and unemployment insurance have been eroded since the 1980s thanks to the rise of neoliberalism, workers have been forced to rely on employer- or union-based benefits. However, in the last year, the economic collapse has exposed the failure of neoliberal capitalism to ensure economic security through either public or private avenues.

While we have yet to witness the recurrence of factory takeovers on a scale akin to the Italian Bienno-Rosso ("Red Year") of 1919-1920, when some 500,000 factory workers seized and operated factories, mostly without official union sanction, today a resurgence of rank-and-file militancy is palpable. Just in the last year, a growing number of workers who had until recently been viewed as conservative and quiescent have begun to take matters into their own hands, engaging in the most militant of activities.

In the United States, the Republic Window and Door sit-down strike in Chicago in December 2008 (see "The Real Audacity of Hope," D&S, January/February 2009) and the threatened factory occupation of Hartmarx, the men's suit manufacturer based in Des Plaines, Ill., in May 2009, have received considerable attention. At Republic the occupation got the workers the back pay and other benefits they were owed; at Hartmarx, where workers had the support of their union, the new SEIU affiliate Workers United, a threatened sit-down helped save some 3,000 jobs.

Notably, in both of these cases, workers took on the banks and creditors who sought to liquidate the firms in order to enhance their own balance sheets. Their move to demand accountability not only from their direct employers but also from financial firms, including some that had received government bailouts, strengthened their case and brought added attention to their struggle. If creditors and manufacturers continue a pattern of arbitrarily shutting down profitable firms to improve their financial ratings, it is likely that a wave of worker factory occupations could occur in the United States.

But it is in Europe that the new militancy is already most pronounced. Varied repertoires of direct action are emerging in different countries, from factory occupations in Britain and Ireland to "bossnappings" in France.

During the first six months of 2009, Unite, the United Kingdom's largest trade union, representing nearly 2 million members, reported that employers laid off over 94,000 members. Formed in 2007 through a merger of the Transport and

General Workers Union and Amicus, Unite represents workers across many industries, from finance to manufacturing.

As the global economic crisis has erupted, Unite has fought mass layoffs while publicly resisting corporate efforts to abuse the so-called "redundancy" system when going into bankruptcy. According to the 1965 Redundancy Payments Act, UK workers with at least two years of service are entitled to a severance payment from their employer. The formula for these payments is based on a number of factors such as age and length of service. The law's provision for financial compensation for laid-off workers, combined with the fact that many employers agreed to provide larger severance packages than the law required, resulted in a drop in worker resistance to mass layoffs. In the ensuing years, the average number of days lost through strikes against mass layoffs in all industries dropped—from 161,744 a year from 1960 to 1965, to 74,473 a year from 1966 to 1969.

However, more recently companies have instead been offering the legal minimum or else going into bankruptcy, in which case plants land in state receivership ("administration"); the state then assumes responsibility for the severance payments. When companies follow this latter strategy, it presents a number of problems for both workers and the economy. The state severance payments come out of a Redundancy Fund financed by a surcharge on the National Insurance Tax, with limits on how much an individual can be paid from that fund. In addition, workers who are forced into a state-funded severance plan lose any pension or other entitlements earned from their term of service.

These were the issues in play this spring, when workers represented by Unite occupied three Visteon auto parts plants in Britain and Ireland—by far the most significant among the recent sit-downs in Europe due to the extensive public support they received and their potential to erupt into a broader movement among workers.

Visteon makes parts for Ford, which spun the parts division off in 2000, one year after GM spun off Delphi. At the time, Ford promised that its wage, pension, and other benefits obligations would be honored by Visteon. Still, many workers viewed these moves as attempts by the auto companies to rid themselves of pension obligations to a segment of their workforce.

On March 31, 2009, workers at Visteon's Belfast plant were given six minutes notice that their services were no longer needed. Stunned by Visteon's arrogance in closing the plant without notice and management's failure to consult workers in any manner, the workers seized control of the plant. Roger Madison, automotive spokesperson for Unite, commented, "Once again we see how cheap and easy it is to sack UK workers. One minute they were working, but six minutes later they were jobless, pensionless, and looking at the state basic in redundancy pay as their company was placed into [bankruptcy receivership]."

Following the Belfast sit-down, workers also occupied Visteon's Basildon and Enfield plants. The arbitrary and abrupt nature of Visteon's mass layoffs traumatized veteran workers. Paul Walker, who had worked at the parts plant in Enfield for 24 years, said the workers wanted to stand firm against global corporations that seek profits at the expense of employees. "This demonstration is to protest how these international companies have treated us. ... We were given six minutes to leave the building, immediate redundancy and that's it. So, we're here for justice for ourselves."

Walker was also struck by how Visteon's abusive treatment developed his working-class consciousness. "It's funny, I was just a worker before. I came to work, I went home. I really didn't pay much attention to anything, but my eyes have been opened up. I think that right now is the right time for this [sit-down strike]."

Visteon had set out to rid itself of nearly 600 workers from the three plants. However, the workers' action forced Visteon and Ford back to the negotiating table. "If we would have walked out, we would have never have gotten [this] far," observed Charlie Maxwell, a Unite representative. The occupations continued for seven weeks when finally members of Unite voted to accept a settlement involving Ford which, according to Madison, was "ten times what people were being offered originally." Visteon agreed to a severance of between six and eighteen months' salary.

The Visteon actions were coordinated and supported by the union to a significantly greater extent than in most other recent cases of militant worker action. They also garnered significant community support, with supporters holding rallies and picketing Ford dealerships throughout Britain and Northern Ireland. Worker and community solidarity was considered the most crucial factor in reaching a settlement at Visteon. At Enfield, the sit-down strike was supported by mass labor and community demonstrations which, according to Ron Clarke, a worker at Enfield, were crucial for the success of the strike: "It took a lot of organizing, but the solidarity of the membership and the people that work [at Enfield] was incredible. It gathered momentum. There was so much support from outside."

The Visteon sit-downs and protests sent shudders through corporate and government leaders in the United States and Europe, who feared they might lead to a militant workers' movement, forcing corporations to take into account the economic and social rights of laid-off employees. On April 28, 2009, the corporate human resources journal Personneltoday.com posted a warning that "employers should beware—if successful today, Visteon workers stand to set a very public and very dangerous precedent. ... [T]he sheer determination of the workers surely stands as a testament to the lengths employees are now willing to go to secure what they believe is a 'fair deal' when they have nothing left to lose."

Sit-Down in Canada

This March, worker resistance resulted in the occupation of the Aradco auto parts plant owned by Catalina Precision Products Ltd. in Windsor, Ontario. Aradco is a privately-owned company that provides parts for Chrysler. The plant shut down after a dispute with Chrysler, which threatened to withdraw from its Canadian operations unless unionized workers made substantial concessions and lowered overall parts costs. In response, twelve workers welded the doors shut from the inside, promising not to leave until they were paid. According to the Canadian UAW, the Aradco workers were owed money for severance pay, vacation pay, and termination pay totaling $1.7 million. After an offer by the plant's owner of four weeks severance pay or about $200,000 in total for all 80 workers was rejected, Chrysler stepped in and doubled it.

Among the other companies in Great Britain and Ireland that have been the targets of militant worker action are auto parts maker Calcast, Waterford Crystal, and Prisme Packaging.

With its skilled labor force and relatively lower wages, Ireland was considered Europe's economic dynamo over the last decade. Now Irish workers facing plant closures have carried out a number of sit-down strikes. In November 2008, Calcast, a subsidiary of the French auto parts manufacturer Montupet SA which produces parts for Audi, Ford, Peugeot, and Renault, announced it was shutting down its plant in Derry and laying off 90 of 102 workers employed there, with the remaining twelve redeployed in jobs elsewhere. Montrupet's plans to close the plant were evident even before the financial meltdown. In August 2008 the company announced plans to move its manufacturing to Ruse, Bulgaria, which was slated to become the firm's primary European factory for auto parts.

After management offered severance packages below what it had previously agreed to, the workers occupied the plant, vowing not to leave until better terms were offered. The sit-in had lasted 72 hours when management made a new offer, which the union membership accepted.

In January 2009, another sit-down strike broke out at the Waterford Crystal Factory in Kilbarry, which employed some 700 workers, including nearly 500 factory workers. Waterford workers were not told directly of the plans for a closure, but only found out after it was leaked that a creditor was imminently planning to close the plant. When workers learned of the creditor's plans, they forced their way into Waterford's Visitors Centre and occupied the building, setting up a rotating shift system in which some 50 to 60 workers controlled the factory at any given time. The following week, thousands of workers, trade unionists, and

TABLE 1: 2008-2009 Sit-Down Strikes in Europe and North America

Location	Plant	Industry	Duration	Union
Nantes, France	Goss International	Printing Press Manufacturing	36 Days	CFDT
Chicago, Illinois	Republic Windows	Energy Conservation	6 Days	UEWU
Derry, Ireland	Calcast Auto Manufacturing	Auto Parts Manufacturing	72 Hours	Unite UK
Kilbarry, Ireland	Waterford Crystal	Glass Manufacturing	51 Days	Unite UK
French Alps	Caterpillar "Boss-nappings"	Tractor Manufacturing	24 Hours	None
Dundee, Scotland	Prisme Meatpacking Plant	Packing Supplies	51 Days	None
Great Britain and Northern Ireland	Visteon Car Plants	Auto Manufacturing	6 Weeks	Unite UK
Mantes-la-Jolie, France	FCI Microconnections	Electronics	34 Days	CGT-CFDT
Winsor, Ontario	Catalina Precision Products	Auto Parts Manufacturing	4 Weeks	Canadian Auto Workers

community allies massed in rallies in the city of Waterford demanding that the plant remain open.

Two major U.S. corporations contended for ownership of the company. One was Clarion Capital, which sought a concessionary pact to reemploy workers at much lower wages and inferior conditions. KPS, the second bidder, had no interest in operating the facility; it was only interested in maintaining Waterford's brand names, product designs, and manufacturing processes. With ongoing financial problems in the company, a significant number of workers were prepared to accept a lay-off. But the closure threatened not only 700 jobs but also the workers' severance payments. The Waterford occupation ended on March 23, when KPS gained control over the company and promised to keep 176 workers. The victory was only partial—while workers gained an additional redundancy payment, the agreement did not prevent Waterford from laying off most of the workers at the plant.

Since the company was in bankruptcy, those workers who lost their jobs would have received the basic national statutory payment for loss of work, rather than the company-promised severance package. KPS offered a 10 million Euro severance package to some 800 workers, including those who had lost their jobs even before the plant closure. This package replaces the company pensions, since Ireland has no pension protection plan for laid-off workers. One worker said: "On the pensions,

TABLE 2: EUROPEAN AND AUSTRALIAN SIT-DOWN STRIKES, 1971–2007

Location	Occupation	Year	Industry	Duration	Union
Glasgow, Scotland	Upper Clyde Shipbuilders	1971	Shipbuilding	11 Months	CSEU
Cambelltown, New South Wales, Australia	Harco Steel Work-In	1971	Steel Manufacturing	4 Weeks	FIA
Kirkby, England	Fisher-Bendix	1972	Washer/Dryer Manufacturing	9 Weeks	AUEW
Besançon, France	LIP Clock Factory	1973	Clock and Watch Manufacturing	5 Months	CGT-CFDT
Greenock, Scotland	Lee Jeans Factory	1981	Clothing	7 Months	NUTG
Dublin, Ireland	Chondalkin Paper Mill	1982	Paper Products	2 Years	Federated Workers Union of Ireland
Uddingston, Scotland	Caterpillar Plant	1987	Tractor/Heavy Machinery	3 Months	Scottish Trade Unions Congress
Saint-Cyr en Val, France	Kimberly-Clark Plant	1998	Paper Products	2 Weeks	FCE-CFDT
Givet, France	Cellatex Chemical Plant	2000	Chemical Technology	13 Days	CGT
Brighton, England	SITA Bin Collectors	2001	Waste Management	5 Days	Unite UK
Grenoble, France	Schneider Electrics	2004	Electronics	15 Days	CGT-CFDT
Viry-Chatillion, France	Buffalo Grill	2007	Hospitality	1 Month	None

everyone has been talking hard but little has really been done. It'll end up in the European courts—which is fine except that people need their pensions today."

Unite, which represented Waterford's laid-off workers, did not press the Irish government to nationalize the plant, but assisted in the process of identifying a private buyer. Even after the buyout, rank-and-file workers maintained the necessity of resisting the layoffs, with or without the union. The Waterford strike helped lay the basis for the Irish Congress of Trade Unions (ICTU) and Unite to call a one day solidarity strike and demonstration on March 30. Strikers and protesters demanded that private and public employers honor the Irish National Wage Agreement, which requires firms to adjust wages to the inflation rate, and protested mass layoffs and Ireland's lack of protection for worker pension plans. The ICTU contends that the Irish government is in "non-compliance with European legislation on pension protection."

Dundee, Scotland was the site of a sit-down strike in March 2009. A small group of 12 workers occupied the Prisme Packaging factory near the city center to force their employer to pay legally required severance payments, following the company's decision to lay off its entire workforce. The workers had been given one hour's notice that the firm was closing. But after receiving notification that the company was planning to withhold severance pay, holiday pay, and back wages, the seven women and five men decided to take control of the factory to prevent the company from removing potentially valuable materials and equipment.

After a 51-day occupation and significant community support in southeastern Scotland, the managing director of Prisme resigned and plans for an independent worker-managed cooperative went into effect. On May 1, Discovery Packaging and Design, Ltd., opened for business with the support of the community and private donations.

In France, worker demands are even more militant than in Britain and Ireland, as workers are demanding that employers keep factories open and challenging owner claims as to the financial viability of firms. Worker direct action has extended beyond occupying factories to blocking roads and to holding factory owners hostage in what have become known as "bossnappings."

Beginning on February 24, 2009, workers at FCI Microconnections, an electronics manufacturer in Mantes-la-Jolie, demanded that management guarantee the future of the plant. Workers believed the company was formulating a plan for mass layoffs. After FCI denied having any layoff plan, over half of the plant's 400 workers went on strike and occupied the factory, preventing any removal of equipment. The occupation continued for the next seven weeks, even after the French government issued a legal order on March 26 for to the workers to end the sit-down strike. Workers intensified the pressure on management to keep the plant open by traveling to the company headquarters in Versailles where they set up a barricade preventing the chief executive and corporate staff from leaving for four hours.

While management continued to insist no closure was planned, CGT, the union representing the workers, produced an internal document showing that FCI had developed a detailed plant-closure plan for November 2009. After the company's plans were revealed and management finally agreed to negotiate the facility's future, striking workers gained greater support from the non-striking workers. A week later negotiations between the CGT and CFDT unions and management culminated in an agreement guaranteeing that the factory will remain open until 2014 with no job cuts before 2011. FCI workers also won payment for 27 of their 34 strike days.

On Friday, March 6, 300 workers at a Goss International plant in Nantes were informed that the newspaper printing machine plant was to be closed and operations transferred to its factory in Montataire, north of Paris. Goss told workers that due to the "financial crisis," downsizing measures were necessary. However, since the plant had experienced rapid growth in production capacity in the preceding 14 years, the workers, in disbelief, insisted that it remain open and that the plant manager, who had refused to order the closure, be reinstated by the company. The occupation lasted for five days, until Goss offered assurances that certain operations at the plant could be maintained and that they would fight to save "as many jobs as possible."

Jean Luc Bonneau, a delegate of the French trade union CFDT, claims that the site is "viable" due to its earnings of "€50 million in dividends to shareholders" in the last five years. According to Bonneau, the "closure has no justification." In fact, the decision to close the factory at Nantes was made by its ownership MatlinPatterson Global Opportunities Partners, which intends to sell off the entire company to raise cash for new investments in "distressed" businesses. MatlinPatterson is one of the leading "vulture funds" that specialize in buying financially weak businesses and selling them off at a high margin after restructuring. The fate of the Goss workers had little to do with the "financial crisis" and everything to do with higher profitability in other markets.

In late March 2009, workers at a Caterpillar plant in the French Alps briefly held five managers captive in a dispute over severance packages. The incident was the third time in three weeks that French Caterpillar workers had detained their bosses to protest job losses. After announcing 22,000 job cuts worldwide in January and February, Caterpillar sought to lay off 733 workers—about a quarter of the work force—at its factories in the towns of Grenoble and Échirolles. Combined with those already laid off and those whose short-term contracts would not be renewed, a total of about 1,000 workers at the French factories were losing their jobs.

Pierre Piccarreta, a CGT union representative, called the actions an effort to apply "pressure" so as to "restart negotiations." He also added, "At a time when the company is making a profit and distributing dividends to shareholders, we want to find a favorable outcome for all the workers and know as quickly as possible where we are going."

The Caterpillar "bossnappings" seemed to inspire other frustrated workers. In the following weeks workers held a 3M executive overnight, forcing management to discuss job cuts. Workers at Sony's French division held a chief executive and director of human relations for a day. Two managers from a Kleber-Michelin machine-parts factory in Toul were also locked up and held by workers demanding negotiations over lay-offs.

These acts of worker resistance are on the rise globally as millions of workers feel anger at corporations that are seemingly using the current financial crisis as a cover for laying off long-term workers and restructuring labor markets through plant relocations and wage cuts. Unite, which itself is under financial stress, has held events to call attention to the need to reform Britain's redundancy laws to prevent employers from using bankruptcy as a means of circumventing severance pay.

The worker actions in Europe represent working-class resistance to employers who arbitrarily shut down plants without the participation of employees. In South America, factory workers have taken the next step by demanding workers' right to control plants that have been shut down by their owners. In Argentina and Venezuela, workers, who have operated some factories without corporate managers for nearly a decade, are demanding that their governments pass legislation legitimizing the expropriation of factories under worker control.

Under the pretext of the financial crisis, finance capitalists are determined to unload the debt burden off their books, and multinational corporations are closing factories to take advantage of lower-wage workers on a global basis. In response, a growing number of workers vulnerable to layoffs across Europe and North America both within and outside of unions are now resisting closures through sit-down strikes and other forms of direct action. Where unions are unwilling to resist the corporate assault on labor, militant workers are engaging in direct action through factory occupations and mass insurrections demanding that plants be reopened or lay-off benefits improved. The wave of factory occupations continuing through 2009 may represent only the beginning of a broader sit-down movement throughout the world, and, following examples in Latin America, demands for worker control over factories. ❑

Sources: K. Baker, "Visteon Dispute: A Dangerous Precedent to be Set?" April 16, 2009, www.personneltoday.com blog; *Oh Sit Down! Accounts of Sitdown Strikes and Workplace Occupations in the UK and around the World*, compilation by libcom.org, www.libcom.org; R. Rosewell, "Work-ins, Sit-ins and Redundancy," *International Socialism*, No. 50, Jan.-March 1972; L. Root, "Britain's Redundancy Payments for Displaced Workers," *Monthly Labor Review*, June 1987; H. Kahn, Repercussions of Redundancy, Allen and Unwin, 1964; "Recession Update May 2009," Unite the Union, June 10, 2009, www.unitetheunion.com; "Factory Occupied for a Second Night," *BBC News*, June 11, 2009; D. Scheherazade, "French Bossnapper Release Hostage Pair," *Financial Times*, April 22, 2009; B. Groom, "Why Sit-Ins Are So 1970s," *Financial Times*, April 7, 2009; J. Reed and J.M. Brown, "Visteon Protestors Face Deadline to Leave," *Financial Times*, April 9, 2009.

Article 9.5

GREECE AS A DEMONSTRATION PROJECT
Will the Black Sheep Bite Back? Will the PIIGS? What about US?

BY MIKE-FRANK EPITROPOULOS
May/June 2010

There has been an avalanche of coverage on Greece's economic situation in the past few months. Most of the coverage rightly attempts to diagnose the underlying problems of Greece's government deficit and national debt, and how they might affect the value of the euro and the integrity of the eurozone. But, as anyone who has followed this story knows, Greece is not alone in this precarious situation. It is lumped into a group of EU countries that have been labeled the "PIIGS"—Portugal, Ireland, Italy, Greece, and Spain. Additionally, it is known that some of the other countries in this group have worse problems and are larger than Greece, which could have an even greater negative impact on the EU and the value of the euro. So, why the focus on Greece?

The Greek situation is both complicated and simple.

Greece has long had a bloated public sector that has employed disproportionate numbers of the population. This system has not operated on market or even traditional public sector principles, but rather on *rousféti*, or patronage. This means that there have typically been more civil servants employed than necessary, with shorter working hours and more lax conditions of service. All of these things have become targets for neoliberal reform around the world, as we are seeing harsh, IMF-style austerity measures once again being pushed as conditions on countries that find themselves in a bind.

Next, the Greek state has long been known as a bastion of corruption. In the financial press, Greece is often described as a leader in black-market economic activity. In 2006, under the conservative New Democracy (ND) government (recently voted out of office), Finance Minister Giorgos Alogoskoufis "redefined" the always-problematic measure of social and economic well-being, Gross Domestic Product (GDP), by essentially adding an estimate of Greece's well-known "black market" activities. In doing so, the government proudly announced that Greece and Greeks were 25% wealthier overnight! More importantly, the Greek government got on board with the global neoliberal program, catering to both domestic and foreign capital, and Washington.

Beyond this, Greece is at the top of the list in military spending as a percentage of GDP in the EU. At the same time, Greek teachers are next to last in salaries in the EU. In the past few years, riot police have beaten and tear-gassed teachers and students more frequently than any other groups. Both the ND and their competitors in Greece's two-party stranglehold, the Pan-Hellenic Socialist Movement (PASOK), have consistently been more in line with the neoliberal economic agenda and tougher in the social arena than their reputation in the West as the "black sheep" of Europe would suggest.

In December 2008, a police officer shot and killed 15-year-old Alexis Grigoropoulos in Athens. Since the shooting occurred in the Exarchia neighborhood of the capital, many identified the incident with the anarchists, for whom Exarchia is a traditional center of activity. The police's claims that the youth had attacked them, however, did not jibe with eyewitness accounts of the event. Greek society was outraged by the incident, and protests ensued across the country, lasting for weeks. The murder of Alexi was the spark that triggered the demonstrations and riots, but the causes were many and had been simmering under the surface of Greek daily life for a long time. Among those were the neoliberal policies of the ND government, such as the privatization of public services and cuts in social spending, in addition to police brutality, overt corruption and scandals, and poor job prospects and working conditions for youth, to name just a few.

While youth and students from universities down through the elementary schools took the lead in organizing and conducting the demonstrations—many of which caused significant property damage, leading to a backlash against the protesters in some circles—a broad spectrum of Athenian society, including left political parties, unions, parents, and immigrant groups also joined in. It was this broad-based anti-government and anti-brutality outpouring that acted as a check against abuse and misrepresentation of events by the mainstream media in Greece. When the media portrayals of events didn't correlate with what the people in the streets and their families directly experienced, the media's credibility suffered. Mainstream news organizations were forced to modify or retract earlier reports of events. The legitimacy of both the media and the government suffered as parents listened to their kids, and as people from all walks of life and classes condemned the killing of Alexi, the government crackdown on dissent, and the sensationalized and inaccurate media depictions of the protests.

In the past few years, Europe has faced serious riots not just in Greece, but also in France, England, and Italy. Government elites in both Europe and the United States have expressed overt concern about these uprisings, especially with the backdrop of the greatest economic downturn since the Great Depression. In France, President Nicolas Sarkozy backed down on education reforms, saying that, "We don't want a European May '68 in the middle of Christmas." Alluding to the increasing number of Greek youth who are relegated to low-wage, part-time, no-benefit jobs, he added, "...The slogan of the Greek students about 'the 600 euro generation' could easily catch on here."

For U.S. intelligence and security officials, Greece has long been a focus of attention, going back to the U.S. government's *de facto* support for Greece's military junta (1967-1974). Today, the United States views Greece as a centerpiece of "counterinsurgency" doctrine, especially with regard to suppressing leftist and anarchist forces. Among the more familiar tactics employed in such counterinsurgency efforts is infiltrating opposition groups with provocateurs. In the context of the December 2008 riots in Greece, Paul J. Watson of Prison Planet reported that

> police masquerading as anarchists were committing acts of wanton violence to inflame tensions and provide a pretext for a brutal crackdown on legitimate demonstrators protesting against police brutality and the mishandling of the economic crisis.

These are the kinds of tactics that lie at the heart of manycounterinsurgency strategies, and can be expected as government responses to anti-authoritarian dissent, especially during a period of economic crisis. Recently, José Trabanco, an independent writer based in Mexico, reported in an article on the website of the Centre for

Research on Globalization on official concerns about potential civil unrest in the United States, as elites begin to grasp the magnitude of the economic crisis. This may not square with recent positive economic news, but we should be just as wary of numbers and projections from the White House as we are of bond ratings from credit-rating agencies.

And this is the crux of why Greece is in the spotlight now.

Greeks, like other Europeans, have a history of bold protest, direct action, and civil disobedience. They have shown willingness to fight for their own class interests, time and again. And this current crisis is no different. It is fine that Greek Prime Minister George Papandreou, German Chancellor Angela Merkel, and even U.S. President Barack Obama pay lip service to cracking down on financial speculators and the big banks. But none of them has moved seriously to regulate, restrict, or punish them. In the United States, we bailed the banks out with taxpayer money. In Greece, the government is introducing punitive austerity measures on the working and middle classes to pay for the "accounting magic" that Wall Street consultants, like Goldman Sachs and JP Morgan, provided to the previous government.

Americans should arguably be *more* angry about the bailout of Wall Street than they already are. U.S. taxpayers are funding not only TARP and other corporate bailouts, but even the largesse of the Greek business and political elite. How? It was Goldman Sachs and J.P. Morgan that were hired to hide the magnitude of the Greek debt. Meanwhile, the executives on Wall Street continue to get paid spectacularly generous bonuses and serious financial regulatory reform is not currently on the radar in Washington. So it should also be clear is that these global bankers' actions have global consequences.

Why *shouldn't* we Americans feel slighted? Barack Obama won the presidency on the slogans of "Hope" and "Change," but the system continues to work for elites at the expense of ordinary people, here and abroad. On recent TV panel discussions in Greece, the mainstream political parties present the austerity measures as "necessary" and "responsible" solutions to a national problem. The government has even characterized the austerity drive as a "war effort," arguing that Greeks should rally together to help pay for the crisis and return to traditional, hard-working Greek ways. Some are even resorting to invoking Barack Obama's slogan of "Hope"!

Yet the government is trying to impose the costs of the crisis squarely on the worse-off. The Bank of Greece recently admitted that the lion's share of public revenues is collected from working- and middle-class households, while the rich and super-rich evade taxes. Meanwhile, it is precisely the working and middle classes that are targeted by the austerity measures. Besides that, austerity measures are arguably the *opposite* of what is needed during recessions and looming depressions.

The real issue, then, is *resistance*. The Greek unions and public have been striking and demonstrating against the austerity measures by stating in clear class terms that, "We are not sacrificing to pay interest to the leaders!" The mainstream and business media analyses of the crisis in Greece and the PIIGS have focused on the potential impact on the euro. Given the choice, however, between the currency (and the perpetrators that created the crisis) bearing the adjustment costs and pain, or the Greek people paying for those costs in prolonged unemployment and poverty, who can reasonably argue for the latter? There are indications that mainstream union leadership will compromise with the government on austerity measures that cut wages and benefits. The question is whether the traditionally protest-oriented and militant Greek people will meekly accept what they see as an unjust solution to this difficult problem.

The global banks, corrupt politicians, and financial speculators are engaging in real economic warfare by betting against Greece and the euro. As one PASOK parliamentarian, Mimis Androulakis, pointed out, "...the often-used casino analogy is faulty because a problem gambler at a casino is betting *his own* money, while these guys are using *other people's* money!"

Mainstream apologists argue that "there is no alternative" but for the working and middle classes to pay for the damage the banks and politicians have left. Greeks, however, are giving a class-conscious response. It's not that they don't want to deal with the crisis, but that many insist on taking it out of the hides of the perpetrators.

So why has the focus been on Greece? To see if public-relations media blitzes, calls to national unity and patriotism, along with fear and repression, can squelch a traditionally militant and class-conscious working class. The Greek workers have historically been willing to take to the streets to defend their own material interests—their pay, their education, their healthcare, and their pensions. They know that saying "Hope!" is not enough, especially when the perpetrators of the current global economic catastrophe continue to operate unencumbered and unscathed.

If the Greeks do not quietly accept the austerity measures, as the American public seems to be doing once again, there may have to be a more forceful *demonstration effect* in the form of violent confrontation between the people and the state. Whose state is it after all? And whose "mess" is this? The working people of Greece—or anywhere in the world, for that matter—should not have to pay or suffer for the crimes and risks of global financial speculators.

Big business does not desire and will not stand for insubordination at this juncture. The non-productive paper economy that has taken control of the global economy is not sustainable for people or governments. There is frustration across the ideological spectrum around the world. The selfish interests that global financial capital is pursuing are naked. We must demand that these people be reined in. It is time for the "black sheep" to bite back. But then there are the PIIGS of Europe and us, here, in the United States. Let us recall the late Howard Zinn and ask: Which is worse at this moment in history—civil disobedience or civil *obedience*? ❏

Sources: Peter Boone and Simon Johnson, "Greece Saved For Now—Is Portugal Next?" Huffington Post, April 11, 2010, co-posted on BaselineScenario.com; Peter Boone and Simon Johnson, "Standing at Thermopylae: Greek Economic Situation Worsening Fast,," Huffington Post, April 8, 2010; Peter Boone and Simon Johnson, "Greece And The Fatal Flaw In An IMF Rescue," Huffington Post, April 8, 2010; Kevin Gallagher, "The Tyranny of Bond Markets: Credit rating agencies helped cause the financial crisis—and as they rear their heads again, it's time for Obama to get tough." The Guardian, April 9, 2010; Diana Johnstone, "The Fall of Greece: Yes, It Really is a Capitalist Plot," CounterPunch, March 10, 2010; Paul Krugman, "Learning from Greece," New York Times, April 10, 2010; Landon Thomas, Jr., "As Greek Bond Rates Soar, Bankruptcy Looms,," New York Times, April 6, 2010; Paul J. Watson, "CIA Preparing To Install Military Government In Greece?" PrisonPlanet.org; Robert Wielaard, "Europe Offers Greece 30 Billion Euros in Loans to Deal With Debt Crisis" Associated Press, April 11, 2010.

Article 9.6

SHOULD WE BE TALKING ABOUT LIVING WAGES *NOW*?

BY JEANNETTE WICKS-LIM
March/April 2009

The Department of Labor announced in January that the U.S. economy shed 2.8 million jobs in 2008, bringing the national unemployment rate to 7.2%—its highest level in 16 years. In today's economic climate, the worst since the Great Depression, are the raises demanded by living-wage campaigns a luxury? Should living-wage campaigns take a back seat to pulling the economy out of recession?

For many, the answer is no. Campaigns across the country continue to build on the widespread success of a movement that has put into place more than 140 living-wage laws since the mid-1990s. Take the Hartford Living Wage Task Force in Connecticut, which is trying to expand the number of workers guaranteed a living wage under its original 1997 law. Or Santa Fe's Living Wage Network, which fought for, and won, a cost-of-living increase to its living wage rate for 2009. Or the Nashville Movement in Tennessee, a group laying the groundwork for a campaign to establish a brand new ordinance.

They are right. Today's economic turmoil challenges us to create practical policies to meet the *heightened* imperative of living wages, not to abandon them.

Why do we need living-wage campaigns? Let's consider first the current legal wage floor. At $7.25 per hour, the federal minimum wage as of July 2009, a full-time year-round worker will bring home $15,080—less than the official poverty threshold of $17,330 for a family of three.

Moreover, poverty experts roundly criticize that official poverty line as too severe. According to the National Survey of American Families, nearly two-thirds of people in households with incomes above the poverty line but below twice that level reported serious economic hardships—failing to pay their rent, having their phone disconnected, worrying about running out of food, or relying on the emergency room for routine medical care.

Consider a more realistic poverty line: the "basic budget" thresholds developed by the Economic Policy Institute as a measure of the income required for "a safe and decent standard of living." These range between two and three times the official poverty line depending on local living costs such as housing. For a family of three, a full-time year-round worker would need to earn between $16 and $24 an hour to reach these basic budget thresholds. Two workers would each need to earn between $8 and $12 per hour. The living-wage ordinances enacted in recent years have typically required rates in this range—on average $10.80, or about 50% above the federal minimum wage.

These basic budgets, however, leave out not only extras such as restaurant meals, but also essential, if not immediate, items such as savings for education, retirement, or even emergencies. Any cut in hours or spell of unemployment can immediately compromise these families' ability to meet their basic needs. Unfortunately, these will be all-too-common occurrences in today's economic climate, which will expose the lowest-paid workers to increasingly severe hardships. This is because businesses tend to let the wages of the lowest-paid workers stagnate or fall unless prodded by a minimum-wage hike or a near-full-employment economy. In the 1980s, for instance, the federal minimum wage remained the same for ten years. Over this period, the lowest-paid workers saw their real (i.e., inflation-adjusted) wages *fall* by 15%.

In other words, to put living-wage campaigns on hold would not simply mean that conditions for low-wage workers and their families would not improve. Instead, these families would face worsening economic hardships.

But perhaps that's inevitable during a recession. Today, with economic indicators falling by the day, can businesses afford to pay a living wage without slashing jobs?

We can learn from the experience of New Jersey's state minimum-wage hikes in the early 1990s: from $3.35 to $3.80 in 1990, then to $4.25 in 1991, and finally to $5.05 in 1992. These three raises, about 10% to 20% each, amounted to a 40% overall rise in the wage floor once adjusted for inflation. The first hike took place in April 1990 when the economy was nearing a business cycle peak. The second and third hikes, however, took place on the heels of the 1990 recession. Economists studied their effects extensively among the businesses likely to be hit hardest—fast-food restaurants—and found no significant negative impact on employment.

One reason businesses can absorb these costs is that for most, minimum-wage hikes require only modest adjustments. For example, in 2003 Santa Fe passed an $8.50 citywide minimum wage. The average low-wage worker, who earned $6.91, received about a 23% raise. The resulting cost increases for restaurants—the most heavily affected businesses—equaled 3% of their sales revenue. In other words, a typical restaurant could offset the entire expense of the minimum-wage hike with a 3% price increase, say, 60¢ on a $20 meal. Unsurprisingly, the city's new wage floor appears to have had no negative impact on jobs.

Even in today's sharp downturn, businesses can likely absorb similar minimum-wage hikes. To see this, consider that U.S. restaurant sales rose by 2.8% between November 2007 and November 2008, almost two percentage points faster than inflation. This is despite a 5% rise in restaurant prices over the same period. In other words, overall sales in this sector grew, albeit sluggishly, even as restaurants raised their prices *and* the recession deepened.

Based on the Santa Fe experience, and using extremely pessimistic assumptions about future sales trends, I estimate that a 20% minimum-wage hike would require, as before, just a 3% price increase to cover these businesses' higher costs.

What can living-wage campaigns draw from these experiences, given that transforming a minimum wage into a living wage requires more dramatic raises on the order of 50%? An obvious possibility is to structure a living-wage ordinance as a series of raises, 10% to 20% each, which gradually achieve an adequate living-wage rate. An added precaution may be in order since we simply do not have extensive data on the impact of minimum-wage hikes during similar economic conditions: each raise could be followed by a year of evaluation, used in turn to adjust future raises up or down. This, by the way, is another lesson Santa Fe's experience offers: the city required exactly such an evaluation before raising its initial $8.50 minimum to $9.50 in 2006.

To turn the economy around we need a significant boost in economic activity—an increase in the demand for businesses' goods and services, not minor adjustments to business costs. This is the logic behind President Obama's stimulus package.

Widespread public support for raising minimum-wage rates (in 2006, more than 60% of voters in six states passed state minimum-wage hikes) suggests, however, that we want not only decent schools, decent medical care, decent roads, and a decent environment, but also decent-paying jobs. To create such jobs, living-wage requirements must be tied to the stimulus plan's funding. Without such mandates, private sector businesses that are the main focus for job creation are unlikely to pass some of that stimulus money along in the form of raises for their lowest-paid workers. Current living-wage laws provide a model: these laws impose living-wage requirements on businesses that contract with, or receive subsidies from, local governments.

Today's economic crisis highlights the vulnerability of the lowest-paid workers and virtually ensures that their living standards will worsen. These facts compel us to pursue living-wage policies with even greater force. Two policy prescriptions are especially important. First, the economic recovery plan, with its extensive government subsidies, provides a tool to impose living-wage requirements. Second, a broader, longer term living-wage policy of multi-step raises guided by interim economic impact studies will allow us to sensibly wean our economy off of poverty wages. Past experience tells us that our economy, even today, can adjust to such a policy. ❑

Article 9.7

ON STRIKE IN CHINA
A Chinese New Deal in the making?

BY CHRIS TILLY AND MARIE KENNEDY
September/October 2010

> *"[There will] never be a strike [at the Hyundai plant in Beijing]. Strikes in China would jeopardize the company's reputation."*
> —Zhang Zhixiong, deputy chairman of the union at that plant, 2003

> *"About 1,000 workers at Hyundai's auto parts factory [in Beijing] staged a two-day strike and demanded wage increases. The action only ended when bosses offered an initial 15% pay rise followed by another 10% in July."*
> —China Daily/Asia News Network, June 4, 2010

Workers in China are on the move. The media initially fixed on the downward trajectory of desperate workers jumping from the roofs of Foxconn, the enormous electronics manufacturer that assembles the iPhone and numerous other familiar gadgets, but soon shifted to the upward arc of strike activity concentrated in the supply chains of Honda and Toyota.

But the auto-sector strikes in China's industrialized Southeast, as well as in the northeastern city of Tianjin, are just the tip of the iceberg. June strikes also pulled out thousands of workers at Brother sewing machine factories and a Carlsberg brewery in the central part of the country; machinery, LCD, and rubber parts plants in the east-central Shanghai area; a shoe manufacturer further inland in Jiujiang; and apparel and electronics workers outside the auto sector in the Southeast and Tianjin. "There are fifteen factories launching strikes now," Qiao Jian of the Chinese Institute of Industrial Relations (CIIR) told us in mid-June. Since that time, still more strikes have been reported, and many others are likely going unreported by Chinese media, which despite their growing independence remain sensitive to government pressure. None of the strikes had approval by the All China Federation of Trade Unions (ACFTU), the only labor movement authorized by Chinese law.

This explosion of wildcat walkouts prompts several questions. Why did it happen? What do the strikes mean for China's low-wage, low-cost manufacturing model? Equally important, what do they imply for China's party- and state-dominated labor relations? China's labor relations scholars—an outspoken bunch—are animatedly discussing that last question in public and in private.

What Happened and Why

The spark for the recent strike wave was the May 17th walkout of hundreds of workers from a Honda transmission plant in Nanhai, near Guangzhou in the Southeast. According to research by Wang Kan of CIIR, the strike was an accident: two employees embroiled in a dispute with Honda consulted a lawyer who advised them to threaten a strike as a bluff and even drew up a set of demands for them. They apparently were as shocked as anyone when workers spontaneously walked out. Accident or not, the workers demanded a 67% raise. Two weeks later, they agreed to return to work with a 42% wage increase. By that time, copycat strikes had erupted at other Honda suppliers in the Southeast and at Hyundai; workers at Toyota suppliers soon followed suit, as did employees from other sectors and regions. Most of these actions won wage settlements in the twenty-percent range.

Why did this strike wave happen now? The first thing to understand is that strikes in China did not begin in 2010. As Berkeley doctoral student Eli Friedman points out, "the number of strikes and officially mediated labor disputes in China [has] been increasing rapidly for at least fifteen years." So-called "mass incidents," of which experts estimate about a third to be strikes, numbered 87,000 in 2005, and were unofficially pegged at 120,000 in 2008. Mediated labor disputes, many of which only involve an individual, have grown even faster, rising in round figures from 19,000 in 1994 to 135,000 in 2000, 350,000 in 2007, and 700,000 in 2008. The huge increase in 2008 is due at least in part to new laws on labor contracts and labor mediation passed that year that bolster workers' ability to bring complaints.

Still, "the Honda strike marks a turning point," in the words of law professor Liu Cheng of Shanghai Normal University. "Previous strikes were mainly about enforcing labor law. This is the first successful strike about collective bargaining." Anita Chan, a labor researcher at the University of Technology in Sydney, agrees, saying the current strikers "are negotiating for their interests and not for their rights—it's a very different set of stakes." The Nanhai Honda action was also a breakthrough in that for the first time strikers demanded the right to elect their own union representatives—a demand to which the provincial union federation has agreed, though the election has not yet taken place. Many subsequent strikes reiterated this demand, although they have focused more on economic issues. Even the economic demands extend beyond wages: at Honda Lock, strikers demanded noise reduction measures to improve the work environment.

The long-term growth in strike activity owes much to demographic changes. Predominantly women, China's industrial workers hail overwhelmingly from the ranks of rural migrants, 140 million of whom live and work in the cities but lack long-term permission to stay there or receive social benefits there. When Deng Xiaoping's market liberalization first spurred rapid industrial growth in the 1980s, migrants were willing to "eat bitterness," enduring hardships and low wages to send remittances home to families who were worse off than they. This stoic attitude and decades of policies aimed at growth at almost any cost are reflected in the decline of labor's share of total national income from 57% in 1983 to 37% in 2005. Unpaid or underpaid overtime and only one or two days off a month—violations of Chinese law—became common in China's manufacturing sector.

But the new generation of migrants, reared in a time of relative prosperity and comparing themselves to their peers in the cities, expect more. "Our demands are higher because we have higher material and spiritual needs," a young Honda striker who identified himself only as Chen told Agence France-Presse. "Our strike demands are based on our need to maintain our living standards." With urban housing costs soaring, this has become a pressing issue. "I dream of one day buying a car or apartment," said Zhang, a 22-year-old man working at the same plant, "but with the salary I'm making now, I will never succeed."

Another long-run factor is the government's new willingness to tolerate strikes as long as they stay within bounds, in contrast to the harsh repression meted out in the 1980s and early 1990s.

Still the "Workshop of the World"?

The current wave of strikes owes its energy, too, to the lopsided policies China's government adopted in response to the global economic crunch. "With the global financial crisis, the income gap and social disparities worsened," commented Qiao of the CIIR. Panicking at the fall-off in demand for Chinese exports, authorities froze the minimum wage in 2009 even as the cost of living continued its upward march. They also put hundreds of billions of dollars into loans to help exporters and allowed employers to defer their tax payments and social insurance contributions.

Perhaps most important for workers' quality of life, provincial and local governments relaxed their enforcement of labor regulations—at a time when examples of hard-pressed businesses closing down and cheating workers out of months of back pay were becoming increasingly common. In Foshan, a government official declared in 2009 that employers violating the Labor Contract Law protecting basic worker rights would "not be fined, and will not have their operating licenses revoked." A year later, Honda workers in the city walked off the job.

But the business-friendly, worker-unfriendly government response to the crisis does not explain why *autoworkers* went out. "I don't know why the Honda workers went on strike, because their salaries and conditions are better than ours," Chen Jian, a 24-year-old worker at Yontai Plastics, not far from the Nanhai Honda plant, said to the *Guardian* newspaper. "We are not satisfied, but we will not go on strike. Some workers tried that last year and they were all fired. That is normal."

Despite Chen's puzzlement, his comments touch on the reason autoworkers led the way: power rooted in the specifics of the auto production process. Autoworkers wield a degree of skill that makes them more difficult to replace. Assembly line technology within the plant, and a division of labor that often locates fabrication of a particular part in a single plant, make it possible for a small number of strategically located workers to shut down the whole production process, a fact exploited by autoworkers around the world going back to the Flint sit-down strike in 1937. And Japanese-initiated just-in-time techniques have cut down inventories, speeding up the impact of strikes. Friedman reports that by the fourth day of the Nanhai strike, work at all four Honda assembly plants in China had ground to a halt due to lack of transmissions.

Pundits have speculated on whether the Chinese workforce's new demands will upend China's export machine. Andy Xie, a Hong Kong-based economist and business analyst formerly with Morgan Stanley, remarks, "To put it bluntly, the key competence of a successful [manufacturer] in China is to squeeze labor to the maximum extent possible." But in fact, Chinese manufacturing wages had already begun rising significantly in the years before the crisis—in part because of earlier strikes and protests. Some companies had already begun relocating work to Vietnam or

Bangladesh. Most observers, including Xie, expect incremental adjustment by businesses, not a stampede. Limited worker demands could even play into the Chinese government's goal of increasing productivity and shifting into higher value-added manufacturing, as well as expanding the buying power of Chinese consumers. But as James Pomfret and Kelvin Soh of Reuters write, China's Communist Party "has faced a policy tightrope. It must also ensure that strikes don't proliferate and scare investors or ignite broader confrontation that erodes Party rule."

"Taking the Same Boat Together to Protect Growth"

Where was the All China Federation of Trade Unions as the working class rose up? Friedman points out that though ACFTU leaders were concerned about defending worker interests in the crisis, they were equally concerned with defending employers' interests. The result was what the ACFTU called "mutually agreed upon actions," which combined promises to desist from job actions with what Friedman describes as "weakly worded requests for employers." "Taking the same boat together to protect growth," a joint March 2009 release by government, unions, and the employer association in Guangdong, was typical, imploring businesses to "work hard" to avoid layoffs and wage cuts—an appeal that seems to have had little real impact on employers.

This ACFTU stance grows directly out of the federation's longstanding focus on "harmonious enterprises," which is rooted in the unions' historic role in state enterprises. "Each trade union is under the control of the local Party branch," Lin Yanling of the CIIR told us. "So, Party, company, and union leadership are often the same." Indeed, the ACFTU typically invites companies to name their union officials; as a result, middle managers often hold those posts. Along the same lines, Shanghai Normal's Liu Cheng stated, "These company unions don't work. They have nothing to do but entertainment. In the summer, they buy watermelon for the workers to celebrate the festivals." Lin Yanling concluded, "Now is the time to change trade unions in China!"

Recommendations for change circulating within China vary widely. "Some local trade union leaders say to reform the trade union, you must sever the relation between the trade union and the local Party branch," said Lin. "If the local union would only listen to upper trade union officials, the problem could be solved." Local state and Party representatives are particularly closely tied to the local businesses, whereas the national officialdom has more often advocated for workers' interests, for example through the new 2008 labor laws. He Zengke, executive director of the Center for Comparative Politics and Economics, expressed support for shifting control to the national level: "Local government has historically supported business, but the [Party Secretary] Hu government is now asking them to pursue a balanced policy—also pro-people, pro-poor."

But Lin is skeptical of this limited fix, arguing that "if you want the unions to change, you need the workers to elect the trade union chairperson." Liu Cheng agrees, but also advocates for unions to have the right to litigate on behalf of workers. Liu argues it is premature to push for the right to strike, whereas Zheng Qiao of CIIR holds that this is a good opportunity to define that right. Qiao Jian of CIIR advocates democratizing unions within a revitalized tripartite (union federation/

employer association/government) system, but his colleague Lin insists, "That system will not function," because the unions don't yet have enough independence within the triad to adequately represent workers. The disagreements are passionate, if good-humored, since these scholars see the future of their country at stake.

Western observers, and some Hong Kong-based worker-rights groups, have gone farther to call for the right for workers to form their own independent unions—what the International Labor Organization calls "freedom of association." But labor relations experts within mainland China, and the strikers themselves, have so far steered clear of such radical proposals. Liu Cheng commented, "Without reform of the unions, I think freedom of association would result in disorder, and destroy the process of evolution. I don't like revolution—with most revolutions, there is no real progress, just a change of emperors." However, he did express the view that as the Chinese labor movement matures, it will reach a point when freedom of association will be possible and desirable.

"If People Are Oppressed, They Must Rebel"

But *will* the unions change—and will the Party and state let them? The question is complicated by the conflicting currents within the union federation itself and within China's official ideology. The same Party that promotes "harmonious enterprises" also enshrines Mao Zedong's dictum, "It's right to rebel." So perhaps it's not surprising that Li, a young striker at Honda's exhaust plant, told Agence France-Presse, "Safeguarding your own rights is always legitimate ... . If people are oppressed they must rebel. This is only natural."

ACFTU responses to date, reported by Friedman and labor activist and blogger Paul Garver, reflect this mixed consciousness. At the Nanhai Honda strike that inaugurated the current wave, the local ACFTU leadership sent a group of 100 people with union hats and armbands to persuade the strikers to stand down. Whether by design or not, the conversation degenerated into a physical confrontation in which some strikers were injured, none severely. On the other hand, provincial-level union leaders then agreed to the strikers' demands to elect their own representatives. The top two Guangdong ACFTU officials, Deng Weilong and Kong Xianghong, subsequently spoke out in favor of the right to strike and pledged to replace current management-appointed officials with worker-elected ones.

When workers at the Denso (Nansha) car-parts factory in Guangzhou (also in Guangdong province) later went on strike, the local union response was different from that in Nanhai. The municipal union federation publicly supported the strikers, refusing to mediate between labor and management. There have even been signs of life from unions in other sectors: about a month after the Nanhai strike, the municipal union federation in Shenyang, in the far northeast of the country, hammered out the nation's first collective bargaining contract with KFC (whose fast-food restaurants blanket China), including a wage increase of nearly 30%.

On the government side, authorities in many provinces have responded to the strike wave with a wave of minimum-wage hikes. Premier Wen Jiabao declared in a June address to migrant workers, "Your work is a glorious thing, and it should be respected by society," and in August told the Japanese government that its companies operating in China should raise wages. Acknowledging that "a wide range of social conflicts have occurred recently," Zhou Yongkang, another top Party official, stated, "Improving people's livelihoods should be the starting and end point of all our work." In August, *BusinessWeek* reported that Guangdong's state legislature was discussing a law formalizing collective bargaining, empowering workers to elect local representatives, and even recognizing the right to strike—particularly noteworthy since Guangdong is China's industrial heartland. Still, pro-worker rhetoric is nothing new, the Guangdong provincial union federation is more progressive and powerful than most, and right around the time of Wen's June speech the Chinese government shut down a website calling for ACFTU democratization.

Amidst these cross-currents, China's labor relations scholars, aware that their own role is "marginal," as one of them put it, remain cautiously optimistic. "I think the situation will lead to union reform," said the CIIR's Zheng Qiao. When asked how activists in the United States can support the Chinese workers, her colleague Lin suggested, "Ask the big American brands to give a larger percentage back to the workers at their suppliers!" At Shanghai Normal, Liu Cheng reasoned through the prospects for change. "If the ACFTU does not do more, there will be more and more independent strikes, and in the end some kind of independent union. So the ACFTU will be scared, and the party will be angry with the ACFTU."

"So," Liu Cheng concluded, "the strike wave is a very good thing." ❑

Sources: Eli Friedman, "Getting through hard times together? Worker insurgency and Chinese unions' response to the economic crisis," paper presented at the International Sociological Association annual conference, Gothenburg, Sweden, July 2010; LabourStart page on China labor news, www.labourstart.org; James Pomfret and Kelvin Soh, "Special Report: China's new migrant workers pushing the line," Reuters, July 5, 2010; "The right to strike may be coming to China," *Bloomberg Businessweek*, August 5, 2010; ITUC/GUF Hong Kong Liaison Office, "A political economic analysis of the strike in Honda and the auto parts industry in China," July 2010..

Chapter 7

THE INTERNATIONAL CRISIS

Article 10.1

THE GIANT POOL OF MONEY

BY ARTHUR MacEWAN
September/October 2009

> Dear Dr. Dollar:
> *On May 9, the public radio program This American Life broadcast an explana-*
> *tion of the housing crisis with the title: "The Giant Pool of Money." With too*
> *much money looking for investment opportunities, lots of bad investments were*
> *made—including the bad loans to home buyers. But where did this "giant pool*
> *of money" come from? Was this really a source of the home mortgage crisis?*
> —Gail Radford, Buffalo, N.Y.

The show was both entertaining and interesting. A good show, but maybe a bit more explanation will be useful.

There was indeed a "giant pool of money" that was an important part of the story of the home mortgage crisis—well, not "money" as we usually think of it, but financial assets, which I'll get to in a moment. And that pool of money is an important link in the larger economic crisis story.

The giant pool of money was the build-up of financial assets—U.S. Treasury bonds, for example, and other assets that pay a fixed income. According to the program, the amount of these assets had grown from roughly $36 trillion in 2000 to $70 trillion in 2008. That's $70 *trillion*, with a T, which is a lot of money, roughly the same as total world output in 2008.

These financial assets built up for a number of reasons. One was the doubling of oil prices (after adjusting for inflation) between 2000 and 2007, largely due to the U.S. invasion of Iraq. This put a lot of money in the hands of governments in oil-producing countries and private individuals connected to the oil industry.

A second factor was the large build up of reserves (i.e., the excess of receipts from exports over payments for imports) by several low-income countries, most notably China. One reason some countries operated in this manner was simply to keep the cost of their currency low in terms of U.S. dollars, thus maintaining demand for their exports. (Using their own currencies to buy dollars, they were increasing both the supply of their currencies and the demand for dollars; this pushed the price of their currencies down and of dollars up.) But another reason was to protect themselves from the sort of problems they had faced in the early 1980s, when world recession cut their export earnings and left them unable to meet their import costs and pay their debts—thus the debt crisis of that era.

This build-up of dollar reserves by governments (actually, central banks) of other countries was also a result of the budgetary deficits of the Bush administration. Spending more than it was taking in as taxes (after the big tax cuts for the wealthy and with the heavy war spending), the Bush administration needed to borrow. Foreign governments, by buying the U.S. securities, were providing the loans.

Still a third factor explaining the giant pool of financial assets was the high level of inequality within the United States and elsewhere in the global economy. Since 1993, half of all income gains in the United States have gone to the highest-income 1% of households. While the very rich spend a good share of their money on mansions, fancy cars, and other luxuries, there was plenty more money for them to put into investments—the stock market but also fixed-income securities (i.e., bonds).

So there is the giant pool of money or, again, of financial assets.

The financial assets became a problem for two connected reasons. First, in the recovery following the 2001 recession, economic growth was very slow; there were thus very limited real investment opportunities. Between 2001 and 2007, private fixed investment (adjusted for inflation) grew by only 11%, whereas in the same number of years following the recession of the early 1990s, investment grew by 59%.

Second, in an effort to stimulate more growth, the Federal Reserve kept interest rates very low. But the low interest rates meant low returns on financial assets—U.S. government bonds in particular, but financial assets in general. So the holders of financial assets went searching for new investment opportunities, which, as the radio program explained, meant pushing money into high-risk mortgages. The rest, as they say, is history.

So the giant pool of money was the link that tied high inequality, the war, and rising financial imbalances in the world economy (caused in large part by the U.S. government's budgetary policies) to the housing crisis and thus to the more general financial crisis. ❏

Article 10.2

W(H)ITHER THE DOLLAR?

The U.S. trade deficit, the global economic crisis, and the dollar's status as the world's reserve currency.

BY KATHERINE SCIACCHITANO
May/June 2010

For more than half a century, the dollar was both a symbol and an instrument of U.S. economic and military power. At the height of the financial crisis in the fall of 2008, the dollar served as a safe haven for investors, and demand for U.S. Treasury bonds ("Treasuries") spiked. More recently, the United States has faced a vacillating dollar, calls to replace the greenback as the global reserve currency, and an international consensus that it should save more and spend less.

At first glance, circumstances seem to give reason for concern. The U.S. budget deficit is over 10% of GDP. China has begun a long-anticipated move away from Treasuries, threatening to make U.S. government borrowing more expensive. And the adoption of austerity measures in Greece—with a budget deficit barely 3% higher than the United States—hovers as a reminder that the bond market can enforce wage cuts and pension freezes on developed as well as developing countries.

These pressures on the dollar and for fiscal cut-backs and austerity come at an awkward time given the level of public outlays required to deal with the crisis and the need to attract international capital to pay for them. But the pressures also highlight the central role of the dollar in the crisis. Understanding that role is critical to grasping the link between the financial recklessness we've been told is to blame for the crisis and the deeper causes of the crisis in the real economy: that link is the outsize U.S. trade deficit.

Trade deficits are a form of debt. For mainstream economists, the cure for the U.S. deficit is thus increased "savings": spend less and the bottom line will improve. But the U.S. trade deficit didn't balloon because U.S. households or the government went on a spending spree. It ballooned because, from the 1980s on, successive U.S. administrations pursued a high-dollar policy that sacrificed U.S. manufacturing for finance, and that combined low-wage, export-led growth in the Global South with low-wage, debt-driven consumption at home. From the late nineties, U.S. dollars that went out to pay for imports increasingly came back not as demand for U.S. goods, but as demand for investments that fueled U.S. housing and stock market bubbles. Understanding the history of how the dollar helped create these imbalances, and how these imbalances in turn led to the housing bubble and sub-prime crash, sheds important light on how labor and the left should respond to pressures for austerity and "saving" as the solution to the crisis.

Gold, Deficits, and Austerity

A good place to start is with the charge that the Federal Reserve triggered the housing bubble by lowering interest rates after the dot-com bubble burst and plunged the country into recession in 2001.

In 2001, manufacturing was too weak to lead a recovery, and the Bush administration was ideologically opposed to fiscal stimulus other than tax cuts for the wealthy. So the real question isn't why the Fed lowered rates; it's why it was able to. In 2000, the U.S. trade deficit stood at 3.7% of GDP. Any other country with this size deficit would have had to tighten its belt and jump-start exports, not embark on stimulating domestic demand that could deepen the deficit even more.

The Fed's ability to lower interest rates despite the U.S. trade deficit stemmed from the dollar's role as the world's currency, which was established during the Bretton Woods negotiations for a new international monetary system at the end of World War II.

A key purpose of an international monetary system—Bretton Woods or any other—is to keep international trade and debt in balance. Trade has to be mutual. One country can't do all the selling while other does all the buying; both must be able to buy and sell. If one or more countries develop trade deficits that persist, they won't be able to continue to import without borrowing and going into debt. At the same time, some other country or countries will have corresponding trade surpluses. The result is a global trade imbalance. To get back "in balance," the deficit country has to import less, export more, or both. The surplus country has to do the reverse.

In practice, economic pressure is stronger on deficit countries to adjust their trade balances by importing less, since it's deficit countries that could run out of money to pay for imports. Importing less can be accomplished with import quotas (which block imports over a set level) or tariffs (which decrease demand for imports by imposing a tax on them). It can also be accomplished with "austerity"—squeezing demand by lowering wages.

Under the gold standard, this squeezing took place automatically. Gold was shipped out of a country to pay for a trade deficit. Since money had to be backed by gold, having less gold meant less money in domestic circulation. So prices and wages fell. Falling wages in turn lowered demand for imports and boosted exports. The deficit was corrected, but at the cost of recession, austerity, and hardship for workers. In other words, the gold standard was deflationary.

Bretton Woods

The gold standard lasted until the Great Depression, and in fact helped to cause it. Beyond the high levels of unemployment, one of the most vivid lessons from the global catastrophe that ensued was the collapse of world trade, as country after country tried to deal with falling exports by limiting imports. After World War II, the industrialized countries wanted an international monetary system that could correct trade imbalances without imposing austerity and risking another depression. This was particularly important given the post-war levels of global debt and deficits, which could have suppressed demand and blocked trade again. Countries pursued these aims at the Bretton Woods negotiations in 1944, in Bretton Woods, New Hampshire.

John Maynard Keynes headed the British delegation. Keynes was already famous for his advocacy of government spending to bolster demand and maintain employment during recessions and depressions. England also owed large war debts to the United States and had suffered from high unemployment for over two decades. Keynes therefore had a keen interest in creating a system that prevented the build-up of global debt and avoided placing the full pressure of correcting trade imbalances on debtor countries.

His proposed solution was an international clearing union—a system of accounts kept in a fictitious unit called the "bancor." Accounts would be tallied each year to see which countries were in deficit and which were in surplus. Countries with trade deficits would have to work to import less and export more. In the mean-time, they would have the unconditional right—for a period—to an "overdraft" of bancors, the size of the overdraft to be based on the size of previous surpluses. These overdrafts would both support continued imports of necessities and guarantee unin-terrupted global trade. At the same time, countries running trade surpluses would be expected to get back in balance too by importing more, and would be fined if their surpluses persisted.

Keynes was also adamant that capital controls be part of the new system. Capital controls are restrictions on the movement of capital across borders. Keynes wanted countries to be able to resort to macroeconomic tools such as deficit spending, lowering interest rates, and expanding money supplies to bolster employment and wages when needed. He worried that without capital controls, capital flight—investors taking their money and running—could veto economic policies and force countries to raise interest rates, cut spending, and lower wages instead, putting downward pressure on global demand as the gold standard had.

Keynes's system wouldn't have solved the problems of capitalism—in his terms, the problem of insufficient demand, and in Marx's terms the problems of overpro-duction and under-consumption. But by creating incentives for surplus countries to import more, it would have supported global demand and job growth and made the kind of trade imbalances that exist today—including the U.S. trade deficit—much less likely. It would also have taken the pressure off deficit countries to adopt auster-ity measures. And it would have prevented surplus countries from using the power of debt to dictate economic policy to deficit countries.

At the end of World War II, the United States was, however, the largest sur-plus country in the world, and it intended to remain so for the foreseeable future. The New Deal had lowered unemployment during the Depression. But political opposition to deficit spending had prevented full recovery until arms production for the war restored manufacturing. Many feared that without continued large U.S. trade surpluses and expanded export markets, unemployment would return to Depression-era levels.

The United States therefore blocked Keynes' proposal. Capital controls were permitted for the time being, largely because of the danger that capital would flee war-torn Europe. But penalties for surplus countries were abandoned; pressures remained primarily on deficit countries to correct. Instead of an international clear-ing union with automatic rights to overdrafts, the International Monetary Fund (IMF) was established to make short-term loans to deficit countries. And instead of the neutral bancor, the dollar—backed by the U.S. pledge to redeem dollars with gold at $35 an ounce—would be the world currency.

Limits of the System

The system worked for just over twenty-five years, not because trade was balanced, but because the United States was able and willing to recycle its huge trade surpluses. U.S. military spending stayed high because of the U.S. cold-war role as "global cop." And massive aid was given to Europe to rebuild. Dollars went out as foreign aid and military spending (both closely coordinated). They came back as demand for U.S. goods.

At the same time, memory of the Depression created a kind of Keynesian consensus in the advanced industrial democracies to use fiscal and monetary policy to maintain full employment. Labor movements, strengthened by both the war and the post-war boom, pushed wage settlements and welfare spending higher. Global demand was high.

Two problems doomed the system. First, the IMF retained the power to impose conditions on debtor countries, and the United States retained the power to control the IMF.

Second, the United States stood outside the rules of the game: The larger the world economy grew, the more dollars would be needed in circulation; U.S. trade deficits would eventually have to provide them. Other countries would have to correct their trade deficits by tightening their belts to import less, exporting more by devaluing their currencies to push down prices, or relying on savings from trade surpluses denominated in dollars (known as "reserves") to pay for their excess of imports over exports. But precisely because countries needed dollar reserves to pay for international transactions and to provide cushions against periods of deficits, other countries would need to hold the U.S. dollars they earned by investing them in U.S. assets. This meant that U.S. dollars that went out for imports would come back and be reinvested in the United States. Once there, these dollars could be used to finance continued spending on imports—and a larger U.S. trade deficit. At that point, sustaining world trade would depend not on recycling U.S. surpluses, but on recycling U.S. deficits. The ultimate result would be large, destabilizing global capital flows.

The Crisis of the Seventies

The turning point came in the early seventies. Europe and Japan had rebuilt from the war and were now export powers in their own right. The U.S. trade surplus was turning into a deficit. And the global rate of profit in manufacturing was falling. The United States had also embarked on its "War on Poverty" just as it increased spending on its real war in Vietnam, and this "guns and butter" strategy—an attempt to quell domestic opposition from the civil right and anti-war movements while maintaining global military dominance—led to high inflation.

The result was global economic crisis: the purchasing power of the dollar fell, just as more and more dollars were flowing out of the United States and being held by foreigners.

What had kept the United States from overspending up to this point was its Bretton Woods commitment to exchange dollars for gold at the rate of $35 an ounce. Now countries and investors that didn't want to stand by and watch as the purchasing power of their dollar holdings fell—as well as countries that objected to the Vietnam War—held the United States to its pledge.

There wasn't enough gold in Ft. Knox. The United States would have to retrench its global military role, reign in domestic spending, or change the rules of the game. It changed the rules of the game. In August 1971, Nixon closed the gold window; the United States would no longer redeem dollars for gold. Countries and individuals would have to hold dollars, or dump them and find another currency that was more certain to hold its value. There was none.

The result was that the dollar remained the global reserve currency. But the world moved from a system where the United States could spend only if could back its spending by gold, to a system where its spending was limited only by the quantity of dollars the rest of the world was willing to hold. The value of the dollar would fluctuate with the level of global demand for U.S. products and investment. The value of other currencies would fluctuate with the dollar.

Trading Manufacturing for Finance

The result of this newfound freedom to spend was a decade of global inflation and crises of the dollar. As inflation grew, each dollar purchased less. As each dollar purchased less, the global demand to hold dollars dropped—and with it the dollar's exchange rate. As the exchange rate fell, imports became even more expensive, and inflation ratcheted up again. The cycle intensified when OPEC—which priced its oil in dollars—raised its prices to compensate for the falling dollar.

Owners of finance capital were unhappy because inflation was eroding the value of dollar assets. Owners of manufacturing capital were unhappy because the global rate of profit in manufacturing was dropping. And both U.S. politicians and elites were unhappy because the falling dollar was eroding U.S. military power by making it more expensive.

The response of the Reagan administration was to unleash neoliberalism on both the national and global levels—the so-called Reagan revolution. On the domestic front, inflation was quelled, and the labor movement was put in its place, with high interest rates and the worst recession since the Depression. Corporate profits were boosted directly through deregulation, privatization, and tax cuts, and indirectly by attacks on unions, unemployment insurance, and social spending.

When it was over, profits were up, inflation and wages were down, and the dollar had changed direction. High interest rates attracted a stream of investment capital into the United States, pushing up demand for the currency, and with it the exchange rate. The inflows paid for the growing trade and budget deficits—Reagan had cut domestic spending, but increased military spending. And they provided abundant capital for finance and overseas investment. But the high dollar also made U.S. exports more expensive for the rest of the world. The United States had effectively traded manufacturing for finance and debt.

Simultaneously, debt was used as a hammer to impose neoliberalism on the Third World. As the price of oil rose in the seventies, OPEC countries deposited their growing trade surpluses—so-called petro-dollars—in U.S. banks, which in turn loaned them to poor countries to pay for the soaring price of oil. Initially set at very low interest rates, loan payments skyrocketed when the United States jacked up its rates to deal with inflation. Third World countries began defaulting, starting with Mexico in 1981. In response, and in exchange for more loans, the U.S.-controlled IMF imposed austerity programs, also known as "structural adjustment programs."

The programs were similar to the policies in the United States, but much more severe, and they operated in reverse. Instead of pushing up exchange rates to attract finance capital as the United States had done, Third World countries were told to devalue their currencies to attract foreign direct investment and export their way out of debt. Capital controls were dismantled to enable transnational corporations to enter and exit at will. Governments were forced to slash spending on social programs and infrastructure to push down wages and demand for imports. Services were privatized to create opportunities for private capital, and finance was deregulated.

Policies dovetailed perfectly. As the high dollar hollowed out U.S. manufacturing, countries in the global South were turned into low-wage export platforms. As U.S. wages stagnated or fell, imports became cheaper, masking the pain. Meanwhile, the high dollar lowered the cost of overseas production. Interest payments on third world debt—which continued to grow—swelled the already large capital flows into the United States and provided even more funds for overseas investment.

The view from the heights of finance looked promising. But Latin America was entering what became known as "the lost decade." And the United State was shifting from exporting goods to exporting demand, and from recycling its trade surplus to recycling its deficit. The world was becoming dependent on the United States as the "consumer of last resort." The United States was becoming dependent on finance and debt.

Consolidating Neoliberalism

The growth of finance in the eighties magnified its political clout in the nineties. With the bond market threatening to charge higher rates for government debt, Clinton abandoned campaign pledges to invest in U.S. infrastructure, education, and industry. Instead, he balanced the budget; he adopted his own high-dollar policy, based on the theory that global competition would keep imports cheap, inflation low, and the living standard high—regardless of sluggish wage growth; and he continued deregulation of the finance industry—repealing Glass-Steagall and refusing to regulate derivatives. By the end of Clinton's second term, the U.S. trade deficit had hit a record 3.7% of GDP; household debt had soared to nearly 69% of GDP and financial profits had risen to 30% of GDP, almost twice as high as they had been at any time up to the mid 1980s.

Internationally, Clinton consolidated IMF-style structural adjustment policies under the rubric of "the Washington Consensus," initiated a new era of trade agreements modeled on the North American Free Trade Agreement, and led the charge to consolidate the elimination of capital controls.

The elimination of capital controls deepened global economic instability in several ways.

First, eliminating restrictions on capital mobility made it easier for capital to go in search of the lowest wages. This expanded the globalization of production, intensifying downward pressure on wages and global demand.

Second, removing capital controls increased the political power of capital by enabling it to "vote with its feet." This accelerated the deregulation of global finance and—as Keynes predicted—limited countries' abilities to run full-employment policies. Regulation of business was punished, as was deficit spending, regardless of its purpose. Low inflation and deregulation of labor markets—weakening unions and making wages more "flexible"—were rewarded.

Finally, capital mobility fed asset bubbles and increased financial speculation and exchange rate volatility. As speculative capital rushed into countries, exchange rates rose; as it fled, they fell. Speculators began betting more and more on currencies themselves, further magnifying rate swings. Rising exchange rates made exports uncompetitive, hurting employment and wages. Falling exchange rates increased the competitiveness of exports, but made imports and foreign borrowing more expensive, except for the United States, which borrows in its own currency. Countries could try to prevent capital flight by raising interest rates, but only at the cost of dampening growth and lost of jobs. Lacking capital controls, there was little countries could do to prevent excessive inflows and bubbles.

Prelude to a Crash

This increased capital mobility, deregulation, and speculation weakened the real economy, further depressed global demand, and greatly magnified economic instability. From the eighties onward, international financial crises broke out approximately every five years, in countries ranging from Mexico to the former Soviet Union.

By far the largest crisis prior to the sub-prime meltdown took place in East Asia in the mid-nineties. Speculative capital began flowing into East Asia in the mid nineties. In 1997, the bubble burst. By the summer of 1998, stock markets around the world were crashing from the ripple effects. The IMF stepped in with $40 billion in loans, bailing out investors but imposing harsh conditions on workers and governments. Millions were left unemployed as Asia plunged into depression.

When the dust settled, Asian countries said "never again." Their solution was to build up large dollar reserves—savings cushions—so they would never have to turn to the IMF for another loan. To build up reserves, countries had to run large trade surpluses. This meant selling even more to the United States, the only market in the world able and willing to run ever-larger trade deficits to absorb their exports.

In addition to further weakening U.S. manufacturing, the Asia crisis set the stage for the sub-prime crisis in several ways.

First, as capital initially fled Asia, it sought out the United States as a "safe haven," igniting the U.S. stock market and nascent housing bubbles.

Second, the longer-term recycling of burgeoning Asian surpluses ensured an abundant and ongoing source of capital to finance not only the mounting trade deficit, but also the billowing U.S. consumer debt more generally.

Third, preventing their exchange rates from rising with their trade surpluses and making their exports uncompetitive required Asian central banks to print money, swelling global capital flows even more.

Between 1998 and 2007, when the U.S. housing bubble burst, many policy makers and mainstream economists came to believe this inflow of dollars and debt would never stop. It simply seemed too mutually beneficial to end. By financing the U.S. trade deficit, Asian countries guaranteed U.S. consumers would continue to purchase their goods. The United States in turn got cheap imports, cheap money for consumer finance, and inflated stock and real estate markets that appeared to be self-financing and to compensate for stagnating wages. At the same time, foreign holders of dollars bought increasing quantities of U.S. Treasuries, saving the U.S. government from having to raise interest rates to attract purchasers, and giving the United States cheap financing for its budget deficit as well.

It was this ability to keep interest rates low—in particular, the Fed's ability to lower rates after the stock market bubble collapsed in 2000—that set off the last and most destructive stage of the housing bubble. Lower interest rates simultaneously increased the demand for housing (since lower interest rates made mortgages cheaper) and decreased the returns to foreign holders of U.S. Treasuries. These lower returns forced investors to look for other "safe" investments with higher yields. Investors believed they found what they needed in U.S. mortgage securities.

As Wall Street realized what a lucrative international market they had, the big banks purposefully set out to increase the number of mortgages that could be repackaged and sold to investors by lowering lending standards. They also entered into complicated systems of private bets, known as credit default swaps, to insure against the risk of defaults. These credit default swaps created a chain of debt that exponentially magnified risk. When the bubble finally burst, only massive stimulus spending and infusions of capital by the industrialized countries into their banking systems kept the world from falling into another depression.

Deficit Politics

The political establishment—right and center—is now licking its chops, attacking fiscal deficits as if ending them were a solution to the crisis. The underlying theory harks back to the deflationary operation of the gold standard and the conditions imposed by the IMF: Government spending causes trade deficits and inflation by increasing demand. Cutting spending will cut deficits by diminishing demand.

Like Clinton before him, Obama is now caving in to the bond market, fearful that international lenders will raise interest rates on U.S. borrowing. He has created a bi-partisan debt commission to focus on long-term fiscal balance—read: cutting Social Security and Medicare—and revived "PAYGO," which requires either cuts or increases in revenue to pay for all new outlays, even as unemployment hovers just under 10%.

By acquiescing, the U.S. public is implicitly blaming itself for the crisis and offering to pay for it twice: first with the millions of jobs lost to the recession, and again by weakening the safety net. But the recent growth of the U.S. budget deficit principally reflects the cost of cleaning up the crisis and of the wars in Iraq and Afghanistan. Assumptions of future deficits are rooted in projected health-care costs in the absence of meaningful reform. And the U.S. trade deficit is driven mainly by the continued high dollar.

The economic crisis won't be resolved by increasing personal savings or enforcing fiscal discipline, because its origins aren't greedy consumers or profligate governments. The real origins of the crisis are the neoliberal response to the crisis of the 1970s—the shift from manufacturing to finance in the United States, and the transformation of the Global South into a low-wage export platform for transnational capital to bolster sagging profit rate. The U.S. trade and budget deficits may symbolize this transformation. But the systemic problem is a global economic model that separates consumption from production and that has balanced world demand—not just the U.S. economy—on debt and speculation.

Forging an alternative will be the work of generations. As for the present, premature tightening of fiscal policy as countries try to "exit" from the crisis will simply drain global demand and endanger recovery. Demonizing government spending will erode the social wage and undermine democratic debate about the public investment needed for a transition to an environmentally sustainable global economy.

In the United States, where labor market and financial deregulation have garnered the most attention in popular critiques of neoliberalism, painting a bulls-eye on government spending also obscures the role of the dollar and U.S. policy in the crisis. For several decades after World War II, U.S. workers benefited materially as the special status of the dollar helped expand export markets for U.S. goods. But as other labor movements throughout the world know from bitter experience, it's the dollar as the world's currency, together with U.S. control of the IMF, that ultimately provided leverage for the United States to create the low-wage export model of growth and financial deregulation that has so unbalanced the global economy and hurt "first" and "third" world workers alike.

Looking Ahead

At the end of World War II, John Maynard Keynes proposed an international monetary system with the bancor at its core; the system would have helped balance trade and avoid the debt and deflation in inherent in the gold standard that preceded the Great Depression. Instead, Bretton Woods was negotiated, with the dollar as the world's currency. What's left of that system has now come full circle and created the very problems it was intended to avoid: large trade imbalances and deflationary economic conditions.

For the past two and a half decades, the dollar enabled the United States to run increasing trade deficits while systematically draining capital from some of the poorest countries in the world. This money could have been used for development in the Global South, to replace aging infrastructure in the United States, or to prepare for and prevent climate change. Instead, it paid for U.S. military interventions, outsourcing, tax cuts for the wealthy, and massive stock market and housing bubbles.

This mismanagement of the dollar hasn't served the long-term interests of workers the United States any more than it has those in of the developing world. In domestic terms, it has been particularly damaging over the last three decades to U.S.

manufacturing, and state budgets and workers are being hit hard by the crisis. Yet even manufacturing workers in the United States cling to the high dollar as if it were a life raft. Many public sector workers advocate cutting back on government spending. And most people in the United States would blame bankers' compensation packages for the sub-prime mess before pointing to the dismantling of capital controls.

After suffering through the worst unemployment since the Depression and paying for the bailout of finance, U.S. unions and the left are right to be angry. On the global scale, there is increased space for activism. Since the summer of 2007, at least 17 countries have imposed or tightened capital controls. Greek workers have been in the streets protesting pension cuts and pay freezes for months now. And a global campaign has been launched for a financial transactions tax that would slow down speculation and provide needed revenue for governments. Together, global labor and the left are actively rethinking and advocating reform of the global financial system, the neoliberal trade agreements, and the role and governance of the International Monetary Fund. And there is increasing discussion of a replacement for the dollar that won't breed deficits, suck capital out of the developing world, impose austerity on deficit countries—or blow bubbles.

All these reforms are critical. All will require more grassroots education. None will come without a struggle. ❏

Sources: C. Fred Bergsten, "The Dollar and the Deficits: How Washington Can Prevent the Next Crisis," Peterson Institute for International Economics, *Foreign Affairs*, Volume 88 No. 6, November 2009; Dean Baker, "The Budget, the Deficit, and the Dollar," Center for Economic Policy and Research, www.cepr.net; Martin Wolf, "Give us fiscal austerity, but not quite yet," *Financial Times* blogs, November 24, 2009; Tom Palley, "Domestic Demand-led Growth: A New Paradigm for Development," paper presented at the Alterantives to Neoliberalism Conference sponsored by the New Rules for Global Finance Coalition, May 21-24, 2002, www. economicswebinstitute.org; Sarah Anderson, "Policy Handcuffs in the Financial Crisis: How U.S. Government And Trade Policy Limit Government Power To Control Capital Flows, " Institute for Policy Studies, February 2009; Susan George, "The World Trade Organisation We Could Have Had," *Le Monde Diplomatique*, January 2007.

Article 10.3

PUTTING THE "GLOBAL" IN THE GLOBAL ECONOMIC CRISIS

BY SMRITI RAO
November/December 2009

There is no question that the current economic crisis originated in the developed world, and primarily in the United States. Much of the analysis of the crisis has thus focused on institutional failures within the United States and there is, rightly, tremendous concern here about high rates of domestic unemployment and under-employment. But after three decades of globalization, what happens in the United States does not stay in the United States; the actions of traders in New York City will mean hunger for children in Nairobi. We now know what crisis looks like in the age of globalization and it is not pretty.

This crisis is uniquely a child of the neoliberal global order. For developing countries the key elements of neoliberalism have consisted of trade liberalization and an emphasis on exports; reductions in government social welfare spending; a greater reliance on the market for determining the price of everything from the currency exchange rate to water from the tap; and, last but not least, economy-wide privatization and deregulation. In each case, the aim was also to promote cross-border flows of goods, services, and capital—and, to a far lesser degree, of people.

Despite Thomas Friedman's assertions of a "flat" world, this age of globalization did not in fact eliminate global inequality. Indeed if we exclude China and India, inequality between countries actually increased during this period. The globalization of the last 30 years was predicated upon the extraction by the developed world of the natural resources, cheap labor, and, in particular, capital of the developing world, the latter via financial markets that siphoned the world's savings to pay for U.S. middle-class consumption. What could be more ironic than the billions of dollars in capital flowing every year from developing countries with unfunded domestic needs to developed countries, which then failed to meet even their minimum obligations with respect to foreign aid? Africa, for example, has actually been a net creditor to the United States for some time, suggesting that the underlying dynamic of the world economy today is not that different from the colonialism of past centuries.

These "reverse flows" are partly the result of attempts by developing countries to ward off balance-of-payment crises by holding large foreign exchange reserves. Within the United States, this capital helped sustain massive borrowing by house-holds, corporations, and governments, exacerbating the debt bubble of the last eight years. Meanwhile, the global "race to the bottom" among developing-county export-ers ensured that the prices of most manufactured goods and services remained low, taking the threat of inflation off the table and enabling the U.S. Federal Reserve to keep interest rates low and facilitate the housing bubble.

Now that this debt bubble has finally burst, it is no surprise that the crisis has been transmitted back to the global South at record speed.

Measuring the Impact

A country-by-country comparison of the growth in real (i.e., inflation-adjusted) GDP from 2007 to 2008 against the average annual growth of the preceding three years (2005-2007) gives us a picture of the differential impact of the economic crisis—at least in its early stages—on various countries. Consistent data are available for 178 developed and developing countries.

Overall, GDP growth for these 178 countries was down by 1.3 percentage points in 2008 compared to the average for 2005-2007. Of course, the financial crisis only hit in full force in September 2008, so the 2009 data will give us a more complete picture of the impact of the crisis. The International Monetary Fund (IMF) estimates that global GDP will decline in 2009 for the first time since World War II. Currently, the IMF is expecting a 1.4% contraction this year. According to the International Labor Organization, global unemployment increased by 10.7 million in 2008, with a further increase of 19 million expected in 2009 by relatively conservative estimates. As a result, the number of people living in poverty will increase by an estimated 46 million this year according to the World Bank.

The initial impact in 2008 was greatest in Eastern Europe and Central Asia: six of the ten countries with the steepest declines in real GDP growth were from the Eastern Europe/Central Asia region (see Table 1). Joined by Ireland, this is a list of global high-fliers—countries with very high rates of growth (before 2008, that is) that had globalized rapidly and enthusiastically in the last decade and a half. Singapore of course was an early adopter of globalization, touted by the IMF as a model for other small countries, while Seychelles has depended heavily on international tourism. Myanmar would seem to be the exception to this pattern of intensive globalization, given its political isolation. From an economic perspective, however, this was a country whose economic growth depended heavily on the rising prices of its commodity exports (natural gas and gems).

Indeed, if we rank these 178 countries by the share of their GDP represented by exports before the crisis, we find a correlation between dependence on exports and steeper declines in GDP growth. The 50 most export-dependent countries actually saw larger declines in GDP in 2008 than those less dependent on exports (see Table 2). Likewise with certain other key markers of neoliberal globalization.

That globalizers appear to be most affected by the crisis is no accident. It turns out that each of the three primary channels through which the crisis has been transmitted from the United States to other countries is a direct outcome of the policy choices that developing countries were urged and sometimes coerced into making—with assurances that this particular form of globalization was the best way to build a healthy and prosperous economy.

Transmission Channels of the Crisis

Lowered exports and remittances. The recession in the United States and Europe has hit exports from the developing world hard. Globally, trade in goods and services did rise by 3% in 2008, but that was compared to 10% and 7% in the previous two years. Trade is expected to decline by a sharp 12% in 2009. The United States, the world's most important importer, has seen imports drop by an unprecedented 30% since July 2008. For countries ranging from Pakistan to Cameroon, this has meant lower foreign exchange earnings, slower economic growth, and higher unemployment.

Meanwhile, for many developing countries, the emphasis on export promotion meant the increasing export not of goods and services but of people, who sought work in richer countries and sent part of their earnings back home. Remittance flows from temporary and permanent migrants accounted for 25% of net inflows of private capital to the global South in 2007. These flows are also affected by the crisis, although they have proved more resilient than other sources of private capital.

Migrant workers in construction, in particular, find that they are no longer able to find work and send money back home, and countries in Latin America have seen sharp declines in remittance inflows. However, as Indian economist Jayati Ghosh points out, women migrants working as maids, nurses, and nannies in the West have not been as hard hit by the recession. This has meant that remittance flows to countries with primarily female migrants, such as Sri Lanka and the Philippines, are not as badly affected. The Middle Eastern countries that are important host countries for many Asian migrants have also been relatively shielded from the crisis. As a result, for the developing world as a whole, remittances actually rose in 2008. Because other private capital flows declined sharply post-crisis, remittances accounted for 46% of net private capital inflows to the developing world in 2008.

Outflows of portfolio capital. In the boom years up to 2007, developing countries were encouraged to liberalize their financial sectors. This meant removing regulatory barriers to the inflow (and outflow) of foreign investors and their money. While

TABLE 1: STEEPEST DECLINES IN ECONOMIC GROWTH

Top ten countries by decline in 2008 real GDP growth vs. 2005-07 annual average.		
	Country	Change in 2008 real GDP growth compared to 2005-07 average(in percentage points)
1	Latvia	−15.56
2	Azerbaijan	−14.44
3	Estonia	−12.26
4	Georgia	−8.42
5	Myanmar	−8.32
6	Ireland	−8.30
7	Seychelles	−7.62
8	Armenia	−6.85
9	Singapore	−6.66
10	Kazakhstan	−6.57

Source: Author's calculations based on data from World Development Indicators online, World Bank, June 2009.

some foreign investors did buy factories and other actual physical assets in the developing world, a substantial portion of foreign capital came in the form of portfolio capital—short-term investments in stock and real estate markets. Portfolio capital is called "hot money" for a reason: it tends to be incredibly mobile, and its mobility has been enhanced by the systematic dismantling of various government restrictions ("capital controls") that formerly prevented this money from entering or leaving countries at the volume and speed it can today.

Around the time of the collapse of Bear Stearns in the United States in early 2008, various global financial powerhouses began pulling their money out of developing-country markets. The pace of the pullout only accelerated after the crash that September. One consequence for developing countries was a fall in their stock market indices, which in turn depressed growth. Another was that as foreign investors converted their krona, rupees, or rubles into dollars in order to leave, the value of the local currency got pushed down.

The IMF has long touted the virtues of allowing freely floating exchange rates, where market forces determine the value of each currency. In the aftermath of the

TABLE 2: EXPORTS AND FOREIGN INVESTMENT

Change in 2008 real GDP growth compared to 2005-07 average (in percentage points) for countries ranked by:		
	Export share of GDP	FDI share of GDP
Average for top 50 countries	−2.25	−1.85
Average for countries ranked 51-100	−1.50	−1.70
Average for the remaining countries	−0.88	−1.07
Total number of countries	167	171

TABLE 3: EXCHANGE RATE AND FISCAL POLICY

Average change in 2008 real GDP growth compared to 2005-07 average (in percentage points) for country groupings:			
Exchange Rate Policy		Fiscal Policy	
Countries with fixed exchange rate	−1.19	Countries with no inflation targeting	−1.18
Countries with managed float or other mixed policy	−1.19	Countries with inflation targeting	−2.35
Countries with freely floating exchange rate	−2.04		
Total number of countries	**178**		**171**

Sources: Author's calculations based on data from World Development Indicators online, World Bank, June 2009 and De Facto Classification of Exchange Rate Regimes and Monetary Policy Frameworks as of April 31, 2008,IMF.

financial crisis, this meant a sharp depreciation in the value of many local currencies relative to the dollar. This in turn meant that every gallon of oil priced in dollars would cost that many more, say, rupees. Similarly, any dollar-denominated debt a country held became harder to repay. The dollar cost of imports and debt servicing went up, just as exports and remittances—the ability to earn those dollars—were falling. Predictably, countries with floating (i.e., market-determined) exchange rates were harder hit in 2008 (see Table 3).

Falling flows of FDI and development aid. Meanwhile, one other source of foreign exchange, foreign investment in actual physical assets such as factories (known as foreign direct investment, or FDI), is stagnant and likely to fall as companies across the world shelve expansion plans. The signs of vulnerability are evident in the fact that countries most dependent upon FDI inflows (as a percentage of GDP) between 2005 and 2007 suffered greater relative GDP declines in 2008 (see Table 2).

Developed countries are also cutting back on foreign aid budgets, citing the cost of domestic stimulus programs and reduced tax revenues. Such cuts particularly affect the poorest countries. With the economic slowdown their governments are losing domestic tax and other revenues, so falling aid flows are likely to hurt even more. The importance of continued aid flows can be seen in the fact that higher levels of aid per capita from 2005 to 2007 were actually associated with more mild drops in GDP growth in 2008 (see Table 2). This may be partly due to the fact that these countries already had low or negative rates of GDP growth so that 2008 declines appear smaller relative to that baseline. Nevertheless, aid flows appear to have protected the most vulnerable countries from even greater economic disaster. In fact the so-called HIPC group (highly indebted poor countries) actually saw an increase of one percentage point in GDP growth rates when compared to the 2005-2007 average.

Both FDI and aid work their way into and out of economies more slowly, so we may have to wait for 2009 data to estimate the full impact of the crisis via this channel.

The simultaneous transmission of the crisis through these three channels has left developing countries reeling. What makes the situation even worse is that unlike developed countries, developing countries are unlikely to be able to afford generous stimulus packages (China is an important exception). Meanwhile, the IMF and its allies, rather than supporting developing-country governments in their quest to stimulate domestic demand and investment, are hindering the process by insisting on the same old policy mix of deficit reductions and interest rate hikes. In an illustration of how ruinous this policy mix can be, countries that had followed IMF advice and adopted "inflation targeting" before the crisis suffered greater relative GDP declines once the crisis hit (see Table 3).

The tragedy of course is that while the remnants of the welfare state still protect citizens of the developed world from the very worst effects of the crisis, developing countries have been urged for two decades to abandon the food and fuel subsidies and public sector provision of essential services that are the only things that come close to resembling a floor for living standards. They were told they didn't need that safety net, that it only got in the way; now, of course, they are free to fall.

For those unwilling to let this tragedy unfold, this is the time to apply pressure on developed-country governments to maintain aid flows. Even more importantly, this is the time to apply pressure on the IMF and the other multilateral development banks, and on their supporters in the halls of power, so that they offer developing countries a genuine chance to survive this crisis and begin to rebuild for the future.

It is worth recalling that the end of the previous "age of globalization," signaled by the Great Depression, led to a renewed role for the public sector the world over and an attempt to achieve growth alongside self-reliance. In the years after World War II, led by Latin America, newly independent developing countries attempted to prioritize building a domestic producer and consumer base. In the long run, perhaps this crisis will result in a similar rethinking of the currently dominant model of development. In the short run, however, the world seems ready to stand by and watch while the poor and vulnerable in developing countries, truly innocent bystanders, suffer. ❑

Sources: Dilip Ratha, Sanket Mohapatra, and Ani Silwal, "Migration and Development Brief 10," Migration and Remittances Team, Development Prospects Group, World Bank, July 13, 2009; Atish R. Ghosh et al. 2009, "Coping with the Crisis: Policy Options for Emerging Market Countries," IMF Staff Position Note, SPN/09/08, April 23, 2009; World Bank, "Swimming Against the Tide: How Developing Countries Are Coping with the Global Crisis," Background Paper prepared by World Bank Staff for the G20 Finance Ministers and Central Bank Governors Meeting, Horsham, United Kingdom on March 13-14, 2009; Jayati Ghosh, "Current Global Financial Crisis: Curse or Blessing in Disguise for Developing Countries?" Presentation prepared for the IWG-GEM Workshop, Levy Economics Institute, New York, June 29-July 10, 2009.

Article 10.4

(ECONOMIC) FREEDOM'S JUST ANOTHER WORD FOR...CRISIS-PRONE

BY JOHN MILLER
September/October 2009

In "Capitalism in Crisis," his May op-ed in the *Wall Street Journal*, U.S. Court of Appeals judge and archconservative legal scholar Richard Posner argued that "a capitalist economy, while immensely dynamic and productive, is not inherently stable." Posner, the long-time cheerleader for deregulation added, quite sensibly, "we may need more regulation of banking to reduce its inherent riskiness."

That may seem like a no-brainer to you and me, right there in the middle of the road with yellow-lines and dead armadillos, as Jim Hightower is fond of saying. But *Journal* readers were having none of it. They wrote in to set Judge Posner straight. "It is not free markets that fail, but government-controlled ones," protested one reader.

And why wouldn't they protest? The *Journal* has repeatedly told readers that "economic freedom" is "the real key to development." And each January for 15 years now the *Journal* tries to elevate that claim to a scientific truth by publishing a summary of the Heritage Foundation Index of Economic Freedom, which they assure readers proves the veracity of the claim. But in the hands of the editors of the *Wall Street Journal* and the researchers from the Heritage Foundation, Washington's foremost right-wing think tank, the Index of Economic Freedom is a barometer of corporate and entrepreneurial freedom from accountability rather than a guide to which countries are giving people more control over their economic lives and over the institutions that govern them.

This January was no different. "The 2009 Index provides strong evidence that the countries that maintain the freest economies do the best job promoting prosperity for all citizens," proclaimed this year's editorial, "Freedom is Still the Winning Formula." But with economies across the globe in recession, the virtues of free markets are a harder sell this year. That is not lost on *Wall Street Journal* editor Paul Gigot, who wrote the foreword to this year's report. Gigot allows that, "ostensibly free-market policymakers in the U.S. lost their monetary policy discipline, and we are now paying a terrible price." Still Gigot maintains that, "the *Index of Economic Freedom* exists to chronicle how steep that price will be and to point the way back to policy wisdom."

What the Heritage report fails to mention is this: while the global economy is in recession, many of the star performers in the Economic Freedom Index are tanking. Fully one half of the ten hardest-hit economies in the world are among the 30 "free" and "mostly free" economies at the top of the Economic Freedom Index rankings of 179 countries.

Here's the damage, according to the IMF. Singapore, the Southeast Asian trading center and perennial number two in the Index, will suffer a 10.0% drop in output this year. Slotting in at number four, Ireland, the so-called Celtic tiger, has seen its rapid export-led growth give way to an 8.0% drop in output. Number 13 and number 30, the foreign-direct-investment-favored Baltic states, Estonia and Lithuania, will each endure a 10.0% loss of output this year. Finally, the economy of Iceland, the loosely regulated European banking center that sits at number 14 on the Index, will contract 10.6% in 2009.

As a group, the Index's 30 most "free" economies will contract 4.1% in 2009. All of the other groups in the Index ("moderately free," "mostly unfree," and "repressed" economies) will muddle through 2009 with a much smaller loss of output or with moderate growth. The 67 "mostly unfree" countries in the Index will post the fastest growth rate for the year, 2.3%.

So it seems that if the Index of Economic Freedom can be trusted, then Judge Posner was not so far off the mark when he described capitalism as dynamic but "not inherently stable." That wouldn't be so bad, one *Journal* reader pointed out in a letter: "Economic recessions are the cost we pay for our economic freedom and economic prosperity is the benefit. We've had many more years of the latter than the former."

Not to be Trusted

But the Index of Economic Freedom cannot and should not be trusted. How free or unfree an economy is according to the Index seems to have little do with how quickly it grows. For instance, economist Jeffery Sachs found "no correlation" between a country's ranking in the Index and its per capita growth rates from 1995 to 2003. Also, in this year's report North America is the "freest" of its six regions of the world, but logged the slowest average rate over the last five years, 2.7% per annum. The Asia-Pacific region, which is "less free" than every other region except Sub-Saharan Africa according to the Index, posted the fastest average growth over the last five years, 7.8% per annum. That region includes several of fastest growing of the world's economies, India, China, and Vietnam, which ranked 123, 132, and 145 respectively in the Index and were classified as "mostly unfree." And there are plenty of relatively slow growers among the countries high up in the Index, including Switzerland (which ranks ninth).

The Heritage Foundation folks who edited the Index objected to Sachs' criticisms, pointing out that they claimed "a close relationship" between *changes* in

ECONOMIC FREEDOM AND ECONOMIC GROWTH IN 2009	
Degree of Economic Freedom	IMF Projected Growth Rate for 2009
"Free" (7 Countries)	-4.54%
"Mostly Free" (23 Counties)	-3.99%
"Moderately Free" (53 Countries)	-0.92%
"Mostly Unfree" (67 Countries)	+2.31%
"Repressed" (69 Counties)	+1.65%

Sources: International Monetary Fund, *World Economic Outlook,: Crisis and Recovery*, April 2009, Tables A1, A2, A3; Terry Miller and Kim R. Holmes, eds., *2009 Index of Economic Freedom*, heritage.org/Index/, Executive Summary.

economic freedom, not the *level* of economic freedom, and growth. But even that claim is fraught with problems. Statistically it doesn't hold up. Economic journalist Doug Henwood found that improvements in the index and GDP growth from 1997 to 2003 could explain no more than 10% of GDP growth. In addition, even a tight correlation would not resolve the problem that many of the fastest growing economies are "mostly unfree" according to the Index.

But even more fundamental flaws with the Index render any claim about the relationship between prosperity and economic freedom, as measured by the Heritage Foundation, questionable. Consider just two of the ten components the Economic Freedom Index uses to rank countries: fiscal freedom and government size.

Fiscal freedom (what we might call the "hell-if-I'm-going-to-pay-for-government" index) relies on the top income tax and corporate income tax brackets as two of its three measures of the tax burden. These are decidedly flawed measures even if all that concerned you was the tax burden of the rich and owners of corporations (or the super-rich). Besides ignoring the burden of other taxes, singling out these two top tax rates don't get at effective corporate and income tax rates, or how much of a taxpayer's total income goes to paying these taxes. For example, on paper U.S. corporate tax rates are higher than those in Europe. But nearly one half of U.S. corporate profits go untaxed. The effective rate of taxation on U.S. corporate profits currently stands at 15%, far below the top corporate tax rate of 35%. And relative to GDP, U.S. corporate income taxes are no more than half those of other OECD countries.

Even their third measure of fiscal freedom, government tax revenues relative to GDP, bears little relationship to economic growth. After an exhaustive review, economist Joel Selmrod, former member of the Reagan Treasury Department, concludes that the literature reveals "no consensus" about the relationship between the level of taxation and economic growth.

The Index's treatment of government size, which relies exclusively on the level of government spending relative to GDP, is just as flawed as the fiscal freedom index. First, "richer countries do not tax and spend less" than poorer countries, reports economist Peter Lindhert. Beyond that, this measure does not take into account how the government uses its money. Social spending programs—public education, child-care and parental support, and public health programs—can make people more productive and promote economic growth. That lesson is not lost on Hong Kong and Singapore, number one and number two in the index. They both provide universal access to health care, despite the small size of their governments.

The size-of-government index also misses the mark because it fails to account for industrial policy. This is a serious mistake, because it overestimates the degree to which some of the fastest growing economies of the last few decades, such as Taiwan and South Korea, relied on the market and underestimates the positive role that government played in directing economic development in those countries by guiding investment and protecting infant industries.

This flaw is thrown into sharp relief by the recent report of the World Bank's Commission on Growth and Development. That group studied 13 economies that grew at least 7% a year for at least 25 years since 1950. Three of the Index's "free" and "mostly free" countries made the list (Singapore, Hong Kong, and Japan) but so did three of the index's "mostly unfree" countries (China, Brazil, and Indonesia). While these rapid growers were all export-oriented, their governments "were not free-market purists," according the Commission's report. "They tried a variety of policies to help diversify exports or sustain competitiveness. These included industrial policies to promote new investments."

Still More

Beyond all that, the Index says nothing about political freedom. Consider once again the two city-states, Hong Kong and Singapore, which top their list of free countries. Both are only "partially free" according to Freedom House, which the editors have called "the Michelin Guide to democracy's development." Hong Kong is still without direct elections for it legislatures or its chief executive and a proposed internal security laws threaten press and academic freedom as well as political dissent. In Singapore, freedom of the press and rights to demonstrate are limited, films, TV, and the like are censored, and preventive detention is legal.

So it seems that the Index of Economic Freedom in practice tells us little about the cost of abandoning free market policies and offers little proof that government intervention into the economy would either retard economic growth or contract political freedom. In actuality, this rather objective-looking index is a slip-shod measure that would seem to have no other purpose than to sell the neoliberal policies that brought on the current crisis, and to stand in the way of policies that might correct the crisis. ❑

Sources: "Capitalism in Crisis," by Richard A Posner, *Wall Street Journal*, 5/07/09; "Letters: Recessions are the Price We Pay for Economic Freedom," *Wall Street Journal*, 5/19/09/; "Freedom is Still the Winning Formula," by Terry Miller, *Wall Street Journal*, 1/13/09 ; "The Real Key to Development," by Mary Anastasia O'Grady, *Wall Street Journal*, 1/15/08; Terry Miller and Kim R. Holmes, eds., *2009 Index of Economic Freedom*, heritage.org/Index/; Freedom House, "Freedom in the World 2009 Survey," freedomhouse.org; Joel Selmrod and Jon Bakija, *Taxing Ourselves: A Citizen's Guide to the Debate over Taxes*, MIT Press, 2008; International Monetary Fund, *World Economic Outlook,: Crisis and Recovery*, April 2009; Peter H. Lindert, *Growing Public*, Cambridge University Press, 2004; Doug Henwood, "*Laissez-faire* Olympics: An LBO Special Report," leftbusinessobserver.com, March 26, 2005; Jeffrey Sachs, *The End of Poverty: Economic Possibilities for Our Time*, Penguin, 2005.

Article 10.5

TAX HAVENS AND THE FINANCIAL CRISIS

From offshore havens to financial centers, banking secrecy faces scrutiny.

BY RACHEL KEELER
May/June 2009

When an entire global financial system collapses, it is reasonable to expect some bickering over the ultimate fixing of things. Rumors of dissention and talk of stimulus-paved roads to hell made everyone squeamish going into the April summit of the G20 group of large and industrialized nations in London. French President Nicolas Sarkozy even threatened to walk out on the whole thing if he didn't get his way.

The French were perhaps right to be nervous: they were taking a somewhat socialist stand, declaring that unregulated shadow banking and offshore tax havens were at the heart of the financial crisis and had to be either controlled or eradicated. They were doing it in a city at the center of the shadow system, and at a summit chaired by British Prime Minister Gordon Brown, a man recently described by the *Financial Times* as "one of the principal cheerleaders for the competitive international deregulation of international financial markets."

But Gordon Brown had already announced his intention to lead the global crackdown on tax havens as a first step toward global financial recovery. German Chancellor Angela Merkel had long backed France in calling for regulation of hedge funds, the poster boys of shadow banking charged with fostering the crisis. And, to Sarkozy's delight, everyone kept their promises at the G20.

"Major failures in the financial sector and in financial regulation and supervision were fundamental causes of the crisis," read the summit's reassuringly clear communiqué. World leaders agreed to regulate all systemically important financial institutions, including hedge funds and those located in tax havens, under threat of sanctions for noncompliance. "The era of banking secrecy is over," they concluded, as close to united as anyone could have dreamed.

But unity that looks good on paper is always more difficult to achieve in reality. The lingering questions post-summit are the same ones Sarkozy may have pondered on his way to London: will leaders from countries made rich from offshore banking follow through to shut it down? What is at stake, and what will the globally coordinated regulation everyone agrees is necessary actually look like? Not surprisingly, there are no easy answers.

Nature of the Beast

Over the years, trillions of dollars in both corporate profits and personal wealth have migrated "offshore" in search of rock bottom tax rates and the comfort of no questions asked. Tax havens and other financial centers promoting low tax rates, light regulation, and financial secrecy include a long list of tropical nations like the Cayman Islands as well as whole mainland economies from Switzerland to Singapore.

Tax Justice Network, an international non-profit advocating tax haven reform, estimates one- third of global assets are held offshore. The offshore world harbors $11.5 trillion in individual wealth alone, representing $250 billion in lost annual tax revenue. Treasury figures show tax havens sucking $100 billion a year out of U.S. coffers. And these numbers have all been growing steadily over the past decade. A *Tax Notes* study found that between 1999 and 2002, the amount of profits U.S. companies reported in tax havens grew from $88 billion to $149 billion.

With little patience left for fat-cat tax scams, the public is finally cheering for reform. Tax havens, it seems, have become the perfect embodiment of suddenly unfashionable capitalist greed. Unemployed workers and unhappy investors grow hot with anger as they imagine exotic hideouts where businessmen go to sip poolside martinis and laugh off their national tax burden.

Reformers have tried and failed in the past to shut down these locales. But analysts say 2008, the year the global financial system finally collapsed under its own liberalized weight, made all the difference. Not only are governments now desperate for tax revenue to help fund bailouts, but a recognition of the role offshore financial centers played in the system's implosion is dawning.

Along with the G20 fanfare, economists and policymakers including Treasury Secretary Timothy Geithner have pointed to the shadow banking system as a root cause of the global crisis. They're talking about the raft of highly-leveraged, virtually unregulated investment vehicles developed over the last 20 years: hedge funds, private equity, conduits, structured investment vehicles (SIVs), collateralized debt obligations (CDOs), and other wildly arcane investment banker toys.

While most of these innovations were born of Wall Street imaginations, few found their home in New York. Seventy-five percent of the world's hedge funds are based in four Caribbean tax havens: the Cayman Islands, Bermuda, the British Virgin Islands, and the Bahamas. The two subprime mortgage-backed Bear Stearns funds that collapsed in 2007, precipitating the credit crisis, were incorporated in the Caymans. Jersey and Guernsey, offshore financial centers in the Channel Islands, specialize in private equity. Many SIVs were created offshore, far from regulatory eyes.

We now know that hedge funds made their record profits from offshore bases by taking long-term gambles with short-term loans. The risky funds were often backed by onshore banks but kept off those institutions' books as they were repackaged and sold around the world. Regulators never took much notice: one, because lobbyists told them not to; two, because the funds were so complex that George Soros barely understood them; and three, because many of the deals were happening offshore.

Beneath regulatory radar, shadow bankers were able to scrap capital cushions, conceal illiquidity, and muddle debt accountability while depending on constant refinancing to survive. When the bubble burst and investors made a run for their money, panicked fund managers found it impossible to honor their debts, or even figure out how to price them as the markets crumbled.

William Cohan writes in his new book on the Bear Stearns collapse (*House of Cards: A Tale of Hubris and Wretched Excess on Wall Street*) that it took the brokerage three weeks working day and night to value illiquid securities when two of its Cayman-based hedge funds fell apart in 2007. In the end, the firm realized it was off by $1 billion from its original guesstimate, on just $1.5 billion in funds.

Mortgage-backed securities that once flourished in offshore tax havens are now the toxic assets that U.S. taxpayers are being asked to salvage through the trillion-dollar TARP and TALF programs.

Last Laughs

This convoluted network of offshore escapades is what world leaders have vowed to bring under global regulatory watch in order to restore worldwide financial stability. To their credit, the crackdown on banking secrecy has already begun in a big way.

In February, secret Swiss bank accounts were blown open to permit an unprecedented Internal Revenue Service probe. Europe's UBS bank has admitted to helping wealthy Americans evade what prosecutors believe to be $300 million a year in taxes.

Switzerland, the world's biggest tax haven where at least $2 trillion in offshore money is stashed, has long refused to recognize tax evasion as a crime. Every nation has the sovereign right to set its own tax code, which is why regulators have had such a hard time challenging offshore banking in the past. The dirty secret of tax havens, as President Obama once noted, is that they're mostly legal.

Under U.S. law, tax avoidance (legal) only becomes tax evasion (illegal) in the absence of other, more credible perks. In other words, a company is free to establish foreign subsidiaries in search of financial expertise, global reach, convenience, etc., just so long as tax dodging does not appear to be the sole reason for relocation.

The IRS will tax individual American income wherever it's found, but finding it is often the key. To access account information in Switzerland, authorities had to have proof not merely of tax evasion but of fraud, which is what much white-knuckled investigation finally produced on UBS. In the wake of this success, and under threat of landing on the OECD's new list of "uncooperative" tax havens, all of Europe's secrecy jurisdictions—Liechtenstein, Andorra, Austria, Luxembourg, and Switzerland—have signed information-sharing agreements.

Following the blood trail, congressional investigators descended on the Cayman Islands in March to tour the infamous Ugland House: one building supposedly home to 12,748 U.S. companies. The trip was an attempt to verify some of the implicit accusations made by a Government Accountability Office report in January which found that 83 of the United States' top 100 companies operate subsidiaries in tax havens.

Many of those, including Citigroup (which holds 90 subsidiaries in the Cayman Islands alone), Bank of America, and AIG, have received billions in taxpayer-funded bailouts. But the report failed to establish whether the subsidiaries were set up for the sole purpose of tax evasion.

Offshore Arguments

Politicians are already patting themselves on the back for their success in tackling tax crime. Everyone is making a big deal of the new tax information-exchange standard that all but three nations (Costa Rica, Malaysia, and the Philippines—the OECD's freshly minted blacklist) have agreed to implement in the wake of the G20 meeting. What leaders aren't saying is that before it became a G20 talking point, tax information exchange was actually tax haven *fans'* favored reform measure.

The first thing most offshore officials claim when confronted with criticism is that their countries are not, indeed, tax havens. Since the OECD launched a tax policy campaign in 1996, many of the offshore centers have been working to clean up their acts. A hoard of information-exchange agreements with onshore economies were signed even before Switzerland took the plunge. Geoff Cook, head of Jersey Finance, says Jersey's agreements with the United States, Germany, Sweden, and others have long outpaced what banks in Switzerland and Singapore traditionally maintained. "Our only fear in this is that people wouldn't look into the subject deep enough to draw those distinctions," Cook said.

But analysts say the agreements lack teeth. To request information from offshore, authorities must already have some evidence of misconduct. And the information-exchange standard still only covers illegal tax evasion, not legal tax avoidance. More importantly, what is already evident is that these agreements don't change much about the way offshore financial centers function. Offshore centers that agree to open up their books still have the luxury of setting their own regulatory standards and will continue to attract business based on their shadow banking credentials.

The G20 decided that shadow banking must be subjected to the same regulation as onshore commercial activity, which will also see more diligent oversight. Financial activity everywhere will be required to maintain better capital buffers, they said, monitored by a new Financial Stability Board; and excessive risk-taking will be rebuked. But the push for harmonized regulation across all financial centers revokes a degree of local liberty. Big ideas about state sovereignty and economic growth are at stake, which is probably what made Sarkozy so nervous about taking his regulatory demands global.

"People come here for expertise and knowledge," argues head of Guernsey Finance Peter Niven, and he may have a point. Many in finance think it's wrong to put all the blame on private funds and offshore centers for a crisis of such complex origins. Havens say stripping away their financial freedoms is hypocritical and shortsighted. "It's really not about the Cayman Islands, it's about the U.S. tax gap—and we're the collateral damage," said one frustrated Cayman Island official, adding: "Everybody needs liquidity and everyone needs money. That's what we do."

Predictably, reform critics warn that responding to the global crisis with "too much" regulation will stifle economic growth, something they know world leaders are quite conscious of. "International Financial Centres such as Jersey play an important role as conduits in the flow of international capital around the world by providing liquidity in neighbouring (often onshore) financial centres, the very lubrication which markets now need," wrote Cook in a recent statement.

Overall, attempting to move beyond paltry information exchange to implementing real regulation of shadow banking across national jurisdictions promises to be extremely difficult.

Real Reform

Part of the solution starts at home. Offshore enthusiasts might be the first to point out that the Securities and Exchange Commission never had the remit to regulate *onshore* hedge funds because Congress didn't give it to them. Wall Street deregulation is often cited in Europe as the base rot in the system.

But demanding more regulation onshore won't do any good if you can't regulate in the same way offshore. A serious aspect of the tax haven problem is a kind of global regulatory arbitrage: widespread onshore deregulation over the last 20 years came alongside an affinity for doing business offshore where even less regulation was possible, which in turn encouraged tax haven-style policies in countries like Britain, the United States, Singapore, and Ireland, all fighting to draw finance back into their economies.

President Obama has long been a champion of both domestic and offshore financial reform, and a critic of the deregulation popular during the Bush years. But for global action to happen, Obama needs Europe's help (not to mention cooperation from Asia and the Middle East) and no one knows how deep Gordon Brown's commitment runs. It is only very recently that Brown transformed himself from deregulation cheerleader as chancellor of the exchequer under Tony Blair to global regulatory savior as Britain's new prime minister.

In an interview late last year, Tax Justice Network's John Christensen predicted Britain could become a barrier to reform. "Britain, I think, will become increasingly isolated, particularly in Europe where the City of London is regarded as a tax haven," he said. Even if Gordon Brown is on board, Britain's finance sector hates to see itself sink. Moreover, some say the UK's lax financial regulatory system has saved the wider economy from decay. When British manufacturing declined, the City of London became the nation's new breadwinner. It grew into the powerhouse it is today largely by luring business away from other centers with the promise of adventurous profit-making and mild public oversight.

The City now funnels much of its business through British overseas territories that make up a big faction in the world's offshore banking club. Many offshore officials have accused Britain of making a show of tax haven reform to deflect attention from its own dirty dealings onshore.

Other obstacles to reform could come from Belgium and Luxembourg, which each hold important votes at the Basel Committee on Banking Supervision (a leading international regulatory voice) and the EU. Neither country has shown much enthusiasm for Europe's reform agenda. And no one will soon forget that China nearly neutered the G20 communiqué when it refused to "endorse" an OECD tax haven blacklist that would allow Europe to chastise financial activities in Hong Kong and Macau.

Still, the regulatory tide is strong and rising; even global financial heavyweights may find it unwise or simply impossible to swim against it. For perhaps the first time since the end of World War II, the world appears open to the kind of global cooperation necessary to facilitate global integration in a socially responsible way.

But the tiny nations that have built empires around unfettered financial services will surely continue to fight for their place in the sun. Some may go the way of Darwinian selection. Declining tourism is already crippling economies across the Caribbean. But many more are optimistic about their ability to hang on. Guernsey is pursuing Chinese markets. Jersey claims business in private equity remains strong. Bermuda still has insurance and hopes to dabble in gambling. Many offshore say they welcome the coming reforms.

"We look forward to those challenges" said Michael Dunkley, leader of the United Bermuda Party, noting that Bermuda, a tiny island with a population of just 66,000 people, is not encumbered by big bureaucracy when it comes to getting things done. Whatever new regulations come up, he said: "Bermuda would be at the cutting edge of making sure it worked."

Accusations of capitalist evil aside, one can't help but admire their spirit. ❑

Sources: Willem Buiter, "Making monetary policy in the UK has become simpler, in no small part thanks to Gordon Brown," *Financial Times*, October 26, 2008; G20 Final Communiqué, "The Global Plan for Recovery and Reform," April 2, 2009; Tax Justice Network, taxjustice.net; Martin Sullivan, Data Shows Dramatic Shift of Profits to Tax Havens, *Tax Notes*, September 13, 2004; William Cohan, *House of Cards: A Tale of Hubris and Wretched Excess on Wall Street*, March 2009; U.S. Government Accountability Office, "International Taxation: Large US corporations and federal contractors in jurisdictions listed as tax havens or financial privacy jurisdictions," December 2008; Organisation for Economic Co-operation and Development. "A Progress Report on the Jurisdictions Surveyed by the OECD Global Forum in Implementing the Internationally Agreed Tax Standard," April 2, 2009; Geoff Cook, Response to *Financial Times* Comment, mail. jerseyfinance.je; March 5, 2009; William Brittain-Catlin, "How offshore capitalism ate our economies—and itself," *The Guardian*, Feb. 5, 2009.

Article 10.6

BEYOND THE WORLD CREDITORS' CARTEL
In Latin America and elsewhere, the IMF may be re-emerging—but in a changed landscape.

BY DARIUSH SOKOLOV
September/October 2009

One group of financiers seems to be doing nicely out of the global recession: the International Monetary Fund and other international financial institutions (IFIs) are enjoying a return to relevance and lining up for increased funding.

The London G20 Summit in April was the IMF's big comeback gig. In 2007 the fund's loan book was down to just $20 billion; now its capital is set to triple to $750 billion, plus permission to issue $250 billion in "special drawing rights" (the fund's quasi-currency which allows member countries to borrow from each others' reserves). Since September 2008 a range of East European and ex-Soviet states have taken out new loans. So too have Pakistan, El Salvador, and Iceland—the fund's first Western European client since Britain in 1976.

The World Bank and regional development banks are also getting in on the party. In Latin America, the World Bank's regional vice president Pamela Cox says she expects lending to triple in 2009 to $14 billion. The Inter-American Development Bank (IDB), the most active IFI in the region, expects to lend $18 billion—its typical loan portfolio is under $8 billion. And the development banks are queuing up behind the IMF with their caps out for capital increases: the Asian Development Bank wants to triple its capital to $165 billion; the IDB is asking for an extra $50 to $80 billion on top of its current $101 billion.

Why now? The IFIs, says Vince McElhinny of the Bank Information Center, a group that monitors them, are opportunists at heart. Just like any private bank or corporation they fight for market share, and as the world economy and global capital markets grow they need to increase their lending apace or lose relevance. The freezing of world capital markets, particularly severe in emerging markets, has created a need which they can seize as opportunity. The Institute of International Finance predicts private net capital flows to emerging markets of $141 billion in 2009, down from $392 billion in 2008, after a record $890 billion in 2007. The IFIs see themselves helping to fill this gap.

But the issues at stake here go beyond the IFIs' own agendas. On the one hand, their revival implies a reassertion of U.S. and global North dominance. They aren't called "Washington-based" just as a matter of real estate: the United States has a 17% voting share on the IMF and World Bank, enough to give it a veto on some major changes; Europe and the United States control the top management positions.

On the other hand, the story underscores how parts of the global South are gaining in economic power. In the crises of the 1990s, or so the neoliberal story went, the IMF stepped in to clean up the messes made when fragile Third World economies exploded. This time around things are very different: the mess is in the North, and the likelihood is that the emerging economies of Asia and Latin America will emerge from it stronger and more independent. (It's important to note, though, that large areas in the South, notably Africa, are not part of this story—nor is Eastern Europe.) The so-called BRIC nations in particular (Brazil, Russia, India, China) are getting the bargaining power to back up their claims on the global financial system. Will these claims be met within the existing institutions, or by creating a new financial architecture that bypasses Washington altogether? The future of the IFIs is a key arena in which global rebalancing of economic power is playing out.

New Financial Architecture?

In May 2007 finance ministers from Brazil, Argentina, Venezuela, Bolivia, and Ecuador signed the "Quito declaration" in the Ecuadorian capital. The plan includes a regional monetary fund and moves toward a South American single currency, but the first step is the creation of the Banco del Sur, a new regional development bank. While the bank's launch is behind schedule, this March its constitution was agreed to, with an initial capitalization of $7 billion. Besides the original five, Paraguay and Uruguay are also members. (Even Colombia had announced its support before its late-2007 row with Venezuela over hostages.)

The aim of Banco del Sur is to replace the Washington-based lenders altogether with institutions run by and for South America. Maria Jose Romero, who researches the IFIs at the Third World Institute in Montevideo, encapsulates this spirit. "In responding to the crisis Latin American countries have two options," she says. "We can return to the old institutions and the failed recipes of the 1990s, or we can move forward with alternatives."

For many Latin American countries a return to the IMF is politically out of the question. According to Mark Weisbrot, co-director of the Center for Economic and Policy Research in Washington, the decline of the IMF started with the Asian financial crisis over a decade ago. After the fund's failure to act as emergency lender of last resort to Asian banking systems in 1997, those states moved to build up sizeable currency reserves, determined not to be dependent on the fund again; others followed suit.

This turning away has been more dramatic in Latin America, where IMF policies are blamed for precipitating the 1998 crisis in Argentina which led to the collapse of its banking system and eventually to its 2002 default. Argentina and Bolivia both paid off the last of their debts to the fund in 2006; in April 2007 Ecuador announced it had paid off its IMF loans and requested the fund withdraw its country manager; the same month Venezuela announced itself debt-free, and a few weeks later said it would withdraw from fund membership altogether. When Daniel Ortega won the Nicaraguan presidential election in May 2007 he promised the country would be "free from the fund" within five years.

How has this freedom-from-Washington line held in the current crisis? U.S.-friendly Mexico was the first to sign up for the new Flexible Credit Lines the IMF is granting without conditions to "pre-approved" governments, followed by Colombia—though neither has yet drawn on them. So far only El Salvador and Costa Rica have taken out new loans. In sharp contrast to Eastern Europe, most Latin American states had healthy reserve cushions coming into the crunch. And with commodity prices now rising again, it may be that the region's anti-IMF resolve is not going to face the test many had anticipated.

As for Banco del Sur, the arrival of crisis no doubt slowed the process: domestic firefighting comes before regional cooperation. But, according to Romero, in the medium term it will help push change:

"The crisis has focused attention to the failings of the existing financial system," she says. "It is helping build the impetus for Banco del Sur, as well as for moves to settle bilateral trade in local currencies [rather than dollars], which is the first step towards monetary union, and for broader South-South cooperation initiatives."

To be fair, Banco del Sur may not live up to proponents' hopes. With just $7 billion in capital, the bank won't be in the same league as the Washington-based IFIs. Nor is there any immediate plan to create an emergency monetary fund—an Ecuadorian proposal to that effect has been dropped. And the principle of one country one vote, perhaps the biggest rallying point of all, has been modified: equal votes will apply only on loans under $70m, above which approval is required from members with two-thirds of the capital contributions.

Finally, there is still no clarity on the focus of lending. Campaigners hope for a true emphasis on poverty reduction and projects to build regional cooperation, and have scored the provision of a socially focused "audit board." But some fear that more conservative members (read: Brazil) could push Banco del Sur toward being just one more development bank.

Across Asia, there are parallel developments. A proposal by Japan to set up an Asian Monetary Fund met the same fate as an earlier Malaysian-backed scheme called the East Asian Economic Caucus—both were dropped after expressions of disapproval from the IMF and U.S. officials. But now the Chiang Mai Initiative, a longstanding plan for a system of swap arrangements between the central banks of the southeast Asian countries plus China, Japan, and South Korea is expected to come on line this year, and the proposed size of the scheme was upped to $120 billion in February. Chiang Mai is linked to the IMF (members need IMF agreements in place to withdraw more than 20% of the total), but some see it leading towards an eventual independent regional fund. For now, though, at least officially, the talk is usually of "complementing," not supplanting, the IMF.

Rise of the BRICs

If the Quito project is the idealistic side of the regionalization movement, the BRIC bloc is global power shift as realpolitik. The BRICs together now account for 22% of world production (by purchasing power parity), up from 16% ten years ago and rising.

Even as they move ahead with building regional institutions independent of the IFIs, the BRICs are pushing for more power within the Washington-based institutions. Increased say at the IMF is one of the four governments' main demands. In March 2008 China's vote share was raised all the way up to 3.7%—putting the world's most populous country on a par with Belgium plus the Netherlands, combined population 27 million. The BRICs jointly muster a 9.82% quota.

According to Vince McElhinny, the BRICs' contributions to the fund's current capital boost are aimed at bolstering their demands for more say in IFI governance.

When, a week before the BRIC summit, Brazil's President Lula announced a $10 billion contribution, he talked of thereby gaining "moral authority to keep pushing for changes needed at the IMF."

The IMF's desire to placate emerging powers such as the BRICs may explain the makeover it has displayed in its current comeback—dubbed "IMF 2.0" by *Time* magazine. Managing director Dominique Strauss-Kahn has called for the fund to spend against recession: less structural adjustment, more counter-cyclical stimulus. But the changes may be largely cosmetic. According to a study by the Third World Network, the actual conditions of recent IMF loans to Pakistan, Hungary, Ukraine, and other countries are familiar: the borrowers must reduce their fiscal deficits through public spending cuts, wage freezes, higher fuel tariffs, and interest rate hikes.

What real changes are the BRICs really likely to get? There's plenty of gossip flying around: some are touting Lula as the next World Bank president; perhaps China will get to pick Strauss-Kahn's successor.

Mark Weisbrot, however, does not see the U.S. government giving any ground on voting shares. "The U.S. would rather walk away from the IMF than give up control," he says.

Beyond the Cartel

Weisbrot describes the IMF as "the most important instrument of influence the U.S. government has in developing countries—beyond the military, beyond the CIA. Or, at least, that's the role it's played for most of the last 30 years. A good part of that influence has been lost recently; now they're trying to get it back."

The IMF's power has never really been about its own lending, however. Its influence over countries' economic policies is far greater than would be suggested by its share in overall capital flows. The real issue is the fund's role as "gatekeeper" of a global "creditors' cartel."

Multilateral loans from the World Bank and regional development banks and bilateral loans from the wealthy countries typically come with some form of "cross-conditionality" clause. You only get your loan if you first have an IMF agreement in place; installments only keep flowing so long as you stick to it. Similar conditions can also apply in private capital transactions. For instance, Venezuela's 2007 threat to give up its IMF membership triggered a market sell-off because under covenants written into its sovereign bonds, a break with the fund would count as a "technical default."

Now, though, recent shifts in Latin America have dealt what Weisbrot says could be "a final blow to the IMF creditors' cartel in middle-income countries."

This is a continental tale, but Argentina is a good place to begin. The country cut itself off from international capital markets with its 2002 default, and is still being chased by "hold-out" bond investors in the New York courts. Yet Argentina grew at almost 9% a year from 2003 through 2007—the country's most rapid growth in 50 years, and some of the fastest growth rates on the continent. This expansion has been funded largely by selling bonds to another emerging regional power, Venezuela. These bond transfers are no subsidies—Argentina pays commercial interest rates—but they do come free of Washington conditions. For Weisbrot, "Venezuela's offers of credit, without policy conditions, to Argentina, Bolivia, Ecuador, Nicaragua, and other countries has changed the equation."

It's true that easy Venezuelan credit dried up early on in the crisis as oil prices plummeted. It's also true that Argentina is now allowing IMF staff in to monitor its economy and taking out new loans from the World Bank and the IDB. But it's telling that Argentina got these loans without any IMF agreement in place: the cartel, at least in its old form, appears to be broken. And then there's the other plank in Argentina's current crisis management strategy: a $10.2 billion swap line direct with China.

In short, the IMF and allied institutions have regained some lost ground in the crisis, but forms of "South-South cooperation" that stand to weaken the Washington-based creditors' cartel have kept on building too.

According to one very plausible interpretation, this crisis has been about the consequences of the rich countries' capital piling into the financial services sphere to compensate for the loss of manufacturing production to the Third World. Control of the world's financial capital flows was one last highly profitable channel where Northern capital still ruled unopposed. Increasingly, though, global-South states and corporations are cutting out the middle man to trade directly with each other. It's against the background of these new possibilities that the next chapter in the story of the IFIs will play out. ❑

Article 10.7

NO BAILOUT FOR AIDS

Are cuts to health care a necessary part of "fiscal reform," or a continuation of decades of neglect?

BY MARA KARDAS-NELSON
July/August 2009

Despite trillions being spent on bank bailouts, the world's AIDS programs are facing billion-dollar deficits in order to continue lifesaving prevention, care, and treatment initiatives. Both domestic and donation governments cite the global financial downturn to explain the significant decrease in funding for AIDS and other health programs in the past year. While a fall-off in government revenue is undeniable, activists condemn the justification of the likely illness and death of millions in the name of "fiscal reform." Some even claim that the economic crisis is simply an excuse for governments to continue decades of AIDS neglect.

Nearly 40 million people are living with HIV worldwide, with 2.7 million new infections and two million people dying of AIDS-related illnesses every year. Sub-Saharan Africa is the hardest-hit region. According to the African Union, the region "faces a grim scenario with respect to the health of its people. [It is] ... home to 12 percent of the world's population [yet] accounts for 22 percent of the total global disease burden, and more than 68 percent of the people living with HIV/AIDS. [This] poor health status is mirrored by crises in health financing and human resources for health. With only 2% of the global health workforce and only 1% of the world's health expenditures, Sub-Saharan African countries are ill-equipped to adequately address their health problems."

In light of the global economic downturn, such indicators will only get worse. The World Bank has gloomily predicted that "the global economic crisis will cause an additional 22 children to die per hour, throughout all of 2009 ... it's possible that the toll will be twice that: an additional 400,000 child deaths, or an extra child dying every 79 seconds."

Unequal Cutbacks

Government-funded health care programs will no doubt be cut during the recession. Such cutbacks are seen as an unfortunate side effect of fiscal reform. According to a recent World Bank report: "Governments tend to expand social expenditures during times of economic expansion and decrease them during times of economic recession." Regardless of whether some cutbacks are necessary, the proportional cuts in funding for social programs historically have not reflected actual decreases in government revenues, thus undermining the argument that governments are "forced" to cut back on health spending. Data from Mexico between 1994 and 1996 show a 4.9% fall in GDP met "by a 23.7% fall in targeted spending per poor person." More damning is the example of Argentina where, "from the end of 2001 to the middle of 2002, preventive health care for children dropped 38% in the general population, but 57% in the poorest households." The World Bank report goes on to point out: "general strategies to maintain government social spending have often failed to protect poor people's access to essential social services during financial emergencies and ended up helping better-off groups in society instead."

These decreases in health spending come at a time when public health programs are most in need. As a statement issued by the South African non-profit Treatment Action Campaign puts it, "reduced income makes people less likely to seek medical attention when they are sick as they can no longer afford to travel. It also forces people to buy cheaper, less nutritious food which leads to an increase in malnutrition.... Despite the fact that clinic visits may contract in times of economic recession, the actual demand for these services increases as people face greater difficulties in accessing adequate food and housing."

One Step Forward, Two Steps Back

Since the beginning of the AIDS epidemic, governments worldwide, with a few notable exceptions, have inadequately funded prevention and treatment efforts. This is true for both domestic funding and for large donor countries like the United States and Britain which, because of their immense political and economic power, have been expected to help fund programs for countries far less economically or politically stable. Until recently, governments did not recognize the urgency or financial support that the epidemic requires.

Finally, in the early and mid-2000s, after decades of campaigning and millions of deaths, domestic and foreign governments began to recognize the importance of funding a variety of programs. Most significantly, the Global Fund to Fight AIDS, Tuberculosis, and Malaria was founded in 2001 as a public-private partnership to direct funding, provided by wealthy countries, foundations, and the private sector, to poorer countries. In 2007, after years of chronic under-financing, the Fund's board voted to triple the size of the effort from $2-3 billion per year in aid to $6-8 billion per year.

In the wake of the economic crisis, the Fund has reneged on this promise. It now faces a $5 billion funding gap, and the board has already responded by delaying the next round of funding applications by six months and cutting budgets for projects currently underway by 10%, warning that it may have to cut their future years' funding by 25%.

A decrease in foreign donations could substantially affect AIDS programs, especially within Africa. According to the World Bank, 28 African states are dependent on external sources for over 11% of their health expenditures; of these, six depend on foreign spending for 41-60% of their health funding. Such "highly donor dependent countries" are "especially vulnerable to aid cuts." Therefore, the sustainability of these countries' AIDS programs, including the critically important provision of antiretroviral treatment to those already infected, depends on their ability to find alternate sources of funding, primarily internal sources.

But countries are already reporting domestic funding cuts for AIDS programs, again blaming the economy. In March of this year, the Botswana government warned that it "may have to cut or completely withdraw its HIV/AIDS funding, despite the rising number of people needing treatment, as the…crisis takes a toll on the vitally important diamond-mining sector…[the country's] most important revenue source." Government funding provides 80% of the cost of Botswana's AIDS programs, with donors making up the remainder. The country's treatment program is considered one of the best in Africa, with the U.N. AIDS agency (UNAIDS) estimating that 94% of those in need have access to antiretrovirals.

Recession, or Continued Neglect?

While the World Bank asserts that the current funding crisis for the Global Fund and other international and domestic AIDS programs can be attributed to the global recession, others are more skeptical. Regarding the Global Fund's current $5 billion shortfall, U.S.-based AIDS non-profit Health Gap contends: "The increase in the size and quality of proposals was exactly in line with what the Board had voted for in 2007. But, the tripling of demand from poor countries [coincided] with a global financial crisis. It's important to note that the…funding gap was not caused by the … crisis."

While the crisis may affect governments' willingness to give to the Fund and other AIDS programs, it does not necessarily affect their ability to do so. As Jeffrey Sachs of Columbia University argues: "There is no shortage of funds at the moment when in three months the rich world has found … $3 trillion of funding for bank bailouts and in which there have been $18 billion of Christmas bonuses for Wall Street supported by bailout legislation." Health Gap agrees: "The total amount of money that went to bail out banks from all the rich countries in the world is 1,000 times more than the amount needed to fill the gap in funding for the Global Fund." Furthermore, "the Global Fund has been successful, whereas banks failed and caused this crisis."

For many, such a gap is simply a continuation of chronic under-funding of health systems, especially AIDS programs. In 2007, before the crisis hit and when most developed economies were booming, "the difference between UNAIDS' estimates of resource needs compared to resources available … was at least $8 billion."

The Global Fund especially has been shortchanged, most notably by the United States. Each contributing country is supposed to donate according to its percentage of the global economy. Thus, the United States should fill one-third of the current funding gap, since it accounts for one-third of the global economy. Such a stipulation is also written into U.S. law. But according to Health Gap, "the United States has historically not contributed its fair share to the Global Fund. After the Fund announced it intended to distribute $10 billion per year, President Bush made the paltry first contribution of $200 million. As a result, the Global Fund has been smaller than anticipated and has had to grow over time instead of starting out large." Today the United States continues to fail its one-third commitment. If the Fund is to keep its pledge to increase funding—a pledge the U.S. government agreed to—then the country must give $2.7 billion for 2010. For 2009 it has given only $900 million to date, $1 billion short of its fair share.

The legitimacy of domestic cuts is also in question. While the Ugandan government has blamed severe shortages of AIDS and TB drugs in the Gulu region on "delays in the disbursement of money from the Global Fund," according to the online HIV/AIDS news service PlusNews, observers point to mismanagement and, at times, corruption as factors. When the parliament's budget committee recommended cutting funding for antiretroviral drugs nearly in half next year, one local AIDS activist pointed out that the government is still finding plenty of money for the defense ministry and for politicians' perks.

Paula Akugizibwe of the AIDS and Rights Alliance of Southern Africa says that while a decrease in government revenue must be taken into consideration, it does not diminish governments' responsibility for public health. "We need to ensure that African lives do not become a silent casualty of the global financial downturn. Our lives are not cheap or expendable. The crisis does not absolve governments of the responsibility to fund essential programmes that they've promised. They must look at how they can re-allocate the money that they do have. We expect health to be prioritised over weapons, sports and lavish politics." Rebecca Hodes of the Treatment Action Campaign adds, "HIV and TB are not in recession." ❑

Sources: "2008 Report on the Global AIDS Epidemic," UNAIDS; African Union Paper (CAMH/EXP/13a(IV)), AU Ministers of Health Conference, Ethiopia, May 2009; Nicholas D. Kristof, "At Stake Are More Than Banks," *The New York Times*, April 1 2009; The World Bank's Human Development Network, "Averting a Human Crisis During the Global Downturn," The World Bank, March 2009; "TAC statement on new cabinet appointments and resources for health," The Treatment Action Campaign, May 12, 2009; "Fact Sheet on Global Fund $5 billion shortfall," Health GAP; "Botswana: Bleak Outlook for Future AIDS Funding," PlusNews, February 20, 2009; Rosanne Skirbel, "Economic Downturn Threatens Global Fund for AIDS, TB, Malaria," VOA News, February 4, 2009. "About Pepfar," from pepfar.gov; Neil MacFarquhar, "Obama Picks Leader for Global AIDS effort," *The New York Times*, April 27, 2009; Amanda Cary, "Repealing the Global Gage Rule: Obama takes Action to Combat AIDS," Physicians for Human Rights, January 23, 2009; "A New and Improved Pepfar Under Obama?" South African Business Coalition on HIV/AIDS, January 21, 2009; Sheryl Gay Stolberg, "Obama Seeks a Global Health Plan Broader Than Bush's AIDS Effort," *The New York Times*, May 5, 2009; Derek Kilner, "AIDS Activists Criticize Obama Budget for HIV," VOA News, May 19 2009.

Article 10.9

THE BEIJING STATEMENT
The Global Economic Crisis: An Historic Opportunity for Transformation
An initial response from individuals, social movements, and non-governmental
organizations in support of a transitional program for radical economic
transformation, Asia-Europe People's Forum, Beijing, October 15, 2008.

Preamble

Taking advantage of the opportunity of so many people from movements gathering in Beijing during the Asia-Europe People's Forum, the
Transnational Institute and Focus on the Global South convened informal
nightly meetings between October 13 and 15, 2008. We took stock of the
meaning of the unfolding global economic crisis and the opportunity it presents for us to put into the public domain some of the inspiring and feasible
alternatives many of us have been working on for decades. This statement
represents the collective outcome of our Beijing nights. We, the initial signa-
tories, mean this to be a contribution towards efforts to formulate proposals
around which our movements can organize as the basis for a radically different
kind of political and economic order.

The Crisis

The global financial system is unraveling at great speed. This is happening in the
midst of a multiplicity of crises in relation to food, climate, and energy. It severely
weakens the power of the United States and the EU, and the global institutions they
dominate, particularly the International Monetary Fund, the World Bank, and the
World Trade Organization. Not only is the legitimacy of the neoliberal paradigm in
question, but so is the very future of capitalism itself.

Such is the chaos in the global financial system that Northern governments have
resorted to measures progressive movements have advocated for years, such as nationalization of banks. These moves are intended, however, as short-term stabilization
measures and once the storm clears, they are likely to return the banks to the private
sector. We have a short window of opportunity to mobilize so that they are not.

The Challenge and the Opportunity

We are entering uncharted terrain with this conjuncture of profound crises—the fallout from the financial crisis will be severe. People are being thrown into a deep sense of
insecurity; misery and hardship will increase for many poorer people everywhere. We
should not cede this moment to fascist, right-wing populist, xenophobic groups, who
will surely try to take advantage of people's fear and anger for reactionary ends.

Powerful movements against neoliberalism have been built over many decades.
This will grow as critical coverage of the crisis enlightens more people, who are
already angry at public funds being diverted to pay for problems they are not

responsible for creating, and already concerned about the ecological crisis and rising prices—especially of food and energy. The movements will grow further as recession starts to bite and economies start sinking into depression.

There is a new openness to alternatives. To capture people's attention and support, they must be practical and immediately feasible. We have convincing alternatives that are already underway, and we have many other good ideas attempted in the past, but defeated. Our alternatives put the well-being of people and the planet at their center. For this, democratic control over financial and economic institutions are required. This is the "red thread" connecting up the proposals presented below.

Proposals for Debate, Elaboration, and Action

Finance

- Introduce full-scale socialization of banks, not just nationalization of bad assets.
- Create people-based banking institutions and strengthen existing popular forms of lending based on mutuality and solidarity.
- Institutionalize full transparency within the financial system through the opening of the books to the public, to be facilitated by citizen and worker organizations.
- Introduce parliamentary and citizens' oversight of the existing banking system.
- Apply social (including labor conditions) and environmental criteria to all lending, including for business purposes.
- Prioritize lending, at minimum rates of interest, to meet social and environmental needs and to expand the already growing social economy.
- Overhaul central banks in line with democratically determined social, environmental, and expansionary (to counter the recession) objectives, and make them publicly accountable institutions.
- Safeguard migrant remittances to their families and introduce legislation to restrict charges and taxes on transfers.

Taxation

- Close all tax havens.
- End tax breaks for fossil fuel and nuclear energy companies.
- Apply stringent progressive tax systems.
- Introduce a global taxation system to prevent transfer pricing and tax evasion.
- Introduce a levy on nationalized bank profits with which to establish citizen investment funds (see below).
- Impose stringent progressive carbon taxes on those with the biggest carbon footprints.
- Adopt controls, such as Tobin taxes, on the movements of speculative capital.
- Re-introduce tariffs and duties on imports of luxury goods and other goods already produced locally as a means of increasing the state's fiscal base, as well as a means to support local production and thereby reduce carbon emissions globally.

Public Spending and Investment

- Radically reduce military spending.
- Redirect government spending from bailing out bankers to guaranteeing basic incomes and social security, and providing universally accessible basic social services such as housing, water, electricity, health, education, child care, and access to the Internet and other public communications facilities.
- Use citizen funds (see above) to support very poor communities.
- Ensure that people at risk of losing their homes due to defaults on mortgages caused by the crisis are offered renegotiated terms of payment.
- Stop privatizations of public services.
- Establish public enterprises under the control of parliaments, local communities and/or workers to increase employment.
- Improve the performance of public enterprises through democratizing management—encourage public service managers, staff, unions, and consumer organizations to collaborate to this end.
- Introduce participatory budgeting over public finances at all feasible levels.
- Invest massively in improved energy efficiency, low carbon emitting public transport, renewable energy, and environmental repair.
- Control or subsidize the prices of basic commodities.

International Trade and Finance

- Introduce a permanent global ban on short-selling of stock and shares.
- Ban on trade in derivatives.
- Ban all speculation on staple food commodities.
- Cancel the debt of all developing countries—debt is mounting as the crisis causes the value of Southern currencies to fall.
- Support the United Nations call to be involved in discussions about how the to resolve the crisis, which is going to have a much bigger impact on Southern economies than is currently being acknowledged.
- Phase out the World Bank, International Monetary Fund, and World Trade Organization.
- Phase out the U.S. dollar as the international reserve currency.
- Establish a people's inquiry into the mechanisms necessary for a just international monetary system.
- Ensure aid transfers do not fall as a result of the crisis.
- Abolish tied aid.
- Abolish neo-liberal aid conditionalities.
- Phase out the paradigm of export-led development, and refocus sustainable development on production for the local and regional market.
- Introduce incentives for products produced for sale closest to the local market.
- Cancel all negotiations for bilateral free trade and economic partnership agreements.
- Promote regional economic cooperation arrangements, such as UNASUR, the Bolivarian Alternative for the Americas (ALBA), the Trade Treaty of the Peoples, and others, that encourage genuine development and an end to poverty.

Environment

- Introduce a global system of compensation for countries which do not exploit fossil fuel reserves in the global interests of limiting effects on the climate, such as Ecuador has proposed.
- Pay reparations to Southern countries for the ecological destruction wrought by the North to assist peoples of the South to deal with climate change and other environmental crises.
- Strictly implement the "precautionary principle" of the UN Declaration on the Right to Development as a condition for all developmental and environmental projects.
- End lending for projects under the Kyoto Protocol's "Clean Development Mechanism" that are environmentally destructive, such as monoculture plantations of eucalyptus, soya, and palm oil.
- Stop the development of carbon trading and other environmentally counterproductive techno-fixes, such as carbon capture and sequestration, agrofuels, nuclear power, and "clean coal" technology.
- Adopt strategies to radically reduce consumption in the rich countries, while promoting sustainable development in poorer countries.
- Introduce democratic management of all international funding mechanisms for climate change mitigation, with strong participation from Southern countries and civil society.

Agriculture and Industry

- Phase out the pernicious paradigm of industry-led development, where the rural sector is squeezed to provide the resources necessary to support industrialization and urbanization.
- Promote agricultural strategies aimed at achieving food security, food sovereignty, and sustainable farming.
- Promote land reforms and other measures which support small-holder agriculture and sustain peasant and indigenous communities.
- Stop the spread of socially and environmentally destructive mono-cultural enterprises.
- Stop labor-law reforms aimed at extending hours of work and making it easier for employers to fire or retrench workers.
- Secure jobs through outlawing precarious low-paid work.
- Guarantee equal pay for equal work for women—as a basic principle and to help counter the coming recession by increasing workers' capacity to consume.
- Protect the rights of migrant workers in the event of job losses, ensuring their safe return to and reintegration into their home countries. For those who cannot return, there should be no forced return, their security should be guaranteed, and they should be provided with employment or a basic minimum income.

Conclusion

These are all practical, common sense proposals. Some are initiatives already under-way and demonstrably feasible. Their successes need to be publicized and popular-ized so as to inspire reproduction. Others are unlikely to be implemented on their objective merits alone. Political will is required. By implication, therefore, every proposal is a call to action.

We have written what we see as a living document to be developed and enriched by us all. Please sign on to this statement at the bottom of the page.

A future occasion to come together to work on the actions needed to make these ideas and others a reality will be the World Social Forum in Belem, Brazil at the end of January 2009.

We have the experience and the ideas—let's meet the challenge of the present ruling disorder and keep the momentum towards an alternative rolling!! ❑

Initial Signatories

Organizations:

Transnational Institute, Netherlands
Focus on the Global South
Red Pepper magazine, United Kingdom
Institute for Global Research and Social Movements, Russia
Ecologistas en Acción, Spain
JS-Asia/Pacific Movement on Debt and Development (JS APMDD), Asia
RESPECT Network Europe, Europe
Commission for Filipino Migrant Workers (CFMW), Netherlands
The Movement for a Just World, Malaysia
Nord-Sud XXI, Switzerland
Europe Solidaire Sans Frontières (ESSF), France
Indian Social Action Forum (INSAF), Inadi
Movimiento Madre Tierra, Honduras
Asian Bridge, South Korea/ Philippines
Center for Encounter and Active Non-Violence, Austria
The Alliance of Progressive Labor (APL)
Pakistan Institute of Labour Education and Research (PILER), Pakistan
Pambansang Katipunan ng Makabayang Magbubukid
National Federation of Patriotic Peasant (PKMM), Phillipines
Proresibong Alyansa ng mga Mangingisda
Progresive Alliance of Fisher (PANGISDA), Philippines
WomanHealth, Philippines
Kilusan para sa Pambansang Demokrasya (KPD), Philippines
Fisherfolk Movement, Philippines
Democratic Socialist Perspective, Australia
Resistance & Alternative, Mauritius
Observatori del Deute en la Globalització, Spain
African Journalists on Trade and Development
Centre for Education and Communication (CEC), India

Individuals:

Fiona Dove, South Africa; Walden Bello, Philippines/Thailand; Hilary Wainwright, United Kingdom; Boris Kagarlitsky, Russia; Achin Vanaik, India; Dot Keet, South Africa; Brid Brennan, Ireland; Pietje Vervest, Netherlands; Cecilia Olivet, Uruguay; Ramon Fernandez, Spain; Pierre Rousset, France; Rodney Bickerstaffe, United Kingdom; Von Francis C Mesina, Philippines; Al D. Senturias, Jr., Philippines; Sammy Gamboa, Philippines; Fe Jusay, Philippines; Nonoi Hacbang, Philippines; Lidy Nacpil, Philippines; Tom Kucharz, Spain; Herbert Docena, Philippines; Seema Mustafa, India; Kenneth Haar, Denmark; Wolfram Schaffar, Germany; Christa Wichterich, Germany; Isabelle Duquesne, France; Adhemar Mineiro, Brazil; Benny Kuruvilla, India; Aehwa Kim, South Korea; Manjette Lopez, Philippines; Bonn Juego, Philippines; Rasti Delizo, Philippines; James Miraflor, Philippines; Miquel Ortega Cerda, Spain; David Llistar, Spain; Alpo Ratia, Finland; Mira Kakonen, Finland; Hilary Chiew, Malaysia; Celeste Fong, Malaysia; Tatcee Macabuag, Philippines; Teodoro M. de Mesa, Philippines; Uwe Hoering, Germany; Asad Rehman, UK; Andy Rutherford, UK; Debbie Valencia, Greece; Petra Snelders, Netherlands; Etta P. Rosales, Philippines; Pete Pinlac, Philippines; Ute Hausrnann, Germany; Alain Baron, France; Hanneke van Eldik Thieme, Netherlands; Dorothy Guerrero, Philippines; Ric Reyes, Philippines; Chandra Muzaffar, Malaysia; Ahmad Soueissi, Switzerland; Elias Davidsson, Germany; Juan Almendares, Honduras; Pierre Rousset, France; Tom Kucharz, Spain; Herbert Docena, Philippines; Carlos Ruiz; Alexis Passadakis; Sally Rousset; D.W. Karuna; Hyowoo Na, South Korea; Sung-Hee Choi, Korea; Marko Ulvila, Finland; Matthias Reichl, Austria; Orsan Senalp, Turkey/ The Netherlands; Tamra Gilbertson, United States; Kamal Mitra Chenoy, India; Anuradha Chenoy, India; Gilbert Achcar, UK; Richel "Ching" M. Borres, Philippines; Helen Mendoza, Philippines; Sukla Sen, India; Olli-Pekka Haavisto, Finland; Amira Armenta, Colombia; William K. Carroll, United States; Gigi Francisco, Philippines; Sylvia Estrada Claudio, Philippines; Pablo Rosales, Philippines; Alice Raymundo, Philippines; Maris dela Cruz, Philippines; Terry Townsend, Australia; Ashok Subron, Mauritius; Ko Ko Thett; Einar Ólafsson, Iceland.

Article 10.10

THE CARACAS STATEMENT
Text of the final declaration from the International Political Economy Conference, Caracas, October 11, 2008.

Academics and researchers from Argentina, Australia, Belgium, Canada, Chile, China, Cuba, Ecuador, France, Mexico, Peru, Philippines, South Korea, Spain, United Kingdom, United States, Uruguay, and Venezuela participated in The International Political Economy Conference: Responses from the South to the Global Economic Crisis, held in Caracas, October 8-11, 2008. The conference stimulated a wide-ranging debate on the current economic and financial health of the global economy and the new perspectives on the challenges to the governments and peoples of the South posed by the international financial crisis.

The meeting concluded that the situation has worsened in the last few weeks. It has progressed rapidly from being a series of crises in the financial markets of countries in the center and has turned into an extremely serious international crisis. This means that countries in the South are in a very difficult situation.

The crisis threatens the real economy and, if energetic and effective actions are not taken immediately, all peoples in the world could be drastically punished, especially the least protected and most neglected sectors.

The vulnerability of our currencies, the financial imbalances, and the serious recession that looms large give the lie to the neoliberal myth about the benefits of deregulating markets and the solidity and trustworthiness of the existing financial institutions; the former also clearly bring into question the foundations of the current capitalist system.

The contributions made to the conference shone the spotlight on the way the crisis, which began in August 2007, has developed and on the failure of the ever larger concessions, bailouts, and privileges provided by state intervention in developed capitalist countries to save the dregs of an already non-functional world financial system.

We denounce the attempt to make the overall world system carry the cost of the financial bailout thus aggravating the situation of poverty, unemployment, and exploitation experienced by the world's workers and peoples.

Neither the colossal state interventionism seen over the last few weeks to rescue institutions dismembered and drained dry by speculation, nor massive public indebtedness are plausible ways to get out of the crisis. The existing dynamic encourages new rounds of capital concentration and, if the peoples do not firmly oppose this, it is becoming perilously likely that restructuring will occur simply to save privileged sectors. This could mean there is a danger of capitalism returning to an authoritarian way of functioning, since in the North an increase in discrimination and racism towards immigrants from countries in the South has already been noted—which is something extremely regressive.

If the current restructuring the capitalist system continues down the same road, there will be enormous productive and social costs and the already fragile sustainability of the environment may suffer even more damage.

The need to reform the international economic and financial structure is today unavoidable. Those who think this also believe that it is necessary to find a post-capitalist solution; in Venezuela this is referred to as "21st-Century Socialism."

In a moment as critical as this, national and regional policies must give priority to social spending and to protecting natural and productive resources. States must introduce urgent financial regulation measures to protect savings, to keep stimulating production and must fight off the dangers implicit in a lack of regulation by immediately implementing exchange and capital movement controls.

It will therefore be essential to develop the highest possible degree of balanced regional complementation and trade integration by reinforcing industrial, agricultural, energy, and infrastructural capacities. Initiatives such as ALBA [Alianza Bolivariana para los Pueblos de Nuestra América] and the Bank of the South must extend their radius of action and move their perspective towards that of an alternative form of greater integration that includes a new common currency. This is so we can move towards creating a new world financial architecture which will make it viable for the south to be involved in a different way in the international division of labor.

In this context it is necessary to evaluate a series of contributions and proposals from the social economy that seek to dignify labor and encourage local coordination to combat the impact of the crisis.

On an international level, we must not cease to demand a far-reaching reform of the international monetary and financial system; this entails defending savings and channeling investments into serving the peoples' essential needs. The continued re-emergence of a system which favors the central role of speculation, increases economic differences, and especially punishes those countries and sectors that are least protected must be prevented.

Therefore new (multilateral) economic institutions must be created on new bases; they must have the authority and the instruments to be able to act against the anarchy of speculation. Hence it has become indispensable that national authorities intervene urgently in ways that challenge the basic workings of the market and protect the finances of the peoples affected. The crisis has created common interests among the peoples of all nations.

Based on these analyses and considerations, The International Political Economy Conference: Responses from the South to the Global Economic Crisis has reached the following conclusions and recommendations.

Conclusions and Recommendations for Action

We begin with the following characterization of the international economic situation:

1. We find ourselves in an unprecedented international situation. The economic and financial crisis has worsened and accelerated greatly in the last few days. Its future development, as well as being difficult to foresee could take on, from one day to the next, dramatic overtones.

2. The initial epicenter of the crisis was in the United States and on the stock markets but the crisis is now a world crisis which is affecting the whole financial system and is increasingly contaminating the productive apparatus. The crisis is having a particular impact now on Eastern and Western Europe.

3. In spite of the initial expectations that Latin America could remain outside the crisis and that it is "shielded," there are already very convincing signs that the sub continent is certain to be affected. We cannot only expect a prolonged decrease in foreign trade but are certain to be hit by a very violent financial crash—and soon. The more internationalized the banking system and stock exchange the greater its fragility.

We are making these suggestions well aware that in any crisis there are always winners and losers. We are strongly in favor of taking those measures that ensure the welfare and rights of our peoples, of citizens in general, and not in favor of coming to the aid of the bankers responsible for the crisis as they are doing in Europe and the United States.

Given this new situation and the fact that it is worsening at an accelerated rate we think it is necessary to make the following recommendations for action, some of which will have to be implemented by taking urgent political decisions at the very highest levels.

Therefore, consideration should be given to calling an immediate Extraordinary Summit of Latin American and Caribbean presidents or at least of those of UNASUR. Either or both of these would be presided over by a large popular mobilization of our peoples.

On the Banking System

- Given the collapse of the international financial system, states in the region should immediately take charge of their banking systems using controls, intervention, and nationalization without compensation following the principle enshrined in the new Ecuadorian constitution which forbids the state to accept responsibility for private debts. (Article 290, point 7: "it is forbidden for the state to accept responsibility for private debts.")
- The reason for these measures is to prevent capital fleeing abroad, a run on currencies, the transference of funds from the branches of foreign banks to their head offices and to prevent banks from freezing credit by not lending the funds they receive.
- The off-shore banking systems of every country must be shut down, for under current circumstances, when liquidity problems are causing money to be siphoned off from the periphery, they are an extremely dangerous haven from regulations and fiscal controls.
- The banks' books must be opened; bank oversight must be strengthened as must the mechanisms of strict regulation which make the real situation of national banking systems transparent for they are the institutions into which the populations' savings are deposited. Given that financial services are public services, one of these measures must guarantee there is a minimum amount of domestic investment in the liquid assets of the system (coefficient of domestic liquidity).
- Popular economic activities for development and not for profit must be encouraged and administered by populations living in the areas where such bodies are located.
- If the state does intervene they must recover the costs of the bailout from the

banks' property and have the right to do so from the property of the shareholders and managers.

The New Financial Architecture

- The lack of coordinated monetary policies causes a "competitive devalua-
tions" war which makes the crisis worse and unleashes rivalry between our
economies thus preventing a coordinated response from the region and even
creates structural threats to the progress of initiative towards integration, such
as UNASUR. Therefore, clear signs that there will be a Latin American monetary agreement should be given which will straight away make evident the
additional opportunities for "shielding" our macroeconomies. Thus, defining a
system of payment settlements based on a basket of Latin American monies will
provide each country with additional sources of liquidity which will allow them
to distance themselves from the logic of the dollar crisis.
- Along the same lines as creating institutions to "shield" our economies we will
need more coordination between our central banks and must go beyond neoliberal dogma by managing our international reserves in a much more efficient
and timely way. So it is important to move forward on the proposal for a Fund
of the South that is an alternative to the IMF with liquidity available for emergencies in exchequers (national treasuries) or balance of payments.

  Making good use of the bigger surplus reserves of each country brought
about by the creation of a payment settlement system (regional credit transfer rights) and by the existence of the Common Fund of the South, resources
can be mobilized to get the Bank of the South up and running straightaway
ensuring that it will function democratically and not reproduce the logic of the
multilateral financial credit organizations. This bank must be the heart of this
process of transforming the already existing network of Latin American *bancos
de fomento* whose mission is the reproduction of productive apparatuses based
on fundamental human rights. We understand all of the foregoing in way something similar to what was emphasized in the Quito Ministerial Declaration of
May of this year where it said: "The peoples gave their governments the mandate to provide the region with new tools for integration for development. These
should be designed on transparent, participatory bases and accountable to those
who issued the mandate."
- It is essential to ratify exchange controls in the countries where they exist and to
establish them where there don't to protect reserves and prevent capital outflows.
- In the context of the suspension of payments imposed by the crisis on the
international financial system it is imperative that the countries of the region
consider suspending payment of public debt. This measure is intended to
temporarily protect sovereign resources threatened by the crisis and avoid an
emptying out of the national treasuries.

  Latin America and the Caribbean should learn from what is happening
in Europe where each country is trying to solve the crisis on its own. This
makes it imperative to bolster the mechanisms of integration being developed
in the region.

Social Emergency

- We propose that the widest possible degree of national and peoples' sovereignty be exercised over natural resources, in order that they be rationally exploited and their prices defended to benefit the peoples.
- We propose setting up a Regional Social Emergency Fund to ensure food and energy sovereignty right away and to deal with the acute problems of migrations and reduction in remittances. This fund could operate out of the Bank of the South or the Alba Bank.
- Pursuant to the principle of not rescuing bankers but rather our populations, public budgets must be maintained for social spending and we must contemplate an increase in these budgets to combat the imminent effects of the international crisis on our peoples; our priorities are employment security, universal income, public health and education, housing.
- Establishing anti-inflationary mechanisms, such as price controls which conserve and increment low wages and pensions, subsidies etc, which play a role in redistributing income and wealth.

Financial Organizations

The international financial crisis has revealed the complicity of the IMF, the World Bank and the IDB with transnational bankers who have caused the current collapse with its horrific social consequences. The loss of prestige of these bodies is obvious. This is the opportunity for the countries in the region to follow Bolivia's example and withdraw from ICSID (International Center for the Settlement of Investment Disputes) and to take up Venezuela's call to withdraw from the IMF and the World Bank and begin to help to build a new international financial architecture.

We convene a second International Political Economy Conference: Responses from the South to the Global Economic Crisis, to be held in the first four months of 2009. ❏

Signatories, Caracas, October 11, 2008:

Argentina: Luis Bilbao, Julio Gambina, Jorge Marchini, Claudio Katz,
Australia: Tim Anderson
Belgium: Olivier Bonfond, Eric Toussaint,
Canada: Pablo Heidrich, Michael Lebowitz
South Korea: Hi Yeon Cho
Chile: Orlando Caputo. Jaime Estay Marta Harnecker
China: Gao Xian
Cuba: Luis Fernando Becerra, Gladis Hernández Pedraza
Ecuador: Fernando López Romero Delfa Mantilla. Pedro Paez Pérez Hugo Arias Palacios
Egypt: Samir Amín
France: Eric Berr
Great Britain: Patrick Devine
Mexico: Julio Huato

Peru: Alex Julca
Philippines: Sithy Reihana Mohideen
Spain: José Deniz Espinos, Armando Fernández Steinko, Víctor Ríos
United States: Donald Campbell
Uruguay: Antonio Elías Dultra.
Venezuela: Servando Álvarez, Víctor Álvarez Rodríguez, Luis Bonilla, Molina Haiman El Troudi.

CONTRIBUTORS

Randy Albelda, a *Dollars & Sense* Associate, teaches economics at the University of Massachusetts-Boston.

Sylvia A. Allegretto, Ph.D. is an economist and deputy chair of the Center on Wage and Employment Dynamics at the Institute for Research on Labor and Employment, University of California, Berkeley.

Dean Baker is co-director of the Center for Economic and Policy Research (www.cepr.net) in Washington, D.C.

William K. Black is an associate professor of economics and law at the University of Missouri-Kansas City.

Mary Bottari is director of the Real Economy Project of the Center for Media and Democracy.

Heather Boushey is a senior economist at the Center for American Progress.

Roger Bybee is the former editor of the union weekly *Racine Labor* and is now a consultant and freelance writer whose work has appeared in *Z Magazine, The Progressive, Extra!,* and other national publications and websites.

Jim Campen is professor emeritus of economics at University of Massachusetts-Boston and a *Dollars & Sense* Associate.

James M. Cypher is a *Dollars & Sense* Associate. He is a professor at California State University-Fresno and at Universidad Autónoma de Zacatecas, Mexico.

Jane D'Arista is a Research Associate at the Political Economy Research Institute at the University of Massachusetts at Amherst. She served as a staff economist for the Banking and Commerce Committees of the U.S. House of Representatives and as a principal analyst in the international division of the Congressional Budget Office.

Ryan A. Dodd is a Ph.D. student in economics and a research associate at the Center for Full Employment and Price Stability at the University of Missouri-Kansas City.

Tamara Draut is director of the Economic Opportunity Program at Demos and author of *Strapped: Why America's 20- and 30-Somethings Can't Get Ahead.*

Marie Duggan is an associate professor of economics at Keene State College in New Hampshire.

Mike-Frank Epitropoulos teaches sociology at the University of Pittsburgh.

Katherine Faherty, a former *Dollars & Sense* intern, recently graduated from Hobart and William Smith Colleges with a B.A. in economics.

Daniel Fireside is the former *Dollars & Sense* book editor.

Gerald Friedman, a co-editor of this volume, is a professor of economics at the University of Massachusetts at Amherst.

Heidi Garrett-Peltier is a research associate at the Political Economy Research Institute in Amherst, Mass.

William Greider has been a political journalist for more the 35 years. He is currently the National Arrairs Correspondent for *The Nation* magazine.

Marianne Hill, an economist and former *D&S* collective member, has published articles in the *Journal of Human Development, Feminist Economics,* and other economics journals. She also writes for the American Forum and the Mississippi Forum.

Mara Kardas-Nelson is a freelance writer currently based in Capetown, South Africa. She has written on health, the environment, and human rights for the *Globe & Mail* and the *Mail & Guardian.*

Howard Karger is a professor of social policy at the University of Houston.

Rachel Keeler is a freelance international business journalist. She holds an MSc in Global Politics from the London School of Economics.

Steve Keen is an associate professor of economics and finance at the University of Western Sydney.

Marie Kennedy teaches at the UCLA Department of Urban Planning.

David Kotz is a professor of economics at the University of Massachusetts at Amherst.

Dan LaBotz is the author of several books on labor and politics in the United States, Mexico, and Indonesia. He is a member of the editorial board of *New Politics*.

Rob Larson is an assistant professor of economics at Ivy Tech Community College in Bloomington, Ind.

Kari Lydersen is the Midwest correspondent for the *Washington Post*. She is a co-author of *Shoot an Iraqi: Art Life and Resistance Under the Gun*.

Arthur MacEwan is professor emeritus of economics at UMass-Boston and is a *Dollars & Sense* Associate.

Stacy Warner Maddern is a PhD candidate in political science at the University of Connecticut.

Paul Mattick is professor of philosophy at Adelphi University. He was editor of the *International Journal of Political Economy* from 1987 to 2004.

John Miller is a member of the *Dollars & Sense* collective and teaches economics at Wheaton College.

Fred Moseley, a co-editor of this volume, is a professor of economics at Mt. Holyoke College.

Immanuel Ness is professor of political science at Brooklyn College-City University of New York. He is author of *Immigrants, Unions, and the New U.S. Labor Market* and editor of *WorkingUSA: The Journal of Labor and Society*.

Thomas I. Palley is an economist who has held positions at the AFL-CIO, Open Society Institute, and the U.S.-China Economic and Security Review Commission.

Steven Pitts is a labor policy specialist at the University of California Berkeley Center for Labor Research and Education, where he focuses on strategies for worker organizing and labor-community alliances.

Robert Pollin teaches economics and is co-director of the Political Economy Research Institute at the University of Massachusetts-Amherst. He is also a *Dollars & Sense* Associate.

Smriti Rao teaches economics at Assumption College in Worcester, Mass., and is a member of the *Dollars & Sense* collective.

Alejandro Reuss, an economist and historian, is a former co-editor of *Dollars & Sense* and a current member of the *D&S* collective.

Adria Scharf, a former co-editor of *Dollars & Sense*, is director of the Richmond Peace Education Center and a *D&S* Associate.

Katherine Sciacchitano is a former labor lawyer and organizer. She teaches political economy at the National Labor College.

Orlando Segura, Jr. has worked for an Atlanta-based global management consulting compnay that consults for private equity firms, and for a private equity firm based in Boston.

Dariush Sokolov is an activist and independent journalist based in Argentina. He writes about political philosophy, anarchist economics, and global finance.

Chris Sturr, a co-editor of this volume, is co-editor of *Dollars & Sense*.

Chris Tilly teaches at the UCLA Department of Urban Planning and is director of the UCLA Institute for Research on Labor and Employment. He is also a *Dollars & Sense* Associate.

James Tracy is a San Francisco-based economic justice organizer and writer. He is a co-author of the forthcoming book *Keep on the Firing Line: Working Class Whites, Radical Politics and the Original Rainbow Coalition*

Ramaa Vasudevan is as assistant professor of economics at Colorado State University and a member of the *Dollars & Sense* collective.

Jeannette Wicks-Lim is an economist and research fellow at the Political Economy Research Institute at the Univeristy of Massachusetts-Amherst.

Richard D. Wolff teaches economics at the University of Massachusetts-Amherst and author of *Capitalism Hits the Fan: The Global Economic Meltdown and What to Do About It*.

Marty Wolfson teaches economics at the University of Notre Dame and is a former economist with the Federal Reserve Board in Washington, D.C.

CPSIA information can be obtained at www.ICGtesting.com
Printed in the USA
269486BV00004B/2/P